A Problem Solving Approach to
Mathematics for Elementary School Teachers
Second Edition

Rick Billstein

Shlomo Libeskind

Johnny W. Lott

University of Montana
Missoula, Montana

The Benjamin/Cummings Publishing Company
Menlo Park, California • Reading, Massachusetts
London • Amsterdam • Don Mills, Ontario • Sydney

To our families: Jane and Carolyn, Molly, Karly,
Ran, Nureet, and John; and to Linda Price,
without whose help we wouldn't have made it.

Sponsoring Editors: Sally Elliott and James W. Behnke
Production Coordinator: Susan Harrington
Copy Editor: Linda Thompson
Book and Cover Designer: John Edeen

Library of Congress Cataloging in Publication Data
Billstein, Rick.
    A problem solving approach to mathematics for
elementary school teachers.

    Includes bibliographies and index.
    1. Mathematics—Study and teaching (Elementary)
2. Mathematics—1961–   . 3. Problem solving.
I. Libeskind, Shlomo.   II. Lott, Johnny W., 1944–
III. Title.
QA135.5.B49   1984   327.7   83-15785
ISBN 0-8053-0856-3

FGHIJ-DO-89876

The Benjamin/Cummings Publishing Company, Inc.
2727 Sand Hill Road
Menlo Park, California 94025

Preface

It is in response to the overwhelmingly enthusiastic reception of the first edition of our book—and to our readers' thoughtful comments—that we have written the second edition of *A Problem Solving Approach to Mathematics for Elementary School Teachers*.

We have taken those suggestions to heart, and have used our own experiences in teaching from the text as well, in preparing this edition, with the goal of making the second edition of our book even more suitable to our readers' needs than the first. We have also considered carefully the recent changes in both the elementary mathematics curriculum and the suggested changes in the teacher preparation program as outlined by the Committee on the Undergraduate Program in Mathematics (CUPM) of the Mathematical Association of America.

OUR GOALS

Although we have expanded and updated the book for the second edition, our primary goals remain the same:

- To survey the appropriate mathematics in a way that is both intelligible and entertaining
- To present and use the heuristics of problem solving as an integral part of mathematics
- To encourage our students to extend their learning beyond the classroom by providing a diversity of problems (both elementary and challenging), discussion topics, and bibliographies for further reading

PROBLEM SOLVING IN THE SECOND EDITION

The first recommendation of the National Council of Teachers of Mathematics (NCTM) is that "problem solving be the focus of school mathematics in the 1980's" (*An Agenda for Action: Recommendations for School Mathematics of the 1980's*). This edition reflects an even greater commitment to that goal than the first. We have emphasized problem solving wherever possible:

- *Two complete chapters* (Chapters 1 and 14) are devoted to the problem solving techniques used throughout the text. Chapter 1 develops a four-step problem solving method, based upon Polya's work:

Understanding the problem

Devising a plan

Carrying out the plan

Looking back

This chapter presupposes only minimal mathematics skills from students. Chapter 14 reviews problem solving strategies and presents challenging problems based upon topics covered in the preceding chapters.

- *A preliminary problem* begins Chapters 1 through 13. Each problem poses a question that students can answer after mastering the material in the chapter. We encourage our students to attempt to solve the preliminary problem before starting the chapter so that they might develop a sense of what is needed to solve the problem. The final section of each of these chapters gives a solution to the preliminary problem using the four-step method presented in Chaper 1.
- *New problems* have been introduced throughout the text. These problems are solved in detail using the four-step problem solving format.

FEATURES

Wherever possible, we have presented new topics in ways that could be used in an actual classroom. In addition, we have included a number of study aids and incorporated end-of-section, end-of-chapter, and design features to make the book as useful and interesting as possible.

Study Aids

COMPUTER CORNER

BRAIN TEASER

- *Sample textbook pages* from several elementary mathematics series are reproduced throughout the book. These pages show how various topics are introduced to students in kindergarten through eighth grade.
- *Computer Corners* are included throughout the book. These illustrate content in the corresponding sections and are written in BASIC or Logo.
- *Brain Teasers* supplement many of the problem sets. They are challenging and entertaining problems related to the subject matter of the sections in which they appear. Solutions to the Brain Teasers are in the Instructor's Resource Manual.
- *Cartoons* are included throughout the book to add a lighter touch to the text and to illustrate the content in sections.
- Problems emphasizing *calculator usage* are indicated in problem sets by a calculator symbol ▦ .

End-of-Section Features

- *Laboratory activities* are suggested at the end of many sections. These may be used to aid in the learning or in the eventual teaching of mathematics content.
- *Problem sets* at the end of each section include large numbers of problems generally arranged in order of increasing difficulty. Stars ★ indicate the most *challenging problems.*
- *Review problems,* a new feature of the second edition, are included in problem sets. The review problems constitute a basic review of material from previous sections in the chapter.
- *Answers* to odd-numbered problems (except Chapter 13) are included in the back of the book. Only selected answers for Chapter 13 are included.

End-of-Chapter Features

- *Questions From the Classroom* sections appear at the end of each of Chapters 2–13. They are collections of some questions students might ask their teachers about the material presented in that chapter. The questions can be discussed in class or assigned as research questions. Our students have found that the questions provide valuable preparation for their future teaching. This feature is based upon *Mathematical Questions from the Classroom* by Richard Crouse and Clifford Sloyer (Prindle, Weber, Schmidt, 1977). Suggested answers to these questions are available in the *Instructor's Guide.*
- *Chapter outlines* are included to help students review the chapter.
- *Chapter Tests* provide an opportunity for students to test themselves on important concepts developed in each chapter.
- A *Selected Bibliography* concludes each chapter except Chapters 13 and 14. The articles or books in these bibliographies can be assigned for outside reading or extra credit; they can be used as references for answering many of the Questions From the Classroom; or they can complement the text for those students who wish to read further on a particular topic.

Design Features

- *Key terms, definitions, theorems,* and other important concepts are highlighted in boldface type. Key terms are repeated in the margins to help students review the material.
- A functional *use of color* in the text material and illustrations helps to emphasize various concepts.
- *Graphs, charts, geometric drawings, cartoons,* and other kinds of illustrations reinforce the content presented.

CONTENT

Because the mathematics preparations of students who take this course vary widely, we have written the book so that the material can be used by students with diverse backgrounds. We have built in flexibility for instructors: We have included enough topics to allow instructors to adapt the text to a variety of course lengths and organizations, including sections preceded by asterisks (*) that are optional and can be omitted without loss of continuity.

As we mentioned previously, Chapters 1 and 14 provide an explanation and review of problem solving. Further chapters cover the following topics:

Sets and relations.   We present these topics (Chapter 2) in a way that allows instructors to cover less than the complete chapter if they wish. Chapter 2 has been reorganized with several sections combined. The work on functions has been expanded.

Numeration systems and whole numbers.   The discussion of whole number operations (Chapter 3) has been reordered and many new models for operations have been added.

Integers.   The development of the system of integers (Chapter 4) has been made less formal.

Number theory.   Number theory concepts (Chapter 5) afford an excellent opportunity to develop the concept of proof. We have developed many of the properties in this chapter in a way that we believe is most meaningful to students at this level.

Rational and irrational numbers.   Chapter 6 of the first edition has been divided into two chapters. The new Chapter 6 deals primarily with fractions and Chapter 7 deals with decimals. Material on percent has been greatly expanded and an optional section on computing interest has been added.

Probability and statistics.   Probability and statistics have been combined into one chapter (Chapter 8). Topics in probability are presented through the use of tree diagrams. Formulas for combinations and permutations are also developed in this chapter. Statistics is presented with an emphasis on organizing, presenting, and interpreting data.

Geometry.   Chapters 9, 10, 11, and 12 cover informal geometry. Chapter 9 introduces basic concepts of geometry. Motion geometry and geometric constructions are taught in Chapter 10 by using compass and straightedge, paper folding, and Miras. Work with Miras can be omitted if they are not available. Chapter 11 deals with the Pythagorean Theorem and notions of measurement.

Chapter 12 presents the fundamentals of coordinate geometry. Appendix III, which is new, provides a summary of the basic compass and straightedge constructions.

Metric measurement.   We integrate metric measures with other geometric concepts and emphasize metric units throughout the text. Metric estimation exercises are included, conversions are metric-to-metric, rather than metric to English and vice versa.

Computers.   A new chapter on computers (Chapter 13) appears in this edition. The chapter is split into two parts, one of which covers BASIC and the other Logo. BASIC is and has for years been the computer language learned by college-bound students and college students. Logo, a language developed at The Massachusetts Institute of Technology, is rapidly being assimilated into the elementary school curriculum.

Logic.   *Appendix I: Informal Logic* is a brief, self-contained overview of logic that emphasizes the precise use of language. We have included this appendix for those instructors who believe that an introduction to logic is necessary in this course. Appendix I can be taught at any time during the course or omitted entirely without any loss of continuity.

Calculator usage.   The third recommendation of the National Council of Teachers of Mathematics states that "mathematics programs must take full advantage of the power of calculators and computers at all grade levels." Appendix II discusses features of calculators and what to look for when you choose a calculator. The calculator symbol ▦ appearing in many problem sets refers to problems where the calculator would be very useful. In this edition, calculator problems have been incorporated into the problem sets.

THE INSTRUCTOR'S GUIDE

This supplement includes

- Answers to odd- and even-numbered problems
- Complete solutions to the problems in Chapters 13 and 14
- Sample chapter tests that may be used as test questions or as make-up tests
- Suggested answers to Questions from the Classroom
- Solutions to Brain Teasers

ACKNOWLEDGMENTS

We would like to thank the students we have taught over the past several years for their patience and suggestions as we have class-tested and refined this text. Our sincere thanks also go to Linda Price for her excellent manuscript preparation. The reviewers of our work (listed below) offered us valuable guidance, and we are grateful to them for the care they took with their reviews. Finally, we would like to thank the staff at Benjamin/Cummings, who have worked extremely hard on both editions of this text and continue to share the excitement we have about this project.

Rick Billstein
Shlomo Libeskind
Johnny W. Lott

Reviewers

Leon J. Ablon, College of Staten Island (CUNY)
G. L. Alexanderson, University of Santa Clara
James R. Boone, Texas A and M University
Louis J. Chatterley, Brigham Young University
Donald J. Dessart, University of Tennessee, Knoxville
Glenadine Gibb, University of Texas, Austin
Boyd Henry, College of Idaho
Allan Hoffer, University of Oregon
E. John Hornsby, Jr., University of New Orleans
Wilburn C. Jones, Western Kentucky University
Robert Kalin, Florida State University
Herbert E. Kasube, Bradley University
Sarah Kennedy, Texas Tech University
Steven D. Kerr, Weber State College
Leland W. Knauf, Youngstown State University
Barbara Moses, Bowling Green State University
Gary Musser, Oregon State University
Keith Peck, Northeast Missouri State University
Helen R. Santiz, University of Michigan, Dearborn
Glenn L. Pfeifer, University of New Mexico
Joe K. Smith, Northern Kentucky University
Virginia Strawderman, Georgia State University
C. Ralph Verno, West Chester State College
John Wagner, Michigan State University
Mark F. Weiner, West Chester State College
Grayson Wheatley, Purdue University
Jerry L. Young, Boise State University

Brief Contents

Detailed Contents

Laboratory Activities are on pages 95, 104, 114, 121

4 THE INTEGERS   132

BRAIN TEASERS
Pages 144, 149, 151, 160

COMPUTER CORNER
Page 144

5 NUMBER THEORY   166

BRAIN TEASERS
Pages 175, 183, 196

COMPUTER CORNER
Page 184

6 RATIONAL NUMBERS AS FRACTIONS   200

BRAIN TEASERS
Pages 215, 227, 233

COMPUTER CORNER
Page 214

7 DECIMALS   245

BRAIN TEASERS
Pages 256, 273

COMPUTER CORNER
Pages 264, 279

A Laboratory Activity is on page 270

8 PROBABILITY AND STATISTICS   297

BRAIN TEASERS
Pages 307, 318, 332,
352

COMPUTER CORNER
Page 314

9 INTRODUCTORY GEOMETRY   360

BRAIN TEASERS
Pages 381, 390, 403

COMPUTER CORNER
Page 394

10 CONSTRUCTIONS, CONGRUENCE, AND SIMILARITY   415

BRAIN TEASERS
Pages 434, 444, 451,
473, 481

COMPUTER CORNER
Pages 427, 434, 452,
459

11 CONCEPTS OF MEASUREMENT   491

BRAIN TEASERS
Pages 500, 513, 522, 527

COMPUTER CORNER
Page 507

A Laboratory Activity is on page 546

12 COORDINATE GEOMETRY   555

BRAIN TEASERS
Pages 583, 593

COMPUTER CORNER
Page 575

13

14

Appendices

I

II

▐▐▐   BASIC CONSTRUCTIONS   679

ANSWER SECTION   683

INDEX   716

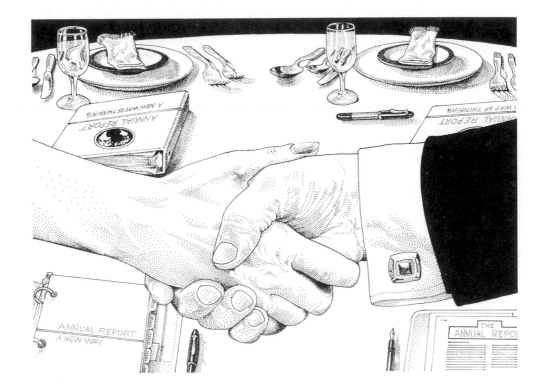

PRELIMINARY PROBLEM

At a convention dinner, twenty people who did not know each other sat at a round table. People shook hands with the people on their immediate right and immediate left. At the end of the dinner, everybody got up and shook hands with every guest except with those with whom they had shaken hands earlier. How many handshakes took place after dinner?

INTRODUCTION

We urge you to spend some time trying to discover a strategy for solving the preliminary problem. If you do not see an immediate solution to the problem, do not give up convinced that the problem is beyond your capabilities. In many cases, problem solving does take time. If you try to solve the problem but are unable to do so, the solution is presented at the end of the chapter.

In this chapter, we present various strategies to help you develop problem-solving skills. Most of the examples in this text are mathematical, but many of the problem-solving techniques can be applied to situations outside mathematics. What is a problem for one person may be an exercise for another. Solving **exercises** involves performing a routine procedure for finding solutions. On the other hand, according to the National Council of Supervisors of Mathematics (1977), solving problems involves "applying previously acquired knowledge to new and unfamiliar situations." For example, solving $12 \times 4 = \square$ is an exercise for most eighth graders, but it is a problem for most second graders. In the cartoon, Peppermint Patty tries to substitute another kind of exercise for a problem.

exercises

© 1978 United Feature Syndicate, Inc.

People rarely encounter computational exercises outside the classroom, but they do encounter problems. Thus, problem-solving skills are important for their success. A well-known mathematician and educator, George Polya, describes the experience of problem solving in his book, *How To Solve It*.

A great discovery solves a great problem but there is a grain of discovery in the solution of any problem. Your problem may be modest; but if it challenges your curiosity and brings into play your inventive facilities, and if you solve it by your own means, you may experience the tension and enjoy the triumph of discovery. Such experiences at a susceptible age may create a taste for mental work and leave their imprint on mind and character for a lifetime.

One way to become a good problem solver is by attempting a variety of problems. Techniques developed in solving these problems can be used to help solve new problems. As part of his work in problem solving, Polya developed a four-step process similar to the following:

1. Understanding the Problem
   (a) Can you state the problem in your own words?
   (b) What are the unknowns?
   (c) What information do you obtain from the problem?
   (d) What information, if any, is missing or not needed?
2. Devising a Plan
   The following list of strategies, although not exhaustive, is very useful.
   (a) Look for a pattern.
   (b) Examine related problems and determine if the same technique can be applied.
   (c) Examine a simpler or special case of the problem to gain insight into the solution of the original problem.
   (d) Make a table, diagram, or model.
   (e) Write an equation.
   (f) Use trial and error.
   (g) Work backwards.
   (h) Identify a subgoal.
3. Carrying Out the Plan
   Perform the necessary computations.
4. Looking Back
   (a) Check the results in the original problem. (In some cases, this will require a proof.)
   (b) Interpret the solution in terms of the original problem.
   (c) Determine whether there is another solution, perhaps a more direct one.
   (d) Determine whether there is another method of finding the solution.
   (e) If possible, determine other related or more general problems for which the techniques will work.

Step 4, Looking Back, is an important step for developing students' problem-solving skills. At this stage, students examine and describe their own thinking. Not only do those students benefit, but other students who hear the description will benefit.

It is not necessary to memorize these four problem-solving steps. They will come naturally with practice. Problem solving is not a spectator sport. You will be asked to use the strategies discussed in this chapter, but not always in the detail seen here. This four-step process does not assure a solution to a problem, but it gives valuable guidelines when there is no obvious way to proceed. Most of the problems presented in this chapter are solved without algebra, because many students in this course do not have the necessary algebraic skills.

1-1   EXPLORATION WITH PATTERNS

inductive reasoning

conjecture

Discovering patterns is a very important strategy in problem solving. In mathematics, we refer to examining a variety of cases, discovering patterns, and forming conclusions based on these patterns as **inductive reasoning.** Scientists use inductive reasoning when they perform a number of experiments to discover various laws of nature. Statisticians use inductive reasoning when they form conclusions based on collected data. Inductive reasoning usually leads to what mathematicians call a **conjecture,** a statement thought to be true but not yet proven as either true or false. Inductive reasoning is an extremely helpful technique, but it should be used cautiously. Later, we will see examples where a certain pattern works for a number of cases but eventually breaks down.

Many problems encountered in grade school involve the strategy of looking for patterns. For example, the student page shown on page 5 is a sample involving patterns from the Addison-Wesley series *Mathematics in Our World,* 1978, Grade 3.

The student pictured on the sample page is faced with finding the next term of the given pattern. She probably notices that the first digit in each number increased by one, while the second digit remained constant at one. Another student may notice that each number is ten greater than the preceding one. Thus, we see that different methods can be used to arrive at the same pattern.

Study the following examples and problems and look for some special property that all terms share. Different people may observe different patterns.

Example 1-1

Find the next three terms to complete a pattern.

1, 2, 4, _____, _____, _____

Solution

The difference between the first two terms is 1; the difference between the second two terms is 2; consequently, the difference between the next two terms might be 3, then 4, and so on. Thus, the completed sequence might appear as follows.

1, 2, 4, 7, 11, 16

Another property that 1, 2, and 4 share is that each term is twice the preceding one; that is, $2 = 2 \cdot 1$ and $4 = 2 \cdot 2$. Thus, the next terms could be $2 \cdot 4$, or 8, $2 \cdot 8$, or 16, and $2 \cdot 16$, or 32. Hence, the completed sequence might appear as follows.

1, 2, 4, 8, 16, 32

It is evident that more than one pattern is possible based on the given information.

Example 1-2

Find the next three terms to complete a pattern.

□, △, △, □, △, △, □, _____, _____, _____

For fun

Finding the Pattern

The last card in each row is turned down.
Can you tell what number is hidden?

Example:

1, 2, 3, 4, 5, 6, 7, 81

1. 2 4 6 8 10 12 14 ?

2. 3 8 13 18 23 28 33 ?

3. 1 2 4 8 16 32 64 ?

4. 1 6 7 12 13 18 19 ?

5. 1 2 4 7 11 16 22 ?

Solution | Notice that between two squares, there are two consecutive triangles. Based on this observation, the next three terms are two triangles followed by a square. Thus, the completed sequence might appear as follows.

□, △, △, □, △, △, □, △, △, □

Example 1-3 | Find the next three terms in the sequence.

1, 4, 7, 10, 13, _____, _____, _____

Solution | Each term is 3 units greater than the previous term.

Sequence   1 ⌣ 4 ⌣ 7 ⌣ 10 ⌣ 13
Difference   3   3   3   3

If this pattern continues, the next three terms will be 16, 19, and 22.

In each example, the terms were given in an ordered arrangement. The word **sequence** is used to describe terms given in a definite order. If each successive term in a sequence is obtained from the previous term by the addition of a fixed number, then the sequence is called an **arithmetic sequence.** The sequence in Example 1-3 is an arithmetic sequence. The fixed number is 3. Neither pattern in Example 1-1 illustrates an arithmetic sequence because no fixed number has been added.

It is often useful to predict the terms in a sequence. Tables are helpful problem-solving aids for finding such values. Table 1-1 shows the sequence in Example 1-3. The column headed *Number of Term* refers to the order of the term in the sequence. The column headed *Term* lists the accompanying terms of the sequence. We use an **ellipsis,** denoted by three dots, to indicate that the sequence continues in the same manner.

sequence

arithmetic sequence

ellipsis

TABLE 1-1

Number of Term	Term
1	1
2	$4 = 1 + 3$
3	$7 = 1 + 3 + 3 = 1 + 2 \cdot 3$
4	$10 = 1 + 3 + 3 + 3 = 1 + 3 \cdot 3$
5	$13 = 1 + 3 + 3 + 3 + 3 = 1 + 4 \cdot 3$
.	.
.	.
.	.

Notice that the number of 3s in each term is one less than the number of the term. Assuming this pattern continues, the tenth term is $1 + 9 \cdot 3$, or 28, and the 100th term is $1 + 99 \cdot 3$, or 298.

nth term

The general term of a sequence is called the ***n*th term.** Knowing the general term enables us to find any term given the number of the term. In the above sequence, the nth term is $1 + (n - 1) \cdot 3$. Thus, for example, the 200th term can be obtained by substituting 200 for n. The 200th term is $1 + (200 - 1) \cdot 3$, or $1 + 199 \cdot 3$, or 598.

A different type of sequence is investigated in the following discussion. A child in a family has 2 parents, 4 grandparents, 8 great-grandparents, 16 great-great-grandparents, and so on. Assuming that none of the ancestors in the family married a relative, we see that the numbers of ancestors from previous generations form the sequence 2, 4, 8, 16, 32, ... This type of sequence is called a **geometric sequence.** Each successive term of a geometric sequence is obtained from its predecessor by multiplying by a fixed number. In this example, the fixed number is 2. To find the nth term, examine Table 1-2.

geometric sequence

TABLE 1-2

Number of Term	Term
1	$2 = 2^1$
2	$4 = 2 \cdot 2 = 2^2$
3	$8 = 2 \cdot (2 \cdot 2) = 2^3$
4	$16 = 2 \cdot (2 \cdot 2 \cdot 2) = 2^4$
5	$32 = 2 \cdot (2 \cdot 2 \cdot 2 \cdot 2) = 2^5$
.	.
.	.
.	.

The table reveals a pattern: When the given term is written as a power of 2, the number of the term is the exponent of 2. Following this pattern, the tenth term is 2^{10}, or 1024, the one-hundredth term is 2^{100}, and the nth term is 2^n. Thus, the number of ancestors in the nth previous generation is 2^n.

Example 1-4

The Greeks were fascinated by the way numbers appear geometrically. The following arrays represent the first four terms of what sequence of numbers? What is the nth term in the sequence?

1 dot   4 dots   9 dots   16 dots

Solution

square numbers

Notice that each array is square. The sequence of numbers suggested is that of the **square numbers,** namely, $1^2, 2^2, 3^2, 4^2, \ldots$. If the pattern continues, the tenth term will be 10^2, the one-hundredth term will be 100^2, and the nth term will be n^2.

Example 1-5 | Find the first four terms of a sequence whose *n*th term is given by: (a) $4 \cdot n + 3$; (b) $n^2 - 1$.

Solution | (a) To find the first term, we substitute $n = 1$ in the formula $4 \cdot n + 3$ to obtain $4 \cdot 1 + 3$, or 7. Similarly, substituting $n = 2, 3, 4$, we obtain $4 \cdot 2 + 3$, or 11, $4 \cdot 3 + 3$, or 15, and $4 \cdot 4 + 3$, or 19, respectively. Hence, the first four terms of the sequence are 7, 11, 15, 19.
(b) Substituting $n = 1, 2, 3, 4$ in the formula $n^2 - 1$, we obtain $1^2 - 1$, or 0, $2^2 - 1$, or 3, $3^2 - 1$, or 8, $4^2 - 1$, or 15, respectively. Thus, the first four terms of the sequence are 0, 3, 8, 15.

Example 1-6 | Find the seventh term in the following sequence.

5, 6, 14, 29, 51, 80, . . .

Solution | The pattern for the differences between successive terms is not easily recognizable.

Sequence   5   6   14   29   51   80
Difference   1   8   15   22   29

To discover a pattern for the original sequence, the strategy of *identifying a subgoal* is used. That is, we try to find a pattern for the sequence of differences 1, 8, 15, 22, 29, ... This sequence is an arithmetic sequence with fixed difference 7. This is shown below.

Sequence   5   6   14   29   51   80
First difference   1   8   15   22   29
Second difference   7   7   7   7

Thus, the sixth term in the first difference row is $29 + 7$, or 36, and hence the seventh term in the original sequence is $80 + 36$, or 116. What number follows 116?

Remark | The general term for this sequence can be found algebraically to be $(7/2)n^2 - (19/2)n + 11$. However, justifying the general term for this particular sequence is beyond the scope of this text.

Example 1-7 | Find the seventh term in the following sequence.

2, 3, 9, 23, 48, 87, . . .

Solution | As in the previous example, we find the first and second differences. Since the second difference is not a fixed number, we go on to the third difference, as shown.

Sequence	2 3 9 23 48 87
First difference	1 6 14 25 39
Second difference	5 8 11 14
Third difference	3 3 3

Since the third difference is a fixed number, the second difference is an arithmetic sequence. The fifth term in the second difference sequence is $14 + 3$, or 17, the sixth term in the first difference sequence is $39 + 17$, or 56, and the seventh term in the original sequence is $87 + 56$, or 143.

When asked to find a pattern for a given sequence, first look for some easily recognizable pattern. If none exists, determine whether the sequence is either arithmetic or geometric. If a pattern is still unclear, taking successive differences may help. It is possible that none of the methods described will reveal a pattern.

PROBLEM SET 1-1

1. List the terms that complete a possible pattern. Then describe the pattern.
   (a) 1×2, 2×3, 3×4, 4×5, ____, ____, ____
   (b) □, 00, □ □ □, 0000, □ □ □ □ □, ____, ____, ____
   (c) 61, 57, 53, 49, ____, ____, ____
   (d) 5, 6, 8, 11, ____, ____, ____
   (e) 2, 5, 10, 17, ____, ____, ____
   (f) X, Y, X, X, Y, X, X, ____, ____, ____
   (g) 1, 3, 1, 8, 1, 13, ____, ____, ____
   (h) 1, 1, 2, 3, 5, 8, 13, 21, ____, ____, ____
   (i) 1, 11, 111, 1111, 11111, ____, ____, ____
   (j) 1, 12, 123, 1234, 12345, ____, ____, ____
   (k) 1×2, 2×2^2, 3×2^3, 4×2^4, 5×2^5, ____, ____, ____
   (l) $2, 2^2, 2^4, 2^8, 2^{16}$, ____, ____, ____
2. Which of the following sequences are arithmetic, which are geometric, and which are neither? In each case, list terms that complete a possible pattern.
   (a) 1, 3, 5, 7, 9, ____, ____, ____
   (b) 0, 50, 100, 150, 200, ____, ____, ____
   (c) 3, 6, 12, 24, 48, ____, ____, ____
   (d) 10, 100, 1000, 10000, 100000, ____, ____, ____
   (e) $5^2, 5^3, 5^4, 5^5, 5^6$, ____, ____, ____
   (f) 11, 22, 33, 44, 55, ____, ____, ____
   (g) $2^1, 2^3, 2^5, 2^7, 2^9$, ____, ____, ____
   (h) 9, 13, 17, 21, 25, 29, ____, ____, ____
   (i) 1, 8, 27, 64, 125, ____, ____, ____
   (j) 2, 6, 18, 54, 162, ____, ____, ____
3. The following geometric arrays suggest a sequence of numbers.

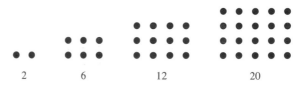

   (a) Find the next three terms.
   (b) Find the one-hundredth term.
   ★ (c) Find the nth term.
4. List the next three terms to complete a pattern in each of the following. (Finding differences may be helpful.)
   (a) 5, 6, 14, 32, 64, 115, 191, ____, ____, ____
   (b) 0, 2, 6, 12, 20, 30, 42, ____, ____, ____
   ★ (c) 10, 8, 3, 0, 4, 20, 53, ____, ____, ____

5. (a) Consider the following geometric arrays of pentagonal numbers. The numbers are formed by counting the dots. Find the first six numbers suggested by this sequence.

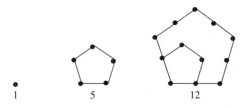

1   5   12

   ⋆ (b) What is the 100th pentagonal number?
6. An employee is paid $1200 at the end of the first month on the job. Each month after that, the worker is paid $20 more than in the preceding month.
   (a) What is the employee's monthly salary at the end of the second year on the job?
   (b) How much will the employee have earned after 6 months?
   (c) After how many months will the employee's monthly salary be $3240?
7. The following is an example of term-by-term addition of two arithmetic sequences.

$$1, 3, \quad 5, \quad 7, \quad 9, 11, \ldots$$
$$+\ 2, 4, \quad 6, \quad 8, 10, 12, \ldots$$
$$\overline{\quad 3, 7, 11, 15, 19, 23, \ldots\quad}$$

Notice that the resulting sequence is also arithmetic. Investigate if this happens again by trying two other examples.
8. Find the first five terms of the sequence with the nth term given as follows.
   (a) $n^2 + 2$
   (b) $5n - 1$
   (c) $10^n - 1$

9. Find the 100th term and the nth term in each of the sequences of Problem 2.
10. The sequence 1, 1, 2, 3, 5, 8, 13, 21, . . . , in which each term starting with the third one is the sum of the two preceding terms, is called a *Fibonacci sequence*. This sequence is named after the great Italian mathematician Leonardo Fibonacci, who lived in the twelfth and thirteenth centuries.
   (a) Write the first 12 terms of the sequence.
   (b) Notice that the sum of the first 3 terms in the sequence is one less than the fifth term of the sequence. Does a similar relationship hold for the sum of the first 4 terms, 5 terms, and 6 terms?
   (c) Guess the sum of the first 10 terms of the sequence.
   ⋆ (d) Make a conjecture concerning the sum of the first n terms of the sequence.
11. Suppose that a pair of rabbits is mature enough to reproduce after the second month of their life. Also suppose that from then on, every month they produce a new pair of mated rabbits. If each new pair of rabbits behaves in the same way and none die, how many pairs of rabbits will there be at the beginning of each month for the first 12 months?
12. How many terms are there in the following sequences?
   (a) 1, 2, 3, 4, . . . , 100
   (b) 51, 52, 53, 54, . . . , 151
   (c) 2, 4, 6, 8, . . . , 200
   (d) 1, 2, 2^2, 2^3, . . . , 2^{60}
   (e) 10, 20, 30, 40, . . . , 2000
⋆ 13. (a) If a fixed number is added to each term of an arithmetic sequence, is the resulting sequence an arithmetic sequence? Justify your answer.
   (b) If each term of an arithmetic sequence is multiplied by a fixed number, will the resulting sequence always be an arithmetic sequence? Justify your answer.
⋆ 14. Answer the questions in Problem 13 for a geometric sequence.

COMPUTER CORNER

Computers are invaluable problem-solving tools, but we have to learn how to communicate with them. A computer understands instructions coded in machine language, the fundamental language understood by an individual computer. Machine language consists of numeric codes in the form of binary numbers, sequences of 0s and 1s, that instruct the computer to perform its basic functions. Because machine languages are hard for people to use, computer scientists developed easier languages to communicate with computers. BASIC (Beginners' All-purpose Symbolic Instruction Code) is one such language. It was developed in the mid-sixties at Dartmouth College and was originally intended to be used for instructional purposes. Because of its simplicity, BASIC became available on almost all computers, both large and small. Many companies adopted BASIC for their data-processing needs, and the language is being taught to high school students, as well as elementary students.

Logo, a new computer language, was developed at the Massachusetts Institute of Technology (MIT) Artificial Intelligence Laboratory. According to Seymour Papert, its inventor, Logo was created with young children in mind. The language is simple enough that preschoolers can learn some aspects of it, but—at the same time—it is rich enough to make it suitable for students of all ages. In his book *Mindstorms,* Papert says that through Logo, learning to communicate with a computer can be a natural process "more like learning French by living in France than like trying to learn it through the unnatural process of American foreign-language instruction in classrooms. . . . We are learning how to make computers with which children love to communicate. When this communication occurs, children learn mathematics as a living language."

1-2 USING THE PROBLEM-SOLVING PROCESS

FIGURE 1-1

If you follow only certain patterns in attacking problems, there is a danger that you may form a *mind set*. A mind set occurs when you draw a faulty conclusion by assuming that you know the answer to a problem without really examining the problem. For example, spell the word "spot" three times aloud. "S-P-O-T! S-P-O-T! S-P-O-T!" Now answer the question: "What do you do when you come to a green light?" Write your answer. If you answered "Stop," you may be guilty of forming a mind set. You do not stop at a *green* light.

Examine Figure 1-1. Do you see anything unusual? Many people do not notice that "the" appears twice in the sign. They have formed a mind set.

Consider the following problem: "A man had 36 sheep. All but 10 died. How many lived?"

Did you answer "10"? If you did, you are catching on and are ready to try some problems. If you did not answer "10," then you should reread the problem and make sure you really understand the question. The next series of problems illustrates how Polya's four-step problem solving process can be used.

PROBLEM 1

FIGURE 1-2
Karl Gauss

When the famous German mathematician Karl Gauss (1777–1855), shown on the stamp in Figure 1-2, was a child, his teacher became infuriated with his class. According to legend, the teacher required the students to find the sum of the first 100 natural numbers as punishment. The teacher expected this problem to keep the class occupied for a considerable amount of time. Gauss gave the answer almost immediately. Can you?

Understanding the Problem

The natural numbers are 1, 2, 3, 4, ... Thus, the problem is to find the sum $1 + 2 + 3 + 4 + \cdots + 100$.

Devising a Plan

Gauss may have used the strategy of *looking for a pattern*. By considering $1 + 100, 2 + 99, 3 + 98, \ldots, 50 + 51$, it is evident that there are 50 pairs of numbers, each with a sum of 101, as shown in Figure 1-3.

FIGURE 1-3

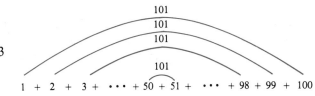

Carrying Out the Plan

There are 50 pairs, each with the sum 101. Thus, the total sum is 50(101), or 5050.

Looking Back

It is easy to check the computation involved. It is also easy to see that the method is mathematically correct because addition can be performed in any order, and multiplication is repeated addition. A more general problem is to find the sum of the first n numbers, $1 + 2 + 3 + 4 + 5 + \cdots + n$, where n is any natural number. We use the same plan as before and notice the relationship in Figure 1-4.

FIGURE 1-4

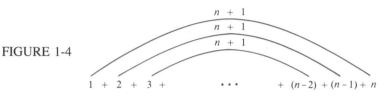

If n is an even natural number, there are $n/2$ pairs of numbers. The sum of each pair is $n + 1$. Therefore, the sum $1 + 2 + 3 + \cdots + n$ is given by $(n/2)(n + 1)$. Does the same formula work if n is odd?

PROBLEM 2

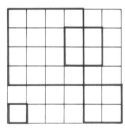

FIGURE 1-5

Using the existing lines in Figure 1-5, how many different squares are there?

Understanding the Problem

Before proceeding, it is important to know what is meant by square and, also, what is meant by "different squares." A square is a four-sided figure whose sides are line segments of equal length and whose adjacent sides meet at right angles. Two squares are different if they have either different dimensions or different locations. For example, the colored lines in Figure 1-6 show four different squares.

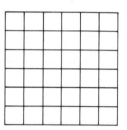

FIGURE 1-6

Devising a Plan

The strategy of *looking at simpler cases* is one of the most important strategies in problem solving and will be used repeatedly in this text. This strategy appears to be appropriate here. The simplest case to consider is given in Figure 1-7(a). How many different squares are there in a 1×1 grid? This is very easy—only one. Now consider the 2×2 grid in Figure 1-7(b). There are four 1×1 squares and one 2×2 square, for a total of five squares. How many squares are in a 3×3 grid? As can be determined from Figure 1-7(c), there are nine 1×1 squares, four 2×2 squares, and one 3×3 square for a total of 14 squares. How many squares are in Figure 1-7(d)?

The problem now becomes more involved. Table 1-3 records information obtained from Figure 1-7.

FIGURE 1-7

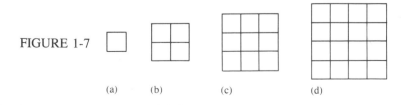

(a)   (b)   (c)   (d)

TABLE 1-3

Grid Size	1 × 1 Squares	2 × 2 Squares	3 × 3 Squares	4 × 4 Squares	Total Squares
1 × 1	1, or 1^2				1
2 × 2	4, or 2^2	1, or 1^2			5
3 × 3	9, or 3^2	4, or 2^2	1, or 1^2		14
4 × 4	16, or 4^2	9, or 3^2	4, or 2^2	1, or 1^2	30

Notice that each total is a sum of perfect squares and that the total of 30 is obtained by finding $1^2 + 2^2 + 3^2 + 4^2$. The table reveals a pattern that is very helpful for counting squares with larger grids. Thus, in a 5 × 5 grid, the total is given by $1^2 + 2^2 + 3^2 + 4^2 + 5^2$; in a 6 × 6 grid, the total is $1^2 + 2^2 + 3^2 + 4^2 + 5^2 + 6^2$.

Carrying Out the Plan

The only computation involved is finding $1^2 + 2^2 + 3^2 + 4^2 + 5^2 + 6^2$, which equals 91.

Looking Back

The more general problem is to find the number of squares in an $n \times n$ grid. Following the preceding pattern, it seems that the number of squares in such a grid is $1^2 + 2^2 + 3^2 + \cdots + n^2$. However, we cannot be absolutely certain of this answer since the observation of a pattern from a few cases does not assure that the pattern always holds. As problem solvers learn more mathematics, they will be able to complete proofs. *Observing a pattern from a few cases does not constitute a proof*. This problem, with a proof of the result, is discussed in detail in the article "Checkerboard Mathematics" by Billstein.

PROBLEM 3

How many ways are there to make change for a quarter using only dimes, nickels, and pennies?

Understanding the Problem

There are no limits on the number of coins to be used. Nickels, dimes, and pennies need not all be used; that is, 25 pennies is an acceptable answer, as is 2 dimes and 1 nickel.

Devising a Plan

In this problem the strategy of *making a table* is used to keep a record of all possibilities as they are examined. First, consider the possibilities when the number of nickels and dimes is zero and the number of pennies is 25. Continue the chart by trading nickels for pennies, as shown in Table 1-4. Are there other combinations? What about dimes? To finish the problem, consider all possibilities using dimes.

TABLE 1-4

D	N	P
0	0	25
0	1	20
0	2	15
0	3	10
0	4	5
0	5	0

Carrying Out the Plan

Start with combinations using one dime. With one dime, the greatest number of pennies possible is 15. Next, trade nickels for pennies, as shown in Table 1-5.

TABLE 1-5

D	N	P
1	0	15
1	1	10
1	2	5
1	3	0

The last case to consider is possibilities with 2 dimes. Proceeding as before, we obtain Table 1-6.

TABLE 1-6

D	N	P
2	0	5
2	1	0

All three cases are shown in Table 1-7.

TABLE 1-7

D	N	P
0	0	25
0	1	20
0	2	15
0	3	10
0	4	5
0	5	0
1	0	15
1	1	10
1	2	5
1	3	0
2	0	5
2	1	0

Thus, there are 12 ways to make change for a quarter using only dimes, nickels, and pennies.

Looking Back

Check each row of Table 1-7 to see that it shows change for a quarter. The systematic listing used in the table shows that all cases have been considered. The problem can be extended easily by starting with an initial amount other than one quarter.

Another interesting, related problem is as follows. Given the number of coins it takes to make change for a quarter, is it possible to determine exactly which coins they are? (*Hint:* Look at Table 1-7 listing the 12 different combinations. Is the number of coins in each combination different?) If you think you know the answer, try it with a friend to see if it works.

PROBLEM 4

A bottle costs 96¢ more than a cork. The bottle and the cork together cost $1.00. How much does the cork cost?

Understanding the Problem

We are asked to find the cost of a cork. We know that the combined cost of the cork and the bottle is $1.00. We also know that the bottle costs 96¢ more than the cork. A first glance might lead us to believe that the cork costs 4¢. If this were true, the bottle would cost $1.00, which contradicts the fact that the bottle and the cork together cost $1.00.

Devising a Plan

The strategy of *writing an equation* may be used. To write an equation, we denote the cost of the cork by c. Then the cost of the bottle in cents is $96 + c$. Because the combined cost of the bottle and the cork is $1 (or 100¢), we obtain:

$$96 + c + c = 100$$

To find the cost of the cork, we must solve the equation; that is, we must find the value of c that makes the equation true.

Carrying Out the Plan

We must solve the equation $96 + c + c = 100$. Since we know that $96 + 4 = 100$, then $c + c = 4$ and c must be 2. Thus, the price of the cork is 2¢.

Looking Back

We can check that 2¢ is the correct price of the cork. Because the bottle costs 96¢ more than the cork and the cork costs 2¢, the bottle costs 98¢. These values satisfy the statement that the bottle and the cork together cost $1.00.

Calculators can be invaluable in problem solving and can be used to reinforce mathematical learning. For example, suppose we press the buttons $\boxed{4}$ $\boxed{+}$ $\boxed{6}$ and then repeatedly press the $\boxed{=}$ button. Many calculators will generate the arithmetic sequence 10, 16, 22, 28, 34, ... If we continue in this way, will the number 616 ever appear? Can this question be answered without pushing the buttons on the calculator?

Problem 5 shows how to use a calculator in problem solving when using the trial-and-error strategy.

PROBLEM 5

Sara and David were reading the same novel. When Sara asked David what page he was reading, he replied that the product of the page number he was reading and the next page number was 98,282. On what page was David reading?

Understanding the Problem

We know that the product of the page number on which David was reading and the next page number is 98,282. We are asked to find the number of the page on which David was reading.

Devising a Plan

Adjacent pages must have consecutive numbers. If we denote the page number David was on by x, then the next page number is $x + 1$. The product of these page numbers is 98,282, so we write the equation as $x \cdot (x + 1) = 98{,}282$. The solution to this equation is not easily recognizable. To solve the equation, we use the *trial-and-error* strategy. A calculator is used as a tool to multiply various consecutive numbers, trying to obtain the product 98,282. Each new trial should be based upon the information obtained from previous trials.

Carrying Out the Plan

Table 1-8 shows a series of trials.

TABLE 1-8

x	$x + 1$	$x \cdot (x + 1)$
100	101	$100 \cdot 101$, or 10,100
200	201	$200 \cdot 201$, or 40,200
300	301	$300 \cdot 301$, or 90,300
400	401	$400 \cdot 401$, or 160,400

From Table 1-8, we see that the desired page number must be closer to 300 than 400. Trying $x = 310$ yields $310 \cdot 311 = 96{,}410$, which shows that 310 is too small for the solution. Successive trials reveal that $313 \cdot 314 = 98{,}282$, so David was reading page 313.

Looking Back

An alternate solution is possible using the concept of square root (see Chapter 7). Consequently, the desired page number is close to the number which, when multiplied times itself, yields the product 98,282. This number is called the *square root* of 98,282. Using a calculator, we push the buttons $\boxed{9}\,\boxed{8}\,\boxed{2}\,\boxed{8}\,\boxed{2}\,\boxed{\sqrt{}}$. This yields 313.4996. Thus, a good guess for the desired page number is 313.

PROBLEM 6

Charles and Cynthia play a game called NIM. Each has a box of matchsticks. They take turns putting 1, 2, or 3 matchsticks in a common pile. The person who is able to add a number of matchsticks to the pile to make a total of 24 wins the game. What should be Charles' strategy to be sure he wins the game?

Understanding the Problem

Each of the players chooses 1, 2, or 3 matchsticks to place in the pile. If Charles puts 3 matchsticks in the pile, Cynthia may put 1, 2, or 3 matchsticks in the pile, which makes a total of 4, 5, or 6. It is now Charles' turn. Whoever makes a total of 24 wins the game.

Devising a Plan

Here the strategy of *working backwards* can be used. If there are 21, 22, or 23 matchsticks in the pile, Charles would like it to be his turn because he can win by adding 3, 2, or 1 matchsticks, respectively. However, if there are 20 matchsticks in the pile, Charles would like for it to be Cynthia's turn because she must add 1, 2, or 3, which would give a total of 21, 22, or 23. A *subgoal* for Charles is to reach 20 matchsticks, which forces Cynthia's total to be 21, 22, or 23. The subgoal of 20 matchsticks can be reached if there are 17, 18, or 19 matchsticks in the pile when Cynthia has completed her turn. For this to happen, there should be 16 matchsticks in the pile when Charles has completed his turn. Hence, a new subgoal for Charles is to reach 16 matchsticks. By similar reasoning, we see that Charles' additional subgoals are to reach 12, 8, and 4 matchsticks.

Carrying Out the Plan

Using the reasoning developed in Devising a Plan, we see that the winning strategy for Charles is to be the person who creates a total of 4 matchsticks and then makes the totals of 8, 12, 16, 20, and 24 on successive turns. To do this, Charles should play second; if Cynthia puts 1, 2, or 3 matchsticks in the pile, Charles should add 3, 2, or 1, respectively, to make a total of 4. The totals 8, 12, 16, 20, and 24 can be achieved in a similar fashion.

Looking Back

A related problem is to solve the game in which the person who reaches 24 or more matchsticks loses. Now what is the winning strategy? Other related games can be examined in which different numbers are used as goals or different numbers of matchsticks are allowed to be added. For example, suppose the goal is 21 and 1, 3, or 5 matchsticks can be added each time.

PROBLEM 7

Find the following sum.

$$1 + 4 + 7 + 10 + 13 + \cdots + 3004$$

Understanding the Problem

From our experience with patterns in Section 1-1, we recognize the sequence 1, 4, 7, 10, 13, . . . , 3004 as an arithmetic sequence whose fixed difference is 3. We are asked to find the sum of the numbers in this sequence.

Devising a Plan

A *related problem* is Gauss' problem of finding the sum $1 + 2 + 3 + 4 + \cdots + 100$. In that problem, we paired 1 with 100, 2 with 99, 3 with 98, and so on and observed that there were 50 pairs of numbers, each with a sum of 101. A similar approach in the present problem yields a sum of 3005, as shown in Figure 1-8.

FIGURE 1-8

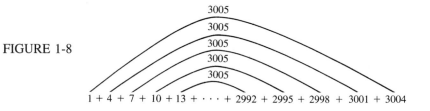

$$3005$$
$$3005$$
$$3005$$
$$3005$$
$$3005$$
$$1 + 4 + 7 + 10 + 13 + \cdots + 2992 + 2995 + 2998 + 3001 + 3004$$

To find the total, we need to know the number of pairs in Figure 1-8 that have a sum of 3005. We could find the number of pairs if we knew the number of terms in the sequence. Thus we have identified a *subgoal,* which is to find the number of terms in the sequence. In previous related problems, we used tables to find a given term or *n*th term. Try a similar approach and make Table 1-9.

TABLE 1-9

Number of Term	Term
1	1
2	$4 = 1 + 3$
3	$7 = 1 + 3 + 3 = 1 + 2 \cdot 3$
4	$10 = 1 + 3 + 3 + 3 = 1 + 3 \cdot 3$
5	$13 = 1 + 3 + 3 + 3 + 3 = 1 + 4 \cdot 3$
.	.
.	.
.	.
?	3004

From Table 1-9, we see that the number of 3s in a term is one less than the number of the term, or the number of each term is one more than the number of 3s in the term. Thus, if we can write 3004 as 1 plus some number of 3s, we can find the number of the term. We see that $3004 = 1 + 3003 = 1 + 1001 \cdot 3$. Thus, the number of terms is 1002, and there are 1002 terms in the given sequence.

Carrying Out the Plan

Because the number of terms is 1002, there are 501 pairs whose sum is 3005. Therefore, the total is 501 · 3005, or 1,505,505.

Looking Back

Using the outlined procedure, we should be able to find the sum of any arithmetic sequence in which we know the first two terms and the last term. Can you find the sum of the first n terms of the arithmetic sequence whose first term is a and whose fixed difference is d?

PROBLEM 8

Choose 12 points on a circle in such a way that when you connect the points two at a time with segments in all possible ways, the greatest number of nonoverlapping regions is formed. How many such nonoverlapping regions are formed? How many such regions are formed for n points?

Understanding the Problem

To better understand what is meant by nonoverlapping regions, consider Figure 1-9. All possible segments joining 2 distinct points separate the circle into 2 regions. With 3 distinct points, 4 regions are formed. With 4 distinct points, 8 regions are formed. The problem is to find the number of regions formed when there are 12 distinct points on a circle connected in pairs by segments in all possible ways. We are then to generalize the problem to n points.

FIGURE 1-9

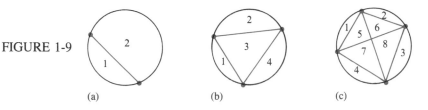

(a)　　　　(b)　　　　(c)

Devising a Plan

One possible strategy to use for 12 points is to *draw a diagram*. To do this, we construct a circle, mark the points, draw the segments, and count the regions. This strategy is not very helpful because the picture is complicated by many segments and regions.

Another strategy, which is suggested by Figure 1-9, is to examine simpler problems and look for a pattern. The first three cases are recorded in Table 1-10.

TABLE 1-10

Number of Points	Number of Regions
2	2
3	4
4	8

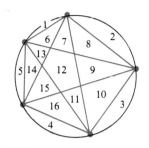

FIGURE 1-10

It appears that as the number of points increases by 1, the number of regions doubles. Based on this observation, it appears that 5 points would yield 16 regions. This is true, as shown in Figure 1-10.

Based on the pattern established, the number of regions for 6 points is 32. To solve the original problem, we could extend Table 1-11 to 12 points and generalize to n points.

TABLE 1-11

Number of Points	Number of Regions
2	2, or 2^1
3	4, or 2^2
4	8, or 2^3
5	16, or 2^4
6	32, or 2^5

Carrying Out the Plan

According to the pattern suggested by the preceding table, the number of regions for 12 points is 2^{11}, or 2048, and the number of regions for n points is 2^{n-1}.

If you are convinced at this point that the problem has been solved, recall that a pattern is very helpful—but there is always a possibility that the pattern may break down, unless we can prove that it works for all cases. A pattern in mathematics leads to an educated guess, not to a sure solution, as discussed in the Looking Back step.

Looking Back

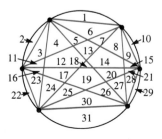

FIGURE 1-11

Part of Looking Back is checking the answer to make sure that it is correct. Because it is very time consuming to count the number of regions formed by 12 points, we check the answer for the number of regions formed by 6 points. The maximum number of regions for 6 points is shown in Figure 1-11. In reality, the answer is *not* 32, as we expected, but 31. Hence, the conclusions for 12 points and n points are not valid. This may be shocking to most of us, who put our complete faith in the continuation of a simple pattern once we have been fortunate enough to discover it.

Although the sequence 1, 2, 4, 8, 16, 32, . . . does not work in the given problem, there is a pattern to the sequence 1, 2, 4, 8, 16, 31, ... The problem was presented as an example of a pattern leading to an incorrect conclusion. It is possible, although somewhat difficult, to find the solution. The complete solution is beyond the scope of this text, but can be found in *Mathematical Morsels* by R. Honsberger, listed in the Selected Bibliography at the end of this chapter.

PROBLEM 9

It is the first day of class for the course in mathematics for elementary school teachers, and there are 20 people present in the room. To become acquainted with one another, each person shakes hands just once with everyone else. How many handshakes take place?

Understanding the Problem

There are 20 people in the room, and each person shakes hands with each other person only once. It takes two people for one handshake; that is, if Maria shakes hands with John and John shakes hands with Maria, this counts as one handshake, not two. The problem is to find the number of handshakes that take place.

Devising a Plan

One plan that would certainly work is to take 20 people and actually count the handshakes. Although this plan provides a solution, it would be nice to find a less elaborate one. First, look at some simpler problems. With one person in the room there are no handshakes. If a second person enters the room, there is 1 handshake (remember, 2 persons shaking hands counts as 1 handshake). If a third person enters the room, he or she shakes hands with each of the other persons present, so there are 2 additional handshakes for a total of $1 + 2$. If a fourth person enters the room, he or she shakes hands with each of the other three members present, so there is an addition of 3 shakes for a total of $1 + 2 + 3$. If a fifth person enters the room, an additional 4 shakes take place.

In Table 1-12 we record the number of handshakes.

TABLE 1-12

Number of People	Number of Handshakes
1	0
2	1
3	$1 + 2 = 3$
4	$1 + 2 + 3 = 6$
5	$1 + 2 + 3 + 4 = 10$

Notice that the last number in the sum, $1 + 2 + 3 + 4$, is one less than the number of people shaking hands. Following this pattern, the answer for 20 people is given by $1 + 2 + 3 + 4 + \cdots + 19$.

Carrying Out the Plan

The technique used by Gauss (Section 1-2) to find certain sums is very useful in completing the problem.

$$1 + 2 + 3 + 4 + \cdots + 19 = \frac{19(20)}{2} = 190$$

Looking Back

Another way of working this problem is to use the strategy of *drawing diagrams* rather than tables. A diagram showing a handshake between persons A and B can be indicated by a line segment connecting A and B as shown.

FIGURE 1-12

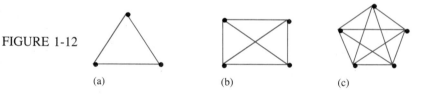

(a)   (b)   (c)

Diagrams showing handshakes for three, four, and five people are given in Figure 1-12. From the diagrams, we see that the problem becomes one of counting the different line segments needed to connect various numbers of points. In looking at the problem for five people (Figure 1-12(c)), we see that A shakes hands with persons $B, C, D,$ and E (4 handshakes). Also, B shakes hands with $A, C, D,$ and E (4 handshakes). In fact, each person shakes hands with 4 other people. Therefore, it appears that there are $5 \cdot 4$, or 20, handshakes. However, notice that the handshake between A and B is counted twice. This dual counting occurs for all 5 people. Consequently, each handshake was counted twice; thus, to obtain the answer, we must divide by 2. The answer is $\frac{(5 \cdot 4)}{2}$, or 10. This approach leads to the answer of 190 handshakes for 20 people and can be generalized for any number of people.

The discussions in this section demonstrate many of the possible problem-solving strategies that can be taught in the elementary grades. The general ideas can be used at almost any grade level. Variations or combinations of these strategies are adaptable to problems encountered in everyday life.

PROBLEM SET 1-2

The first thirteen problems are warm-up problems or puzzles that have been around in one form or another for many years. They will help you begin to think and to understand what is really being asked in a problem. Beware of mind sets. (The strategies discussed in Chapter 1 will be useful in Problems 14–43.)

1. How much dirt is in a hole 2 feet long, 3 feet wide, and 2 feet deep?
2. Two U.S. coins have a total value of 55¢. One coin is not a nickel. What are the two coins?
3. Walter had a dozen apples in his office. He ate all but 4. How many were left?
4. Divide 30 by $\frac{1}{2}$. Add 12. What is the answer?
5. Sal owns 20 blue and 20 brown socks, which he keeps in a drawer in complete disorder. What is the minimum number of socks that he must pull out of the drawer on a dark morning to be sure he has a matching pair?
6. A heavy smoker wakes up in the middle of the night and finds herself out of cigarettes. The stores are closed, so she looks through all the ashtrays for butts. She figures that with five butts she can make one new cigarette. She finds 25 butts and decides they will last her till morning if she smokes only one cigarette every hour. How long does her supply last?
7. You have 8 sticks. Four of them are exactly half the length of the other 4. Enclose 3 squares of equal size with them.
8. Suppose you have only one 5-L (liter) container and one 3-L container. How can you measure exactly 4 L of water if neither container is marked for measuring?
9. It takes 1 hour 20 minutes to drive to the airport, yet the return trip takes only 80 minutes using the same route and driving at what seems to be the same speed. How can this be?
10. What is the minimum number of pitches possible for a pitcher to make in a major league baseball game, assuming he plays the entire game and it is not called prior to completion?
11. Consider the following banking transaction. Deposit $50 and withdraw it as follows:

withdraw $20	leaving $30
withdraw 15	leaving 15
withdraw 9	leaving 6
withdraw 6	leaving 0
$\overline{\$50}$	$\overline{\$51}$

Where did the extra dollar come from? To whom does it belong?

12. John rode out on Wednesday to go hunting. Twenty-three days later, John returned on Wednesday. How is this possible?
13. A businessman bought four pieces of solid-gold chain, each consisting of three links.

He wanted to keep them as an investment, but his wife felt that, joined together, the pieces would make a lovely necklace. A jeweler charges $10.50 to break a link and $10.50 to melt it together again. What is the minimum charge possible to form a necklace using all the pieces?

14. An alternate version of the story of Gauss computing $1 + 2 + 3 + \cdots + 100$ reports that he simply listed the numbers in the following way to discover the sum.

$$
\begin{array}{r}
1 + 2 + 3 + 4 + 5 + \cdots + 98 + 99 + 100 \\
\underline{100 + 99 + 98 + 97 + 96 + \cdots + 3 + 2 + 1} \\
101 + 101 + 101 + 101 + 101 + \cdots + 101 + 101 + 101
\end{array}
$$

Does this method give the same answer? Discuss the advantages of this method over the one described in the text.

15. How many different squares are in the following figure?

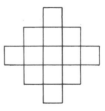

16. What is the largest sum of money—all in coins and no silver dollars—that I could have in my pocket without being able to give change for a dollar, a half-dollar, a quarter, a dime, or a nickel?

17. Arrange the numbers 1 through 9 into a square arranged like the one shown so that the sums of every

row, column, and diagonal are the same. (The result is called a *magic square*.)

18. Molly is building a staircase out of blocks in the pattern shown. How many blocks will it take to build a staircase that is 25 blocks high?

19. How can you cook an egg for exactly 15 minutes if all you have are a 7-minute and an 11-minute timer?
20. How many different ways can you make change for a $50 bill using $5, $10, and $20 bills?
21. How many four-digit numbers have the same digits as 1984?
22. There are four volumes of Shakespeare's collected works on a shelf. The volumes are in order from left to right. The pages of each volume are exactly 2 inches thick. The covers are each $\frac{1}{6}$ inch thick. A bookworm started eating at page 1 of Volume I and ate through to the last page of Volume IV. What is the distance the bookworm traveled?
23. Looking out in the backyard one day, I saw an assortment of boys and dogs. Counting heads, I got 22. Counting feet, I got 68. How many boys and how many dogs were in the yard?
24. A compass and a ruler together cost $4. The compass costs 90¢ more than the ruler. How much does the compass cost?
25. A cat is at the bottom of an 18-foot well. Each day it climbs up 3 feet, and each night it slides back 2 feet. How long will it take the cat to get out of the well?
26. A pioneer moving west had a goose, a bag of corn, and a fox. He came to a river. The ferry was large enough to carry him and one of his possessions. If he were to leave the fox and the goose alone, the fox would eat the goose. If he were to leave the goose and corn alone, the goose would eat the corn. How did he get himself and his possessions across the river?

27. In a horse race:
    (a) Fast Jack finished a length ahead of Lookout.
    (b) Lookout did not finish in last place.
    (c) Null Set finished 7 lengths ahead of Bent Leg.
    (d) Fast Jack finished 7 lengths behind Applejack.
    (e) Bent Leg finished 3 lengths behind Fast Jack.
    What was the finishing position of each horse?
28. Eight marbles all look alike, but one is slightly heavier than the others. By using a balance scale, how can you determine the heavier one in exactly:
    (a) 3 weighings?   (b) 2 weighings?
29. Marc went to the store with $1.00 in change. He had at least one of each coin less than a half-dollar, but he did not have a half-dollar coin.
    (a) What is the least number of coins he could have?
    (b) What is the greatest number of coins he could have?
30. A farmer needs to fence a rectangular piece of land. She wants the length of the field to be 80 feet longer than the width. If she has 1080 feet of fencing material, what should the length and the width of the field be?
31. In the song "The Twelve Days of Christmas," the person received a partridge in a pear tree the first day, two turtle doves and a partridge in a pear tree the second day, three French hens, two turtle doves, and a partridge in a pear tree the third day, and so on. How many gifts did the person receive the twelfth day? What is the total number of gifts the person received in "The Twelve Days of Christmas"?
32. You are given a checkerboard with the two squares on opposite corners removed and a set of dominoes such that each domino can cover two squares on the board. Can the dominoes be arranged in such a way that all of the 62 remaining squares on the board can be covered? If not, why not?

★ 33. Ten women are fishing all in a row in a boat. One seat in the center of the boat is empty. The five women in the front of the boat want to change seats with the five women in the back of the boat. A person can move from her seat to the next empty seat or she can step over one person without capsizing the boat. What is the minimum number of moves needed for the five women in front to change places with the five in back?

34. How many terms are there in the following sequences?
    (a) 1, 3, 5, 7, 9, . . . , 2001
    (b) 2, 5, 8, 11, 14, . . . , 899
    (c) 5, 9, 13, 17, 21, . . . , 601

35. Find the following sums.
    (a) $2 + 4 + 6 + 8 + 10 + \cdots + 1020$
    (b) $1 + 6 + 11 + 16 + 21 + \cdots + 1001$
    (c) $3 + 7 + 11 + 15 + 19 + \cdots + 403$

36. Would you rather work for a month (31 days) and get one million dollars or be paid 1¢ the first day, 2¢ the second day, 4¢ the third day, 8¢ the fourth day, and so on?

37. The following is one version of a game called NIM. Two players and one calculator are needed. Player 1 pushes $\boxed{1}$ or $\boxed{2}$ and $\boxed{+}$. Player 2 pushes $\boxed{1}$ or $\boxed{2}$ and $\boxed{+}$. The players take turns until the target number of 21 is reached. The first player to make the display read 21 is the winner. Determine a strategy for deciding who always wins.

38. Try a game of NIM (see Problem 37) using the digits 1, 2, 3, and 4, with a target number of 104. The first player to reach 104 wins. What is the winning strategy?

39. Try a game of NIM using the digits 3, 5, and 7, with target number 73. The first player to exceed 73 loses. What is the winning strategy?

40. In the game of NIM in Problem 37, two players and one calculator are needed. Player 1 pushes $\boxed{1}$ or $\boxed{2}$ and $\boxed{+}$. Player 2 pushes $\boxed{1}$ or $\boxed{2}$ and $\boxed{+}$, and both try to reach the target number of 21. Now, play Reverse NIM. Instead of $\boxed{+}$, use $\boxed{-}$. Put 21 on the display. Let the new target number be 0. Determine a strategy for winning Reverse NIM.

41. Try Reverse NIM using the digits 1, 2, and 3, starting with 24 on the display. The target number is 0. What is the winning strategy?

42. Try Reverse NIM using the digits 3, 5, and 7, starting with 73 on the display. The first player to display a negative number loses. What is the winning strategy?

★ 43. Find a simple expression for the sum

$$1 + 2 + 2^2 + 2^3 + \cdots + 2^{n-1}$$

(*Hint:* Use the strategy of examining a simpler case.)

Laboratory Activity

Place a half-dollar, a quarter, and a nickel in position A as shown in the figure. Try to move these coins, one at a time, to position C. At no time may a larger coin be placed on a smaller coin. Coins may be placed in position B. How many moves does it take? Now, add a penny to the pile and see how many moves it takes. This is a simple case of the famous Tower of Hanoi problem, in which ancient Brahman priests were required to move a pile of 64 disks of decreasing size, after which the world would end. How long would this take at a rate of one move per second?

SOLUTION TO THE PRELIMINARY PROBLEM

Understanding the Problem

There were 20 people at a round table for dinner, who shook hands with the people on their immediate right and left. At the end of the dinner, each person got up and shook hands with everybody except with thc people who sat to the immediate right or left at dinner. We are asked to find the number of handshakes that took place after dinner.

Devising a Plan

One way to solve the problem is to consider a related problem. One related problem is Problem 9, where—in a group of 20 people—each person shakes hands with everyone else. In order to solve the present problem, we need to subtract the number of handshakes that took place during dinner from the answer to Problem 9. To determine how many handshakes took place during dinner, we first consider the simpler problem of how many hands a single person shook. For example, if Rachel sat between David and Jonathan, she shook hands with each of them, which counts as two handshakes. Similarly, each of the guests made two handshakes at dinner, so 20 guests made $20 \cdot 2$, or 40, handshakes. However, in this way each handshake was counted twice because, for example, Rachel's handshake with David is the same as David's handshake with Rachel. Each of these handshakes was counted among the 40 handshakes at dinner. Thus, the actual number of handshakes during dinner is half of 40, or 20.

Carrying Out the Plan

From Problem 9, we know that if 20 people shook hands with each other, the number of handshakes would have been 190. Because the number of handshakes at the dinner table was 20, the number of handshakes that took place after dinner was $190 - 20$, or 170.

Looking Back

Another way of approaching this problem is to use the strategy of drawing a diagram. We may represent the 20 people sitting at a round table by 20 points on a circle. If we connect each point to its neighboring two points, we obtain a figure with 20 sides, as shown in Figure 1-13. The sides of the figure represent the handshakes that took place during dinner. Since the figure has 20 sides, we subtract 20 from the 190 total handshakes found in Problem 9 and obtain 170 for the answer to the problem.

Another approach to the problem, which does not use the result of Problem 9, is as follows. After dinner, all the people shook hands with everybody except

FIGURE 1-13

with themselves and their two neighbors (one who sat on the left and one on the right). Hence, each person shook hands with $20 - 3$, or 17, people. Because there are 20 people, we may count $20 \cdot 17$ handshakes. However, every handshake is counted twice; therefore, the actual number of handshakes is $\dfrac{20 \cdot 17}{2}$, or 170.

CHAPTER OUTLINE

I. Mathematical patterns
  A. Patterns are an important part of problem solving.
  B. Patterns are used in **inductive reasoning** to form conjectures. A **conjecture** is a statement that is thought to be true but has not yet been proven.
  C. A **sequence** is a group of terms in a definite order.
    1. **Arithmetic sequence:** Each successive term is obtained from the previous one by the addition of a fixed number.
    2. **Geometric sequence:** Each successive term is obtained from its predecessor by multiplying it by a fixed number.
    3. Finding differences for a sequence is one technique for finding the next terms.
II. Problem solving
  A. Problem solving should be guided by the following four-step process:

  1. Understanding the Problem
  2. Devising a Plan
  3. Carrying Out the Plan
  4. Looking Back
  B. Important problem-solving strategies include:
    1. Look for a pattern.
    2. Examine related problems and determine if the same technique can be applied.
    3. Examine a simpler or special case of the problem to gain insight to the solution of the original problem.
    4. Make a table, diagram, or model.
    5. Write an equation.
    6. Use trial and error.
    7. Work backwards.
    8. Identify a subgoal.
  C. Beware of mind sets!

SELECTED BIBLIOGRAPHY

Selected references are given. An excellent bibliography is available in *Problem Solving in School Mathematics,* 1980 *Yearbook,* published by National Council of Teachers of Mathematics.

Bernard, J. "Creating Problem-Solving Experiences with Ordinary Arithmetic Processes." *Arithmetic Teacher* 30 (September 1982):52–53.

Billstein, R. "Checkerboard Mathematics." *The Mathematics Teacher* 86 (December 1975):640–646.

Bruni, J. "Problem Solving for the Primary Grades." *Arithmetic Teacher* 29 (February 1982):10–15.

Burns, M. "How to Teach Problem Solving." *Arithmetic Teacher* 29 (February 1982):46–49.

De Vault, M. "Doing Mathematics is Problem Solving." *Arithmetic Teacher* 28 (April 1981):40–43.

Duea, J., and E. Ockenga. "Classroom Problem Solving with Calculators." *Arithmetic Teacher* 29 (February 1982):50–51.

Fisher, B. "Calculator Games: Combining Skills and Problem Solving." *Arithmetic Teacher* 27 (December 1979):40–41.

Gathany, T. "Involving Students in Problem Solving." *The Mathematics Teacher* 72 (November 1979):617–621.

Green, D. "Ant, Aardvark and Fudge Brownies." *Arithmetic Teacher* 27 (March 1979):38–39.

Greenes, C., R. Spungin, and J. Dombrowski. *Problem-mathics.* Palo Alto, Calif.: Creative Publications, 1977.

Greenes, C., J. Gregory, and D. Seymour. *Successful Problem-Solving Techniques.* Palo Alto, Calif.: Creative Publications, 1977.

Hecht, A. "Environmental Problem Solving," *Arithmetic Teacher* 27 (December 1979):42–43.

Honsberger, R. *Mathematical Morsels.* Washington, D. C.: The Mathematical Association of America, 1978.

Hughes, B. *Thinking Through Problems.* Palo Alto, Calif.: Creative Publications, 1976.

Krulik, S. "Problem Solving: Some Considerations." *Arithmetic Teacher* 25 (December 1977):51–52.

LeBlanc, J. "You Can Teach Problem Solving." *Arithmetic Teacher* 25 (November 1977):16–19.

LeBlanc, J. "Teaching Textbook Story Problems." *Arithmetic Teacher* 29 (February 1982):52–54.

Lee, K. "Guiding Young Children in Successful Problem Solving." *Arithmetic Teacher* 29 (January 1982):15–17.

Liedtke, W. "The Young Child as a Problem Solver." *The Arithmetic Teacher* 25 (April 1977):333–338.

Linquist, M. "Problem Solving with Five Easy Pieces." *Arithmetic Teacher* 25 (November 1977):7–10.

Lott, J. "Behold! A Magic Square." *The Arithmetic Teacher* 24 (March 1977):228–229.

Maletsky, E. "Problem Solving for the Junior High School." *Arithmetic Teacher* 29 (February 1982):20–24.

Masse, M. "More Problems Please." *Arithmetic Teacher* 26 (December 1978):11–14.

Morris, J. "Problem Solving with Calculators." *Arithmetic Teacher* 25 (April 1978):24–26.

Papert, S. *Mindstorms*. New York: Basic Books, 1980.

Polya, G. *How to Solve It*. Princeton, N.J.: Princeton University Press, 1957.

Polya, G. *Mathematical Discovery*. Vol. I. New York: John Wiley & Sons, 1962.

Polya, G. *Mathematical Discovery*. Vol. II, New York: John Wiley & Sons, 1965.

Spencer, J., and F. Lester. "Second Graders Can be Problem Solvers." *Arithmetic Teacher* 29 (September 1981):15–17.

Schmalz, S. "Classroom Activities for Problem Solving." *Arithmetic Teacher* 29 (September 1981):42–43.

Suydam, M., and F. Weaver. "Research on Problem Solving: Implications for Elementary School Classrooms." *Arithmetic Teacher* 25 (November 1977):40–42.

Szetela, W. "Analogy and Problem Solving: A Tool for Helping Children to Develop a Better Concept of Capacity." *Arithmetic Teacher* 27 (March 1980):18–22.

Thomas, D. "Geometry in the Middle School: Problem Solving with Trapezoids." *Arithmetic Teacher* 26 (February 1979): 20–21.

Underhill, R. "Teaching Word Problems to First Graders." *Arithmetic Teacher* 25 (November 1977):54–56.

Walter, M. "Frame Geometry: An Example in Posing and Solving Problems." *Arithmetic Teacher* 28 (October 1980):16–18.

Wheatley, G. "The Right Hemisphere's Role in Problem Solving." *Arithmetic Teacher* 25 (November 1977):36–39.

Whitin, D. "Patterns with Square Numbers." *Arithmetic Teacher* 27 (December 1979):38–39.

Wickelgren, W. *How to Solve Problems*. San Francisco: W. H. Freeman, 1974.

Worth, J. "Problem Solving in the Intermediate Grades: Helping Your Students Learn to Solve Problems." *Arithmetic Teacher* 29 (February 1982):16–19.

Zalewski, D. "Magic Triangles—More Discoveries!" *Arithmetic Teacher* 27 (September 1979): 46–47.

Zur, M. and F. Silverman. "Problem Solving for Teachers." *Arithmetic Teacher* 28 (October 1980):48–50.

Zweng, M. "The Problem of Solving Story Problems." *Arithmetic Teacher* 27 (September 1979):2–3.

Sets and Relations 2

PRELIMINARY PROBLEM

At the end of a tour of the Grand Canyon, several guides were talking about the people on the latest British-American tour. The guides could not remember the total number in the group; however, together they compiled the following statistics about the group. It contained 26 British females, 17 American women, 17 American males, 29 girls, 44 British citizens, 29 women, and 24 British adults. Find the total number of people in the group.

INTRODUCTION

set theory

It was George Cantor, in the years 1871–1884, who created a new and special area of mathematics called **set theory.** Cantor was born in Russia and educated in Germany. Much of his professional life was spent at the University of Halle, now in East Germany. Cantor's later years were spent in controversy over his work on set theory, causing him to spend some time in a mental institution. He finally won recognition for his work before he died. His theories have had a profound effect on mathematical research and on the teaching of mathematics.

The language of set theory was introduced into elementary schools in the 1960s in the post-Sputnik era. It contained words such as *set, subset, union,* and *intersection.* In the 1970s, numerous people felt that the new language caused confusion for children, as well as for teachers and other adults. The cartoon illustrates the feelings of many of these people.

© 1965 United Feature Syndicate, Inc.

However, the basic set concepts clarify many mathematical ideas and, in an appropriate form, are simple enough to be taught in the early grades.

2-1   DESCRIBING SETS

set
elements
members

In mathematics, undefined terms are usually terms that are very basic, and we usually have a clear picture of them. The word *set* is such a term. In mathematics, a **set** is any collection or group of objects. The individual objects in a set are called **elements,** or **members,** of the set. If we are speaking of the set of students in your mathematics class, each student is an element or a member of that set. If we consider the set of letters in the English alphabet, each letter is an element of that set. We let capital letters stand for sets and use braces to enclose the elements of the set. The set of letters of the English alphabet can be written as

$A = \{a, b, c, d, e, f, g, h, i, j, k, l, m, n, o, p, q, r, s, t, u, v, w, x, y, z\}$

The set consisting of the first four counting numbers can be written as

$B = \{1, 2, 3, 4\}$

The order in which the elements are written makes no difference, and each element is listed only once. The set of letters in the word "book" could be written as $\{b, o, k\}$.

well defined

For a given set to be useful in mathematics, it must be **well defined.** This means that if we are given a set and some particular object, the object does or does not belong to the set. For example, the set of all citizens of Hong Kong who ate rice on January 1, 1984, is well defined. We do not know if a particular resident of Hong Kong ate rice or not, but we do know that person either did or did not.

Consider the set A consisting of the letters of the English alphabet. This set is well defined. We know that m is an element of set A. This can be written in symbols as $m \in A$. The number 12 is not an element of A. This is written as $12 \notin A$.

Consider the set of all the tall students in your mathematics class. This set is not well defined because the decision as to whether a student belongs to this set can be left to personal opinion. Different people have different views on what it means to be tall. Similarly, the set of good mathematics teachers is not well defined because not everyone agrees on the definition of a good mathematics teacher.

natural numbers
counting numbers

We use sets to define mathematical terms. For example, the set of **natural, or counting, numbers** is defined by the following.

$$N = \{1, 2, 3, 4, \ldots\}$$

infinite set

The three ellipsis dots indicate that this sequence continues indefinitely. The set of natural numbers N is an example of an infinite set. An **infinite set,** informally described, is a set that contains an unlimited number of elements. In contrast, a set

finite set

is called a **finite set** if the number of elements in the set is zero or a natural number. For example, the set of letters in the English alphabet is a finite set because it contains exactly 26 elements.

equal sets

Two sets are **equal** if they contain exactly the same elements. The order in which the elements are listed does not matter. If A and B are equal, written $A = B$, then every element of A is an element of B, *and* every element of B is an element of A. If A does not equal B, we write $A \neq B$.

Example 2-1

Tell which of the following pairs of sets are equal.

(a) $A = \{a, b, c\}$ and $B = \{b, c, a\}$
(b) $C = \{a, 1, 2\}$ and $D = \{a, 1, 3\}$
(c) $E = \{2, 4, 6\}$ and $G = \{2, 4, 6, 8, 10\}$

Solution

(a) $A = B$ (b) $C \neq D$ (c) $E \neq G$

set-builder notation

Sometimes the individual elements of a set are not known or they are too numerous to list. In these cases the elements are indicated using **set-builder notation.** The set of animals in the San Diego Zoo can be written as

$$Z = \{x \mid x \text{ is an animal in the San Diego Zoo}\}$$

This is read, "Z is the set of all elements x such that x is an animal in the San Diego Zoo." The vertical line is read, "such that."

Example 2-2

Write the following sets using set-builder notation.

(a) {51, 52, 53, 54, . . . , 498, 499}
(b) {2, 4, 6, 8, 10, . . .}

Solution

(a) $\{x \mid x$ is a natural number greater than 50 and less than 500$\}$
(b) $\{x \mid x$ is an even natural number$\}$

Two examples of sets with no elements are the following.

$F = \{x \mid x$ was a female president of the United States before 1900$\}$

$G = \{x \mid x$ is a natural number less than 1$\}$

empty set
null set

    A set that contains no elements is called an **empty set,** or **null set.** The empty set is designated by the symbols $\varnothing$ or { }. The empty set is often incorrectly recorded as $\{\varnothing\}$. This set is not empty. It contains one element, namely, $\varnothing$. Likewise, {0} does not represent the empty set.

universal set
universe

    The **universal set,** or the **universe,** is the set that contains all elements being considered in a given discussion. The universal set is denoted by U. While the empty set never changes, the universal set may vary from one discussion to another. For this reason, you should be aware of what the universal set is in any given problem. Suppose $U = \{x \mid x$ is a person living in California$\}$ and $F = \{x \mid x$ is a female living in California$\}$. The universal set and set F can be represented by a diagram. The universal set is usually indicated by a large rectangle, and particular sets are indicated by geometric figures inside the rectangle as shown in Figure 2-1. This figure is an example of a **Venn diagram,** named after the Englishman John Venn, who used diagrams like Figure 2-1 to illustrate ideas in logic.

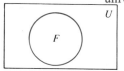

FIGURE 2-1

Venn diagram

    Suppose $U = \{1, 2, 3, 4, 5, 6\}$ and $A = \{1, 3, 5\}$. The set of all the elements of the universe that are *not* in A is {2, 4, 6} and is called the **complement** of A.

complement

DEFINITION

The **complement** of a set A, written $\bar{A}$, is the set of all elements in the universal set U that are not in A.

Using set-builder notation, $\bar{A} = \{x \mid x \in U$ and $x \notin A\}$.

Example 2-3

If $U = \{a, b, c, d\}$ and $B = \{c, d\}$, find: (a) $\bar{B}$; (b) $\bar{U}$; (c) $\bar{\varnothing}$.

Solution

(a) $\bar{B} = \{a, b\}$ (b) $\bar{U} = \varnothing$ (c) $\bar{\varnothing} = U$

Example 2-4

If $U = \{x \mid x$ is an animal in the zoo$\}$ and $S = \{x \mid x$ is a snake in the zoo$\}$, find $\bar{S}$.

Solution | Because the individual animals in the zoo are not known, $\bar{S}$ must be described using set-builder notation.

$$\bar{S} = \{x \mid x \text{ is an animal in the zoo that is not a snake}\}$$

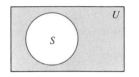

FIGURE 2-2

Venn diagrams can also be used to represent complements. The shaded region in Figure 2-2 represents $\bar{S}$.

Consider the sets $U = \{1, 2, 3, 4, 5, 6, 7, 8, 9, 10\}$, $A = \{1, 2, 3, 4, 5, 6\}$, and $B = \{2, 4, 6\}$. Notice that all the elements of B are contained in A. We say that

subset | B is a **subset** of A and write $B \subseteq A$. In general, we have the following definition.

DEFINITION | B is a **subset** of A, written $B \subseteq A$, if and only if every element of B is also an element of A.

This definition allows B to be equal to A. The definition is written with the phrase "if and only if," which means "if B is a subset of A, then every element of B is also an element of A, and if every element of B is also an element of A, then B is a subset of A. (All definitions can be written using "if and only if.")

proper subset | If B is a subset of A and B is not equal to A, then B is called a **proper subset** of A, written $B \subset A$. This means that every element of B is contained in A and there exists at least one element of A that is not in B.

Example 2-5 | Given $U = \{1, 2, 3, 4, 5\}$, $D = \{1, 3, 5\}$, and $E = \{1, 3\}$.

(a) Which sets are subsets of each other?
(b) Which sets are proper subsets of each other?

Solution | (a) $D \subseteq U$, $E \subseteq U$, $E \subseteq D$, $D \subseteq D$, $E \subseteq E$, and $U \subseteq U$.
(b) $D \subset U$, $E \subset U$, and $E \subset D$.

When a set A is not a subset of another set B, we write $A \not\subseteq B$. To show that $A \not\subseteq B$, we must find at least one element of A that is not in B. If $A = \{1, 3, 5\}$ and $B = \{1, 2, 3\}$, then A is not a subset of B because there is an element—namely, 5—belonging to A but not to B. Likewise, $B \not\subseteq A$ because there exists an element—namely, 2—belonging to B but not to A. (Note that $\{2\} \subseteq \{1, 2\}$ and $2 \in \{1, 2\}$, but $\{2\} \notin \{1, 2\}$ and $2 \not\subseteq \{1, 2\}$.)

We now use the techniques of Chapter 1 to investigate two problems involving sets.

PROBLEM 1

Of which sets, if any, is the empty set a subset?

Solution

To investigate this problem, we use the strategy of looking at a special case. For example, is it true that $\varnothing \subseteq \{1, 2\}$? Suppose $\varnothing \nsubseteq \{1, 2\}$. Then there must be some element in $\varnothing$ that is not in $\{1, 2\}$. Since the empty set has no elements, there cannot be an element in the empty set that is not in $\{1, 2\}$. Consequently, $\varnothing \nsubseteq \{1, 2\}$ is false, and therefore $\varnothing \subseteq \{1, 2\}$, is true. The same reasoning can be applied in the case of the empty set and any other set. *Thus, for any set A, $\varnothing \subseteq A$.* In particular, $\varnothing \subseteq \varnothing$.

PROBLEM 2

How many subsets does a set with n elements have?

To emphasize the problem-solving process, we outline the solution using the four problem-solving steps.

Understanding the Problem

There are n elements in a set. We are to determine a formula for finding the number of subsets for this set, no matter what n is.

Devising a Plan

To obtain a general formula, try some simple cases first.

1. If $B = \{a\}$, then B has 2 subsets, $\varnothing$ and $\{a\}$.
2. If $C = \{a, b\}$, then C has 4 subsets, namely, $\varnothing$, $\{a\}$, $\{b\}$, and $\{a, b\}$.
3. If $D = \{a, b, c\}$, then D has 8 subsets, namely, $\varnothing$, $\{a\}$, $\{b\}$, $\{c\}$, $\{a, b\}$, $\{a, c\}$, $\{b, c\}$, and $\{a, b, c\}$.

Using the information from these cases, we make a table and search for a pattern.

TABLE 2-1

Number of Elements	Number of Subsets
1	2, or 2^1
2	4, or 2^2
3	8, or 2^3
.	.
.	.
.	.

Table 2-1 suggests that for 4 elements, there are 2^4, or 16, subsets. Is this guess correct? If $E = \{a, b, c, d\}$, then all the subsets of $D = \{a, b, c\}$ are also subsets of E. Eight new subsets are also formed by adjoining the element d to each of the 8 subsets of D. The 8 new subsets are $\{d\}$, $\{a, d\}$, $\{b, d\}$, $\{c, d\}$, $\{a, b, d\}$, $\{a, c, d\}$, $\{b, c, d\}$, and $\{a, b, c, d\}$. Thus, there are twice as many subsets of set E (with 4 elements) as there are of set D (with 3 elements). There are indeed 16, or 2^4, subsets of a set with 4 elements. Extending the pattern, there are 2^5, or 32, subsets of a set with 5 elements, and 2^6, or 64, subsets of a set with 6 elements.

Carrying Out the Plan

Notice that in each case the number of elements and the power of 2, which is used to obtain the number of subsets, match exactly. Thus, if there are n elements in a set, there are 2^n subsets that can be formed.

Looking Back

In this problem, the answer is based on more than simply observing patterns in a table. It was observed that adding one more element to a set doubled the number of possible subsets. The formula 2^n for the number of subsets of a set with n elements is based on this doubling factor. If we apply this formula to the empty set—that is, when $n = 0$—then $2^0 = 1$ because the empty set has only one subset. The fact that $a^0 = 1$, $a \in N$, is investigated in Chapter 6. Another question this problem suggests is: Given a set with n elements, how many subsets, each having exactly one element, exactly two elements, exactly three elements, and—in general—exactly k elements, are there?

PROBLEM SET 2-1

1. Which of the following sets are well defined?
   (a) The set of wealthy school teachers.
   (b) The set of great books.
   (c) The set of natural numbers greater than 100.
2. Write the following sets by listing the members or using set-builder notation.
   (a) The set of letters in the word *mathematics*.
   (b) The set of pink elephants taking this class.
   (c) The set of months whose names begin with J.
   (d) The set of natural numbers greater than 20.
   (e) The set of states in the United States.

3. Rewrite the following statements using mathematical symbols.
   (a) B is equal to the set whose elements are x, y, z, and w.
   (b) 3 is not an element of set B.
   (c) The set consisting of the elements 1 and 2 is a proper subset of the set consisting of the elements 1, 2, 3, and 4.
   (d) The set D is not a subset of set E.
   (e) The set A is not a proper subset of set B.
4. Describe three sets of which you are a member.

5. If U is the set of all college students and A is the set of all college students with a straight-A average, describe $\overline{A}$.

6. Indicate which symbol, $\in$ or $\notin$, makes each of the following statements true.
   (a) 3 _____ $\{1, 2, 3\}$ (b) 2 _____ $\{2\}$
   (c) 0 _____ $\varnothing$ (d) a _____ $\varnothing$
   (e) $\{1\}$ _____ $\{1, 2\}$ (f) $\varnothing$ _____ 1
   (g) $\varnothing$ _____ $\varnothing$ (h) $\{1, 2\}$ _____ $\{1, 2\}$
   (i) $\{1\}$ _____ $\{\{1\}, \varnothing\}$ (j) $\{1, 2\}$ _____ $\{1\}$

7. Indicate which symbol, $\subseteq$ or $\nsubseteq$, makes each part of Problem 6 true.

8. Find the set of all subsets of $\{x, y, z\}$.

9. (a) If $A = \{a, b, c, d, e, f\}$, how many subsets does A have? How many proper subsets does A have?
   (b) If a set B has n elements where n is some natural number, how many proper subsets does B have?

10. Which of the following represent equal sets?

$A = \{a, b, c, d\}$

$B = \{x, y, z, w\}$

$C = \{c, d, a, b\}$

$D = \{x \mid x$ is one of the first four letters of the English alphabet$\}$

$E = \varnothing$

$F = \{\varnothing\}$

$G = \{0\}$

$H = \{\ \}$

11. If $B \subset C$, what is the least possible number of elements in C? Why?

12. If $C \subseteq D$ and $D \subseteq C$, what other relationship exists between C and D?

13. Is $\varnothing$ a proper subset of every set? Why?

14. Is it always true that $A \nsubseteq B$ implies $B \subseteq A$? Why?

15. Classify each of the following as true or false. If you answer "false," tell why.
    (a) $\{\ \} = \varnothing$
    (b) $\{\varnothing\} = \{\ \}$
    (c) If $A = B$, then $A \subseteq B$
    (d) If $A \subseteq B$, then $A \subset B$
    (e) If $A \subset B$, then $A \subseteq B$
    (f) If $A \subseteq B$, then $A = B$

The brain teaser is a version of Russell's paradox, named after Bertrand Russell. Russell's paradox was one of the causes of controversy over Cantor's set theory.

BRAIN TEASER

A soldier, Joe, was ordered to shave those soldiers, and only those soldiers, of his platoon who did not shave themselves. Let $A = \{x \mid x$ is a soldier who shaves himself$\}$ and $B = \{x \mid x$ is a soldier who does not shave himself$\}$. Notice that every soldier must belong to one set or the other. To which set does Joe belong?

2-2   OPERATIONS AND PROPERTIES OF SETS

Suppose that during the fall quarter, one high school wants to mail a survey to all students who are enrolled in both algebra and biology classes. To do this, the school officials must identify these students. If A is the set of students taking algebra courses during the fall quarter and B is the set of students taking biology courses during the fall quarter, then the desired set of students for the survey is

intersection   called the **intersection** of A and B.

DEFINITION

> The **intersection** of two sets A and B, written $A \cap B$, is the set of all elements common to both A and B.

Using set-builder notation, we write this definition as

$$A \cap B = \{x \mid x \in A \text{ and } x \in B\}$$

Example 2-6

Find the intersections for each of the following pairs of sets.

(a) $A = \{$Charlie, Snoopy, Lucy$\}$ and $B = \{$Snoopy, Lucy, Linus$\}$
(b) $M = \{1, 2, 3, 4, 5\}$ and $N = \{6, 7, 8\}$
(c) $H = \{1, 2, 3, 4\}$ and $J = \varnothing$
(d) $F = \{1, 2, 3\}$ and $G = \{1, 2, 3, 4, 5\}$

Solution

(a) $A \cap B = \{$Snoopy, Lucy$\}$ (b) $M \cap N = \varnothing$
(c) $H \cap J = \varnothing$ (d) $F \cap G = \{1, 2, 3\}$

disjoint sets

When sets such as M and N in Example 2-6(b) have no elements in common, we call them **disjoint sets.** In other words, two sets A and B are disjoint if and only if $A \cap B = \varnothing$.

commutative property
of set intersection

In Example 2-6(d), $F \cap G = \{1, 2, 3\}$. The same result is obtained by finding $G \cap F$; that is, $F \cap G = G \cap F = \{1, 2, 3\}$. This is an example of the **commutative property of set intersection.** This property holds in general.

Property

> **Commutative Property of Set Intersection.** For all sets A and B:
>
> $A \cap B = B \cap A$

Venn diagrams can be used to picture the intersection of sets. If the exact elements of two sets A and B are unknown, a figure like Figure 2-3(a) is used to depict the sets. Set A is indicated by horizontal lines. Set B is indicated by vertical lines. The intersection of two sets is indicated by the shading.

FIGURE 2-3

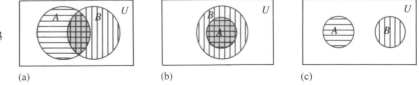

(a)   (b)   (c)

If we know that $A \subseteq B$, then Figure 2-3(b) may be used to show that $A \cap B = A$. If we know that sets A and B are disjoint, then Figure 2-3(c) may be used to show that $A \cap B = \varnothing$.

We can also form a new set from two given sets using an operation called union. For example, if A is the set of students taking algebra courses during the fall quarter and B is the set of students taking biology courses during the fall quarter, then the set of students taking either algebra or biology or both is the union of sets A and B.

DEFINITION

> The **union** of two sets A and B, written $A \cup B$, is the set of all elements in A or in B or in both A and B.

Using set-builder notation, we write this definition as $A \cup B = \{x \mid x \in A \text{ or } x \in B\}$.

The key word in the definition of union is "or." In everyday language, the word "or" usually means one thing or another but not both, as in "I am going to the ball game or to the play." In mathematics, "or" usually means "one or the other or both."

Example 2-7

Find the union of the sets in each of the following pairs.

(a) $A = \{$Charlie, Snoopy, Lucy$\}$ and $B = \{$Snoopy, Lucy, Linus, Schroeder$\}$
(b) $E = \{1, 2, 3\}$ and $F = \{2, 3, 4, 5\}$
(c) $C = \{1, 2\}$ and $D = \varnothing$
(d) $X = \{1, 2, 3, 4\}$ and $Y = \{5, 6, 7, 8\}$
(e) $F = \{2, 3, 4, 5\}$ and $E = \{1, 2, 3\}$

Solution

(a) $A \cup B = \{$Charlie, Snoopy, Lucy, Linus, Schroeder$\}$
(b) $E \cup F = \{1, 2, 3, 4, 5\}$
(c) $C \cup D = \{1, 2\} = C$
(d) $X \cup Y = \{1, 2, 3, 4, 5, 6, 7, 8\}$
(e) $F \cup E = \{1, 2, 3, 4, 5\}$

Although some elements are listed in both sets, they are listed only once in the union of the sets. Set union is also a commutative operation. Example 2-7(b) and (e) shows $E \cup F = F \cup E$. The **commutative property of set union** also holds in general.

commutative property
of set union

Property

> **Commutative Property of Set Union.** For all sets A and B:
>
> $A \cup B = B \cup A.$

Venn diagrams showing the union of sets A and B for three different conditions are given in Figure 2-4. In each case, the union is indicated by the shaded region.

In Figure 2-4(c), $A \subseteq B$ and $A \cup B = B$.

FIGURE 2-4

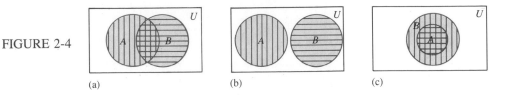

(a)   (b)   (c)

Example 2-8

Draw a Venn diagram for $\overline{A \cup B}$.

Solution

Since the complement bar is over the expression $A \cup B$, first find $A \cup B$ and then find its complement. $\overline{A \cup B}$ is the shaded portion of Figure 2-5.

FIGURE 2-5

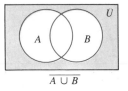

$\overline{A \cup B}$

complement of A relative to B

If A is the set of students taking algebra classes during fall quarter and B is the set of students taking biology classes, then the set of all the students taking biology classes but not algebra classes is called the **complement of A relative to B.**

DEFINITION

The **complement of A relative to B,** written $B - A$, is the set of all elements in B that are not in A.

The expression $B - A$ is also read, "the set difference of B and A." Using set-builder notation, $B - A = \{x \mid x \in B \text{ and } x \notin A\}$. A Venn diagram representing $B - A$ is shown in Figure 2-6(a). A Venn diagram for $B \cap \overline{A}$ is given in Figure 2-6(b). These diagrams imply $B - A = B \cap \overline{A}$.

FIGURE 2-6

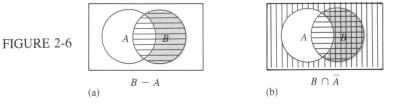

$B - A$ $B \cap \overline{A}$

(a)   (b)

Example 2-9

If $U = \{a, b, c, d, e, f, g\}$, $A = \{d, e, f\}$, and $B = \{a, b, c, d, e\}$, find:

(a) $B - A$ (b) $A - B$ (c) $A \cap \overline{B}$ (d) $A - A$

Solution

(a) $B - A = \{a, b, c, d, e\} - \{d, e, f\} = \{a, b, c\}$
(b) $A - B = \{d, e, f\} - \{a, b, c, d, e\} = \{f\}$
(c) $A \cap \bar{B} = \{d, e, f\} \cap \{f, g\} = \{f\}$
(d) $A - A = \{d, e, f\} - \{d, e, f\} = \varnothing$

Is grouping important when two different set operations are involved? For example, is it true that $A \cap (B \cup C) = (A \cap B) \cup C$? To investigate this, let $A = \{a, b, c, d\}$, $B = \{c, d, e\}$, and $C = \{d, e, f, g\}$.

$$A \cap (B \cup C) = \{a, b, c, d\} \cap (\{c, d, e\} \cup \{d, e, f, g\})$$
$$= \{a, b, c, d\} \cap \{c, d, e, f, g\}$$
$$= \{c, d\}$$

$$(A \cap B) \cup C = (\{a, b, c, d\} \cap \{c, d, e\}) \cup \{d, e, f, g\}$$
$$= \{c, d\} \cup \{d, e, f, g\}$$
$$= \{c, d, e, f, g\}.$$

In this case, $A \cap (B \cup C) \neq (A \cap B) \cup C$. We have found what is called a

counterexample

counterexample in mathematics, that is, an example that illustrates that a general statement is not always true. One counterexample is enough to make a conjecture false. Thus, in general, $A \cap (B \cup C) \neq (A \cap B) \cup C$. (Drawing Venn diagrams to show that $A \cap (B \cup C) \neq (A \cap B) \cup C$ and $A \cup (B \cap C) \neq (A \cup B) \cap C$ is left as an exercise.)

To discover an expression that is equal to $A \cap (B \cup C)$, consider the Venn diagram for $A \cap (B \cup C)$ shown by the shaded region in Figure 2-7. According to the figure, two regions, $A \cap C$ and $A \cap B$, are parts (subsets) of the shaded region. The union of these two regions is the entire shaded region of the figure. Thus, this shaded region can be identified as $(A \cap C) \cup (A \cap B)$. Consequently, $A \cap (B \cup C) = (A \cap B) \cup (A \cap C)$. A similar approach illustrates that $A \cup (B \cap C) = (A \cup B) \cap (A \cup C)$. These properties that relate intersection and union are called

distributive properties

distributive properties.

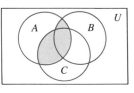

FIGURE 2-7

Properties

For all sets A, B, and C:
1. **Distributive property of set intersection over union.**

   $$A \cap (B \cup C) = (A \cap B) \cup (A \cap C)$$

2. **Distributive property of set union over intersection.**

   $$A \cup (B \cap C) = (A \cup B) \cap (A \cup C)$$

Example 2-10

If $A = \{a, b, c\}$, $B = \{b, c, d\}$, and $C = \{d, e, f, g\}$, verify the distributive property of intersection over union for these sets.

Solution

$$A \cap (B \cup C) = \{a, b, c\} \cap (\{b, c, d\} \cup \{d, e, f, g\})$$
$$= \{a, b, c\} \cap \{b, c, d, e, f, g\}$$
$$= \{b, c\}$$
$$(A \cap B) \cup (A \cap C) = (\{a, b, c\} \cap \{b, c, d\}) \cup (\{a, b, c\} \cap \{d, e, f, g\})$$
$$= \{b, c\} \cup \varnothing$$
$$= \{b, c\}$$

Thus, $A \cap (B \cup C) = (A \cap B) \cup (A \cap C)$.

The following properties of set operations can also be verified.

Properties

1. **Associative Properties**   For all sets A, B, and C:
   (a) $(A \cap B) \cap C = A \cap (B \cap C)$ Associative property of set intersection.
   (b) $(A \cup B) \cup C = A \cup (B \cup C)$ Associative property of set union.
2. **Identity Properties**   For every set A and the universe U:
   (a) $A \cap U = U \cap A = A$ U is the identity for set intersection.
   (b) $A \cup \varnothing = \varnothing \cup A = A$ $\varnothing$ is the identity for set union.
3. **Complement Properties**   For every set A and the universe U:
   (a) $\overline{U} = \varnothing$ (b) $\overline{\varnothing} = U$ (c) $A \cap \overline{A} = \varnothing$
   (d) $A \cup \overline{A} = U$ (e) $\overline{\overline{A}} = A$

Venn diagrams can be used as problem-solving tools, as shown in the examples below. In these examples, the given information is modeled using diagrams.

Example 2-11

Use set notation to describe the shaded portions of the Venn diagrams in Figure 2-8(a) and (b).

FIGURE 2-8

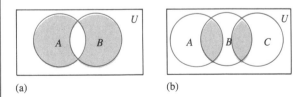

(a)   (b)

Solution

The solutions can be described in many different, but equivalent, forms.

(a) $(A \cup B) \cap (\overline{A \cap B})$, or $(A \cup B) - (A \cap B)$
(b) $(A \cap B) \cup (B \cap C)$, or $B \cap (A \cup C)$

Example 2-12

Suppose M is the set of all students taking mathematics and E is the set of all students taking English. Identify the students described by each region in Figure 2-9.

FIGURE 2-9

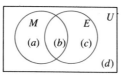

Solution

Region (*a*) contains all students taking mathematics but not English.
Region (*b*) contains all students taking both mathematics and English.
Region (*c*) contains all students taking English but not mathematics.
Region (*d*) contains all students taking neither mathematics nor English.

Example 2-13

Suppose a survey was taken of college freshmen to determine something about their high school backgrounds. The following information was gathered from interviews with 110 students:

25 took physics
45 took biology
48 took mathematics
10 took physics and mathematics
 8 took biology and mathematics
 6 took physics and biology
 5 took all three subjects

How many students took biology, but neither physics nor mathematics? How many did not take any of the three subjects?

Solution

To solve this problem, build a model using sets. Because there are three distinct subjects, three circles should be used. The maximum number of regions of a Venn diagram using three circles is 8. In Figure 2-10, P is the set of students taking physics, B is the set taking biology, and M is the set taking mathematics. The shaded region represents the 5 students who took all three subjects. The lined region represents the students who took physics and mathematics, but who did not take biology.

Because a total of 10 students took physics and mathematics, and because 5 of those also took biology, $10 - 5$, or 5, students took physics and math, but not biology. The other numbers in the diagram were derived using similar reasoning. After completing the diagram, we interpret the results. Of all the students, 36 took biology, but neither physics nor mathematics; 11 did not take any of the three subjects.

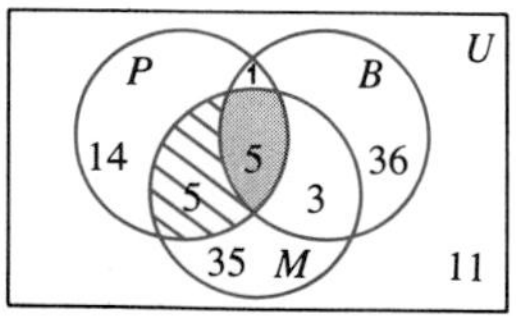

FIGURE 2-10

PROBLEM SET 2-2

1. Given $U = \{f, i, n, a, l, s, o, v, e, r\}$ and $A = \{f, i, n, a, l, s\}$, $B = \{a, r, e\}$, and $C = \{o, v, e, r\}$, find each of the following.
   (a) $A \cup B$ (b) $A \cap B$
   (c) $\overline{A} \cup C$ (d) $A \cap C$
   (e) $(A \cup B) \cup C$ (f) $B \cap \overline{C}$
   (g) $\overline{C} \cup \overline{A}$ (h) $\overline{C - A}$

2. Tell whether each of the following is true or false. If false, give a counterexample.
   (a) For all sets A, $A \cup \varnothing = A$.
   (b) For all sets A and B, $A - B = B - A$.
   (c) For all sets A, $A \cup A = A$.
   (d) For all sets A and B, $\overline{A \cap B} = \overline{A} \cap \overline{B}$.
   (e) For all sets A and B, $A \cap B = B \cap A$.
   (f) For all sets A, B, and C, $(A \cup B) \cup C = A \cup (B \cup C)$.
   (g) For all sets A, $A - \varnothing = A$.

3. If $B \subseteq A$, find a simpler expression for each.
   (a) $A \cap B$ (b) $A \cup B$

4. For each of the following, indicate the portion of the Venn diagram that illustrates the set.
   (a) $A \cup B$ (b) $\overline{A} \cap B$
   (c) $A \cap \overline{B}$ (d) $(A \cup B) \cap \overline{C}$
   (e) $\overline{A} \cap B$ (f) $(A \cap B) \cup C$
   (g) $(A \cap B) \cup (A \cap C)$ (h) $(\overline{A} \cap B) \cup C$

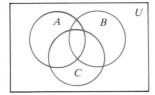

5. Use set notation to identify each of the following shaded regions.

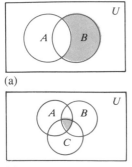

(a)

(b)

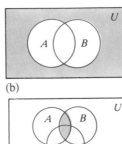

(c)

(d)

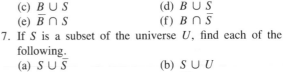

(e)

(f)

6. Given that the universe is the set of all humans, $B = \{x \mid x$ is a college basketball player$\}$, and $S = \{x \mid x$ is a college student more than 200 cm tall$\}$, describe each of the following in words.
   (a) $B \cap S$ (b) $\overline{S}$
   (c) $B \cup S$ (d) $\overline{B \cup S}$
   (e) $\overline{B} \cap S$ (f) $B \cap \overline{S}$

7. If S is a subset of the universe U, find each of the following.
   (a) $S \cup \overline{S}$ (b) $S \cup U$
   (c) $\varnothing \cup S$ (d) $\overline{U}$
   (e) $S \cap U$ (f) $\overline{\varnothing}$
   (g) $S \cap \overline{S}$ (h) $S - \overline{S}$
   (i) $U \cap \overline{S}$ (j) $\overline{\overline{S}}$

8. Answer each of the following and justify your answer.
   (a) If $a \in A \cap B$, is it true that $a \in A \cup B$?
   (b) If $a \in A \cup B$, is it true that $a \in A \cap B$?

9. For each of the following conditions, find $A - B$.
   (a) $A \cap B = \varnothing$ (b) $B = U$
   (c) $A = B$ (d) $A \subseteq B$

10. For each of the following, draw a Venn diagram so that sets A, B, and C satisfy the given conditions.
    (a) $A \cap B \neq \varnothing$, $C \subset (A \cap B)$
    (b) $A \cap C \neq \varnothing$, $B \cap C \neq \varnothing$, $A \cap B = \varnothing$
    (c) $A \subset B$, $C \cap B \neq \varnothing$, $A \cap C = \varnothing$

11. Shade the portion of the diagram that represents the given sets.

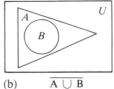

(a) $A \cap \overline{B}$ (b) $\overline{A \cup B}$

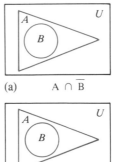

(c) $(A \cap B) \cup \overline{A}$

12. (a) If A has 3 elements and B has 2 elements, what is the greatest number of elements possible in (i) $A \cup B$; (ii) $A \cap B$?
   (b) If A has n elements and B has m elements, what is the greatest number of elements in (i) $A \cup B$; (ii) $A \cap B$?

13. Try examples or use Venn diagrams to determine if each of the following is true.
   (a) $A \cup (B \cap C) = (A \cup B) \cap C$
   (b) $A \cap (B \cup C) = (A \cap B) \cup C$

14. Use Venn diagrams to verify the associative property of union; that is, show $A \cup (B \cup C) = (A \cup B) \cup C$.

15. Investigate the following properties of the set difference operation.
   (a) Is it commutative, that is, does $A - B = B - A$?
   (b) Is it associative, that is, does $A - (B - C) = (A - B) - C$?
   (c) Does the distributive property of set difference over union hold, that is, does $A - (B \cup C) = (A - B) \cup (A - C)$?

16. Suppose $U = \{e, q, u, a, l, i, t, y\}$, $A = \{l, i, t, e\}$, $B = \{t, i, e\}$, and $C = \{q, u, e\}$. Decide whether the following pairs of sets are equal.
   (a) $A \cap B$ and $B \cap A$
   (b) $A \cup B$ and $B \cup A$
   (c) $A \cup (B \cup C)$ and $(A \cup B) \cup C$
   (d) $A \cup \varnothing$ and A
   (e) $(A \cap A)$ and $(A \cap \varnothing)$
   (f) $\overline{\overline{C}}$ and C

17. The equations $\overline{A \cup B} = \overline{A} \cap \overline{B}$ and $\overline{A \cap B} = \overline{A} \cup \overline{B}$ are referred to as *DeMorgan's laws* in honor of the famous British mathematician who first discovered them. Use Venn diagrams to show each of the following.
   (a) $\overline{A \cup B} = \overline{A} \cap \overline{B}$ (b) $\overline{A \cap B} = \overline{A} \cup \overline{B}$
   (c) Verify (a) and (b) for specific sets A and B.

18. If $A \cap B = A \cup B$, how are A and B related?

19. Suppose P is the set of all eighth-grade students at the Paxson school, with B the set of all students in the band and C the set of all students in the choir. Identify in words the students described by each region of the diagram.

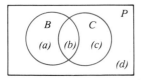

20. Of the eighth graders at the Paxson school, there were:
   7 who played basketball
   9 who played volleyball
   10 who played soccer
   1 who played basketball and volleyball only
   1 who played basketball and soccer only
   2 who played volleyball and soccer only, and
   2 who played volleyball, basketball and soccer
   How many played one or more of the three sports?

21. In a fraternity with 30 members, 18 take mathematics, 5 take both mathematics and biology, and 8 take neither mathematics nor biology. How many take biology but not mathematics?

22. Three types of antigens are looked for in blood tests; they are A, B, and Rh. Whenever the antigen A or B is present, it is listed, but if both these antigens are absent, the blood is said to be type O. If the Rh antigen is present, the blood is said to be positive; otherwise it is negative. Thus, the main blood types are:

$$\{A^+, A^-, B^+, B^-, AB^+, AB^-, O^+, O^-\}$$

A Venn diagram for blood types is shown.

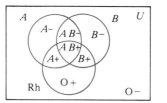

   (a) Indicate the area representing the people who react positively to the A antigen but not the B antigen nor the Rh antigen.
   (b) Suppose a laboratory technician reports the following results after testing the blood samples of 100 people. How many of the 100 people were classified as O negative?

Number of Samples	Antigens in Blood
40	A
18	B
82	Rh
5	A and B
31	A and Rh
11	B and Rh
4	A, B, and Rh

* 23. A paper carrier delivers 31 copies of the Town Gazette and 37 copies of the Daily Flyer each day to 60 houses. If no house received 2 copies of the same paper, answer the following.
  (a) What is the least number of houses to which 2 papers could have been delivered?
  (b) What is the greatest number of houses to which 2 papers could have been delivered?

* 24. Two families each having three children are assembled for a birthday party. Each of the six children has either blue or brown eyes and brown or blond hair. Children in one family may differ by at most one characteristic. The following are descriptions of the six children.

  Tom: blue eyes, brown hair

  Dick: brown eyes, blond hair
  Mary: brown eyes, brown hair
  Harry: blue eyes, blond hair
  Jane: blue eyes, brown hair
  Abby: blue eyes, blond hair

  Separate the children into two families.

* 25. Using set notation, describe the shaded region shown.

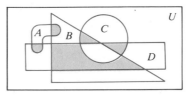

* * * * * * * REVIEW PROBLEMS * * * * * * *

26. List all the subsets of $A = \{a, b, c\}$.
27. Are the following two sets equal?

    $\{2, 4, 6, 8, 10, \ldots\}$
    $\{x \mid x = 2n, n \in N\}$

28. Given $B = \{p, q, r, s\}$, list the nonempty, proper subsets of B.
29. Write the set of states of the United States that begin with the letter M by:
    (a) listing them
    (b) using set-builder notation

BRAIN TEASER

Every doodad is a doohickey. Half of all thingamajigs are doohickeys. Half of all doohickeys are doodads. There are 30 thingamajigs and 20 doodads. No thingamajig is a doodad. How many doohickeys are neither doodads nor thingamajigs?

2-3 CARTESIAN PRODUCTS AND RELATIONS

Cartesian product

Two ways that a third set can be created from two given sets are by forming the union of the two sets or by forming the intersection of the two sets. Another way to produce a set from two given sets is by forming the **Cartesian product.** The Cartesian product involves pairing the elements of one set with the elements of another set. For example, suppose a person has three pairs of pants, $P = \{$blue, white, green$\}$, and two shirts, $S = \{$blue, red$\}$. How many different pant-and-shirt combinations does the person have? The possible combinations follow, with the color of pants listed first and the color of shirt listed second.

| blue—blue | white—blue | green—blue |
| blue—red | white—red | green—red |

Six combinations are possible. The combination of pants and shirts forms a set of all possible pairs in which the first member of the pair is an element of set P, and the second member is an element of set S. The set of all possible combinations is

{(blue, blue), (blue, red), (white, blue), (white, red), (green, blue), (green, red)}

Because the first component in each pair represents pants and the second component in each pair represents shirts, the order in which the components are written is important. Thus, (green, blue) represents green pants and a blue shirt, whereas (blue, green) represents blue pants and green shirt. Therefore, the two pairs represent different outfits. Because the order in each pair is important,
ordered pairs   the pairs are called **ordered pairs.** The positions that the ordered pairs occupy
components   within the set of outfits is immaterial. Only the order of the **components** within each pair is significant.

An ordered pair (x, y) is formed by choosing x from one set and y from another set in such a way that x is designated as the first component and y is designated as the second component. By definition, $(x, y) = (m, n)$ if and only if $x = m$ and $y = n$. Thus, (green, blue) $\neq$ (blue, green), although {green, blue} = {blue, green}.

A set consisting of ordered pairs such as the ones in the pants-and-shirt example is the Cartesian product of the set of pants and the set of shirts.

DEFINITION

> For any sets A and B, the **Cartesian product** of A and B, written $A \times B$, is the set of all ordered pairs such that the first element of each pair is an element of A and the second element of each pair is an element of B.

Remark

> Using set notation, $A \times B = \{(x, y) \mid x \in A \text{ and } y \in B\}$. Also, $A \times B$ is commonly read as "A cross B." Be careful not to say "A times B." We multiply numbers, but we take Cartesian products of sets.

Example 2-14

> If $A = \{a, b, c\}$ and $B = \{1, 2, 3\}$, find each of the following.
>
> (a) $A \times B$ (b) $B \times A$ (c) $A \times A$

Solution

> (a) $A \times B = \{(a, 1), (a, 2), (a, 3), (b, 1), (b, 2), (b, 3), (c, 1), (c, 2), (c, 3)\}$
> (b) $B \times A = \{(1, a), (1, b), (1, c), (2, a), (2, b), (2, c), (3, a), (3, b), (3, c)\}$
> (c) $A \times A = \{(a, a), (a, b), (a, c), (b, a), (b, b), (b, c), (c, a), (c, b), (c, c)\}$

It is possible to form a Cartesian product involving the null set. Suppose $A = \{1, 2\}$. Because there are no elements in $\varnothing$, no ordered pairs (x, y) with $x \in A$ and $y \in \varnothing$ are possible, so $A \times \varnothing = \varnothing$. This is true for all sets A. Similarly, $\varnothing \times A = \varnothing$ for all sets A.

relation   A subset of a Cartesian product is called a **relation.** Before formally examining this mathematical concept, let us examine nonmathematical relations. The word "relations" brings to mind members of a family—parents, brothers, sisters, grandfathers, aunts, and so on. If we say Billy is the brother of Jimmy, "is the brother of" expresses the relation between Billy and Jimmy.

Other familiar relations occur in everyday life. For example, 543-8975 is the telephone number of Rick. "Is the telephone number of" expresses the relation between the number and Rick. Other examples of relations include the following.

"is the daughter of"   "is the hometown of"
"is the same color as"   "is the author of"
"sits in the same row as" "is the social security number of"

Examples of relations in mathematics are

"is less than"   "is three more than"
"is parallel to"   "is the area of"

To illustrate relations, a diagram like Figure 2-11 is useful.

FIGURE 2-11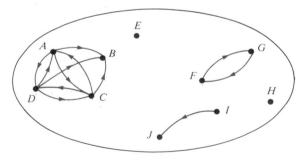

Suppose that each point in Figure 2-11 represents a child on a playground, the letters represent their names, and an arrow going from I to J means that I "is the sister of" J.

If all sister relationships are indicated in Figure 2-11, can you tell which of the children are boys and which are girls? Try to answer this question before reading further.

The information in Figure 2-11 indicates that A, C, D, F, G, and I are definitely girls and that B and J are definitely boys. Why? It also indicates that H and E have no sisters on the playground, but it does not indicate the gender of H and E.

Another way to exhibit the relation "is a sister of" is by using the same set twice, with arrows, as in Figure 2-12.

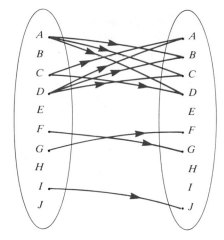

FIGURE 2-12

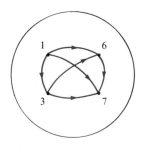

FIGURE 2-13

Still another way to show the relation "is a sister of" is to write the relation "*A* is a sister of *B*" as an ordered pair (A, B). Notice that (B, A) means that *B* is a sister of *A*. Using this method, the relation "is a sister of" can be described for the children on the playground as the set

$\{(A, B), (A, C), (A, D), (C, A), (C, B), (C, D), (D, A), (D, B), (D, C), (F, G),$
$(G, F), (I, J)\}$

Next, we illustrate this idea with Figure 2-13, and let the arrows represent "is less than." The relation could also be shown by using two sets with the arrows as shown in Figure 2-14.

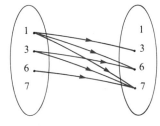

FIGURE 2-14

Ordered pairs also can be used to describe the relation pictured in Figures 2-13 and 2-14. The relation "is less than" on the set $\{1, 3, 6, 7\}$ would appear as

$\{(1, 3), (1, 6), (1, 7), (3, 6), (3, 7), (6, 7)\}$

Example 2-15

The pairs (Helena, Montana), (Denver, Colorado), (Springfield, Illinois), (Juneau, Alaska) are included in some relation. Give a rule that describes the relation.

Solution

One possible rule is that the ordered pair (x, y) indicates that x is the capital of y.

A relation is a pairing of elements of two sets according to some criterion. In Example 2-15, the first components of the ordered pairs are state capitals; the second components are states of the United States. Each ordered pair in the example is an element of the Cartesian product $A \times B$, where A is the set of state capitals and B is the set of states in the United States. Notice that not all the possible ordered pairs in $A \times B$ are in the relation in Example 2-15.

DEFINITION

> Given any two sets A and B, a **relation** from A to B is a subset of $A \times B$; that is, if R is a relation, then $R \subseteq A \times B$.

relation on A

In the definition, the phrase "from A to B" means that the first components in the ordered pairs are elements of A and the second components are elements of B. If $A = B$, we say that the **relation is on A.**

one-to-one correspondence

Consider the set of people $P = \{$Tomas, Dick, Mari$\}$ and the set of numbers $S = \{1, 2, 3\}$. To show that each person receives a number, we pair the elements of the two sets. Such pairing is called **one-to-one correspondence.** One way to exhibit a one-to-one correspondence is shown in Figure 2-15.

FIGURE 2-15

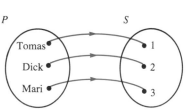

An equivalent notation is: Tomas $\leftrightarrow$ 1, Dick $\leftrightarrow$ 2, Mari $\leftrightarrow$ 3.

DEFINITION

> Two sets A and B are said to be in **one-to-one correspondence** (or matched) if and only if the elements of A and B can be paired so that for each element of A there is exactly one element of B, and for each element of B there is exactly one element of A.

Other possible one-to-one correspondences exist between the sets P and S given earlier. There are several schemes for exhibiting them. For example, all six possible one-to-one correspondences for sets P and S can be listed as follows.

Tomas ↔ 1	Tomas ↔ 2	Tomas ↔ 3
Dick ↔ 2	Dick ↔ 1	Dick ↔ 1
Mari ↔ 3	Mari ↔ 3	Mari ↔ 2
Tomas ↔ 1	Tomas ↔ 2	Tomas ↔ 3
Dick ↔ 3	Dick ↔ 3	Dick ↔ 2
Mari ↔ 2	Mari ↔ 1	Mari ↔ 1

It is not always possible to set up a one-to-one correspondence between two sets. For example, let $Q = \{$Tomas, Dick, Mari, Harry$\}$ and $S = \{1, 2, 3\}$. In any attempted one-to-one correspondence between Q and S, one person will be without a number. This is true regardless of how the elements are paired. One example of a pairing is

$$Q = \{\text{Tomas, Dick, Mari, Harry}\}$$
$$\updownarrow \quad \updownarrow \quad \updownarrow$$
$$S = \{\ 1, \quad 2, \quad 3\}$$

In this case, we say that S has *fewer,* or *less,* elements than Q.

When two sets A and B are compared, one of three possible conditions exists.

A has as many elements as B and can be put in one-to-one correspondence with B.

The number of elements in A is *greater than* the number of elements in B.

The number of elements in A is *less than* the number of elements in B.

These comparisons can be made without counting. In fact, children who do not know how to count can often tell which set contains more elements.

equivalent sets

Suppose a room contains 20 chairs and one student is sitting in each chair with no one standing. There is a one-to-one correspondence between the set of chairs and the set of students in the room. In this case, the set of chairs and the set of students are **equivalent sets.**

DEFINITION

> Two sets A and B are said to be **equivalent,** written $A \sim B$, if and only if there exists a one-to-one correspondence between the sets.

The term *equivalent* should not be confused with *equal.* The difference should be made clear by the following example.

Example 2-16 | Let

$$A = \{1, 2, 3, 4, 5\}$$
$$B = \{a, b, c\}$$
$$C = \{x, y, z\}$$
$$D = \{b, a, c\}$$

Compare the sets using the terms *equal* and *equivalent*.

Solution | Sets A and B are not equivalent $(A \nsim B)$ and not equal $(A \ne B)$.
Sets A and C are not equivalent $(A \nsim C)$ and not equal $(A \ne C)$.
Sets A and D are not equivalent $(A \nsim D)$ and not equal $(A \ne D)$.
Sets B and C are equivalent $(B \sim C)$, but not equal $(B \ne C)$.
Sets B and D are equivalent $(B \sim D)$ and equal $(B = D)$.
Sets C and D are equivalent $(C \sim D)$, but not equal $(C \ne D)$.

Remark | Observe that if two sets are equal, they are equivalent; however, if two sets are equivalent, they are not necessarily equal.

Consider the five sets $\{a, b\}$, $\{1, 2\}$, $\{x, y\}$, $\{b, a\}$, and $\{*, \#\}$. How are these sets related? They are equivalent to each other. In fact, they are equivalent in a special way; they share the property of "twoness." In mathematics, we say that these sets have the same cardinal number, namely, 2. The **cardinal number** of a set X, denoted by $n(X)$, indicates the number of elements in the set X. If $D = \{a, b, c\}$, we say that the cardinal number of D is 3 and write $n(D) = 3$.

cardinal number

Note that if A is equivalent to B, then A and B have the same cardinal number; that is, $n(A) = n(B)$. Also, if $n(A) = n(B)$, the two sets are equivalent, but not necessarily equal. Furthermore, if $A = B$, then $A \sim B$ and $n(A) = n(B)$.

PROBLEM SET 2-3

1. Let $A = \{x, y\}$, $B = \{a, b, c\}$, and $C = \{0\}$. Find each of the following.
   (a) $A \times B$
   (b) $C \times B$
   (c) $B \times A$
   (d) $B \times \varnothing$
   (e) $C \times C$
   (f) $\varnothing \times C$
   (g) $(A \times C) \cup (B \times C)$
   (h) $(A \cup B) \times C$
   (i) $A \times (B \cap C)$
   (j) $(A \times B) \cap (A \times C)$

2. For each of the following, the Cartesian product, $C \times D$, is given by the following sets. Find C and D.
   (a) $\{(a, b), (a, c), (a, d), (a, e)\}$
   (b) $\{(1, 1), (1, 2), (1, 3), (2, 1), (2, 2), (2, 3)\}$
   (c) $\{(0, 1), (0, 0), (1, 1), (1, 0)\}$

3. Answer each of the following.
   (a) If A has 3 elements and B has 1 element, how many elements are in $A \times B$?
   (b) If A has 3 elements and B has 2 elements, how many elements are in $A \times B$?
   (c) If A has 3 elements and B has 3 elements, how many elements are in $A \times B$?
   (d) If A has 5 elements and B has 4 elements, how many elements are in $A \times B$?
   (e) If A has m elements and B has n elements, how many elements are in $A \times B$?
   (f) If A has m elements, B has n elements, and C has p elements, how many elements are in $(A \times B) \times C$?

4. If $A = \{1, 2, 3\}$, $B = \{0\}$, and $C = \varnothing$, find the number of elements in each of the following.
   (a) $A \times B$ (b) $A \times C$ (c) $B \times C$
5. If the number of elements in set B is 3 and the number of elements in $(A \cup B) \times B$ is 24, what is the number of elements in A if $A \cap B = \varnothing$?
6. If A and B are nonempty sets such that $A \times B = B \times A$, does $A = B$?
7. Suppose you can choose one piece of fruit from the set {apple, orange, banana} and one piece of candy from the set {sucker, jawbreaker, candy kiss, licorice}. How many different combinations could you choose?
8. If there are 6 teams in the Alpha league and 5 teams in the Beta league, and if each team from one league plays each team from the other league exactly once, how many games are played?
9. José has 4 pairs of slacks, 5 shirts, and 3 sweaters. From how many different combinations can he choose if he chooses a pair of slacks, a shirt, and a sweater each time?
10. (a) Is the operation of forming Cartesian products commutative?
    (b) Is the operation of forming Cartesian products associative?
11. Each of the following gives pairs that are included in some relation. Give a rule or phrase that could describe each relation and list two more pairs that could be included in the relation.
    (a) (1, 1), (2, 4), (3, 9), (4, 16)
    (b) (Blondie, Dagwood), (Martha, George), (Rosalyn, Jimmy), (Flo, Andy), (Scarlett, Rhett), (Nancy, Ronald)
    (c) (a, A), (b, B), (c, C), (d, D)
    (d) (3 candies, 10¢), (6 candies, 20¢)
12. Let $X = \{a, b, c\}$ and $Y = \{m, n\}$, and suppose X and Y represent two sets of students. The students in X point to the shorter students in Y. The following diagrams list two possiblities. Tell as much as you can about the students in each diagram.

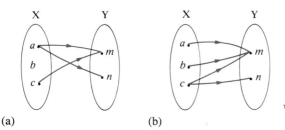

(a)   (b)

13. Write three ordered pairs that satisfy the relation "is owned by."
14. The following are the ages of the children in a family: Bill, 17; Becky, 14; John, 9; Abby, 3; Karly, 1. Draw an arrow diagram showing the names of the children and the relation "is younger than."
15. Which of the following pairs of sets can be placed in one-to-one correspondence?
    (a) $\{1, 2, 3, 4, 5\}$ and $\{m, n, o, p, q\}$
    (b) $\{m, a, t, h\}$ and $\{f, u, n\}$
    (c) $\{a, b, c, d, e, f, \ldots, m\}$ and $\{1, 2, 3, 4, 5, 6, \ldots, 13\}$
    (d) $\{x \mid x$ is a letter in the word "mathematics"$\}$ and $\{1, 2, 3, 4, \ldots, 11\}$
    (e) $\{\bigcirc, \triangle\}$ and $\{2\}$
16. Show all possible one-to-one correspondences between the sets A and B if $A = \{1, 2\}$ and $B = \{a, b\}$.
17. How many different one-to-one correspondences are there in each case?
    (a) Between two sets with four elements each.
    (b) Between two sets with five elements each.
    (c) Between two sets with n elements each.
18. Classify each of the following statements as true or false.
    (a) If $A \sim B$, then $B \sim A$.
    (b) If $A \sim B$ and $B \sim C$, then $A \sim C$.
    (c) If $A = B$, then $A \sim B$.
    (d) $\varnothing \sim \varnothing$.
19. Cardinal numbers answer the question "How many?" **Ordinal numbers** are used to describe the relative position an element can occupy in an ordered set rather than the number of elements in the set. For example, we might say that Carla sits in the *fourth* row and she is reading page 87 of this book. These are examples of ordinal numbers, rather than cardinal numbers, because they refer to position or order. Ordinal numbers answer the question "Which one?" Indicate whether a cardinal number or an ordinal number is used in each of the following cases.
    (a) The book has 562 pages.
    (b) Christmas falls on December 25.
    (c) Turn to page 125.
    (d) She paid $15 for the book.
    (e) Our class will take four tests and we just finished the first one.
20. How many subsets of $A = \{a, b, c, d\}$ have cardinal number 3?
★ 21. A set A can be defined to be **infinite** if and only if it can be put into a one-to-one correspondence with a proper

subset of itself. For example, the one-to-one correspondence below shows that N is an infinite set.

$$N = \{1, 2, 3, 4, \ 5, \ldots, \ n, \ldots\}$$
$$\updownarrow \ \updownarrow \ \updownarrow \ \updownarrow \ \updownarrow \qquad \updownarrow$$
$$E = \{2, 4, 6, 8, 10, \ldots, 2n, \ldots\}$$

Use this definition to show that the following sets are infinite.
(a) $\{1, 3, 5, 7, 9, \ldots\}$
(b) $\{100, 101, 102, 103, \ldots\}$

22. Classify the following sets as finite or infinite.
(a) $\{1, 2, 3, 4, \ldots, 999, 1000\}$
(b) $\{x \mid x$ was a sixth-grade student in the state of New York on January 20, 1984$\}$

(c) $\{1, 4, 7, 10, 13, 16, \ldots\}$
(d) $\{x \mid x$ is the number of seconds in 1,000,000 years $\}$

★ 23. In the book *Stories About Sets,* Vilenkin writes about an extraordinary hotel with an infinite number of rooms. At a convention, all the rooms were filled. To make room for one more person, the manager moved the guest in room 1 to room 2, the guest in room 2 to room 3, and so on. After all the grumbling about moving was done, everyone was happy.
(a) Suppose 999,999 more guests arrive. Could a similar solution be obtained?
(b) Suppose the guests in all the even-numbered rooms check out. Could the guests be shifted so that all the rooms in the hotel would be filled?

* * * * * * * REVIEW PROBLEMS * * * * * * * *

24. How many proper subsets does $A = \{a, b, c, d, e, f\}$ have?
25. Use set-builder notation to write a set that is well defined.
26. Given $U = \{1, 2, 3, 4, 5, 6, 7, 8\}$, $A = \{1, 2, 3\}$, $B = \{2, 3\}$, and $C = \{5\}$. Find each of the following.
(a) $A \cap B$ (b) $B \cup C$ (c) $A \cup \overline{B}$
(d) $\overline{A \cup B}$ (e) $A - B$
27. Draw a Venn diagram to show $\overline{(A \cap B)} \cup C$.
28. Illustrate the commutative property of set intersection using sets $A = \{a, b, c, d\}$ and $B = \{b, c, d\}$.
29. The given Venn diagram contains the cardinal numbers (not elements) of the different regions. For example, the cardinal number of $A \cap B \cap C$ is 3; that is, $n(A \cap B \cap C) = 3$. Complete the following.

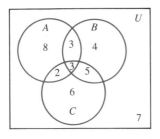

(a) $n(A) = $ _____
(b) $n(B) = $ _____

(c) $n(B \cup C) = $ _____
(d) $n(B \cap C) = $ _____
(e) $n((A \cup B) \cap \overline{C}) = $ _____
(f) $n(A \cup B \cup C) = $ _____
(g) $n(A - B) = $ _____

30. A school is planning a bus trip, which will include the math club, the English club, and the computer club. Eighteen students belong to both the math club and the English club, 12 belong to both the math club and the computer club, 14 belong to both the English club and the computer club, and 5 belong to all three clubs. If there are 30 students in the math club, 40 students in the English club, and 50 students in the computer club, how many bus seats are needed?

31. Howie, O.J., and Frank each tried to predict the winners of Sunday's professional football games. The only team not picked that is playing Sunday was the Giants. The choices for each person were as follows.

> Howie: Cowboys, Steelers, Vikings, Bills
> O.J.: Steelers, Packers, Cowboys, Redskins
> Frank: Redskins, Vikings, Jets, Cowboys

If the only teams playing Sunday are those just mentioned, which teams will play which other teams?

BRAIN TEASER

Only 10 rooms were vacant in the Village Hotel. Eleven men went into the hotel at the same time, each wanting a separate room. The clerk, settling the argument, said: "I'll tell you what I'll do. I'll put two men in Room 1 with the understanding that I will come back and get one of them a few minutes later." The men agreed to this. The clerk continued: "I will put the rest of you men in rooms as follows: the 3rd man in Room 2, the 4th man in Room 3, the 5th man in Room 4, the 6th man in Room 5, the 7th man in Room 6, the 8th man in Room 7, the 9th man in Room 8, and the 10th man in Room 9."
Then the clerk went back and got the extra man he had left in Room 1 and put him in Room 10. Everybody was happy. What is wrong with this plan?

2-4   FUNCTIONS

function

The following is an example of a game called "guess my rule." The game is one way a special kind of relation, called a **function,** is often introduced in elementary school.

> When Tom said 2, Noah said 5. When Dick said 4, Noah said 7. When Mary said 10, Noah said 13. When Liz said 6, what did Noah say? What is Noah's rule?

The answer to the first question may be 9, and the rule could be "take the original number and add 3"; that is, for any number n, Noah's answer is $n + 3$.

Example 2-17

Guess the teacher's rule for the following responses.

(a)

You	Teacher
1	3
0	0
4	12
10	30

(b)

You	Teacher
2	5
3	7
5	11
10	21

(c)

You	Teacher
2	0
4	0
7	1
21	1

Solution

(a) The teacher's rule could be "multiply the given number n by 3"; that is, $n \cdot 3$.

(b) The teacher's rule could be "double the original number n and add 1"; that is, $2n + 1$.

(c) The teacher's rule could be "if the number n is even, answer 0; if the number is odd, answer 1."

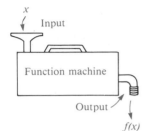

FIGURE 2-16

Another way to prepare students for the formal idea of a function is by using a "function machine." A machine such as the one in Figure 2-16 consists of an input unit where items are entered, a processing unit, and an output unit where results are obtained. The function machine is similar to actual vending machines with which many children are familiar.

In a function machine, for any input element x there is an output element denoted by $f(x)$, read "f of x." A function machine is a machine that associates *exactly one output with each input* according to some rule. That is, if you enter some number x as input and obtain some number $f(x)$ as output, then *every* time you enter that same x as input, you will obtain that same $f(x)$ as output.

Example 2-18

Consider the function machine shown.

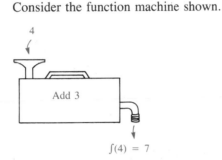

What will happen if the numbers 0, 1, 3, and 6 are entered?

Solution

Each time a number is entered as input, the machine adds 3 to it. The numbers corresponding to the inputs 0, 1, 3, and 6 are 3, 4, 6, and 9.

If the numbers output in Example 2-18 are denoted by $f(x)$, the corresponding values can be described using Table 2-2.

TABLE 2-2

x	$f(x)$
0	3
1	4
3	6
6	9

To describe the function in Example 2-18 in general, we can write an equation. If the input is x, the output is $x + 3$; that is, $f(x) = x + 3$. Note that the output values can be obtained by substituting the values 0, 1, 3, and 6 for x in $f(x) = x + 3$, as shown.

$f(0) = 0 + 3 = 3$
$f(1) = 1 + 3 = 4$
$f(3) = 3 + 3 = 6$
$f(6) = 6 + 3 = 9$

Still another way to describe the function in Example 2-18 is by a graph. A graph for this function is given in Figure 2-17(a).

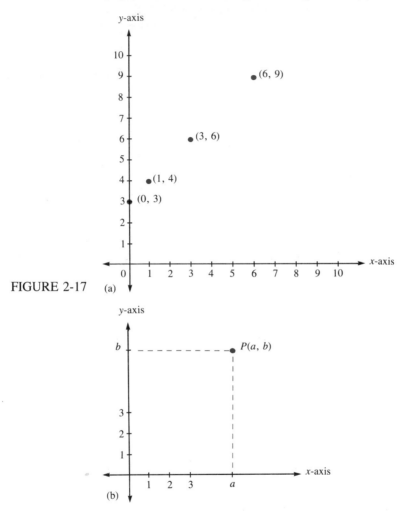

FIGURE 2-17   (a)

(b)

Graphing a function, as in Figure 2-17(a), requires some knowledge of coordinate systems (discussed in detail in Chapter 12). A coordinate system can be constructed by drawing two perpendicular lines. The horizontal line is called the *x*-axis   *y*-axis   **x-axis,** the vertical line is called the **y-axis,** and the point of intersection is called origin   the **origin.**

Figure 2-17(b) shows that the location of any point *P* on a graph can be described by an ordered pair. If a perpendicular from *P* to the *x*-axis intersects the *x*-axis at *a* and a perpendicular from *P* to the *y*-axis intersects the *y*-axis at *b*, then coordinates   we say that point *P* has **coordinates** (a, b). In Figure 2-17, each value of *x* is associated with exactly one value of *y*. This and the idea of a function machine associating exactly one output with each input according to some rule leads us to the definition given below.

DEFINITION

A **function** from A to B is a relation from A to B in which each element of A is paired with one *and only one* element of B.

domain
range

The set of all first components, all the elements of A, is called the **domain.** The set of the second components, a subset of B, is called the **range.** In terms of a function machine, the domain is the set of all possible input values. The range is the set of all output values.

Example 2-19

Suppose a given machine is a doubling machine; that is, for any given input, it will produce its double as output. If the domain is the set of natural numbers, describe the range.

Solution

The range is the set of all even natural numbers (all multiples of two).

A calculator (see Appendix II) can be used as a function machine. For example, a student can make up a rule such as "times 9." The student then enters $\boxed{9}\ \boxed{\times}\ \boxed{K}$ on the calculator using the constant button $\boxed{K}$. The student then presses $\boxed{0}$ and hands the calculator to another student. The other student is to determine the rule by entering various numbers, followed by the $\boxed{=}$ button.

Are all input-output machines function machines? Consider the machine shown below. For any natural-number input, x, the machine outputs a number y that is less than x.

If, for example, you input the number 10, the machine may output 9 since 9 is less than 10. If you input 10 again, the machine may output 3, since 3 is less than 10. This clearly violates the definition of a function, since 10 can be paired with more than one element. The machine is not a function machine.

Consider the relations described in Figure 2-18. Do they illustrate functions?

FIGURE 2-18

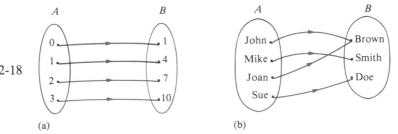

(a)   (b)

In Figure 2-18(a), for every element belonging to the domain A, there is one and only one element belonging to B. Thus, this relation is a function from A to B. A diagram, then, shows a function from A to B if there is one and only one arrow leaving each element of the domain pointing to an element of B. Figure 2-18(b) also illustrates a function since there is only one arrow leaving each element in A. It does not matter that an element of set B, Brown, has two arrows pointing to it.

Example 2-20 | Which, if any, of the following three diagrams exhibits a function from A to B?

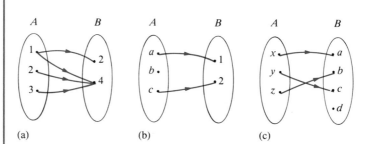

(a) (b) (c)

Solution | (a) This diagram does not define a function from A to B since the element 1 is paired both with 2 and 4.
(b) This diagram does not define a function from A to B since the element b is not paired with any element of B. (It is a function from a subset of A to B).
(c) This diagram does define a function from A to B since there is one and only one arrow leaving each element of A. The fact that d, an element of B, is not paired with any element in the domain does not violate the definition.

Consider the relation $\{(a, b), (b, c), (c, d), (d, e)\}$. Since each first component of the ordered pairs is associated with one and only one second component, this relation is a function from the set $\{a, b, c, d\}$ of the first components to the set $\{b, c, d, e\}$ of the second components.

Example 2-21 | Determine whether the following relations are functions from the set of first components to the set of second components.

(a) $\{(1, 2), (2, 5), (3, 7), (1, 4), (4, 8)\}$
(b) $\{(1, 2), (2, 2), (3, 2), (4, 2)\}$

Solution | (a) This is not a function since the first component, 1, is associated with two different second components, namely, 2 and 4.
(b) This is a function from $\{1, 2, 3, 4\}$ to $\{2\}$, since each first component is associated with exactly one second component. The fact that the second component, 2, is associated with more than one first component does not matter.

Example 2-22 | Determine whether each of the following graphs describes a function.

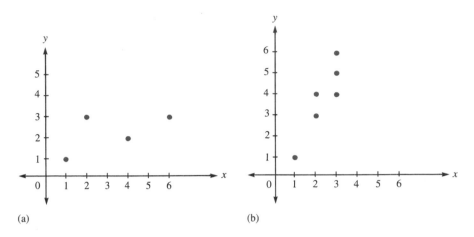

(a)   (b)

Solution | (a) This graph determines a function from {1, 2, 4, 6} to {1, 2, 3} because each value of x is associated with exactly one value of y.
(b) The graph does not determine a function because some x-values are associated with more than one y-value. For example, 2 is associated with 3 and 4.

The concept of a function appears in many real-life applications. For example, on direct-dial, long-distance calls, you pay only for the minutes you talk. The initial rate period is 1 minute. Suppose the weekday rate for a long-distance phone call from Missoula, Montana, to Butte, Montana, is 50¢ for the first minute and 30¢ for each additional minute or part of a minute. We have seen that one way to describe a function is by writing an equation. The equation in this case is $C = 50 + 30(t - 1)$, where C is the cost of the call in cents and t is the length of the call in minutes. This could also be written as $f(t) = 50 + 30(t - 1)$, where $f(t)$ is the cost of the call.

We restrict the time in minutes to the first five natural numbers. The function can be described as shown in Figure 2-19 using (a) a table, (b) a graph, and (c) ordered pairs.

FIGURE 2-19

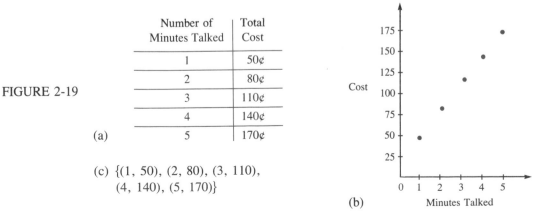

Number of Minutes Talked	Total Cost
1	50¢
2	80¢
3	110¢
4	140¢
5	170¢

(a)

(c) {(1, 50), (2, 80), (3, 110), (4, 140), (5, 170)}

(b)

PROBLEM SET 2-4

1. For each of the following, guess a teacher's rule.

(a)
You	Teacher
3	8
4	11
5	14
10	29

(b)
You	Teacher
0	1
3	10
5	26
8	65

(c)
You	Teacher
6	42
0	0
8	72
2	6

2. The following sets of ordered pairs are functions. Give a rule that describes each function. For example, in $\{(1, 3), (3, 9), (5, 15), (7, 21)\}$, the rule is $f(x) = 3x$, where $x \in \{1, 3, 5, 7\}$.
   (a) $\{(2, 4), (3, 6), (9, 18), (12, 24)\}$
   (b) $\{(5, 3), (7, 5), (11, 9), (14, 12)\}$
   (c) $\{(2, 8), (5, 11), (7, 13), (4, 10)\}$
   (d) $\{(2, 5), (3, 10), (4, 17), (5, 26)\}$

3. Following are five relations from the set $\{1, 2, 3\}$ to the set $\{a, b, c, d\}$. Which are functions? (A diagram may help.) If the relation is not a function, tell why it is not.
   (a) $\{(1, a), (2, b), (3, c), (1, d)\}$
   (b) $\{(1, c), (3, d)\}$
   (c) $\{(1, a), (2, b), (3, a)\}$
   (d) $\{(1, a), (1, b), (1, c)\}$

4. State the domain and range for each function in Problem 3.

5. Does the diagram define a function from A to B? Why or why not?

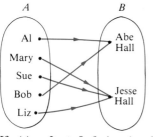

6. If $g(x) = 3x + 5$, find each value.
   (a) $g(0)$ (b) $g(2)$
   (c) $g(10)$ (d) $g(a)$

7. The domain of a function f is $\{1, 10, 11\}$. If $f(x) = 4x + 1$, what is the range of f?

8. Draw a diagram of a function with domain $\{1, 2, 3, 4, 5\}$ and range $\{a, b\}$. (There are many possibilities.)

9. Tell which of the relations shown are functions and why.

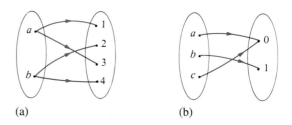

(a)   (b)

10. Suppose $f(x) = 2x + 1$ and the domain is $\{0, 1, 2, 3, 4\}$. Describe the function in the following ways.
    (a) Draw an arrow diagram involving two sets.
    (b) Use ordered pairs.
    (c) Make a table.
    (d) Draw a graph.

11. Which of the following graphs do not describe functions? Why?

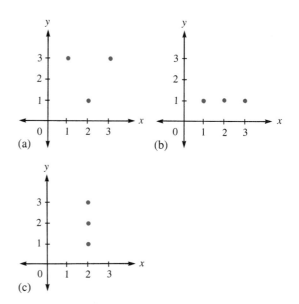

12. Consider the two function machines, which are placed as shown.

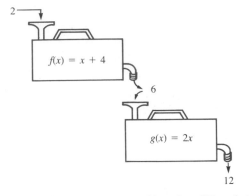

If 2 is entered in the top machine, then $f(2) = 2 + 4 = 6$; 6 is then entered in the second machine and $g(6) = 2 \cdot 6 = 12$. Find the final output for each of the following.

(a) 0   (b) 3   (c) 10

13. The rule for computing the cost of a first-class letter is a function of its weight. Suppose the rule is that the first ounce costs 20¢ and each additional ounce up to 13 ounces costs 15¢.
   (a) What is the cost of an 11-ounce letter?
   (b) Find the equation relating the cost, C, of the letter to its weight, W.

14. According to wildlife experts, the rate at which crickets chirp is a function of the temperature; namely, $C = T - 40$, where C is the number of chirps every 15 seconds and T is the temperature in degrees Fahrenheit.
   (a) How many chirps does the cricket make per second if the temperature is 70°F?
   (b) What is the temperature if the cricket chirps 40 times in 1 minute?

15. If taxi fares are 95¢ for the first half mile and 40¢ for each additional quarter mile, what is the fare for a 2-mile trip?

* * * * * * * REVIEW PROBLEMS * * * * * * * *

16. Suppose U is the set of natural numbers, $\{1, 2, 3, 4, \ldots\}$. Write each of the following using set notation.
   (a) The set of even numbers greater than 12.
   (b) The set of numbers less than 14.

17. If $U = \{a, b, c, d\}$, $A = \{a, b, c\}$, $B = \{b, c\}$, and $C = \{d\}$, find each of the following.
   (a) $A \cup \overline{B}$ (b) $\overline{A \cap B}$ (c) $A \cap \varnothing$
   (d) $B \cap C$ (e) $B - A$

18. If $A = \{\text{cow, dog}\}$ and $B = \{\text{boy, girl}\}$, find each of the following.
   (a) $A \times B$ (b) $B \times A$
   (c) $A \times \varnothing$ (d) $n(A \times B)$

19. Write two sets with three elements each and establish a one-to-one correspondence between them.

20. If $A = \{a, b\}$ and $B = \{c\}$, write the proper subsets of $A \times B$.

21. Write a set that is equivalent to, but not equal to, the set $\{5, 6, 7, 8\}$.

22. How many different one-to-one correspondences are possible between $A = \{a, b, c\}$ and $B = \{1, 2, 3\}$?

23. Illustrate the associative property of set union with the sets $U = \{h, e, l, p, m, n, o, w\}$, $A = \{h, e, l, p\}$, $B = \{m, e\}$, and $C = \{n, o, w\}$.

SOLUTION TO THE PRELIMINARY PROBLEM

Understanding the Problem

The problem is to determine the total number of people who had been on a tour of the Grand Canyon. Guides for the tour remembered that there had been 26 British females, 17 American women, 17 American males, 29 girls, 44 British citizens, 29 women, and 24 British adults. The sets of people are not disjoint. For example, there are 26 British females and 29 girls, and some of the British females may be girls. Thus, we need to sort and classify the data.

Devising a Plan

The Venn diagram is used in this chapter as a tool for classifying and sorting objects. If we could distinguish disjoint sets among the data where the union of the disjoint sets is the union of the set of people on the tour, we might be able to use the strategy of drawing a diagram to answer the question.

If the set of people on the tour is the universal set, then the sets of British citizens and American citizens are complementary sets. Because we know that there are 44 British citizens, the problem would be solved if we could determine the number of Americans. Because there are 17 American males, we need to find only the number of American females. We know that the tour had 17 American women; consequently, to find the number of American females, we must determine the number of American girls. We know that there are 29 girls altogether—British and American. If we can draw a Venn diagram that sorts the British girls from the American girls, then the number of American girls can be found and, as a result, the total number on the tour can be found.

Carrying Out the Plan

The number of American girls is not apparent from the information given, but we do have information about the numbers of some females on the tour. To sort out the American girls, we draw a Venn diagram that concentrates only on the females. If we use the set of all females as the universal set and denote the set of all girls as G, then $\overline{G}$ is the set of all women. Further, because the American females and the set of British females are complementary sets in the set of all females, we let A represent the set of American females to obtain the Venn diagram in Figure 2-23. For discussion purposes, we designate the disjoint regions in Figure 2-23 by small letters in parentheses.

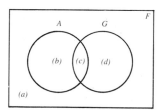

FIGURE 2-23

The regions may be identified as follows:

(a) The set of British women.
(b) The set of British girls.
(c) The set of American girls.
(d) The set of American women.

We use the information from the guides to obtain the number of people in each region. A study of the data reveals that because there are 29 women in regions (a) and (d), with 17 American women in the region marked (d), there must be 29 − 17, or 12, British women in the region marked (a). Also, because there are 26 British females—of whom there are 12 women—there are 26 − 12, or 14, British girls in the region marked (b). Because there are 29 girls in all, there must be 29 − 14, or 15, American girls in the region marked (c).

To complete the solution of the problem, we use the facts that there were 44 British citizens, 17 American males, 17 American women, and 15 American girls for a total of 44 + 17 + 17 + 15, or 93, people on the tour.

Looking Back

As an alternate approach to the problem, we could have used a Venn diagram involving other sets. For example, the Venn diagram in Figure 2-24 could be used. If A represents the set of adults, then B represents the set of British citizens and F represents the set of females. It is left for you to sort the information based upon this diagram.

FIGURE 2-24

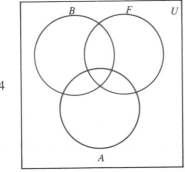

QUESTIONS FROM THE CLASSROOM

1. A student argues that $\{\varnothing\}$ is the proper notation for the empty set. What is your response?
2. A student does not believe that the empty set is a subset of every set. What is your response?
3. A student asks if $A = \{a, b, c\}$ and $B = \{b, c, d\}$, why isn't it true that $A \cup B = \{a, b, c, b, c, d\}$? What is your response?
4. A student asks, "How can I tell if a set is infinite?" What is your response?
5. A student asks, "Are any two infinite sets equivalent?" What is your response?
6. A student claims that a finite set of numbers is any set that has a largest element. Do you agree?
7. A student claims that the complement bar can be broken over the operation of intersection; that is, $\overline{A \cap B} = \overline{A} \cap \overline{B}$. What is your response?
8. A student claims that $\overline{A} \cap B$ includes all elements that are not in A. What is your response?
9. A student asks whether a formula and a function are the same. What is your response?
10. A student asks whether all functions are relations. What is your reply?
11. A student states that either $A \subseteq B$ or $B \subseteq A$. Is the student correct?

CHAPTER OUTLINE

I. Set definitions and notations
   A. A **set** can be described as any collection of objects.
   B. Sets should be **well defined**; that is, it is possible to determine whether or not an object belongs to the set.
   C. An **element** is any member of the set, for example, $a \in \{a, b\}$.

D. Sets can be specified by either listing all the elements or using **set-builder notation.**

E. The **empty set,** written ∅, contains no elements.

F. The **universal set** contains all the elements being discussed.

II. Relationships and operations on sets

A. Two sets are **equal** if and only if they have exactly the same elements.

B. Two sets A and B are in **one-to-one correspondence** if and only if each element of A can be paired with exactly one element of B and each element of B can be paired with exactly one element of A.

C. Two sets are **equivalent** if and only if their elements can be placed into one-to-one correspondence (written $A \sim B$).

D. Set A is a **subset** of B if and only if every element of A is an element of B (written $A \subseteq B$).

E. Set A is a **proper subset** of B if and only if every element of A is an element of B and there is at least one element of B that is not in A (written $A \subset B$).

F. The **union** of two sets A and B, is the set of all elements in A, in B, or in both A and B (written $A \cup B$).

G. The **intersection** of two sets A and B is the set of all elements belonging to both A and B (written $A \cap B$).

H. The **complement** of a set A is the set consisting of the elements of the universal set not in A (written $\overline{A}$).

I. The **complement of set A relative to set B** (set difference) is the set of all elements in B that are not in A (written $B - A$).

J. The **Cartesian product** of sets A and B is the set of all ordered pairs such that the first element of each pair is an element of A and the second element of each pair is an element of B (written $A \times B$).

K. **Venn diagrams** are useful in determining relationships between sets.

III. Properties of set operations

For all sets A, B, C, and the universal set U, the following properties hold.

A. $A \cap B = B \cap A$; commutative property of set intersection

B. $A \cup B = B \cup A$; commutative property of set union

C. $(A \cap B) \cap C = A \cap (B \cap C)$; associative property of set intersection

D. $(A \cup B) \cup C = A \cup (B \cup C)$; associative property of set union

E. $A \cap (B \cup C) = (A \cap B) \cup (A \cap C)$; distributive property of set intersection over union

F. $A \cup (B \cap C) = (A \cup B) \cap (A \cup C)$; distributive property of set union over intersection

G. $A \cap U = U \cap A = A$; U is the identity for set intersection

H. $A \cup \varnothing = \varnothing \cup A = A$; $\varnothing$ is the identity for set union

IV. Relations and functions

A. A **relation** R from set A to set B is a subset of $A \times B$; that is, if R is a relation, then $R \subseteq A \times B$.

B. A **function** from set A to set B is a relation from A to B in which each element of A is paired with one and only one element of B.

1. The set of all first components of a function, all the elements of A, is called the **domain** of the function.

2. The set of all second components of a function, a subset of B, is called the **range** of the function.

CHAPTER TEST

1. Write the set of letters of the English alphabet using set-builder notation.

2. List all the subsets of $\{m, a, t, h\}$.

3. Let

$U = \{x \mid x$ is a person living in Montana$\}$
$A = \{x \mid x$ is a person 30 years or older$\}$
$B = \{x \mid x$ is a person less than 30 years old$\}$
$C = \{x \mid x$ is a person who owns a gun$\}$

Describe in words each of the following.

(a) $\overline{A}$ (b) $A \cap C$ (c) $A \cup B$
(d) $\overline{C}$ (e) $\overline{A \cap C}$

4. Let

$U = \{u, n, i, v, e, r, s, a, l\}$
$A = \{r, a, v, e\}$ $C = \{l, i, n, e\}$
$B = \{a, r, e\}$ $D = \{s, a, l, e\}$

Find each of the following.
(a) $A \cup B$
(b) $C \cap D$
(c) $\overline{D}$
(d) $A \cap \overline{D}$
(e) $\overline{B \cup C}$
(f) $(B \cup C) \cap D$
(g) $(\overline{A} \cup B) \cap (C \cap \overline{D})$
(h) $(C \cap D) \cap A$
(i) $n(\overline{C})$
(j) $n(C \times D)$

5. Indicate the following sets by shading.

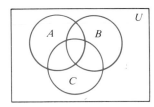

(a) $A \cap (B \cup C)$

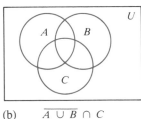

(b) $\overline{A \cup B} \cap C$

6. Let $A = \{s, e, t\}$ and $B = \{i, d, e, a\}$. Find each of the following.
(a) $B \times A$ (b) $A \times A$
(c) $n(A \times \varnothing)$ (d) $n(B - A)$

7. If $C = \{e, q, u, a, l, s\}$, how many proper subsets does C have?

8. Show one possible one-to-one correspondence between sets D and E if $D = \{t, h, e\}$ and $E = \{e, n, d\}$. How many different one-to-one correspondences between sets D and E are possible?

9. Use a Venn diagram to determine whether $A \cap (B \cup C) = (A \cap B) \cup C$ for all sets A, B, and C.

10. Describe, using symbols, the shaded portion in each of the following.

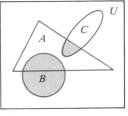

(a)

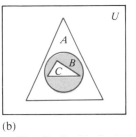

(b)

11. Which of the following relations are functions from the set of first components to the set of second components?
(a) $\{(a, b), (c, d), (e, a), (f, g)\}$
(b) $\{(a, b), (a, c), (b, b), (b, c)\}$
(c) $\{(a, b), (b, a)\}$

12. If $f(x) = 3x + 7$, find each of the following.
(a) $f(0)$ (b) $f(8)$ (c) $f(10)$

13. Given the following function rules and the domains, find the associated ranges.
(a) $f(x) = x + 3$ domain $= \{0, 1, 2, 3\}$
(b) $f(x) = 3x - 1$ domain $= \{5, 10, 15, 20\}$
(c) $f(x) = x^2$ domain $= \{0, 1, 2, 3, 4\}$
(d) $f(x) = x^2 + 3x + 5$ domain $= \{0, 1, 2\}$

14. If $A = \{1, 2, 3\}$, $B = \{2, 3, 4, 5\}$, and $C = \{3, 4, 5, 6, 7\}$, illustrate the associative property of intersection of sets. Using sets A and B, illustrate the commutative property of union of sets.

15. Classify each of the following as true or false. If false, tell why.
(a) For all sets A and B, either $A \subseteq B$ or $B \subseteq A$.
(b) The empty set is a proper subset of every set.
(c) For all sets A and B, if $A \sim B$, then $A = B$.
(d) The set $\{5, 10, 15, 20, \ldots\}$ is a finite set.
(e) No set is equivalent to a proper subset of itself.
(f) If A is an infinite set and $B \subseteq A$, then B also is an infinite set.
(g) For all finite sets A and B, if $A \cap B \neq \varnothing$, then $n(A \cup B) \neq n(A) + n(B)$.

(h) If A and B are sets such that $A \cap B = \varnothing$, then $A = \varnothing$ or $B = \varnothing$.

(i) $\varnothing \in \varnothing$

(j) If A and B are sets such that $A \times B = \varnothing$, then $A = \varnothing$ or $B = \varnothing$.

16. In a student survey, it was found that 16 students liked history, 19 liked English, 18 liked mathematics, 8 liked mathematics and English, 5 liked history and English, 7 liked history and mathematics, 3 liked all three subjects, and every student liked at least one of the subjects. Draw a Venn diagram describing this information and answer the following questions.

(a) How many students were in the survey?

(b) How many students liked only mathematics?

(c) How many students liked English and mathematics but not history?

SELECTED BIBLIOGRAPHY

Blomgrem, G. "What's in the Box-Subsets!" *The Arithmethic Teacher* 17 (March 1970):242.

Brieske, T. "Functions, Mappings, and Mapping Diagrams." *The Mathematics Teacher* 66 (May 1973):463–468.

Bruni, J., and H. Silverman. "Using Classification to Interpret Consumer Information." *The Arithmetic Teacher* 24 (January 1977):4–12.

Cetorelli, N. "Teaching Function Notation." *The Mathematics Teacher* 72 (November 1979):590–591.

Coltharp, F. "Mathematical Aspects of the Attribute Games." *The Arithmetic Teacher* 21 (March 1974):246–251.

Cruikshank, D. "Sorting, Classifying and Logic." *The Arithmetic Teacher* 21 (November 1974):588–598.

Geddes, D., and S. Lipsey, "The Hazards of Sets." *The Mathemetics Teacher* 62 (October 1969): 454.

Gilbert, R. "Hey Mister! It's Upside Down!" *Arithmetic Teacher* 25 (December 1977):18–19.

Lettieri, F. "Meet the Zorkies: A New Attribute Material." *Arithmetic Teacher* 26 (September 1978):36–39.

Liedtke, W. "Experiences with Blocks in Kindergarten," *The Arithmetic Teacher* 22 (May 1975):406–412.

Liedtke, W. "Rational Counting." *Arithmetic Teacher* 26 (October 1978):20–26.

National Council of Teachers of Mathematics. *Topics in Mathematics for Elementary School Teachers.* Booklet Number 1. Sets. 1964.

Papy, F. *Graphs and The Child.* New Rochelle, N.Y.: Cuisenaire Company of America, Inc., 1970.

Papy, F. *Mathematics and The Child.* New Rochelle, N.Y.: Cuisenaire Company of America, Inc., 1971.

Pereira-Mendoza, L. "Graphing and Prediction in the Elementary School." *The Arithmetic Teacher* 24 (February 1977):112–113.

Peterson, J., and G. Dolson. "Property Games." *The Arithmetic Teacher* 24 (January 1977):36–38.

Schoen, H. "Some Difficulty in the Language of Sets." *The Arithmetic Teacher* 21 (March 1974):236–237.

Silverman, H. "Teacher Made Materials for Teaching Numbers and Counting." *The Arithmetic Teacher* 19 (October 1972):431–433.

Vance, J. "The Large-Blue-Triangle: A Matter of Logic." *The Arithmetic Teacher* 22 (March 1975):237–240.

Vilenkin, N. *Stories about Sets.* New York and London: Academic Press, 1969.

Numeration Systems and Whole Numbers 3

PRELIMINARY PROBLEM

In a small rural community, the elementary school had no refrigerators. Through a federally financed program, the school provided 1 cup of milk per day for each student. Milk for the day was purchased at the local store each morning. The milk was available in gallons, half-gallons, quarts, pints, or cups, and the larger containers were better buys. If 1 gallon, 1 quart, and 1 pint of milk were purchased on Tuesday, how many students were at school that day? On Wednesday, 31 students were at school. How much milk was purchased on Wednesday to make the best buy?

INTRODUCTION

Early people needed only a few numbers for their daily activities. With the coming of civilization, people needed to invent a system to handle greater numbers. Such a system did not come readily, but developed over centuries. In this chapter we examine different numeration systems from a historical perspective. This will help us to develop an appreciation for the simplicity and efficiency of our present numeration system.

After investigating other systems, we examine the Hindu-Arabic system, a base ten system. Algorithms for the operations of addition, subtraction, multiplication, and division of whole numbers in base ten numeration are considered. Finally, properties and algorithms in number bases other than ten will be discussed as another mechanism for developing an understanding of our present system.

3-1   NUMERATION SYSTEMS

The earliest numerals were strokes drawn on a wall. They represented animals such as mammoths and deer, and each stroke represented one animal. Since that time, numerals have changed extensively. Figure 3-1 shows some changes leading to our present-day Hindu-Arabic system. Even today there are variations in the Hindu-Arabic symbols used around the world. For example, Arabs use 0 for 5 and . for 0.

FIGURE 3-1

(Hindu 300 B.C.)

(Hindu 876 A.D.)

(Hindu 11th century)

(West Arabic 11th century)

(East Arabic 1575)

(European 15th century)

(European 16th century)

As you can see, different symbols can be used to represent the same quantity. For example, 3 and III both represent the quantity we call three. The symbols 3 and III are called numerals. Strictly speaking, a **numeral** is a written symbol used to represent a quantity or number. A **number** is an abstract concept used to describe quantity. You can see a numeral but not a number. In this text, we distinguish between number and numeral only if the distinction clarifies a concept.

Many civilizations developed **numeration systems,** that is, logically structured methods of denoting numbers. Some early systems—such as the Egyptian system, which dates back to about 3400 B.C.—were based on tally marks. Tally marks are scratches or marks that represent the items being counted. One tally mark is used for each object being counted, so that a one-to-one correspondence exists between tally marks and the objects. The Egyptian system was a very simple, but inefficient, system for recording large numbers. Later improvements on the tally-mark system led to new numerals for certain groupings. For example, the Egyptians used a heel bone symbol, ∩ , to stand for a grouping of ten tally marks.

IIIIIIIII ⟶ ∩

Other numerals which the Egyptians used in their system are given in Table 3-1.

(margin labels: numeral, number, numeration systems)

TABLE 3-1

Egyptian Numeral	Description	Hindu-Arabic Face Value
I	Vertical staff	1
∩	Heel bone	10
9	Scroll	100
⌔	Lotus flower	1000
⌀	Pointing finger	10,000
⌕	Polliwog or burbot	100,000
⌦	Astonished man	1,000,000

The Egyptian system involved an additive property in which the value of a number was the sum of the values of the numerals. An example is given below.

⌕	represents	100,000	
999	represents	300	(100 + 100 + 100)
∩∩	represents	20	(10 + 10)
II	represents	2	(1 + 1)

⌕999∩∩II   represents   100,322

In the Egyptian system, 100,322 could also have been written as 999∩∩⌕II . The order of the numerals made no difference.

The Babylonian system was developed at about the same time as the Egyptian system. Records of the Babylonian system have been preserved for centuries because the Babylonians used clay tablets. The tablets were indented with a stylus and baked in the sun. The Babylonian system used the symbols given in Table 3-2.

TABLE 3-2

Babylonian Numeral	Hindu-Arabic Face Value
▼	1
<	10

The Babylonian numerals 1 through 59 were similar to the Egyptian numerals, but the staff and the heel bone were replaced by the symbols in Table 3-2. For example, ≪ ▼▼ represented 22. For numbers greater than 59, the Babylonians used place value. Numbers greater than 59 used repeated groupings of sixty, much as we use groupings of ten today. For example, ▼▼ ≪<▼▼ represents $2 \cdot 60 + 22$, or 142. The space indicates that ▼▼ represents $2 \cdot 60$ rather than 2. Numerals to the left of a second space have a value $60 \cdot 60$ times their face value, and so on.

≪ ▼   represents $20 \cdot 60 + 1$, or 1201

<▼ <▼ ▼   represents $11 \cdot 60 \cdot 60 + 11 \cdot 60 + 1$, or 40,261

▼ <▼ <▼ ▼   represents $1 \cdot 60 \cdot 60 \cdot 60 + 11 \cdot 60 \cdot 60 + 11 \cdot 60 + 1$, or 256,261

The Babylonian system was superior to the Egyptian system, but inadequacies still existed. For example, the symbol ▼▼ could have represented 2 or $2 \cdot 60$ because the Babylonian system lacked a symbol for the very important number zero.

Another system without a symbol for zero was the Roman numeration system, which remains in use today. Roman numerals appear on cornerstones, on the opening pages of books, and on the faces of clocks. The basic Roman numerals are pictured in Table 3-3.

TABLE 3-3

Roman Numeral	Hindu-Arabic Face Value
I	1
V	5
X	10
L	50
C	100
D	500
M	1000

Roman numerals can be combined using the additive property. The additive property applies to Roman numerals listed in decreasing order from left to right. For example, MDCLXVI represents $1000 + 500 + 100 + 50 + 10 + 5 + 1 = 1666$, CCCXXVIII represents 328, and VI represents 6. However, if the numerals are not listed in decreasing order from left to right, then a subtractive property applies. For example, I is less than V, so if it is to the left of V, it is subtracted. Thus, IV has a value of $5 - 1$, or 4, and XC represents $100 - 10$, or 90. The only allowed pairings of symbols based on the subtractive property are given in Table 3-4.

TABLE 3-4

Roman Numeral	Hindu-Arabic Face Value
IV	$5 - 1$, or 4
IX	$10 - 1$, or 9
XL	$50 - 10$, or 40
XC	$100 - 10$, or 90
CD	$500 - 100$, or 400
CM	$1000 - 100$, or 900

Some extensions of the subtractive property could lead to ambiguous results. For example, IXC could be 91 or 89. By custom, 91 is written XCI, and 89 is written LXXXIX. In general, only one smaller symbol can be to the left of a larger symbol, and the pair must be one of those listed in Table 3-4.

The Romans adopted the use of bars to write large numbers. The use of bars is based on a multiplicative property. A bar over a symbol or symbols indicates that the value is multiplied by 1000. For example, $\overline{V}$ represents $5 \cdot 1000$, or 5000, and $\overline{CDX}$ represents $410 \cdot 1000$, or 410,000. To indicate even greater numbers, more bars appear. For example, $\overline{\overline{V}}$ represents $5 \cdot 1000 \cdot 1000$, or 5,000,000; $\overline{\overline{\overline{CXI}}}$ represents $111 \cdot 1000 \cdot 1000 \cdot 1000$ or 111,000,000,000; and $\overline{CX}I$ represents $110 \cdot 1000 + 1$, or 110,001.

The properties of numeration systems illustrated in this section are not definitive, but several of them are used in the Hindu-Arabic system. The Hindu-Arabic numeration system we use today has ten basic symbols, called **digits**: 0, 1, 2, 3, 4, 5, 6, 7, 8, 9. The system uses place value. The value of a digit in a given numeral depends on the placement of the digit with respect to other digits in the numeral. Each place in a Hindu-Arabic numeral represents a power of 10. Thus, the system is called a **decimal system,** after the Latin word *decem* for ten.

A special feature of the Hindu-Arabic system is a place-holding symbol, 0. It represents the absence of a power of 10. For example, in 403, the 0 indicates that there are *no* tens. None of the other three systems—Egyptian, Babylonian, or Roman—had this feature. One of the first systems to utilize a symbol for zero was the Mayan system.

PROBLEM SET 3-1

1. For each of the following, tell which numeral represents the greater number and why.
   (a) $\overline{\text{MCDXXIV}}$ and $\overline{\overline{\text{MCDXXIV}}}$
   (b) 4632 and 46,032
   (c) ＜▼▼ and ＜ ▼▼
   (d) 999∩∩‖ and ⟨ᶠ∩|

2. For each of the following, name both the succeeding and preceding numerals (one more and one less).
   (a) MCMXLIX   (b) $\overline{\text{MI}}$ (c) CMXCIX
   (d) ＜＜ ＜▼   (e) ⟨ᶠ99

3. For each of the following systems, discuss how you might add 245 and 989.
   (a) Babylonian   (b) Egyptian   (c) Roman

4. Write each of the following in Roman symbols.
   (a) 121   (b) 42   (c) 89   (d) 5282

5. Could 6000 be written using Babylonian symbols? Why or why not?

6. Write each of the following using Egyptian symbols.
   (a) 52   (b) 103   (c) 100,003   (d) 38

7. How might you perform the following subtraction problem using Egyptian numerals?

$$\begin{array}{r} ⟨∩∩||| \\ -∩∩∩∩∩|||||| \\ \hline \end{array}$$

8. Complete the following chart, which compares symbols for numbers in different numeration systems.

Hindu-Arabic	Babylonian	Egyptian	Roman
72			
	＜ ▼▼		
		⟨ᶠ99∩∩‖‖	
			DCLXVII

9. (a) Create a numeration system of your own with unique symbols and write a paragraph explaining the properties of your system.
   (b) Complete the chart below using your system.

Hindu-Arabic Numeral	Your System Numeral	Hindu-Arabic Numeral	Your System Numeral
1		100	
5		5,000	
10		10,000	
50		15,280	

3-2 WHOLE NUMBERS AND THE OPERATIONS OF ADDITION AND SUBTRACTION

Many children learn to count before they begin school. At first they recite the names—one, two, three, four, and so on—without knowing what the names mean. Typically, children do not understand place value. For example, when asked the significance of 3 in the numeral 37, they may have no response. Place value has been very important in the evolution of numeration systems, and the use of zero is essential. When zero is joined with the natural numbers, the set

whole numbers $N = \{1, 2, 3, 4, 5, \ldots\}$, we have the set of numbers we call **whole numbers,** denoted by W. In the base ten number system, we have $W = \{0, 1, 2, 3, 4, 5, \ldots\}$, or $W = \{0\} \cup N$. An alternate way of defining a whole number is to define it as the cardinal number of a finite set.

In the base ten system, we can write a numeral to represent any number of objects using only ten digits, 0 through 9. Numbers in the system are based on groupings of ten; ten groups of tens, or hundreds; ten groups of hundreds, or thousands; and so on. In the system the value of a digit in a given numeral depends on the placement of the digit with respect to the other digits in the numeral. The value of a number is determined by multiplying each digit times its place value and finding the sum of these products. Chip trading and multibase blocks are excellent aids for teaching these concepts to children.

A calculator can be used to reinforce the concepts of place value. Students can be asked to enter numbers on the calculator as the teacher says them orally. For example, if the teacher says, "five thousand nine hundred eighty four," the student enters $\boxed{5}$ $\boxed{9}$ $\boxed{8}$ $\boxed{4}$. The 5 represents 5 thousands; the 9 represents 9 hundreds; the 8 represents 8 tens; and the 4 represents 4 units, as shown in Figure 3-2.

FIGURE 3-2

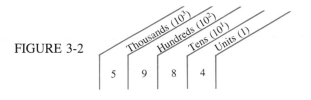

Hence, $5984 = 5 \cdot 1000 + 9 \cdot 100 + 8 \cdot 10 + 4$. This representation is called the **expanded form** of the number. Using exponents, products such as $10 \cdot 10 \cdot 10$ and $10 \cdot 10$ can be written as 10^3 and 10^2, respectively; in each case, 10 is called a **factor** of the products. Thus, 5984 can be written using exponents as $5 \cdot 10^3 + 9 \cdot 10^2 + 8 \cdot 10 + 4$, which is another way of writing the expanded form of 5984. The notion of exponents can be generalized as shown below.

expanded form

factor

DEFINITION

> If a is any number and n is any natural number, then a^n is defined by the following equation.
>
> $$a^n = \underbrace{a \cdot a \cdot a \cdot \ldots \cdot a}_{n \text{ factors}}$$

*n*th power of *a*
exponent
base

a^n is called the ***n*th power of a;** n is called the **exponent;** a is called the **base.**

In Chapter 6 the definitions and properties of exponents are discussed in detail. It is shown there why it is useful to define a^0 as 1 if $a \neq 0$.

Computations involving exponents can be made using a calculator. If the calculator has an automatic constant, the following steps will compute $5^4 = 625$.

Some calculators have an exponential button, which looks like this: $\boxed{y^x}$. This button computes some number y raised to the x power. For example, to compute 5^4 we push $\boxed{5}$ $\boxed{y^x}$ $\boxed{4}$ $\boxed{=}$.

Addition and Subtraction of Whole Numbers

The concept of addition of whole numbers is normally introduced to children using the notion of "combining." Suppose Jane has 4 pencils in one pile and 3 pencils in another. If she combines the two groups of pencils into one pile, how many pencils are in the combined pile? Figure 3-3 shows the solution as it might appear in an elementary school textbook.

FIGURE 3-3

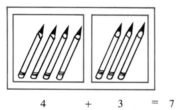

4   +   3   =   7

Addition of whole numbers can be used to describe the situation in Figure 3-3. The combined set of pencils is the union of the set of 4 pencils and the set of 3 pencils. Thus, the notion of combining two groups can be expressed mathematically as the union of two disjoint sets.

DEFINITION

> Let A and B be two disjoint sets. If $n(A) = a$ and $n(B) = b$, then $a + b = n(A \cup B)$.

addends   sum

The numbers a and b in this definition are the **addends**; $(a + b)$ is the **sum.** Addition is a *binary operation* because a sum involves two numbers.

The importance of A and B being disjoint in this definition is explored in the problem set. This definition is a generalization of the situation described in Figure 3-3. However, most elementary students need not be exposed to such a formal definition.

In elementary school classrooms, a number line can be used to model whole numbers. Any line marked with two fundamental points, one representing 0 and the other representing 1, can be turned into a number line. For example, on a horizontal line, choose an arbitrary point and label the point 0. Then choose any other point on the line to the right of the point labeled 0, and label this point 1. The points representing 0 and 1 mark the ends of a **unit segment.** Other points are marked and labeled as shown in Figure 3-4. Any two consecutive points in Figure 3-4 mark the ends of a segment that has the same length as the unit segment.

unit segment

FIGURE 3-4

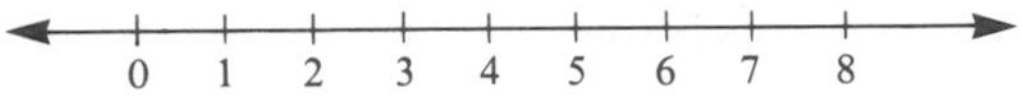

Any given number can be represented by a directed arrow of a given length. For example, Figure 3-5 shows several directed arrows that represent 2.

FIGURE 3-5

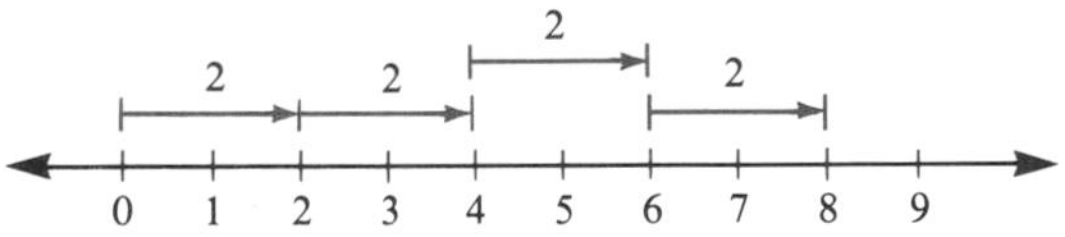

Using directed arrows on the number line, it is possible to model additional problems. For example, the sum of $4 + 3$ is shown in Figure 3-6. Arrows representing the addends, 4 and 3, are combined into one arrow representing the sum.

FIGURE 3-6

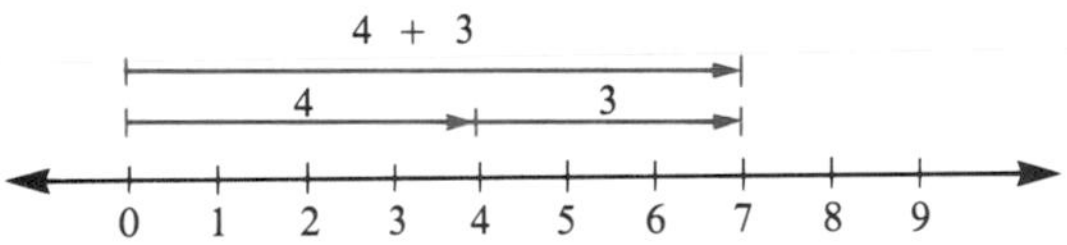

greater than   less than

A number line can also be used to describe **greater than** and **less than** relations. For example, in Figure 3-6, notice that 7 is to the right of 4 on the number line. We say, "seven is greater than four," and we write $7 > 4$. Since 7 is to the right of 4, there is a number that can be added to 4 to get 7, namely, 3. Thus, $7 > 4$ since $7 = 4 + 3$. We can generalize to form a definition for greater than.

DEFINITION

> For any whole numbers a and b, a is **greater than** b, written $a > b$, if and only if there exists a natural number k such that $a = b + k$.

greater than or equal to
less than or equal to

The expression $a > b$ can also be read from right to left. From right to left, it reads "b is less than a," and this can be written as $b < a$. For example, 7 is greater than 3 implies that 3 is less than 7. Sometimes equality is combined with the inequalities greater than and less than to give **greater than or equal to** or **less than or equal to** relations, denoted by $\geq$ and $\leq$. Note that $5 \geq 3$ and $3 \geq 3$ are both true statements.

We now examine properties of whole-number addition. These properties will be used to develop algorithms for more complicated addition. The first property says that when two whole numbers are added, the result is a unique whole number. This property is called the *closure property for addition of whole numbers,* and we say, "The set of whole numbers is closed under addition." This is summarized in the following property.

Property | **Closure Property for Addition of Whole Numbers**   If *a* and *b* are any whole numbers, then *a* + *b* is a unique whole number.

With some sets, the addition of two numbers from the set results in a number that does not belong to the set. In this case, we say the set is *not closed* under addition. For example, the set {0, 1, 2, 3} is not closed under addition because we can find a sum—for example, 2 + 3 = 5—that is not an element of the given set.

Example 3-1 | Which of these sets are closed under addition?

(a) {0, 1}   (b) {*x* | *x* is an even whole number}
(c) {*x* | *x* is an odd whole number}

Solution | (a) This set is not closed under addition. Although the sum of two different numbers such as 0 and 1 belongs to the set {0, 1}, it is not true for all sums involving numbers from the set. For example, 1 + 1 = 2 and 2 ∉ {0, 1}.
(b) This set is closed under addition because the sum of any two even whole numbers is always an even whole number. For example, 8 + 10 = 16.
(c) This set is not closed under addition because the sum of two odd numbers is an even number. For example, 5 + 3 = 8.

The closure property for addition can be extended to any finite sum of whole numbers. For example, if *a*, *b*, *c*, and *d* are whole numbers, then *a* + *b* + *c* + *d* is a unique whole number.

Figure 3-7 shows two additions. Pictured above the number line is 3 + 5, and below the number line is 5 + 3. The sums are exactly the same. This demonstrates that 3 + 5 = 5 + 3. This idea that two whole numbers can be added in either order is true for any two whole numbers *a* and *b*. (This can be easily proved using the definition of addition of whole numbers and the fact that $A \cup B = B \cup A$). This property is called the *commutative property for addition of whole numbers* and we say, "The set of whole numbers is commutative under addition."

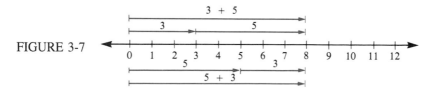

FIGURE 3-7

Property | **Commutative Property for Addition of Whole Numbers**   If *a* and *b* are any whole numbers, then *a* + *b* = *b* + *a*.

The commutative property for addition of whole numbers is not obvious to many children. They may be able to find the sum 9 + 2 and not be able to find the sum 2 + 9. (Why?)

When adding three or more numbers, it is necessary to select the order in which to add the numbers. For example, consider $4 + 8 + 2$. One person might group the 4 and the 8 together and do the computation as $4 + 8 + 2 = (4 + 8) + 2 = 12 + 2 = 14$. The parentheses indicate that the first two numbers are grouped together. Another person might recognize that it is easy to add any number to 10 and work the problem as $4 + 8 + 2 = 4 + (8 + 2) = 4 + 10 = 14$. Thus, we see that $4 + 8 + 2 = (4 + 8) + 2 = 4 + (8 + 2)$. This example illustrates the *associative property for addition of whole numbers* and we say, "The set of whole numbers is associative under addition."

Property | **Associative Property for Addition of Whole Numbers**   If a, b, and c are any whole numbers, then $(a + b) + c = a + (b + c)$.

When several numbers are being added, the parentheses are usually omitted because the grouping does not alter the result. The commutative and associative properties for addition are often used together. For example, to find the sum $20 + 5 + 60 + 4$, we group the addends as $(20 + 60) + (5 + 4)$ to obtain $80 + 9$, or 89.

Another property of addition of whole numbers is seen when one addend is 0. In Figure 3-8, set A has 5 blocks and set B has 0 blocks. The union of sets A and B has only 5 blocks.

FIGURE 3-8

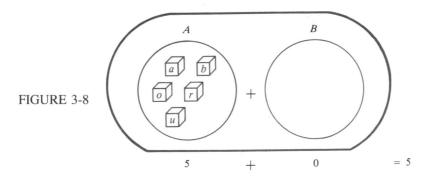

$$5 \qquad + \qquad 0 \qquad = 5$$

This example illustrates yet another general property, as follows.

Property | **Identity Property for Addition for Whole Numbers**   There is a unique whole number 0 such that for any whole number a, $a + 0 = a = 0 + a$.

Remark
additive identity | The number 0 is called the **additive identity** for whole numbers.

Example 3-2 | Which of the properties for whole number addition are used in each of the following?

(a) $5 + 7 = 7 + 5$
(b) $1001 + 733$ is a whole number.

(c) $(3 + 5) + 7 = (5 + 3) + 7$
(d) $(8 + 5) + 2 = 8 + (5 + 2)$
(e) $0 + 8 = 8$
(f) $(10 + 5) + (10 + 3) = (10 + 10) + (5 + 3)$

Solution

(a) Commutative property for addition.
(b) Closure property for addition.
(c) Commutative property for addition.
(d) Associative property for addition.
(e) Identity property for addition.
(f) Commutative and associative properties for addition.

In the cartoon, Peppermint Patty reacts to the operation of subtraction, which we investigate next.

© 1978 United Feature Syndicate, Inc.

One way to think about subtraction is this: Instead of a second set of objects being joined to a first set, as in addition, the second set is being "taken away" from a first set. For example, suppose we have 8 blocks and we take away 3 of them, as shown in Figure 3-9.

FIGURE 3-9 ⬦ ⬦ ⬦ ⬦ ⬦ ⬦ ⬦ ⬦ → Take away these.

We record this process as $8 - 3$. Because 5 blocks remain, we write $8 - 3 = 5$.

A second way to consider subtraction is by using a "comparison" model. Suppose we have 8 blocks and 3 balls and we would like to know how many more blocks we have than balls. We can pair the blocks and balls, as shown in Figure 3-10, take away the paired objects, and determine that there are 5 more blocks than balls. We also write this as $8 - 3 = 5$.

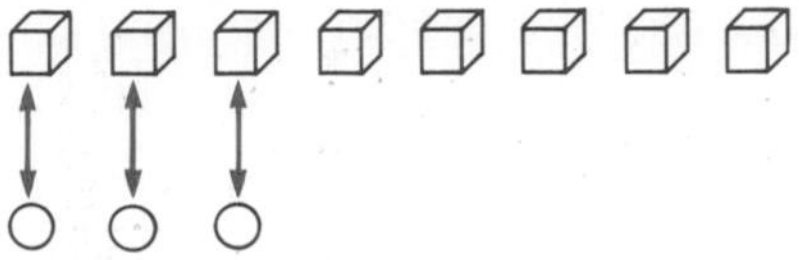

FIGURE 3-10

A third model for subtraction, the "missing-addend" model, relates subtraction and addition. Recall that in Figure 3-9, $8 - 3$ is pictured with blocks as 8 blocks "take away" 3 blocks. The number of blocks left is the number $8 - 3$, or 5. This can also be thought of as the number of blocks that could be added to 3 blocks in order to get 8 blocks; that is,

$$\boxed{8 - 3} + 3 = 8$$

Thus, $8 - 3$ can be thought of as the number that can be added to 3 to obtain 8. The number $8 - 3$, or 5, is called the **missing addend** in the equation $\square + 3 = 8$. This idea can be generalized for whole numbers a and b as shown below.

missing addend

DEFINITION

> For any whole numbers a and b, $a - b$ is the unique whole number c such that $c + b = a$; that is, $a - b = c$ if and only if $a = b + c$.

Remark

minuend   subtrahend
difference

The notation $a - b$ is read "a subtract b" or "a minus b." The number a is called the **minuend;** b is called the **subtrahend;** c is called the **difference.**

For $a - b$ to be meaningful for whole numbers, b must be less than or equal to a. Consider the difference $3 - 5$. Using the definition of subtraction, $3 - 5 = c$ means $c + 5 = 3$. Since there is no whole number c that satisfies the equation, the solution for $3 - 5$ cannot be found in the set of whole numbers. This means that the set of whole numbers is *not* closed under subtraction. In Chapter 4 we consider the set of integers, which is closed under subtraction. Showing that the set of whole numbers does not have the commutative, associative, or identity properties under subtraction is left as an exercise.

Subtraction of whole numbers can be modeled using a number line. For example, $5 - 3$ is shown in Figure 3-11. Observe that an arrow extends 5 units to the right from 0. Because the operation is subtraction, the second arrow extends 3 units to the left. Thus, we see that $5 - 3 = 2$.

FIGURE 3-11

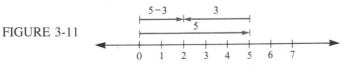

An alternate way to find $5 - 3$ using a number line is to determine the missing number that must be added to 3 to obtain the sum of 5. In Figure 3-12, the missing number is 2, and we have $5 - 3 = 2$.

FIGURE 3-12

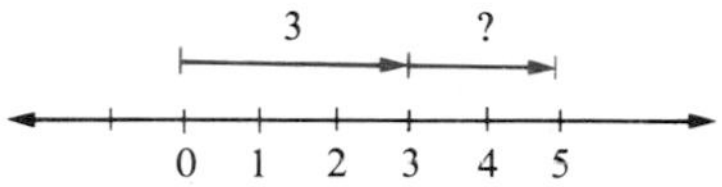

PROBLEM SET 3-2

1. For each of the following decimal numerals, give the place value of the underlined numeral.
   (a) 827,<u>3</u>67
   (b) 8,421,<u>0</u>00
   (c) 97,<u>9</u>98
   (d) 810,48<u>5</u>
   (e) <u>1</u>6,450
   (f) a,<u>b</u>cd,efg
2. The following are numerals written using expanded form. Rewrite each as it is usually seen.
   (a) $3 \cdot 10^6 + 4 \cdot 10^3 + 5$
   (b) $2 \cdot 10^4 + 1$
   (c) $3 \cdot 10^3 + 5 \cdot 10^2 + 6 \cdot 10$
   (d) $9 \cdot 10^6 + 9 \cdot 10 + 9$
3. Use a number line to explain why $5 < 7$ and why $6 > 3$.
4. Explain why $5 < 7$ and why $6 > 3$ by finding natural numbers k such that each is true.
   (a) $5 + k = 7$
   (b) $6 = 3 + k$
5. In the definition of "greater than," can the natural number k be replaced by the whole number k? Why or why not?
6. Give an example to show why, in the definition of addition, sets A and B must be disjoint.
7. Use the number line model to illustrate $6 + 3 = 9$.
8. For each of the following, indicate which whole numbers will make the statements true.
   (a) $2 + \square = 7$
   (b) $\square + 4 = 6$
   (c) $3 + \square \leq 5$
   (d) $\square + 6 \geq 9$
9. Tell whether or not the following sets are closed under addition. Why or why not?
   (a) $B = \{0\}$
   (b) $T = \{0, 3, 6, 9, 12, \ldots\}$
   (c) $N = \{1, 2, 3, 4, 5, \ldots\}$
   (d) $V = \{3, 5, 7\}$

10. Each of the following is an example of one of the properties for addition of whole numbers. Identify the property illustrated.
    (a) $7 + 0 = 7$
    (b) $6 + 3 = 3 + 6$
    (c) $(6 + 3) + 5 = 6 + (3 + 5)$
    (d) $(6 + 3) + 5 = (3 + 6) + 5$
    (e) $12 + 0 = 12$
    (f) If $q, r, s \in W$, $(q + r) + s = q + (r + s)$
11. For each of the following, use the underlined expressions to illustrate that English expressions are not always commutative.
    (a) Siamese <u><u>cat</u> <u>show</u></u>
    (b) <u>Going to school</u> <u>I saw the birds</u>.
12. For each of the following, use the three words to illustrate that English expressions are not always associative.
    (a) dog house broken
    (b) short story writer
13. For each of the following, find the whole numbers to make the statements true, if possible.
    (a) $8 - 5 = \square$
    (b) $8 - \square = 5$
    (c) $\square - 4 = 9$
    (d) $a - 0 = \square$
    (e) $a - \square = a$
    (f) $\square - 3 \leq 6$
    (g) $\square - 3 > 6$
14. Jill lost 7 pounds, while Jack lost only 3. How much more weight did Jill lose than Jack?
15. Rewrite each of the following subtraction problems as an addition problem.
    (a) $x - 119 = 213$
    (b) $213 - x = 119$
    (c) $213 - 119 = x$

16. Use a number line to illustrate each of the following subtractions.
    (a) $11 - 3$
    (b) $8 - 4$
17. Illustrate $9 - 2$ using each of the models listed below.
    (a) Take-away model.
    (b) Comparison model.
    (c) Missing-addend model.
18. Show that, in general, each of the following is false for the set of whole numbers.
    (a) $a - b = b - a$
    (b) $(a - b) - c = a - (b - c)$
    (c) $a - 0 = 0 - a = a$
19. For each of the following, determine possible whole numbers a, b, and c for which the statement is true.
    (a) $a - b = b - a$
    (b) $(a - b) - c = a - (b - c)$
    (c) $a - 0 = 0 - a = a$
    (d) $a(b - c) = ab - ac$
20. Suppose $A \subseteq B$. If $n(A) = a$ and $n(B) = b$, then $b - a$ could be defined as $n(B - A)$. Choose two sets A and B and illustrate this definition.
21. A palindrome is any number that reads the same backward and forward—for example, 121 and 2332. Try the following. Begin with any number. Is it a palindrome? If not, reverse the digits and add this new number to the original number. Is this a palindrome? If not, repeat the above procedure until a palindrome is obtained. For example, start with 78. Because 78 is not a palindrome, we add: $78 + 87 = 165$. Because 165 is not a palindrome, we add: $165 + 561 = 726$. Again, 726 is not a palindrome, so we add $726 + 627$ to obtain 1353. Finally, $1353 + 3531$ yields 4884, which is a palindrome.
    (a) Try the above method with the following numbers.
        (i) 93   (ii) 588   (iii) 2003
    (b) Find a number for which the procedure described takes more than five steps to form a palindrome.
22. A magic square is an array of numbers in which the sum of every row, column, and diagonal is the same.

Make each of the following a magic square.

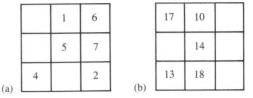

(a)   (b)

23. Angelo read 6 pages of *Black Beauty* on Monday. He had read a total of 15 pages before Wednesday. How many pages did he read on Tuesday?
24. Find the next three terms in each of the following sequences.
    (a) 8, 13, 18, 23, 28, _____, _____, _____
    (b) 98, 91, 84, 77, 70, 63, _____, _____, _____
25. Make a calculator display numbers that have the following values.
    (a) Seven tens   (b) Nine thousands
    (c) Eleven hundreds   (d) Fifty-six tens
    (e) Three hundred forty-seven tens
26. Use only the buttons $\boxed{1}$, $\boxed{2}$, $\boxed{3}$, $\boxed{4}$, $\boxed{5}$, $\boxed{6}$, $\boxed{7}$, $\boxed{8}$, and $\boxed{9}$ for each of the following.
    (a) Fill the display to show the greatest number possible; each button may be used only once.
    (b) Fill the display to show the least number possible; each button may be used only once.
    (c) Fill the display to show the greatest number possible if a button may be used more than once.
    (d) Fill the display to show the smallest number possible if a button may be used more than once.
27. Display the greatest number that has exactly seven digits with no two digits repeated.
28. Make a calculator count to 100. (Use a constant operation if available.)
    (a) By 1s   (b) By 2s   (c) By 5s
29. Make a calculator count backward to 0 from 27. (Use a constant operation if possible.)
    (a) By 1s   (b) By 3s   (c) By 9s
30. If a calculator is made to count by 2s starting at 2, what is the thirteenth number in the sequence?

* * * * * * * REVIEW PROBLEMS * * * * * * *

31. Write the number that precedes each of the following.
    (a) CMLX   (b) XXXIX
32. What are the advantages of the Babylonian system over the Egyptian system?

BRAIN TEASER

Place the numbers 1 through 11 in the circles shown so that the sums are the same in each direction.

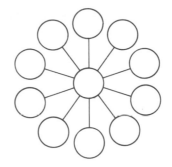

3-3   MULTIPLICATION AND DIVISION OF WHOLE NUMBERS

Multiplication of whole numbers is related to addition of whole numbers. It is very important that addition be mastered before multiplication is introduced. Multiplication of whole numbers is usually introduced in elementary school as a shorthand method of writing repeated addition. This will be explored in the following example.

Example 3-3

Looking at her empty classroom before the first bell, a mathematics teacher noticed that there were 6 rows of chairs with 4 chairs in each row. When the bell rang, each chair was occupied by a student. How many students were present?

Solution

A strategy here is to reduce the problem to one that we know how to solve. In this case, the problem can be rewritten as an addition problem. Since each chair is occupied, there are 6 rows of students with 4 students in each row for a total of

$$\underbrace{4 + 4 + 4 + 4 + 4 + 4}_{\text{six 4s}} = 24$$

We use the notation 6×4, or $6 \cdot 4$, to mean six 4s are added. Multiplication of whole numbers is defined in many grade school books as repeated addition.

DEFINITION

> For any whole numbers n and a,
>
> $$n \cdot a = \underbrace{a + a + \cdots + a}_{n \text{ terms}}$$

Note that if $n = 0$, then $0 \cdot a$ means there are 0 terms. This is interpreted to mean $0 \cdot a = 0$.

A calculator can be used to show that multiplication and repeated addition yield the same result. For example, to compute $6 \cdot 9$ we may use the constant button, as follows.

(Remember, different calculators have different constant features.) If we push $\boxed{6}$ $\boxed{\times}$ $\boxed{9}$ $\boxed{=}$, we obtain the same result.

Multiplication of whole numbers can be modeled on a number line. For example, the number line model for $5 \cdot 4$ is shown in Figure 3-13.

FIGURE 3-13

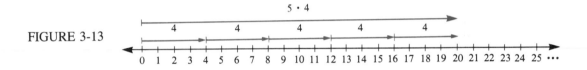

The following problem suggests another model for multiplication of whole numbers.

PROBLEM 1

At a health food bar, you can order a soyburger on dark or light bread with any one of the following: mustard, mayonnaise, or horseradish. How many different soyburgers can a waiter call out to the cook?

Understanding the Problem

The problem asks for the number of combinations of bread and condiments, where the bread is chosen from a set $B = \{$light, dark$\}$ and the condiment is chosen from a set $C = \{$mustard, mayonnaise, horseradish$\}$.

Devising a Plan

One strategy is to list all possibilities in an organized manner. A model called a *tree diagram* can be used to accomplish this, as shown in Figure 3-14. To solve the problem, simply count the items under "What the cook hears."

FIGURE 3-14

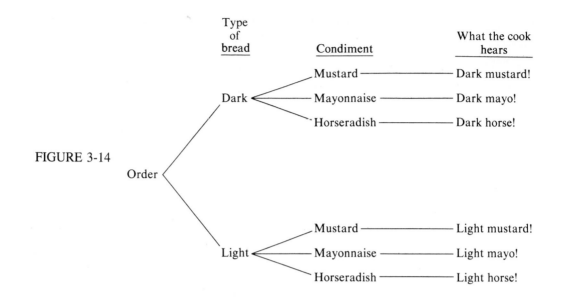

Carrying Out the Plan

All the possible ways of ordering the soyburgers are listed in Figure 3-14, so we see there are six orders that can be called out by the waiter.

Looking Back

We could investigate problems involving different numbers of available breads and condiments at this point in order to find out if there is a general formula for finding the number of different orders the cook hears. What the cook hears could be written as ordered pairs—for example, (dark, mustard). The entire set of ordered pairs formed is the Cartesian product, $B \times C$, of sets $B = \{$light, dark$\}$ and $C = \{$mustard, mayonnaise, horseradish$\}$. The number of ordered pairs in $B \times C$ is the answer to the problem. Because the answer is $2 \cdot 3$, we see that $2 \cdot 3 = n(B) \cdot n(C) = n(B \times C)$.

The approach in Looking Back of Problem 1 leads us to an alternate definition of multiplication of whole numbers.

DEFINITION

For finite sets A and B, if $n(A) = a$ and $n(B) = b$, then $a \cdot b = n(A \times B)$.

product   multiplier
multiplicand

Note that in this definition, sets A and B do not have to be disjoint. The expression $a \cdot b$ is called the **product** of a and b, a is called the **multiplier,** and b is called the **multiplicand.** Also, note that $A \times B$ indicates the Cartesian product, not multiplication. We multiply numbers, not sets.

As with addition, multiplication on the set of whole numbers has the closure, commutative, associative, and identity properties.

Property | **Closure Property for Multiplication of Whole Numbers** For any whole numbers a and b, $a \cdot b$ is a unique whole number.

Property | **Commutative Property for Multiplication of Whole Numbers** For any whole numbers a and b, $a \cdot b = b \cdot a$.

Property | **Associative Property for Multiplication of Whole Numbers** For any whole numbers a, b, and c, $(a \cdot b) \cdot c = a \cdot (b \cdot c)$.

Property | **Identity Property for Multiplication of Whole Numbers** There is a unique whole number 1 such that for any whole number a, $a \cdot 1 = a = 1 \cdot a$.

The commutative property for multiplication of whole numbers is easily illustrated by building a 3 by 5 grid and then turning it sideways, as shown in Figure 3-15. We see that the number of one-by-one squares present in either case is 15—that is, $3 \cdot 5 = 15 = 5 \cdot 3$. The commutative property can be verified in general by recalling that $n(A \times B) = n(B \times A)$.

FIGURE 3-15

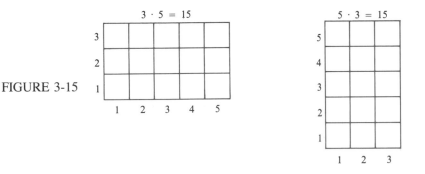

The associative property for multiplication of whole numbers can be illustrated as follows. Suppose $a = 3$, $b = 5$, and $c = 4$. Compare $3 \cdot (5 \cdot 4)$ and $(3 \cdot 5) \cdot 4$. First, $5 \cdot 4$ is illustrated with blocks, as shown in Figure 3-16(a). Then 3 stacks of $(5 \cdot 4)$ blocks are pictured in Figure 3-16(b). Finally, we see $3 \cdot (5 \cdot 4)$ blocks in Figure 3-16(c).

FIGURE 3-16

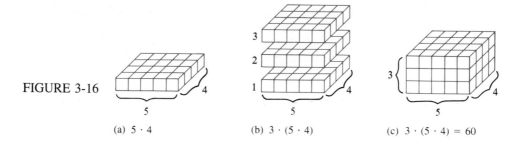

(a) $5 \cdot 4$ (b) $3 \cdot (5 \cdot 4)$ (c) $3 \cdot (5 \cdot 4) = 60$

In Figure 3-17, the blocks are combined in a different way to show $(3 \cdot 5) \cdot 4$. In Figures 3-16(c) and 3-17(c), the same set of blocks is used. Hence, $3 \cdot (5 \cdot 4) = (3 \cdot 5) \cdot 4$.

FIGURE 3-17

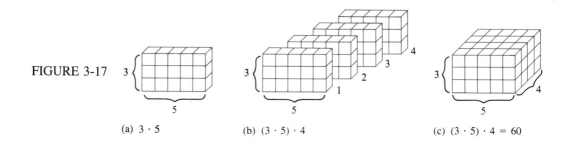

(a) $3 \cdot 5$ (b) $(3 \cdot 5) \cdot 4$ (c) $(3 \cdot 5) \cdot 4 = 60$

multiplicative identity

The **multiplicative identity** for whole numbers is 1. For example, $3 \cdot 1 = 1 + 1 + 1 = 3$. In general, for any whole number a,

$$a \cdot 1 = \underbrace{1 + 1 + 1 + \cdots + 1}_{a \text{ terms}} = a$$

Thus, $a \cdot 1 = a$, which—along with the commutative property for multiplication—implies that $a \cdot 1 = a = 1 \cdot a$.

We have seen that 0 is the additive identity for whole numbers and 1 is the multiplicative identity for whole numbers. The number 0 has special properties in multiplication. For example, consider $6 \cdot 0$. We see that $6 \cdot 0 = 0 + 0 + 0 + 0 + 0 + 0 = 0$. Thus, we see that multiplying 0 by 6 yields a product of 0. This is true in general and can be stated as follows.

Property | **Zero Multiplication Property of Whole Numbers**   For any whole number a, $a \cdot 0 = 0 = 0 \cdot a$.

The zero multiplication property of whole numbers can also be verified using the definition of multiplication in terms of Cartesian products. Let A be any set such that $n(A) = a$. Then, $a \cdot 0 = n(A \times \varnothing) = n(\varnothing) = 0$.

The next property that we investigate involves the use of both addition and multiplication. For example, in Figure 3-18, $5 \cdot (3 + 4) = (5 \cdot 3) + (5 \cdot 4)$.

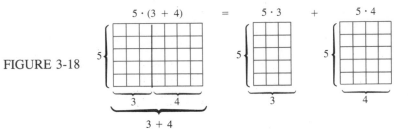

FIGURE 3-18

The properties of addition and multiplication also can be used to justify this result.

$$5 \cdot (3 + 4) = \underbrace{(3 + 4) + (3 + 4) + (3 + 4) + (3 + 4) + (3 + 4)}_{5 \text{ terms}}$$

Multiplication is repeated addition.

$$= (3 + 3 + 3 + 3 + 3) + (4 + 4 + 4 + 4 + 4)$$

Commutative and associative properties of addition.

$$= 5 \cdot 3 + 5 \cdot 4$$

Multiplication is repeated addition.

This example illustrates the *distributive property of multiplication over addition* for whole numbers, which is stated in general as follows.

Property

Distributive Property for Multiplication over Addition of Whole Numbers For any whole numbers a, b, and c,

$$a \cdot (b + c) = a \cdot b + a \cdot c$$

Because the commutative property for multiplication of whole numbers holds, the distributive property for multiplication over addition can be rewritten as $(b + c) \cdot a = b \cdot a + c \cdot a$. The distributive property can be generalized to any finite number of terms. For example, $a \cdot (b + c + d) = a \cdot b + a \cdot c + a \cdot d$.

Example 3-4

Rename each of the following using the distributive property.

(a) $3 \cdot (x + y)$ (b) $(x + 1) \cdot x$
(c) $3 \cdot (2x + y + 3)$ (d) $a \cdot x + a \cdot y$
(e) $a \cdot x + a$ (f) $(x + 2) \cdot 5 + (x + 2) \cdot a$

Solution

(a) $3 \cdot (x + y) = 3 \cdot x + 3 \cdot y = 3x + 3y$
(b) $(x + 1) \cdot x = x \cdot x + 1 \cdot x = x^2 + x$
(c) $3 \cdot (2x + y + 3) = 3 \cdot (2x) + 3 \cdot y + 3 \cdot 3 = (3 \cdot 2) \cdot x + 3 \cdot y + 9$
$= 6x + 3y + 9$

(d) $a \cdot x + a \cdot y = a \cdot (x + y) = a(x + y)$
(e) $a \cdot x + a = a \cdot x + a \cdot 1 = a \cdot (x + 1) = a(x + 1)$
(f) $(x + 2) \cdot 5 + (x + 2) \cdot a = (x + 2) \cdot (5 + a) = (x + 2)(5 + a)$

Remark

Where there is no ambiguity, we omit the multiplication dot and, for example, write $3x$ rather than $3 \cdot x$. Furthermore, an expression such as $2 \cdot (a \cdot b)$ can be written as $2ab$.

Example 3-5

Using the distributive property, simplify $(a + b)^2$.

Solution

By the definition of exponents, $(a + b)^2 = (a + b)(a + b)$. Consider the first term, $(a + b)$ as a single whole number and apply the distributive property. You should supply the reasons for each step given below.

$$
\begin{aligned}
(a + b)(a + b) &= (a + b)a + (a + b)b \\
&= (aa + ba) + (ab + bb) \\
&= (a^2 + ba) + (ab + b^2) \\
&= a^2 + (ba + ab) + b^2 \\
&= a^2 + (ab + ab) + b^2 \\
&= a^2 + 1(ab) + 1(ab) + b^2 \\
&= a^2 + (1 + 1)(ab) + b^2 \\
&= a^2 + 2ab + b^2
\end{aligned}
$$

Difficulties involving the order of operations sometimes arise. For example, many students will treat $2 + 3 \cdot 6$ as $(2 + 3) \cdot 6$, while others will treat it as $2 + (3 \cdot 6)$. In the first case, the value is 30. In the second case, the value is 20. In order to avoid confusion, mathematicians agree that when no parentheses are present, multiplications are performed *before* additions. Thus, $2 + 3 \cdot 6 = 2 + 18 = 20$. This order of operations is not built into many calculators, which display the incorrect answer of 30. Do you see how a calculator could arrive at an answer of 30?

Division of Whole Numbers

Subtraction has been defined in terms of addition. Similarly, multiplication can be used to define a new operation called *division*. One approach to division is illustrated in Example 3-6.

Example 3-6

Benny Crocker baked 18 cookies. He decided to give an equal number of cookies to each of his three best friends, Bob, Charlie, and Dean. How many did each friend receive?

Solution

If we use the strategy of drawing a picture, we see that we can divide (or partition) the 18 cookies into three sets, with an equal number of cookies in each set. Figure 3-19 shows that each friend received 6 cookies.

FIGURE 3-19

Bob   Dean   Charlie

The solution to Example 3-6 can be designated using the division symbol, $\div$; that is, $18 \div 3 = 6$. Thus, $18 \div 3$ in Example 3-6 is the number of cookies in each of three disjoint sets whose union is 18 cookies. In this approach to division, we partition a set into a number of equivalent subsets.

Another strategy for solving Example 3-6 is to write an equation. Suppose that each friend receives c cookies. Then the three friends receive $3 \cdot c$ cookies, or 18 cookies. Hence $3 \cdot c = 18$. Since $3 \cdot c = 18$, then $c = 6$. We have solved the division problem using multiplication. This leads us to the following definition of division of whole numbers.

DEFINITION

> For any whole numbers a and b with $b \neq 0$, $a \div b$ is the unique whole number c, if it exists, such that $b \cdot c = a$; that is, $a \div b = c$ if and only if $a = b \cdot c$.

Remark

dividend divisor
quotient

If the whole number c in the definition does not exist, then $a \div b$ is not defined in the set of whole numbers. The notation $a \div b = c$ is read "a divided by b is equal to c." The number a is called the **dividend,** b is called the **divisor,** and c is called the **quotient.** Note that $a \div b$ can also be written as $\frac{a}{b}$ or $b)\overline{a}$.

The relationship between division and multiplication is shown in a portion of a student page from *Holt School Mathematics,* 1974, Grade 6.

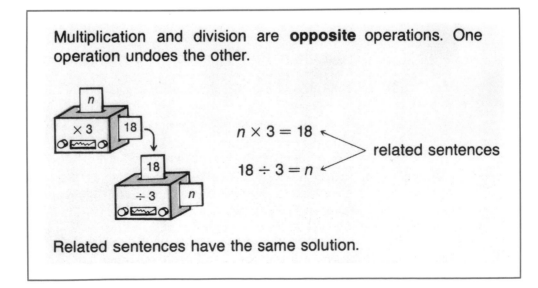

Multiplication and division are **opposite** operations. One operation undoes the other.

$n \times 3 = 18$

$18 \div 3 = n$

related sentences

Related sentences have the same solution.

Just as subtraction of whole numbers is not always meaningful, division of whole numbers is not always meaningful. For example, to find $5 \div 3$, we look for a whole number c such that

$$3 \cdot c = 5$$

There is no whole number c that satisfies this equation, so $5 \div 3$ has no meaning in the set of whole numbers. Thus, the set of whole numbers is not closed under division. (Other properties of division on the set of whole numbers are investigated in the exercises.)

It is not always easy to tell by looking that a division is meaningful on the set of whole numbers. Consider $383 \div 57$. To find a solution to this division, we need to find a number c such that $57 \cdot c = 383$. Table 3-5 shows several products of whole numbers times 57. Since 383 is between 342 and 399, there is no whole number c such that $57 \cdot c = 383$.

TABLE 3-5

$57 \cdot 1$	$57 \cdot 2$	$57 \cdot 3$	$57 \cdot 4$	$57 \cdot 5$	$57 \cdot 6$	$57 \cdot 7$
57	114	171	228	285	342	399

remainder

division algorithm

In the real world, if 383 apples were to be divided among 57 students, then the division would have a solution; each student would receive 6 apples, and 41 apples would remain. The number 41 is called the **remainder.** Thus 383 contains six 57s with a remainder of 41. Observe that the remainder is a whole number less than 57. The concept illustrated is called the **division algorithm.**

DIVISION
ALGORITHM

> Given any whole numbers a and b with $b \neq 0$, there exist unique whole numbers q (quotient) and r (remainder) such that
>
> $a = b \cdot q + r$ with $0 \le r < b$

Remark | The quotient q is the greatest whole number of bs in a.

Example 3-7 | Find whole numbers q and r such that $16 = 3q + r$ with $0 \le r < 3$.

Solution | $16 = 15 + 1 = 3 \cdot 5 + 1$. Thus, $q = 5$ and $r = 1$.

Remark | Note that $16 = 3 \cdot 4 + 4$ is not the correct form of the division algorithm because the remainder cannot be greater than 3.

The whole numbers 0 and 1 deserve special attention with respect to division of whole numbers. Before reading on, try finding the values of the following three expressions:

(a) $3 \div 0$

(b) $0 \div 3$

(c) $0 \div 0$

Consider the following explanations:

(a) By definition, $3 \div 0 = c$ if there is a unique number c such that $0 \cdot c = 3$. Since the zero property of multiplication states that $0 \cdot c = 0$ for any whole number c, there is no whole number c such that $0 \cdot c = 3$. Thus, $3 \div 0$ is undefined.

(b) By definition, $0 \div 3 = c$ if there exists a unique number c such that $3 \cdot c = 0$. The zero property of multiplication states that any number times 0 is 0. Since $3 \cdot 0 = 0$, then $c = 0$ and $0 \div 3 = 0$. Note that $c = 0$ is the only number that satisfies $3 \cdot c = 0$.

(c) By definition, $0 \div 0 = c$ if there is a unique whole number c such that $0 \cdot c = 0$. Notice that for *any* c, $0 \cdot c = 0$. According to the definition of division, c must be unique. Since there is *no* unique number c such that $0 \cdot c = 0$, it follows that $0 \div 0$ is indeterminate, or undefined.

Division involving 0 may be summarized as follows.

Let n be any natural number. Then:

(a) $n \div 0$ is undefined;

(b) $0 \div n = 0$;

(c) $0 \div 0$ is indeterminate, or undefined.

Recall that $n \cdot 1 = n$ for any whole number n. Thus, by the definition of division, $n \div 1 = n$. For example, $3 \div 1 = 3$, $1 \div 1 = 1$, and $0 \div 1 = 0$.

PROBLEM SET 3-3

1. Use the number line model to illustrate why $3 \cdot 5 = 15$.

2. For each of the following, find the whole numbers that make the equations true.

   (a) $2 \cdot \square = 10$ (b) $\square \cdot 3 = 21$

   (c) $3 \cdot \square = 15$ (d) $\square \cdot 4 = 12$

3. Each ticket to the band concert costs $2.00. How much do 8 tickets cost?

4. Tell whether or not the following sets are closed under multiplication.

   (a) $\{0, 1\}$ (b) $\{0\}$

   (c) $\{2, 4, 6, 8, 10, \ldots\}$ (d) $\{1, 3, 5, 7, 9, \ldots\}$

   (e) $\{1, 4, 7, 10, 13, 16, \ldots\}$

   (f) $\{0, 1, 2\}$

5. Use the distributive property to describe how you might find the product $8 \cdot 3$ if you know only the addition table and the two and six multiplication facts.

6. Identify the property being illustrated in each of the following.

   (a) $3 \cdot 2 = 2 \cdot 3$ (b) $3(2 \cdot 4) = (3 \cdot 2)4$

   (c) $3(2 + 3) = 3(3 + 2)$ (d) $8 \cdot 0 = 0$

   (e) $1 \cdot 8 = 8$ (f) $6(3 + 5) = (3 + 5)6$

   (g) $6(3 + 5) = 6 \cdot 3 + 6 \cdot 5$

   (h) $(3 + 5)6 = 3 \cdot 6 + 5 \cdot 6$

   (i) $1(a + b) = a + b$ (j) $(a + b)0 = 0$

7. Rename each of the following using the distributive property for multiplication over addition so that there are no parentheses in the final answer.

   (a) $3(100 + 1)$ (b) $(a + b)(c + d)$

   (c) $3(x + y + 5)$ (d) $\square(\triangle + \bigcirc)$

   (e) $(x + y)(x + y + z)$

8. For each of the following, find—if possible—the whole numbers that make the equations true.
   (a) $3 \cdot \square = 15$ (b) $18 = 6 + 3 \cdot \square$
   (c) $\square \cdot \square = 25$
   (d) $\square \cdot (5 + 6) = \square \cdot 5 + \square \cdot 6$

9. Rename each of the following using the distributive property for multiplication over addition and whole number addition, if appropriate.
   (a) $2x + 3x$ (b) $x + 5x + 8x$
   (c) $2(x + 1) + 3(x + 1)$ (d) $ab + a$
   (e) $mb + mc + m$ (f) $2(x + 3) + x(x + 3)$

10. Perform each of the following computations.
    (a) $2 \cdot 3 + 5$ (b) $2(3 + 5)$
    (c) $2 \cdot 3 + 2 \cdot 5$ (d) $3 + 2 \cdot 5$

11. The generalized distributive property for three terms states that for any whole numbers a, b, c, and d, $a(b + c + d) = ab + ac + ad$. Justify this property using the distributive property for two terms.

12. The FOIL method is often used as a shortcut to multiply expressions like $(m + n)(x + y)$.

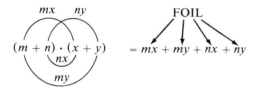

$$(m + n) \cdot (x + y) = mx + my + nx + ny$$

   where F   stands for product of the *first* terms, mx
        O   stands for product of the *outer* terms, my
        I   stands for product of the *inner* terms, nx
        L   stands for product of the *last* terms, ny
   (a) Use the FOIL method on each of the following.
        (i) $(a + b)(a + b)$
        (ii) $(50 + 8)(20 + 6)$
   (b) Use the distributive property to show why the FOIL method works.

13. For each of the following, find the whole numbers to make the statement true, if possible.
    (a) $18 \div 3 = \square$
    (b) $\square \div 76 = 0$
    (c) $28 \div \square = 7$

14. Rewrite each of the following division problems as a multiplication problem.
    (a) $40 \div 8 = 5$ (b) $326 \div 2 = x$
    (c) $48 \div x = 16$ (d) $x \div 5 = 17$
    (e) $a \div b = c$ (f) $(48 - 36) \div 6 = x$

15. Show that, in general, each of the following is false if a, b, and c are whole numbers.
    (a) $a \div b = b \div a$

(b) $(a \div b) \div c = a \div (b \div c)$
(c) $a \div (b + c) = (a \div b) + (a \div c)$
(d) $a \div b$ is a whole number.

16. Use the definition of division to justify that for any whole numbers a and b, where $b \neq 0$, $(ab) \div b = a$.

17. Because the Jones' water meter was stuck, they were billed the same amount for water each month for 5 months. If they paid $160, what was the monthly bill?

18. If Charlie drove 200 km (kilometers) in 4 hours at a constant speed, at what speed was he traveling?

19. There were 17 sandwiches for 7 people on a picnic. How many whole sandwiches were there for each person if they were divided equally? How many were left over?

20. If it takes 1 minute per cut, how long will it take to cut a 10-foot log into 10 equal pieces?

21. For each of the following, name all the possible pairs of replacements for $\square$ and $\triangle$.
    (a) $34 = \square \cdot 8 + \triangle$
    (b) $\triangle = 4 \cdot 16 + 2$
    (c) $28 = \square \cdot \triangle + 3$

22. Find all the pairs of whole numbers whose product is 36.

23. A new model of a car is available in four different exterior colors and three different interior colors. How many different color schemes are possible for the car?

24. Paul has sold eight $3 tickets and eight $5 tickets for the raffle. How much money has he collected?

25. Tony has 5 ways to get from his home to the park. He has 6 ways to get from the park to the school. How many ways can Tony get from his home to school by way of the park?

26. Use the constant feature on a calculator to determine the value of $9 \times 9 \times 9 \times 9 \times 9 \times 9 \times 9$, or 9^7.

27. The division algorithm states that for any two whole numbers a and b with $a \geq b$, $a = b \cdot q + r$, where $0 \leq r < b$.

    Example: To find $7 \div 5$ on the calculator, push $\boxed{7}$ $\boxed{\div}$ $\boxed{5}$ $\boxed{=}$, which yields 1.4. To find the whole number remainder, ignore the decimal portion of 1.4, multiply $5 \cdot 1$, and subtract this product from 7. The result is the remainder. Use a calculator to find the whole number remainder for each of the following divisions.
    (a) $28 \div 5$ (b) $32 \div 10$ (c) $29 \div 3$
    (d) $41 \div 7$ (e) $49,382 \div 14$

28. In the problems below, use only the designated number keys. Use any function keys on the calculator.
    (a) Use the calculator buttons $\boxed{1}$, $\boxed{9}$, $\boxed{7}$ exactly once each in any order and use any operations available to write as many of the whole numbers as

possible from 1 to 20. For example, $9 - 7 - 1 = 1$ and $1 \cdot 9 - 7 = 2$.

(b) Use the button $\boxed{4}$ as many times as desired with any operations to display 13.

(c) Use the button $\boxed{2}$ three times with any operations to display 24.

(d) Use the button $\boxed{1}$ five times with any operations to display 100.

* * * * * * REVIEW PROBLEMS * * * * * * *

29. Write 75 using Egyptian, Roman, and Babylonian numerals.
30. Write 35,206 in expanded form.
31. Give a set that is not closed under addition.

32. Are the whole numbers commutative under subtraction? If not, give a counterexample.
33. Illustrate $11 - 3$ using a number-line model.

Laboratory Activity

Enter a number less than 20 on the calculator. If the number is even, divide it by 2; if it is odd, multiply it by 3 and add 1. Next, use the number on the display. Follow the given directions. Repeat the process again:

1. Will the display eventually reach 1?
2. Which number less than 20 takes the most steps in order to reach 1?
3. Do even or odd numbers reach 1 more quickly?
4. Investigate what happens with numbers greater than 20.

3-4 ALGORITHMS FOR WHOLE NUMBER ADDITION AND SUBTRACTION

algorithm

An **algorithm** (named for the Arabian mathematician, Al-Khowarizmi) is a step-by-step procedure used to accomplish a mathematical operation. It is valuable for every prospective elementary teacher to know more than one algorithm to do operations. Not all students learn in the same manner, and the shortest, most efficient algorithms may not be the best for every individual. Not only should teachers know alternative algorithms, but they should also know why each algorithm works. A teacher who understands algorithms will be better equipped to respond to new algorithms or methods that students develop. Single-digit addition and subtraction facts, the properties of addition, and the meaning of place value are prerequisites for understanding the algorithms in this section.

Addition Algorithms

The use of concrete teaching aids—such as chip trading, bean sticks, an abacus, or multibase blocks—helps provide insight into the creation of algorithms for addition. A set of multibase blocks, shown in Figure 3-20, consists of *units, longs, flats,* and *blocks,* representing 1, 10, 100, and 1000, respectively.

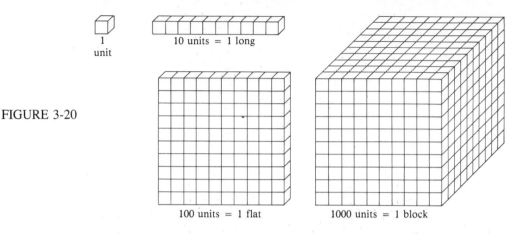

FIGURE 3-20

1 unit

10 units = 1 long

100 units = 1 flat

1000 units = 1 block

Students trade blocks by regrouping, that is, they take a set of multibase blocks representing a number and trade them until they have the fewest possible pieces representing the same number. For example, suppose you have 58 units and want to trade them. What is the smallest number of pieces you can receive in exchange? The units can be grouped into tens to form longs. Five sets of 10 units each can be traded for 5 longs. Thus, 58 units can be traded for 5 longs and 8 units. In terms of numbers, this is analogous to rewriting 58 as $5 \cdot 10 + 8$. You cannot receive flats or blocks. The smallest number of pieces you can receive is 13.

Example 3-8

Suppose you have 11 flats, 17 longs, and 16 units. What is the smallest number of pieces you can receive in exchange?

Solution

The 16 units can be traded for 1 long and 6 units.

11 flats	17 longs	~~16 units~~	(16 units = 1 long and 6 units)
	1 long	6 units	(Trade)
11 flats	18 longs	6 units	(After the first trade)

The 18 longs can be traded for 1 flat and 8 longs.

11 flats	~~18 longs~~	6 units	(18 longs = 1 flat and 8 longs)
1 flat	8 longs		(Trade)
12 flats	8 longs	6 units	(After the second trade)

The 12 flats can be traded for 1 block and 2 flats.

	~~12 flats~~	8 longs	6 units	(12 flats = 1 block and 2 flats)
1 block	2 flats			(Trade)
1 block	2 flats	8 longs	6 units	(After the third trade)

The smallest number of pieces is $1 + 2 + 8 + 6$ or 17; that is, 1 block, 2 flats, 8 longs, and 6 units. In terms of numbers, this is analogous to rewriting $11 \cdot 10^2 + 17 \cdot 10 + 16$ as $1 \cdot 10^3 + 2 \cdot 10^2 + 8 \cdot 10 + 6$, which implies that there are 1286 units.

We now use multibase blocks to help develop an algorithm for whole number addition. Suppose we wish to add $14 + 23$. We show this computation using a concrete model in Figure 3-21(a), then an introductory algorithm in Figure 3-21(b), and—finally—the familiar algorithm in Figure 3-21(c).

(a)

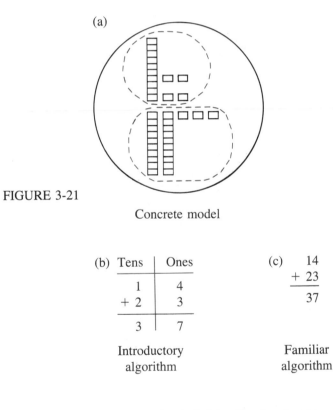

FIGURE 3-21

Concrete model

(b)

Tens	Ones
1	4
+ 2	3
3	7

Introductory
algorithm

(c)
$$\begin{array}{r} 14 \\ + 23 \\ \hline 37 \end{array}$$

Familiar
algorithm

A mathematical justification for this addition is the following.

$14 + 23 = (1 \cdot 10 + 4) + (2 \cdot 10 + 3)$	Place value.
$\quad = (1 \cdot 10 + 2 \cdot 10) + (4 + 3)$	Commutative and associative properties of addition.
$\quad = (1 + 2) \cdot 10 + (4 + 3)$	Distributive property of multiplication over addition.
$\quad = 3 \cdot 10 + 7$	Single-digit addition facts.
$\quad = 37$	Place value.

Adding with regrouping

In this example, 10 ones are regrouped for 1 ten.

Step 1. Add ones.   **Step 2.** Regroup.   **Step 3.** Add tens.

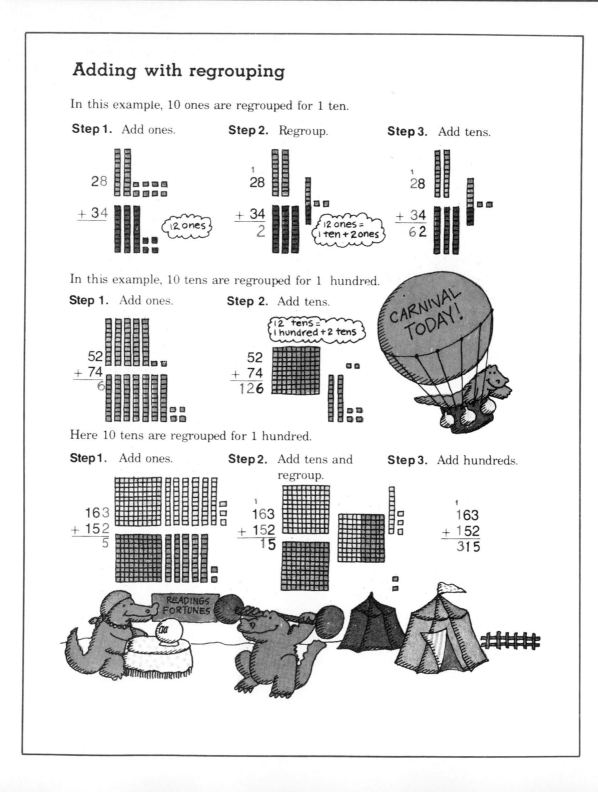

28
+ 34

12 ones

28
+ 34
   2

12 ones = 1 ten + 2 ones

28
+ 34
  62

In this example, 10 tens are regrouped for 1 hundred.

Step 1. Add ones.   **Step 2.** Add tens.

52
+ 74
   6

12 tens = 1 hundred + 2 tens

52
+ 74
 126

CARNIVAL TODAY!

Here 10 tens are regrouped for 1 hundred.

Step 1. Add ones.   **Step 2.** Add tens and regroup.   **Step 3.** Add hundreds.

163
+ 152
    5

163
+ 152
   15

163
+ 152
  315

READINGS FORTUNES

Although this mathematical justification is not usually presented in the elementary school, the ideas and properties shown are necessary to understand why the algorithm works. Some problems are more involved than this one because they involve "regrouping," or "carrying," in which students trade by regrouping. This is described in terms of the concrete multibase blocks on the student page on page 98 from *Heath Mathematics,* 1979, Grade 4.

After using concrete aids, children are ready to complete a computation such as 28 + 34 as shown in Figure 3-22(a); after some practice, they can complete the computation as shown in Figure 3-22(b).

FIGURE 3-22

(a)

Tens	Ones	
2	8	
+ 3	4	
5	$\cancel{12}$	(Add)
+ 1	2	(Regroup)
6	2	

(b)
$$
\begin{array}{r}
\overset{1}{2}8 \\
+\ 34 \\
\hline
62
\end{array}
$$

The following is a mathematical justification for this addition.

$$28 + 34 = (2 \cdot 10 + 8) + (3 \cdot 10 + 4) \qquad \text{Place value.}$$
$$= (2 \cdot 10 + 3 \cdot 10) + (8 + 4) \qquad \text{Commutative and associative properties of addition.}$$
$$= (2 \cdot 10 + 3 \cdot 10) + 12 \qquad \text{Single-digit addition fact.}$$
$$= (2 \cdot 10 + 3 \cdot 10) + (1 \cdot 10 + 2) \qquad \text{Place value}$$
$$= (2 \cdot 10 + 3 \cdot 10 + 1 \cdot 10) + 2 \qquad \text{Associative property of addition.}$$
$$= (2 + 3 + 1) \cdot 10 + 2 \qquad \text{Distributive property of multiplication over addition.}$$
$$= 6 \cdot 10 + 2 \qquad \text{Associative property and single-digit addition facts.}$$
$$= 62 \qquad \text{Place value.}$$

scratch addition

An alternative algorithm for addition, called **scratch addition,** is shown for 87 + 65 + 49. This algorithm allows students to do complicated additions by doing a series of additions involving only two single digits.

1.

$$
\begin{array}{cc}
8 & 7 \\
6 & \cancel{5}_2 \\
4 & 9 \\
\hline
\end{array}
$$

1. Add the numbers in the units place starting at the top. When the sum is 10 or more, record this sum by scratching a line through the last number added and writing the number of units next to the scratched number. For example, since 7 + 5 = 12, the "scratch" represents 10 and the 2 written down represents the units.

2.   8 7   2. Continue adding the units. When the addition again
        6 $\cancel{3}$2   results in a sum of 10 or more, repeat the process
        4 $\cancel{9}$ı   described in (1); 2 + 9 = 11.

3. $\overset{2}{8}$ 7   3. When the first column of additions is completed, write
        6 $\cancel{3}$2   the number of units, 1, below the addition line. Count
        4 $\cancel{9}$ı   the number of scratches, 2, and add this number to the
        ___   second column.
           1

4. $\overset{2}{\cancel{8}0}$ 7   4. Repeat the procedure for each successive column.
        6 $\cancel{3}$2
        $\cancel{4}0$ $\cancel{9}$ı
        _____
      2 0 1

Example 3-9 | Compute the following additions using the scratch algorithm.

(a)   296   (b)   1369
        840   4813
     +   27   5879
                                    + 6183

Solution | (a)

     $\overset{ı}{2}$ $\overset{ı}{\cancel{9}0}$ 6   (b) $\overset{2}{1}$ $\overset{2}{3}$ $\overset{2}{6}$ 9
   $\cancel{8}$ı 4 0   4 $\cancel{8}3$ 1 $\cancel{3}2$
   +   2 $\cancel{7}$3 $\cancel{3}2$ $\cancel{8}$ı $\cancel{7}6$ $\cancel{9}$ı
   _____   +   6 1 $\cancel{8}4$ 3
   1 1 6 3   _____
                                         1 8 2 4 4

Subtraction Algorithms

As with addition, the use of multibase blocks can provide a concrete model for subtraction. Consider 36 − 24. We do this computation in Figure 3-23(a) using multibase blocks, in Figure 3-23(b) using an introductory algorithm based on the blocks, and finally in Figure 3-23(c) using the familiar algorithm.

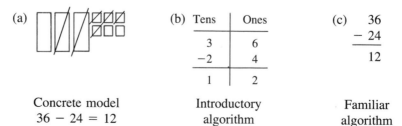

FIGURE 3-23

(a) Concrete model
36 − 24 = 12

(b)
Tens	Ones
3	6
−2	4
1	2

Introductory algorithm

(c)   36
      − 24
        12

Familiar algorithm

Notice that this subtraction problem can be checked using the definition of subtraction: $36 - 24 = 12$ because $12 + 24 = 36$.

Subtractions become more involved when renaming is necessary, as in $56 - 29$. The three stages for working this problem are shown in Figure 3-24.

(a)

$\rightarrow 56 - 29 = 27$

Concrete Model

FIGURE 3-24

(b)
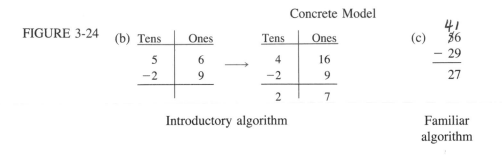

Tens	Ones		Tens	Ones
5	6		4	16
−2	9	→	−2	9
			2	7

Introductory algorithm

(c)
$$\begin{array}{r} {}^{4}\!\!\!\not5\,{}^{1}\!\!\!\not6 \\ -\ 29 \\ \hline 27 \end{array}$$

Familiar algorithm

The "cashier's algorithm" for subtraction is closely related to the formal definition of subtraction; that is, $a - b = c$ if and only if $b + c = a$. An example of the cashier's algorithm follows.

Example 3-10

Noah owed $11 for his groceries. He used a $50 check to pay the bill. While handing Noah the change, the cashier said, "$11, $12, $13, $14, $15, $20, $30, $50. Thank you. Have a good day." How much change did Noah receive?

Solution

Table 3-6 shows what the cashier said and how much money Noah received each time. Since $11 plus $1 is $12, Noah must have received $1 when the cashier said $12. The same reasoning follows for $13, $14, and so on. Thus, the total amount of change that Noah received is given by

$$\$1 + \$1 + \$1 + \$1 + \$5 + \$10 + \$20 = \$39$$

In other words, $\$50 - \$11 = \$39$ because $\$39 + \$11 = \$50$.

TABLE 3-6

What the cashier said	$11	$12	$13	$14	$15	$20	$30	$50
Amount of money Noah received each time	0	$1	$1	$1	$1	$5	$10	$20

PROBLEM SET 3-4

1. Perform the following additions using both the scratch and conventional algorithms.
   (a)   3789
          9296
        + 6843
   (b)   3004
        + 987
   (c)   524
          328
          567
        + 135

2. Explain why the scratch addition algorithm works.

3. An addition algorithm from an elementary text follows. Explain why it works.

2	7
+ 6	8
1	5
8	
9	5

4. Find the missing numbers in each of the following.
   (a)   _ _ 1
        + 4 2 _
        _ 4 0 2

   (b)   _ 0 2 5
          1 1 _ 6
        + 3 1 4 8
          6 _ 6 _

   (c)   1 _ 6 9
          2 _ 9 4
          9 5 4 6
          9 _ _ 3
        + 7 _ 6 4
          2 8 7 7 6

   (d)   2 _ 1
          4 5 _
        + _ 8 4
          1 3 2 6

5. Perform the following subtractions. Verify your answers by using the definition of subtraction.
   (a)   436
        − 79
   (b)   1001
        −   99
   (c)   3003
        − 129

6. Find the missing numbers for each of the following.
   (a)   8 7 6 9 3
        − _ _ _ _ _
          4 1 2 7 9

   (b)   8 1 3 5
        − 4 6 8 2
          _ _ _ _

   (c)   3 _ _
        − 1 5 9
          _ 2 4

   (d)   1 _ _ _ 6
        −   8 3 0 9
          4 9 8 7

7. Place the digits 7, 6, 8, 3, 5, 2 in the boxes to obtain: (a) the greatest sum; (b) the least sum.

8. Place the digits 7, 6, 8, 3, 5, 2 in the boxes to obtain: (a) the greatest difference; (b) the least difference.

9. Naomi has 537 marbles. Jeff has 103. How many more marbles does Naomi have?

10. Paul went to the basketball game. There were 8767 people who purchased tickets for the game. The field house holds 9200 people. How many seats were not sold?

11. At the beginning of the year, the library had 15,282 books. During fall quarter 125 books were added, during winter quarter 137 were added, and during spring quarter 238 were added. How many books did the library have at the end of the school year?

12. Find the next three numbers in each of the sequences given below.
    (a) 9, 14, 19, 24, 29, _____, _____, _____
    (b) 97, 94, 91, 88, 85, _____, _____, _____

13. Charles has 45¢. He needs 92¢ to buy a new toy. How many more cents does he need?

14. Maria goes into a store with 87¢. If she buys a candy bar for 25¢, a balloon for 15¢, and a comb for 17¢, how much money does she have left?

15. Tom's diet allows only 1500 calories per day. For breakfast, Tom had skim milk (90 calories), a waffle with no syrup (120 calories), and a banana (119 calories). For lunch, he had $\frac{1}{2}$ cup of salad (185 calories) with mayonnaise (110 calories), tea (0 calories), and then he "blew it" with pecan pie (570 calories). Can he have dinner? Can he have a steak (250 calories), a salad with no mayonnaise, and tea?

16. *M*, *A*, *T*, and *H* each stand for a different natural number. What are possible values for *H*?

$$
\begin{array}{r}
M\ M\ M \\
A\ A\ A \\
+\ T\ T\ T \\
\hline
H\ H\ H
\end{array}
$$

17. Consider the following subtraction algorithm, called the "equal-additions" algorithm.

$$
\begin{array}{r}
836 = \quad 8 \cdot 10^2 + 3 \cdot 10 + 6 \\
-\ 584 = -\ (5 \cdot 10^2 + 8 \cdot 10 + 4) \\
\hline
\end{array}
$$

In order to subtract $8 \cdot 10$ from $3 \cdot 10$, add ten 10s to the minuend and $1 \cdot 10^2$ (or ten 10s) to the subtrahend. Thus,

$$
\begin{array}{r}
8 \cdot 10^2 + 3 \cdot 10 + 6 \\
-\ (5 \cdot 10^2 + 8 \cdot 10 + 4) \\
\hline
\end{array}
$$

becomes

$$
\begin{array}{r}
8 \cdot 10^2 + 13 \cdot 10 + 6 \\
-\ (6 \cdot 10^2 + \ \ 8 \cdot 10 + 4) \\
\hline
2 \cdot 10^2 + \ \ 5 \cdot 10 + 2\ = 252
\end{array}
$$

Notice that the problem is changed, but 252 is the answer to the original problem. Will this algorithm work in general? Why or why not?

18. Given the following addition problem, replace nine digits with 0s so that the sum of the numbers is 1111.

$$
\begin{array}{r}
999 \\
777 \\
555 \\
333 \\
111 \\
\hline
\end{array}
$$

19. Arrange eight 8s so that the sum is 1000.

20. (a) Use a calculator to place the whole numbers 24, 25, 26, 27, 28, 29, 30, 31, and 32 in the empty circles so that the sum of the values of the numbers in the circles connected by each line is the same. Each number may be used exactly once.
    (b) How many different numbers can be placed in the middle to obtain a solution?

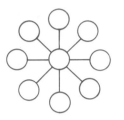

21. The following is a supermagic square taken from an engraving called *Melancholia* by Dürer (1514).

16	3	2	13
5	10	11	8
9	6	7	12
4	15	14	1

(a) Find the sum of each row, the sum of each column, and the sum of each diagonal.
(b) Find the sum of the four numbers in the center.
(c) Find the sum of the four numbers in each corner.
(d) Add 11 to each number in the square above. Is the square still a magic square? Explain your answer.
(e) Subtract 11 from each number in the square above. Is the square still a magic square?

22. Consider the following sums.

$$
\begin{array}{l}
1 + 11 = \\
1 + 11 + 111 = \\
1 + 11 + 111 + 1111 =
\end{array}
$$

(a) What is the pattern?
(b) How many addends are there the first time the pattern no longer works?

* * * * * * * REVIEW PROBLEMS * * * * * * *

23. Write 5280 in expanded form.
24. Give an example of the associative property of addition for whole numbers.
25. Illustrate $11 + 8$ using a number-line model.
26. Is the set $\{0, 1\}$ closed with respect to multiplication? Why or why not?
27. What is the value of $\overline{MCDX}$ in Hindu-Arabic numerals?

28. Rename the following using the distributive property of multiplication over addition.

    (a) $ax + a$ (b) $3(x + y) + a(x + y)$

29. Jim has 5 new shirts and 3 new pairs of pants. How many combinations of new shirts and pants does he have?

Laboratory Activity

12	7	5
5	4	1
7	3	4

FIGURE 3-25

1. For each of the following, subtract the numbers in each row and column, as shown in Figure 3-25. Investigate why this works.

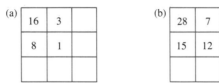

(a)
16	3	
8	1	

(b)
28	7	
15	12	

2. The Chinese abacus, *suan pan* (see Figure 3-26), is still in use today. A bar separates two sets of bead counters. Each counter above the bar represents five times the counter below the bar. Numbers are illustrated by moving the counter toward the bar. The number 7362 is pictured. Practice demonstrating numbers and adding on the *suan pan*.

FIGURE 3-26

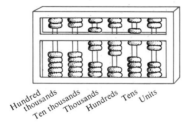

Hundred thousands Ten thousands Thousands Hundreds Tens Units

3-5 ALGORITHMS FOR WHOLE NUMBER MULTIPLICATION AND DIVISION

To aid in developing algorithms for multiplying multidigit whole numbers, we use the strategy of examining simpler computations first. Consider $4 \cdot 12$. Because we have seen that multiplication can be thought of as repeated addition, this computation could be pictured as in Figure 3-27—that is, as 4 rows of 12 dots, or 48 dots.

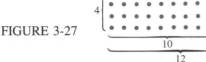

FIGURE 3-27

The dots in Figure 3-27 can also be partitioned to show that $4 \cdot 12 = 4 \cdot (10 + 2) = 4 \cdot 10 + 4 \cdot 2$. The numbers $4 \cdot 10$ and $4 \cdot 2$ are called *partial products*. We know that $4 \cdot 2 = 8$ from previous work with single-digit multiplication facts. Also, using the additive identity and place value, $4 \cdot 10 = 4 \cdot 10 + 0 = 40$. Thus, $40 \cdot 12 = 4 \cdot (10 + 2) = 4 \cdot 10 + 4 \cdot 2 = 40 + 8 = 48$.

Figure 3-27 illustrates the distributive property of multiplication over addition on the set of whole numbers, a property essential to the development and understanding of multiplication algorithms. The process leading to an algorithm for multiplying $4 \cdot 12$ is:

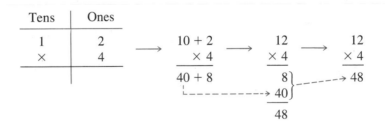

A mathematical justification for this multiplication is as follows.

$$4 \cdot 12 = 4 \cdot (1 \cdot 10 + 2) \qquad \text{Place value.}$$
$$= 4 \cdot (1 \cdot 10) + 4 \cdot 2 \qquad \text{Distributive property of multiplication over addition.}$$
$$= (4 \cdot 1) \cdot 10 + 4 \cdot 2 \qquad \text{Associative property of multiplication.}$$
$$= 4 \cdot 10 + 8 \qquad \text{Single-digit multiplication facts.}$$
$$= 48 \qquad \text{Place value.}$$

The partial product $4 \cdot 10$ illustrates that the multiplication of 4 by 10 results in annexing a zero to 4. This is also true when other whole numbers are multiplied by 10. It can be shown that multiplication by 10^2 results in annexing two zeros, and, in general, *multiplication by 10^n, where n is a natural number, results in annexing n zeros to the multiplicand.*

When multiplying powers of 10, an extension of the definition of exponents is used. For example, $10^2 \cdot 10^1 = (10 \cdot 10) \cdot 10 = 10^3$. Observe that $10^3 = 10^{2+1}$. In general, where a is a natural number and m and n are whole numbers, $a^m \cdot a^n$ is given by the following.

$$a^m \cdot a^n = \underbrace{(a \cdot a \cdot a \cdot \ldots \cdot a)}_{m \text{ factors}}\underbrace{(a \cdot a \cdot a \cdot \ldots \cdot a)}_{n \text{ factors}}$$

$$= \underbrace{a \cdot a \cdot a \cdot \ldots \cdot a}_{m + n \text{ factors}} = a^{m+n}$$

Consequently, $a^m \cdot a^n = a^{m+n}$.

To compute products involving powers of 10, such as $3 \cdot 500$ or $3 \cdot (5 \cdot 10^2)$, we proceed as follows.

$$3 \cdot 500 = 3 \cdot (5 \cdot 10^2)$$
$$= (3 \cdot 5) \cdot 10^2$$
$$= 15 \cdot 10^2$$
$$= 1500$$

Example 3-11

Multiply:

(a) $10^5 \cdot 36$ (b) $10^3 \cdot 279$ (c) $10^{13} \cdot 10^8$ (d) $7 \cdot 200$

Solution

(a) $10^5 \cdot 36 = 3,600,000$ (b) $10^3 \cdot 279 = 279,000$
(c) $10^{13} \cdot 10^8 = 10^{13+8} = 10^{21}$
(d) $7 \cdot 200 = 7 \cdot (2 \cdot 10^2) = (7 \cdot 2) \cdot 10^2 = 1400$

We now consider the multiplication of a single-digit number and a three-digit number. For example, to compute $6 \cdot 431$ we apply the distributive property of multiplication over addition and use the algorithms just developed.

Hundreds	Tens	Ones
4	3	1
×		6

$\longrightarrow$

$$400 + 30 + 1$$
$$\underline{\times 6}$$
$$2400 + 180 + 6$$

$\longrightarrow$

$$431$$
$$\underline{\times 6}$$
$$\begin{aligned}6\\180\\2400\end{aligned}$$

$\longrightarrow$

$$431$$
$$\underline{\times 6}$$
$$2586$$

$$2586$$

Next, we consider computations with two-digit multipliers, such as $14 \cdot 23$. We know how to multiply by 10 and by a single-digit number, so we write 14 as $10 + 4$ and use the distributive property of multiplication over addition.

$$14 \cdot 23 = (10 + 4) \cdot 23$$
$$= 10 \cdot 23 + 4 \cdot 23$$
$$= 230 + 92$$

This leads to an algorithm for multiplication.

```
   23              10 + 4            23
 × 14                              × 14
 ─────                             ─────
   92    (4 · 23)      or            92
  230   (10 · 23)                    23
 ─────                             ─────
  322                               322
```

We are accustomed to seeing this last step of the algorithm written without a zero.

When children first learn multiplication algorithms, they should be encouraged not to omit the zero in order to avoid errors and promote better understanding. The use of the zeros is shown on the student page from *Scott, Foresman Mathematics,* 1980, Grade 5 (page 108).

lattice multiplication

An alternative to the conventional algorithm for multiplying 68 and 27 follows. It is called **lattice multiplication.** (Determining the reasons why lattice multiplication works is left as an exercise.)

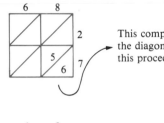

This computation is 7 · 8. The tens go above the diagonal and the units below. Continue this procedure for all the blocks.

Once the multiplication is complete, add along the diagonals. It is necessary in this example to "carry" 1 to the hundreds.

Division Algorithms

Algorithms for division can be developed using repeated subtraction. Consider the following problem.

PROBLEM 2

A shopkeeper is packaging soda pop in cartons that hold 6 bottles each. She has 726 bottles. How many cartons does she need?

Multiplying a Three-Digit Number by a Three-Digit Number

A. The park district ordered 268 boxes of envelopes to mail letters. Each box contains 144 envelopes. How many envelopes did the park district order?

Find 268 × 144.

$$
\begin{array}{r}
144 \\
\times\,268 \\
\hline
1152 \\
8640 \\
28800 \\
\hline
38592
\end{array}
$$

200 + 60 + 8

8 × 144
60 × 144
200 × 144

The park district ordered 38,592 envelopes.

B. Find 300 × 256.

$$
\begin{array}{r}
256 \\
\times\,300 \\
\hline
76800
\end{array}
$$

Multiply by 0 ones and 0 tens.
Then multiply by 3 hundreds.

C. Find 204 × 137.

$$
\begin{array}{r}
137 \\
\times\,204 \\
\hline
548 \\
27400 \\
\hline
27948
\end{array}
$$

200 + 4

4 × 137
200 × 137

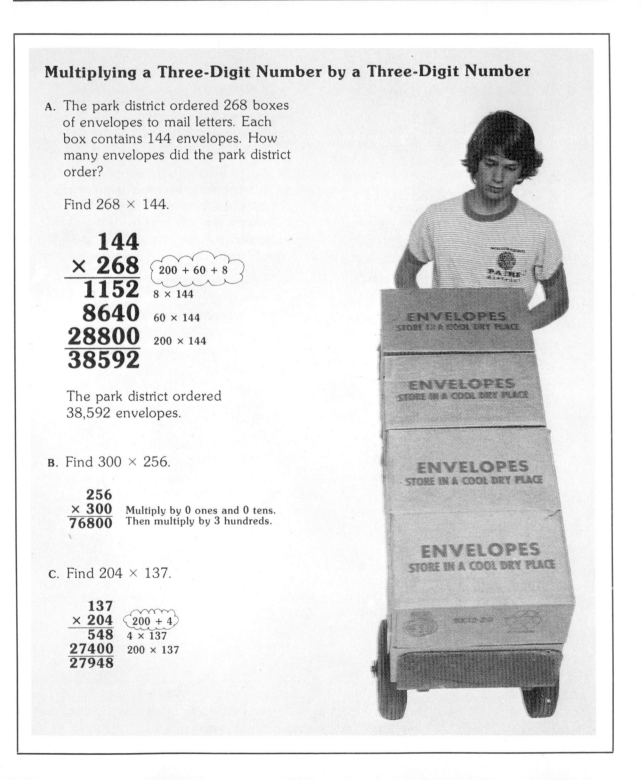

Solution

We might reason that if 1 carton holds 6 bottles, then 10 cartons hold 60 bottles and 100 cartons hold 600 bottles. If 100 cartons are filled, there are $726 - 100 \cdot 6$, or 126, bottles remaining. If 10 more cartons are filled, then $126 - 10 \cdot 6$, or 66, bottles remain. Similarly, if 10 more cartons are filled, $66 - 10 \cdot 6$, or 6, bottles remain. Finally, 1 carton will hold the remaining 6 bottles. The total number of cartons necessary is $100 + 10 + 10 + 1$, or 121. This procedure is summarized in Figure 3-28(a).

FIGURE 3-28

```
(a)  6)726                           (b)  6)726
     - 600    100 sixes                   - 600    100 sixes
     -----                                -----
      126                                   126
     -  60     10 sixes                   - 120      20 sixes
     -----                                -----
       66                                     6
     -  60     10 sixes                   -   6       1 six
     -----                                -----
        6                                     0      121 sixes
     -   6      1 six
     -----
        0      121 sixes
```

A more efficient way to determine the number of cartons is shown in Figure 3-28(b). Efficiency comes with practice.

Divisions such as the one in Figure 3-28 are usually shown in elementary school texts in more efficient form, as in Figure 3-29(a), and in the most efficient form, as in Figure 3-29(b), in which the numbers in color are omitted.

FIGURE 3-29

```
(a)        1 ⎤                        (b)        121
          2 0 ⎬ 121                             6)726
          1 00 ⎦                                - 6
          6)726                                 ----
          - 6 00                                  12
          ------                                - 12
           12 6                                 ----
          - 12 0                                   6
          ------                                -  6
              6                                 ----
          -   6                                    0
          ------
              0
```

Two-Digit Divisors, Zeros in the Quotient

A. All 73 rooms in the Ridgeland Hotel were decorated for a total cost of $59,057. What was the average cost for each room?

Find 59,057 ÷ 73.

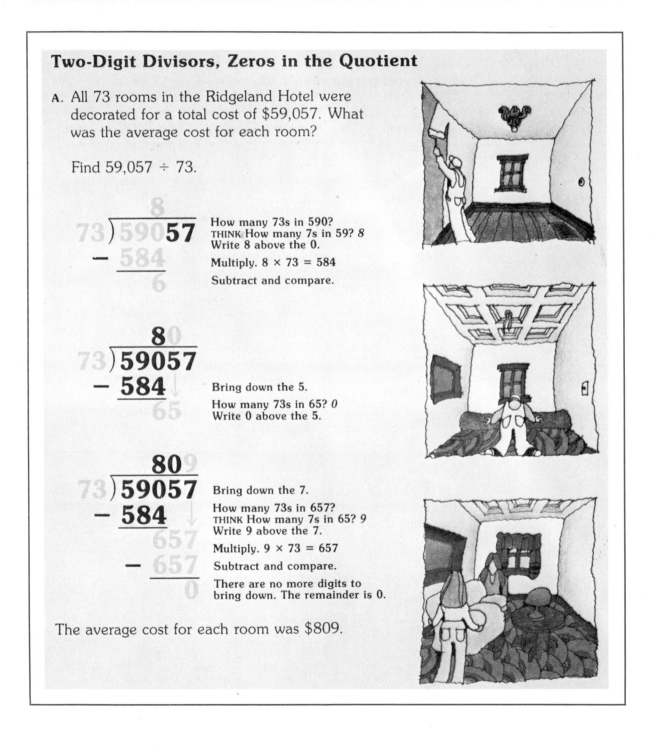

$$\begin{array}{r} 8 \\ 73\overline{)590} \\ -584 \\ \hline 6 \end{array}$$

How many 73s in 590?
THINK How many 7s in 59? *8*
Write 8 above the 0.

Multiply. 8 × 73 = 584

Subtract and compare.

$$\begin{array}{r} 8 \\ 73\overline{)59057} \\ -584\downarrow \\ \hline 65 \end{array}$$

Bring down the 5.

How many 73s in 65? *0*
Write 0 above the 5.

$$\begin{array}{r} 809 \\ 73\overline{)59057} \\ -584\downarrow \\ \hline 657 \\ -657 \\ \hline 0 \end{array}$$

Bring down the 7.

How many 73s in 657?
THINK How many 7s in 65? *9*
Write 9 above the 7.

Multiply. 9 × 73 = 657

Subtract and compare.

There are no more digits to bring down. The remainder is 0.

The average cost for each room was $809.

Example 3-12 | Divide $32\overline{)463}$.

Solution | The repeated subtraction method is shown on the left and the conventional algorithm is shown on the right.

$$
\begin{array}{r}
32\overline{)463} \\
-\ 320 \\
\hline
143 \\
-\ 128 \\
\hline
15
\end{array}
\quad
\begin{array}{l}
\\
\text{10 thirty-twos} \\
\\
\text{4 thirty-twos} \\
\text{14 thirty-twos}
\end{array}
$$

Place to represent $1 \cdot 10$.

$$
\begin{array}{r}
14 \\
32\overline{)463} \\
32 \\
\hline
143 \\
128 \\
\hline
15
\end{array}
$$

Place to represent $32 \cdot 10$.

The division algorithm verifies the solution, $463 = 14 \cdot 32 + 15$.

Good estimations are important when using a division algorithm efficiently. This is illustrated on the student page from *Scott, Foresman Mathematics*, 1980, Grade 5, on page 110.

Calculators can be used to show that division and repeated subtraction yield the same result. For example, consider $135 \div 15$. If the calculator has a constant button, push $\boxed{1}\ \boxed{5}\ \boxed{-}\ \boxed{K}\ \boxed{1}\ \boxed{3}\ \boxed{5}\ \boxed{=}\ .\ .\ .$, and then count how many times you must push the equal button in order to make the display read 0. (Calculators with a different constant feature may require a different sequence of entries.) Compare your answer with the one achieved by pushing this sequence of keys.

$\boxed{1}\ \boxed{3}\ \boxed{5}\ \boxed{\div}\ \boxed{1}\ \boxed{5}\ \boxed{=}$

PROBLEM SET 3-5

1. Perform the following multiplications, using both the conventional and lattice multiplication algorithms.

   (a) $\begin{array}{r} 728 \\ \times\ 94 \\ \hline \end{array}$
   (b) $\begin{array}{r} 306 \\ \times\ 24 \\ \hline \end{array}$

2. Explain why the lattice multiplication algorithm works.

3. Use the distributive property to explain why $386 \cdot 10,000 = 3,860,000$.

4. Fill in the missing numbers for each of the following.

   (a) $\begin{array}{r} 4\_6 \\ \times\ 783 \\ \hline 1\_78 \\ 3408\ \\ \_982\ \ \\ \hline 3335\_8 \end{array}$
   (b) $\begin{array}{r} 327 \\ \times\ 9\_1 \\ \hline 327 \\ 1\_08\ \\ \_9\_3\ \ \\ \hline 30\_\_07 \end{array}$

5. Simplify each of the following, using properties of exponents.

   (a) $5^7 \cdot 5^{12}$
   (b) $6^{10} \cdot 6^2 \cdot 6^3$
   (c) $10^{296} \cdot 10^{17}$
   (d) $2^7 \cdot 10^5 \cdot 5^7$

6. The following chart gives water usage for one person for one day.

Use	Average Amount
Taking bath	110 L (liters)
Taking shower	75 L
Flushing toilet	22 L
Washing hands, face	7 L
Getting a drink	1 L
Brushing teeth	1 L
Doing dishes (one meal)	30 L
Cooking (one meal)	18 L

   (a) Use the chart to calculate how much water you use each day.
   (b) The average American uses approximately 200 L of water per day. Are you average?
   (c) If there are 215,000,000 people in the United States, approximately how much water is used in the United States per day?

7. How many seconds are in a day? A week? A year?

8. The given model illustrates 23 · 14.

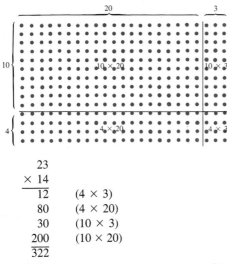

$$
\begin{array}{rl}
23 & \\
\times\ 14 & \\
\hline
12 & (4 \times 3) \\
80 & (4 \times 20) \\
30 & (10 \times 3) \\
200 & (10 \times 20) \\
\hline
322 &
\end{array}
$$

Draw similar models illustrating each of the following.
   (a) 6 · 23   (b) 18 · 25

9. In a certain book, 2981 digits were used to print the page numbers. How many pages are in the book?

10. Consider the following.

$$
\begin{array}{rl}
476 & \\
\times\ 293 & \\
\hline
952 & (2 \cdot 476) \\
4284 & (9 \cdot 476) \\
1428 & (3 \cdot 476) \\
\hline
139468 &
\end{array}
$$

   (a) Show that by using the conventional algorithm, the answer is correct.
   (b) Explain why the algorithm works.
   (c) Try the method to multiply 84 × 363.

11. The Russian peasant algorithm for multiplying 27 × 68 follows. (Disregard remainders when halving.)

	Halves	Doubles	
	⟶ 27	× ⑥⑧	
Halve 27	⟶ 13	⑬⑥	Double 68.
Halve 13	6	272	Double 136.
Halve 6	⟶ 3	⑤④④	Double 272.
Halve 3	⟶ 1	⑩⑧⑧	Double 544.

In the "Halves" column, choose the odd numbers. In the "Doubles" column, choose the numbers paired with the odds from the "Halves" column. Add the circled numbers.

$$
\begin{array}{r}
68 \\
136 \\
544 \\
1088 \\
\hline
1836
\end{array}
$$

This is the product 27 · 68.

Try this algorithm for 17 · 63 and other numbers. For an explanation of why the Russian peasant algorithm works, read "Understanding the Russian Peasant" by C. Reardin.

12. Compute 6 · 411, showing the mathematical justification for each step.

13. Perform each division using both the repeated subtraction and familiar algorithms.
   (a) $8\overline{)623}$ (b) $36\overline{)298}$ (c) $391\overline{)4001}$

14. Use the digits 7, 6, 8, and 3 and place them in the boxes to determine: (a) the greatest quotient; (b) the least quotient.

   $\Box\overline{)\Box\ \Box\ \Box}$

15. If the astronauts from Apollo-Saturn 10 traveled 720 km in 1 minute at reentry, how far did they travel in 1 second?

16. The Wright brothers flew approximately 50 m in 10 seconds. How far did they fly in 1 second?

17. Jack watched 492 minutes of television last week. How many hours and minutes did Jack watch television?

18. Place the digits 7, 6, 8, and 3 in the boxes to obtain: (a) the greatest product; (b) the least product.

$$
\begin{array}{r}
\Box\ \Box\ \Box \\
\times \qquad \Box \\
\end{array}
$$

19. Place the digits 7, 6, 8, 3, and 2 in the boxes to obtain: (a) the greatest product; (b) the least product.

$$
\begin{array}{r}
\Box\ \Box\ \Box \\
\times \quad \Box\ \Box \\
\end{array}
$$

20. If a cow produces 700 pounds (lb) of hamburger, and there are 4 Quarter Pounders to a pound, how many cows would it take to produce 21 billion hamburgers, assuming they each weigh a quarter pound?

21. Use a calculator to find the missing numbers.

$$
\begin{array}{lll}
\text{(a)} &
\begin{array}{r}
3\ 7 \\
\times\ 4\ 3 \\
\hline
-\ -\ - \\
-\ -\ -\ - \\
\hline
5\ 9\ 1
\end{array}
& \text{(b)} \quad
\begin{array}{r}
-\ - \\
\times\ 3\ 6 \\
\hline
5\ 5\ 8 \\
2\ 7\ 9\ 0 \\
\hline
-\ -\ -\ -
\end{array}
\end{array}
$$

(c)
$$
\begin{array}{r}
\_\ \_\ \_ \\
\times\ 2\ 1 \\
\hline
1\ 5\ 7\ 2 \\
3\ 1\ 4\ 4\ 0 \\
\hline
3\ 3\ 0\ 1\ 2
\end{array}
$$

(d)
$$
\begin{array}{r}
\_\ \ 3 \\
\times\ 5\ \_ \\
\hline
2\ 5\ 8 \\
2\ 1\ 5\ 0 \\
\hline
2\ 4\ 0\ 8
\end{array}
$$

22. Given the following problems, find all the possible whole number divisors.

(a)
$$
\begin{array}{r}
\overline{)123} \\
-\ 9 \\
\hline
33 \\
-\ 27 \\
\hline
6
\end{array}
$$

(b)
$$
\begin{array}{r}
\overline{)147} \\
-\ 10 \\
\hline
47 \\
-\ 45 \\
\hline
2
\end{array}
$$

(c)
$$
\begin{array}{r}
\overline{)146} \\
\\
\hline
3
\end{array}
$$

(d)
$$
\begin{array}{r}
\overline{)335} \\
\\
\hline
2
\end{array}
$$

23. Describe the pattern in the answers to the following products.

$$1 \times 1$$
$$11 \times 11$$
$$111 \times 111$$
$$1111 \times 1111$$

Through how many steps does this pattern continue?

24. How many 7s are in 98?
    (a) Use the constant feature to count backward from 98 to 0 by 7s, and count the number of 7s subtracted.
    (b) Count forward from 0 to 98 by 7s.
    (c) Use a calculator to find $98 \div 7$.

25. Estimate which of the following division problems have quotients between 20 and 50. Use a calculator to verify the answers.
    (a) $436 \div 13$
    (b) $4368 \div 131$
    (c) $4368 \div 13$
    (d) $436 \div 131$

26. Investigate the following numbers.

    $$2^{(3^7)} \quad \text{and} \quad (2^3)^7$$

    Are they equal? Is exponentiation associative?

27. Suppose a person can spend $1 per second. How much can that person spend in a minute? An hour? A day? A week? A month? A year? Twenty years?

28. Compare $2^{12} + 2^{12}$ and 2^{24}. Which is greater?

29. Suppose a friend chooses a number between 250,000 and 1,000,000. What is the fewest number of questions that must be asked in order to guess the number if the friend answers only yes or no to the questions?

* * * * * * * REVIEW PROBLEMS * * * * * * *

30. Write the number succeeding 673 in Egyptian numerals.
31. Write $3 \cdot 10^5 + 2 \cdot 10^2 + 6 \cdot 10$ as a Hindu-Arabic numeral.
32. Illustrate the identity property of addition for whole numbers.
33. Rename each of the following using the distributive property of multiplication over addition.

    (a) $ax + bx + 2x$
    (b) $3(a + b) + x(a + b)$

34. At the beginning of the trip, the odometer registered 52,281. At the end of the trip, the odometer registered 59,260. How many miles were traveled on this trip?
35. The registration for the computer conference was 192 people on Thursday, 215 on Friday, and 317 on Saturday. What was the total registration?

BRAIN TEASER

For each of the following, replace the letters with digits in such a way that the computation is correct. A single letter may represent only one digit.

$$
\begin{array}{r}
\text{LYNDON} \\
\times\ \text{B} \\
\hline
\text{JOHNSON}
\end{array}
$$

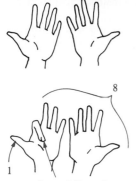

Second finger bent

Laboratory Activity

1. Finger multiplication has long been popular in many parts of the world. Multiplication of single digits by 9 is very simple using the following steps.
   (a) Place your hands next to each other as shown below.
   (b) To multiply 2 by 9, bend down the second finger from the left. The remaining fingers show the product.
   (c) Similarly, to multiply 3 by 9, bend down the third finger from the left. The remaining fingers will show the product $3 \times 9 = 27$. Try this procedure with other multiplications by 9.
2. "Napier's bones" were a set of multiplication tables, originally constructed on bones or ivory. The method for using them is similar to lattice multiplication. Find 4×1783 on the bones below.

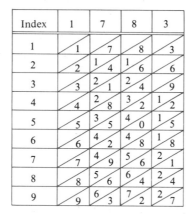

Index	1	7	8	3
1	1	7	8	3
2	2	1/4	1/6	6
3	3	2/1	2/4	9
4	4	2/8	3/2	1/2
5	5	3/5	4/0	1/5
6	6	4/2	4/8	1/8
7	7	4/9	5/6	2/1
8	8	5/6	6/4	2/4
9	9	6/3	7/2	2/7

For further reference see "Tangible Arithmetic" by P. Jones.

*3-6   OTHER NUMBER BASES

The Babylonian numeration system was based on 60 and the digital computer is based on 2, while the Hindu-Arabic system is based on 10. Mathematical historians believe that one reason the majority of the world uses the base ten system, with the ten digits 0 through 9, is that most people have ten fingers. When you count with two hands and reach the last finger, you begin using two-digit numbers. Suppose you can use only one hand and the digits available for counting are 0, 1, 2, 3, and 4. In the "one-hand system," you count 1, 2, 3, 4, 10, where 10 represents one hand and no fingers. The one-hand system is a base five system. (Recall that in base ten, 10 represents 1 ten and no units.)

In the one-hand, or base five, system, counting is in groups of five, rather than ten. In Figure 3-30(a), x's are grouped into tens, and in Figure 3-30(b), they are grouped into fives. In Figure 3-30(a), the grouping shows 1 set of ten x's and 9 other x's. This is written as 19_{ten}, or just 19.

FIGURE 3-30

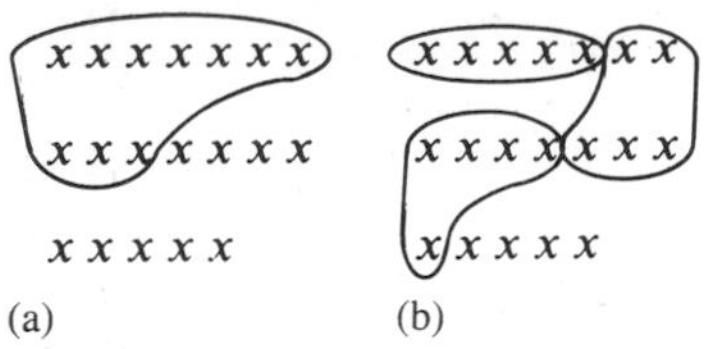

(a)　　　　　(b)

Figure 3-30(b) shows 3 groups of five x's and 4 other x's. This is written as 34_{five}. Thus, $19_{ten} = 34_{five}$. We write the small "five" below the numeral as a reminder that the number is written in base five. Counting in base five proceeds as shown in Figure 3-31.

FIGURE 3-31

Base Five Symbol	Base Five Grouping	One-Hand System
0_{five}		0 fingers
1_{five}	x	1 fingers
2_{five}	xx	2 fingers
3_{five}	xxx	3 fingers
4_{five}	xxxx	4 fingers
10_{five}	(xxxxx)	1 hand and 0 fingers
11_{five}	(xxxxx) x	1 hand and 1 fingers
12_{five}	(xxxxx) xx	1 hand and 2 fingers
13_{five}	(xxxxx) xxx	1 hand and 3 fingers
14_{five}	(xxxxx) xxxx	1 hand and 4 fingers
20_{five}	(xxxxx) (xxxxx)	2 hands
21_{five}	(xxxxx) (xxxxx) x	2 hands and 1 finger

What number follows 44_{five}? There are no more two-digit numbers in the system after 44_{five}. In base ten the same situation occurs at 99. We use 100 to represent ten tens, or one hundred. In the base five system, we need a symbol to represent five fives. To continue the analogy with base ten, we use 100_{five} to represent 1 group of five fives, no groups of five, and no units. To distinguish from "one hundred" in base ten, the name for 100_{five} is "one-zero-zero base five." The number 100_{ten} means $(1 \cdot 10^2 + 0 \cdot 10^1 + 0)_{ten}$, whereas the number 100_{five} means $(1 \cdot 10^2 + 0 \cdot 10^1 + 0)_{five}$, or $(1 \cdot 5^2 + 0 \cdot 5^1 + 0)_{ten}$.

The value of a number is determined by its base. The base ten value of 100_{five} could be computed as follows.

$$100_{\text{five}} = (1 \cdot 10^2 + 0 \cdot 10^1 + 0)_{\text{five}} = (1 \cdot 5^2 + 0 \cdot 5^1 + 0)_{\text{ten}} = 25_{\text{ten}}$$

This illustration shows a method of converting a number in any base to base ten; namely, use powers of the base value and write the number as an expanded base ten number.

Example 3-13

Convert each of the following to base ten: (a) 34412_{five}; (b) 1002_{five}.

Solution

(a) $\begin{aligned} 34412_{\text{five}} &= (3 \cdot 5^4 + 4 \cdot 5^3 + 4 \cdot 5^2 + 1 \cdot 5 + 2)_{\text{ten}} \\ &= (3 \cdot 625 + 4 \cdot 125 + 4 \cdot 25 + 5 + 2)_{\text{ten}} \\ &= (1875 + 500 + 100 + 5 + 2)_{\text{ten}} \\ &= 2482_{\text{ten}} \end{aligned}$

(b) $\begin{aligned} 1002_{\text{five}} &= (1 \cdot 5^3 + 0 \cdot 5^2 + 0 \cdot 5 + 2)_{\text{ten}} \\ &= (1 \cdot 125 + 0 + 0 + 2)_{\text{ten}} \\ &= (125 + 2)_{\text{ten}} \\ &= 127_{\text{ten}} \end{aligned}$

Example 3-13 also suggests a method for changing a base ten number to a base five number. Notice that the conversion involves powers of five. To convert 824_{ten} to base five, we divide by the powers of five: 5^1, or 5; 5^2, or 25; 5^3, or 125; 5^4, or 625; 5^5, or 3125; and so on. For example, the greatest power of 5 contained in 824 is 5^4, or 625. There is $1 \cdot 5^4$, with 199 left over. Thus,

$$824 = 1 \cdot 5^4 + 199$$

The greatest power of 5 contained in 199 is 5^3. There is $1 \cdot 5^3$, with 74 left over, in 199. Thus,

$$824 = 1 \cdot 5^4 + 1 \cdot 5^3 + 74$$

The greatest power of 5 contained in 74 is 5^2. There are $2 \cdot 5^2$ with 24 left over in 74.

$$824 = 1 \cdot 5^4 + 1 \cdot 5^3 + 2 \cdot 5^2 + 24$$

Finally, the greatest power of 5 in 24 is 5^1. There are $4 \cdot 5^1$, with 4 left, in 24, and there are 4 ones in 4. Thus,

$$824 = 1 \cdot 5^4 + 1 \cdot 5^3 + 2 \cdot 5^2 + 4 \cdot 5 + 4 = 11244_{\text{five}}$$

Thus changing from base ten to base five can be accomplished by dividing by successive powers of five. A shorthand method for illustrating this conversion follows.

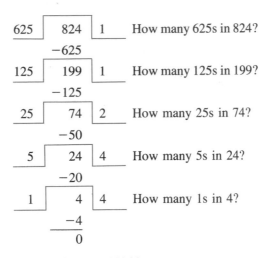

$$625 \overline{)\;824\;} 1 \qquad \text{How many 625s in 824?}$$
$$-625$$
$$125 \overline{)\;199\;} 1 \qquad \text{How many 125s in 199?}$$
$$-125$$
$$25 \overline{)\;74\;} 2 \qquad \text{How many 25s in 74?}$$
$$-50$$
$$5 \overline{)\;24\;} 4 \qquad \text{How many 5s in 24?}$$
$$-20$$
$$1 \overline{)\;4\;} 4 \qquad \text{How many 1s in 4?}$$
$$-4$$
$$0$$

Again, $824_{ten} = 11244_{five}$.

Historians tell of early tribes that used base two. Some Australian tribes still count "one, two, two and one, two twos, two twos and one, ..." Because base two has only two digits, it is called the **binary system.** Base two is especially important because of its use in computers. One of the two digits may be represented by the presence of an electrical signal and the other by the absence of an electrical signal. Although base two works well for computers, it is inefficient for everyday use because multidigit numbers are reached very rapidly in counting, as shown in Figure 3-32.

binary system

Base Two	Base Two Grouping	Base Ten Name	Base Two	Base Two Grouping	Base Ten Name
1_{two}	x	1	101_{two}	(xx)(xx) x	5
10_{two}	(xx)	2	110_{two}	(xx)(xx)(xx)	6
11_{two}	(xx) x	3	111_{two}	(xx)(xx)(xx) x	7
100_{two}	(xx)(xx)	4	1000_{two}	(xx)(xx)(xx)(xx)	8

FIGURE 3-32

The conversions from base two to base ten, and vice versa, may be accomplished in a manner similar to base five conversions.

Example 3-14

Convert 10111_{two} to base ten.

Solution

$$10111_{two} = (1 \cdot 2^4 + 0 \cdot 2^3 + 1 \cdot 2^2 + 1 \cdot 2^1 + 1)_{ten}$$
$$= (16 + 0 + 4 + 2 + 1)_{ten}$$
$$= 23_{ten}$$

Example 3-15 | Convert 27_{ten} to base two.

Solution

16	27	1	How many 16s in 27?
	-16		
8	11	1	How many 8s in 11?
	-8		
4	3	0	How many 4s in 3?
	-0		
2	3	1	How many 2s in 3?
	-2		
1	1	1	How many 1s in 1?
	-1		
	0		

Thus, 27_{ten} is equivalent to 11011_{two}.

Another commonly used number base system is base twelve, or duodecimal, system, known popularly as the "dozens" system. Eggs are bought by the dozens, and pencils are bought by the gross (a dozen dozens). In base twelve, there are twelve digits, just as there are ten digits in base ten, five digits in base five, and two digits in base two. In base twelve, new symbols are needed to represent the following groups of xs.

$$10 \ xs \qquad\qquad\qquad 11 \ xs$$
$$\overbrace{x \ x \ x \ x \ x \ x \ x \ x \ x \ x} \quad \text{and} \quad \overbrace{x \ x \ x \ x \ x \ x \ x \ x \ x \ x \ x}$$

The new symbols chosen are T and E, respectively, so that the base twelve digits are $0, 1, 2, 3, 4, 5, 6, 7, 8, 9, T, E$. Thus, in base twelve you count "1, 2, 3, 4, 5, 6, 7, 8, 9, T, E, 10, 11, 12, . . . , 17, 18, 19, $1T$, $1E$, 20, 21, 22, . . . , 28, 29, $2T$, $2E$, 30, ..." Notice that T_{twelve} is another way of writing 10_{ten} and E_{twelve} is another way of writing 11_{ten}. Also $10_{twelve} = 12_{ten}$.

Example 3-16 | Convert $E2T_{twelve}$ to base ten.

Solution

$$\begin{aligned} E2T_{twelve} &= (11 \cdot 12^2 + 2 \cdot 12^1 + 10)_{ten} \\ &= (11 \cdot 144 + 24 + 10)_{ten} \\ &= (1584 + 24 + 10)_{ten} \\ &= 1618_{ten} \end{aligned}$$

Example 3-17 | Convert 1277_{ten} to base twelve.

Solution

$$\begin{array}{r|r|l} 144 & 1277 & 8 \\ & -1152 & \\ \hline 12 & 125 & T \\ & -120 & \\ \hline 1 & 5 & 5 \\ & -5 & \\ \hline & 0 & \end{array}$$

How many 144s in 1277?

How many 12s in 125?

How many 1s in 5?

Thus, $1277_{ten} = 8T5_{twelve}$.

Example 3-18

The Rattlesnake Elementary School District needs 1000 pencils for students to use while taking standardized tests. The Wegotem Pencil Company sells pencils by the gross, by the dozen, and individually. A 30% discount is given when pencils are bought by the gross, a 20% discount when pencils are bought by the dozen, and no discount when pencils are bought individually. How should the school order exactly 1000 pencils so that the maximum discount is obtained?

Solution

Understanding the Problem

The problem is to obtain a maximum discount when ordering exactly 1000 pencils. To do this, the school must order the greatest number of pencils possible by the gross, then by the dozen, and, finally, individually.

Devising a Plan

Since 1 gross = 144, or 12^2, and 1 dozen = 12^1, we need to find x, y, and z so that $1000 = x \cdot 12^2 + y \cdot 12 + z \cdot 1$. The values for x, y, and z can be found by solving a related problem, converting 1000 to a base twelve number. Once the values of x, y, and z are determined, we can conclude that we should order x gross of pencils, y dozen pencils, and z individual pencils.

Carrying Out the Plan

We can determine the values for x, y, and z by changing 1000 to base twelve.

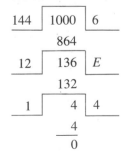

$$\begin{array}{r|r|l} 144 & 1000 & 6 \\ & 864 & \\ \hline 12 & 136 & E \\ & 132 & \\ \hline 1 & 4 & 4 \\ & 4 & \\ \hline & 0 & \end{array}$$

Because $1000 = 6E4_{\text{twelve}}$, this implies that the school district should order 6 gross, 11 dozen, and 4 individual pencils in order to receive the maximum discount.

Looking Back

To make sure that the school district will receive the 1000 pencils, we check that $6 \cdot 144 + 11 \cdot 12 + 4$ is equal to 1000.

PROBLEM SET 3-6

1. Write the first fifteen counting numbers for each of the following bases.
   - (a) base two
   - (b) base three
   - (c) base four
   - (d) base eight

2. Group the x's below to write the number of x's in bases five, three, and eight.
   - (a) x x x x
     x x x x
     x x x
   - (b) x x x x x
     x x x x x
     x x x x
   - (c) x x x x x x x x
     x x x x x x
     x x x x

3. How many different digits are needed for base twenty?

4. Write 2032_{four} in expanded base four notation.

5. What is the greatest three-digit number in each base?
   - (a) base two
   - (b) base six
   - (c) base ten
   - (d) base twelve

6. What, if anything, is wrong with the numerals below?
   - (a) 204_{four}
   - (b) 607_{five}
   - (c) $T12_{\text{three}}$

7. Find the numbers preceding and succeeding each of the following.
   - (a) $EE0_{\text{twelve}}$
   - (b) 100000_{two}
   - (c) 555_{six}
   - (d) 100_{seven}
   - (e) 1000_{five}

8. Convert each of the following base ten numbers to numbers in the indicated bases.
   - (a) 432 to base five
   - (b) 1963 to base twelve
   - (c) 404 to base four
   - (d) 37 to base two
   - (e) $3 \cdot 10^4 + 2 \cdot 10^2 + 4$ to base five
   - (f) $4 \cdot 10^4 + 3 \cdot 10^2$ to base twelve
   - (g) $9 \cdot 12^5 + 11 \cdot 12$ to base twelve

9. Write each of the following numbers in base ten.
   - (a) 432_{five}
   - (b) 101101_{two}
   - (c) $92E_{\text{twelve}}$
   - (d) $T0E_{\text{twelve}}$
   - (e) 111_{twelve}
   - (f) 346_{seven}
   - (g) 551_{six}
   - (h) 3002_{four}

10. Change 42_{eight} to base two.

11. Suppose you have two quarters, four nickels, and two pennies. What is the value of your money in cents? Write a base five representation to indicate the value of your fortune.

12. You are asked to distribute $900 in prize money. The dollar amounts for the prizes are $625, $125, $25, $5, and $1. How should this money be distributed in order to give the fewest number of prizes?

13. What is the minimum number of quarters, nickels, and pennies necessary to make 97¢?

14. Convert each of the following.
    - (a) 58 days to weeks and days
    - (b) 54 months to years and months
    - (c) 29 hours to days and hours
    - (d) 68 inches to feet and inches

15. For each of the following, find b.
    - (a) $b2_{\text{seven}} = 44_{\text{ten}}$
    - (b) $5b2_{\text{twelve}} = 734_{\text{ten}}$
    - (c) $23_{\text{ten}} = 25_b$

16. A bookstore ordered 11 gross, 6 dozen, 6 pencils. Express the number of pencils in base twelve and in base ten.

17. George was cooking an elaborate meal for Thanksgiving. He could only cook one thing at a time in his microwave oven. His turkey takes 75 minutes; the pumpkin pie takes 18 minutes; rolls take 45 seconds; and a cup of coffee takes 30 seconds to heat. How much time did he need to cook the meal?

18. What are the advantages and disadvantages of bases two and twelve over base ten?

19. An inspector of weights and measures has a special set of weights used to check the accuracy of scales. Various weights are placed on a scale to check accuracy of

any amount from 1 ounce through 15 ounces. What is the least number of weights that the inspector needs? What weights are needed to check the accuracy of scales from 1 ounce through 15 ounces? From 1 through 31 ounces?

20. Anna's bank contains only pennies, nickels, and quarters. What is the minimum number of coins she could trade for 117 pennies? If she trades 2 quarters, 4 nickels, and 3 pennies for pennies, how many pennies will she have?

Laboratory Activity

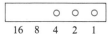

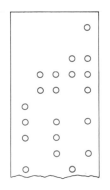

1. Messages can be coded on paper tape using base two. A hole in the tape represents 1, while a space represents 0. The value of each hole depends upon its position, from left to right, 16, 8, 4, 2, 1 (all powers of 2). Using base two, letters of the alphabet may be coded according to their position in the alphabet. For example, G is the seventh letter. Since $7 = 1 \cdot 4 + 1 \cdot 2 + 1$, the holes appear as they do at the left.
   (a) Decode the message on the left.
   (b) Write your name on a tape using base two.
2. The following number game uses base two arithmetic.

Card A		Card B		Card C		Card D		Card E	
16	24	8	24	4	20	2	18	1	17
17	25	9	25	5	21	3	19	3	19
18	26	10	26	6	22	6	22	5	21
19	27	11	27	7	23	7	23	7	23
20	28	12	28	12	28	10	26	9	25
21	29	13	29	13	29	11	27	11	27
22	30	14	30	14	30	14	30	13	29
23	31	15	31	15	31	15	31	15	31

Suppose a person's age appears on cards A, C, and D. Then, the person is 22. Can you discover how this works and why?

*3-7 COMPUTATIONS IN DIFFERENT BASES

One reason for studying computations in different number bases is to enhance our understanding of base ten computations. Another reason is to put you, as a prospective teacher, in somewhat the same role as a child studying arithmetic. We hope that by studying bases other than ten, you will better understand the problems that the children encounter learning place value and computational skills.

Recall that before studying algorithms in base ten, you had to assume a knowledge of the basic addition and multiplication facts. The same is true for other bases.

Addition and Subtraction in Different Bases

A table of basic addition facts for base five can be developed using the number line or other models similar to the models used for base ten numbers. A number line for base five illustrating $4_{\text{five}} + 3_{\text{five}}$ is shown in Figure 3-33. Thus, $4_{\text{five}} + 3_{\text{five}} = 12_{\text{five}}$.

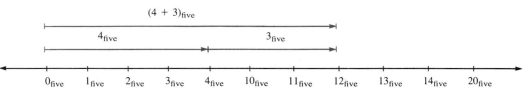

FIGURE 3-33

Using a number line such as the one pictured in Figure 3-33, we could construct the base five addition table shown in Table 3-7.

TABLE 3-7

+	0	1	2	3	4
0	0	1	2	3	4
1	1	2	3	4	10
2	2	3	4	10	11
3	3	4	10	11	12
4	4	10	11	12	13

Addition Table (Base Five)

Using the addition facts in Table 3-7, we can begin to develop algorithms for base five addition similar to those for base ten addition. Concrete teaching aids, such as multibase blocks, chip trading, and bean sticks, can also be used to develop these algorithms.

Suppose we wish to add $12_{\text{five}} + 31_{\text{five}}$. We show the problem using a concrete model in Figure 3-34(a), an introductory algorithm in Figure 3-34(b), and the familiar algorithm in Figure 3-34(c).

FIGURE 3-34

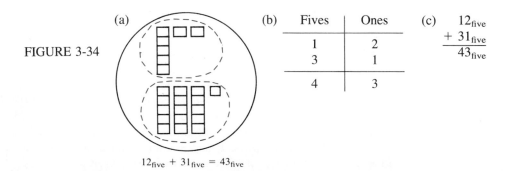

$12_{\text{five}} + 31_{\text{five}} = 43_{\text{five}}$

Addition problems that involve carrying can also be handled similarly to base ten problems. For example, $414_{\text{five}} + 23_{\text{five}}$ can be worked initially as shown in Figure 3-35(a); after more practice, it can be worked as shown in Figure 3-35(b).

FIGURE 3-35

(a)

Twenty-fives	Fives	Ones	
4	1	4	
+	2	3	
4	3	1̷2̷	Add.
	1	2	Trade.
4	4	2	Add.

(b)
$$414_{\text{five}}$$
$$+\ 23_{\text{five}}$$
$$\overline{442_{\text{five}}}$$

Additions in other number bases can be handled the same way, as shown in Example 3-19. Scratch addition can also be used to add numbers in various number bases. This will be explored in the problem set.

Example 3-19

Add each of the following.

(a)
$$101_{\text{two}}$$
$$111_{\text{two}}$$
$$+\ 110_{\text{two}}$$

(b)
$$E2T_{\text{twelve}}$$
$$389_{\text{twelve}}$$
$$+\ 2T0_{\text{twelve}}$$

Solution

(a)
$$11$$
$$101_{\text{two}}$$
$$111_{\text{two}}$$
$$+\ 110_{\text{two}}$$
$$\overline{10010_{\text{two}}}$$

(b)
$$1\ 1$$
$$E2T_{\text{twelve}}$$
$$389_{\text{twelve}}$$
$$+\ 2T0_{\text{twelve}}$$
$$\overline{1597_{\text{twelve}}}$$

Subtractions such as $12_{\text{five}} - 4_{\text{five}}$ can be modeled using a number line, as shown in Figure 3-36.

FIGURE 3-36

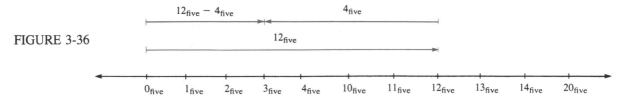

Thus, we see that $12_{\text{five}} - 4_{\text{five}} = 3_{\text{five}}$. The subtraction facts for base five can also be derived from the addition facts table by using the definition of subtraction. For example, to find $(12 - 4)_{\text{five}}$, recall that $(12 - {}'4)_{\text{five}} = c_{\text{five}}$ if and only if $(c + 4)_{\text{five}} = 12_{\text{five}}$. From Table 3-7, $c = 3_{\text{five}}$. More involved subtraction problems can be performed using the same ideas developed for base ten.

An example of subtraction involving borrowing, $32_{five} - 14_{five}$, is developed in Figure 3-37.

(a)

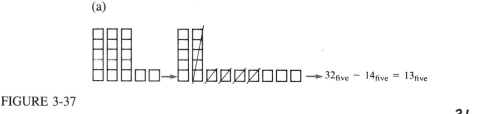

FIGURE 3-37

(b)

	Fives	Ones			Fives	Ones	
	3	2	$\longrightarrow$		2	12	
	-1	4			-1	4	
					1	3	

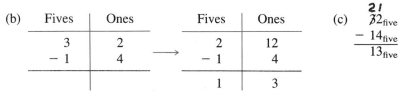

Subtraction in other number bases can be handled similarly, as shown in Example 3-20.

Example 3-20 Subtract:

(a) $\begin{array}{r} 1010_{two} \\ -\ 111_{two} \\ \hline \end{array}$ (b) $\begin{array}{r} 2E3_{twelve} \\ -\ 1T9_{twelve} \\ \hline \end{array}$

Solution (a) $\begin{array}{r} 1010_{two} \\ -\ 111_{two} \\ \hline 11_{two} \end{array}$ (b) $\begin{array}{r} 2E3_{twelve} \\ -\ 1T9_{twelve} \\ \hline 106_{twelve} \end{array}$

Multiplication and Division in Different Bases

As with addition and subtraction, the basic facts of multiplication must be learned before algorithms can be used. The multiplication facts for base five are given in Table 3-8. These facts can be derived by using repeated addition. (A number line may be helpful, too.)

TABLE 3-8

$\times$	0	1	2	3	4
0	0	0	0	0	0
1	0	1	2	3	4
2	0	2	4	11	13
3	0	3	11	14	22
4	0	4	13	22	31

Multiplication Table (Base Five)

There are various ways to do the multiplication $21_{\text{five}} \cdot 3_{\text{five}}$.

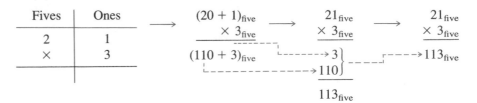

The multiplication of a two-digit number by a two-digit number is developed next.

$$
\begin{array}{r}
23_{\text{five}} \\
\times\ 14_{\text{five}} \\
\hline
22 \\
130 \\
30 \\
200 \\
\hline
432_{\text{five}}
\end{array}
\qquad
\begin{array}{l}
(10 + 4)_{\text{five}} \\
(4 \cdot 3)_{\text{five}} \\
(4 \cdot 20)_{\text{five}} \\
(10 \cdot 3)_{\text{five}} \\
(10 \cdot 20)_{\text{five}}
\end{array}
\qquad
\begin{array}{r}
{}^{2}23_{\text{five}} \\
\times\ 14_{\text{five}} \\
\hline
202 \\
230 \\
\hline
432_{\text{five}}
\end{array}
$$

Multiplication involving different number bases is demonstrated in Example 3-21.

Example 3-21

Multiply:

(a) $\quad 101_{\text{two}}$
    $\underline{\times\ 11_{\text{two}}}$

(b) $\quad E29_{\text{twelve}}$
    $\underline{\times\ T3_{\text{twelve}}}$

Solution

(a) $\quad 101_{\text{two}}$
    $\underline{\times\ 11_{\text{two}}}$
    $\quad\ 101$
    $\underline{\ 101}$
    $\ 1111_{\text{two}}$

(b) $\quad E29_{\text{twelve}}$
    $\underline{\times\ T3_{\text{twelve}}}$
    $\quad 2983$
    $\underline{9436}$
    97123_{twelve}

Lattice multiplication can also be used to multiply numbers in various number bases. This will be explored in the problem set.

Division in different bases can be performed using the multiplication facts and the definition of division. For example, $22_{\text{five}} \div 3_{\text{five}} = c$ if and only if $c \cdot 3_{\text{five}} = 22_{\text{five}}$. From Table 3-8, we see that $c = 4_{\text{five}}$. As with base ten, computing multidigit divisions efficiently in different bases requires practice. The ideas behind the algorithms for division can be developed using repeated subtraction, just as they were for base ten. For example, $3241_{\text{five}} \div 43_{\text{five}}$ is shown using the repeated subtraction technique in Figure 3-38(a) and the conventional algorithm in Figure 3-38(b).

$$
\begin{array}{ll}
\text{(a)} \quad 43_{\text{five}}\overline{)3241_{\text{five}}} & \\
\phantom{43_{\text{five}})}\underline{-\ 430} & (10 \cdot 43)_{\text{five}} \\
\phantom{43_{\text{five}})}2311 & \\
\phantom{43_{\text{five}})}\underline{-\ 430} & (10 \cdot 43)_{\text{five}} \\
\phantom{43_{\text{five}})}1331 & \\
\phantom{43_{\text{five}})}\underline{-\ 430} & (10 \cdot 43)_{\text{five}} \\
\phantom{43_{\text{five}})}401 & \\
\phantom{43_{\text{five}})}\underline{-\ 141} & (2 \cdot 43)_{\text{five}} \\
\phantom{43_{\text{five}})}210 & \\
\phantom{43_{\text{five}})}\underline{-\ 141} & (2 \cdot 43)_{\text{five}} \\
\phantom{43_{\text{five}})}14 & \overline{(34 \cdot 43)_{\text{five}}}
\end{array}
$$

FIGURE 3-38

$$
\begin{array}{l}
\text{(b)} \qquad\qquad\quad 34_{\text{five}} \\
\phantom{\text{(b)} }43_{\text{five}}\overline{)3241_{\text{five}}} \\
\phantom{\text{(b)} 43_{\text{five}})}\underline{-\ 234} \\
\phantom{\text{(b)} 43_{\text{five}})}401 \\
\phantom{\text{(b)} 43_{\text{five}})}\underline{-\ 332} \\
\phantom{\text{(b)} 43_{\text{five}})}14
\end{array}
$$

Thus, $3241_{\text{five}} \div 43_{\text{five}} = 34_{\text{five}}$ with remainder 14_{five}.

Base two division is much simpler than base five division, because the partial quotients are either 1 or 0, as Example 3-22 demonstrates.

Example 3-22

Divide:

$$101_{\text{two}}\overline{)110110_{\text{two}}}$$

Solution

$$
\begin{array}{l}
\phantom{101_{\text{two}})}1010_{\text{two}} \\
101_{\text{two}}\overline{)110110_{\text{two}}} \\
\phantom{101_{\text{two}})}\underline{-\ 101} \\
\phantom{101_{\text{two}})1}111 \\
\phantom{101_{\text{two}})1}\underline{-\ 101} \\
\phantom{101_{\text{two}})11}100
\end{array}
$$

PROBLEM SET 3-7

1. Perform each of the following operations using the bases shown.
   (a) $43_{\text{five}} + 23_{\text{five}}$ (b) $43_{\text{five}} - 23_{\text{five}}$
   (c) $432_{\text{five}} + 23_{\text{five}}$ (d) $42_{\text{five}} - 23_{\text{five}}$
   (e) $110_{\text{two}} + 11_{\text{two}}$ (f) $10001_{\text{two}} - 111_{\text{two}}$

2. Construct addition and multiplication tables for base eight.

3. Perform each of the following operations.

   (a)   3 hours 36 minutes 58 seconds
       $\underline{+\ 5 \text{ hours } 56 \text{ minutes } 27 \text{ seconds}}$

   (b)   5 hours 36 minutes 38 seconds
       $\underline{-\ 3 \text{ hours } 56 \text{ minutes } 58 \text{ seconds}}$

4. Perform each of the following operations (2 cups = 1 pint, 2 pints = 1 quart, 4 quarts = 1 gallon).
   (a)   1 quart 1 pint 1 cup   (b)   1 quart 1 cup
       $\underline{+\qquad\quad 1 \text{ pint } 1 \text{ cup}}$ $\underline{-\ 1 \text{ pint } 1 \text{ cup}}$

   (c)   1 gallon 3 quarts 1 cup
       $\underline{-\qquad\quad 4 \text{ quarts } 2 \text{ cups}}$

5. Use scratch addition to perform the following.

$$
\begin{array}{r}
32_{\text{five}} \\
13_{\text{five}} \\
22_{\text{five}} \\
43_{\text{five}} \\
23_{\text{five}} \\
\underline{+\ 12_{\text{five}}}
\end{array}
$$

6. Perform each of the following operations.
   (a)   4 gross 4 dozen 6 ones
      −   5 dozen 9 ones
      ─────────────────────

   (b)   2 gross 9 dozen 7 ones
      + 3 gross 5 dozen 9 ones
      ─────────────────────

7. What is wrong with the following?

   22_{five}
   $+\ 33_{\text{five}}$
   ─────
   55_{five}

8. Fill in the missing numbers in each of the following.
   (a) $2\ \_\ \_{\text{five}}$ (b) $2\ 0\ 0\ 1\ 0_{\text{three}}$
      $+\ \ 2\ 2_{\text{five}}$ $-\ \ \ 2\ \_\ 2\ \_{\text{three}}$
      ───────   ───────
      $\_\ 0\ 3_{\text{five}}$ $1\ \_\ 2\ \_\ 1_{\text{three}}$

9. Perform each of the following operations using the bases shown.
   (a) $(32_{\text{five}}) \cdot (4_{\text{five}})$ (b) $32_{\text{five}} \div 4_{\text{five}}$

   (c) $(43_{\text{five}}) \cdot (23_{\text{five}})$ (d) $143_{\text{five}} \div 3_{\text{five}}$
   (e) $(13_{\text{eight}}) \cdot (5_{\text{eight}})$ (f) $67_{\text{eight}} \div 4_{\text{eight}}$
   (g) $10010_{\text{two}} \div 11_{\text{two}}$ (h) $(10110_{\text{two}}) \cdot (101_{\text{two}})$

10. For what possible bases are each of the following computations correct?
    (a)   213   (b)   322
       + 308   − 233
       ─────   ─────
         522   23

    (c)   213   (d)   101
       × 32   11)1111
       ─────   − 11
         430   ───
       1043   11
       ─────   − 11
      11300   ───
                             0

11. Compute the following subtractions and leave your answers in base eight.
    (a) $463_{\text{eight}} - 1011_{\text{two}}$ (b) $32_{\text{eight}} - 101_{\text{two}}$

12. Use lattice multiplication to compute $(323_{\text{five}}) \cdot (42_{\text{five}})$.

SOLUTION TO THE PRELIMINARY PROBLEM

Understanding the Problem

A rural elementary school provided 1 cup of milk for each student each day. Milk was cheaper when purchased in large quantities, but the exact amount had to be purchased each day. Milk could be bought in gallons, half-gallons, quarts, pints, and cups. If 1 gallon, 1 quart, and 1 pint were bought on Tuesday, we are to find the number of students that were present on Tuesday. In addition, we are to find out how much milk was purchased if there were 31 students present on Wednesday.

Devising a Plan

There is one other bit of information required before a solution is found. Each child is to have 1 cup of milk per day, but the quantities to be bought are not only cups but also pints, quarts, half-gallons, and gallons. We need the following information:

1 pint = 2 cups
1 quart = 2 pints = 2 · (2 cups) = 4 cups
1 half-gallon = 2 quarts = 2 · (4 cups) = 8 cups
1 gallon = 2 half-gallons = 2 · (8 cups) = 16 cups

A table is helpful in answering the first question. The fact that 1 gallon, 1 quart, and 1 pint were bought is recorded in Table 3-9, along with the equivalent number of cups.

TABLE 3-9

Amount bought	1 gallon	0 half-gallons	1 quart	1 pint	0 cups
No. of cups in quantity	$1 \cdot (16$ cups$)$	$0 \cdot (8$ cups$)$	$1 \cdot (4$ cups$)$	$1 \cdot (2$ cups$)$	$0 \cdot (1$ cup$)$

Carrying Out the Plan

The total number of cups bought on Tuesday is $16 + 0 + 4 + 2 + 0 = 22$. Since each student received 1 cup, there were 22 students present.

To determine what combinations of containers of milk must be bought for 31 students, we use the number of cups in each quantity. Thirty-one students require 31 cups of milk. Since 1 gallon = 16 cups, then 31 cups = 1 gallon + 15 cups. Since 1 half-gallon = 8 cups, then 31 cups = 1 gallon + 1 half-gallon + 7 cups. Since 1 quart equals 4 cups, 31 cups = 1 gallon + 1 half-gallon + 1 quart + 3 cups. Since 1 pint equals 2 cups, 31 cups = 1 gallon + 1 half-gallon + 1 quart + 1 pint + 1 cup. Therefore, 31 cups is equivalent to 1 gallon, 1 half-gallon, 1 quart, 1 pint, and 1 cup.

Looking Back

Questions like those in this problem can be modeled in the base two number system. To understand the problem, we looked back at powers of 2 to determine the number of cups in each of the quantities that could be purchased. In the base two setting, the first question of converting 1 gallon, 0 half-gallons, 1 quart, 1 pint, and 0 cups to cups becomes a question of converting 10110_{two} to base ten. The second question becomes one of converting 31_{ten} to base two.

QUESTIONS FROM THE CLASSROOM

1. A student asks, "Does $2 \cdot (3 \cdot 4)$ equal $(2 \cdot 3) \cdot (2 \cdot 4)$?" Is there a distributive property of multiplication over multiplication?
2. Since $39 + 41 = 40 + 40$, is it true that $39 \cdot 41 = 40 \cdot 40$?
3. The division algorithm, $a = bq + r$, holds for $a > b$; $a, b, q, r \in W$. Is this true when $a < b$?
4. A student asks if 5 times 4 is the same as 5 multiplied by 4. How do you respond?
5. Can we define $0 \div 0$ as 1? Why or why not?

6. A student divides as follows. How do you help?

$$6\overline{)36}$$
$$\begin{array}{r} 15 \\ \underline{6} \\ 30 \\ \underline{30} \end{array}$$

7. When using Roman numerals, a student asks whether or not it is correct to write $\bar{\text{II}}$, as well as MI, for 1001. How do you respond?

8. A student says that $(x + 7) \div 7 = x + 1$. What is that student doing wrong?
9. A student says $x \div x$ is always 1. Is the student correct?
10. What is the difference in the expressions $(2^3)^2$ and $2^{(3^2)}$?

11. A student asks if division on the set of whole numbers is distributive over subtraction. How do you respond?
12. A student says that 0 is the identity for subtraction. How do you respond?
13. A student asks if zero is the same as nothing. What is your answer?

CHAPTER OUTLINE

I. Numeration systems
  A. Studying numeration systems, including those with bases other than ten, provides insight into the Hindu-Arabic system (base ten) of numbers.
  B. Properties of numeration systems give basic structure to the systems.
    1. Additive property
    2. Place-value property
    3. Subtractive property
    4. Multiplicative property

II. Exponents
  A. For any whole number a and any natural number n,

$$a^n = \underbrace{a \cdot a \cdot a \cdot \ldots \cdot a}_{n \text{ factors}}$$

where a is the **base** and n is the **exponent.**
  B. For any natural number a with whole numbers m and n, $a^m \cdot a^n = a^{m+n}$.

III. Whole numbers
  A. The set of whole numbers W is $\{0, 1, 2, 3, \ldots\}$.
  B. The basic operations for whole numbers are addition, subtraction, multiplication, and division.
    1. Addition: If $n(A) = a$ and $n(B) = b$, where $A \cap B = \varnothing$, then $a + b = n(A \cup B)$. The numbers a and b are **addends** and $a + b$ is the **sum.**
    2. Subtraction: If a and b are any whole numbers, then $a - b$ is the unique whole number c such that $b + c = a$. The number a is the **minuend;** b is the **subtrahend;** and c is the **difference.**
    3. Multiplication: If a and b are any whole numbers, then $a \cdot b =$

$$\underbrace{b + b + b + \cdots + b}_{a \text{ terms}}$$

a is the **multiplier;** b is the **multiplicand;** and $a \cdot b$ the **product.**

4. Multiplication: If A and B are sets such that $n(A) = a$ and $n(B) = b$, then $a \cdot b = n(A \times B)$.
5. Division: If a and b are any whole numbers with $b \neq 0$, $a \div b$ is the unique whole number c such that $b \cdot c = a$. The number a is the **dividend;** b is the **divisor;** and c is the **quotient.**
6. Division algorithm: Given any whole numbers a and b with $b \neq 0$, there exist unique whole numbers q and r such that $a = b \cdot q + r$ with $0 \leq r < b$.

C. Properties of addition and multiplications of whole numbers
  1. Closure: If $a, b \in W$, then $a + b \in W$ and $a \cdot b \in W$.
  2. Commutative: If $a, b \in W$, then $a + b = b + a$ and $a \cdot b = b \cdot a$.
  3. Associative: If $a, b, c \in W$, then $(a + b) + c = a + (b + c)$ and $a \cdot (b \cdot c) = (a \cdot b) \cdot c$.
  4. Identity: 0 is the unique identity element for addition of whole numbers; 1 is the unique identity element for multiplication.
  5. Distributive property of multiplication over addition. If $a, b, c \in W$, then $a \cdot (b + c) = a \cdot b + a \cdot c$.

D. Summary of properties for whole numbers.

	Addition	Subtraction	Multiplication	Division
Closure	Yes	No	Yes	No
Associative	Yes	No	Yes	No
Commutative	Yes	No	Yes	No
Identity	Yes	No	Yes	No

E. Relations on whole numbers
  1. $a < b$ if and only if there is a natural number c such that $a + c = b$.
  2. $a > b$ if and only if there is a natural number c such that $a = b + c$.

CHAPTER TEST

1. Convert each of the following to base ten.
   (a) $\overline{\text{CDXLIV}}$ * (b) 432_{five} * (c) $ET0_{\text{twelve}}$
   *(d) 1011_{two} *(e) 4136_{seven}

2. Convert each of the following base ten numbers to numbers in the indicated system.
   (a) 999 to Roman
   * (b) 346_{ten} to base five
   * (c) 1728_{ten} to base twelve
   * (d) 27_{ten} to base two
   * (e) 928_{ten} to base nine
   * (f) 13_{eight} to base two

3. Simplify each of the following, if possible. Write your answers in exponential form, a^b.
   (a) $3^4 \cdot 3^7 \cdot 3^6$ (b) $2^{10} \cdot 2^{11}$
   (c) $3^4 + 2 \cdot 3^4$

4. For each of the following, identify the properties of the operation(s) for whole numbers illustrated.
   (a) $3 \cdot (a + b) = 3 \cdot a + 3 \cdot b$
   (b) $2 + a = a + 2$
   (c) $16 \cdot 1 = 1 \cdot 16 = 16$
   (d) $6 \cdot (12 + 3) = 6 \cdot 12 + 6 \cdot 3$
   (e) $3 \cdot (a \cdot 2) = 3 \cdot (2 \cdot a)$
   (f) $3 \cdot (2 \cdot a) = (3 \cdot 2) \cdot a$

5. Using the definitions of less than or greater than, prove that each of the following inequalities is true.
   (a) $3 < 13$ (b) $12 > 9$

6. Explain why the product of $1000 \cdot 483$, namely, 483,000, has 0 for the hundreds, tens, and units digits.

7. Use both the scratch and traditional algorithms to perform each of the following.
   (a)   316   * (b) 316_{twelve}
          712   712_{twelve}
      + 91   + 913_{twelve}

8. Use both the traditional and lattice multiplication algorithms to perform each of the following.
   (a)   613   * (b) 216_{eight}
      × 98   × 54_{eight}

9. Use both the repeated subtraction and the conventional algorithms to perform each of the following.
   (a) $912\overline{)4803}$ (b) $11\overline{)1011}$
   * (c) $23_{\text{five}}\overline{)3312_{\text{five}}}$

10. Use the division algorithm to check your answers in Problem 9.

11. For each of the following base ten numbers, tell the place value for each of the circled digits.
    (a) $4\circled{3}2$ (b) $\circled{3}432$ (c) $19\circled{3}24$

12. For each of the following, find all possible whole number replacements that make the following true statements.
    (a) $4 \cdot \square - 36 < 27$ (b) $398 = \square \cdot 37 + 28$
    (c) $\square \cdot (3 + 4) = \square \cdot 3 + \square \cdot 4$
    (d) $42 - \square \geq 16$

13. Use a number line to perform each of the following operations.
    (a) $27 - 15$ (b) $17 + 2$
    * (c) $3_{\text{five}} + 11_{\text{five}}$ * (d) $12_{\text{three}} + 2_{\text{three}}$

14. Use the distributive property of multiplication and addition facts if possible to rename each of the following.
    (a) $3a + 7a + 5a$ (b) $3x^2 + 7x^2 - 5x^2$
    (c) $x(a + b + y)$ (d) $(x + 5)3 + (x + 5)y$

15. For each of the following, decide which operations apply and then solve the problems.
    (a) Mary had 5 apples, 14 oranges, and 6 raisins. How many fruits did she have?
    (b) Carlos had 32 apricots and 4 friends. If he wished to give each friend an equal number of apricots, how many did each receive?
    (c) Joe had 6 books, each with 12 chapters. How many chapters were there in all?
    (d) Jerry paid $24 for a shirt with a $50 bill. How much change did he receive?

16. You had a balance in your checking account of $720 before writing checks for $162, $158, and $33 and making a deposit of $28. What is your new balance?

17. Jim was paid $320 a month for 6 months and $410 a month for 6 months. What were his total earnings for the year?

18. A soft drink manufacturer produces 15,600 cans of his product each hour. Cans are packed 24 to a case. How many cases are produced in 4 hours?

19. A limited partnership of 120 investors sold a piece of land for $461,040. How much did each investor receive?

SELECTED BIBLIOGRAPHY

Anderson, A. "Why the Continuing Resistance to the Use of Counting Sticks?" *Arithmetic Teacher* 25 (March 1978):18.

Bachrach, B. "Using Money to Clarify the Decomposition Subtraction Algorithm." *The Arithmetic Teacher* 33 (April 1976):244–246.

Balin, F. "Finger Multiplication." *Arithmetic Teacher* 26 (March 1979):34–37.

Beard, E., and R. Polis. "Subtraction Facts with Pattern Explorations." *Arithmetic Teacher* 29 (December 1981):6–9.

Bernard, J. "Creating Problem-Solving Experiences with Ordinary Arithmetic Process." *Arithmetic Teacher* 30 (September 1982):52–53.

Bolduc, E., Jr. "Genaille Division Sticks." *Arithmetic Teacher* 28 (January 1979):12–13.

Boykin, W. "The Russian–Peasant Algorithm: Rediscovery and Extension." *The Arithmetic Teacher* 20 (January 1973):29–32.

Bradford, J. "Methods and Materials for Learning Subtraction." *Arithmetic Teacher* 25 (February 1978):19–21.

Brulle, A., and C. Brulle. "Basic Computational Facts: A Problem and a Procedure." *Arithmetic Teacher* 29 (March 1982):34–36.

Davidson, P., G. Galton and A. Fair. *Chip Trading Activities*. Fort Collins, Colo.: Scott Resources, Inc., 1972. (Scott Resources, Inc., P. O. Box 2121, Fort Collins, CO 80522.)

Dunkels, A. "More Popsicle-Stick Multiplication." *Arithmetic Teacher* 29 (March 1982):20–21.

Engelhardt, J. "Using Computational Errors in Diagnostic Teaching." *Arithmetic Teacher* 29 (April 1982):16–19.

Ferguson, A. "The Stored-Ten Method of Subtraction." *Arithmetic Teacher* 29 (December 1981):15–18.

Granito, D. "Number Patterns and the Addition Operation." *The Arithmetic Teacher* 23 (October 1976):432–434.

Hall, D., and C. Hall. "The Odometer in the Addition Algorithm." *The Arithmetic Teacher* 24 (January 1977):18–21.

Jones, P. "Tangible Arithmetic, I-Napier's and Genaille's Rods." *The Mathematics Teacher* 48 (November 1954):482–487.

Keller, R. "A Discovery Approach with Ancient Numeration Systems." *The Arithmetic Teacher* 19 (November 1972):543–544.

Kulm, G. "Multiplication and Division Algorithms in German Schools." *Arithmetic Teacher* 27 (May 1980):26–27.

Laing, R., and R. Meyer. "Transitional Division Algorithms." *Arithmetic Teacher* 29 (May 1982):10–12.

Lazerick, B. "Mastering Basic Facts of Addition: An Alternate Strategy." *Arithmetic Teacher* 28 (March 1981):20–24.

Lee, J. "Changing Bases by Direct Computation." *The Mathematics Teacher* 65 (December 1972):752–753.

Leutzinger, L., and G. Nelson. "Let's Do It: Using Addition Facts to Learn Subtraction Facts." *Arithmetic Teacher* 27 (December 1979):8–13.

Logan, H. "Renaming with a Money Model." *Arithmetic Teacher* 26 (September 1978):23–24.

Marcy, S., and J. Marcy. *Mathimagination, Books A–F*. Palo Alto, Calif.: Creative Publications, Inc., 1973. (Creative Publications, Inc., P. O. Box 10328, Palo Alto, CA 94303.)

McKellep, W. "Computational Skill in Division: Results and Implications from National Assessment." *Arithmetic Teacher* 28 (March 1981):34–35.

Merriell, D. "Nim and Natural Numbers." *The Mathematics Teacher* 64 (April 1971):342–344.

Moser, J. "Dear Kathy's Teacher." *Arithmetic Teacher* 29 (April 1982):26.

Murray, P. "Addition Practice Through Partitioning of Sets of Numbers." *The Arithmetic Teacher* 23 (October 1976):430–431.

Musser, G. "Let's Teach Mental Algorithms for Addition and Subtraction." *Arithmetic Teacher* 29 (April 1982):40–42.

O'Neil, D., and R. Jenson. "Some Aids for Teaching Place Value." *Arithmetic Teacher* 29 (December 1981):6–9.

O'Neil, D., and R. Jenson. "Strategies for Learning the Basic Facts." *Arithmetic Teacher* 29 (December 1981):6–9.

Reardin, C., Jr. "Understanding the Russian Peasant." *The Arithmetic Teacher* 20 (January 1973):33–35.

Robitaille, D. "An Investigation of Some Numerical Properties." *Arithmetic Teacher* 29 (May 1982):13–15.

Schultz, J. "Using a Calculator to Do Arithmetic in Bases Other than Ten." *Arithmetic Teacher* 26 (September 1978):25–27.

Seymour, D., M. Laycock, B. Larsen, R. Heller, and V. Holmberg. *Aftermath, Volumes 1–4*. Palo Alto, Calif.: Creative Publications, Inc., 1971. (Creative Publications, Inc., P. O. Box 10328, Palo Alto, CA 94303.)

Shaw, J., and M. Cliatt. "Number Walks." *Arithmetic Teacher* 28 (May 1981):9–12.

Shokoohi, G-H. "Manipulative Devices for Teaching Place Value." *Arithmetic Teacher* 25 (March 1978):49–51.

Smith, K. "Inventing a Numeration System." *The Arithmetic Teacher* 20 (November 1973):550–553.

Spitler, G. "Painless Division with Doc. Spitler's Magic Division Estimator." *Arithmetic Teacher* 28 (March 1981):34–35.

Stuart, M., and B. Bestgen. "Productive Pieces: Exploring Multiplication on the Overhead." *Arithmetic Teacher* 29 (January 1982): 22–23.

Thompson, C., and J. Babcock. "A Successful Strategy for Teaching Missing Addends." *Arithmetic Teacher* 26 (December 1978):38–41.

Thompson, C., and J. Van de Walle. "Transition Boards: Moving from Materials to Symbols in Subtraction." *Arithmetic Teacher* 28 (January 1981):4–7.

Tucker, B. "Give and Take: Getting Ready to Regroup." *Arithmetic Teacher* 28 (April 1981):24–26.

Unenge, J. "Introducing the Binary System in Grades Four to Six." *The Arithmetic Teacher* 20 (March 1973):182–183.

Van de Walle, J., and C. Thompson. "Give Bean Sticks a New Look." *Arithmetic Teacher* 28 (March 1981):6–12.

Wenner, W. "Compound Subtraction—An Easier Way." *Arithmetic Teacher* 25 (January 1978):33–34.

Wheatley, C., and G. Wheatley. "How Shall We Teach Column Addition? Some Evidence." *Arithmetic Teacher* 25 (January 1978):18–19.

Wolfers, E. "The Original Counting Systems of Papua and New Guinea." *The Arithmetic Teacher* 18 (February 1971):77–83.

Woodward, E. "Calculators with a Constant Arithmetic Feature." *Arithmetic Teacher* 29 (October 1981):40–41.

PRELIMINARY PROBLEM

Mary, a ten-year-old calculator genius, announced a discovery to her classmates one day. She said, "I have found a special five-digit number I call *abcde*. If I enter 1 and then the number on my calculator and then multiply by 3, the result is the number with 1 on the end!"

Mary's discovery is shown in the figure below. Can you find her number?

a	b	c	d	e	1

INTRODUCTION

The Chinese used red rods for positive numbers and black rods for negative numbers in calculations possibly as early as 500 B.C. Brahmagupta, a seventh-century Hindu mathematician, wrote, "Positive divided by positive, or negative by negative, is affirmative." However, as late as the eighteenth century, some mathematicians worried about whether two negative numbers could be multiplied. As we can see, the process of change in mathematics is usually neither rapid nor easy. Kline, in *Mathematics for Liberal Arts,* described the process as follows.

> The history of mathematics illustrates the rather significant observation that it is more difficult to get a truth accepted than to discover it. The mathematician to whom "number" meant whole numbers and fractions found it hard to accept negative numbers as true numbers. They [sic], too, failed to realize for centuries that mathematical concepts are man-made abstractions which can be introduced at will if they can serve useful purposes.

Negative numbers do serve useful purposes in everyday life. For example, they are used to report losses on the stock market, to record below-zero temperatures, and even to report lost yardage in a football game.

In mathematics, the need for negative numbers arises because subtractions cannot always be performed using only whole numbers. The cartoon depicts Linus attempting a subtraction using only whole numbers.

To compute $4 - 6$ using the definition of subtraction for whole numbers, a whole number a must be found such that $6 + a = 4$. Because there is no whole number a such that $6 + a = 4$, Linus' subtraction is not possible using only whole numbers. In order to perform the computation in the cartoon, a new number must be invented. This number, written as $^{-}2$, is called a negative integer. This chapter deals with the creation of negative integers, operations involving these numbers, and their properties.

4-1   INTEGERS AND THE OPERATIONS OF ADDITION AND SUBTRACTION

If we attempt the subtraction $4 - 6$ on a number line, as we did with whole numbers, we see that it is necessary to draw intervals to the left of 0.

On the extended number line in Figure 4-1, $4 - 6$ is pictured as an arrow that starts at 0 and ends two units to the left of 0.

FIGURE 4-1

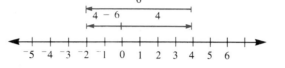

negative integers

The name that we give to the new number that corresponds to a point 2 units to the left of 0 is *negative two*, which is symbolized by $^-2$. Other numbers to the left of zero are created similarly. The new set of numbers, $\{^-1, \ ^-2, \ ^-3, \ ^-4, \ ^-5, \ . . .\}$ is called the set of **negative integers.** Unfortunately, the symbol "$-$" is used to indicate both a subtraction and a negative sign. To reduce confusion between the uses of this symbol, it is customary initially to use a raised "$-$" sign for negative numbers, as in $^-2$, in contrast to the ordinary minus sign for subtraction, as in $4 - 6$. To emphasize that an integer is positive, some people use a raised plus sign, as in $^+3$. In this text, we use the plus sign for addition only and write $^+3$ simply as 3.

The negative integers are pictured with the whole numbers on the number line in Figure 4-2.

FIGURE 4-2

integers

The union of the set $\{^-1, \ ^-2, \ ^-3, \ ^-4, \ ^-5, \ . . .\}$ and the set of whole numbers, $\{0, 1, 2, 3, \ . . .\}$, is called the set of **integers.** The set of integers is denoted by I:

$$I = \{. \ . \ . \ , \ ^-5, \ ^-4, \ ^-3, \ ^-2, \ ^-1, \ 0, \ 1, \ 2, \ 3, \ 4, \ 5, \ . \ . \ .\}$$

Frequently, it is convenient to partition the set of integers into the three subsets $\{1, 2, 3, 4, \ . . .\}$, $\{0\}$, and $\{^-1, \ ^-2, \ ^-3, \ ^-4, \ . . .\}$. The three subsets are called the *positive integers, zero,* and the *negative integers,* respectively. *Zero is neither positive nor negative.*

In Figure 4-2, the position of the negative integers can be described as mirror images of the positive integers, assuming the mirror is placed at 0 perpendicular to the number line. For example, the mirror image of 5 is $^-5$, and the mirror image of 0 is 0.

Similarly, the positive integers can be described as mirror images of the negative integers. For example, 4 is the mirror image of $^-4$. Another term for opposite   "mirror image of" is "**opposite** of." Thus, the opposite of 4 is denoted by ⁻4, and the opposite of ⁻4 can be denoted as ⁻(⁻4), or 4. In general, we have the following definition.

DEFINITION

If n is an integer, then the unique integer ^-n is called the opposite of n, and n is called the opposite of ^-n.

Example 4-1   Find the opposite of each of the following integers.

(a) 3 (b) ⁻5 (c) 0 (d) ⁻a

Solution   (a) ⁻3 (b) 5 (c) 0 (d) a

Example 4-2   For each of the following, find the value of ^-x.

(a) $x = 3$ (b) $x = {}^-5$ (c) $x = 0$

Solution   (a) $^-x = {}^-3$ (b) $^-x = {}^-(^-5) = 5$ (c) $^-x = {}^-0 = 0$

Remark   *Notice that ^-x does not necessarily represent a negative integer.* For example, the value of ^-x in Example 4-2(b) is 5.

As we mentioned, 4 and ⁻4 are opposites of each other. As such, they are on opposite sides of 0 on the number line and are the same distance—4 units—from 0, as shown in Figure 4-3.

FIGURE 4-3

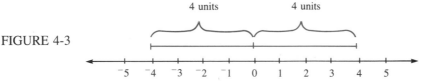

Distance is always a positive number or zero. The distance between the points corresponding to an integer and 0 is called the **absolute value** of the integer. Thus, the absolute value of both 4 and ⁻4 is 4, written as $|4| = 4$ and $|^-4| = 4$, respectively. (A more formal definition of absolute value is given in Problem 22 of Problem Set 4-1.)

absolute value

Example 4-3   Evaluate each of the following.

(a) $|20|$ (b) $|^-5|$ (c) $|0|$ (d) $^-|^-3|$

Solution   (a) $|20| = 20$ (b) $|^-5| = 5$ (c) $|0| = 0$ (d) $^-|^-3| = {}^-3$

Absolute values can be used to define addition of integers, but we consider more informal approaches first. The following model from the stock market illustrates integer addition using gains and losses:

1. A stock gains 7 points on Monday and 6 points on Tuesday. Interpreting both gains as positive numbers, the net gain can be written as $7 + 6 = 13$.
2. A stock dropped 10 points on Monday and then dropped an additional 15 points on Tuesday. We think about the total loss in points as $^-10 + {}^-15$. Because the total loss is 25 points, we record this as $^-10 + {}^-15 = {}^-25$.
3. A stock dropped 10 points on Monday and then gained 10 points on Tuesday. The net gain is 0. Thus, $^-10 + 10 = 0$.
4. A stock gains 8 points on Monday and drops 5 points on Tuesday. The net gain is $8 - 5 = 3$. We interpret a gain of 8 points as (positive) 8 and a loss of 5 points as $^-5$, so the net gain can be written as $8 + {}^-5$. Thus, $8 + {}^-5 = 8 - 5 = 3$.
5. A stock gained 10 points on Monday and then dropped 25 points on Tuesday. We think of the total loss in points as $10 + {}^-25$. Because the total loss is 15 points, we record this as $10 + {}^-25 = {}^-15$. Because $25 - 10 = 15$, we see that $10 + {}^-25 = {}^-(25 - 10)$.

Another model for addition of integers involves a number line. Consider Example 4-4, which involves a thermometer with a scale in the form of a vertical number line.

Example 4-4

The temperature was $^-4°C$. In an hour, it rose $10°C$. What is the new temperature?

Solution

Figure 4-4 shows that the new temperature is $6°C$ and that $^-4 + 10 = 6$.

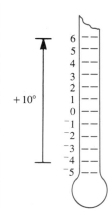

FIGURE 4-4

On a horizontal number line, we can picture a positive integer as an arrow pointing to the right and a negative integer as an arrow pointing to the left. For example, $^-3$ can be pictured using any of the arrows in Figure 4-5.

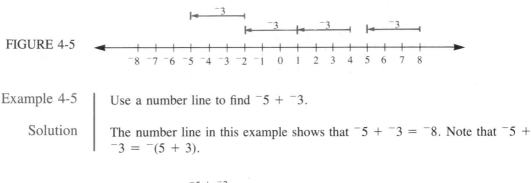

FIGURE 4-5

Example 4-5

Use a number line to find ⁻5 + ⁻3.

Solution

The number line in this example shows that ⁻5 + ⁻3 = ⁻8. Note that ⁻5 + ⁻3 = ⁻(5 + 3).

Figure 4-6 shows how to find 8 + ⁻5 on a number line. Place the starting end of the arrow representing the second number, ⁻5, at the point of the arrow representing the first number, 8. An arrow from 0 to the tip of the second arrow represents the sum of the two integers. Notice that the representation of 8 + ⁻5 is the same as that of 8 − 5.

FIGURE 4-6

From the gain-loss model, we see that 8 + ⁻5 is 8 − 5, or 3. Also, from the number-line model of Figure 4-6, we see that 8 + ⁻5 is represented by an arrow of length 3 to the right. Thus, 8 + ⁻5 = 8 − 5, or 3. To explain these models, absolute value may be used. In both models, a difference involving the whole numbers 8 and 5 is found. Because 8 and 5 are the absolute values of 8 and ⁻5, respectively, the pattern appears to be one of finding the difference of the absolute values of these integers. In fact, this pattern is true and is summarized in general as follows:

To add integers with unlike signs, subtract the lesser of the two absolute values of the integers from the greater. The sum has the same sign as the integer with the greater absolute value. If the two integers with unlike signs have equal absolute values, their sum is 0.

The pattern for addition of integers with like signs can also be summarized using absolute values:

To add integers with like signs, add the absolute values of the integers. The sum has the same sign as the integers.

Example 4-6 | Use the procedures for adding integers to find each of the following sums.

(a) $9 + {}^-4$ (b) ${}^-5 + {}^-8$ (c) ${}^-5 + 5$ (d) $3 + {}^-10$

Solution |
(a) $9 + {}^-4 = 5$ (b) ${}^-5 + {}^-8 = {}^-13$
(c) ${}^-5 + 5 = 0$ (d) $3 + {}^-10 = {}^-7$

In Example 4-6(b), ${}^-5 + {}^-8 = {}^-13$. Notice that ${}^-13$ is also equal to ${}^-(5 + 8)$. Hence, ${}^-5 + {}^-8 = {}^-(5 + 8)$. This is true in general. Thus, for any integers a and b,

$${}^-a + {}^-b = {}^-(a + b)$$

The justification of this equation is left as an exercise.

Integer addition has all the properties of whole number addition. These properties are summarized below.

Properties |
Given any two integers a and b:

Closure Property for Addition of Integers $a + b$ is a unique integer.

Commutative Property for Addition of Integers $a + b = b + a$.

Associative Property for Addition of Integers $(a + b) + c = a + (b + c)$.

Identity Element for Addition of Integers 0 is the unique integer such that for all integers a, $0 + a = a = a + 0$.

additive inverse
Unlike the set of whole numbers, the set of integers has the property that each of its members has an opposite. In mathematics, the opposite is also called the **additive inverse.** The fact that the set of integers has an additive inverse for each element in the set is recorded in the following property.

Property |
Additive Inverse Property For every integer a, there exists a unique integer ${}^-a$, called the additive inverse of a, such that $a + {}^-a = 0 = {}^-a + a$.

Observe that the additive inverse of ${}^-a$ can be written as ${}^-({}^-a)$, or a. Because the additive inverse of ${}^-a$ must be unique, we have ${}^-({}^-a) = a$.

Example 4-7 | Find the additive inverse of each of the following.

(a) ${}^-(3 + x)$ (b) $(a + {}^-4)$ (c) ${}^-3 + ({}^-x)$

Solution |
(a) $3 + x$
(b) ${}^-(a + {}^-4)$, which can be written as ${}^-(a) + {}^-({}^-4)$, or ${}^-a + 4$.
(c) ${}^-[{}^-3 + ({}^-x)]$, which can be written as ${}^-({}^-3) + {}^-({}^-x)$, or $3 + x$.

Subtraction of integers can be defined in terms of addition. This can be done in two different ways. One way is analogous to the definition of subtraction for whole numbers, and the other uses the concept of additive inverse. The subtraction $15 - 6$ was computed by finding a whole number n as follows.

$15 - 6 = n$ if and only if $6 + n = 15$

Because $6 + 9 = 15$, then $n = 9$.

Similarly, we may compute $3 - 5$ using the missing-addend approach.

$3 - 5 = n$ if and only if $5 + n = 3$

To find n in the equation $5 + n = 3$, we use a number line, as shown in Figure 4-7.

FIGURE 4-7

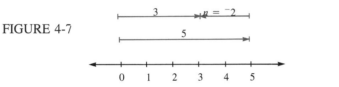

Hence, $3 - 5 = {}^-2$. In general for integers a and b, we have the following missing-addend approach to subtraction.

$a - b = n$ **if and only if** $b + n = a$

From our previous work with addition of integers, we know that $3 + {}^-5 = {}^-2$. Hence, $3 - 5 = 3 + {}^-5$. In general, for all integers a and b, the following is true.

$a - b = a +$ **(the additive inverse of b)**

   or

$a - b = a + ({}^-b)$

Example 4-8

Use the missing-addend approach to subtraction to compute the following.

(a) $3 - 10$ (b) ${}^-2 - 10$

Solution

(a) Let $3 - 10 = n$. Then $10 + n = 3$, so $n = {}^-7$. Therefore, $3 - 10 = {}^-7$.
(b) Let ${}^-2 - 10 = n$. Then $10 + n = {}^-2$, so $n = {}^-12$. Therefore, ${}^-2 - 10 = {}^-12$.

Example 4-9

Compute each of the following using the fact that $a - b = a + ({}^-b)$.
(a) $2 - 8$ (b) $2 - ({}^-8)$ (c) ${}^-12 - ({}^-5)$ (d) ${}^-12 - 5$

Solution

(a) $2 - 8 = 2 + {}^-8 = {}^-6$
(b) $2 - ({}^-8) = 2 + {}^-({}^-8) = 2 + 8 = 10$
(c) ${}^-12 - ({}^-5) = {}^-12 + {}^-({}^-5) = {}^-12 + 5 = {}^-7$
(d) ${}^-12 - 5 = {}^-12 + {}^-5 = {}^-17$

12–3 Subtracting Integers

Subtraction and addition are inverse operations.
You can subtract by writing and solving an addition equation.

$$^+5 - {}^-3 = n \text{ can be thought of as } {}^-3 + n = {}^+5.$$

Use a number line to solve for n.

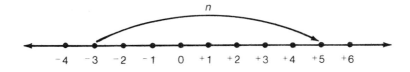

What do you add to $^-3$ to get $^+5$? $^-3 + \ n = {}^+5$
By counting, $n = {}^+\mathbf{8}$. $^-3 + {}^+\mathbf{8} = {}^+5$

Now the subtraction equation is solved.

$$^+5 - {}^-3 = \ n$$
$$^+5 - {}^-3 = {}^+\mathbf{8}$$

Notice that the answer is the same in these two examples.

$$^+5 - {}^-3 = {}^+8 \qquad\qquad {}^+5 + {}^+3 = {}^+8 \qquad\qquad {}^-3 \text{ and } {}^+3 \text{ are opposites.}$$

Compare these examples.

Subtraction   **Addition**

$$^+5 - {}^-4 = {}^+9 \longrightarrow {}^+5 + {}^+4 = {}^+9 \qquad {}^-4 \text{ and } {}^+4 \text{ are opposites.}$$
$$^-4 - {}^+5 = {}^-9 \longrightarrow {}^-4 + {}^-5 = {}^-9 \qquad {}^+5 \text{ and } {}^-5 \text{ are opposites.}$$

> **Subtracting an integer is the
> same as adding its opposite.**

$$^-3 - {}^+5 = {}^-3 + {}^-5 = {}^-8 \qquad\qquad {}^+7 - {}^-4 = {}^+7 + {}^+4 = {}^+11$$

$$^-8 - {}^-2 = {}^-8 + {}^+2 = {}^-6 \qquad\qquad {}^+9 - {}^+3 = {}^+9 + {}^-3 = {}^+6$$

Most calculators have a change-of-sign key, either $\boxed{\text{CHS}}$ or $\boxed{+/-}$, which allows for computation with integers. For example, to compute $^-8 - (^-3)$, we would push $\boxed{8}\ \boxed{+/-}\ \boxed{-}\ \boxed{3}\ \boxed{+/-}\ \boxed{=}$.

Subtraction of integers is developed on page 140, which is from *McGraw-Hill Mathematics,* 1981, Grade 7; it uses both approaches and a number line. (Note that a plus sign is used to denote positive integers.)

Subtraction on the set of integers has only a few properties. However, the set of integers is closed under subtraction.

Property | **Closure Property for Subtraction of Integers** For any integers a and b, $a - b$ is a unique integer.

Subtraction on the set of integers is neither commutative nor associative, as illustrated in these counterexamples.

$$5 - 3 \neq 3 - 5 \quad \text{because} \quad 2 \neq {}^-2$$

$$(3 - 15) - 8 \neq 3 - (15 - 8) \quad \text{because} \quad {}^-20 \neq {}^-4$$

Remember, if parentheses are present in an arithmetic expression, any computations within parentheses must be completed before other computations.

An expression such as $3 - 15 - 8$ is ambiguous unless there is agreement about the order in which subtractions are performed. Mathematicians agree that $3 - 15 - 8$ means $(3 - 15) - 8$; that is, the subtractions in $3 - 15 - 8$ are performed in the order of their appearance from left to right. Similarly, $3 - 4 + 5$ means $(3 - 4) + 5$ and not $3 - (4 + 5)$. Thus, $(a - b) - c$ may be written without parentheses as $a - b - c$.

Example 4-10 | Compute each of the following.

(a) $2 - 5 - 5$ (b) $3 - 7 + 3$ (c) $3 - (7 + 3)$

Solution | (a) $2 - 5 - 5 = {}^-3 - 5 = {}^-8$
(b) $3 - 7 + 3 = {}^-4 + 3 = {}^-1$
(c) $3 - (7 + 3) = 3 - 10 = {}^-7$

Finding an equivalent expression without parentheses for $a - (b - c)$ can be completed as follows. Give reasons for each of the steps.

$$
\begin{aligned}
a - (b - c) &= a + {}^-(b - c) \\
&= a + {}^-(b + {}^-c) \\
&= a + [{}^-b + {}^-({}^-c)] \\
&= a + ({}^-b + c) \\
&= (a + {}^-b) + c \\
&= (a - b) + c \\
&= a - b + c
\end{aligned}
$$

Hence, $a - (b - c) = a - b + c$.

In the process of showing that $a - (b - c) = a - b + c$, it was necessary to show that $^-(b - c) = ^-b + c$. Because $^-b + c = c + ^-b = c - b$, we have $^-(b - c) = c - b$; that is, $b - c$ and $c - b$ are additive inverses of each other.

Example 4-11 | Simplify each of the following.

(a) $2 - (5 - x)$ (b) $5 - (x - 3)$ (c) $^-(x - y) - y$

Solution | (a) $2 - (5 - x) = 2 - 5 + x = ^-3 + x$
(b) $5 - (x - 3) = 5 - x + 3 = 8 - x$
(c) $^-(x - y) - y = (^-x + y) - y = ^-x + (y - y) = ^-x$

PROBLEM SET 4-1

1. Find the opposites of each of the following integers. Write your answer in the simplest possible form.
   (a) 2   (b) $^-5$ (c) m
   (d) 0   (e) ^-m (f) $a + b$
2. Simplify each of the following.
   (a) $^-(^-2)$
   (b) $^-(^-m)$
   (c) $^-0$
3. Evaluate each of the following.
   (a) $|^-5|$ (b) $|10|$ (c) $|2 + ^-5|$
   (d) $|^-3 + ^-4|$ (e) $^-|^-5|$
4. Add each of the following.
   (a) $10 + ^-3$ (b) $10 + ^-12$
   (c) $10 + ^-10$ (d) $^-10 + 10$
   (e) $^-2 + ^-8$ (f) $(^-2 + ^-3) + 7$
   (g) $^-2 + (^-3 + 7)$
5. Demonstrate each addition on a number line.
   (a) $5 + ^-3$ (b) $^-2 + 3$ (c) $^-3 + 2$
   (d) $^-3 + ^-2$ (e) $(2 + ^-4) + ^-3$
6. Write an addition fact corresponding to each of the following sentences, and then answer the question.
   (a) A certain stock dropped 17 points and the following day gained 10 points. What was the net change in the stock's worth?
   (b) The temperature was $^-10°C$, and then it rose 8°C. What is the new temperature?
   (c) The plane was at 5000 feet and dropped 100 feet. What is the new altitude of the plane?
   (d) A visitor in a Las Vegas casino lost $200, won

$100, and then lost $50. What was the change in the gambler's net worth?
   (e) In four downs, the football team lost 2 yards, gained 7 yards, gained 0 yards, and lost 8 yards. What was the total gain or loss?
7. On January 1, Jane's bank balance was $300. During the month, she wrote checks for $45, $55, $165, $35, and $100 and made deposits of $75, $25, and $400.
   (a) If a check is represented by a negative integer and a deposit by a positive integer, express Jane's transactions as a sum of positive and negative integers.
   (b) What was the balance in Jane's account at the end of the month?
8. Evaluate each of the following using the definition of subtraction.
   (a) $2 - 11$ (b) $^-3 - 7$
   (c) $5 - (^-8)$ (d) $0 - 4$
9. Use the missing-addend approach to compute each of the following.
   (a) $3 - 15$ (b) $^-2 - 5$
   (c) $^-3 - (^-15)$ (d) $0 - 4$
10. Perform each of the following.
   (a) $^-2 + (3 - 10)$ (b) $[8 - (^-5)] - 10$
   (c) $(^-2 - 7) + 10$ (d) $^-2 - (7 + 10)$
   (e) $8 - 11 - 10$ (f) $^-2 - 7 + 3$
11. Demonstrate each subtraction below on a number line.
   (a) $5 - 7$ (b) $^-5 - 7$
   (c) $^-5 - ^-7$ (d) $5 - ^-7$

12. A model for subtraction of integers involves charged particles. Write an explanation of each of the three computations in terms of charged particles.

    (a) $^+3 - ^-2 = ^+5$

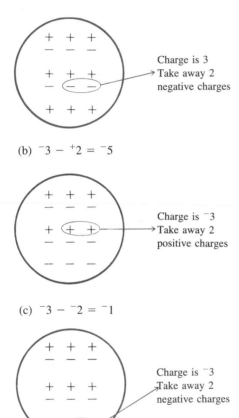

Charge is 3
Take away 2
negative charges

    (b) $^-3 - ^+2 = ^-5$

Charge is $^-3$
Take away 2
positive charges

    (c) $^-3 - ^-2 = ^-1$

Charge is $^-3$
Take away 2
negative charges

13. Consider the expressions $(x + y) - (z + w)$ and $(x - z) + (y - w)$.
    (a) Are the expressions equal for $x = 30$, $y = 4$, $z = 10$, and $w = 7$?
    (b) Are the expressions equal if $x = ^-4$, $y = 5$, $z = ^-9$, and $w = 7$?

14. Let W stand for the set of whole numbers, I the set of integers, I^+ the set of positive integers, and I^- the set of negative integers. Find each of the following.
    (a) $W \cup I$ (b) $W \cap I$ (c) $I^+ \cup I^-$
    (d) $I^+ \cap I^-$ (e) $W - I$ (f) $I - W$
    (g) $W - I^+$ (h) $W - I^-$

15. Complete the magic square using the following integers: $^-13$, $^-10$, $^-7$, $^-4$, 2, 5, 8, 11.

16. In a game of Triominoes, Jack's scores in five successive turns were 17, $^-8$, $^-9$, 14, and 45. What was his total at the end of five turns?

17. The largest bubble chamber in the world is 15 feet in diameter and contains 7259 gallons of liquid hydrogen at a temperature of $^-247°C$. If the temperature is dropped 11°C per hour for 2 consecutive hours, what is the new temperature?

18. The greatest recorded temperature ranges in the world are around the Siberian "cold pole" in the USSR. Temperatures in Verkhoyansk have varied from $^-94°F$ to 98°F. What has been the range in temperature in Verkhoyansk?

19. A turnpike driver had car trouble. He knew that he had driven 12 miles from milepost 68 before the trouble. If he is confused and disoriented when he calls on his CB for help, what are his possible locations?

20. To find the opposite of a number, enter the number on the display and then push the $\boxed{+/-}$ key. For example, entering 7 and pushing $\boxed{+/-}$ yields $^-7$ on the display. Find the opposites for each of the following.
    (a) 14   (b) 24   (c) $^-2$ (d) $^-5$

21. Complete each of the following integer arithmetic problems on the calculator making use of the $\boxed{+/-}$ key. For example, to find $^-5 + ^-4$, enter $\boxed{5}\boxed{+/-}\boxed{+}$ $\boxed{4}\boxed{+/-}\boxed{=}$.
    (a) $^-12 + ^-6$ (b) $^-7 + (^-99)$
    (c) $^-12 + 6$ (d) $27 + (^-5)$
    (e) $3 + (^-14)$ (f) $^-7 - (^-9)$
    (g) $^-12 - 6$ (h) $16 - (^-7)$

★ 22. The following is a definition for the absolute value of an integer x.

    If x is a positive integer or 0, then $|x| = x$.

    If x is a negative integer, then $|x| = ^-x$.

    Use this definition to evaluate each of the following.
    (a) $|5|$ (b) $|^-5|$
    (c) $|0|$ (d) $^-|^-7|$

BRAIN TEASER

If the digits 1 through 9 are written in order, it is possible to place plus and minus signs between the numbers or to use no operation symbol at all to obtain a total of 100. For example,

$$1 + 2 + 3 + {}^-4 + 5 + 6 + 78 + 9 = 100$$

Can you obtain a total of 100 using fewer plus or minus signs than in the given example? Notice that digits, such as 7 and 8, may be combined.

COMPUTER   CORNER

1. Type the BASIC program below on your computer.

```
 10 PRINT "THIS PROGRAM FINDS THE ABSOLUTE VALUE ";
 20 PRINT "OF A NUMBER."
 30 PRINT "AFTER THE QUESTION MARK, TYPE ";
 40 PRINT "YOUR NUMBER."
 50 INPUT N
 60 IF N < 0 GOTO 90
 70 PRINT "THE ABSOLUTE VALUE OF "; N;" IS "; N
 80 GOTO 100
 90 PRINT "THE ABSOLUTE VALUE OF "; N;" IS ";-N
100 PRINT "IF YOU WANT TO FIND ANOTHER ABSOLUTE VALUE, "
110 PRINT "TYPE 1 AFTER THE QUESTION MARK. IF NOT, TYPE 0."
120 INPUT V
130 IF V = 1 GOTO 30
140 END
```

Run this program and input the following values.

(a) ⁻7   (b) 0   (c) 140   (d) ⁻21

2. Type the given Logo program on your computer.

```
TO ABS :X
IF :X < 0 THEN OUTPUT (-:X)
OUTPUT :X
END
```

Run this program and input the following values.

(a) ⁻7   (b) 0   (c) 140   (d) ⁻21

4-2 MULTIPLICATION AND DIVISION OF INTEGERS

We can approach multiplication of a nonnegative integer times any integer through repeated addition, as we did with whole numbers. For example, if E. T. Simpson lost 2 yards on each of three carries in a football game, then E. T. had a net loss of $^-2 + {}^-2 + {}^-2$, or $^-6$, yards. Since $^-2 + {}^-2 + {}^-2$ can be written as $3 \cdot (^-2)$ using repeated addition, we have $3 \cdot (^-2) = {}^-6$.

Next consider a product like $(^-2) \cdot 3$. It is meaningless to say that there are $^-2$ threes in a sum. To develop a feeling for what $(^-2) \cdot 3$ should be, consider this pattern.

$$4 \cdot 3 = 12$$
$$3 \cdot 3 = 9$$
$$2 \cdot 3 = 6$$
$$1 \cdot 3 = 3$$
$$0 \cdot 3 = 0$$
$$^-1 \cdot 3 = \,?$$
$$^-2 \cdot 3 = \,?$$

The first five products, 12, 9, 6, 3, and 0, are terms of an arithmetic sequence with fixed difference $^-3$. If the pattern continues, the next two terms in the sequence are $^-3$ and $^-6$. Thus, it appears that $(^-2) \cdot 3 = {}^-6$. Recall that $3 \cdot (^-2)$ also equals $^-6$. Hence, if $(^-2) \cdot 3 = {}^-6$, we have $(^-2) \cdot 3 = 3(^-2)$. This result is consistent with the commutative property of multiplication developed for whole numbers.

Next consider the product $(^-2) \cdot (^-3)$. Using the previous results, the following pattern can be developed.

$$(^-2) \cdot 3 = {}^-6$$
$$(^-2) \cdot 2 = {}^-4$$
$$(^-2) \cdot 1 = {}^-2$$
$$(^-2) \cdot 0 = 0$$
$$(^-2) \cdot (^-1) = \,?$$
$$(^-2) \cdot (^-2) = \,?$$
$$(^-2) \cdot (^-3) = \,?$$

The first four products, $^-6$, $^-4$, $^-2$, and 0, are terms in an arithmetic sequence with fixed difference 2. If the pattern continues, the next three terms in the sequence are 2, 4, and 6. Thus, it appears that $(^-2) \cdot (^-3) = 6$.

From the patterns above, the following general rules appear to be true.

A positive integer times a positive integer is a positive integer.

Any integer times zero is zero.

A positive integer times a negative integer is a negative integer.

A negative integer times a positive integer is a negative integer.

A negative integer times a negative integer is a positive integer.

Remember, patterns can be misleading. However, in this case, patterns lead to the way multiplication of two integers is defined. A more formal mathematical approach to multiplication of two integers is given later in this section, when more properties of integers are available.

Example 4-12

Find each of the following products.

(a) $3 \cdot (^-15)$
(c) $0 \cdot (^-3)$
(e) $(^-5) \cdot (^-7)$

(b) $(^-5) \cdot 7$
(d) $0 \cdot (^-n), n \in W$

Solution

(a) $3 \cdot (^-15) = {}^-45$
(c) $0 \cdot (^-3) = 0$
(e) $(^-5) \cdot (^-7) = 35$

(b) $(^-5) \cdot 7 = {}^-35$
(d) $0 \cdot (^-n) = 0$

The set of integers has properties under multiplication analogous to those of the set of whole numbers under multiplication. These properties are summarized below.

Properties

The set of integers, I, satisfies the following properties of multiplication for all integers $a, b, c, \in I$.

Closure Property for Multiplication of Integers $a \cdot b$ is a unique integer.

Commutative Property for Multiplication of Integers $a \cdot b = b \cdot a$.

Associative Property for Multiplication of Integers $(a \cdot b) \cdot c = a \cdot (b \cdot c)$

Identity Element for Multiplication of Integers 1 is the unique integer such that for all integers a, $1 \cdot a = a = a \cdot 1$.

Distributive Properties of Multiplication over Addition for Integers
$a \cdot (b + c) = a \cdot b + a \cdot c$ and $(b + c) \cdot a = b \cdot a + c \cdot a$

Using the above properties, we formally develop the rules for multiplication of integers. A mathematical approach for showing that $(^-2) \cdot 3 = {}^-(2 \cdot 3)$ uses the uniqueness property of additive inverses. If we can show that $(^-2) \cdot 3$ and $^-(2 \cdot 3)$ are additive inverses of the same number, then they must be equal. By definition, the additive inverse of $(2 \cdot 3)$ is $^-(2 \cdot 3)$. That $(^-2) \cdot 3$ is also the additive inverse of $2 \cdot 3$ can be proved by showing $(^-2) \cdot 3 + 2 \cdot 3 = 0$. The proof follows.

$(^-2) \cdot 3 + 2 \cdot 3 = (^-2 + 2) \cdot 3$ Distributive property of multiplication over addition.

$= 0 \cdot 3$ Additive inverse.

$= 0$ Zero multiplication.

Because $(^-2) \cdot 3$ and $^-(2 \cdot 3)$ are both additive inverses of $(2 \cdot 3)$ and the additive inverse must be unique, $(^-2) \cdot 3 = {}^-(2 \cdot 3)$.
The above proof is true in general for any integers a and b.

Property | For any integers a and b, $(^-a) \cdot b = {}^-(a \cdot b)$.

Similarly, we can prove the following.

Property | For any integers a and b, $(^-a) \cdot (^-b) = a \cdot b$.

Note there is no restriction that a must be positive or that ^-a must be negative.
Another property that can be developed using the distributive property of multiplication over addition is the distributive property of multiplication over subtraction. Consider the following.

$$
\begin{aligned}
a(b - c) &= a(b + {}^-c) \\
&= ab + a(^-c) \\
&= ab + {}^-(ac) \\
&= ab - ac
\end{aligned}
$$

Consequently, $a(b - c) = ab - ac$. Similarly, it can be shown that $(b - c)a = ba - ca$.

Property | **Distributive Property of Multiplication over Subtraction for Integers**   For any integers a, b, and c,

$$a(b - c) = ab - ac$$
$$(b - c)a = ba - ca$$

Example 4-13 |

Simplify each of the following so that there are no parentheses in the final answer.

(a) $(^-3)(x - 2)$ (b) $(a + b)(a - b)$

Solution |

(a) $(^-3)(x - 2) = (^-3)x - (^-3)(2) = {}^-3x - (^-6) = {}^-3x + 6$
(b) $(a + b)(a - b) = (a + b)a - (a + b)b$
$$
\begin{aligned}
&= (a^2 + ba) - (ab + b^2) \\
&= a^2 + ab - ab - b^2 \\
&= a^2 - b^2
\end{aligned}
$$
Thus, $(a + b)(a - b) = a^2 - b^2$.

difference of squares   The result $(a + b)(a - b) = a^2 - b^2$ in Example 4-13(b) generally is called the **difference of squares** formula.

Example 4-14 | Use the difference of squares formula to aid in simplifying the following.

(a) $22 \cdot 18$ (b) $(4 + b)(4 - b)$ (c) $(^-4 + b)(^-4 - b)$

Solution | (a) $22 \cdot 18 = (20 + 2)(20 - 2) = 20^2 - 2^2 = 400 - 4 = 396$
(b) $(4 + b)(4 - b) = 4^2 - b^2 = 16 - b^2$
(c) $(^-4 + b)(^-4 - b) = (^-4)^2 - b^2 = 16 - b^2$

Both the difference of squares formula and the distributive properties of multiplication over addition and subtraction can be used for factoring.

Example 4-15 | Factor each of the following completely.

(a) $x^2 - 9$ (b) $(x + y)^2 - z^2$ (c) $^-3x + 5xy$ (d) $3x - 6$

Solution | (a) $x^2 - 9 = x^2 - 3^2 = (x + 3)(x - 3)$
(b) $(x + y)^2 - z^2 = (x + y + z)(x + y - z)$
(c) $^-3x + 5xy = x(^-3 + 5y)$
(d) $3x - 6 = 3(x - 2)$

Recall that when addition and multiplication appear in a problem without parentheses, multiplication is done first.

When addition, subtraction, multiplication, and division appear without parentheses, multiplications and divisions are done first in the order of their appearance from left to right and then additions and subtractions in the order of their appearance from left to right. Any arithmetic appearing inside parentheses must be done first.

Example 4-16 | Evaluate each of the following.

(a) $2 - 5 \cdot 4 + 1$ (b) $(2 - 5) \cdot 4 + 1$
(c) $2 - 3 \cdot 4 + 5 \cdot 2 - 1 + 5$

Solution | (a) $2 - 5 \cdot 4 + 1 = 2 - 20 + 1 = {}^-18 + 1 = {}^-17$
(b) $(2 - 5) \cdot 4 + 1 = {}^-3 \cdot 4 + 1 = {}^-12 + 1 = {}^-11$
(c) $2 - 3 \cdot 4 + 5 \cdot 2 - 1 + 5 = 2 - 12 + 10 - 1 + 5 = 4$

Remark | Problems like those in Example 4-16 should be examined by students so that they later realize that $2 - 5x + 1$ is *not* equal to $^-3x + 1$.

Division is the last operation on integers to be considered. Recall that on the set of whole numbers, $a \div b$ where $b \neq 0$ is defined to be the unique whole number c such that $a = bc$. If such a whole number c does not exist, then $a \div b$ is undefined. Division in the set of integers is defined analogously.

DEFINITION	If a and b are any integers with $b \neq 0$, then $a \div b$ is the unique integer c such that $a = bc$.

Example 4-17   Use the definition of division to evaluate each of the following.

(a) $12 \div (^-4)$ (b) $^-12 \div 4$ (c) $^-12 \div (^-4)$

Solution   (a) Let $12 \div (^-4) = c$. Then, $12 = ^-4c$, and consequently, $c = ^-3$. Thus, $12 \div (^-4) = ^-3$.

(b) Let $^-12 \div 4 = c$. Then, $^-12 = 4c$, and therefore, $c = ^-3$. Thus, $^-12 \div 4 = ^-3$.

(c) Let $^-12 \div (^-4) = c$. Then $^-12 = ^-4c$, and consequently, $c = 3$. Thus, $^-12 \div (^-4) = 3$.

Example 4-17 suggests that, if it exists, the quotient of two negative integers is a positive integer and, if it exists, the quotient of a positive and a negative integer or a negative and a positive integer is negative.

BRAIN TEASER

Express each of the numbers from 1 through 10 using four 4s and any operations. For example,

$1 = 44 \div 44$ or
$1 = (4 \div 4)^{44}$ or
$1 = ^-4 + 4 + (4 \div 4)$.

PROBLEM SET 4-2

1. Evaluate each of the following.
   (a) $^-3(^-4)$
   (b) $3(^-5)$
   (c) $(^-5) \cdot 3$
   (d) $^-5 \cdot 0$
   (e) $^-2(^-3 \cdot 5)$
   (f) $[^-2(^-5)](^-3)$
   (g) $(^-4 + 4)(^-3)$
   (h) $(^-5 - ^-3)(^-5 - 3)$
   (i) $^-3(^-3 + ^-7)$

2. Use the definition of division to find each quotient (if possible). If a quotient is not defined, explain why.
   (a) $^-40 \div ^-8$
   (b) $143 \div (^-11)$
   (c) $^-143 \div 13$
   (d) $0 \div (^-5)$
   (e) $^-5 \div 0$
   (f) $0 \div 0$

3. Evaluate each of the following (if possible).
   (a) $(^-10 \div ^-2)(^-2)$
   (b) $(^-40 \div 8)8$
   (c) $(a \div b)b$
   (d) $(^-10 \cdot 5) \div 5$
   (e) $(ab) \div b$
   (f) $(^-8 \div ^-2)(^-8)$
   (g) $(^-6 + ^-14) \div 4$
   (h) $(^-8 + 8) \div 8$
   (i) $^-8 \div (^-8 + 8)$
   (j) $(^-23 - ^-7) \div 4$
   (k) $(^-6 + 6) \div (^-2 + 2)$
   (l) $^-13 \div (^-1)$
   (m) $(^-36 \div 12) \div 3$
   (n) $^-36 \div (12 \div 3)$
   (o) $|^-24| \div (3 - 15)$

4. Compute each of the following if

   $$a^n = \underbrace{a \cdot a \cdot a \cdot \ldots \cdot a,}_{n \text{ factors}} \quad a \in I$$

   (a) $(^-2)^3$
   (b) $(^-2)^4$
   (c) $(^-10)^5 \div (^-10)^2$
   (d) $(^-3)^5 \div (^-3)$
   (e) $(^-1)^{10}$
   (f) $(^-1)^{15}$
   (g) $(^-1)^{50}$
   (h) $(^-1)^{151}$

5. Consider the distributive property of multiplication over addition, $a(b + c) = ab + ac$. Show that this property is true for each of the following values of a, b, and c.
   (a) $a = {}^{-}1$, $b = {}^{-}5$, $c = {}^{-}2$
   (b) $a = {}^{-}3$, $b = {}^{-}3$, $c = 2$
   (c) $a = {}^{-}5$, $b = 2$, $c = {}^{-}6$

6. Prove that the equation $a \div (b + c) = (a \div b) + (a \div c)$ is not true for each of the following values of a, b, and c.
   (a) $a = 12$, $b = {}^{-}2$, $c = 4$
   (b) $a = {}^{-}20$, $b = 4$, $c = {}^{-}5$
   (c) $a = {}^{-}10$, $b = 1$, $c = 1$

7. Consider the statement $(a + b) \div c = (a \div c) + (b \div c)$. Is this statement true for each of the following values of a, b, and c?
   (a) $a = {}^{-}9$, $b = 21$, $c = 3$
   (b) $a = {}^{-}9$, $b = {}^{-}21$, $c = {}^{-}3$
   (c) $a = 9$, $b = {}^{-}21$, $c = {}^{-}3$
   (d) $a = {}^{-}50$, $b = 25$, $c = {}^{-}25$

8. (a) On each of four consecutive plays in a football game, Foo University lost 11 yards. If lost yardage is interpreted as a negative integer, write the information as a product of integers and determine the total number of yards lost.
   (b) If Jack Jones lost a total of 66 yards in 11 plays, how many yards, on the average, did he lose on each play?

9. The temperature has been rising $6°$ each hour. If the temperature is $9°C$ now, what was it 4 hours ago?

10. In 1979, it was predicted that the farmland acreage lost to family dwellings over the next 5 years would be 12,000 acres per year. If this prediction were true, how much acreage would have been lost to homes by 1984?

11. Find a pattern for each of the following and write the next three terms.
    (a) $7, 3, {}^{-}1, {}^{-}5, {}^{-}9,$ _____, _____, _____
    (b) ${}^{-}2, {}^{-}4, {}^{-}6, {}^{-}8, {}^{-}10,$ _____, _____, _____
    (c) $2187, {}^{-}729, 243, {}^{-}81, 27,$ _____, _____, _____
    (d) ${}^{-}20, {}^{-}17, {}^{-}14, {}^{-}11, {}^{-}8$ _____, _____, _____

12. For each of the following, find all integers x (if possible) that make the given equation true.
    (a) ${}^{-}3x = 6$ (b) ${}^{-}3x = {}^{-}6$
    (c) ${}^{-}2x = 0$ (d) $5x = {}^{-}30$
    (e) $x \div 3 = {}^{-}12$ (f) $x \div ({}^{-}3) = {}^{-}2$
    (g) $x \div ({}^{-}x) = {}^{-}1$ (h) $0 \div x = 0$
    (i) $x \div 0 = 1$ (j) $x^2 = 9$
    (k) $x^2 = {}^{-}9$ (l) ${}^{-}x \div {}^{-}x = 1$

13. Use patterns to show that $({}^{-}1)({}^{-}1) = 1$.

14. Compute each of the following.
    (a) ${}^{-}2 + 3 \cdot 5 - 1$
    (b) $10 - 3 \cdot 7 - 4({}^{-}2) + 3$
    (c) $10 - 3 - 12$ (d) $10 - (3 - 12)$
    (e) $({}^{-}3)^2$ (f) ${}^{-}3^2$
    (g) ${}^{-}5^2 + 3({}^{-}2)^2$ (h) ${}^{-}2^3$
    (i) $({}^{-}2)^3$ (j) ${}^{-}2^4$
    (k) $({}^{-}2)^4$

15. If x is an integer and $x \neq 0$, which of the following are always positive and which are always negative?
    (a) ${}^{-}x^2$ (b) x^2 (c) $({}^{-}x)^2$ (d) ${}^{-}x^3$
    (e) $({}^{-}x)^3$ (f) ${}^{-}x^4$ (g) $({}^{-}x)^4$ (h) x^4
    (i) x (j) ${}^{-}x$

16. Which of the expressions in Problem 15 are equal to each other for all values of x except 0?

17. Simplify each of the following expressions.
    (a) $({}^{-}x)({}^{-}y)$ (b) ${}^{-}2x({}^{-}y)$
    (c) ${}^{-}(x + y) + x + y$ (d) ${}^{-}1 \cdot x$
    (e) $x - 2({}^{-}y)$ (f) $a - (a - b)$
    (g) $y - (y - x)$ (h) ${}^{-}(x - y) + x$

18. Multiply each of the following.
    (a) ${}^{-}2(x - 1)$ (b) ${}^{-}2(x - y)$
    (c) $x(x - y)$ (d) ${}^{-}x(x - y)$
    (e) ${}^{-}2(x + y - z)$ (f) ${}^{-}x(x - y - 3)$
    (g) $({}^{-}5 - x)(5 + x)$
    (h) $(x - y - 1)(x + y + 1)$
    (i) $({}^{-}x^2 + 2)(x^2 - 1)$

19. Use the difference of squares formula to simplify each of the following, if possible.
    (a) $52 \cdot 48$ (b) $(5 - 100)(5 + 100)$
    (c) $({}^{-}x - y)({}^{-}x + y)$ (d) $(2 + 3x)(2 - 3x)$
    (e) $(x - 1)(1 + x)$ (f) $213^2 - 13^2$

20. Can $({}^{-}x - y)(x + y)$ be multiplied by using the difference of squares formula? Explain why or why not.

21. Factor each of the following expressions completely and then simplify, if possible.
    (a) $3x + 5x$ (b) $ax + 2x$
    (c) $xy + x$ (d) $ax - 2x$
    (e) $x^2 + xy$ (f) $3x - 4x + 7x$
    (g) $3xy + 2x - xz$ (h) $3x^2 + xy - x$
    (i) $abc + ab - a$
    (j) $(a + b)(c + 1) - (a + b)$
    (k) $16 - a^2$ (l) $x^2 - 9y^2$
    (m) $4x^2 - 25y^2$ (n) $(x^2 - y^2) + x + y$

★22. Prove the following for any integers a and b.
   (a) $(^-a)b = {}^-(ab)$
   (b) $(^-a)(^-b) = ab$
   (c) $^-(a + b) = {}^-a + {}^-b$

23. Use the $\boxed{+/-}$ key on the calculator to compute each of the following.
   (a) $^-27 \times 3$ (b) $^-46 \times {}^-4$
   (c) $^-26 \div 13$ (d) $^-26 \div {}^-13$

* * * * * * * REVIEW PROBLEMS * * * * * * *

24. Compute each of the following.
   (a) $3 - 6$ (b) $8 + {}^-7$
   (c) $5 - {}^-8$ (d) $^-5 - {}^-8$
   (e) $^-8 + 5$ (f) $^-8 + {}^-5$
25. Illustrate $^-8 + {}^-5$ on a number line.

26. Find the opposite of each of the following.
   (a) $^-5$ (b) 7   (c) 0
27. Compute each of the following.
   (a) $|^-14|$ (b) $|^-14| + 7$
   (c) $8 - |^-12|$ (d) $|11| + |^-11|$

BRAIN TEASER

Find the product

$$(x - a)(x - b)(x - c) \cdots (x - z)$$

if $a, \ldots, z$ are integers

4-3   SOLVING EQUATIONS AND INEQUALITIES

The following properties of equality hold for integers.

Property | For any integers a, b, and c:
Reflexive Property $a = a$.
Symmetric Property   If $a = b$, then $b = a$.
Transitive Property   If $a = b$ and $b = c$, then $a = c$.

Property | **The Addition Property of Equality**   For any integers a, b, and c, if $a = b$, then $a + c = b + c$.

According to the addition property of equality, it is possible to add the same integer to both sides of an equation without affecting the equality.

Property | **The Multiplication Property of Equality**   For any integers a, b, and c, if $a = b$, then $ac = bc$.

According to the multiplication property of equality, it is possible to multiply both sides of an equation by the same integer without affecting the equality. Multiplication of both sides by zero is rarely used.

substitution property

In mathematical expressions, it is valid to substitute a number for its equal. This property is referred to as the **substitution property.** Examples of substitution follow:

1. If $a + b = c + d$ and $d = 5$, then $a + b = c + 5$.
2. If $a + b = c + d$, if $b = e$, and if $d = f$, then $a + e = c + f$.
3. If $x = 2$, then $3x = 3 \cdot 2 = 6$.
4. Since $^-2(^-3) = 6$, it is possible to write $6 = 10 + ^-4$ as $^-2(^-3) = 10 + ^-4$.

converse

The addition property of equality was formulated as follows. For any integers a, b, and c, if $a = b$, then $a + c = b + c$. A new statement results from reversing the order of the *if* and *then* parts of this addition property. This new statement is called the **converse** of the original statement. In the case of the addition property, the converse is a true statement. The converse of the multiplication property of equality is also true when $c \neq 0$. These properties, called the *cancellation properties of equality,* are given below.

Property

The Cancellation Properties of Equality for Addition and Multiplication:

1. For any integers a, b, and c, if $a + c = b + c$ then $a = b$.
2. For any integers a, b, and c, with $c \neq 0$, if $ac = bc$, then $a = b$.

Before we consider solving equations and inequalities, we have to develop additional properties of inequalities for integers. As with other whole numbers, "greater than" and "less than" relations can be defined for integers.

DEFINITION

For any integers a and b, a is **greater than** b, written $a > b$, if and only if there exists a positive integer k such that $a = b + k$. Also, b is less than a, written $b < a$, if and only if $a > b$.

By the definition of greater than, $a > b$ if and only if there exists a positive integer k such that $a = b + k$. By the definition of subtraction, $a = b + k$ if and only if $a - b = k$. Thus, because k is positive, $a - b > 0$. We summarize this discussion as follows:

For any two integers a and b, $a > b$ if and only if $a - b > 0$, that is, $a - b$ is positive.

The table compares the properties of the inequality relations with the properties of the equality relation. Assume that a, b, and c represent integers.

TABLE 4-1

Property	Equality	Inequality
Reflexive	$a = a$	—
Symmetric	$a = b$ implies $b = a$	—
Transitive	$a = b$ and $b = c$ implies $a = c$	$a > b$ and $b > c$ implies $a > c$
		$a < b$ and $b < c$ implies $a < c$
Addition	$a = b$ implies $a + c = b + c$	$a > b$ implies $a + c > b + c$
		$a < b$ implies $a + c < b + c$
Multiplication	$a = b$ implies $ac = bc$	$a > b$ and $c > 0$ implies $ac > bc$
		$a > b$ and $c < 0$ implies $ac < bc$
		$a < b$ and $c > 0$ implies $ac < bc$
		$a < b$ and $c < 0$ implies $ac > bc$

Remark | It is possible to combine properties of equality and inequality using the $\geq$ or $\leq$ symbols.

The reflexive property does not hold for inequality. For example, $5 > 5$ is false. Also, the symmetric property does not hold for inequality. For example, while $6 > 2$ is true, $2 > 6$ is false. One way to demonstrate the transitive property for inequality is with temperature. If the temperature in Aberdeen is higher than the temperature in Barstow, and if the temperature in Barstow is higher than the temperature in Cranston, then the temperature in Aberdeen is higher than the temperature in Cranston. In other words, $a > b$ and $b > c$ implies $a > c$.

Examples of the addition property of greater than follow.

$$5 > 2 \quad \text{implies} \quad 5 + 10 > 2 + 10$$
$$^-2 > {}^-5 \quad \text{implies} \quad {}^-2 + 2 > {}^-5 + 2$$
$$x > 3 \quad \text{implies} \quad x + 2 > 3 + 2$$
$$x - 3 > 5 \quad \text{implies} \quad x - 3 + 3 > 5 + 3$$

When both sides of an inequality are multiplied by a positive integer, the direction of inequality is preserved, but if both sides of an inequality are multiplied by a negative integer, the direction of inequality is reversed. Consider the following examples.

$$5 > 3 \quad \text{implies} \quad 5 \cdot 2 > 3 \cdot 2, \text{ but } 5 \cdot (^-2) < 3 \cdot (^-2)$$
$$^-3 > {}^-5 \quad \text{implies} \quad (^-3)2 > (^-5)2, \text{ but } (^-3)(^-2) < (^-5)(^-2)$$
$$x > 3 \quad \text{implies} \quad 2x > 2 \cdot 3, \text{ but } {}^-2x < {}^-2 \cdot 3$$

Properties for subtraction and division of inequalities follow from the addition and multiplication properties of inequality.

Property	If a, b, and c are any integers, then:

1. $a > b$ implies $a - c > b - c$;
2. $a > b$ and $c > 0$ implies $a \div c > b \div c$, provided the divisions are defined;
3. $a > b$ and $c < 0$ implies $a \div c < b \div c$, provided that the divisions are defined.

Example 4-18

Justify each of the following.

(a) $^-2 > {}^-5$ implies $^-7 > {}^-10$
(b) $10 > 6$ implies $5 > 3$
(c) $10 > 6$ implies $^-5 < {}^-3$

Solution

(a) By the subtraction property of inequality, $^-2 > {}^-5$ implies $^-2 - 5 > {}^-5 - 5$; that is, $^-7 > {}^-10$.
(b) By the division property of inequality, $10 > 6$ implies $10 \div 2 > 6 \div 2$; that is, $5 > 3$.
(c) By the division property of inequality, $10 > 6$ implies $10 \div {}^-2 < 6 \div {}^-2$; that is, $^-5 < {}^-3$.

algebra

The study of **algebra** concerns itself with operations on numbers and other elements often represented by symbols. Finding solutions to equations and inequalities is one part of algebra.

solution set

Solving an equation or inequality over a particular domain means finding the set of all possible values of the variable for which the equation or inequality is true. This set is called the **solution set.** For example, suppose a is an integer such that $4a > 12$. Divide both sides of the inequality by 4. Then, $(4a) \div 4 > 12 \div 4$, or $a > 3$. Because a is an integer, the solution set to $4a > 12$ is $\{4, 5, 6, 7, \ldots\}$.

Example 4-19

Solve each of the following for x, where x is an integer.

(a) $x + 4 = {}^-6$ (b) $x + 4 > {}^-6$

Solution

(a)
$$x + 4 = {}^-6$$
$$(x + 4) + {}^-4 = {}^-6 + {}^-4$$
$$x = {}^-10$$

(b)
$$x + 4 > {}^-6$$
$$(x + 4) + {}^-4 > {}^-6 + {}^-4$$
$$x > {}^-10, \quad x \in I$$

Example 4-20 | Solve each of the following for x, where x is an integer.

(a) $^-x - 5 = 8$ (b) $^-x - 5 \geq 8$
(c) $^-2x + 3 = ^-11$ (d) $^-2x + 3 > ^-11$

Solution

(a)
$$^-x - 5 = 8$$
$$(^-x - 5) + 5 = 8 + 5$$
$$^-x = 13$$
$$(^-x)(^-1) = 13(^-1)$$
$$x = ^-13$$

(b)
$$^-x - 5 \geq 8$$
$$(^-x - 5) + 5 \geq 8 + 5$$
$$^-x \geq 13$$
$$(^-x)(^-1) \leq 13(^-1)$$
$$x \leq ^-13, \quad x \in I$$

(c)
$$^-2x + 3 = ^-11$$
$$(^-2x + 3) + ^-3 = ^-11 + ^-3$$
$$^-2x = ^-14$$
$$(^-2x) \div ^-2 = ^-14 \div ^-2$$
$$x = 7$$

(d)
$$^-2x + 3 > ^-11$$
$$(^-2x + 3) + ^-3 > ^-11 + ^-3$$
$$^-2x > ^-14$$
$$(^-2x) \div ^-2 < (^-14) \div ^-2$$
$$x < 7, \quad x \in I$$

Algebra can be used to solve many kinds of word problems. To understand word problems, we first identify what is given and what is to be found. Devising a Plan may involve assigning letters to the unknown quantities and translating the information in the problem into a model involving equations or inequalities. In Carrying Out the Plan, we solve the equations or inequalities. In Looking Back, we check the solution to be sure the original problem is answered. We demonstrate this process in the following problems.

PROBLEM 1

David is thinking of a number. If he multiplies that number by $^-3$ and then adds 6, he has $^-4$ times his original number. What is David's original number?

Understanding the Problem

The problem asks us to find David's number. We are given that the number times $^-3$, plus 6, equals $^-4$ times the number.

Devising a Plan

Let n represent David's number. Now, we translate the information from the problem into mathematical symbols and solve the resulting equation.

Information	*Mathematical Translation*
David is thinking of a number.	n
He multiplies that number by $^-3$.	^-3n
He adds 6.	$^-3n + 6$
He has ($^-4$) times his original number.	$^-3n + 6 = (^-4)n$

Carrying Out the Plan

Solve the equation

$$^-3n + 6 = {}^-4n$$
$$4n + {}^-3n + 6 = 4n + {}^-4n$$
$$n + 6 = 0$$
$$n = {}^-6$$

Thus, the number David is thinking about is $^-6$.

Looking Back

To check that $^-6$ is the correct solution, follow the written information using $^-6$ as David's number. The number, $^-6$, times $^-3$ is 18. Next, 18 plus 6 is 24. Also, $^-4$ times the number, $^-6$, is 24. So the answer is correct.

PROBLEM 2

Beans that cost 75¢ per pound are mixed with beans that cost 95¢ per pound to produce a 20-pound mixture that costs 80¢ per pound. How many pounds of the beans costing 75¢ per pound are used?

Understanding the Problem

The problem asks how many pounds of beans costing 75¢ per pound are necessary to make 20 pounds of a mixture costing 80¢ per pound. To make the 20 pound mixture, beans costing 95¢ per pound are mixed with the beans costing 75¢ per pound. Thus, the number of pounds of the beans costing 95¢ per pound is 20 minus the number of pounds of the beans costing 75¢ per pound. Also, the total cost of the beans costing 75¢ per pound and the beans costing 95¢ per pound must be the cost of 20 pounds of beans costing 80¢ per pound.

Devising a Plan

Let x stand for the number of pounds of the beans costing 75¢ per pound. Using this symbolism, we know that the number of pounds of the beans costing 95¢ per pound is $20 - x$ pounds. Since the rest of the given information involves cost, we need the cost of each type of beans. The cost of x pounds of beans costing 75¢ per pound is $75x$ (in cents). Similarly, the cost of the $20 - x$ pounds of beans costing 95¢ per pound is $95(20 - x)$ (in cents). The total mixture, 20 pounds, costs 80¢ per pound or $80 \cdot 20$ cents. We use this information to write the following equation.

$$75x + 95(20 - x) = 80 \cdot 20$$

We must solve the equation for x. This will give the number of pounds of the beans costing 75¢ per pound.

Carrying Out the Plan

$$
\begin{aligned}
75x + 95(20 - x) &= 80 \cdot 20 \\
75x + 1900 - 95x &= 1600 \\
{}^-20x + 1900 &= 1600 \\
{}^-20x &= {}^-300 \\
x &= 15
\end{aligned}
$$

Thus, 15 pounds of the beans costing 75¢ per pound are required. Because there are 20 pounds of the final mixture, of which 15 pounds are of the beans costing 75¢ per pound, $20 - 15$, or 5, pounds of the beans costing 95¢ per pound are used.

Looking Back

The solution should be checked in the original problem. The cost of 15 pounds of the beans costing 75¢ per pound is $15 \cdot 75$¢, or $11.25. The cost of 5 pounds of the beans costing 95¢ per pound is $5 \cdot 95$¢, or $4.75. The cost of 20 pounds of the final mixture at 80¢ per pound is $20 \cdot 80$¢, or $16.00. The conditions of the problem are satisfied because $11.25 + $4.75 = $16.00.

A different method of solving the problem involves using two unknowns. We let x stand for the number of pounds of 75¢ beans and y stand for the number of pounds of 95¢ beans. Next, we translate the information from the problem into mathematical statements. There are 20 pounds in the blend, so we have $x + y = 20$. The remaining information tells us about the cost per pound of each type of beans. To produce an equation using this information, notice that the value of the beans costing 75¢ per pound plus the value of the beans costing 95¢ per pound equals the value of the 20-pound mixture of beans.

Cost of 75¢ per pound beans plus cost of 95¢ per pound beans = cost of mixture

$$75x \qquad + \qquad 95y \qquad = \qquad 80 \cdot 20$$

The two equations obtained are as follows.

$$x + \quad y = 20$$
$$75x + 95y = 80 \cdot 20$$

We know how to solve equations with one unknown, so we try to combine these two equations into one equation with one unknown. This can be achieved by solving one of the equations for y and then substituting the expression for y in the other equation. Because $x + y = 20$ implies $y = 20 - x$, we substitute $20 - x$ for y in the second equation and solve for x. We then use the value of x obtained to find the value of y.

PROBLEM 3

In a certain factory, machine A produces three times as many bolts as machine B. Machine C produces 13 more bolts than machine A. If the total production is 4997 bolts per day, how many bolts does each machine produce in a day?

Understanding the Problem

The problem asks for the number of bolts that each of machine A, machine B, and machine C produce in 1 day. The problem gives information that compares the production of A to B and of C to A.

Devising a Plan

Let a, b, and c be the number of bolts produced by machines A, B, and C, respectively. We translate the given problem into equations as follows.

Machine A produces 3 times as many bolts as B: $a = 3b$

Machine C produces 13 more bolts than A: $c = a + 13$

Total production is 4997: $a + b + c = 4997$

In order to reduce the number of variables, we substitute $3b$ for a in the second and third equations.

$$c = a + 13 \quad \text{becomes} \qquad\qquad c = 3b + 13$$
$$a + b + c = 4997 \quad \text{becomes} \quad 3b + b + c = 4997$$

Next, we make an equation in one variable, b, by substituting $3b + 13$ for c in the equation $3b + b + c = 4997$, solve for b, and then find a and c.

Carrying Out the Plan

$$3b + b + 3b + 13 = 4997$$
$$7b + 13 = 4997$$
$$7b = 4984$$
$$b = 712$$

Thus, $a = 3b = 3 \cdot 712 = 2136$. Also, $c = a + 13 = 2136 + 13 = 2149$. Machine A produces 2136 bolts, machine B produces 712 bolts, and machine C produces 2149 bolts.

Looking Back

To check the answers, we follow the original information, using $a = 2136$, $b = 712$, and $c = 2149$. The information in the first sentence, "Machine A produces 3 times as many bolts as machine B," checks, since $2136 = 3 \cdot 712$. The second sentence, "Machine C produces 13 more bolts than machine A," is true because $2149 = 13 + 2136$. The information in the last sentence, "The total production was 4997 bolts," checks, since $2136 + 712 + 2149 = 4997$.

An alternate solution to Problem 3 is as follows. Let x be the number of bolts produced by machine B. Then, we express the number of bolts that machines A and C produce in terms of x.

Information	*Mathematical Translation*
The number of items that machine B produces.	x
Machine A produces three times as many items as machine B.	$3x$
Machine C produces 13 more items than machine A.	$3x + 13$
The total production is 4997.	$x + 3x + (3x + 13) = 4997$

Solve the equation.

$$x + 3x + (3x + 13) = 4997$$
$$7x + 13 = 4997$$
$$7x = 4984$$
$$x = 712$$

Hence, machine B produces 712 bolts. Because $3x = 3 \cdot 712 = 2136$, machine A produces 2136 bolts; $3x + 13 = 2136 + 13 = 2149$, so machine C produces 2149 bolts.

If we had let x be the number of bolts that machine A produces, the problem would have been more complicated to solve because machine B then produces $x \div 3$ bolts.

BRAIN TEASER

The following is an argument showing that an ant weighs as much as an elephant. What is wrong?

Let e be the weight of the elephant and a the weight of the ant. Let $e - a = d$. Consequently, $e = a + d$. Multiply each side of $e = a + d$ by $e - a$. Then simplify.

$$e(e - a) = (a + d)(e - a)$$
$$e^2 - ea = ae + de - a^2 - da$$
$$e^2 - ea - de = ae - a^2 - da$$
$$e(e - a - d) = a(e - a - d)$$
$$e = a$$

Thus, the weight of the elephant equals the weight of the ant.

PROBLEM SET 4-3

1. Write each of the following lists of numbers in increasing order.
   (a) $^-13, ^-20, ^-5, 0, 4, ^-3$
   (b) $^-5, ^-6, 5, 6, 0$
   (c) $^-20, ^-15, ^-100, 0, ^-13$
   (d) $13, ^-2, ^-3, 5$
2. Show that each of the following is true.
   (a) $^-3 > ^-5$ (b) $^-6 < 0$
   (c) $^-8 > ^-10$ (d) $^-5 < 4$
3. Solve each of the following if x is an integer.
   (a) $x + 3 = ^-15$ (b) $x + 3 > ^-15$
   (c) $3 - x = ^-15$ (d) $^-x + 3 > ^-15$
   (e) $^-x - 3 = 15$ (f) $^-x - 3 \geq 15$
   (g) $3x + 5 = ^-16$ (h) $3x + 5 < ^-16$
   (i) $^-3x + 5 = 11$ (j) $^-3x + 5 \leq 11$
   (k) $5x - 3 = 7x - 1$ (l) $5x - 3 > 7x - 1$
   (m) $3(x + 5) = ^-4(x + 5) + 21$
   (n) $^-5(x + 3) > 0$
4. Give a counterexample to show that the symmetric property does not hold for the less than relation on the set of integers.
5. Which of the following are true for all possible integer values of x?
   (a) $3(x + 1) = 3x + 3$ (b) $x - 3 = 3 - x$
   (c) $x + 3 = 3 + x$
   (d) $2(x - 1) + 2 = 3x - x$
   (e) $x^2 + 1 > 0$ (f) $3x > 4x - x$
6. For each of the following, which elements of the given set, if any, satisfy the equation or inequality?
   (a) $x^3 + x^2 = 2x$, $\{1, ^-1, ^-2, 0\}$
   (b) $3x - 3 = 24$, $\{^-9, 9\}$
   (c) $^-x \geq 5$, $\{6, ^-6, 7, ^-7, 2\}$
   (d) $x^2 < 16$, $\{^-4, ^-3, ^-2, ^-1, 0, 1, 2, 3, 4\}$

7. Solve each of the following equations. Check your answers by substituting in the given equation. Assume x, y, and z represent integers.
   (a) $^-2x + ^-11 = 3x + 4$ (b) $5(^-x + 1) = 5$
   (c) $^-3y + 4 = y$ (d) $^-3(z - 1) = 8z + 3$
8. If you multiply Tom's age by 3 and add 4, the result is more than 37. What can you tell about Tom's age?
9. If you multiply a number by $^-6$ and then add 20 to the product, the result is 50. What is the number?
10. David has three times as much money as Rick. Together, they have $400. How much does each have?
11. Ran is 4 years older than Nureet. Six years ago Ran was twice as old as Nureet was then. How old are they now?
12. Factory A produces twice as many cars per day as factory B. Factory C produces 300 cars more per day than factory A. If the total production in the three factories is 7300 cars per day, how many cars per day are produced in each factory?
13. Tea that costs 60¢ per pound is mixed with tea that costs 45¢ per pound to produce a 100-pound blend that costs 51¢ per pound. How much of each kind of tea is used?
14. For a certain event, 812 tickets were sold, totaling $1912. If students paid $2 per ticket and nonstudents paid $3 per ticket, how many student tickets were sold?
15. The sum of three consecutive integers is 237. Find the three integers.
16. The sum of three consecutive even integers is 240. Find the three integers.
17. The sum of two numbers is 21. The first number is twice the second number. Find the numbers.

18. A man left an estate of $64,000 to three children. The eldest child received three times as much as the youngest. The middle child received $14,000 more than the youngest. How much did each child receive?

★ 19. (a) Is it always true that for any integers x and y, $x^2 + y^2 \geq 2xy$? Prove your answer.
(b) For which integers x and y is $x^2 + y^2 = 2xy$?

★ 20. If $0 < a < b$ where a and b are integers, prove that $a^2 < b^2$.

★ 21. If $a < b$ where a and b are integers, is it always true that $a^2 < b^2$?

★ 22. If $a < b$ where a and b are integers, prove that $c - b < c - a$, if c is an integer.

★ 23. For each of the following, find all integers x such that the statement is true.
(a) $x + 1 < 3$ and $^-x + 1 < 5$
(b) $2x < ^-6$ or $1 + x < 0$

* * * * * * * REVIEW PROBLEMS * * * * * * *

24. Find the additive inverse of each of the following.
(a) $^-7$
(b) 5
(c) $^-(^-3)$
(d) $3 - (^-7)$

25. Compute each of the following.
(a) $^-3 + ^-7$
(b) $^-3 - ^-7$
(c) $3 + ^-7$
(d) $3 - ^-7$
(e) $^-3 \cdot 7$
(f) $^-3 \cdot ^-7$
(g) $3 - 7$
(h) $^-21 \div 7$
(i) $^-21 \div ^-7$
(j) $7 - 3 - 8$
(k) $8 + 2 \cdot 3 - 7$
(l) $^-8 - 7 - 2 \cdot 3$
(m) $|^-7| \cdot |^-3|$
(n) $|^-7| \cdot |^-8|$
(o) $|^-7| + 8$
(p) $|^-7| - |^-8|$

26. Compute $^-7 + (^-3)$ using a number line.

SOLUTION TO THE PRELIMINARY PROBLEM

Understanding the Problem

Mary found a five-digit number called *abcde*, so that three times the display 1*abcde* gives the display *abcde*1 on the calculator. It will help us to understand the problem if we guess any five-digit number and see if our guess is correct. Suppose we guess 34,578. With 1 after it, it becomes 345,781. With 1 before it, it becomes 134,578. Since $3 \cdot 134,578 \neq 345,781$, our guess is incorrect.

Devising a Plan

We know that three times 1*abcde* is *abcde*1. This can be translated to an equation by letting the unknown number on the display *abcde* be n and using place value. Note that 1*abcde* means $1 \cdot 10^5 + n$, or $100,000 + n$ and *abcde*1 means $n \cdot 10 + 1$, or $10n + 1$. Thus, Mary's computation tells us that

$$3(100,000 + n) = 10n + 1$$

Now all that is necessary to solve the problem is to solve this equation for n.

Carrying Out the Plan

We use properties of equality to solve the equation for n.

$$3(100,000 + n) = 10n + 1$$
$$300,000 + 3n = 10n + 1$$
$$299,999 = 7n$$
$$42,857 = n$$

Consequently, the five-digit number is 42,857.

Looking Back

To check the answer, we compute $3 \cdot 142,857 = 428,571$ and see that the solution is correct. Similar problems can be investigated by asking analogous questions for six-, seven-, or eight-digit numbers. Another generalization is to find a five-digit number, n, such that $k(100,000 + n) = 10n + 1$, where k is different from 3.

An alternate solution to this problem can be found by considering the multiplication one digit at a time. For example, in Figure 4-8(a), we see that $3 \cdot e$ has a 1 in the units digit of the product. Because e is a single digit and 7 is the only single digit that can be multiplied by 3 to yield a product with units digit 1, than e must be 7.

FIGURE 4-8

$$
\begin{array}{r}
1abcde \\
\times\ 3 \\
\hline
abcde1
\end{array}
\qquad
\begin{array}{r}
\overset{2}{} \\
1abcd7 \\
\times\ 3 \\
\hline
abcd71
\end{array}
$$

(a)   (b)

If we substitute 7 for e, as shown in Figure 4-8(b), we see that $3 \cdot d + 2$ has 7 as a units digit, or—equivalently—that $3 \cdot d$ has 5 as units digit. Because d is a single digit and 5 is the only single digit that can be multiplied by 5 to yield a product with a units digit 5, then $d = 5$. Similarly, each of the digits a, b, and c can also be found.

QUESTIONS FROM THE CLASSROOM

1. A student argues that $(^-1)(^-1) = 1$, since $^-(^-1) = 1$. What is your response?

2. A fourth-grade student devised the following subtraction algorithm for subtracting $84 - 27$.
   Four minus seven equals negative three.

$$
\begin{array}{r}
84 \\
-\ 27 \\
\hline
^-3
\end{array}
$$

Eighty minus twenty equals sixty.

$$
\begin{array}{r}
84 \\
-\ 27 \\
\hline
^-3 \\
60
\end{array}
$$

Sixty plus negative three equals fifty-seven.

$$
\begin{array}{r}
84 \\
-\ 27 \\
\hline
^-3 \\
60 \\
\hline
57
\end{array}
$$

Thus, the answer is 57. What is your response as a teacher?

3. A seventh-grade student does not believe that $^-5 < ^-2$. The student argues that a debt of $5 is greater than a debt of $2. How do you respond?

4. An eighth-grade student claims she can prove that subtraction of integers is commutative. She points out that if a and b are integers, then $a - b = a + ^-b$. Since addition is commutative, so is subtraction. What is your response?

5. A student claims that if $x \neq 0$, then $|x| = ^-x$ is never true since absolute value is always positive. What is your response?

6. A student claims that since $(a \cdot b)^2 = a^2 \cdot b^2$, it must also be true that $(a + b)^2 = a^2 + b^2$. How do you respond?

7. A student solves $1 - 2x > x - 5$, where x is an integer, and reports the solution as $x < 2$. The student asks if it is possible to check the answer in a way similar to the method of substitution for equations. What is your response?

8. A student computes $^-8 - 2(^-3)$ by writing $^-10(^-3) = 30$. How would you help this student?

9. A student says that his father showed him a very simple method for dealing with expressions like $^-(a - b + 1)$ and $x - (2x - 3)$. The rule is: If there is a negative sign before the parentheses, change the signs of the expressions inside the parentheses. Thus, $^-(a - b + 1) = ^-a + b - 1$ and $x - (2x - 3) = x - 2x + 3$. What is your response?

10. A student solving word problems always checks her solutions by substituting in equations rather than following the written information. Is this an accurate check for the word problem?

11. A student shows you the following proof that $(^-1)(^-1) = 1$: There are two possibilities, either $(^-1)(^-1) = 1$ or $(^-1)(^-1) = ^-1$. Suppose $(^-1)(^-1) = ^-1$. Since $^-1 = (^-1) \cdot 1$, then $(^-1)(^-1) = ^-1$ can be written as $(^-1)(^-1) = (^-1) \cdot 1$. By the cancellation property of multiplication, it follows that $^-1 = 1$, which is impossible. Hence, $(^-1)(^-1)$ cannot equal $^-1$ and must, therefore, equal 1. What is your reaction?

CHAPTER OUTLINE

I. Basic concepts of integers
  A. The set of **integers**, I, is $\{. . . , ^-3, ^-2, ^-1, 0, 1, 2, 3, . . .\}$.
  B. The distance from any integer to 0 is called the **absolute value** of the integer. The absolute value of an integer x is denoted $|x|$.
  C. Operations with integers
    1. **Addition:**
      (a) To add integers with unlike signs, subtract the lesser of the two absolute values of the integers from the greater. The sum has the same sign as the integer with the greater absolute value.
      (b) To add integers with like signs, add the absolute values of the integers. The sum has the same sign as the integers.
      (c) $^-a + ^-b = ^-(a + b)$
    2. **Subtraction:**
      (a) If a and b are any integers, then $a - b = n$ if and only if $b + n = a$.
      (b) For all integers a and b, $a - b = a + ^-b$.
    3. **Multiplication:** For any integers n and m, $n(^-m) = (^-m)n = ^-(nm)$ and $(^-m)(^-n) = mn$.
    4. **Division:** If a and b are any integers with $b \neq 0$, then $a \div b$ is the unique integer c such that $a = bc$.
    5. **Order of operations:** When addition, subtraction, multiplication and division appear without parentheses, multiplication and divisions are done first in the order of their appearance from left to right and then additions and subtractions in the order of their appearance from left to right. Any arithmetic in parentheses is done first.

II. The system of integers
  A. The set of integers $I = \{. . . , ^-3, ^-2, ^-1, 0, 1, 2, 3, . . .\}$, along with the operations of addition and multiplication satisfy the following properties.

Property	+	×
Closure	Yes	Yes
Commutative	Yes	Yes
Associative	Yes	Yes
Identity	Yes, 0	Yes, 1
Inverse	Yes	No
Distributive Property of Multiplication over Addition		

B. **Addition property of equality:** For any integers a, b, c, if $a = b$, then $a + c = b + c$.

C. **Multiplication property of equality:** For any integers a, b, c, if $a = b$, then $ac = bc$.

D. **Substitution property:** Any number may be substituted for its equal.

E. **Cancellation properties for addition and multiplication:**
   (a) For any integers a, b, and c, if $a + c = b + c$, then $a = b$.
   (b) For any integers a, b, and c, if $c \neq 0$ and $ac = bc$, then $a = b$.

F. For all integers a, b, and c:
   1. $^-(^-a) = a$
   2. $a - (b - c) = a - b + c$
   3. $(a + b)(a - b) = a^2 - b^2$ (Difference-of-squares formula)

III. Inequalities
   A. $a > b$ if and only if there exists a positive integer k such that $a = b + k$. $b < a$ if and only if $a > b$.

B. Let a and b be any two integers. Then, $a > b$ if and only if $a - b > 0$.

C. Properties of inequalities.
   1. **Addition property:** If $a > b$ and c is any integer, then $a + c > b + c$.
   2. **Multiplication properties:**
      (a) If $a > b$ and $c > 0$, then $ac > bc$.
      (b) If $a > b$ and $c < 0$, then $ac < bc$.

IV. Solving word problems
   A. The solution to word problems involves each of the following.
      1. **Understanding the Problem:** Identify what is given and what is to be found.
      2. **Devising a Plan:** Assign letters to the unknown quantities and translate the data into equations or inequalities.
      3. **Carrying Out the Plan:** Solve the equations or inequalities.
      4. **Looking Back:** Check and interpret the solution in terms of the situation given in the problem.

CHAPTER TEST

1. Find the additive inverse of each of the following.
   (a) 3   (b) ^-a (c) 0
   (d) $x + y$ (e) $^-x + y$

2. Perform each of the following operations.
   (a) $(^-2 + {}^-8) + 3$ (b) $^-2 - (^-5) + 5$
   (c) $^-3(^-2) + 2$ (d) $^-3(^-5 + 5)$
   (e) $^-40 \div (^-5)$ (f) $(^-25 \div 5)(^-3)$

3. For each of the following, find all integer values of x (if there are any) that make the given equation true.
   (a) $^-x + 3 = 0$ (b) $^-2x = 10$
   (c) $0 \div (^-x) = 0$ (d) $^-x \div 0 = {}^-1$
   (e) $3x - 1 = {}^-124$ (f) $^-2x + 3x = x$

4. Use a pattern approach to show that $(^-2)(^-3) = 6$.

5. (a) Show that $(x - y)(x + y) = x^2 - y^2$.
   (b) Use the result in part (a) to compute $(^-2 - x)(^-2 + x)$.

6. Simplify each of the following expressions.
   (a) ^-1x (b) $(^-1)(x - y)$
   (c) $2x - (1 - x)$ (d) $(^-x)^2 + x^2$
   (e) $(^-x)^3 + x^3$ (f) $(^-3 - x)(3 + x)$

7. Factor each of the following expressions and then simplify, if possible.

   (a) $x - 3x$ (b) $x^2 + x$
   (c) $5 + 5x$
   (d) $(x - y)(x + 1) - (x - y)$

8. Solve each of the following for x, if x is an integer.
   (a) $^-3x + 7 = {}^-x + 11$ (b) $|x| = 5$
   (c) $^-2x + 1 < 0$
   (d) $^-2(^-3x + 7) < {}^-2(^-x + 11)$

9. A certain college has 5715 undergraduates. There are 115 more seniors than juniors. The number of sophomores is twice the number of seniors, and the number of freshmen is twice the number of juniors. How many freshmen, sophomores, juniors, and seniors attend the college?

10. Classify each of the following as true or false (all letters represent integers.)
   (a) $|x|$ always is positive.
   (b) For all x and y, $|x + y| = |x| + |y|$.
   (c) If $a < {}^-b$, then $a < 0$.
   (d) For all x and y, $(x - y)^2 = (y - x)^2$.
   (e) $(^-a)(^-b)$ is the additive inverse of ab.

11. If the temperature was $^-16°C$ and it rose by $9°C$, what is the new temperature?

12. Find a counterexample to disprove each of the properties on the set of integers.
    (a) Commutative property of division
    (b) Associative property of subtraction
    (c) Closure property for division
    (d) Distributive property of division over subtraction
13. Twice Molly's weight added to 50 pounds is equal to 78 pounds. Find Molly's weight.

14. A truck contains 150 small packages, some weighing 1 kg each and some weighing 2 kg each. How many packages of each weight are in the truck if the total weight of the packages is 265 kg?
15. John has a collection of nickels and dimes. He has three more dimes than twice the number of nickels. If he has $2.05, how many of each type of coin does he have?

SELECTED BIBLIOGRAPHY

Brumfiel, C. "An Introduction to Negative Integers." *The Mathematics Teacher* 49 (November 1956):531–534.

Brumfiel, C. "Teaching the Absolute Value Function." *The Mathematics Teacher* 73 (January 1980):24–30.

Davis, R. (The Madison Project) *Explorations in Mathematics: A Text for Teachers.* Reading, Mass.: Addison-Wesley, 1967, 54–91.

DiDomenico, A. "Discovery of a Property of Consecutive Integers." *The Mathematics Teacher* 72 (April 1979):285–286.

Entwhistle, A. "Subtracting Signed Numbers." *The Mathematics Teacher* 48 (March 1955):1975–1976.

Grady, M. "A Manipulative Aid for Adding and Subtracting Integers." *Arithmetic Teacher* 26 (November, 1978):40.

Jacobs, H. *Algebra.* San Francisco: W. H. Freeman, 1979

Jencks, S., and D. Peck. "Hot and Cold Cubes." *The Arithmetic Teacher* 24 (January 1977):70–71.

Johnson, J. "Working With Integers." *The Mathematics Teacher* 71 (January 1978):31.

Kilhefner, D. "Equation Hangman." *Arithmetic Teacher* 27 (January, 1979):46–47.

Kindle, G. "Droopy, The Number Line, and Multiplication of Integers." *The Arithmetic Teacher* 23 (December 1976): 647–650.

Kline, M. *Mathematics for Liberal Arts.* Reading, Mass.: Addison-Wesley, 1967, pp. 74–75.

Kohn, J. "A Physical Model for Operations with Integers." *The Mathematics Teacher* 71 (December 1978):734–736.

Krause, E. *Mathematics for Elementary Teachers.* Englewood Cliffs, N.J.: Prentice-Hall, 1978.

Morrow, L. "Flow Charts for Equation Solving and Maintenance of Skills." *The Mathematics Teacher* 66 (October 1973): 499–506.

National Council of Teachers of Mathematics. *More Topics in Mathematics for Elementary School Teachers.* Thirtieth Yearbook, 1968.

National Council of Teachers of Mathematics, "The System of Integers." booklet number 9. *Topics in Mathematics for Elementary School Teachers,* 1968.

Peterson, J. "Fourteen Different Strategies for Multiplication of Integers, or Why $(^-1)(^-1) = {}^+1$." *The Arithmetic Teacher* 19 (May 1972):396–403.

Pratt, E. "A Teaching Aid for Signed Numbers." *The Arithmetic Teacher* 13 (November 1966):589–590.

Rheins, J., and G. Rheins. "The Additive Inverse in Elementary Algebra." *The Mathematics Teacher* 54 (November 1961): 538–539.

Richardson, L. "The Role of Strategies for Teaching Pupils to Solve Verbal Problems." *The Arithmetic Teacher* 22 (May 1975):414–421.

Schultz, J. *Mathematics for Elementary School Teachers.* Columbus, Ohio: Charles E. Merrill Publishing Co., 1977.

Sconyers, J. "Something New on Number Lines." *The Mathematics Teacher* 67 (March 1974):253–254.

Shoemaker, R. "Please, My Dear Aunt Sally." *Arithmetic Teacher* 27 (May 1980):34–35.

Uth, C. "Teaching Aid for Developing $(a + b)(a - b)$." *The Mathematics Teacher* 48 (April 1955):247–249.

Williams, K. "The Three Faces of $(-)$." *The Mathematics Teacher* 55 (December 1962):668–669.

Zlot, W., and R. Roberts. "The Multiplication of Signed Numbers." *The Mathematics Teacher* 75 (April 1982):302–304.

Zweng, M. "One Point of View: The Problem of Solving Story Problems." *Arithmetic Teacher* 27 (September 1979):2.

PRELIMINARY PROBLEM

A seventh grade class from Washington Elementary School visited a neighborhood cannery warehouse. The warehouse manager told the class that there were 11,368 cans of juice in the inventory and that the cans were packed in boxes of 6 or 24, depending upon the size of the can. One of the students, Sam, thought for a moment and announced that there was a mistake in the inventory. Is Sam's announcement correct? Why or why not?

INTRODUCTION

Number theory is concerned primarily with relationships among integers. These relationships have fascinated mathematicians for centuries. Number theory is associated with names like Pythagoras (500 B.C.), Euclid (300 B.C.), and Diophantus (A.D. 300).

As a field of study, number theory began to flourish in the seventeenth century with the work of the lawyer Pierre de Fermat (1601–1665), often called the father of number theory. His extensive mathematical notes on the margins of his copy of Bachet's *Diophantus Arithmetica* included a conjecture, now known as *Fermat's Last Theorem*. In the margin of this text next to a problem about finding squares that are sums of two squares (for example, $5^2 = 3^2 + 4^2$ and $13^2 = 12^2 + 5^2$), Fermat wrote,

> On the other hand, it is impossible for a cube to be the sum of two cubes, a fourth power to be the sum of two fourth powers, or, in general, for any number that is a power greater than the second to be the sum of two like powers. I have discovered a truly marvelous demonstration of this proposition that this margin is too narrow to contain.

No one has been able to prove or disprove the conjecture. It remains one of the most prominent unsolved problems of mathematics.

Topics from number theory that appear in elementary school curricula include multiples, factors, divisibility tests, prime numbers, prime factorizations, greatest common divisors, and least common multiples.

5-1   DIVISIBILITY

is divisible by   divisor
divides   multiple   factor

In a division fact such as $12 \div 3 = 4$, where the remainder is zero, we say that 12 **is divisible by** 3, or 3 is a **divisor** of 12, or 3 **divides** 12. Because $12 = 3 \cdot 4$, we also say that 12 is a **multiple** of 3, or 3 is a **factor** of 12. In general, if $a \div b = c$, where a, b, and c are integers, the following are true statements.

a is divisible by b.
b is a divisor of a.
b divides a.
a is a multiple of b.
b is a factor of a.

Each of the statements above can be written as $b \mid a$. The expression $b \mid a$ is usually read, "b divides a." Note that $b \neq 0$ because division by 0 is undefined.

DEFINITION

> If a and b are any integers with $b \neq 0$, then b divides a, written $b \mid a$, if and only if there is unique integer c such that $a = cb$.

Remark | Do not confuse $b \mid a$ with b/a, which is interpreted as $b \div a$. The former, a relation, is either true or false. The latter, an operation, has a numerical value, as shown in Chapter 6.

To symbolize that 12 is not divisible by 5, or 5 does not divide 12, we write $5 \nmid 12$. The notation $5 \nmid 12$ also is used to show that 12 is not a multiple of 5 and 5 is not a factor of 12.

Example 5-1 | Classify each of the following as true or false. Explain your answer.

(a) $^-3 \mid 12$ (b) $0 \mid 3$ (c) $3 \mid 0$ (d) $8 \nmid 2$
(e) For all integers a, $1 \mid a$ (f) For all integers a, $^-1 \mid a$
(g) $0 \mid 0$

Solution | (a) $^-3 \mid 12$ is true because $12 = 4(^-3)$.
(b) $0 \mid 3$ is false because there is no integer c such that $3 = c \cdot 0$.
(c) $3 \mid 0$ is true because $0 = 0 \cdot 3$.
(d) $8 \nmid 2$ is true because there is no integer c such that $2 = c \cdot 8$.
(e) $1 \mid a$ is true for all integers a because $a = a \cdot 1$.
(f) $^-1 \mid a$ is true for all integers a because $a = (^-a)(^-1)$.
(g) $0 \mid 0$ is false because there is no unique integer c such that $0 = c \cdot 0$.

To obtain multiples of any integer, we need only to multiply the integer by another integer. For example, $3 \cdot 3$, $2 \cdot 3$, $0 \cdot 3$, and $^-1 \cdot 3$ are all multiples of 3. We now use multiples of 3 to investigate some properties of divisibility. Consider two bags of apples. Suppose the number of apples in each bag can be equally divided among three students; that is, the number of apples in each bag is a multiple of 3. If all the apples are put in one large bag, it is still possible to divide the apples equally among the three students. Consequently, if the number of apples in the first bag is a and the number of apples in the second bag is b, then we can record the preceding discussion as $3 \mid a$ and $3 \mid b$ implies $3 \mid (a + b)$. If the number of apples in one bag cannot be divided among three students, then the total number of apples cannot be equally divided among three students. That is, if $3 \mid a$ and $3 \nmid b$, then $3 \nmid (a + b)$. These ideas may be generalized in the following

theorem | **theorem.** (A theorem is a statement that can be logically deduced from basic properties and definitions.)

THEOREM 5-1 |

For any integers a, b, and d with $d \neq 0$:

1. If $d \mid a$ and $d \mid b$, then $d \mid (a + b)$.
2. If $d \mid a$ and $d \nmid b$, then $d \nmid (a + b)$.

Since subtraction is defined in terms of addition, a similar theorem holds for subtraction.

THEOREM 5-2

For any integers a, b, and d with $d \neq 0$:

1. If $d \mid a$ and $d \mid b$, then $d \mid (a - b)$.
2. If $d \mid a$ and $d \nmid b$, then $d \nmid (a - b)$.

The proofs of most theorems in this section are left as exercises, but the proof of part 1 of Theorem 5-2 is given as an illustration.

Proof

Because $d \mid a$, we have $a = m \cdot d$, where m is an integer. Similarly, $d \mid b$ implies $b = n \cdot d$, where n is an integer. We would like to show that $d \mid (a - b)$. To do this, we must show that $a - b$ is some integer times d. Substituting for a and b, we obtain $a - b = md - nd$. By the distributive property of multiplication over subtraction, this equation can be rewritten as $a - b = (m - n)d$. Now, $m - n$ is an integer because both m and n are integers, and the set of integers is closed under subtraction. Therefore, $d \mid (a - b)$, and the proof is complete.

Theorems 5-1 and 5-2 can be used to deduce another theorem. Substituting a for b in part 1 of Theorem 5-1, we have: If $d \mid a$ and $d \mid a$, then $d \mid (a + a)$, or $d \mid 2a$. Now, $d \mid a$ and $d \mid 2a$ imply that $d \mid (a + 2a)$, or $d \mid 3a$. Continuing in this way, it is possible to show that if d divides a, then d divides any positive multiple of a. That is, $d \mid a$ implies $d \mid ka$, where k is a positive integer. Similarly, using Theorem 5-2, it can be shown that this statement is also true when k is a negative integer.

THEOREM 5-3

For any integers a and d with $d \neq 0$, if $d \mid a$ and k is any integer, then $d \mid ka$.

Example 5-2

Classify each of the following as true or false where x, y, and z are integers. If a statement is true, prove it. If a statement is false, exhibit a counterexample.

(a) If $3 \mid x$ and $3 \mid y$, then $3 \mid xy$.
(b) If $3 \mid (x + y)$, then $3 \mid x$ and $3 \mid y$.
(c) If $9 \nmid a$, then $3 \nmid a$.

Solution | (a) True. By Theorem 5-3, if $3 \mid x$, then for any integer k, $3 \mid kx$. If $k = y$, then $3 \mid yx$ or $3 \mid xy$. (Notice that $3 \mid xy$ regardless of whether $3 \mid y$ or $3 \nmid y$.)
(b) False. For example, $3 \mid (7 + 2)$ but $3 \nmid 7$ and $3 \nmid 2$. (How does this compare with part 1 of Theorem 5-1?)
(c) False. For example, $9 \nmid 21$, but $3 \mid 21$.

Example 5-3 | Five students found a padlocked money box, which had a deposit slip attached to it. The deposit slip was waterspotted, so the currency total appeared as shown in Figure 5-1. One student remarked that if the money listed on the deposit slip was in the box, it could easily be divided equally among the five students without using coins. How did the student know this?

FIGURE 5-1 |

Solution | The units digit of the amount of the currency is zero. The solution to the problem becomes one of determining whether any natural number whose units digit is 0 is divisible by 5.

One method for attacking this problem is to look for a pattern. Natural numbers whose units digit is zero form a pattern, that is, 10, 20 30, 40, 50, ... These numbers are multiples of 10. We are to determine whether 5 divides all multiples of 10.

We know that the amount of money in the box is a multiple of 10. Since $5 \mid 10$, any multiple of 10 is divisible by 5 by Theorem 5-3. Hence, 5 divides the amount of money in the box, and the student is correct.

Procedures similar to those used in Example 5-3 can be used to investigate divisibility by 2. Consider the number 358, whose expanded form is $3 \cdot 10^2 + 5 \cdot 10 + 8$. Since $2 \mid 10$, then $2 \mid 10^2$ and $2 \mid (5 \cdot 10)$. Likewise, $2 \mid 10^2$ implies that $2 \mid (3 \cdot 10^2)$. Hence, $2 \mid (3 \cdot 10^2 + 5 \cdot 10)$. Now, since $358 = (3 \cdot 10^2 + 5 \cdot 10) + 8$ and $2 \mid 8$, it follows that the sum $[(3 \cdot 10^2 + 5 \cdot 10) + 8]$ is divisible by 2; that is, $2 \mid 358$. The same argument holds if the units digit is any even number. A similar argument shows that 2 does not divide a number whose units digit is odd. For example, consider 357, or $3 \cdot 10^2 + 5 \cdot 10 + 7$. Since $2 \mid (3 \cdot 10^2 + 5 \cdot 10)$ and $2 \nmid 7$, it follows that $2 \nmid (3 \cdot 10^2 + 5 \cdot 10 + 7)$; that is, $2 \nmid 357$. In general, the following divisibility test holds.

Divisibility Test for 2 | An integer is divisible by 2 if and only if the units digit of the integer is divisible by 2.

There are similar tests for divisibility by 5 and 10. The tests follow from the fact that the only positive integers other than 1 and 2 that divide 10 are 5 and 10.

Divisibility Test for 5 | An integer is divisible by 5 if and only if the units digit of the integer is divisible by 5, that is, the units digit is 0 or 5.

Divisibility Test for 10 | An integer is divisible by 10 if and only if the units digit is divisible by 10, that is, the units digit is 0.

Other one-digit numbers that divide powers of 10 are 4 and 8. To develop a divisibility rule for 4, consider any four-digit number n such that $n = a \cdot 10^3 + b \cdot 10^2 + c \cdot 10 + d$. The first step is to write the given number as a sum of two numbers, one of which is as great as possible and divisible by 4. Notice that $4 \nmid 10$ but $4 \mid 10^2$. Consequently, $4 \mid 10 \cdot 10^2$; that is, $4 \mid 10^3$. Now, $4 \mid 10^2$ implies $4 \mid b \cdot 10^2$, and $4 \mid 10^3$ implies $4 \mid a \cdot 10^3$. Finally, $4 \mid a \cdot 10^3$ and $4 \mid b \cdot 10^2$ imply $4 \mid (a \cdot 10^3 + b \cdot 10^2)$. Since $4 \mid (a \cdot 10^3 + b \cdot 10^2)$, the divisibility of $a \cdot 10^3 + b \cdot 10^2 + c \cdot 10 + d$ by 4 depends upon the divisibility of $(c \cdot 10 + d)$ by 4. If $4 \mid (c \cdot 10 + d)$, then 4 divides the given number n. If $4 \nmid (c \cdot 10 + d)$, then 4 does not divide the given number n. Notice that $c \cdot 10 + d$ is the number represented by the last two digits in the given number, n.

Divisibility Test for 4 | An integer is divisible by 4 if and only if the last two digits of the integer represent a number divisible by 4.

To investigate divisibility by 8, we note that the least positive power of 10 divisible by 8 is 10^3. Consequently, all integral powers of 10 greater than 10^3 are divisible by 8. Hence, the following is a divisibility test for 8.

Divisibility Test for 8 | An integer is divisible by 8 if and only if the last three digits of the integer represent a number divisible by 8.

Example 5-4 | (a) Determine whether 97,128 is divisible by 2, 4, and 8.
(b) Determine whether 83,026 is divisible by 2, 4, and 8.

Solution | (a) $2 \mid 97{,}128$ because $2 \mid 8$.
$4 \mid 97{,}128$ because $4 \mid 28$.
$8 \mid 97{,}128$ because $8 \mid 128$.

(b) $2 \mid 83{,}026$ because $2 \mid 6$.
$4 \nmid 83{,}026$ because $4 \nmid 26$.
$8 \nmid 83{,}026$ because $8 \nmid 026$.

Next we consider a divisibility test for 3. We illustrate the procedure on the number 5721, that is, $5 \cdot 10^3 + 7 \cdot 10^2 + 2 \cdot 10 + 1$. No power of 10 is divisible by 3, but there are numbers close to powers of 10 that are divisible by 3. The numbers 9, 99, 999, and so on are such numbers. Although it is not yet possible to determine whether 5721, or $5 \cdot 10^3 + 7 \cdot 10^2 + 2 \cdot 10 + 1$, is divisible by 3, the number $5 \cdot 999 + 7 \cdot 99 + 2 \cdot 9$ is close to 5721 and is divisible by 3. (Why?)

Next, look for a number x to make the following equation true.

$$5721 = 5 \cdot 10^3 + 7 \cdot 10^2 + 2 \cdot 10 + 1 = (5 \cdot 999 + 7 \cdot 99 + 2 \cdot 9) + x$$

What must be added to $5 \cdot 999$ to obtain $5 \cdot 10^3$? Because $5 \cdot 10^3 = 5 \cdot 1000 = 5(999 + 1) = 5 \cdot 999 + 5 \cdot 1$, the answer is 5. Similarly, $7 \cdot 10^2 = 7 \cdot 100 = 7(99 + 1) = 7 \cdot 99 + 7 \cdot 1$, and $2 \cdot 10 = 2 \cdot (9 + 1) = 2 \cdot 9 + 2 \cdot 1$. Thus, the number x is $5 \cdot 1 + 7 \cdot 1 + 2 \cdot 1 + 1$, or $5 + 7 + 2 + 1$. Consequently,

$$5721 = 5 \cdot 10^3 + 7 \cdot 10^2 + 2 \cdot 10 + 1$$
$$= (5 \cdot 999 + 7 \cdot 99 + 2 \cdot 9) + (5 + 7 + 2 + 1)$$

The sum in the first set of parentheses is divisible by 3, so the divisibility of 5721 by 3 depends upon the sum in the second set of parentheses. In this case, $5 + 7 + 2 + 1 = 15$ and $3 \mid 15$. Thus, $3 \mid [(5 \cdot 999 + 7 \cdot 99 + 2 \cdot 9) + (5 + 7 + 2 + 1)]$; that is, $3 \mid 5721$. Hence, to test 5721 for divisibility by 3, simply test $5 + 7 + 2 + 1$ for divisibility by 3. Notice that $5 + 7 + 2 + 1$ is the sum of the digits of 5721. The example suggests the following test for divisibility by 3.

Divisibility Test for 3 | An integer is divisible by 3 if and only if the sum of its digits is divisible by 3.

An argument similar to the one used to demonstrate that $3 \mid 5721$ can be used to prove the test for divisibility by 3 on an integer with any number of digits and in particular for any four-digit number n such that $n = a \cdot 10^3 + b \cdot 10^2 + c \cdot 10 + d$. Even though $a \cdot 10^3 + b \cdot 10^2 + c \cdot 10 + d$ is not necessarily divisible by 3, the number $a \cdot 999 + b \cdot 99 + c \cdot 9$ is close to n and *is* divisible by 3.

$$a \cdot 10^3 = a \cdot 1000 = a(999 + 1) = a \cdot 999 + a \cdot 1$$
$$b \cdot 10^2 = b \cdot 100 = b(99 + 1) = b \cdot 99 + b \cdot 1$$
$$c \cdot 10^1 = c \cdot 10 = c(9 + 1) = c \cdot 9 + c \cdot 1$$

Thus, $n = a \cdot 10^3 + b \cdot 10^2 + c \cdot 10 + d = (a \cdot 999 + b \cdot 99 + c \cdot 9) + (a + b + c + d)$. Because $3 \mid 9$, $3 \mid 99$, and $3 \mid 999$, it follows that $3 \mid (a \cdot 999 + b \cdot 99 + c \cdot 9)$. If $3 \mid (a + b + c + d)$, then $3 \mid [(a \cdot 999 + b \cdot 99 + c \cdot 9) + (a + b + c + d)]$, that is, $3 \mid n$. If, on the other hand, $3 \nmid (a + b + c + d)$, it follows from part 2 of Theorem 5-2 that $3 \nmid n$.

Since $9 \mid 9$, $9 \mid 99$, $9 \mid 999$, and so on, a test similar to that for divisibility by 3 applies to divisibility by 9.

Divisibility Test for 9 | An integer is divisible by 9 if and only if the sum of the digits of the integer is divisible by 9.

Example 5-5 | Use divisibility tests to determine whether each of the following numbers is divisible by 3 and divisible by 9.

(a) 1002   (b) 14,238

Solution | (a) Because $1 + 0 + 0 + 2 = 3$ and $3 \mid 3$, it follows that $3 \mid 1002$. Because $9 \nmid 3$, $9 \nmid 1002$.
(b) Because $1 + 4 + 2 + 3 + 8 = 18$ and $3 \mid 18$, it follows that $3 \mid 14{,}238$. Because $9 \mid 18$, it follows that $9 \mid 14{,}238$.

Divisibility tests can be devised for 7 and 11. We give two such tests, but omit the proofs.

Divisibility Test for 7 | An integer is divisible by 7 if and only if the difference of the integer represented without its units digit and twice the units digit of the original integer is divisible by 7.

Divisibility Test for 11 | An integer is divisible by 11 if and only if the sum of the digits in the places that are odd powers of 10 minus the sum of the digits in the places that are even powers of 10 is divisible by 11.

At this point, the only number less than 11 for which we have no divisibility test is 6. The divisibility test for 6 depends upon the divisibility tests for 2 and 3. We state the test here and justify it in the next section.

Divisibility Test for 6 | An integer is divisible by 6 if and only if the integer is divisible by both 2 and 3.

Example 5-6 | Test each of the following numbers for divisibility by 7, 11, and 6.

(a) 462   (b) 964,194

Solution | (a) $7 \mid (46 - 2 \cdot 2)$, so $7 \mid 462$.
$11 \mid (4 + 2 - 6)$, so $11 \mid 462$.
$2 \mid 462$ and $3 \mid 462$, so $6 \mid 462$.
(b) To determine whether or not 7 divides 964,194, we use the process several times.

$7 \mid 964{,}194$ if and only if $7 \mid (96{,}419 - 2 \cdot 4)$, or $7 \mid 96{,}411$

$7 \mid 96{,}411$ if and only if $7 \mid 9641 - 2 \cdot 1)$, or $7 \mid 9639$

$7 \mid 9639$ if and only if $7 \mid (963 - 2 \cdot 9)$ or $7 \mid 945$

$7 \mid 945$ if and only if $7 \mid (94 - 2 \cdot 5)$, or $7 \mid 84$

Because $7 \mid 84$ is true, then $7 \mid 964{,}194$.

$11 \mid [(9 + 4 + 9) - (4 + 1 + 6)]$, so $11 \mid 964{,}194$.
$2 \mid 964{,}194$ and $3 \mid 964{,}194$, so $6 \mid 964{,}194$.

PROBLEM SET 5-1

1. Classify each of the following as true or false.
   (a) 6 is a factor of 30
   (b) 6 is a divisor of 30
   (c) $6 \mid 30$
   (d) 30 is divisible by 6
   (e) 30 is a multiple of 6
   (f) 6 is a multiple of 30

2. Use part 1 of Theorem 5-1 to complete each of the following sentences. Assume a, b, and d are integers with $d \neq 0$. Simplify your answers, if possible.
   (a) If $7 \mid 14$ and $7 \mid 21$, then _____ .
   (b) If $d \mid (213 - 57)$ and $d \mid 57$, then _____ .
   (c) If $d \mid (a - b)$ and $d \mid b$, then _____ .

3. There are 1379 children signed up to play Little League baseball. If 9 players are assigned to each team, will any teams be short of players?

4. A forester has 43,682 seedlings to be planted. Can these be planted in an equal number of rows with 11 seedlings in each row?

5. For each of the following, state the theorems that justify the given statements assuming a, b, and c are integers. If a statement cannot be justified by one of the theorems in this section, answer "none."
   (a) $4 \mid 20$ implies $4 \mid 113 \cdot 20$.
   (b) $4 \mid 100$ and $4 \nmid 13$ imply $4 \nmid (100 + 13)$.
   (c) $4 \mid 100$ and $4 \nmid 13$ imply $4 \nmid 1300$.
   (d) $3 \mid (a + b)$ and $3 \nmid c$ imply $3 \nmid (a + b + c)$.
   (e) $3 \mid a$ implies $3 \mid a^2$.

6. Classify each of the following as true or false assuming a, b, c, and d are integers with $d \neq 0$. If a statement is true, justify it; if it is false, give a counterexample.
   (a) If $d \mid (a + b)$, then $d \mid a$ and $d \mid b$.
   (b) If $d \mid (a + b)$, then $d \mid a$ or $d \mid b$.
   (c) If $d \mid a$ and $d \mid b$, then $d \mid ab$.
   (d) If $d \mid ab$, then $d \mid a$ or $d \mid b$.
   (e) If $ab \mid c$, $a \neq 0$, and $b \neq 0$, then $a \mid c$ and $b \mid c$.
   (f) $1 \mid a$
   (g) $d \mid 0$

7. (a) If we multiply any odd number by 5, what is the units digit of the product?
   (b) If we multiply any even whole number by 5, what is the units digit of the product?

8. Classify each of the following as true or false.
   (a) If every digit of a number is divisible by 3, the number itself is divisible by 3.
   (b) If a number is divisible by 3, then every digit of the number is divisible by 3.
   (c) A number is divisible by 3 if and only if every digit of the number is divisible by 3.

   (d) If a number is divisible by 6, then it is divisible by 2 and by 3.
   (e) If a number is divisible by 2 and 3, then it is divisible by 6.
   (f) If a number is divisible by 2 and 4, then it is divisible by 8.
   (g) If a number is divisible by 8, then it is divisible by 2 and 4.

9. Devise a test for divisibility by each given number.
   (a) 16
   (b) 25

10. Devise divisibility tests for 12 and 15.

11. Jack owes $7812 on a new car. Can this be paid in 12 equal monthly installments?

12. A group of people ordered No-Cal candy bars. The bill was $2.09. If the original price of each was 12¢ but the price has been inflated, how much does each cost?

13. When the two missing digits in the given number are replaced, the number is divisible by 99. What is the number?

    85_ _1

14. Test each of the following numbers for divisibility by 2, 3, 4, 5, 6, 7, 8, 9, 10, 11, 12, and 15.
    (a) 746,988
    (b) 81,342
    (c) 15,810
    (d) 183,324
    (e) 901,815
    (f) 4,201,012
    (g) 1001
    (h) 10,001

15. Answer each of the following and justify your answer.
    (a) If a number is not divisible by 5, can it be divisible by 10?
    (b) If a number is not divisible by 10, can it be divisible by 5?

16. Fill each blank with the greatest digit that makes the statement true.
    (a) $3 \mid 74\_$
    (b) $9 \mid 83\_45$
    (c) $11 \mid 6\_55$

17. A number in which each digit except 0 appears exactly three times is divisible by 3. For example, 777,555,222 and 414,143,313 are divisible by 3. Explain why this statement is true.

18. Prove the following theorem: For any integers a, b, and c with $a \neq 0$ and $b \neq 0$, if $a \mid b$ and $b \mid c$, then $a \mid c$.

★ 19. Prove each of the following.
    (a) Theorem 5-1
    (b) Theorem 5-2
    (c) Theorem 5-3

★ 20. Prove the test for divisibility by 9 for any five-digit number.

★21. Prove the test for divisibility by 2 for any number n, such that

$$n = a_k 10^k + a_{k-1} 10^{k-1} + \cdots + a_3 10^3 + a_2 10^2 + a_1 10 + a_0$$

22. Enter any three-digit number on the calculator; for example, enter 243. Repeat it: 243,243. Divide by 7. Divide by 11. Divide by 13. What is the answer? Try it again with any other three-digit number. Will this always work? Why?

23. The calculator may be used to test for divisibility of one number by another. Test the divisibility of the first number by the second in each of the following.

(a) 490 by 2   (b) 575 by 5
(c) 353 by 3   (d) 4907 by 7
(e) 4074 by 4   (f) 123,123 by 11

BRAIN TEASER

Joan announced to her friends that she had learned a new number trick. She said that if she picked a whole number, reversed the digits in the number, and took the difference between the two, then 9 would always divide the difference. Is this true?

5-2 PRIME AND COMPOSITE NUMBERS

prime
composite

Some numbers, such as 7 and 13, have exactly two distinct positive factors—namely, 1 and themselves. Any positive integer with exactly two distinct positive factors is called a *prime number,* or a **prime.** Any number that has a positive factor other than 1 and itself is called a *composite number,* or a **composite.** For example, 6 and 10 are composites because they have factors other than 1 and themselves. The number 1 has only one positive factor, so it is neither prime nor composite. (Problem 19 in Problem Set 5-2 deals with the question of why the number 1 is not included among the prime numbers.) The first ten primes are 2, 3, 5, 7, 11, 13, 17, 19, 23, and 29.

Example 5-7

Show that the following numbers are composite.

(a) 1564   (b) 2781   (c) 1001

Solution

(a) Since $2 \mid 4$, 1564 is divisible by 2.
(b) Since $3 \mid (2 + 7 + 8 + 1)$, 2781 is divisible by 3.
(c) Since $11 \mid [(1 + 0) - (0 + 1)]$, 1001 is divisible by 11.

factorization
prime factorization

Composite numbers can be expressed as products of two or more lesser whole numbers. For example, $18 = 2 \cdot 9$, $18 = 3 \cdot 6$, or $18 = 2 \cdot 3 \cdot 3$. Each expression of 18 as a product of factors is called a **factorization.** A factorization containing only prime numbers is called **prime factorization.** To find the prime

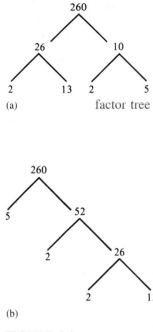

(a)   factor tree

(b)

FIGURE 5-2

factorization of a given composite number, first rewrite the number as a product of two smaller numbers. Continue the process, factoring the lesser numbers until all factors are primes. For example, consider 260.

$$260 = 26 \cdot 10 = 2 \cdot 13 \cdot 2 \cdot 5 = 2 \cdot 2 \cdot 5 \cdot 13 = 2^2 \cdot 5 \cdot 13$$

The procedure for finding the prime factorization of a number can be organized using a model called a **factor tree.** A factor tree is demonstrated in Figure 5-2(a). Notice that the last branches of the trees display the prime factors of 260.

The factorization of 260, or any other composite number, can be started in different ways. A second way for factoring 260 is shown in Figure 5-2(b). The two trees produce the same prime factorization, except for the order in which the primes appear in the products.

To use a more precise algorithmic approach to finding the prime factorization of a number, we start with the smallest prime and check to see if it divides the number. If not, we try the next greater prime and check for divisibility by this prime. Once we find a prime that divides the number in question, then we must find the quotient of the number divided by the prime. Now, we check to see if the prime divides the quotient. If so, we repeat the process. If not, we try the next greater prime and check to see if it divides the quotient. We continue the procedure, using greater primes, until a quotient of 1 is reached. The original number is the product of all the primes used. The prime factorization of 260 using this method is shown in Figure 5-3. Hence, $260 = 2^2 \cdot 5 \cdot 13$.

FIGURE 5-3

$$
\begin{array}{r|r}
2 & 260 \\ \hline
2 & 130 \\ \hline
5 & 65 \\ \hline
13 & 13 \\ \hline
& 1
\end{array}
$$

In general, the prime factorization of a number is unique. The *Fundamental Theorem of Arithmetic,* sometimes called the *Unique Factorization Theorem,* states this fact.

THEOREM 5-4

Fundamental Theorem of Arithmetic   Each composite number has one and only one prime factorization.

Normally, the primes in the prime factorization of a number are listed in increasing order from left to right. If a prime appears in a product more than once, exponential notation is used. Thus, $13 \cdot 2 \cdot 2 \cdot 2 \cdot 5 \cdot 5 \cdot 5 \cdot 7$ is customarily written $2^3 \cdot 5^3 \cdot 7 \cdot 13$.

In determining the factorization of a number such as 8127, observe that $9 \mid 8127$. Hence, $8127 = 9k$, where k is an integer. Because $8127 = 9k$, then k is a factor of 8127 and $k = \frac{8127}{9}$. Theorem 5-5 states the general case.

THEOREM 5-5

> If d is a factor of n, where $n \neq 0$ and $d \neq 0$, then $\dfrac{n}{d}$ is a factor of n.

Remark

> Sometimes we do not obtain a different factor when using this process. This occurs when $\dfrac{n}{d} = d$. For example, 7 is a factor of 49 and so is $\dfrac{49}{7}$, or 7.

To investigate whether a number n is composite, we utilize Theorem 5-5. Suppose p is the *least* prime factor of the number n. If n is prime, then $p = n$, but if n is composite, we have $p \leq \dfrac{n}{p}$ because $\dfrac{n}{p}$ is also a factor of n and p is the least factor of n. Thus, $p^2 \leq n$. This idea is summarized by the following theorem.

THEOREM 5-6

> If n is composite, then n has a prime factor p such that $p^2 \leq n$.

Theorem 5-6 can be used to help determine whether a given number is prime or composite. Consider, for example, the number 109. If 109 is composite, it must have a prime divisor p such that $p^2 \leq 109$. The primes whose squares do not exceed 109 are 2, 3, 5, and 7. Checking for divisibility by these primes reveals that $2 \nmid 109$, $3 \nmid 109$, $5 \nmid 109$, and $7 \nmid 109$. Hence, 109 is prime. The argument used leads to the following theorem.

THEOREM 5-7

> If n is an integer greater than 1 such that n is not divisible by any prime p, where $p^2 \leq n$, then n is a prime.

Example 5-8

> Is 397 composite or prime?

Solution

> The possible primes p such that $p^2 \leq 397$ are 2, 3, 5, 7, 11, 13, 17, and 19. Because $2 \nmid 397$, $3 \nmid 397$, $5 \nmid 397$, $7 \nmid 397$, $11 \nmid 397$, $13 \nmid 397$, $17 \nmid 397$, and $19 \nmid 397$, the number 397 is prime.

One way to find all the primes less than a given number is to use the Sieve of Eratosthenes, named after the Greek mathematician Eratosthenes (200 B.C.). If all the natural numbers greater than 1 are considered (or placed in the sieve), the numbers that are not prime are methodically crossed out (or drop through the holes of the sieve). The remaining numbers are prime. The procedure presented on page 178 is from *McGraw-Hill Mathematics*, 1981, Grade 5. We leave it as an exercise to work through the student page and to explain why, after crossing out all the multiples of 2, 3, 5, and 7, the remaining numbers in the sieve are prime.

Historical Highlight

1	2	3	4	5	6	7	8	9	10
11	12	13	14	15	16	17	18	19	20
21	22	23	24	25	26	27	28	29	30
31	32	33	34	35	36	37	38	39	40
41	42	43	44	45	46	47	48	49	50

The Sieve of Eratosthenes is a way to find prime numbers. Use the table of numbers from 1 to 50.

1. Cross out 1. (1 is not prime.)

2. Circle 2. (2 is prime.)

3. Cross out other multiples of 2. Why are they not prime?

4. Circle 3. (3 is prime.)

5. Cross out other multiples of 3. Why?

6. Circle 5. Circle 7. Cross out their other multiples.

7. The numbers left are prime, or "caught in the sieve." List them.

ERATOSTHENES · GREEK SCHOLAR
ABOUT 275 – 195 B.C.

More About Primes

There are infinitely many whole numbers, infinitely many odd numbers, and infinitely many even numbers. Are there infinitely many primes? Because prime numbers do not appear in any known pattern, the answer to this question is not obvious. Euclid was the first to prove that there are infinitely many primes (see Problem Set 5-2, Problem 21).

PROBLEM 1

Although Euclid proved that there are infinitely many primes, it has been shown that there are strings of as many consecutive composite numbers as desired. Find 1000 consecutive natural numbers that are composite.

Understanding the Problem

The goal is to find 1000 consecutive natural numbers that are not prime. Because the numbers must be consecutive, they can be written in the form $n, n + 1, n + 2, n + 3, \ldots, n + 999$ or in a similar ordering, where n is some natural number. Also, since each of the numbers is to be composite, each must have at least one divisor other than 1 and itself.

Devising a Plan

To find a set of 1000 consecutive composite natural numbers using the Sieve of Eratosthenes would seem to require a large list of numbers. In the sieve on page 178, we can find no more than five consecutive composites. One such group is 24, 25, 26, 27, and 28. Constructing a large sieve and counting the number of composites is very time-consuming; thus, we should try other alternatives.

A possible strategy is to look at a simpler problem. For example, we might consider finding a string of ten consecutive composites, which we can label n, $n + 1, n + 2, \ldots$, and $n + 9$. We would like to choose n so that these ten numbers are composite. The greatest number in the list, $n + 9$, will be composite if n is a multiple of 9. Similarly, $n + 8$ will be composite if n is a multiple of 8. Continuing in this way, the numbers, $n + 7, n + 6, \ldots$, and $n + 2$ will be composite if n is a multiple of $7, 6, \ldots$, and 2, respectively. This process reveals little about $n + 1$, but the process can be used to create the number n. Because n is to be a multiple of $9, 8, 7, 6, \ldots$, and 2, perhaps the simplest value for n is $9 \cdot 8 \cdot 7 \cdot 6 \cdot \ldots \cdot 3 \cdot 2$.

With $n = 9 \cdot 8 \cdot 7 \cdot 6 \cdot \ldots \cdot 3 \cdot 2$, we have $n + 9, n + 8, n + 7, \ldots$, and $n + 2$ as composite numbers. Notice that this process yields eight consecutive composite numbers, rather than ten. Also, observe that to obtain eight consecutive composites, we used $n + 9$ as the greatest number. Similarly, to obtain ten consecutive composites, we choose $n + 11$ as the greatest composite; to obtain 1000 consecutive composites, we use $n + 1001$.

Carrying Out the Plan

Using the process developed above, we consider the 1000 consecutive natural numbers $n + 2, n + 3, \ldots, n + 1000, n + 1001$. We choose $n = 2 \cdot 3 \cdot 4 \cdot \ldots \cdot 1001$. With this choice of n, the 1000 consecutive natural numbers we have just described are composite.

Looking Back

In a similar manner, we can find as many consecutive composite numbers as desired. Though there are infinitely many primes, we can find a million, a billion, or a trillion consecutive composite numbers and, in general, as many as we want.

For centuries, mathematicians have looked for a formula that produces only primes, but no one has ever found one. One such attempt resulted in the expression $n^2 - n + 41$, where n is a whole number. Substituting $0, 1, 2, 3, \ldots,$ 40 for n in the expression always results in a prime number. However, substituting 41 for n gives $41^2 - 41 + 41$, or 41^2, a composite number.

Mersenne primes   Prime numbers of the form $2^p - 1$, where p is a prime, are called **Mersenne primes,** after the French mathematician Marin Mersenne (1588–1648). One of the greatest known primes, which is a Mersenne prime, was discovered at the University of Illinois. It has 3376 digits and can be written in the form $2^{11,213} - 1$. To realize just how great this number is, note that 2^{64} grains of wheat is more wheat than has ever been produced in the history of the world. The University of Illinois advertised the discovery on its postal meter, as shown in Figure 5-4.

FIGURE 5-4

Until recently, the largest known prime was $2^{19,937} - 1$, found in 1971 by Bryant Tuckerman of IBM. However, in 1978, two high school students—Laura Nickel and Curt Noll, from Hayward, California—found a larger prime, $2^{23,209} - 1$, using a computer. Other larger primes have since been discovered, one of the latest being $2^{132,049} - 1$. It too was discovered by a computer. The finding was announced in a national newscast on September 23, 1983.

Goldbach's conjecture   There are many interesting problems concerning primes. For example, Christian Goldbach (1690–1764) asserted that every even integer greater than 2 is the sum of two primes. This statement is known as **Goldbach's conjecture.** For example, $4 = 2 + 2$, $6 = 3 + 3$, $8 = 3 + 5$, $10 = 3 + 7$, $12 = 5 + 7$, and $14 = 3 + 11$. In spite of the simplicity of the statement, no one knows for sure whether or not the statement is true.

PROBLEM 2

A woman with a basket of eggs finds that if she removes the eggs from the basket either 2, 3, 4, 5, or 6 at a time, there is always 1 egg left. However, if she removes the eggs 7 at a time, there are no eggs left. If the basket holds up to 500 eggs, how many eggs does the woman have?

Understanding the Problem

When a woman removes eggs from the basket 2, 3, 4, 5, or 6 at a time, there is always 1 egg left. That means that if the number of eggs is divided by 2, 3, 4, 5, or 6, the remainder is always 1. We also know that when she removes the eggs 7 at a time, there are no eggs left; that is, the number of eggs is a multiple of 7. Finally, we know that the basket holds up to 500 eggs. We have to find the number of eggs in the basket.

Devising a Plan

One way to solve the problem is to write all the multiples of 7 between 7 and 500 and check which ones have a remainder of 1 when divided by 2, 3, 4, 5, or 6. Since this method is tedious, we look for a different approach. Let the number of eggs be n. Then, if n is divided by 2, the remainder is 1. Consequently, $n - 1$ will be divisible by 2. Similarly, 3, 4, 5, and 6 divide $n - 1$.

Since 2 and 3 divide $n - 1$, the primes 2 and 3 appear in the prime factorization of $n - 1$. Note that $4 \mid (n - 1)$ implies that $2 \mid (n - 1)$, and hence, from the information $2 \mid (n - 1)$ and $4 \mid (n - 1)$, we can conclude only that 2^2 appears in the prime factorization of $n - 1$. Since $5 \mid (n - 1)$, 5 appears in the prime factorization of $n - 1$. The fact that $6 \mid (n - 1)$ does not provide any new information, since it only implies that 2 and 3 are prime factors of $n - 1$, which we already know. Now, $n - 1$ may also have other prime factors. Denoting the product of these prime factors by k, we have $n - 1 = 2^2 \cdot 3 \cdot 5 \cdot k = 60k$, where k is some natural number, and so $n = 60k + 1$. We now find all possible values for n in the form $60k + 1$ less than 500 and determine which ones are divisible by 7.

Carrying Out the Plan

Because $n = 60k + 1$ and k is any natural number, we substitute $k = 1, 2, 3, \ldots$ to obtain the following possible values for n that are less than 500:

61, 121, 181, 241, 301, 361, 421, 481

Among these values, only 301 is divisible by 7; hence, 301 is the only possible answer to the problem.

Looking Back

In the preceding situation, we still have to test eight numbers for divisibility by 7. Is it possible to further reduce the computations? We know that $n = 60k + 1$ and that the possible values for k are $k = 1, 2, 3, 4, 5, 6, 7, 8$. We also know that $7 \mid n$; that is, $7 \mid (60k + 1)$. The problem is to find for which of the above values of k,

$7 \mid (60k + 1)$. The question would have been easier to answer if instead of $60k + 1$, we had a smaller number. We know that the multiple of k closest to $60k$ that is divisible by 7 is $56k$. Since $7 \mid (60k + 1)$ and $7 \mid 56k$, we conclude that $7 \mid (60k + 1 - 56k)$; that is, $7 \mid (4k + 1)$. We now see that $7 \mid (60k + 1)$, if and only if $7 \mid (4k + 1)$. The only value of k between 1 and 8 that makes $4k + 1$ divisible by 7 is 5. Consequently, $7 \mid (60 \cdot 5 + 1)$, and 301 is the solution to the problem.

PROBLEM SET 5-2

1. Use a factor tree to find the prime factorization for each of the following.
   (a) 504   (b) 2475   (c) 11,250
2. Which of the following numbers are primes?
   (a) 149   (b) 923   (c) 433
3. What is the greatest prime you must consider to test whether or not 5669 is prime?
4. Explain why, in the Sieve of Eratosthenes on page 178, after crossing out all the multiples of 2, 3, 5, and 7, the remaining numbers are primes.
5. Extend the Sieve of Eratosthenes to find all primes less than 200.
6. Factors of a locker number are 2, 5, and 9. If there are exactly nine other factors, what is the locker number?
7. (a) When the United States flag had 48 stars, the stars were arranged in a 6×8 rectangular array. In what other rectangular arrays could they have been arranged?
   (b) How many different rectangular arrays of stars could there be if there were only 47 states?
8. If the Spanish Armada had 177 galleons, could it have gone to sea in an equal number of small flotillas? If so, how many ships would have been in each?
9. Suppose the 435 members of the House of Representatives are placed on committees with more than 2 members but less than 30 members. Each committee is to have an equal number of members and each member is on only one committee.
   (a) What size committees are possible?
   (b) How many committees are there of each size?
10. Mr. Arboreta wants to set out fruit trees in a rectangular array. For each of the following numbers of trees,

find all possible numbers of rows if each row is to have the same number of trees.
   (a) 36   (b) 28   (c) 17   (d) 144
11. What is the smallest number that has exactly seven positive factors?
12. (a) Find a composite number different from 41^2 that is of the form $n^2 - n + 41$.
   * (b) Prove that there are infinitely many composite numbers of the form $n^2 - n + 41$.
13. Find the least number divisible by each natural number less than or equal to 12.
14. The primes 2 and 3 are consecutive integers. Is there another pair of consecutive integers both of which are prime? Justify your answer.
15. The prime numbers 11 and 13 are called **twin primes** because they differ by 2. Find all the twin primes less than 200. (The existence of infinitely many twin primes has not been proved.)
16. (a) Use the Fundamental Theorem of Arithmetic to justify that if $2 \mid n$ and $3 \mid n$, then $6 \mid n$.
   (b) Is it always true that if $a \mid n$ and $b \mid n$, then $ab \mid n$? Either prove the statement or give a counterexample.
17. In order to test for divisibility by 12, one student checked to determine divisibility by 3 and 4, while another checked for divisibility by 2 and 6. Are both students using a correct approach to divisibility by 12? Why or why not?
18. (a) Is it always true that if $3 \mid ab$, then $3 \mid a$ or $3 \mid b$?
   (b) Is it always true that if $4 \mid ab$, then $4 \mid a$ or $4 \mid b$?
19. Show that if 1 were considered a prime, every number would have more than one prime factorization.

20. (a) Find all the positive divisors of 2^8.
    (b) Find all the positive divisors of 3^5.
    (c) How many positive divisors does $2^8 \cdot 3^5$ have?
    ★ (d) If p and q are primes, how many divisors does $p^k q^m$ have?
★ 21. Complete the details for the following proof, which shows that there are infinitely many prime numbers.
    If the number of primes is finite, then there is a greatest prime denoted by p. Consider the product of all the primes, $2 \cdot 3 \cdot 5 \cdot \ldots \cdot p$, and let $N = (2 \cdot 3 \cdot 5 \cdot \ldots \cdot p) + 1$. Because $N > p$, where p is the greatest prime, N is composite. Because N is composite, there

is a prime, q, among the primes 2, 3, 5, . . . , p such that $q \mid N$. However, none of the primes 2, 3, 5, . . . , p divides N. (Why?)
    Consequently, $q \nmid N$, which is a contradiction. Thus, the assumption that there are finitely many primes is false and the set of primes must be infinite.

22. One formula yielding several primes is $n^2 + n + 17$.
    (a) Substitute $n = 1, 2, 3, \ldots, 17$ in the formula and find which of the resulting numbers are primes and which are composites.
    ★ (b) Find a value of n, $n > 100$, for which $n^2 + n + 17$ yields a prime.

* * * * * * REVIEW PROBLEMS * * * * * * *

23. Classify each of the following as true or false.
    (a) 11 is a factor of 189.
    (b) 1001 is a multiple of 13.
    (c) $7 \mid 1001$ and $7 \nmid 12$ imply $7 \nmid (1001 - 12)$.
    (d) If a number is divisible by both 7 and 11, then its prime factorization contains 7 and 11.

24. Test each of the following for divisibility by 2, 3, 4, 5, 6, 7, 8, 9, 10, and 11.
    (a) 438,162   (b) 2,345,678,910
25. Prove: If a number is divisible by 12, then it is divisible by 3.

BRAIN TEASER

Consider the factorization of numbers in the set, E, of even counting numbers, {2, 4, 6, 8, 10, . . .}. In this set, there are numbers that cannot be written as products of other numbers in the set. For example, 6 is not a product of two other elements of the set (6 = 2 · 3, but 3 is not in E). A number in E that cannot be written as a product of other numbers in E is called an E-prime. A number in E that can be written as a product of

numbers in E is called an E-composite.
(a) List the first 10 E-primes.
(b) Find an even number whose E-prime factorization is not unique, that is, an even number that can be factored into a product of E-primes in more than one way.
(c) Find a test for determining whether or not an even number is an E-prime.

COMPUTER CORNER

The following BASIC program will determine if a positive integer N is prime. Type it into your computer.

```
 10 PRINT "THIS PROGRAM DETERMINES IF A POSITIVE INTEGER IS "
 15 PRINT "PRIME."
 20 PRINT "AFTER THE QUESTION MARK, TYPE A POSITIVE INTEGER."
 30 INPUT N
 40 IF N = 1 GOTO 90
 50 IF N = 2 GOTO 120
 60 FOR K = 2 TO SQR(N)
 70 IF N/K = INT(N/K) THEN 90
 80 GOTO 110
 90 PRINT N; " IS NOT PRIME."
100 GOTO 130
110 NEXT K
120 PRINT N; " IS PRIME."
130 PRINT "IF YOU WANT TO CHECK ANOTHER NUMBER, TYPE 1. IF "
135 PRINT "NOT, TYPE 0."
140 INPUT V
150 IF V = 1 GOTO 20
160 END
```

Run this program using different values for N.

5-3 GREATEST COMMON DIVISOR AND LEAST COMMON MULTIPLE

greatest common divisor (GCD)

The **greatest common divisor (GCD)** of two numbers is the greatest divisor or factor that the two numbers have in common. The concept of GCD is used in Chapter 6 to reduce fractions to lowest terms.

There are several ways to find the GCD of two or more numbers. One way is to list all members of the set of positive divisors of the two numbers, then find the set of all common divisors, and, finally, pick the greatest element in that set. For example, to find the GCD of 20 and 32, denote the sets of divisors of 20 and 32 by D_{20} and D_{32}, respectively.

$D_{20} = \{1, 2, 4, 5, 10, 20\}$

$D_{32} = \{1, 2, 4, 8, 16, 32\}$

The set of all common positive divisors of 20 and 32 is

$D_{20} \cap D_{32} = \{1, 2, 4\}$

Because the greatest number in the set of common positive divisors is 4, the GCD of 20 and 32 is 4, written GCD(20, 32) = 4.

The method for finding the GCD of two numbers just described, called the *intersection-of-sets method,* is rather time-consuming and tedious if the numbers have many divisors. Another, more efficient, method involves finding the prime factorization of each number. To find GCD(180, 168), first notice that $180 = 2 \cdot 2 \cdot 3 \cdot 3 \cdot 5$ and $168 = 2 \cdot 2 \cdot 2 \cdot 3 \cdot 7$. Prime factorization shows that 180 and 168 have two factors of 2 and one of 3 in common. These common primes divide both 180 and 168. In fact, the only numbers other than 1 that divide both 180 and 168 must have no more than two 2s and one 3 and no other prime factors in their prime factorizations. The possible common divisors are 1, 2, 2^2, 3, $2 \cdot 3$, and $2^2 \cdot 3$. Hence, the greatest common divisor of 180 and 168 is $2^2 \cdot 3$. This procedure works in general.

> To find the GCD of two or more numbers, first find the prime factorizations of the given numbers, then take each common prime factor of the given numbers; the GCD is the product of these common factors, each raised to the lowest power of that prime that occurs in either of the prime factorizations.

Example 5-9   Find each of the following.

(a) GCD(108, 72)
(b) GCD(x, y) if $x = 2^3 \cdot 7^2 \cdot 11 \cdot 13$ and $y = 2 \cdot 7^3 \cdot 13 \cdot 17$.
(c) GCD(x, y, z) if $z = 2^2 \cdot 7$, using x and y from part (b).

Solution   (a) Since $108 = 2^2 \cdot 3^3$, and $72 = 2^3 \cdot 3^2$, it follows that GCD(108, 72) = $2^2 \cdot 3^2 = 36$.
(b) GCD(x, y) = $2 \cdot 7^2 \cdot 13 = 1274$.
(c) Because $x = 2^3 \cdot 7^2 \cdot 11 \cdot 13$, $y = 2 \cdot 7^3 \cdot 13 \cdot 17$, and $z = 2^2 \cdot 7$, then GCD(x, y, z) = $2 \cdot 7 = 14$. Notice that GCD(x, y, z) can also be obtained by finding the GCD of z and 1274, the answer from part (b).

If we apply the prime factorization technique to finding GCD(4, 9), we see that 4 and 9 have no common prime factors. Consequently, 1 is the only common divisor, so GCD(4, 9) = 1. Numbers such as 4 and 9, whose GCD is 1, are called

relatively prime   **relatively prime.**

Some numbers are hard to factor. For these numbers another method is more efficient for finding the GCD. For example, suppose we want to find

GCD(676, 221). If we could find two smaller numbers whose GCD is the same as GCD(676, 221), our task would be easier. Observe that GCD(15, 10) = 5 and GCD(15 − 10, 10) = 5. Also, GCD(15, 6) = 3 and GCD(15 − 6, 6) = 3. Similarly, GCD(676, 221) = GCD(676 − 221, 221). From part 1 of Theorem 5-2, every divisor of 676 and 221 is also a divisor of 676 − 221 and 221. Conversely, every divisor of 676 − 221 and 221 is also a divisor of 676 and 221. Thus, the set of all the common divisors of 676 and 221 is the same as the set of all common divisors of 676 − 221 and 221. Consequently, GCD(676, 221) = GCD(676 − 221, 221). This argument holds in general, and we have the following theorem.

THEOREM 5-8

> If a and b are any whole numbers and $a \geq b$, then
>
> GCD(a, b) = GCD($a − b$, b).

Using Theorem 5-8 repeatedly, we can find the GCD of any two numbers; for example, consider GCD(676, 221). By using Theorem 5-8 several times, we have

GCD(676, 221) = GCD(676 − 221, 221)

= GCD(455, 221)	Because 676 − 221 = 455.
= GCD(234, 221)	Because 455 − 221 = 234.
= GCD(13, 221)	Because 234 − 221 = 13.

Notice that we have actually subtracted 3 · 221 from 676, and the difference is 676 − 3 · 221 = 13. Because division can be thought of as repeated subtraction, the three subtractions could have been achieved by dividing 676 by 221 and recording the remainder, as follows.

$$
\begin{array}{r}
3 \\
221\overline{)676} \\
663 \\
\hline
13
\end{array}
$$

It follows that GCD(676, 221) = GCD(13, 221). Since the only divisors of 13 are 1 and 13, the only possible values for GCD(13, 221) are 1 and 13. Because 221 = 17 · 13, we know that 13 | 221, and we have GCD(13, 221) = 13. This implies that GCD(676, 221) = 13. We could continue to use Theorem 5-8 to calculate GCD(13, 221). Because GCD(13, 221) = GCD(221, 13), we can subtract 13 from 221 as many times as needed. If 13 is subtracted from 221 seventeen times, we conclude that GCD(221, 13) = GCD(0, 13). Every integer except 0 divides 0, so GCD(0, 13) = 13. Thus, GCD(221, 13) = 13. Notice that GCD(221, 13) could also have been found using division rather than repeated subtraction:

$$\begin{array}{r} 17 \\ 13\overline{)221} \\ \underline{13} \\ 91 \\ \underline{91} \\ 0 \end{array}$$

Because the remainder in the division is 0, GCD(221, 13) = GCD(0, 13). The process of repeated division ends when we obtain a zero remainder in some division. Because each remainder is smaller than the remainder in a preceding division, we must eventually obtain a remainder of 0.

Based upon this development, Theorem 5-8 can be generalized.

THEOREM 5-9

> If a and b are any whole numbers and $a \geq b$, then GCD(a, b) = GCD(r, b), where r is the remainder when a is divided by b.

Euclidean Algorithm

Finding the GCD of two numbers by the repeated use of Theorem 5-9 until the remainder 0 is reached is referred to as the **Euclidean Algorithm.**

Example 5-10

Use the Euclidean Algorithm to find GCD(10,764, 2300).

Solution

$$\begin{array}{r} 4 \\ 2300\overline{)10{,}764} \\ \underline{9\ 200} \\ 1\ 564 \end{array}$$ Thus, GCD(10764, 2300) = GCD(2300, 1564).

$$\begin{array}{r} 1 \\ 1564\overline{)2300} \\ \underline{1564} \\ 736 \end{array}$$ Thus, GCD(2300, 1564) = GCD(1564, 736).

$$\begin{array}{r} 2 \\ 736\overline{)1564} \\ \underline{1472} \\ 92 \end{array}$$ Thus, GCD(1564, 736) = GCD(736, 92).

$$\begin{array}{r} 8 \\ 92\overline{)736} \\ \underline{736} \\ 0 \end{array}$$ Thus, GCD(736, 92) = GCD(92, 0).

Because GCD(92, 0) = 92, it follows that GCD(10,764, 2300) = 92.

Remark | The procedure for finding the GCD using the Euclidean Algorithm can be stopped at any step at which the GCD is obvious.

least common multiple (LCM)

Another useful number theory concept is least common multiple. This concept is useful for determining the least common denominator of two fractions. The **least common multiple (LCM)** of two natural numbers is the least positive multiple that the two numbers have in common. To find the LCM of two given natural numbers, we can use the intersection-of-sets method. First, find the set of all positive multiples of both the first and second numbers, then find the set of all common multiples of both numbers, and, finally, pick the least element in that set. For example, to find the LCM of 8 and 12, denote the sets of positive multiples of 8 and 12 by M_8 and M_{12}, respectively.

$M_8 = \{8, 16, 24, 32, 40, 48, 56, 64, 72, \ldots\}$

$M_{12} = \{12, 24, 36, 48, 60, 72, 84, 96, 108, \ldots\}$

The set of common multiples is

$M_8 \cap M_{12} = \{24, 48, 72, \ldots\}$

Because the least number in $M_8 \cap M_{12}$ is 24, the LCM of 8 and 12 is 24, written LCM(8, 12) = 24.

The method for finding the LCM described above is often lengthy, especially when finding the LCM of three or more natural numbers. Another, more efficient method for finding the LCM of several numbers involves prime factorization. For example, to find LCM(40, 12), first find the prime factorizations of 40 and 12, namely, $2^3 \cdot 5$ and $2^2 \cdot 3$, respectively.

Next, let $m = $ LCM(40, 12). Because m is a multiple of 40, it must contain both 2^3 and 5 as factors. Also, m is a multiple of 12, so it must contain 2^2 and 3 as factors. Since 2^3 is a multiple of 2^2, then $m = 2^3 \cdot 5 \cdot 3 = 120$. In general, we have the following:

To find the LCM of two natural numbers, first find the prime factorization of each number. Then take each of the primes that are factors of either *of the given numbers. The LCM is the product of these primes, each raised to the greatest power of that prime that occurs in either of the prime factorizations.*

Example 5-11 | Find the LCM of 2520 and 10,530.

Solution |

$$2520 = 2^3 \cdot 3^2 \cdot 5 \cdot 7$$
$$10{,}530 = 2 \cdot 3^4 \cdot 5 \cdot 13$$
$$\text{LCM}(2520, 10{,}530) = 2^3 \cdot 3^4 \cdot 5 \cdot 7 \cdot 13$$

The similarity between the prime factorization algorithms for GCD and LCM suggests a connection. Consider the GCD and LCM of 6 and 9. Because $6 = 2 \cdot 3$ and $9 = 3^2$, it follows that $GCD(6, 9) = 3$ and $LCM(6, 9) = 18$. Notice that $GCD(6,9) \cdot LCM(6, 9) = 3 \cdot 18 = 54$. Observe that 54 is also the product of the original numbers 6 and 9. In general, for any two natural numbers a and b, the connection between their GCD and LCM is given by Theorem 5-10.

THEOREM 5-10

> For any two natural numbers a and b,
>
> $GCD(a, b) \cdot LCM(a, b) = ab$

This result is useful for finding the LCM of two numbers a and b when their prime factorizations are not easy to find. $GCD(a, b)$ can be found by the Euclidean Algorithm, the product ab can be found by simple multiplication, and $LCM(a, b)$ can be found by division.

Example 5-12   Find LCM(731, 952).

Solution   By the Euclidean Algorithm, $GCD(731, 952) = 17$. By Theorem 5-10, $17 \cdot LCM(731, 952) = 731 \cdot 952$. Consequently,

$$LCM(731, 952) = \frac{731 \cdot 952}{17} = 40{,}936$$

Although Theorem 5-10 cannot be used to find the LCM of more than two numbers, it is possible to find the LCM for three or more numbers. For example, to find LCM(12, 108, 120), we can use a method similar to the one for two numbers.

$12 = 2^2 \cdot 3$

$108 = 2^2 \cdot 3^3$

$120 = 2^3 \cdot 3 \cdot 5$

Then, $LCM(12, 108, 120) = 2^3 \cdot 3^3 \cdot 5 = 1080$.

Another procedure for finding the LCM of several natural numbers involves division by primes. For example, to find LCM(12, 75, 120), we start with the least prime that divides at least one of the given numbers and divide as follows.

$2 \underline{\mid 12,\ 75,\ 120}$
  $\ \ \ 6,\ 75,\ \ 60$

Because 2 does not divide 75, simply bring down the 75. In order to obtain the

LCM using this procedure, the division process is continued until the row of answers consists of relatively prime numbers.

$$
\begin{array}{r|rrr}
2 & 12, & 75, & 120 \\
\hline
2 & 6, & 75, & 60 \\
\hline
2 & 3, & 75, & 30 \\
\hline
3 & 3, & 75, & 15 \\
\hline
5 & 1, & 25, & 5 \\
\hline
  & 1, & 5, & 1
\end{array}
$$

Thus, $\text{LCM}(12, 75, 120) = 2 \cdot 2 \cdot 2 \cdot 3 \cdot 5 \cdot 1 \cdot 5 \cdot 1 = 2^3 \cdot 3 \cdot 5^2 = 600$.

PROBLEM SET 5-3

1. Find the GCD and the LCM for each of the following using the intersection-of-sets method.
   (a) 18 and 10   (b) 24 and 36
   (c) 8, 24, and 52
2. Find the GCD and the LCM for each of the following using the prime factorization method.
   (a) 132 and 504   (b) 65 and 1690
   (c) 900, 96, and 630
3. Find the GCD for each of the following using the Euclidean Algorithm.
   (a) 220 and 2924   (b) 14,595 and 10,856
   (c) 122,368 and 123,152
4. Find the LCM for each of the following using any method.
   (a) 24 and 36   (b) 72 and 90 and 96
   (c) 90 and 105 and 315
5. Find the LCM for each of the following pairs of numbers using Theorem 5-10 and the answers from Problem 3.
   (a) 220 and 2924   (b) 14,595 and 10,856
   (c) 122,368 and 123,152
6. Find each of the following by using any method.
   (a) GCD(56, 72)   (b) GCD(84, 92)
   (c) GCD(1804, 328)   (d) LCM(56, 72)
   (e) LCM(24, 82)   (f) LCM(963, 657)
7. Bill and Sue both work at night. Bill has every sixth night off and Sue has every eighth night off. If they are both off tonight, how many nights will it be before they are both off again together?
8. Midas has 120 gold coins and 144 silver coins. He wants to place his gold coins and his silver coins in stacks so that there are the same number of coins in

each stack. What is the greatest number of coins that he can place in each stack?

9. By selling cookies at 24¢ each, José made enough money to buy several cans of pop costing 45¢ per can. If he had no money left over after buying the pop, what is the least number of cookies he could have sold?
10. Bijou I and II start their movies at 7:00 P.M. The movie at Bijou I takes 75 minutes, while the movie at Bijou II takes 90 minutes. If the shows run continuously, when will they start at the same time again?
11. Assume a and b are any natural numbers, and answer each of the following.
    (a) If $\text{GCD}(a, b) = 1$, find $\text{LCM}(a, b)$.
    (b) Find $\text{GCD}(a, a)$ and $\text{LCM}(a, a)$.
    (c) Find $\text{GCD}(a^2, a)$ and $\text{LCM}(a^2, a)$.
    (d) If $a \mid b$, find $\text{GCD}(a, b)$ and $\text{LCM}(a, b)$.
    (e) If a and b are two different primes, find $\text{GCD}(a, b)$ and $\text{LCM}(a, b)$.
    (f) What is the relationship between a and b if $\text{GCD}(a, b) = a$?
    (g) What is the relationship between a and b if $\text{LCM}(a, b) = a$?
12. Classify each of the following as true or false. Justify your answers.
    (a) If $\text{GCD}(a, b) = 1$, then a and b cannot be both even.
    (b) If $\text{GCD}(a, b) = 2$, then both a and b are even.
    (c) If a and b are even, then $\text{GCD}(a, b) = 2$.
    (d) For all natural numbers a and b, $\text{LCM}(a, b) \mid \text{GCD}(a, b)$.
    (e) For all natural numbers a and b, $\text{LCM}(a, b) \mid ab$.
    (f) $\text{GCD}(a, b) \leq a$.   (g) $\text{LCM}(a, b) \geq a$.

13. Find GCD(120, 75, 105) using the Euclidean Algorithm applied to two numbers at a time.
14. Is it true that GCD(a, b, c) · LCM(a, b, c) = abc? Justify your answer.
15. Two bike riders ride around in a circular path. The first rider completes one round in 12 minutes and the second rider completes it in 18 minutes. If they both start at the same place and the same time and go in the same direction, after how many minutes will they meet again at the starting place?
16. (a) Show that 97,219,988,751 and 4 are relatively prime.

(b) Show that 181,345,913 and 11 are relatively prime.
(c) Show that 181,345,913 and 33 are relatively prime.
17. Find all natural numbers x such that GCD(25, x) = 1 and $1 \le x \le 25$.
18. If GCD(a, b) = 1, what can be said about GCD(a^2, b^2)? Justify your answer.
19. One use of GCD is to reduce fractions to lowest terms (see Chapter 6). For example, $\frac{12}{54}$ can be reduced to $\frac{2}{9}$ by dividing both 12 and 54 by GCD(12, 54), or 6. Use the GCD to reduce each of the following.

(a) $\dfrac{28}{48}$ (b) $\dfrac{63}{99}$ (c) $\dfrac{117}{288}$ (d) $\dfrac{65}{260}$

* * * * * * * REVIEW PROBLEMS * * * * * * * *

20. Is 3111 a prime? Prove your answer.
21. Find a number with exactly six prime factors.
22. Produce the least number that is divisible by 2, 3, 4, 5, 6, 7, 8, 9, 10, and 11.

23. What is the greatest prime that must be used to determine if 2089 is prime?

*5-4   CLOCK AND MODULAR ARITHMETIC

The book *Disquisitiones Arithmeticae* is among Karl Friedrich Gauss' great mathematical works. Many problems that had been attacked without success by other mathematicians were solved by Gauss for the first time in this book. In his book, Gauss introduced a new topic, the theory of congruences, which very rapidly gained general acceptance and has since become a foundation for number theory. The basics of the theory of congruences can be understood in elementary school and can provide enrichment for students.

One type of enrichment activity involving congruences uses the arithmetic of a 12-hour clock. For example, if it is 9 o'clock, what time will it be 8 hours later? It is possible to use the clock in Figure 5-5 to determine that 8 hours after 9 o'clock is 5 o'clock. We record this as 9 $\oplus$ 8 = 5, where $\oplus$ denotes clock addition.

The answer, 9 $\oplus$ 8 = 5, can also be obtained by performing the regular addition 9 + 8 = 17 and then subtracting 12 (or by dividing 17 by 12 and taking the remainder). Thus, whenever the sum of two digits on a 12-hour clock under regular addition exceeds 12, add the numbers in the regular way and then subtract 12 to obtain the answer for clock addition.

It is possible to perform other operations on the clock. For example, 2 $\ominus$ 9 on the clock, where $\ominus$ denotes clock subtraction, could be interpreted as the time

FIGURE 5-5

9 hours before 2 o'clock. Counting backward (counterclockwise) 9 units from 2 reveals that $2 \ominus 9 = 5$. If subtraction on the clock is defined in terms of addition, we have $2 \ominus 9 = x$, if and only if $2 = 9 \oplus x$. Consequently, $x = 5$.

Example 5-13

Perform each of the following computations on a 12-hour clock.

(a) $8 \oplus 8$ (b) $4 \ominus 12$ (c) $4 \ominus 4$

Solution

(a) $8 + 8 - 12 = 4$. Hence, $8 \oplus 8 = 4$.

(b) $4 \ominus 12 = 4$, since by counting forward or backward 12 hours, you arrive at the original position.

(c) $4 \ominus 4 = 12$. This should be clear by looking at the clock, but it can also be found using the definition of subtraction in terms of addition.

As with whole numbers, clock multiplication can be defined using repeated addition. For example, $2 \otimes 8 = 8 \oplus 8 = 4$, where $\otimes$ denotes clock multiplication. Similarly, $3 \otimes 5 = (5 \oplus 5) \oplus 5 = 10 \oplus 5 = 3$. As with whole numbers, clock division can be defined in terms of multiplication. For example, $8 \oslash 5 = x$, where $\oslash$ denotes clock division, if and only if $8 = 5 \otimes x$, for a unique x in the set $\{1, 2, 3, \ldots, 12\}$. Because $5 \otimes 4 = 8$, then $8 \oslash 5 = 4$.

Example 5-14

Perform the following operations on a 12-hour clock, if possible.

(a) $3 \otimes 11$ (b) $2 \oslash 7$ (c) $3 \oslash 2$ (d) $5 \oslash 12$

Solution

(a) $3 \otimes 11 = 11 \oplus 11 \oplus 11 = 10 \oplus 11 = 9$

(b) $2 \oslash 7 = x$ if and only if $2 = 7 \otimes x$. Consequently, $x = 2$.

(c) $3 \oslash 2 = x$ if and only if $3 = 2 \otimes x$. Multiplying each of the numbers 1, 2, 3, 4, . . . , 12 by 2 shows that none of the multiplications yield 3. Thus, the equation $3 = 2 \otimes x$ has no solution, and consequently, $3 \oslash 2$ is undefined.

(d) $5 \oslash 12 = x$ if and only if $5 = 12 \otimes x$. However, $12 \otimes x = 12$ for every x in the set $\{1, 3, 4, \ldots, 12\}$. Thus, $5 = 12 \otimes x$ has no solution on the clock, and, therefore, $5 \oslash 12$ is undefined.

On a 12-hour clock, addition, subtraction, and multiplication can be performed for any two numbers but, as shown in Example 5-14, not all divisions can be performed. Division by 12, the additive identity, on a 12-hour clock can either never be performed or is not meaningful, since it does not yield a unique answer. However, there are clocks on which all divisions can be performed, except by the corresponding additive identities. One such clock is a 5-hour clock, shown in Figure 5-6.

On this clock, $3 \oplus 4 = 2$, $2 \ominus 3 = 4$, $2 \otimes 4 = 3$, and $3 \oslash 4 = 2$. Since adding 5 to any number yields the original number, 5 is the additive identity for this 5-hour clock as seen in Table 5-1(a). Consequently, you might suspect that

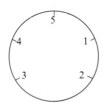

FIGURE 5-6

division by 5 is not possible on a 5-hour clock. To determine which divisions are possible, consider Table 5-1(b), a multiplication table for 5-hour clock arithmetic.

TABLE 5-1 (a)

$\oplus$	1	2	3	4	5
1	2	3	4	5	1
2	3	4	5	1	2
3	4	5	1	2	3
4	5	1	2	3	4
5	1	2	3	4	5

(b)

$\otimes$	1	2	3	4	5
1	1	2	3	4	5
2	2	4	1	3	5
3	3	1	4	2	5
4	4	3	2	1	5
5	5	5	5	5	5

To find $1 \oslash 2$, we write $1 \oslash 2 = x$, which is equivalent to $1 = 2 \otimes x$. The second row of part (b) of the table shows that $2 \otimes 1 = 2$, $2 \otimes 2 = 4$, $2 \otimes 3 = 1$, $2 \otimes 4 = 3$, and $2 \otimes 5 = 5$. The solution of $1 = 2 \otimes x$ is $x = 3$, so $1 \oslash 2 = 3$. The information given in the second row of the table can be used to determine the following divisions.

$2 \oslash 2 = 1$ because $2 = 2 \otimes 1$

$3 \oslash 2 = 4$ because $3 = 2 \otimes 4$

$4 \oslash 2 = 2$ because $4 = 2 \otimes 2$

$5 \oslash 2 = 5$ because $5 = 2 \otimes 5$

According to the table, division by 2 is always possible because every element occurs in the second row. Similarly, division by all other numbers, except 5, is always possible. In the problem set, you are asked to perform arithmetic on different clocks and investigate for which clocks all computations, except division by the additive identity, can be performed.

Many of the concepts for clock arithmetic can be used to work problems involving a calendar. On the calendar in Figure 5-7, notice that the five Sundays have dates 1, 8, 15, 22, and 29. Any two of these dates for Sunday differ by a multiple of 7. The same property is true for any other day of the week. If the second day of the month falls on Monday, then 7 days later the day will be Monday again. In fact, it will be Monday after any multiple of 7 days. For example, the second and thirtieth days fall on the same day since $30 - 2 = 28$ and 28 is a multiple of 7. We say that 30 is congruent to 2, modulo 7, and write $30 \equiv 2 \pmod 7$. Similarly, because 18 and 6 differ by a multiple of 12, we write $18 \equiv 6 \pmod{12}$. This leads to the following definition.

April

S	M	T	W	T	F	S
	1	2	3	4	5	6	7
8	9	10	11	12	13	14
15	16	17	18	19	20	21
22	23	24	25	26	27	28
29	30

FIGURE 5-7

DEFINITION

> For integers a and b, **a is congruent to b modulo m,** written $a \equiv b \pmod m$, if and only if $a - b$ is a multiple of m, where m is a positive integer greater than 1.

Example 5-15

Tell why each of the following is true.

(a) $23 \equiv 3 \pmod{10}$
(b) $23 \equiv 3 \pmod 4$
(c) $23 \not\equiv 3 \pmod 7$
(d) $10 \equiv {}^-1 \pmod{11}$
(e) $25 \equiv 5 \pmod 5$

Solution

(a) $23 \equiv 3 \pmod{10}$, because $23 - 3$ is a multiple of 10.
(b) $23 \equiv 3 \pmod 4$, because $23 - 3$ is a multiple of 4.
(c) $23 \not\equiv 3 \pmod 7$, because $23 - 3$ is not a multiple of 7.
(d) $10 \equiv {}^-1 \pmod{11}$, because $10 - ({}^-1) = 11$ is a multiple of 11.
(e) $25 \equiv 5 \pmod 5$, because $25 - 5 = 20$ is a multiple of 5.

Example 5-16

Find all integers x such that $x \equiv 1 \pmod{10}$.

Solution

$x \equiv 1 \pmod{10}$ if and only if $x - 1 = 10k$, where k is any integer. Consequently, $x = 10k + 1$. Letting $k = 0, 1, 2, 3, \ldots$ yields the sequence $1, 11, 21, 31, 41, \ldots$ Also, letting $k = {}^-1, {}^-2, {}^-3, {}^-4, \ldots$ yields the negative integers ${}^-9, {}^-19, {}^-29, {}^-39, \ldots$ The two sequences can be combined to give the solution set

$$\{\ldots, {}^-39, {}^-29, {}^-19, {}^-9, 1, 11, 21, 31, 41, 51, \ldots\}$$

In Example 5-16, the positive integers obtained, $1, 11, 21, 31, 41, 51, \ldots$, all differ from each other by a multiple of 10 and, hence, are congruent to each other modulo 10. Notice that each of the numbers $1, 11, 21, 31, 41, 51, \ldots$ has a remainder of 1 when divided by 10. In general, two whole numbers are congruent modulo m if and only if their remainders, upon division by m, are the same.

Many properties of congruence are similar to properties for equality. Several of these are listed below.

Property

For all integers a, b, and c:

1. $a \equiv a \pmod m$.
2. If $a \equiv b \pmod m$, then $b \equiv a \pmod m$.
3. If $a \equiv b \pmod m$, and $b \equiv c \pmod m$, then $a \equiv c \pmod m$.
4. If $a \equiv b \pmod m$, then $a + c \equiv b + c \pmod m$.
5. If $a \equiv b \pmod m$, then $ac \equiv bc \pmod m$.
6. If $a \equiv b \pmod m$, and $c \equiv d \pmod m$, then $ac \equiv bd \pmod m$.
7. If $a \equiv b \pmod m$ and k is a natural number, then $a^k \equiv b^k \pmod m$.

With the help of these properties, it is possible to solve many problems. For example, to find the remainder when 2^{96} is divided by 7, find a number less than 2^{96} that has the same remainder upon division by 7, that is, find a lesser number congruent to 2^{96} modulo 7. Because $2^3 = 8$, then $2^3 \equiv 1 \pmod 7$; consequently,

$(2^3)^{32} \equiv (1)^{32} \pmod 7$, or $2^{96} \equiv 1 \pmod 7$. Thus, 2^{96} gives remainder 1 when divided by 7.

Example 5-17 | Find the remainder when 3^{100} is divided by 5.

Solution |
$$3^2 \equiv 4 \pmod 5$$
$$3^3 \equiv 3 \cdot 4 \equiv 2 \pmod 5$$
$$3^3 \equiv 2 \pmod 5$$
$$3^4 \equiv 3 \cdot 2 \equiv 1 \pmod 5$$
$$3^4 \equiv 1 \pmod 5$$
$$(3^4)^{25} \equiv (1)^{25} \pmod 5$$

Therefore, $3^{100} \equiv 1 \pmod 5$. It follows that 3^{100} and 1 have the same remainder when divided by 5. Thus, 3^{100} has remainder 1 when divided by 5.

PROBLEM SET 5-4

1. Perform each of the following operations on a 12-hour clock, if possible.
   (a) $7 \oplus 8$
   (b) $4 \oplus 10$
   (c) $3 \ominus 9$
   (d) $4 \ominus 8$
   (e) $3 \otimes 9$
   (f) $4 \otimes 4$
   (g) $1 \oslash 3$
   (h) $2 \oslash 5$
2. Perform each of the following operations on a 5-hour clock.
   (a) $3 \oplus 4$
   (b) $3 \oplus 6$
   (c) $3 \otimes 4$
   (d) $1 \otimes 4$
   (e) $3 \otimes 4$
   (f) $2 \otimes 3$
   (g) $3 \oslash 4$
   (h) $1 \oslash 4$
3. (a) Construct an addition table for a 7-hour clock.
   (b) Using the addition table in (a), find $5 \ominus 6$ and $2 \ominus 5$.
   (c) Using the addition table in (a), show that subtraction can always be performed on a 7-hour clock.
4. (a) Construct a multiplication table for a 7-hour clock.
   (b) Use the multiplication table in (a) to find $3 \oslash 5$ and $4 \oslash 6$.
   (c) Use the multiplication table to find whether division by numbers different from 7 is always possible.
5. (a) Construct the multiplication tables for 3-, 4-, 6-, and 11-hour clocks.
   (b) On which of the clocks in part (a) can divisions by numbers other than the additive identity always be performed?

(c) How do the multiplication tables of clocks for which division can always be performed (except by an additive identity) differ from the multiplication tables of clocks for which division is not always meaningful?
6. On a 12-hour clock, the additive inverse of m is a number x such that $m \oplus x = 12$. Denote the additive inverse of m by ^-m and find each of the following.
   (a) additive inverse of 2
   (b) additive inverse of 3
   (c) $(^-2) \oplus (^-3)$
   (d) $^-(2 \oplus 3)$
   (e) $(^-2) \ominus (^-3)$
   (f) $(^-2) \otimes (^-3)$
7. If September 3 falls on Monday, on what day of the week will it fall the next year, if next year is a leap year?
8. Show that each of the following statements is true.
   (a) $81 \equiv 1 \pmod 8$
   (b) $81 \equiv 1 \pmod{10}$
   (c) $1000 \equiv {}^-1 \pmod{13}$
   (d) $10^{84} \equiv 1 \pmod 9$
   (e) $10^{100} \equiv 1 \pmod{11}$
   (f) $937 \equiv 37 \pmod{100}$
9. Fill in each blank in such a way that the answer is nonnegative and the least possible number.
   (a) $29 \equiv \underline{\hspace{1cm}} \pmod 5$
   (b) $3498 \equiv \underline{\hspace{1cm}} \pmod 3$
   (c) $3498 \equiv \underline{\hspace{1cm}} \pmod{11}$
   (d) $^-23 \equiv \underline{\hspace{1cm}} \pmod{10}$
10. Show that $a \equiv 0 \pmod m$, if and only if $m \mid a$.

11. Translate each of the following statements into the language of congruences.
    (a) $8 \mid 24$ (b) $3 \mid {}^-90$
    (c) Any nonzero integer n divides itself.
12. (a) Find all x such that $x \equiv 0 \pmod 2$.
    (b) Find all x such that $x \equiv 1 \pmod 2$.
    (c) Find all x such that $x \equiv 3 \pmod 5$.
13. Find the remainder for each of the following.
    (a) 5^{100} is divided by 6.   (b) 5^{101} is divided by 6.
    (c) 10^{99} is divided by 11.
★ 14. (a) Find a negative integer value for x such that $10^3 \equiv x \pmod{13}$ and $|x|$ is the least possible.
    (b) Find the remainder when 10^{99} is divided by 13.

★ 15. Use the fact that $100 \equiv 0 \pmod 4$ to find and prove a test for divisibility by 4.
★ 16. Use congruences to find and prove a divisibility test by 5, 8, 10, and 25.
★ 17. (a) Show that, in general, the cancellation property for multiplication does not hold for congruences; that is, show that $ac \equiv bc \pmod m$ does not always imply $a \equiv b \pmod m$.
    (b) Show that, in general, $a^k \equiv b^k \pmod m$ does not imply $a \equiv b \pmod m$.
★ 18. Prove each of the properties of congruences mentioned in this section.

SOLUTION TO THE PRELIMINARY PROBLEM

Understanding the Problem

A warehouse manager told a group of students that a warehouse contained 11,368 cans of juice packed in boxes of 6 or 24, depending on the size of the can. After a few moments, one of the students, Sam, announced that the total was incorrect. The problem is to determine whether Sam is correct. To solve the problem, we must assume that there are no partial boxes of cans; that is, a box must contain exactly 6 or exactly 24 cans of juice.

Devising a Plan

BRAIN TEASER

How many primes are in the following sequence?

9, 98, 987, 9876, . . . ,
987654321, 9876543219,
98765432198, . . .

We know that the boxes contain either 6 cans or 24 cans, but we do not know how many boxes of each type there are. One strategy for solving this problem is to find an equation that involves the total number of cans in all the boxes.

    The total number of cans, 11,368, equals the number of cans in all the 6-can boxes plus the number of cans in all the 24-can boxes. If there are n boxes containing 6 cans each, there are $6n$ cans altogether in those boxes. Similarly, if there are m boxes with 24 cans each, these boxes contain a total of $24m$ cans. Because the total was reported to be 11,368 cans, we have the equation $6n + 24m = 11{,}368$. Sam claimed that $6n + 24m \neq 11{,}368$.

    One way to show that $6n + 24m \neq 11{,}368$ is to show $6n + 24m$ and 11,368 do not have the same divisors. Both $6n$ and $24m$ are divisible by 6, which implies that $6n + 24m$ must be divisible by 6. If 11,368 is not divisible by 6, then Sam is correct.

Carrying Out the Plan

The divisibility test for 6 states that a number is divisible by 6 if and only if the number is divisible by both 2 and 3. Because 11,368 is an even number, it is divisible by 2. Is it divisible by 3?

The divisibility test for 3 states that a number is divisible by 3 if and only if the sum of the digits in the number is divisible by three. We see that $1 + 1 + 3 + 6 + 8 = 19$, which is not divisible by 3, so 11,368 is not divisible by 3. Hence, Sam is correct.

Looking Back

Suppose 11,368 had been divisible by 6. Would that have implied that the manager was correct? The answer is no; it would have only implied that there was not enough information given to determine the correctness of the manager's statement.

As a further Looking Back activity, suppose the manager is correct. Can we determine values for m and n? This, in fact, can be done, and if a computer is available, a program can be written to determine all possible natural number values of m and n.

In general, when can we be sure that the equation $ax + by = c$, where a, b, and c are integers, has a solution? It can be shown that if d is the greatest common divisor of a and b, then the equation has integer solutions if d divides c. If d does not divide c, there are no solutions.

QUESTIONS FROM THE CLASSROOM

1. A student claims that $a \mid a$ and $a \mid a$ implies $a \mid (a - a)$, and hence, $a \mid 0$. Is the student correct?
2. A student argues that $0 \mid 0$, since $0 = k \cdot 0$ for any integer k. How do you respond?
3. A student writes, "If $d \nmid a$ and $d \nmid b$, then $d \nmid (a + b)$." How do you respond?
4. A seventh-grade teacher just completed a unit on divisibility rules. One of the better students asks why divisibility by numbers other than 3 and 9 cannot be tested by dividing the sum of the digits by the tested number. How should you respond?
5. A student claims that a number with an even number of digits is divisible by 7, if and only if each of the numbers formed by pairing the digits into groups of two is divisible by 7. For example, 49,562,107 is divisible by 7, since each of the numbers 49, 56, 21, and 07 is divisible by 7. Is this true?
6. A sixth-grade student argues that there are infinitely many primes because "there is no end to numbers." How do you respond?
7. A student claims that a number is divisible by 21 if and only if it is divisible by 3 and by 7, and, in general, a number is divisible by $a \cdot b$ if and only if it is divisible by a and by b. What is your response?
8. A student claims that there are no integers x and y that make the equation $12x - 9y = 7$ true. How do you respond?
9. A student claims that the greatest common divisor of two numbers is always less than their least common multiple. Is the student correct?

CHAPTER OUTLINE

I. Divisibility
   A. If a and b are any integers with $b \neq 0$, then b divides a, denoted $b \mid a$, if and only if there is a unique integer c such that $a = cb$.
   B. The following are basic divisibility theorems for integers a, b, and d with $d \neq 0$.
      1. If $d \mid a$ and $d \mid b$, then $d \mid (a + b)$.
      2. If $d \mid a$ and $d \nmid b$, then $d \nmid (a + b)$.
      3. If $d \mid a$ and $d \mid b$, then $d \mid (a - b)$.
      4. If $d \mid a$ and $d \nmid b$, then $d \nmid (a - b)$.
      5. If $d \mid a$ and k is any integer, then $d \mid ka$.
   C. Divisibility tests
      1. An integer is divisible by 2, 5, or 10 if and only if the units digit of the integer is divisible by 2, 5, or 10, respectively.
      2. An integer is divisible by 4 if and only if the last two digits of the integer represent a number divisible by 4.
      3. An integer is divisible by 8 if and only if the last three digits of the integer represent a number divisible by 8.
      4. An integer is divisible by 3 or by 9 if and only if the sum of its digits is divisible by 3 or 9, respectively.
      5. An integer is divisible by 6 if and only if the integer is divisible by both 2 and 3.
      6. An integer is divisible by 7 if and only if the difference of the integer represented without its units digit and twice the units digit of the original number is divisible by 7.
      7. An integer is divisible by 11 if and only if the sum of the digits in the places that are odd powers of 10 minus the sum of the digits in the places that are even powers of 10 are divisible by 11.

II. Prime and composite numbrs
   A. Positive integers that have exactly two positive divisors—namely, 1 and themselves—are called **primes.** Integers greater than 1 that are not primes are called **composites.**
   B. **Fundamental Theorem of Arithmetic:** Every composite number has one and only one prime factorization.
   C. Criterion for determining if a given number n is prime: If n is not divisible by any prime p such that $p^2 \leq n$, then n is prime.

III. Greatest common divisor and least common multiple
   A. The **greatest common divisor (GCD)** of two or more natural numbers is the greatest divisor, or factor, that the numbers have in common.
   B. The **least common multiple (LCM)** of two or more natural numbers is the least positive multiple that the numbers have in common.
   C. **Euclidean Algorithm:** If a and b are whole numbers and $a \geq b$, then GCD$(a, b) =$ GCD(b, r), where r is the remainder when a is divided by b. The procedure of finding the GCD of two numbers a and b by using the above result repeatedly is called the *Euclidean Algorithm.*
   D. GCD$(a, b) \cdot$ LCM$(a, b) = ab$.

* IV. Clock and modular arithmetic
   A. For any integers a and b, **a is congruent to b modulo m** if and only if $a - b$ is a multiple of m, where m is a positive integer greater than 1.
   B. Two integers are congruent modulo m if and only if their remainders upon division by m are the same.

CHAPTER TEST

1. Classify each of the following as true or false.
   (a) $8 \mid 4$ (b) $0 \mid 4$ (c) $4 \mid 0$
   (d) If a number is divisible by 4 and by 6, then it is divisible by 24.
   (e) If a number is not divisible by 12, then it is not divisible by 3.

2. Classify each of the following as true or false. If false, show a counterexample.
   (a) If $7 \mid x$ and $7 \nmid y$, then $7 \nmid xy$.
   (b) If $d \nmid (a + b)$, then $d \nmid a$, and $d \nmid b$.
   (c) If $16 \mid 10^4$, then $16 \mid 10^6$.
   (d) If $d \mid (a + b)$ and $d \nmid a$, then $d \nmid b$.
   (e) If $d \mid (x + y)$ and $d \mid x$, then $d \mid y$.
   (f) If $4 \nmid x$ and $4 \nmid y$, then $4 \nmid xy$.

3. Test each of the following numbers for divisibility by 2, 3, 4, 5, 6, 7, 8, 9, and 11.
   (a) 83,160   (b) 83,193
4. Assume that 10,007 is prime. Without actually dividing 10,024 by 17, prove that 10,024 is not divisible by 17.
5. Prove the test for divisibility by 9 using a three-digit number n such that $n = a \cdot 10^2 + b \cdot 10 + c$.
6. Determine whether each of the following numbers is prime or composite.
   (a) 143   (b) 223
7. How can you tell if a number is divisible by 24? Check 4152 for divisibility by 24.

8. Find the GCD for each of the following.
   (a) 24 and 52   (b) 5767 and 4453
9. Find the LCM for each of the following.
   (a) $2^3 \cdot 5^2 \cdot 7^3$ and $2 \cdot 5^3 \cdot 7^2 \cdot 13$, and $2^4 \cdot 5 \cdot 7^4 \cdot 29$
   (b) 278 and 279
10. Construct a number with exactly five divisors.
11. Find all divisors of 144.
12. Find the prime factorization of each of the following.
   (a) 172   (b) 288   (c) 260   (d) 111
13. Jane and Ramon run 100 laps in the gym. If they start at the same time and place and go in the same direction with Jane running 5 laps per minute and Ramon running 3 laps per minute, how many times are they together at the starting place?

SELECTED BIBLIOGRAPHY

Adams, V. "A Variation on the Algorithm for GCD and LCM." *Arithmetic Teacher* 30 (November 1982):46.

Avital, S. "The Plight and Might of Number Seven." *Arithmetic Teacher* 25 (February 1978):22–24.

Bezuszka, S. "Even Perfect Numbers—An Update." *The Mathematics Teacher* 74 (September 1981):460–463.

Brown, S. *Some Prime Comparisons*. National Council of Teachers of Mathematics, 1978.

Burton, G., and J. Knifong. "Definitions for Prime Numbers." *Arithmetic Teacher* 27 (February 1980):44–47.

Cassidy, C., and B. Hodgson. "Because a Door Has to be Open or Closed. . ." *The Mathematics Teacher* 75 (February 1982):155–158.

Cavanaugh, W. "The Spirograph and the Greatest Common Factor." *The Mathematics Teacher* 68 (February 1975):162–163.

Duncan, D., and B. Litwiller. "A Pattern in Number Theory: Example Generalization Proof." *The Mathematics Teacher* 64 (November 1971):661–664.

Engle, J. "A Rediscovered Test for Divisibility by Eleven." *The Mathematics Teacher* 69 (December 1976):669.

Gullen, G., III. "The Smallest Prime Factor of a Natural Number." *The Mathematics Teacher* 67 (April 1974):329–332.

Hadar, N. "Odd and Even Numbers—Magician's Approach." *The Mathematics Teacher* 75 (May 1982):408–412.

Henry, B. "Modulo 7 Arithmetic—A Perfect Example of Field Properties." *The Mathematics Teacher* 65 (October 1972):525–528.

Henry, L. "Another Look at Least Common Multiple and Greatest Common Factor." *Arithmetic Teacher* 25 (March 1978):52–53.

Hoffer, A. "What You Always Wanted to Know about Six But Have Been Afraid to Ask." *The Arithmetic Teacher* 20 (March 1973):173–180.

Hohfold, J. "An Inductive Approach to Prime Factors." *Arithmetic Teacher* 29 (December 1981):28–29.

Johnson, P. "Understanding the Check of Nines." *Arithmetic Teacher* 26 (November 1978):54–55.

Kennedy, R. "Divisibility for Integers Ending in 1, 3, 7, or 9." *The Mathematics Teacher* 64 (February 1971):137–138.

Lappan, G., and M. Winter. "Prime Factorizations." *Arithmetic Teacher* 27 (March 1980):24–27.

Long, C. "A Simpler '7' Divisibility Rule." *The Mathematics Teacher* 64 (May 1971):473–475.

Mann, N., III. "Modulo Systems: One More Step." *The Mathematics Teacher* 65 (March 1972):207–209.

Ore, O. *Invitation to Number Theory*. New York: Random House, The L. W. Singer Company New Mathematical Library, 1967.

Parkerson, E. "Patterns in Divisibility." *Arithmetic Teacher* 25 (January 1978):58.

Prielipp, R. "Perfect Numbers, Abundant Numbers, and Deficient Numbers." *The Mathematics Teacher* 63 (December 1970):692–696.

Rockwell, C. "Another 'Sieve' for Prime Numbers." *The Arithmetic Teacher* 20 (November 1973):603–605.

Roy, S. "LCM and GCF in the Hundred Chart." *Arithmetic Teacher* 26 (December 1978):53.

Scheuer, D., Jr. "All-Star GCF." *Arithmetic Teacher* 26 (November 1978):34–35.

Sconyers, J. "Prime Numbers—A Locust's View." *The Mathematics Teacher* 74 (February 1981):105–108.

Sherzer, L. "A Simplified Presentation for Finding the LCM and the GCF." *The Arithmetic Teacher* 21 (May 1974):415–416.

Singer, R. "Modular Arithmetic and Divisibility Criteria." *The Mathematics Teacher* 63 (December 1970):653–656.

Smith, L. "A General Test of Divisibility." *The Mathematics Teacher* 71 (November 1978):668–669.

Snover, S., and M. Spikell. "Problem Solving and Programming: The License Plate Curiosity." *The Mathematics Teacher* 74 (November 1981):616–617.

Stock, M. "On What Day Were You Born?" *The Mathematics Teacher* 65 (January 1972):73–75.

Szetela, W. "A General Divisibility Test for Whole Numbers." *The Mathematics Teacher* 73 (March 1980):223–225.

Tucker, B. "The Division Algorithm." *The Arithmetic Teacher* 20 (December 1973):639–646.

White, P. "An Application of Clock Arithmetic." *The Mathematics Teacher* 66 (November 1973):645–647.

Yazbak, N. "Some Unusual Tests of Divisibility." *The Mathematics Teacher* 69 (December 1976):669.

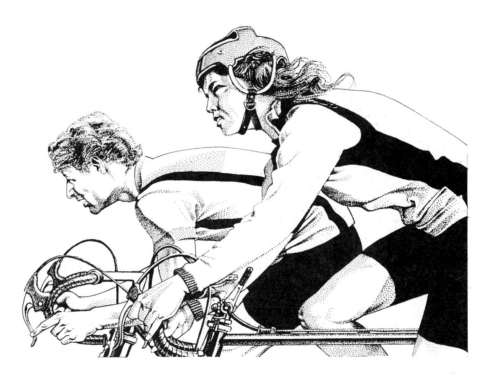

PRELIMINARY PROBLEM

Two cyclists, David and Sara, started riding their bikes at 9:00 A.M. at City Hall. They followed the local bike trail, and returned to City Hall at the same time. However, David rode three times as long as Sara rested on her trip and Sara rode four times as long as David rested on his trip. Assuming that each cyclist rode at a constant speed, who rode faster?

INTRODUCTION

The early Egyptian numeration system had symbols for fractions with numerators of 1. For example, one-third was 𓏢 , and one-tenth was 𓎺 . Most fractions other than unit fractions (fractions with numerators of 1) were expressed as a sum of two different unit fractions; for example, seven-twelfths was one-third plus one-fourth.

Table 6-1 shows how fractions are used in several different ways.

TABLE 6-1

Use	Example
Division problem or solution to a multiplication problem	The solution to $2x = 3$ is $\frac{3}{2}$.
Partition or part of a whole	Joe received one-half of Mary's salary each month for alimony.
Ratio	The ratio of Republicans to Democrats in the Senate is three to five.

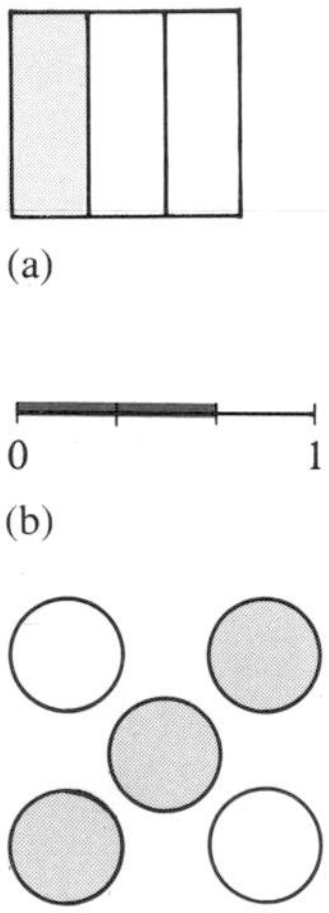

(a)

(b)

(c)

FIGURE 6-1

Figure 6-1 illustrates the use of fractions as a part of a whole and as part of a given set. For example, in Figure 6-1(a), one part out of three congruent parts, or $\frac{1}{3}$ of the rectangle, is shaded. In Figure 6-1(b), two parts out of three parts, or $\frac{2}{3}$ of the unit segment, are shaded. In Figure 6-1(c), three circles out of five circles, or $\frac{3}{5}$ of the circles, are shaded.

6-1 THE SET OF RATIONAL NUMBERS

rational numbers

Numbers represented by fractions such as $\frac{1}{3}$, $\frac{3}{5}$, and $\frac{2}{3}$ belong to the set of **rational numbers.**

DEFINITION

> A rational number is a number that can be represented by $\frac{a}{b}$, where a and b are integers and $b \neq 0$.

numerator

denominator

In the rational number $\frac{a}{b}$, a is called the **numerator** and b is called the **denominator.** The rational number $\frac{a}{b}$ may also be represented as a/b or as $a \div b$.

(a)

(b)

FIGURE 6-2

The set of rational numbers, denoted by Q, can be written as follows.

$$Q = \left\{ \frac{a}{b} \;\middle|\; a \text{ and } b \text{ are integers and } b \neq 0 \right\}$$

If we use the division representation of a fraction, then $a \div 1 = \frac{a}{1}$. Since $a \div 1 - a$, every integer a can be written as $\frac{a}{1}$. This shows that the set of integers is a subset of the set of rational numbers. Also, the set of rational numbers is a proper subset of a set of numbers of the form $\frac{a}{b}$, called *fractions*, where a and b are not necessarily integers. All the properties of rational numbers developed in this chapter also hold for fractions in general.

equivalent

In Figure 6-2(a), one of three congruent parts, or $\frac{1}{3}$, is shaded. Also, in Figure 6-2(a) two of the six congruent parts, or $\frac{2}{6}$, are shaded. Thus, both $\frac{1}{3}$ and $\frac{2}{6}$ represent exactly the same shaded portion. Although $\frac{1}{3}$ and $\frac{2}{6}$ do not look alike, they represent the same rational number. Strictly speaking, $\frac{1}{3}$ and $\frac{2}{6}$ are **equivalent** rational numbers. However, in most applications, we may consider $\frac{1}{3}$ and $\frac{2}{6}$ equal. As a result, we write $\frac{1}{3} = \frac{2}{6}$.

Figure 6-2(b) shows the rectangle subdivided into twelve parts, with four parts shaded. Thus, $\frac{1}{3}$ is equivalent to $\frac{4}{12}$ because the same portion of the model is covered. Similarly, we could illustrate that $\frac{1}{3}$, , $\frac{4}{12}$, $\frac{8}{24}$, . . . are equivalent. In other words, there are infinitely many ways of naming the rational number $\frac{1}{3}$. Similarly, there are infinitely many ways of naming any rational number.

This process of generating fractions equivalent to $\frac{1}{3}$ can be thought of as follows: If each of 3 equally sized parts of a whole are halved, there must be twice as many of the smaller pieces. Hence, $\frac{1}{3} = \frac{2}{6}$. Similarly, $\frac{1}{3} = \frac{4}{12}$ because if each of three equally sized parts of a whole are divided into four equally sized parts, then there must be four times as many of the smaller pieces. In general, we have the following property of fractions, called the *Fundamental Law of Fractions*.

Property

Fundamental Law of Fractions   For any rational number $\frac{a}{b}$ and any integer $c \neq 0$,

$$\frac{a}{b} = \frac{ac}{bc}$$

The Fundamental Law of Fractions may be stated in words as follows: *The value of a fraction does not change if its numerator and denominator are multiplied by the same nonzero number.* However, the Fundamental Law of Fractions does not imply that adding the same nonzero number to the numerator and the denominator results in an equivalent fraction. For example,

$$\frac{1}{2} \neq \frac{1+2}{2+2}, \quad \text{or} \quad \frac{3}{4}$$

Example 6-1	Find a value for x so that $\dfrac{x}{210} = \dfrac{12}{42}$.
Solution	By the Fundamental Law of Fractions,

$$\frac{12}{42} = \frac{12c}{42c} \qquad \text{where } c \text{ is an integer such that } c \neq 0.$$

Let $42c = 210$. Then, $c = 5$. Thus,

$$\frac{12}{42} = \frac{12 \cdot 5}{42 \cdot 5} = \frac{60}{210}$$

Hence, $x = 60$.

Example 6-2	Find the set, S, of all rational numbers, each of whose elements is equivalent to $\frac{3}{5}$.
Solution	

$$\frac{3}{5} = \frac{3 \cdot 2}{5 \cdot 2} = \frac{3 \cdot 3}{5 \cdot 3} = \frac{3 \cdot 4}{5 \cdot 4} = \frac{3 \cdot 5}{5 \cdot 5} = \cdots$$

Also,

$$\frac{3}{5} = \frac{3(^-1)}{5(^-1)} = \frac{3(^-2)}{5(^-2)} = \frac{3(^-3)}{5(^-3)} = \cdots$$

So,

$$S = \left\{ \frac{a}{b} \;\middle|\; \frac{a}{b} = \frac{3c}{5c}, \text{ where } c \text{ is an integer and } c \neq 0 \right\}$$

The Fundamental Law of Fractions implies

$$\frac{ac}{bc} = \frac{a}{b} \qquad \text{where } c \neq 0.$$

This justifies a process often referred to as *reducing fractions*. For example,

$$\frac{60}{210} = \frac{6 \cdot 10}{21 \cdot 10} = \frac{6}{21}$$

Also,

$$\frac{6}{21} = \frac{2 \cdot 3}{7 \cdot 3} = \frac{2}{7}$$

We can reduce $\frac{60}{210}$ because the numerator and denominator have a common factor of 10. Also, we can reduce $\frac{6}{21}$ because 6 and 21 have a common factor of 3. However, we cannot reduce $\frac{2}{7}$ because 2 and 7 have no common factors other than 1. The fraction $\frac{2}{7}$ is called the **simplest form** of $\frac{60}{210}$. In general, $\dfrac{a}{b}$ *is the*

simplest form

simplest form of a fraction if a and b have no common factor other than 1, that is, if a and b are relatively prime. Finding the simplest form of $\frac{60}{210}$ can be achieved with fewer steps by writing

$$\frac{60}{210} = \frac{2 \cdot 30}{7 \cdot 30} = \frac{2}{7}$$

The number 30 is the GCD of 60 and 210. This process amounts to dividing 60 and 210 by their greatest common divisor, 30. In general, the fraction $\frac{a}{b}$ can be reduced to its simplest form by dividing a and b by GCD(a, b).

Example 6-3

Write each of the following in simplest form.

(a) $\dfrac{45}{60}$

(b) $\dfrac{35}{17}$

Solution

(a) GCD(45, 60) = 15, so $\dfrac{45}{60} = \dfrac{3 \cdot 15}{4 \cdot 15} = \dfrac{3}{4}$.

Another method for writing the fraction in simplest form is to find the prime factorization of the numerator and denominator and then to divide both numerator and denominator by common primes.

$$\frac{45}{60} = \frac{3 \cdot 3 \cdot 5}{2 \cdot 2 \cdot 3 \cdot 5} = \frac{3 \cdot 3}{2 \cdot 2 \cdot 3} = \frac{3}{2 \cdot 2} = \frac{3}{4}$$

(b) GCD(35, 17) = 1, so $\frac{35}{17}$ is in simplest form.

It is often possible to reduce an algebraic fraction—that is, a fraction involving variables—to its simplest form. For example,

$$\frac{a^2 b}{ab^2} = \frac{a \cdot (ab)}{b \cdot (ab)} = \frac{a}{b}$$

Example 6-4

Write each of the following in simplest form.

(a) $\dfrac{28ab^2}{42a^2b^2}$ (b) $\dfrac{(a+b)^2}{3a+3b}$ (c) $\dfrac{x^2+x}{x+1}$ (d) $\dfrac{3+x^2}{3x}$ (e) $\dfrac{3+3x^2}{3x}$

Solution

(a) $\dfrac{28ab^2}{42a^2b^2} = \dfrac{2 \cdot (14ab^2)}{3a \cdot (14ab^2)} = \dfrac{2}{3a}$

(b) $\dfrac{(a+b)^2}{3a+3b} = \dfrac{(a+b) \cdot (a+b)}{3 \cdot (a+b)} = \dfrac{a+b}{3}$

(c) $\dfrac{x^2+x}{x+1} = \dfrac{x(x+1)}{x+1} = \dfrac{x \cdot (x+1)}{1 \cdot (x+1)} = \dfrac{x}{1} = x$

(d) $\dfrac{3 + x^2}{3x}$ cannot be further reduced because $3 + x^2$ and $3x$ have no factors in common except 1.

(e) $\dfrac{3 + 3x^2}{3x} = \dfrac{3 \cdot (1 + x^2)}{3 \cdot x} = \dfrac{1 + x^2}{x}$

Two fractions such as $\frac{12}{42}$ and $\frac{10}{35}$ can be shown to be equivalent by several methods.

1. Reduce both fractions to the same simplest form.

$$\dfrac{12}{42} = \dfrac{2^2 \cdot 3}{2 \cdot 3 \cdot 7} = \dfrac{2}{7} \quad \text{and} \quad \dfrac{10}{35} = \dfrac{5 \cdot 2}{5 \cdot 7} = \dfrac{2}{7}$$

Thus,

$$\dfrac{12}{42} = \dfrac{10}{35}$$

2. Rewrite both fractions with a common denominator (not necessarily the least). A common multiple of 42 and 35 may be found by finding the product $42 \cdot 35$ or 1470. Now,

$$\dfrac{12}{42} = \dfrac{420}{1470} \quad \text{and} \quad \dfrac{10}{35} = \dfrac{420}{1470}$$

Hence,

$$\dfrac{12}{42} = \dfrac{10}{35}$$

3. Rewrite both fractions with the same least common denominator. Since the LCM(42, 35) = 210, then

$$\dfrac{12}{42} = \dfrac{60}{210} \quad \text{and} \quad \dfrac{10}{35} = \dfrac{60}{210}$$

Thus,

$$\dfrac{12}{42} = \dfrac{10}{35}$$

The second method suggests a general algorithm for determining if two fractions $\dfrac{a}{b}$ and $\dfrac{c}{d}$ are equal. Rewrite both fractions with common denominator bd. That is,

$$\dfrac{a}{b} = \dfrac{ad}{bd} \quad \text{and} \quad \dfrac{c}{d} = \dfrac{cb}{bd}$$

Because the denominators are the same, $\dfrac{ad}{bd} = \dfrac{cb}{bd}$ if and only if $ad = cb$. For example, $\frac{24}{36} = \frac{6}{9}$ because $24 \cdot 9 = 216 = 36 \cdot 6$. In general, the following property results.

Property | Two rational numbers, $\frac{a}{b}$ and $\frac{c}{d}$, are equal if and only if $ad = bc$.

Using a calculator, we can determine if two fractions are equivalent by using the property that $\frac{a}{b} = \frac{c}{d}$ if and only if $ad = bc$. We see that $\frac{2}{4} = \frac{1098}{2196}$ since both $\boxed{2}\ \boxed{\times}$ $\boxed{2}\ \boxed{1}\ \boxed{9}\ \boxed{6}\ \boxed{=}$ and $\boxed{4}\ \boxed{\times}\ \boxed{1}\ \boxed{0}\ \boxed{9}\ \boxed{8}\ \boxed{=}$ yield a display of 4392.

PROBLEM SET 6-1

1. Write a sentence illustrating $\frac{7}{8}$ used in each of the following ways.
   (a) As a division problem.
   (b) As a part of a whole.
   (c) As a ratio.
2. For each of the following, write a fraction to represent the shaded portion.

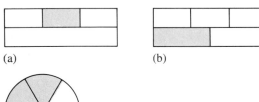

(a)   (b)

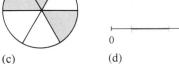

(c)   (d)

3. For each of the following, write three fractions equivalent to the given fraction.
   (a) $\frac{2}{9}$ (b) $\frac{^-2}{5}$ (c) $\frac{0}{3}$ (d) $\frac{a}{2}$

4. Find the simplest form for each of the following fractions.
   (a) $\frac{156}{93}$ (b) $\frac{27}{45}$ (c) $\frac{^-65}{91}$
   (d) $\frac{6629}{70,395}$ (e) $\frac{0}{68}$ (f) $\frac{84^2}{91^2}$

5. Determine if the following pairs are equal by writing each in simplest form.
   (a) $\frac{3}{8}$ and $\frac{375}{1000}$ (b) $\frac{18}{54}$ and $\frac{23}{69}$
   (c) $\frac{6}{10}$ and $\frac{600}{1000}$ (d) $\frac{17}{27}$ and $\frac{25}{45}$
   (e) $\frac{24}{36}$ and $\frac{6}{9}$ (f) $\frac{^-7}{49}$ and $\frac{^-14}{98}$

6. Determine if the following pairs are equal by changing both to the same denominator.
   (a) $\frac{10}{16}$ and $\frac{12}{18}$ (b) $\frac{3}{12}$ and $\frac{41}{154}$
   (c) $\frac{3}{^-12}$ and $\frac{^-36}{144}$ (d) $\frac{^-21}{86}$ and $\frac{^-51}{215}$
   (e) $\frac{6}{10}$ and $\frac{6000}{10,000}$ (f) $\frac{^-a}{b}$ and $\frac{a}{^-b}$

7. (a) If $\frac{a}{c} = \frac{b}{c}$, what must be true?
   (b) If $\frac{a}{b} = \frac{a}{c}$, what must be true?

8. Solve for x in each of the following.
   (a) $\frac{2}{3} = \frac{x}{16}$ (b) $\frac{3}{4} = \frac{^-27}{x}$ (c) $\frac{3}{x} = \frac{3x}{x^2}$

9. Represent each of the following as a fraction.
   (a) The dots inside the circle as a part of all the dots in the figure.
   (b) The dots inside the rectangle as a part of all the dots in the figure.
   (c) The dots in the intersection of the rectangle and the circle as a part of all the dots in the figure.
   (d) The dots outside the circle but inside the rectangle as part of all the dots in the figure.

10. Mr. Gonzales and Ms. Price gave the same test to their fifth-grade classes. In Mr. Gonzales' class, 20 out of 25 students passed the test, and in Ms. Price's class, 24 out of 30 students passed the test. One of Ms. Price's students heard about the results of the tests and claimed that the classes did equally well. Is the student right? Explain.

11. Find the simplest form for each of the following fractions.

(a) $\dfrac{x}{x}$

(b) $\dfrac{14x^2y}{63xy^2}$

(c) $\dfrac{a^2 + ab}{a + b}$

(d) $\dfrac{a^3 + 1}{a^3b}$

(e) $\dfrac{a}{3a + ab}$

(f) $\dfrac{a}{3a + b}$

12. Let W be the set of whole numbers, I be the set of integers, and Q be the set of rational numbers. Classify each of the following as true or false.

(a) $W \subseteq Q$

(b) $(I \cup W) \subset Q$

(c) If Q is the universal set, $\bar{I} = W$.

(d) $Q \cap I = W$

(e) $Q \cap W = W$

13. Use a calculator to check whether each of the following pairs of fractions are equivalent.

(a) $\dfrac{24}{31}$ and $\dfrac{23}{30}$

(b) $\dfrac{86}{75}$ and $\dfrac{85}{74}$

(c) $\dfrac{1513}{1691}$ and $\dfrac{1581}{1767}$

6-2 ADDITION AND SUBTRACTION OF RATIONAL NUMBERS

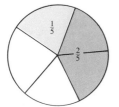

FIGURE 6-3

To be able to describe mathematically the amount of liquid in a cup when $\frac{1}{3}$ cup of water is added to $\frac{1}{2}$ cup of water, it is necessary to add rational numbers. Before adding rational numbers with unlike denominators, we try the simpler problem of adding fractions with like denominators. For example, suppose a pizza is divided into five parts of equal size. If one person ate one piece of the pizza and another ate two pieces of the pizza, then they ate $\frac{1}{5}$ and $\frac{2}{5}$ of the pizza, respectively, as shown in Figure 6-3.

We see from the figure that $\frac{3}{5}$ of the pizza was eaten. That is, $\frac{1}{5} + \frac{2}{5} = \frac{3}{5}$, or

$$\frac{1}{5} + \frac{2}{5} = \frac{1 + 2}{5}$$

In a similar manner, we can find the sum of any two rational numbers, $\dfrac{a}{b}$ and $\dfrac{c}{b}$, where the denominators are the same.

DEFINITION

If $\dfrac{a}{b}$ and $\dfrac{c}{b}$ are rational numbers, then $\dfrac{a}{b} + \dfrac{c}{b} = \dfrac{a + c}{b}$.

Example 6-5

Find each sum.

(a) $\dfrac{4}{6} + \dfrac{5}{6}$

(b) $\dfrac{5}{18} + \dfrac{11}{18}$

Solution

(a) $\dfrac{4}{6} + \dfrac{5}{6} = \dfrac{4 + 5}{6} = \dfrac{9}{6}$

(b) $\dfrac{5}{18} + \dfrac{11}{18} = \dfrac{5 + 11}{18} = \dfrac{16}{18}$

The sum of two rational numbers can also be found using a number line. For example, to compute $\frac{1}{5} + \frac{2}{5}$, we use a number line with one unit divided into fifths, as shown in Figure 6-4.

FIGURE 6-4

To determine how to add two fractions with unequal denominators—for example, $\frac{3}{8} + \frac{1}{6}$—we use the strategy of changing the problem into an equivalent problem that we already know how to do. We know how to add fractions with the same denominators, so we rewrite $\frac{3}{8}$ and $\frac{1}{6}$ with the same denominators. We wrote fractions with the same denominators to determine if fractions were equal. One way to accomplish this is to find the product of the denominators, $6 \cdot 8$ or 48. Because

$$\frac{3}{8} = \frac{3 \cdot 6}{8 \cdot 6} \quad \text{and} \quad \frac{1}{6} = \frac{8 \cdot 1}{8 \cdot 6}$$

we have

$$\frac{3}{8} + \frac{1}{6} = \frac{3 \cdot 6}{8 \cdot 6} + \frac{8 \cdot 1}{8 \cdot 6} = \frac{3 \cdot 6 + 8 \cdot 1}{8 \cdot 6} = \frac{18 + 8}{48} = \frac{26}{48}$$

In general, given two fractions $\frac{a}{b}$ and $\frac{c}{d}$, we may add the fractions as follows.

$$\frac{a}{b} + \frac{c}{d} = \frac{a \cdot d}{b \cdot d} + \frac{b \cdot c}{b \cdot d} = \frac{ad + bc}{bd}$$

We summarize this property below.

Property | If $\frac{a}{b}$ and $\frac{c}{d}$ are any two fractions, then $\frac{a}{b} + \frac{c}{d} = \frac{ad + bc}{bd}$.

Example 6-6 | Find each of the following sums.

(a) $\dfrac{2}{15} + \dfrac{4}{21}$ (b) $\dfrac{2}{-3} + \dfrac{1}{5}$

Solution | (a) $\dfrac{2}{15} + \dfrac{4}{21} = \dfrac{2 \cdot 21 + 15 \cdot 4}{15 \cdot 21} = \dfrac{102}{315}$, or $\dfrac{34}{105}$

(b) $\dfrac{2}{-3} + \dfrac{1}{5} = \dfrac{(2)(5) + (^-3)(1)}{(^-3)(5)} = \dfrac{10 + ^-3}{^-15} = \dfrac{7}{^-15}$

| Remark | Because $\dfrac{7}{-15} = \dfrac{7(^-1)}{-15(^-1)} = \dfrac{^-7}{15}$, then $\dfrac{7}{-15} = \dfrac{^-7}{15}$. Although $\dfrac{7}{-15}$ is an accept-able answer, $\dfrac{^-7}{15}$ is the preferred form for the answer because it is customary to write fractions with positive denominators. (We later show that $\dfrac{^-7}{15} = -\dfrac{7}{15}$.) |

In Example 6-6(a), we used the product of the denominators as a common denominator to add the fractions $\frac{2}{15}$ and $\frac{4}{21}$. We also could find LCM(15, 21), which is the *least common denominator* for these two fractions. Because LCM(15, 21) = 105, we have the following.

$$\frac{2}{15} + \frac{4}{21} = \frac{14}{105} + \frac{20}{105} = \frac{34}{105}$$

mixed number   The sum of an integer and a rational number is often written as a **mixed number.** For example, $1 + \frac{3}{4}$ can be written as $1\frac{3}{4}$. A mixed number can always be written as a rational number in the form $\dfrac{a}{b}$. For example,

$$1\frac{3}{4} = 1 + \frac{3}{4} = \frac{1}{1} + \frac{3}{4} = \frac{1 \cdot 4 + 1 \cdot 3}{1 \cdot 4} = \frac{4 + 3}{4} = \frac{7}{4}$$

improper fraction   Thus, $1\frac{3}{4} = \frac{7}{4}$. A fraction of the form $\dfrac{a}{b}$, where $0 < |b| \leq |a|$, is called an **improper**

proper fraction   **fraction.** A fraction $\dfrac{a}{b}$, where $0 \leq |a| < |b|$, is called a **proper fraction.** For example, $\frac{7}{4}$ and $\frac{4}{4}$ are improper fractions and $\frac{4}{7}$ is a proper fraction. Every improper fraction can be written as a mixed number, and, conversely, every mixed number can be written as an improper fraction. Children sometimes infer that $1\frac{3}{4}$ means 1 times $\frac{3}{4}$, since $y\frac{3}{4}$ means $y \cdot \frac{3}{4}$. This is not the case; $1\frac{3}{4}$ means $1 + \frac{3}{4}$. Also, the number $^-4\frac{3}{4}$ means $^-(4 + \frac{3}{4})$, not $^-4 + \frac{3}{4}$.

Example 6-7	Change each of the following mixed numbers to improper fractions.
	(a) $4\frac{1}{3}$ (b) $^-3\frac{2}{5}$
Solution	(a) $4\frac{1}{3} = 4 + \frac{1}{3} = \frac{4}{1} + \frac{1}{3} = \dfrac{4 \cdot 3 + 1 \cdot 1}{1 \cdot 3} = \dfrac{12 + 1}{3} = \dfrac{13}{3}$
	(b) $^-3\frac{2}{5} = {}^-(3 + \frac{2}{5}) = {}^-\left(\dfrac{3}{1} + \dfrac{2}{5}\right) = {}^-\left(\dfrac{3 \cdot 5 + 1 \cdot 2}{1 \cdot 5}\right) = \dfrac{^-17}{5}$

Example 6-8	Change $\frac{29}{5}$ to a mixed number.
Solution	By the Division Algorithm, $29 = 5 \cdot 5 + 4$. Thus,
	$\dfrac{29}{5} = \dfrac{5 \cdot 5 + 4}{5} = \dfrac{5 \cdot 5}{5} + \dfrac{4}{5} = 5 + \dfrac{4}{5} = 5\dfrac{4}{5}$

In elementary schools, problems like Example 6-8 are usually solved using division.

$$\begin{array}{r} 5 \\ 5\overline{)29} \\ \underline{25} \\ 4 \end{array}$$

Hence, $\frac{29}{5} = 5 + \frac{4}{5} = 5\frac{4}{5}$.

Example 6-9   Find $2\frac{4}{5} + 3\frac{5}{6}$.

Solution   The problem is solved in two ways for comparison.

Change each mixed number into an improper fraction.

$$2\frac{4}{5} + 3\frac{5}{6} = \frac{14}{5} + \frac{23}{6}$$

$$= \frac{14 \cdot 6 + 5 \cdot 23}{5 \cdot 6}$$

$$= \frac{84 + 115}{30}$$

$$= \frac{199}{30}$$

$$= 6\frac{19}{30}$$

Add the integers in the mixed numbers and add the fractional parts of the mixed numbers separately.

$$\begin{array}{rl} 2\frac{4}{5} = & 2\frac{24}{30} \\ + 3\frac{5}{6} = & + 3\frac{25}{30} \\ \hline & 5\frac{49}{30} \end{array}$$

But,

$$\frac{49}{30} = 1\frac{19}{30}$$

so

$$5\frac{49}{30} = 5 + \frac{49}{30} = 5 + 1\frac{19}{30} = 6\frac{19}{30}$$

As with integers, rational numbers have the following properties under addition.

Properties

Closure Property for Addition of Rational Numbers   If $\frac{a}{b}$ and $\frac{c}{d}$ are any rational numbers, then $\frac{a}{b} + \frac{c}{d}$ is a unique rational number.

Commutative Property for Addition of Rational Numbers   If $\frac{a}{b}$ and $\frac{c}{d}$ are rational numbers, then $\frac{a}{b} + \frac{c}{d} = \frac{c}{d} + \frac{a}{b}$.

Associative Property for Addition of Rational Numbers   If $\frac{a}{b}, \frac{c}{d}$, and $\frac{e}{f}$ are rational numbers, then $\left(\frac{a}{b} + \frac{c}{d}\right) + \frac{e}{f} = \frac{a}{b} + \left(\frac{c}{d} + \frac{e}{f}\right)$.

Additive Identity Property of Rational Numbers The number 0 is the unique number such that for every rational number $\frac{a}{b}$, $0 + \frac{a}{b} = \frac{a}{b} = \frac{a}{b} + 0$.

Additive Inverse Property of Rational Numbers   For any rational number $\frac{a}{b}$, the additive inverse is $-\frac{a}{b}$. That is, $-\frac{a}{b}$ is the unique rational number having the property that $\frac{a}{b} + \left(-\frac{a}{b}\right) = 0 = \left(-\frac{a}{b}\right) + \frac{a}{b}$.

Another form of $-\frac{a}{b}$ can be found by considering the sum $\frac{a}{b} + \frac{^-a}{b}$. Because

$$\frac{a}{b} + \frac{^-a}{b} = \frac{a + {^-a}}{b} = \frac{0}{b} = 0$$

$-\frac{a}{b}$ and $\frac{^-a}{b}$ are both additive inverses of $\frac{a}{b}$, so $-\frac{a}{b} = \frac{^-a}{b}$. Also, since $\frac{^-a}{b} = \frac{a}{^-b}$, then $-\frac{a}{b} = \frac{a}{^-b}$.

Example 6-10

Find the additive inverses for each of the following.

(a) $\frac{3}{5}$ (b) $\frac{^-5}{11}$ (c) $4\frac{1}{2}$

Solution

(a) $\frac{^-3}{5}$ or $-\frac{3}{5}$ (b) $-\left(\frac{^-5}{11}\right)$ or $\frac{5}{11}$ (c) $^-4\frac{1}{2}$

Properties of the additive inverse for rational numbers are analogous to those of the additive inverse for integers as shown in Table 6-2.

TABLE 6-2   Properties of Additive Inverse

Integers	Rational Numbers
1. $^-(^-a) = a$	1. $-\left(-\frac{a}{b}\right) = \frac{a}{b}$
2. $^-(a + b) = {^-a} + {^-b}$	2. $-\left(\frac{a}{b} + \frac{c}{d}\right) = \frac{^-a}{b} + \frac{^-c}{d}$

As with the set of integers, the set of rational numbers also has the addition property of equality.

Property

Addition Property of Equality   If $\frac{a}{b}$ and $\frac{c}{d}$ are any rational numbers such that $\frac{a}{b} = \frac{c}{d}$ and if $\frac{e}{f}$ is any rational number, then $\frac{a}{b} + \frac{e}{f} = \frac{c}{d} + \frac{e}{f}$

Subtraction of rational numbers, like subtraction of integers, is defined in terms of addition.

DEFINITION

> **Subtraction of Rational Numbers**   If $\dfrac{a}{b}$ and $\dfrac{c}{d}$ are any rational numbers,
>
> then $\dfrac{a}{b} - \dfrac{c}{d} = \dfrac{e}{f}$ if and only if $\dfrac{a}{b} = \dfrac{c}{d} + \dfrac{e}{f}$.

Subtraction of rational numbers can also be performed by adding the additive inverse. If $\dfrac{a}{b}$ and $\dfrac{c}{d}$ are any rational numbers, then

$$\frac{a}{b} - \frac{c}{d} = \frac{a}{b} + \frac{^{-}c}{d}$$

Using the definition of addition of rational numbers results in the following property.

Property

> If $\dfrac{a}{b}$ and $\dfrac{c}{d}$ are any rational numbers, then
>
> $$\frac{a}{b} - \frac{c}{d} = \frac{ad - bc}{bd}$$

Example 6-11

Find each difference.

(a) $\dfrac{5}{8} - \dfrac{1}{3}$

(b) $5\dfrac{1}{3} - 2\dfrac{3}{4}$

Solution

(a) $\dfrac{5}{8} - \dfrac{1}{3} = \dfrac{5 \cdot 3 - 8 \cdot 1}{8 \cdot 3} = \dfrac{15 - 8}{24} = \dfrac{7}{24}$

(b) Two methods of solution are given, as in Example 6-9.

$$5\frac{1}{3} - 2\frac{3}{4} = \frac{16}{3} - \frac{11}{4}$$

$$= \frac{16 \cdot 4 - 3 \cdot 11}{3 \cdot 4}$$

$$= \frac{64 - 33}{12}$$

$$= \frac{31}{12} \text{ or } 2\frac{7}{12}$$

$$5\frac{1}{3} = 5\frac{4}{12} = 4 + 1\frac{4}{12} = 4\frac{16}{12}$$

$$-2\frac{3}{4} = -2\frac{9}{12} = -2\frac{9}{12} \qquad = -2\frac{9}{12}$$

$$2\frac{7}{12}$$

PROBLEM SET 6-2

1. Use a number line to find $\frac{1}{5} + \frac{2}{3}$.
2. In each case, perform the computation using the least common denominator.

   (a) $\frac{3}{16} + \frac{7}{-8}$ (b) $\frac{4}{12} - \frac{2}{3}$

   (c) $\frac{5}{6} + \frac{-4}{9} + \frac{2}{3}$ (d) $\frac{2}{21} - \frac{3}{14}$

3. Use the definition of addition to find each of the following.

   (a) $\frac{6}{5} + \frac{-11}{4}$ (b) $\frac{4}{5} + \frac{6}{7}$

   (c) $\frac{-7}{8} + \frac{2}{5}$ (d) $\frac{5}{x} + \frac{-3}{y}$

4. Add the following rational numbers. Write your answers in the simplest form.

   (a) $\frac{6}{7} + \frac{3}{14}$ (b) $\frac{-2}{3} + \frac{-4}{7} + \frac{3}{21}$

   (c) $\frac{-3}{2x} + \frac{3}{2y} + \frac{-1}{4xy}$ (d) $\frac{-3}{2x^2y} + \frac{5}{6xy^2} + \frac{7}{x^2}$

5. Change each of the following improper fractions to mixed numbers.

   (a) $\frac{56}{3}$ (b) $\frac{14}{5}$

   (c) $-\frac{293}{100}$ (d) $-\frac{47}{8}$

6. Change each of the following mixed numbers to improper fractions.

   (a) $6\frac{3}{4}$ (b) $7\frac{1}{2}$

   (c) $^{-}3\frac{5}{8}$ (d) $^{-}4\frac{2}{3}$

7. Compute the following.

   (a) $2\frac{1}{3} - 1\frac{3}{4}$ (b) $2\frac{1}{3} + 1\frac{3}{4}$ (c) $3\frac{5}{6} - 2\frac{1}{8}$

   (d) $\frac{5}{6} + 2\frac{1}{8}$ (e) $^{-}4\frac{1}{2} - 3\frac{1}{6}$ (f) $^{-}4\frac{3}{4} + 2\frac{5}{6}$

8. Joe lives $\frac{4}{10}$ mile from the university, and Mary lives $\frac{1}{6}$ mile away. How much further from school does Joe live than Mary?

9. A clerk sold three pieces of ribbon. One piece was $\frac{1}{3}$ yard long, another piece was $2\frac{3}{4}$ yards long, and the third was $3\frac{1}{2}$ yards long. What was the total length of ribbon sold?

10. What, if anything, is wrong with each of the following?

    (a) $2 = \frac{6}{3} = \frac{3+3}{3} = \frac{3}{3} + 3 = 1 + 3 = 4$

    (b) $1 = \frac{4}{2+2} = \frac{4}{2} + \frac{4}{2} = 2 + 2 = 4$

    (c) $\frac{ab + c}{a} = \frac{\not{a}b + c}{\not{a}} = b + c$

    (d) $\frac{a^2 - b^2}{a - b} = \frac{a \cdot \not{a} - b \cdot \not{b}}{\not{a} - \not{b}} = a - b$

    (e) $\frac{a + c}{b + c} = \frac{a + \not{c}}{b + \not{c}} = \frac{a}{b}$

11. Express each of the following as a rational number.

    (a) $\frac{5}{2^4 \cdot 3^2} - \frac{1}{2^3 \cdot 3^4}$ (b) $\frac{11}{2^3 \cdot 5^4 \cdot 7^5} + \frac{3}{2^4 \cdot 5^3 \cdot 7}$

    (c) $11 - \left(\frac{3}{5} + \frac{-4}{45}\right)$ (d) $\frac{3}{4} - \left(2\frac{3}{4} - 1\frac{1}{2}\right)$

12. Does each of the following properties hold for subtraction of rational numbers? Justify your answer.

    (a) Closure   (b) Commutative
    (c) Associative   (d) Identity
    (e) Inverse
    (f) Subtraction property of equality

13. Perform the indicated operations on the following rational numbers. Write your answers in simplest form.

    (a) $\frac{d}{bc} - \frac{a}{bc}$ (b) $\frac{d}{b} + \frac{a}{bc}$

    (c) $\frac{7}{a - b} + \frac{5}{a + b}$ (d) $\frac{a^2b}{c} - \frac{bc}{ad}$

    (e) $\frac{a}{a - b} + \frac{b}{a + b}$ (f) $\frac{a}{a^2 - b^2} - \frac{b}{a - b}$

14. Demonstrate by example that each of the following properties of rational numbers holds.

    (a) Closure property of addition
    (b) Commutative property of addition
    (c) Addition property of equality
    (d) Associative property of addition

15. In a certain Swiss city, each resident speaks only one language: $\frac{3}{4}$ speak German, $\frac{1}{8}$ speak French, and $\frac{1}{16}$ speak Italian. What fraction of the residents speak neither German, French, nor Italian?

16. (a) Check that each of the following is true.

    $$\frac{1}{3} = \frac{1}{4} + \frac{1}{3 \cdot 4} \qquad \frac{1}{4} = \frac{1}{5} + \frac{1}{4 \cdot 5}$$

    $$\frac{1}{5} = \frac{1}{6} + \frac{1}{5 \cdot 6}$$

    (b) Based on the examples in part (a), write $\frac{1}{n}$ as a sum of two unit fractions, that is, fractions with numerator 1.

    ★ (c) Prove your answer in (b).

★ 17. The following are the first three terms of a sequence.

$$\frac{1}{1 \cdot 2} + \frac{1}{2 \cdot 3}, \quad \frac{1}{1 \cdot 2} + \frac{1}{2 \cdot 3} + \frac{1}{3 \cdot 4},$$

$$\frac{1}{1 \cdot 2} + \frac{1}{2 \cdot 3} + \frac{1}{3 \cdot 4} + \frac{1}{4 \cdot 5}$$

(a) Write each of the first three terms in the simplest form.

(b) Find the simplest form of the following.

$$\frac{1}{1 \cdot 2} + \frac{1}{2 \cdot 3} + \frac{1}{3 \cdot 4} + \frac{1}{4 \cdot 5} + \cdots$$
$$+ \frac{1}{n \cdot (n + 1)}$$

★★ (c) Prove your answer to part (b).

* * * * * * * REVIEW PROBLEMS * * * * * * * *

18. Reduce each of the following fractions to its simplest form.

(a) $\dfrac{14}{21}$ (b) $\dfrac{117}{153}$ (c) $\dfrac{5^2}{7^2}$

(d) $\dfrac{a^2 + a}{1 + a}$ (e) $\dfrac{a^2 + 1}{a + 1}$

19. Determine if each of the following pairs of fractions is equivalent.

(a) $\dfrac{3}{17}$ and $\dfrac{69}{391}$ (b) $\dfrac{^-145}{261}$ and $\dfrac{155}{279}$

(c) $\dfrac{a^2}{b}$ and $\dfrac{a^2 b^2}{b^3}$ (d) $\dfrac{377}{400}$ and $\dfrac{378}{401}$

(e) $\dfrac{0}{10}$ and $\dfrac{0}{^-10}$

(f) $\dfrac{a}{b}$ and $\dfrac{a + 1}{b + 1}$, where $a \neq b$

COMPUTER   CORNER

The following is a BASIC program for adding two rational numbers and obtaining the result in the simplest form. The program may be used as a drill for addition of fractions. Type this program into your computer and run it to add the following.

(a) $\dfrac{2}{5} + \dfrac{8}{10}$ (b) $\dfrac{3}{4} + \dfrac{1}{3}$

```
10 REM ADDITION OF FRACTIONS
15 PRINT "THIS PROGRAM IS AN ADDITION OF FRACTIONS DRILL."
20 PRINT "ENTER THE NUMERATOR AND DENOMINATOR OF"
30 PRINT "THE FIRST FRACTION SEPARATED BY A COMMA."
40 INPUT A, B
50 PRINT "ENTER THE NUMERATOR AND DENOMINATOR OF"
60 PRINT "THE SECOND FRACTION SEPARATED BY A COMMA."
70 INPUT C, D
80 LET N = D * A + B * C
```

```
 90 LET E = B * D
100 REM REDUCE THE FRACTION N/E
110 IF N < E THEN M = N
115 IF N > = E THEN M = E
120 FOR I = M TO 1 STEP -1
130 IF N/I = INT (N/I) AND E/I = INT (E/I) THEN 150
140 NEXT I
150 REM GCD = I
160 LET N = N/I
170 LET E = E/I
180 PRINT
190 PRINT "ENTER NUMERATOR AND DENOMINATOR OF THE"
200 PRINT "SUM IN LOWEST TERMS"
210 INPUT X, Y
220 IF X = N AND Y = E THEN PRINT "CORRECT" GOTO 240
230 PRINT "NO, THAT IS WRONG."
240 PRINT "DO YOU WANT TO ADD OTHER FRACTIONS (YES OR NO)"
250 INPUT Q$
260 IF Q$ = "YES" THEN 15
270 END
```

BRAIN TEASER

When Professor Sum was asked by Mr. Little how many students were in his classes, he answered, "All of them study either languages, physics, or not at all. One-half of them study languages only, one-fourth of them study French, one-seventh of them study physics only, and there are 20 who do not study at all." How many students does Professor Sum have?

6-3 MULTIPLICATION AND DIVISION OF RATIONAL NUMBERS

To motivate the definition of multiplication of rational numbers, consider $8 \cdot \frac{1}{4}$. Using repeated addition, $8 \cdot \frac{1}{4}$ can be interpreted as follows:

$$8 \cdot \frac{1}{4} = \frac{1}{4} + \frac{1}{4} + \frac{1}{4} + \frac{1}{4} + \frac{1}{4} + \frac{1}{4} + \frac{1}{4} + \frac{1}{4} = \frac{8}{4} = 2$$

If the commutative property of multiplication for rational numbers is to be true, then $8 \cdot \frac{1}{4} = \frac{1}{4} \cdot 8 = 2$. The product $\frac{1}{4} \cdot 8$ may be thought of as $\frac{1}{4}$ of 8, because if 8 is divided into four equal parts, the result is also 2. Similarly we can interpret $\frac{1}{4} \cdot \frac{1}{3}$ as $\frac{1}{4}$ of $\frac{1}{3}$—that is, one part when $\frac{1}{3}$ is divided into four equal parts. Suppose the entire rectangular region in Figure 6-5(a) represents one unit. The shaded section represents $\frac{1}{3}$ of the rectangle. Figure 6-5(b) shows the rectangle further separated into four congruent parts with $\frac{1}{4}$ of these parts shaded. The crosshatched portion represents $\frac{1}{4}$ of $\frac{1}{3}$, and is $\frac{1}{12}$ of the entire one-unit region. Thus, we interpret $\frac{1}{4} \cdot \frac{1}{3}$ as $\frac{1}{12}$.

FIGURE 6-5

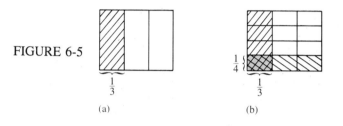

(a)   (b)

Figure 6-6(a) shows a one-unit rectangle separated into fifths, with $\frac{2}{5}$ shaded. Figure 6-6(b) shows the rectangle further separated into thirds, with $\frac{2}{3}$ shaded. The crosshatched portion represents 4 parts out of 15, or $\frac{4}{15}$ of the rectangle. Thus,

$$\frac{2}{3} \cdot \frac{2}{5} = \frac{4}{15} = \frac{2 \cdot 2}{3 \cdot 5}$$

FIGURE 6-6

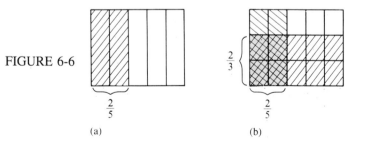

(a)   (b)

This discussion leads to the following definition.

DEFINITION

If $\frac{a}{b}$ and $\frac{c}{d}$ are any rational numbers, then $\frac{a}{b} \cdot \frac{c}{d} = \frac{a \cdot c}{b \cdot d}$.

Example 6-12 | Find each of the following products.

(a) $\dfrac{5}{6} \cdot \dfrac{7}{11}$ (b) $6 \cdot \dfrac{1}{5}$ (c) $2\dfrac{1}{3} \cdot 3\dfrac{1}{5}$

Solution | (a) $\dfrac{5}{6} \cdot \dfrac{7}{11} = \dfrac{5 \cdot 7}{6 \cdot 11} = \dfrac{35}{66}$

(b) $6 \cdot \dfrac{1}{5} = \dfrac{6}{1} \cdot \dfrac{1}{5} = \dfrac{6 \cdot 1}{1 \cdot 5} = \dfrac{6}{5}$

(c) $2\dfrac{1}{3} \cdot 3\dfrac{1}{5} = \dfrac{7}{3} \cdot \dfrac{16}{5} = \dfrac{7 \cdot 16}{3 \cdot 5} = \dfrac{112}{15} = 7\dfrac{7}{15}$

Multiplication of rational numbers has the following properties.

Properties | **Closure Property for Multiplication of Rational Numbers**   If $\dfrac{a}{b}$ and $\dfrac{c}{d}$ are any rational numbers, then $\dfrac{a}{b} \cdot \dfrac{c}{d}$ is a rational number.

Commutative Property for Multiplication of Rational Numbers   If $\dfrac{a}{b}$ and $\dfrac{c}{d}$ are any rational numbers, then

$$\frac{a}{b} \cdot \frac{c}{d} = \frac{c}{d} \cdot \frac{a}{b}$$

Associative Property for Multiplication of Rational Numbers   If $\dfrac{a}{b}, \dfrac{c}{d},$ and $\dfrac{e}{f}$ are any rational numbers, then

$$\left(\frac{a}{b} \cdot \frac{c}{d}\right) \cdot \frac{e}{f} = \frac{a}{b} \cdot \left(\frac{c}{d} \cdot \frac{e}{f}\right)$$

Multiplicative Identity of Rational Numbers   The number 1 is the unique number such that for every rational number $\dfrac{a}{b}$,

$$1 \cdot \left(\frac{a}{b}\right) = \frac{a}{b} = \left(\frac{a}{b}\right) \cdot 1$$

Multiplicative Inverse of Rational Numbers   For any nonzero rational number $\dfrac{a}{b}, \dfrac{b}{a}$ is the unique rational number such that $\dfrac{a}{b} \cdot \dfrac{b}{a} = 1 = \dfrac{b}{a} \cdot \dfrac{a}{b}$. The

reciprocal | multiplicative inverse of $\dfrac{a}{b}$ is also called the **reciprocal** of $\dfrac{a}{b}$.

Distributive Property for Multiplication over Addition of Rational Numbers   If $\dfrac{a}{b}, \dfrac{c}{d},$ and $\dfrac{e}{f}$ are any rational numbers, then

$$\frac{a}{b}\left(\frac{c}{d} + \frac{e}{f}\right) = \left(\frac{a}{b} \cdot \frac{c}{d}\right) + \left(\frac{a}{b} \cdot \frac{e}{f}\right)$$

Verifications of these properties are left as exercises.

Example 6-13   Find the multiplicative inverse of each of the following rational numbers.

(a) $\dfrac{2}{3}$ (b) $\dfrac{^-2}{5}$ (c) 4   (d) 0   (e) $6\dfrac{1}{2}$

Solution   (a) $\dfrac{3}{2}$ (b) $\dfrac{5}{^-2}$, which can be written as $\dfrac{^-5}{2}$.

(c) Because $4 = \dfrac{4}{1}$, the multiplicative inverse of 4 is $\dfrac{1}{4}$.

(d) Even though $0 = \dfrac{0}{1}$, $\dfrac{1}{0}$ is undefined, so there is no multiplicative inverse of 0.

(e) Because $6\dfrac{1}{2} = \dfrac{13}{2}$, the multiplicative inverse of $6\dfrac{1}{2}$ is $\dfrac{2}{13}$.

Additional properties for multiplication on the set of rational numbers are the following.

Properties   **Multiplication Property of Equality for Rational Numbers**   If $\dfrac{a}{b}$ and $\dfrac{c}{d}$ are any rational numbers such that $\dfrac{a}{b} = \dfrac{c}{d}$ and $\dfrac{e}{f}$ is any rational number, then $\dfrac{a}{b} \cdot \dfrac{e}{f} = \dfrac{c}{d} \cdot \dfrac{e}{f}$.

Multiplication Property of Zero for Rational Numbers   If $\dfrac{a}{b}$ is any rational number, then $\dfrac{a}{b} \cdot 0 = 0 = 0 \cdot \dfrac{a}{b}$.

Example 6-14   Solve for x, where x is a rational number.

(a) $\dfrac{3}{2}x = \dfrac{3}{4}$ (b) $\dfrac{2}{3}x - \dfrac{1}{5} = \dfrac{3}{4}$

Solution   (a) The reciprocal of a fraction times the fraction yields 1, so we multiply both sides of the equation by $\frac{2}{3}$, the reciprocal of $\frac{3}{2}$.

$$\dfrac{3}{2}x = \dfrac{3}{4}$$

$$\dfrac{2}{3} \cdot \dfrac{3}{2}x = \dfrac{2}{3} \cdot \dfrac{3}{4}$$

$$1 \cdot x = \dfrac{2 \cdot 3}{3 \cdot 4}$$

$$x = \dfrac{1}{2}$$

(b) We would like to "eliminate" $-\frac{1}{5}$ from the left side of the equation. To achieve this goal, we add $\frac{1}{5}$ to both sides of the equation and proceed using the technique of part (a).

$$\frac{2}{3}x - \frac{1}{5} = \frac{3}{4}$$

$$\frac{2}{3}x - \frac{1}{5} + \frac{1}{5} = \frac{3}{4} + \frac{1}{5}$$

$$\frac{2}{3}x = \frac{19}{20}$$

$$\frac{3}{2} \cdot \frac{2}{3}x = \frac{3}{2} \cdot \frac{19}{20}$$

$$x = \frac{57}{40}$$

Remark | In part (a) of Example 6-14, $\frac{3}{2}x$ can be treated as $\frac{3}{2} \cdot \frac{x}{1}$, or $\frac{3 \cdot x}{2 \cdot 1} = \frac{3x}{2}$.

Hence, $\frac{3}{2}x = \frac{3x}{2}$.

PROBLEM 1

A castle in the faraway land of Aluossim was surrounded by four moats. One day the castle was besieged by a fierce tribe from the north. Guards were stationed at each bridge. Prince Juanaricmo was allowed to take a number of bags of gold from the castle as he went into exile. However, the guard at the first bridge demanded half the bags of gold plus one more bag. Prince Juanaricmo met this demand and proceeded to the next bridge. The guards at the second, third, and fourth bridges made identical demands, all of which the prince met. When the prince finally crossed all the bridges, he had a single bag of gold left. With how many bags did he start?

Understanding the Problem

To help explain the problem, suppose the prince had 18 bags of gold. To the first guard, he gave $\frac{1}{2} \cdot 18$ or 9 bags plus one more bag. Because he gave the guard 10 bags, he had 8 bags left to proceed to the next bridge. This process is continued as in the statement of the problem until only one bag is left.

Devising a Plan

We can solve this problem by setting up an equation that satisfies the conditions of the problem. We write an algebraic expression for the number of bags of gold the prince had after crossing the first bridge. Using this expression, we write a similar expression for the number of bags of gold he had after crossing the second bridge, and so on. Then we set the expression representing the number of bags that the prince had after crossing the final bridge equal to 1. The solution to the resulting equation is the answer to the problem.

Carrying Out the Plan

Let n be the number of bags of gold with which the prince started. We summarize what happened at each bridge in Table 6-3.

TABLE 6-3

	Number of Bags Each Guard Took	Number of Bags the Prince Had After Crossing
First bridge	$\frac{1}{2}n + 1$	$n - \left(\frac{1}{2}n + 1\right) = \frac{1}{2}n - 1$
Second bridge	$\frac{1}{2}\left(\frac{1}{2}n - 1\right) + 1 = \frac{1}{4}n + \frac{1}{2}$	$\frac{1}{2}n - 1 - \left(\frac{1}{4}n + \frac{1}{2}\right) = \frac{1}{4}n - \frac{3}{2}$
Third bridge	$\frac{1}{2}\left(\frac{1}{4}n - \frac{3}{2}\right) + 1 = \frac{1}{8}n + \frac{1}{4}$	$\frac{1}{4}n - \frac{3}{2} - \left(\frac{1}{8}n + \frac{1}{4}\right) = \frac{1}{8}n - \frac{7}{4}$
Fourth bridge	$\frac{1}{2}\left(\frac{1}{8}n - \frac{7}{4}\right) + 1 = \frac{1}{16}n + \frac{1}{8}$	$\frac{1}{8}n - \frac{7}{4} - \left(\frac{1}{16}n + \frac{1}{8}\right) = \frac{1}{16}n - \frac{15}{8}$

Because the prince had only one bag left after crossing the fourth bridge, we have

$$\frac{1}{16}n - \frac{15}{8} = 1$$
$$\frac{1}{16}n = 1 + \frac{15}{8}$$
$$\frac{1}{16}n = \frac{23}{8}$$
$$n = \frac{23}{8} \cdot 16$$
$$n = 46$$

Looking Back

Another way of finding the solution is to "work backwards." In the preceding solution, observe that after crossing each bridge, the prince was left with half the number of bags he had previously minus one additional bag of gold. To determine the number he had prior to crossing the bridge, we can use the inverse operations; that is, add 1 and multiply by 2. The prince had one bag left after crossing the fourth bridge. He must have had two before he gave the guard the extra bag. Finally he must have had four bags before he gave the guard at the fourth bridge any bags. The entire procedure is summarized in Table 6-4.

TABLE 6-4

Bridge	Bags After Crossing	Bags Before Guard Given Extra	Bags Prior to Crossing
Fourth	1	2	4
Third	4	5	10
Second	10	11	22
First	22	23	46

We define division for rational numbers in terms of multiplication in the same way as we define division for integers.

DEFINITION

If $\frac{a}{b}$ and $\frac{c}{d}$ are any rational numbers and $\frac{c}{d}$ is not zero, then $\frac{a}{b} \div \frac{c}{d} = \frac{e}{f}$ if and only if $\frac{e}{f}$ is the unique rational number such that $\frac{c}{d} \cdot \frac{e}{f} = \frac{a}{b}$.

Remark

In the definition of division, $\frac{c}{d}$ is not zero because division by zero is impossible. Also, $\frac{c}{d} \neq 0$ implies that $c \neq 0$.

Recall that the set of integers is not closed under division. However, the set of rational numbers is closed under division as long as we do not divide by 0. To find an algorithm for rational-number division, examine the following examples.

Example 6-15 | Find $1 \div \frac{2}{3}$.

Solution | By definition $1 \div \frac{2}{3} = x$ if and only if $\frac{2}{3} \cdot x = 1$. Since $\frac{2}{3}$ and x must be multiplicative inverses of each other, $x = \frac{3}{2}$. Thus, $1 \div \frac{2}{3} = \frac{3}{2}$.

Example 6-16 | Find $\frac{2}{3} \div \frac{5}{7}$.

Solution | Let $\frac{2}{3} \div \frac{5}{7} = x$. Then $\frac{5}{7} \cdot x = \frac{2}{3}$. To solve for x, multiply both sides of the equation by the reciprocal of $\frac{5}{7}$, namely, $\frac{7}{5}$. Thus,

$$\frac{7}{5}\left(\frac{5}{7}x\right) = \frac{7}{5} \cdot \frac{2}{3}$$

Hence,

$$x = \frac{7}{5} \cdot \frac{2}{3} = \frac{14}{15}$$

The procedures in Examples 6-15 and 6-16 suggest using an extension of the Fundamental Law of Fractions, $\frac{a}{b} = \frac{ac}{bc}$, where a, b, and c are all fractions.

$$\frac{2}{3} \div \frac{5}{7} = \frac{\frac{2}{3}}{\frac{5}{7}} = \frac{\frac{2}{3}}{\frac{5}{7}} \cdot \frac{\frac{7}{5}}{\frac{7}{5}} = \frac{\frac{2}{3} \cdot \frac{7}{5}}{\frac{5}{7} \cdot \frac{7}{5}} = \frac{\frac{2}{3} \cdot \frac{7}{5}}{1} = \frac{2}{3} \cdot \frac{7}{5}$$

Thus,

$$\frac{2}{3} \div \frac{5}{7} = \frac{2}{3} \cdot \frac{7}{5}$$

The preceding equations illustrate the standard algorithm, "invert and multiply," taught to elementary school students.

$$\frac{a}{b} \div \frac{c}{d} = \frac{a}{b} \cdot \frac{d}{c}$$

Examples of this algorithm are seen on page 223, from the Addison-Wesley series, *Mathematics in Our World*, 1978, Grade 6.

Example 6-17 | Perform each of the following divisions and write your answers in simplest form.

(a) $\dfrac{^-5}{6} \div \dfrac{^-3}{8}$ (b) $5\frac{1}{6} \div 4\frac{2}{3}$ (c) $\dfrac{\frac{1}{4} + \frac{^-3}{2}}{\frac{5}{6} + \frac{7}{8}}$

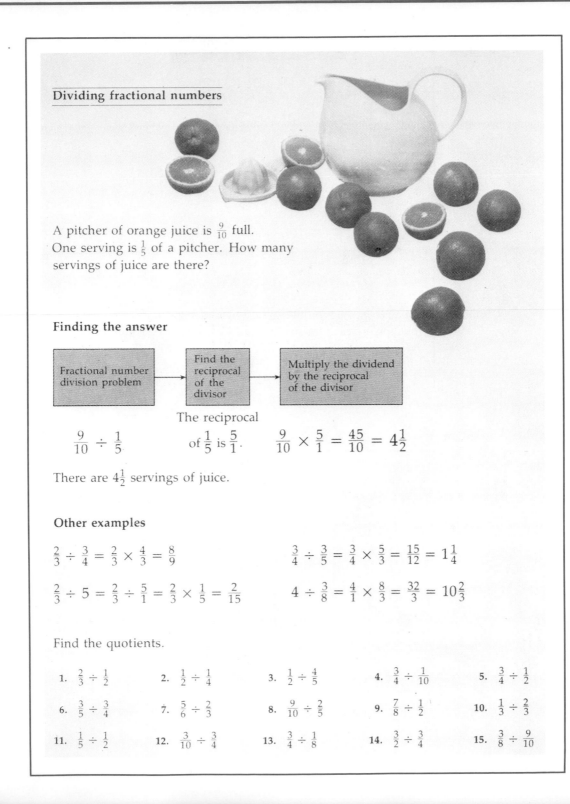

Dividing fractional numbers

A pitcher of orange juice is $\frac{9}{10}$ full. One serving is $\frac{1}{5}$ of a pitcher. How many servings of juice are there?

Finding the answer

| Fractional number division problem | → | Find the reciprocal of the divisor | → | Multiply the dividend by the reciprocal of the divisor |

The reciprocal

$$\frac{9}{10} \div \frac{1}{5} \qquad \text{of } \frac{1}{5} \text{ is } \frac{5}{1}. \qquad \frac{9}{10} \times \frac{5}{1} = \frac{45}{10} = 4\frac{1}{2}$$

There are $4\frac{1}{2}$ servings of juice.

Other examples

$$\frac{2}{3} \div \frac{3}{4} = \frac{2}{3} \times \frac{4}{3} = \frac{8}{9} \qquad\qquad \frac{3}{4} \div \frac{3}{5} = \frac{3}{4} \times \frac{5}{3} = \frac{15}{12} = 1\frac{1}{4}$$

$$\frac{2}{3} \div 5 = \frac{2}{3} \div \frac{5}{1} = \frac{2}{3} \times \frac{1}{5} = \frac{2}{15} \qquad\qquad 4 \div \frac{3}{8} = \frac{4}{1} \times \frac{8}{3} = \frac{32}{3} = 10\frac{2}{3}$$

Find the quotients.

1. $\frac{2}{3} \div \frac{1}{2}$ 2. $\frac{1}{2} \div \frac{1}{4}$ 3. $\frac{1}{2} \div \frac{4}{5}$ 4. $\frac{3}{4} \div \frac{1}{10}$ 5. $\frac{3}{4} \div \frac{1}{2}$

6. $\frac{3}{5} \div \frac{3}{4}$ 7. $\frac{5}{6} \div \frac{2}{3}$ 8. $\frac{9}{10} \div \frac{2}{5}$ 9. $\frac{7}{8} \div \frac{1}{2}$ 10. $\frac{1}{3} \div \frac{2}{3}$

11. $\frac{1}{5} \div \frac{1}{2}$ 12. $\frac{3}{10} \div \frac{3}{4}$ 13. $\frac{3}{4} \div \frac{1}{8}$ 14. $\frac{3}{2} \div \frac{3}{4}$ 15. $\frac{3}{8} \div \frac{9}{10}$

Solution

(a) $\dfrac{^-5}{6} \div \dfrac{^-3}{8} = \dfrac{^-5}{6} \cdot \dfrac{8}{^-3} = \dfrac{^-40}{^-18} = \dfrac{20}{9}$

(b) $5\dfrac{1}{6} \div 4\dfrac{2}{3} = \dfrac{31}{6} \div \dfrac{14}{3} = \dfrac{31}{6} \cdot \dfrac{3}{14} = \dfrac{93}{84} = \dfrac{31}{28}$, or $1\dfrac{3}{28}$

(c) We first perform the additions and then the division.

$$\dfrac{1}{4} + \dfrac{^-3}{2} = \dfrac{1}{4} + \dfrac{^-6}{4} = \dfrac{^-5}{4}$$

$$\dfrac{5}{6} + \dfrac{7}{8} = \dfrac{20}{24} + \dfrac{21}{24} = \dfrac{41}{24}$$

Hence

$$\dfrac{\frac{1}{4} + \frac{^-3}{2}}{\frac{5}{6} + \frac{7}{8}} = \dfrac{\frac{^-5}{4}}{\frac{41}{24}} = \dfrac{^-5}{4} \cdot \dfrac{24}{41} = \dfrac{^-30}{41}$$

Remark

Another method for dividing the two fractions in Example 6-17(c) is based on multiplying each fraction by the LCM of their denominators. Thus,

$$\dfrac{\frac{^-5}{4}}{\frac{41}{24}} = \dfrac{\frac{^-5}{4} \cdot 24}{\frac{41}{24} \cdot 24} = \dfrac{^-5 \cdot 6}{41} = \dfrac{^-30}{41}$$

PROBLEM SET 6-3

1. In the following figures, a unit rectangle is used to illustrate the product of two fractions. Name the fractions and their product.

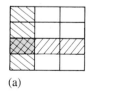

(a)

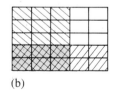

(b)

2. Use a rectangular region to illustrate each of the following products.

(a) $\dfrac{3}{4} \cdot \dfrac{1}{3}$ (b) $\dfrac{1}{5} \cdot \dfrac{2}{3}$

3. Find each product of rational numbers. Write your answers in simplest form.

(a) $\dfrac{10}{9} \cdot \dfrac{27}{40}$ (b) $\dfrac{^-3}{5} \cdot \dfrac{^-15}{24}$ (c) $\dfrac{49}{65} \cdot \dfrac{26}{98}$

(d) $\dfrac{a}{b} \cdot \dfrac{b^2}{a^2}$ (e) $\dfrac{2a}{3b} \cdot \dfrac{^-5ab}{2ab}$ (f) $\dfrac{xy}{z} \cdot \dfrac{z^2a}{x^3y^2}$

4. Find each product. Write your answers as mixed numbers.

(a) $2\dfrac{1}{3} \cdot 3\dfrac{3}{4}$ (b) $^-5\dfrac{1}{6} \cdot 4\dfrac{1}{2}$

(c) $\dfrac{22}{7} \cdot 4\dfrac{2}{3}$ (d) $\dfrac{^-5}{2} \cdot 2\dfrac{1}{2}$

5. Use the distributive property to find each product.

(a) $4\dfrac{1}{2} \cdot 2\dfrac{1}{3}$ $\left[\text{Hint: } \left(4 + \dfrac{1}{2}\right) \cdot \left(2 + \dfrac{1}{3}\right). \right]$

(b) $3\dfrac{1}{3} \cdot 2\dfrac{1}{2}$

6. Find the multiplicative inverse for each of the following.

(a) $\dfrac{^-1}{3}$

(b) $\dfrac{3}{5}$

(c) $\dfrac{14}{7}$

(d) $3\dfrac{1}{3}$

(e) $\dfrac{x}{y}$, if $x \neq 0$ and $y \neq 0$

(f) $^-7$

7. Perform each of the following divisions and write your answers in simplest form.

(a) $3 \div \dfrac{1}{9}$

(b) $\dfrac{2}{3} \div \dfrac{7}{12}$

(c) $\dfrac{^-3}{4} \div \dfrac{7}{8}$

(d) $\dfrac{x}{y} \div \dfrac{x^2}{y^2}$, where $x, y \neq 0$

(e) $\dfrac{\frac{3}{16}}{\frac{4}{9}}$

(f) $\dfrac{\frac{3}{16}}{\frac{9}{4}}$

(g) $\dfrac{\frac{8}{7}}{\frac{3}{4}}$

(h) $\dfrac{\frac{^-3}{5}}{\frac{^-6}{7}}$

(i) $\dfrac{^-3}{1\frac{1}{14}}$

8. Express each of the following as a fraction in simplest form.

(a) $\dfrac{2\frac{3}{4}}{1\frac{1}{4}}$

(b) $2\dfrac{3}{4} \cdot 1\dfrac{4}{3}$

(c) $(3\frac{2}{5} + 1)(4\frac{1}{3} - 2\frac{2}{3})$

(d) $1\dfrac{1}{2} \cdot 1\dfrac{1}{3} \cdot 1\dfrac{1}{4}$

(e) $\dfrac{\frac{1}{2} + \frac{1}{3}}{\frac{1}{2} - \frac{1}{3}}$

(f) $\dfrac{\frac{1}{4} + \frac{3}{2}}{\frac{5}{6} + \frac{^-7}{8}}$

(g) $\dfrac{1\frac{1}{2} - 2\frac{3}{4}}{\frac{1}{4} + \frac{^-7}{8}}$

(h) $\dfrac{\frac{x}{y}}{\frac{x}{z}}$

9. Solve each of the following for x and write your answer in simplest form.

(a) $\dfrac{1}{3}x = \dfrac{7}{8}$

(b) $\dfrac{2}{5} \cdot \dfrac{3}{6} = x$

(c) $\dfrac{1}{5} = \dfrac{7}{3} \cdot x$

(d) $x \div \dfrac{3}{4} = \dfrac{5}{8}$

(e) $\dfrac{1}{2}x - 7 = \dfrac{3}{4}x$

(f) $2\dfrac{1}{3}x + 7 = 3\dfrac{1}{4}$

(g) $\dfrac{2}{3}\left(\dfrac{1}{2}x - 7\right) = \dfrac{3}{4}x$

(h) $\dfrac{^-2}{5}(10x + 1) = 1 - x$

(i) $\dfrac{1}{x} + \dfrac{1}{3} = \dfrac{1}{5}$

10. Write each of the following in simplest form.

(a) $\dfrac{x}{y} \cdot \dfrac{yz}{x}$

(b) $x \cdot \dfrac{5}{xy} \cdot \dfrac{y}{x}$

(c) $\dfrac{x^2y^3}{z^3} \cdot \dfrac{z^2}{xy^2}$

11. Find two consecutive integers, x and $x + 1$, such that one-half of the greater integer exceeds one-third of the lesser integer by 9.

12. The sum of the ages of a father and his son is 75 years. Five years later the son's age is one-fourth of the father's age. Find their ages.

13. Skip A. Little was absent one-fourth of the school year. If there are 180 days in the school year, how many days was he absent?

14. Di Paloma University had a faculty reduction and lost one-fifth of its faculty. If there were 320 faculty members left after the reduction, how many members were there originally?

15. Ten minutes is what part of an hour? Of a week?

16. Alberto owns five-ninths of the stock in the North West Tofu company. His sister, Renatta, owns half as much stock as Alberto. What part of the stock is owned by neither Alberto nor by Renatta?

17. A person has $29\frac{1}{2}$ yards of material available to make uniforms. Each uniform requires $\frac{3}{4}$ yard of material.
(a) How many uniforms can be made?
(b) How much material will be left over?

18. Show that the following properties do *not* hold for division of rational numbers.
(a) Commutative
(b) Associative
(c) Identity
(d) Inverse

19. Peppermint Patty is frustrated with a problem. Help her solve it.

★ 20. If Sherwin can paint the house in 2 days working by himself and William can paint the house in 4 days working by himself, how many days would it take Sherwin and William working together?

★ 21. If Mary and Carter can paint a house in 5 hours, while Mary alone can do the same job in 8 hours, how long will it take Carter working alone?

★ 22. Prove the following properties of rational numbers.
(a) Closure for multiplication
(b) Commutative for addition
(c) Associative for multiplication
(d) Multiplication property of zero
(e) Distributive property of multiplication over addition

★ 23. Prove that if x, y, and z are rational numbers and $z \neq 0$, then $(x \cdot y) \div z = x \cdot (y \div z)$.

★ 24. Investigate under what conditions, if any,
$$\frac{a}{b} = \frac{a + c}{b + c}.$$

★★ 25. Consider these products.

First product: $\left(1 + \frac{1}{1}\right)\left(1 + \frac{1}{2}\right)$

Second product: $\left(1 + \frac{1}{1}\right)\left(1 + \frac{1}{2}\right)\left(1 + \frac{1}{3}\right)$

Third product: $\left(1 + \frac{1}{1}\right)\left(1 + \frac{1}{2}\right)\left(1 + \frac{1}{3}\right)\left(1 + \frac{1}{4}\right)$

(a) Calculate the value of each product. Based on the pattern in your answers, guess the value of the fourth product; then check to determine if your guess is correct.

(b) Guess the value of the 100th product.
(c) Find as simple expression as possible for the nth product.

★ 26. Let $S = \frac{1}{2} + \frac{1}{2^2} + \frac{1}{2^3} + \cdots + \frac{1}{2^{64}}$.
(a) Use the distributive property of multiplication over addition to find an expression for $2S$.
(b) Show that $2S - S = S = 1 - (\frac{1}{2})^{64}$.
(c) Find a simple expression for the sum

$$\frac{1}{2} + \frac{1}{2^2} + \frac{1}{2^2} + \cdots + \frac{1}{2^n}$$

27. Recall the procedure for multiplying fractions.

$$\frac{a}{b} \cdot \frac{c}{d} = \frac{a \cdot c}{b \cdot d}$$

To multiply fractions on a calculator, the following sequence may be used.

Try this technique with each of the following problems.

(a) $\frac{2}{3} \cdot \frac{1}{5}$

(b) $\frac{1}{19} \cdot \frac{4}{17}$

(c) $\frac{3}{1} \cdot \frac{2}{3}$

(Note that the answer on the display may not be accurate, depending on rounding.)

* * * * * * * REVIEW PROBLEMS * * * * * * * *

28. Perform each of the following computations. Leave your answers in the simplest form.

(a) $\frac{^-3}{16} + \frac{7}{4}$

(b) $\frac{1}{6} + \frac{^-4}{9} + \frac{5}{3}$

(c) $\frac{^-5}{2^3 \cdot 3^2} - \frac{^-5}{2 \cdot 3^3}$

(d) $3\frac{4}{5} + 4\frac{5}{6}$

(e) $5\frac{1}{6} - 3\frac{5}{8}$

(f) $-4\frac{1}{3} - 5\frac{5}{12}$

29. Each student at Sussex Elementary School takes one foreign language. Two-thirds of the students take Spanish, $\frac{1}{9}$ take French, $\frac{1}{18}$ take German, and the rest take some other foreign language. If there are 720 students in the school, how many do not take Spanish, French, or German?

30. Perform the indicated operations and write your answers in simplest form.

(a) $\frac{^-3}{5x} + \frac{1}{x} - \frac{^-2}{3x}$

(b) $\frac{^-2}{2xy^2} + \frac{3}{x^2y} - \frac{1}{xy}$

BRAIN TEASER

A woman's will decreed that her cats would be shared among her three daughters as follows: $\frac{1}{2}$ of the cats to the eldest daughter, $\frac{1}{3}$ of the cats to the middle daughter, and $\frac{1}{9}$ of the cats to the youngest daughter. Since the woman had 17 cats, the daughters decided that they could not carry out their mother's wishes. The judge who held the will agreed to lend the daughters a cat so they could share the cats as their mother wished. Now, $\frac{1}{2}$ of 18 is 9; $\frac{1}{3}$ of 18 is 6; and $\frac{1}{9}$ of 18 is 2. Since $9 + 6 + 2 = 17$, the daughters were able to divide the 17 cats and return the borrowed cat. They obviously did not need the extra cat to carry out the mother's will, but they could not divide 17 into halves, thirds, and ninths. Has the woman's will really been followed?

6-4   SOME PROPERTIES OF RATIONAL NUMBERS

Ordering of Rational Numbers

The greater than and less than relations for rational numbers are defined in such a way that the definitions of these relations for integers are still true. Thus, if $\frac{a}{b}$ and $\frac{c}{d}$ are rational numbers, then $\frac{a}{b} > \frac{c}{d}$ if and only if there is a positive rational number k such that $\frac{c}{d} + k = \frac{a}{b}$. Since $\frac{c}{d} + k = \frac{a}{b}$, then $\frac{a}{b} - \frac{c}{d} = k$. Consequently, since $k > 0$, $\frac{a}{b} > \frac{c}{d}$ if and only if $\frac{a}{b} - \frac{c}{d} > 0$. If the denominators are the same, that is, if $b = d$, then $\frac{a}{b} > \frac{c}{b}$ if and only if $\frac{a-c}{b} > 0$. If, in addition, the denominator b is positive, then $a - c > 0$, or $a > c$. Thus, we have the following criterion for determining which of two rational numbers is greater.

Property | If $b > 0$, then $\frac{a}{b} > \frac{c}{b}$ if and only if $a > c$.

Consider $\frac{3}{-7}$ and $\frac{2}{-7}$. In spite of the fact that $3 > 2$, $\frac{3}{-7}$ is not greater than $\frac{2}{-7}$. This is easy to see if we write equivalent fractions with positive denominators. Thus,

$$\frac{3}{-7} = \frac{3 \cdot (^-1)}{^-7 \cdot (^-1)} = \frac{^-3}{7}$$

and, similarly, $\frac{2}{-7} = \frac{-2}{7}$. Since $^-2 > ^-3$, we have $\frac{-2}{7} > \frac{-3}{7}$.

Example 6-18

Determine which fraction in each of the given pairs is greater.

(a) $\dfrac{8}{15}$ and $\dfrac{15}{31}$

(b) $\dfrac{-5}{12}$ and $\dfrac{1}{-2}$

Solution

(a) $\dfrac{8}{15} = \dfrac{8 \cdot 31}{15 \cdot 31} = \dfrac{248}{465}$ and $\dfrac{15}{31} = \dfrac{15 \cdot 15}{15 \cdot 31} = \dfrac{225}{465}$.

Because $248 > 225$, it follows that $\dfrac{248}{465} > \dfrac{225}{465}$, so $\dfrac{8}{15} > \dfrac{15}{31}$.

(b) $\dfrac{1}{-2} = \dfrac{1 \cdot (^-6)}{^-2 \cdot (^-6)} = \dfrac{^-6}{12}$

Because $^-5 > ^-6$, $\dfrac{^-5}{12} > \dfrac{^-6}{12}$; therefore, $\dfrac{^-5}{12} > \dfrac{1}{^-2}$.

A general criterion for the greater-than relation on rational numbers can be developed for the case when the denominators are positive. Using the common denominator bd, the fractions $\dfrac{a}{b}$ and $\dfrac{c}{d}$ can be written as $\dfrac{ad}{bd}$ and $\dfrac{bc}{bd}$. Because $b > 0$ and $d > 0$, $bd > 0$ and $\dfrac{ad}{bd} > \dfrac{bc}{bd}$ if and only if $ad > bc$.

Property

For any rational numbers $\dfrac{a}{b}$ and $\dfrac{c}{d}$, with b and d positive integers, $\dfrac{a}{b} > \dfrac{c}{d}$ if and only if $ad > bc$. Similarly, $\dfrac{a}{b} < \dfrac{c}{d}$ if and only if $ad < bc$.

Example 6-19

Prove that the following order relations are true.

(a) $\dfrac{8}{9} > \dfrac{16}{19}$

(b) $\dfrac{-7}{8} < \dfrac{14}{15}$

(c) $\dfrac{1}{-4} < \dfrac{2}{11}$

Solution

(a) $\dfrac{8}{9} > \dfrac{16}{19}$ because $8 \cdot 19 > 9 \cdot 16$, or $152 > 144$.

(b) $\dfrac{-7}{8} < \dfrac{14}{15}$ because $^-7 \cdot 15 < 8 \cdot 14$, or $^-105 < 112$.

(c) $\dfrac{1}{-4} < \dfrac{2}{11}$ because $\dfrac{1}{-4} = \dfrac{-1}{4}$ and $\dfrac{-1}{4} < \dfrac{2}{11}$, because a negative number is less than a positive number.

The proofs of the following properties of the greater-than relation on rational numbers are similar to those involving integers and are left as exercises. Similar properties hold for $<$, $\le$, and $\ge$.

THEOREM 6-1

Transitive Property of Greater Than   For any rational numbers $\frac{a}{b}, \frac{c}{d}$, and $\frac{e}{f}$, if $\frac{a}{b} > \frac{c}{d}$ and $\frac{c}{d} > \frac{e}{f}$, then $\frac{a}{b} > \frac{e}{f}$.

THEOREM 6-2

Addition Property of Greater Than   For any rational numbers $\frac{a}{b}, \frac{c}{d}$, and $\frac{e}{f}$, if $\frac{a}{b} > \frac{c}{d}$, then $\frac{a}{b} + \frac{e}{f} > \frac{c}{d} + \frac{e}{f}$.

THEOREM 6-3

Multiplication Property of Greater Than   For any rational numbers $\frac{a}{b}, \frac{c}{d}$, and $\frac{e}{f}$:

1. If $\frac{a}{b} > \frac{c}{d}$ and $\frac{e}{f} > 0$, then $\frac{a}{b} \cdot \frac{e}{f} > \frac{c}{d} \cdot \frac{e}{f}$.

2. If $\frac{a}{b} > \frac{c}{d}$ and $\frac{e}{f} < 0$, then $\frac{a}{b} \cdot \frac{e}{f} < \frac{c}{d} \cdot \frac{e}{f}$.

Example 6-20

Solve for x, where x is a rational number.

(a) $\frac{3}{2} x < \frac{3}{4}$

(b) $\frac{1}{4}x + \frac{1}{5} \geq \frac{2}{3}x - \frac{1}{7}$

Solution

(a)
$$\frac{3}{2}x < \frac{3}{4}$$
$$\left(\frac{2}{3}\right)\left(\frac{3}{2}x\right) < \left(\frac{2}{3}\right)\left(\frac{3}{4}\right)$$
$$x < \frac{6}{12}, \text{ or } x < \frac{1}{2}$$

(b)
$$\frac{1}{4}x + \frac{1}{5} \geq \frac{2}{3}x - \frac{1}{7}$$
$$\frac{1}{4}x + \frac{1}{5} + \frac{^-1}{5} \geq \frac{2}{3}x - \frac{1}{7} + \frac{^-1}{5}$$
$$\frac{1}{4}x \geq \frac{2}{3}x - \frac{12}{35}$$
$$\frac{^-2}{3}x + \frac{1}{4}x \geq \frac{^-2}{3}x + \frac{2}{3}x - \frac{12}{35}$$
$$\left(\frac{^-2}{3} + \frac{1}{4}\right)x \geq \frac{^-12}{35}$$
$$\frac{^-5}{12}x \geq \frac{^-12}{35}$$
$$\left(\frac{^-12}{5}\right)\left(\frac{^-5}{12}x\right) \leq \left(\frac{^-12}{5}\right)\left(\frac{^-12}{35}\right)$$
$$x \leq \frac{144}{175}$$

Often there is more than one way to solve an inequality. Two alternate methods for solving the second inequality in Example 6-20 follow.

1. First, add the fractions on each side of the inequality. Then, solve the resulting inequality.

$$\frac{1}{4}x + \frac{1}{5} \geq \frac{2}{3}x - \frac{1}{7}$$

$$\frac{5x + 4}{20} \geq \frac{14x - 3}{21}$$

$$21(5x + 4) \geq 20(14x - 3)$$

$$105x + 84 \geq 280x - 60$$

$$^-175x \geq ^-144$$

$$\left(\frac{^-1}{175}\right)(^-175x) \leq \left(\frac{^-1}{175}\right)(^-144)$$

$$x \leq \frac{144}{175}$$

2. First, multiply both sides of the inequality by the LCM of all the denominators. (This gives an inequality that does not involve fractions.) Then, solve the resulting inequality.

$$\frac{1}{4}x + \frac{1}{5} \geq \frac{2}{3}x - \frac{1}{7}$$

Since LCM(4, 5, 3, 7) = 420,

$$420\left(\frac{1}{4}x + \frac{1}{5}\right) \geq 420\left(\frac{2}{3}x - \frac{1}{7}\right)$$

$$105x + 84 \geq 280x - 60$$

$$^-175x \geq ^-144$$

$$x \leq \frac{144}{175}$$

Denseness Property

denseness property

The set of rational numbers has a very special property called the **denseness property**. Neither the set of whole numbers nor the set of integers has this property. *Given any two rational numbers $\frac{a}{b}$ and $\frac{c}{d}$, there is another rational number between these two.* Also, between $\frac{a}{b}$ and the new rational number, there is another rational number. Continuing this process shows that between any two rational numbers $\frac{a}{b}$ and $\frac{c}{d}$ there are infinitely many other rational numbers. For example, consider $\frac{1}{2}$ and $\frac{2}{3}$. To find a rational number between $\frac{1}{2}$ and $\frac{2}{3}$, we first rewrite the fractions with a common denominator, as $\frac{3}{6}$ and $\frac{4}{6}$. Because there is no whole number between the numerators 3 and 4, we next find two fractions equivalent to $\frac{1}{2}$ and $\frac{2}{3}$ with greater denominators. For example, $\frac{1}{2} = \frac{6}{12}$ and $\frac{2}{3} = \frac{8}{12}$, and $\frac{7}{12}$ is between the two fractions $\frac{6}{12}$ and $\frac{8}{12}$. So, $\frac{7}{12}$ is between $\frac{1}{2}$ and $\frac{2}{3}$.

Another way to find a rational number between two given rationals $\frac{a}{b}$ and $\frac{c}{d}$ is to find the average of the two numbers. For example, the average of $\frac{1}{2}$ and $\frac{2}{3}$ is $\frac{1}{2}\left(\frac{1}{2} + \frac{2}{3}\right)$, or $\frac{7}{12}$. The proof that the average of two given rational numbers always is between them is left as an exercise.

Ratio and Proportion

ratio   One of the primary uses of fractions is as ratios. For example, there may be a two-to-three ratio of Democrats to Republicans on a certain legislative committee, a friend may be given a speeding ticket for driving 63 miles per hour, or eggs are 98¢ per dozen. Each of these illustrates a **ratio**, or a quotient. A 1-to-2 ratio of males to females means that the number of males is $\frac{1}{2}$ the number of females or that there is 1 male for every 2 females. The ratio 1 to 2 can be written as $\frac{1}{2}$ or 1:2. In general, a ratio is denoted by $\frac{a}{b}$ or $a{:}b$, where $b \neq 0$.

Example 6-21

There were 7 males and 12 females in the Dew Drop Inn on Monday evening. In the Game Room, next door, there were 14 males and 24 females.

(a) Express the number of males to females in the Inn as a ratio.
(b) Express the number of males to females in the Game Room as a ratio.

Solution

(a) The ratio is $\dfrac{7}{12}$.   (b) The ratio is $\dfrac{14}{24}$.

proportional   The ratios $\frac{7}{12}$ and $\frac{14}{24}$ in Example 6-21 are said to be proportional to one another. In general, two ratios are **proportional** if and only if the fractions proportion   representing them are equal. Two equal ratios are said to form a **proportion**. For rational numbers, $\frac{a}{b} = \frac{c}{d}$ if and only if $ad = bc$. Thus, $\frac{a}{b} = \frac{c}{d}$ is a proportion if and only if $ad = bc$. For example, $\frac{14}{24} = \frac{7}{12}$ is a proportion, because $14 \cdot 12 = 24 \cdot 7$.

Frequently, one term in a proportion is missing, as in

$$\frac{3}{8} = \frac{x}{16}$$

Finding x requires solving an equation. The definition of equality of rational numbers can be used to solve such an equation.

$$\frac{3}{8} = \frac{x}{16}$$

$$3 \cdot 16 = 8 \cdot x$$

$$48 = 8 \cdot x$$

$$6 = x$$

Example 6-22	If there should be 3 calculators for every 4 students in an elementary class, how many calculators are needed for 44 students?	
Solution	Set up a table (Table 6-5). The ratio of calculators to students should always be the same.	

TABLE 6-5

Number of Calculators	3	x
Number of Students	4	44

$$\frac{3}{4} = \frac{x}{44}$$

$$3 \cdot 44 = 4 \cdot x$$

$$132 = 4x$$

$$33 = x$$

Thus, 33 calculators are needed.

Example 6-23

Suppose a car travels 50 km/hour.

(a) How far will it travel in $3\frac{1}{2}$ hours?
(b) How long will it take the car to travel 1300 km?

Solution

(a) Again, set up a table (Table 6-6).

TABLE 6-6

Distance (km)	50	x
Number of Hours	1	$3\frac{1}{2}$

$$\frac{50}{1} = \frac{x}{3\frac{1}{2}}$$

$$50(3\tfrac{1}{2}) = 1 \cdot x$$

$$175 = x$$

Therefore, the distance traveled in $3\frac{1}{2}$ hours is 175 km.

TABLE 6-7

(b)

Distance (km)	50	1300
Number of Hours	1	x

$$\frac{50}{1} = \frac{1300}{x}$$

$$50x = 1300$$

$$x = 26$$

Thus, to travel 1300 km requires 26 hours.

Consider the proportion $\frac{15}{30} = \frac{3}{6}$. Because the ratios in the proportion are equal fractions and equal fractions have equal reciprocals, then $\frac{30}{15} = \frac{6}{3}$.

THEOREM 6-4

For any rational numbers $\frac{a}{b}$ and $\frac{c}{d}$ with $a \neq 0$ and $c \neq 0$, $\frac{a}{b} = \frac{c}{d}$ if and only if $\frac{b}{a} = \frac{d}{c}$.

Using the properties of rational numbers, $\frac{15}{30} = \frac{3}{6}$ if and only if $15 \cdot 6 = 30 \cdot 3$. Also, $\frac{15}{3} = \frac{30}{6}$ if and only if $15 \cdot 6 = 3 \cdot 30$. Hence $\frac{15}{30} = \frac{3}{6}$ if and only if $\frac{15}{3} = \frac{30}{6}$. This result is generalized in the following theorem.

THEOREM 6-5

For any rational numbers $\frac{a}{b}$ and $\frac{c}{d}$ with $c \neq 0$, $\frac{a}{b} = \frac{c}{d}$ if and only if $\frac{a}{c} = \frac{b}{d}$.

BRAIN TEASER

Find the exact time between 2 o'clock and 3 o'clock when the hands of a clock coincide.

PROBLEM SET 6-4

1. For each of the following pairs of fractions, replace the comma with the correct symbol ($<$, $=$, $>$) to make a true statement.

   (a) $\dfrac{7}{8}, \dfrac{5}{6}$ (b) $2\dfrac{4}{5}, 2\dfrac{3}{6}$ (c) $\dfrac{-7}{8}, \dfrac{-4}{5}$

   (d) $\dfrac{1}{-7}, \dfrac{1}{-8}$ (e) $\dfrac{2}{5}, \dfrac{4}{10}$ (f) $\dfrac{0}{7}, \dfrac{0}{17}$

2. Arrange each of the following in decreasing order.

   (a) $\dfrac{11}{22}, \dfrac{11}{16}, \dfrac{11}{13}$ (b) $\dfrac{33}{16}, \dfrac{23}{12}, 3$

   (c) $\dfrac{-1}{5}, \dfrac{-19}{36}, \dfrac{-17}{30}$

3. Find the solution sets for each of the following.

   (a) $\dfrac{2}{3}x - \dfrac{7}{8} \le \dfrac{1}{4}$ (b) $\dfrac{1}{5}x - 7 \ge \dfrac{2}{3}$

   (c) $x - \dfrac{1}{3} < \dfrac{2}{3}x + \dfrac{4}{5}$ (d) $5 - \dfrac{2}{3}x \le \dfrac{1}{4}x - \dfrac{7}{8}$

4. For each of the following, find two rational numbers between the given fractions.

   (a) $\dfrac{3}{7}$ and $\dfrac{4}{7}$ (b) $\dfrac{-7}{9}$ and $\dfrac{-8}{9}$

   (c) $\dfrac{5}{6}$ and $\dfrac{83}{100}$ (d) $\dfrac{-1}{3}$ and $\dfrac{3}{4}$

5. (a) If $b < 0$ and $d > 0$, is it true that $\dfrac{a}{b} > \dfrac{c}{d}$ if and only if $ad > bc$? Explain your answer.

   (b) If $b < 0$ and $d < 0$, is it true that $\dfrac{a}{b} > \dfrac{c}{d}$ if and only if $ad > bc$? Explain your answer.

6. The difference between one-fifth of a certain number and one-ninth of the number is less than 4. Find all possible rational numbers that satisfy this sentence.

7. Twice the number of pupils in a certain class is less than three times the number minus 39. Four times the number plus 20 is greater than 5 times the number minus 21. Find the number of pupils in the class.

8. (a) Explain why the system of whole numbers does not have the denseness property.

   (b) Explain why the system of integers does not have the denseness property.

9. If there are 18 poodles and 12 cocker spaniels in a dog show, what is the ratio of poodles to cockers?

10. If a 4-ounce can of pepper costs 98¢, what is the cost per ounce?

11. If a new car is 8 feet long and $4\dfrac{1}{2}$ ft high, what is the ratio of length to height?

12. Solve for x in each proportion.

    (a) $\dfrac{12}{x} = \dfrac{18}{45}$ (b) $\dfrac{x}{7} = \dfrac{-10}{21}$

    (c) $\dfrac{5}{7} = \dfrac{3x}{98}$ (d) $3\dfrac{1}{2}$ is to 5 as x is to 15

13. There are five adult drivers for each teenage driver in Aluossim. If there are 12,345 adult drivers in Aluossim, how many teenage drivers are there?

14. If 3 grapefruit sell for 79¢, how much do 18 grapefruit cost?

15. On a map, $\dfrac{1}{3}$ inch represents 5 miles. If New York and Aluossim are 18 inches apart on the map, what is the actual distance between them?

16. Prove: For any rational numbers $\dfrac{a}{b}$ and $\dfrac{c}{d}$, if $\dfrac{a}{b} = \dfrac{c}{d}$ where $a \ne 0$ and $c \ne 0$, then $\dfrac{b}{a} = \dfrac{d}{c}$.

17. Prove that the product of two proper fractions greater than 0 is less than either of the fractions.

18. (a) In Room A of the University Center there are one man and two women; in Room B there are two men and four women; and in Room C there are five men and ten women. If all the people in Rooms B and C go to Room A, what will be the ratio of men to women in Room A?

    ★ (b) Prove the following generalization of the proportions used in part (a).

    If $\dfrac{a}{b} = \dfrac{c}{d} = \dfrac{e}{f}$, then $\dfrac{a}{b} = \dfrac{c}{d} = \dfrac{e}{f} = \dfrac{a+c+e}{b+d+f}$.

19. (a) Prove that if

    $\dfrac{a}{b} = \dfrac{c}{d}$, then $\dfrac{a+b}{b} = \dfrac{c+d}{d}$

    $\left(Hint: \dfrac{a}{b} + 1 = \dfrac{c}{d} + 1.\right)$

    ★ (b) Prove that if

    $\dfrac{a}{b} = \dfrac{c}{d}$, then $\dfrac{a-b}{a+b} = \dfrac{c-d}{c+d}$

★ 20. Prove: (a) Theorem 6-1;   (b) Theorem 6-2;   (c) Theorem 6-3.

★ 21. Show that the average of two rational numbers is between the two numbers, that is, for $0 < \frac{a}{b} < \frac{c}{d}$, prove that $0 < \frac{a}{b} < \frac{1}{2}\left(\frac{a}{b} + \frac{c}{d}\right) < \frac{c}{d}$

★ 22. If the same positive number is added to the numerator and denominator of a positive proper fraction, is the new fraction greater than, less than, or equal to the original fraction? Justify your answer.

* * * * * * * REVIEW PROBLEMS * * * * * * *

23. Write each of the following in simplest form.

(a) $3\frac{5}{8}$

(b) $3\frac{5}{8} \div 2\frac{5}{6}$

(c) $\frac{-5}{12} \div \frac{-12}{5}$

(d) $\frac{(x-y)^2}{x^2 - y^2} \cdot \frac{x+y}{x-y}$

24. For each of the following pairs of fractions, use a calculator and the method in Example 6-19 to replace the comma with the correct symbol ($<, =, >$) to make a true statement.

(a) $\frac{169}{170}, \frac{170}{171}$

(b) $\frac{13}{91}, \frac{91}{637}$

(c) $\frac{174}{315}, \frac{217}{618}$

(d) $\frac{135}{171}, \frac{137}{173}$

25. Solve each of the following for x and write your answer in simplest form.

(a) $\frac{-3}{4}x = 1$

(b) $^-x - \frac{3}{4} = \frac{5}{8}$

(c) $\frac{3}{4}x = \frac{-2}{3}x + 2$

(d) $\frac{3}{4}\left(1 - \frac{2}{3}x\right) = \frac{-3}{4}x$

26. The distance from Albertson to Florance is $28\frac{3}{4}$ miles. Roberto walks at the rate of $4\frac{1}{2}$ miles per hour. How long will it take him to walk from Albertson to Florance?

6-5 EXPONENTS REVISITED

Recall that for whole numbers a, m, and n, with $a \neq 0$, the following properties hold:

1. $a^m = \underbrace{a \cdot a \cdot a \cdot \ldots \cdot a}_{m \text{ factors}}$

2. $a^m \cdot a^n = a^{m+n}$
3. $a^0 = 1$ where $a \neq 0$

Property (3) is consistent with Property (2). If $m = 0$, then $a^m \cdot a^n = a^{m+n}$ becomes $a^0 \cdot a^n = a^{0+n} = a^n$ and 1 is the only number that, upon multiplying by a^n, gives a^n. The above notions can be extended for rational number values of a. For example, consider the following.

$$\left(\frac{2}{3}\right)^4 = \frac{2}{3} \cdot \frac{2}{3} \cdot \frac{2}{3} \cdot \frac{2}{3}$$

$$\left(\frac{2}{3}\right)^2 \cdot \left(\frac{2}{3}\right)^3 = \left(\frac{2}{3} \cdot \frac{2}{3}\right) \cdot \left(\frac{2}{3} \cdot \frac{2}{3} \cdot \frac{2}{3}\right) = \left(\frac{2}{3}\right)^{2+3} = \left(\frac{2}{3}\right)^5$$

$$\left(\frac{2}{3}\right)^0 = 1$$

Exponents can also be extended to negative integers as follows.

$10^3 = 10 \cdot 10 \cdot 10$

$10^2 = 10 \cdot 10$

$10^1 = 10$

$10^0 = 1$

Notice that as the exponents decrease by one, the numbers on the right are divided by 10. Thus, the pattern might be continued as

$$10^{-1} = \frac{1}{10} = \frac{1}{10^1}$$

$$10^{-2} = \frac{1}{10} \cdot \frac{1}{10} = \frac{1}{10^2}$$

$$10^{-3} = \frac{1}{10^2} \cdot \frac{1}{10} = \frac{1}{10^3}$$

If the pattern is extended, then we would predict that $10^{-n} = \dfrac{1}{10^n}$. This is true, and—in general—for any nonzero number a, $a^{-n} = \dfrac{1}{a^n}$.

Another explanation for the definition of a^{-n} is as follows. If the property $a^m \cdot a^n = a^{m+n}$ is to hold for all integer exponents, then $a^{-n} \cdot a^n = a^{-n+n} = a^0 = 1$. Thus, a^{-n} is the multiplicative inverse of a^n, and, consequently, $a^{-n} = \dfrac{1}{a^n}$.

Consider whether the property $a^m \cdot a^n = a^{m+n}$ can be extended to include all powers of a, where the exponents are integers. For example, is it true that $2^4 \cdot 2^{-3} = 2^{4+^-3} = 2^1$? The definitions of 2^{-3} and the properties of nonnegative exponents assure that this is true.

$$2^4 \cdot 2^{-3} = 2^4 \cdot \frac{1}{2^3} = \frac{2^4}{2^3} = \frac{2^1 \cdot 2^3}{2^3} = 2^1$$

Also, $2^{-4} \cdot 2^{-3} = 2^{-4+^-3} = 2^{-7}$ is true because

$$2^{-4} \cdot 2^{-3} = \frac{1}{2^4} \cdot \frac{1}{2^3} = \frac{1 \cdot 1}{2^4 \cdot 2^3} = \frac{1}{2^{4+3}} = \frac{1}{2^7} = 2^{-7}$$

In general, with integer exponents the following property holds.

Property | For any nonzero rational number a and any integers m and n, $a^m \cdot a^n = a^{m+n}$.

Other properties of exponents can be developed using the notions of rational numbers.

$$\frac{2^5}{2^3} = \frac{2^3 \cdot 2^2}{2^3} = 2^2 = 2^{5-3} \qquad \frac{2^5}{2^8} = \frac{2^5}{2^5 \cdot 2^3} = \frac{1}{2^3} = 2^{-3}$$

Thus, for any rational number a such that $a \neq 0$ and for integers m and n such that

$m > n$, $\dfrac{a^m}{a^n} = a^{m-n}$. Now, consider the case when $m < n$, such as $\dfrac{2^5}{2^8}$. If the property $\dfrac{a^m}{a^n} = a^{m-n}$ is to hold, then $\dfrac{2^5}{2^8} = 2^{5-8} = 2^{-3}$. This is true as above. Since a similar argument holds if $m = n$, we have the following property.

Property | For any rational number a such that $a \neq 0$ and for any integers m and n,
$$\frac{a^m}{a^n} = a^{m-n}.$$

Suppose a is a nonzero rational number and m and n are positive integers.

$$(a^m)^n = \underbrace{a^m \cdot a^m \cdot a^m \cdot \ldots \cdot a^m}_{n \text{ factors}} = \overbrace{a^{m+m+\cdots+m}}^{n \text{ terms}} = a^{nm} = a^{mn}$$

Thus, $(a^m)^n = a^{mn}$. For example, $(2^3)^4 = 2^{3\cdot4} = 2^{12}$.

Does this property hold for negative integer exponents? For example, does $(2^3)^{-4} = 2^{(3)(-4)} = 2^{-12}$? The answer is yes, because $(2^3)^{-4} = \dfrac{1}{(2^3)^4} = \dfrac{1}{2^{12}} = 2^{-12}$. Also, $(2^{-3})^4 = \left(\dfrac{1}{2^3}\right)^4 = \dfrac{1}{2^3} \cdot \dfrac{1}{2^3} \cdot \dfrac{1}{2^3} \cdot \dfrac{1}{2^3} = \dfrac{1^4}{(2^3)^4} = \dfrac{1}{2^{12}} = 2^{-12}$.

Property | For any rational number $a \neq 0$ and integers m and n, $(a^m)^n = a^{mn}$.

Using the definitions and properties developed, additional properties can be derived. Notice, for example, that

$$\left(\frac{2}{3}\right)^4 = \frac{2}{3} \cdot \frac{2}{3} \cdot \frac{2}{3} \cdot \frac{2}{3} = \frac{2 \cdot 2 \cdot 2 \cdot 2}{3 \cdot 3 \cdot 3 \cdot 3} = \frac{2^4}{3^4}$$

Property | For any nonzero rational number $\dfrac{a}{b}$ and any integer m,
$$\left(\frac{a}{b}\right)^m = \frac{a^m}{b^m}$$

Note that from the definition of negative exponents, the above property, and division of fractions, we have

$$\left(\frac{a}{b}\right)^{-m} = \frac{1}{\left(\frac{a}{b}\right)^m} = \frac{1}{\frac{a^m}{b^m}} = \frac{b^m}{a^m} = \left(\frac{b}{a}\right)^m$$

Consequently, $\left(\dfrac{a}{b}\right)^{-m} = \left(\dfrac{b}{a}\right)^m$.

A property similar to this holds for multiplication. For example,

$$(2 \cdot 3)^{-3} = \frac{1}{(2 \cdot 3)^3} = \frac{1}{2^3 \cdot 3^3} = \left(\frac{1}{2^3}\right) \cdot \left(\frac{1}{3^3}\right) = 2^{-3} \cdot 3^{-3}$$

and in general, it is true that $(a \cdot b)^m = a^m \cdot b^m$ if a and b are rational numbers and m is an integer.

The definitions and properties of exponents are summarized in the following list:

1. $a^m = \underbrace{a \cdot a \cdot a \cdot \ldots \cdot a}_{m \text{ factors}}$, where m is a positive integer

2. $a^0 = 1$, where $a \neq 0$

3. $a^{-m} = \dfrac{1}{a^m}$, where $a \neq 0$

4. $a^m \cdot a^n = a^{m+n}$

5. $\dfrac{a^m}{a^n} = a^{m-n}$, where $a \neq 0$

6. $(a^m)^n = a^{mn}$

7. $\left(\dfrac{a}{b}\right)^m = \dfrac{a^m}{b^m}$, where $b \neq 0$

8. $(ab)^m = a^m \cdot b^m$

Observe that all the properties of exponents refer to powers with either the same base or the same exponent. Hence, to evaluate expressions using exponents where different bases or powers are used, perform all the computations or rewrite the expressions using either the same base or exponent if possible. For example, $\dfrac{27^4}{81^3}$ can be rewritten as $\dfrac{27^4}{81^3} = \dfrac{(3^3)^4}{(3^4)^3} = \dfrac{3^{12}}{3^{12}} = 1$.

| Example 6-24 | Write each of the following in the simplest form using positive exponents in the final answer. |

(a) $16^2 \cdot 8^{-3}$ (b) $20^2 \div 2^4$

(c) $(3x)^3 + 2y^2x^0 + 5y^2 + x^2 \cdot x$, where $x \neq 0$

(d) $(a^{-3} + b^{-3})^{-1}$

Solution

(a) $16^2 \cdot 8^{-3} = (2^4)^2 \cdot (2^3)^{-3} = 2^8 \cdot 2^{-9} = 2^{8+{-9}} = 2^{-1} = \dfrac{1}{2}$

(b) $\dfrac{20^2}{2^4} = \dfrac{(2^2 \cdot 5)^2}{2^4} = \dfrac{2^4 \cdot 5^2}{2^4} = 5^2$

(c) $(3x)^3 + 2y^2x^0 + 5y^2 + x^2 \cdot x = 27x^3 + 2y^2 \cdot 1 + 5y^2 + x^3$

$\qquad\qquad = (27x^3 + x^3) + (2y^2 + 5y^2) = 28x^3 + 7y^2$

(d) $(a^{-3} + b^{-3})^{-1} = \left(\dfrac{1}{a^3} + \dfrac{1}{b^3}\right)^{-1} = \left(\dfrac{b^3 + a^3}{a^3b^3}\right)^{-1} = \dfrac{1}{\dfrac{a^3 + b^3}{a^3b^3}} = \dfrac{a^3b^3}{a^3 + b^3}$

PROBLEM SET 6-5

1. Write each of the following in the simplest form with positive exponents in the final answer.
   (a) $3^{-7} \cdot 3^{-6}$
   (b) $3^7 \cdot 3^6$
   (c) $5^{15} \div 5^4$
   (d) $5^{15} \div 5^{-4}$
   (e) $(^{-}5)^{-2}$
   (f) $\dfrac{a^2}{a^{-3}}$, where $a \neq 0$
   (g) $\dfrac{a}{a^{-1}}$, where $a \neq 0$

2. Write each of the following in the simplest form using positive exponents in the final answer.
   (a) $\left(\dfrac{1}{2}\right)^3 \cdot \left(\dfrac{1}{2}\right)^7$
   (b) $\left(\dfrac{1}{2}\right)^9 \div \left(\dfrac{1}{2}\right)^6$
   (c) $\left(\dfrac{2}{3}\right)^5 \cdot \left(\dfrac{4}{9}\right)^2$
   (d) $\left(\dfrac{3}{5}\right)^7 \div \left(\dfrac{3}{5}\right)^7$
   (e) $\left(\dfrac{3}{5}\right)^{-7} \div \left(\dfrac{5}{3}\right)^4$
   (f) $\left[\left(\dfrac{5}{6}\right)^7\right]^3$

3. If a and b are rational numbers with $a \neq 0$ and $b \neq 0$, m and n are integers, which of the following are true and which are false? Justify your answer.
   (a) $a^m \cdot b^n = (ab)^{m+n}$
   (b) $a^m \cdot b^n = (ab)^{mn}$
   (c) $a^m \cdot b^m = (ab)^{2m}$
   (d) $a^0 = 0$
   (e) $(a + b)^m = a^m + b^m$
   (f) $(a + b)^{-m} = \dfrac{1}{a^m} + \dfrac{1}{b^m}$
   (g) $a^{mn} = a^m \cdot a^n$
   (h) $\left(\dfrac{a}{b}\right)^{-1} = \dfrac{b}{a}$

4. Solve for the integer n in each of the following.
   (a) $2^n = 32$
   (b) $n^2 = 36$
   (c) $2^n \cdot 2^7 = 2^5$
   (d) $2^n \cdot 2^7 = 8$
   (e) $(2 + n)^2 = 2^2 + n^2$
   (f) $3^n = 27^5$

5. A human has approximately 25 trillion $(25 \cdot 10^{12})$ red blood cells, each with an average radius of $4 \cdot 10^{-3}$ mm (millimeters). If these cells were placed end to end in a line, how long would the line be in millimeters? If 1 km is 10^6 mm, how long will the line be in kilometers?

6. Solve each of the following inequalities for x, where x is an integer.
   (a) $3^x \leq 81$
   (b) $4^x < 8$
   (c) $3^{2x} > 27$
   (d) $2^x > 1$

7. Rewrite the following expressions using positive exponents and expressing all fractions in the simplest form.
   (a) $x^{-1} - x$
   (b) $x^2 - y^{-2}$
   (c) $y^{-3} + y^3$
   (d) $2x^2 + (2x)^2 + 2^2x$
   (e) $\dfrac{3a - b}{(3a - b)^{-1}}$
   (f) $(2x)^2 + (4a)^3 + a^2 \cdot 3a + 4x^2$
   (g) $(x^{-2} + 3y^{-1})^{-1}$

8. Which of the fractions in each pair is greater?
   (a) $\left(\dfrac{1}{2}\right)^3$ or $\left(\dfrac{1}{2}\right)^4$
   (b) $\left(\dfrac{3}{4}\right)^{10}$ or $\left(\dfrac{3}{4}\right)^8$
   (c) $\left(\dfrac{4}{3}\right)^{10}$ or $\left(\dfrac{4}{3}\right)^8$
   (d) $\left(\dfrac{3}{4}\right)^{10}$ or $\left(\dfrac{4}{5}\right)^{10}$
   (e) $\left(\dfrac{4}{3}\right)^{10}$ or $\left(\dfrac{5}{4}\right)^{10}$
   (f) $\left(\dfrac{3}{4}\right)^{100}$ or $\left(\dfrac{3}{4} \cdot \dfrac{9}{10}\right)^{100}$

* * * * * * * REVIEW PROBLEMS * * * * * * *

9. Arrange each of the following in increasing order.
   (a) $\dfrac{-2}{5}, \dfrac{-3}{5}, 0, \dfrac{1}{5}, \dfrac{2}{5}$
   (b) $\dfrac{7}{12}, \dfrac{13}{18}, \dfrac{13}{24}$

10. Find the solution sets for each of the following.
    (a) $\dfrac{3}{4}x - \dfrac{5}{8} \geq \dfrac{1}{2}$
    (b) $\dfrac{-x}{5} + \dfrac{1}{10} < \dfrac{-1}{2}$
    (c) $\dfrac{-2}{5}(10x + 1) < 1 - x$
    (d) $\dfrac{2}{3}\left(\dfrac{1}{2}x - 7\right) \geq \dfrac{3}{4}x$

11. For each of the following, find three rational numbers between the given fractions.
    (a) $\dfrac{1}{3}$ and $\dfrac{2}{3}$
    (b) $\dfrac{-5}{12}$ and $\dfrac{-1}{18}$

SOLUTION TO THE PRELIMINARY PROBLEM

Understanding the Problem

David and Sara started riding their bikes at 9:00 A.M. at City Hall. They followed the local bike trail and returned to City Hall at the same time. David rode three times as long as Sara rested and Sara rode four times as long as David rested. We know that each rode at a constant speed and we want to find who rode faster.

Devising a Plan

Since we are not asked how fast each cyclist rode, we do not need to find their exact speeds. Both cyclists covered the same distance, so it follows that the one who rode longer is the slower one. If we denote David's riding time in hours (or any other unit of time) by d and Sara's riding time, also in hours, by s, it would be sufficient to determine if $d < s$. For that purpose, we use the strategy of writing an equation. We translate the given information in terms of s and d and try to find an equation involving s and d. If we can express d in terms of s, or vice versa, we should be able to deduce which is greater.

Carrying Out the Plan

Because David rode three times as long as Sara rested, we can deduce that Sara rested one-third as long as David rode, that is, $\dfrac{d}{3}$ hours. Similarly, because Sara rode four times as long as David rested, we can deduce that David rested one-fourth as long as Sara rode her bike, that is, $\dfrac{s}{4}$. Using the expressions $\dfrac{d}{3}$ and $\dfrac{s}{4}$, we can write expressions for the total time of the trip, as shown in Table 6-8.

TABLE 6-8

	Riding Time	Resting Time	Total Time of Trip
David	d	$\dfrac{s}{4}$	$d + \dfrac{s}{4}$
Sara	s	$\dfrac{d}{3}$	$s + \dfrac{d}{3}$

Both cyclists started and returned at the same time, so their total trip times are the same. As shown in Table 6-8, David's total trip time is $d + \dfrac{s}{4}$ and Sara's total trip time is $s + \dfrac{d}{3}$. Consequently, we have the following equation and solution in terms of s.

$$d + \frac{s}{4} = s + \frac{d}{3}$$

$$d - \frac{d}{3} = s - \frac{s}{4}$$

$$\frac{2}{3}d = \frac{3}{4}s$$

$$d = \frac{3}{2} \cdot \frac{3}{4}s$$

$$d = \frac{9}{8}s$$

Because $\dfrac{9}{8} > 1$, it follows that $\dfrac{9}{8}s > s$, or that $d > s$. Thus, it took David longer to travel the same distance as Sara traveled, so Sara rode faster than David.

Looking Back

The problem could have also been solved by using all four variables mentioned in the question—that is, each cyclist's riding and resting times. By proper substitutions, we should obtain the same relation between d and s.

QUESTIONS FROM THE CLASSROOM

1. A student wrote the solution set to the equation $\dfrac{x}{7} - 2 < {}^{-}3$ as $\{{}^{-}8, {}^{-}9, {}^{-}10, {}^{-}11, \ldots\}$. Is the student correct?

2. A student reduced the fraction $\dfrac{(m + n)}{(p + n)}$ to $\dfrac{m}{p}$. Is that student correct?

3. A student asks if the reason we "invert and multiply" when dividing fractions is because division is the inverse of multiplication. Is this argument valid? Explain your answer.

4. When working on the problem of simplifying $\frac{3}{4} \cdot \frac{1}{2} \cdot \frac{2}{3}$, a student did the following.

$$\frac{3}{4} \cdot \frac{1}{2} \cdot \frac{2}{3} = \left(\frac{3 \cdot 1}{4 \cdot 2}\right)\left(\frac{3 \cdot 2}{4 \cdot 3}\right) = \frac{3}{8} \cdot \frac{6}{12} = \frac{18}{96}$$

What was the error?

5. A student asks, "If the ratio of boys to girls in the class is $\dfrac{2}{3}$, and 4 boys and 6 girls join the class, then the new ratio is $\dfrac{(2 + 4)}{(3 + 6)}$, or $\dfrac{6}{9}$. Since $\dfrac{2}{3} + \dfrac{4}{6} = \dfrac{(2 + 4)}{(3 + 6)}$, can all fractions be added in the same way?

6. Is $\dfrac{0}{6}$ in simplest form? Why or why not?

7. A student says that taking one-half of a number is the same as dividing the number by one-half. Is this correct?

8. A student writes $\dfrac{15}{53} < \dfrac{1}{3}$ because $3 \cdot 15 < 53 \cdot 1$. Another student writes $\dfrac{15}{53} = \dfrac{1}{3}$. Where is the fallacy?

9. On a test, a student wrote the following.

$$\frac{x}{7} - 2 < {}^-3$$

$$\frac{x}{7} < {}^-1$$

$$x > {}^-7$$

What is the error?

10. A student claims that each of the following is an arithmetic sequence. Is the student right?

(a) $\dfrac{1}{2}, \dfrac{2}{3}, \dfrac{3}{4}, \dfrac{4}{5}, \dfrac{5}{6}, \dfrac{6}{7}, \dfrac{7}{8}, \ldots$

(b) $\dfrac{1}{2}, \left(\dfrac{1}{2}\right)^{-2}, \left(\dfrac{1}{2}\right)^{-5}, \left(\dfrac{1}{2}\right)^{-8}, \left(\dfrac{1}{2}\right)^{-11}, \ldots$

11. A student claims that she found a new way to obtain a fraction between two positive fractions: If $\dfrac{a}{b}$ and $\dfrac{c}{d}$ are two positive fractions, then $\dfrac{a+c}{b+d}$ is between these fractions. Is she right?

12. A student claims that if $\dfrac{a}{b} = \dfrac{c}{d}$, then $\dfrac{a+c}{b+d} = \dfrac{a}{b} = \dfrac{c}{d}$. Is he right?

13. A student claims that $\dfrac{1}{x} < \dfrac{1}{y}$ if and only if $x > y$. Assuming that $x \neq 0$ and $y \neq 0$, is this right?

CHAPTER OUTLINE

I. Rational numbers

  A. Numbers of the form $\dfrac{a}{b}$, where a and b are integers and $b \neq 0$, are called **rational numbers.**

  B. A rational number can be used as:
    1. A division problem or the solution to a multiplication problem.
    2. A partition, or part, of a whole.
    3. A ratio.

  C. Two rational numbers $\dfrac{a}{b}$ and $\dfrac{c}{d}$ are **equal** if and only if $ad = bc$.

  D. If GCD$(a, b) = 1$, then $\dfrac{a}{b}$ is said to be in **simplest form.**

  E. If $0 < |b| \leq |a|$, then $\dfrac{a}{b}$ is called an **improper fraction.**

  F. If $0 < a < b$, then $\dfrac{a}{b}$ is called a **proper fraction.**

II. Operations on rational numbers

  A. $\dfrac{a}{b} + \dfrac{c}{b} = \dfrac{a+c}{b}$

  B. $\dfrac{a}{b} + \dfrac{c}{d} = \dfrac{ad+bc}{bd}$

  C. $\dfrac{a}{b} - \dfrac{c}{d} = \dfrac{ad-bc}{bd}$

  D. $\dfrac{a}{b} \cdot \dfrac{c}{d} = \dfrac{ac}{bd}$

  E. $\dfrac{a}{b} \div \dfrac{c}{d} = \dfrac{a}{b} \cdot \dfrac{d}{c} = \dfrac{ad}{bc}$, where $c \neq 0$

III. Properties of rational numbers

  A.

	Addition	Subtraction	Multiplication	Division
Closure	Yes	Yes	Yes	Yes, except for division by 0
Commutative	Yes	No	Yes	No
Associative	Yes	No	Yes	No
Identity	Yes	No	Yes	No
Inverse	Yes	No	Yes, except 0	No

  B. **Distributive property for multiplication over addition** of rational numbers x, y, and z: $x(y + z) = xy + xz$.

  C. **Denseness property:** Between any two rational numbers, there is another rational number.

IV. Ratio and proportion
    A. A quotient $a \div b$ is a **ratio.**
    B. A **proportion** is an equation of two ratios.
    C. Properties of proportions
        1. If $\dfrac{a}{b} = \dfrac{c}{d}$, then $\dfrac{b}{a} = \dfrac{d}{c}$, where $a \neq 0$ and $c \neq 0$.
        2. If $\dfrac{a}{b} = \dfrac{c}{d}$, then $\dfrac{a}{c} = \dfrac{b}{d}$, where $c \neq 0$.

V. Exponents
    A. $a^m = \underbrace{a \cdot a \cdot a \cdot \ldots \cdot a}_{m \text{ factors}}$, where m is a

        positive integer and a is a rational number.

B. Properties of exponents involving rational numbers
    1. $a^0 = 1$, where $a \neq 0$
    2. $a^{-n} = \dfrac{1}{a^n}$, where $a \neq 0$ and n is any rational number
    3. $a^m \cdot a^n = a^{m+n}$
    4. $(a^m)^n = a^{mn}$
    5. $(ab)^m = a^m b^m$
    6. $\left(\dfrac{a}{b}\right)^m = \dfrac{a^m}{b^m}$
    7. $\dfrac{a^m}{a^n} = a^{m-n}$

CHAPTER TEST

1. For each of the following, draw a diagram illustrating the fraction.
    (a) $\dfrac{3}{4}$ (b) $\dfrac{2}{3}$

2. Write three rational numbers equal to $\dfrac{5}{6}$.

3. Reduce each of the following rational numbers to simplest form.
    (a) $\dfrac{24}{28}$ (b) $\dfrac{ax^2}{bx}$ (c) $\dfrac{0}{17}$
    (d) $\dfrac{45}{81}$ (e) $\dfrac{b^2 + bx}{b + x}$ (f) $\dfrac{16}{216}$

4. Replace the comma with $>$, $<$, or $=$ in each of the following pairs to make a true statement.
    (a) $\dfrac{6}{10}, \dfrac{120}{200}$ (b) $\dfrac{-3}{4}, \dfrac{-5}{6}$
    (c) $\left(\dfrac{4}{5}\right)^{10}, \left(\dfrac{4}{5}\right)^{20}$ (d) $\left(1 + \dfrac{1}{3}\right)^2, \left(1 + \dfrac{1}{3}\right)^3$

5. Perform each of the following computations.
    (a) $\dfrac{5}{6} + \dfrac{4}{15}$ (b) $\dfrac{4}{25} - \dfrac{3}{35}$
    (c) $\dfrac{5}{6} \cdot \dfrac{12}{13}$ (d) $\dfrac{5}{6} \div \dfrac{12}{15}$
    (e) $\left(5\dfrac{1}{6} + 7\dfrac{1}{3}\right) \div 2\dfrac{1}{4}$
    (f) $\left(-5\dfrac{1}{6} + 7\dfrac{1}{3}\right) \div \dfrac{-9}{4}$

6. Find the additive and multiplicative inverses for each of the following:
    (a) 3 (b) $3\dfrac{1}{7}$ (c) $\dfrac{5}{6}$ (d) $-\dfrac{3}{4}$

7. Simplify each of the following. Write your answer in the form $\dfrac{a}{b}$, where a and b are integers and $b \neq 0$.
    (a) $\dfrac{\frac{1}{2} - \frac{3}{4}}{\frac{5}{6} - \frac{7}{8}}$ (b) $\dfrac{\frac{3}{4} \cdot \frac{5}{6}}{\frac{1}{2}}$ (c) $\dfrac{(\frac{1}{2})^2 - (\frac{3}{4})^2}{\frac{1}{2} + \frac{3}{4}}$

8. Solve each of the following for x, where x is a rational number.
    (a) $\dfrac{1}{4} x - \dfrac{3}{5} \leq \dfrac{1}{2} (3 - 2x)$
    (b) $\dfrac{x}{3} - \dfrac{x}{2} \geq \dfrac{-1}{4}$
    (c) $\dfrac{2}{3} \left(\dfrac{3}{4} x - 1\right) = \dfrac{2}{3} - x$
    (d) $\dfrac{5}{6} = \dfrac{4 - x}{3}$

9. Justify the invert-and-multiply algorithm for division of rational numbers.

10. If the ratio of boys to girls in Mr. Good's class is 3 to 5, the ratio of boys to girls in Ms. Garcia's is the same, and you know that there are 15 girls in Ms. Garcia's class, how many boys are in her class?

11. Write each of the following in simplest form with nonnegative exponents in the final answer.

(a) $\left(\frac{1}{2}\right)^4\left(\frac{1}{2}\right)^7$

(b) $5^{-16} \div 5^4$

(c) $\left[\left(\frac{2}{3}\right)^7\right]^{-4}$

(d) $3^{16} \cdot 3^2$

12. John has $54\frac{1}{4}$ yards of material. If he needs to cut the cloth into pieces that are $3\frac{1}{12}$ yards long, how many pieces can be cut? How much material will be left over?

SELECTED BIBLIOGRAPHY

Bennett, A., Jr., and P. Davidson. *Fraction Bars*. Palo Alto, Calif.: Creative Publications.

Brown, C. "Fractions on Grid Paper." *Arithmetic Teacher* 27 (January 1979):8–10.

Bruni, J., and H. Silverman. "Let's Do It: Using Rectangles and Squares to Develop Fraction Concepts." *The Arithmetic Teacher* 24 (February 1977):96–102.

Carlisle, E. "Fractions and Popsicle Sticks." *Arithmetic Teacher* 27 (February 1980):50–51.

Coxford, A., and L. Ellerbruch. "Fractional Numbers." In *Mathematics Learning in Early Childhood*, 37th Yearbook of the National Council of Teachers of Mathematics. Reston, Va.: The National Council of Teachers of Mathematics, 1975.

Ellerbruch, L., and J. Payne. "A Teaching Sequence from Initial Concepts Through the Addition of Unlike Fractions." In *Developing Computational Skills*, 1978 Yearbook of the National Council of Teachers of Mathematics. Reston, Va.: The National Council of Teachers of Mathematics, 1978.

Feinberg, M. "Is It Necessary to Invert?" *Arithmetic Teacher* 27 (January 1980):50–52.

Jencks, S., D. Peck, and L. Chatterley. "Why Blame the Kids? We Teach Mistakes." *Arithmetic Teacher* 28 (October 1980): 38–42.

Leutzinger, L., and G. Nelson. "Let's Do It–Fractions With Models." *Arithmetic Teacher* 27 (May 1980):6–11.

Miller, A. "Teaching the Concept of $\frac{1}{2}$ in the Primary Grades." *Arithmetic Teacher* 25 (March 1978):57–58.

Moulton, J. "A Working Model for Rational Numbers." *The Arithmetic Teacher* 22 (April 1975):328–332.

Payne, J. "One Point of View: Sense and Nonsense about Fractions and Decimals." *Arithmetic Teacher* 27 (January 1980):4–7.

Post, T. "Fractions: Results and Implications from National Assessment." *Arithmetic Teacher* 28 (May 1981):26–31.

Sanok, G. "Mathematics and Saltine Crackers." *Arithmetic Teacher* 28 (December 1980):36.

Scott, W. "Fractions Taught by Folding Paper Strips." *Arithmetic Teacher* 28 (January 1981):18–21.

Shookoohi, G-H. "Readiness of Eight-Year-Old Children to Understand the Division of Fractions." *Arithmetic Teacher* 27 (March 1980):40–43.

Thiessen, D. "David's Algorithm for the L.C.D." *Arithmetic Teacher* 28 (March 1981):18.

Wassmansdorf, M. "Reducing Fractions Can Be Easy, Maybe Even Fun." *The Arithmetic Teacher* 21 (February 1974):99–102.

PRELIMINARY PROBLEM

Howard entered a store and said to the owner, "Give me as much money as I have with me and I will spend 80% of the total." After this was done, Howard repeated the operation at a second store and at a third store and was finally left with $12. With how much money did he start?

INTRODUCTION

Although the Hindu-Arabic numeration system discussed in Chapter 3 was perfected around the sixth century, the extension of the system to decimals did not take place until about a thousand years later. Suggestions for decimals were recorded long before the Dutch scientist Simon Stevin was credited as being responsible for their invention. In 1585, Stevin wrote *La Disme,* a work that gave rules for computing with decimals. The only significant improvement in Stevin's original ideas has been in notation. Even today there is no universally accepted form of writing a decimal point. For example, in the United States we write 6.75; in England this number is written as 6·75 and in Germany and France it is written 6,75.

Today, the increased use of the metric system and the emergence of calculators and computers make a knowledge of decimals even more important in schools and in homes. The full impact of these developments on the teaching of decimals is not yet known.

7-1 DECIMALS AND DECIMAL OPERATIONS

The word *decimal* comes from the Latin *decem,* which means ten. Many students first see decimals when dealing with our notation for money. For example, even young children realize that a sign that says that a doll costs $9.95 means that they must pay nine whole dollars and some part of a dollar. The digits to the left of the dot, called the **decimal point,** form the integer part of the decimal. The digits to the right represent the sum of a set of rational numbers whose numerators are the given digits and whose denominators are successive powers of ten starting with 10^1. For example, 562.681 represents

decimal point

$$562 + \frac{6}{10^1} + \frac{8}{10^2} + \frac{1}{10^3} = 562 + \frac{6}{10} + \frac{8}{100} + \frac{1}{1000}$$

or $562 \frac{681}{1000}$. The decimal 562.681 is read "five hundred sixty-two and six hundred eighty-one thousandths." The decimal point is read as "and." Each place to the right of a decimal point may be named by its power of 10. For example, the places of 12.61843 can be named as shown in Table 7-1.

TABLE 7-1

1	2	.	6	1	8	4	3
Tens	Units	And	Tenths	Hundredths	Thousandths	Ten-thousandths	Hundred-thousandths

Table 7-2 shows other examples.

TABLE 7-2

Decimal	Meaning	Fraction
5.3	$5 + \dfrac{3}{10}$	$5\dfrac{3}{10}$, or $\dfrac{53}{10}$
0.02	$0 + \dfrac{0}{10} + \dfrac{2}{100}$	$\dfrac{2}{100}$
0.58	$0 + \dfrac{5}{10} + \dfrac{8}{100}$	$\dfrac{58}{100}$
2.0103	$2 + \dfrac{0}{10} + \dfrac{1}{100} + \dfrac{0}{1000} + \dfrac{3}{10,000}$	$2\dfrac{103}{10,000}$, or $\dfrac{20,103}{10,000}$
−3.6	$-\left(3 + \dfrac{6}{10}\right)$	$-3\dfrac{6}{10}$, or $-\dfrac{36}{10}$

Every decimal can also be written in expanded form using place value and negative exponents. Thus, 12.61843 may be written as $1 \cdot 10^1 + 2 \cdot 10^0 + 6 \cdot 10^{-1} + 1 \cdot 10^{-2} + 8 \cdot 10^{-3} + 4 \cdot 10^{-4} + 3 \cdot 10^{-5}$. However, to avoid negative exponents, most elementary texts use fractional notation. The decimal 12.61843 could be written as

$$12.61843 = 10 + 2 + \frac{6}{10} + \frac{1}{100} + \frac{8}{1000} + \frac{4}{10,000} + \frac{3}{100,000}$$

or

$$12.61843 = 1 \cdot 10^1 + 2 \cdot 10^0 + 6\left(\frac{1}{10}\right) + 1\left(\frac{1}{100}\right) + 8\left(\frac{1}{1000}\right) + 4\left(\frac{1}{10,000}\right)$$
$$+ 3\left(\frac{1}{100,000}\right)$$

Both forms are acceptable, and we use them interchangeably.

Example 7-1 shows how to convert rational numbers whose denominators are powers of 10 to a decimal.

Example 7-1

Convert each of the following to decimals.

(a) $\dfrac{56}{100}$　　　　　(b) $\dfrac{326}{10}$　　　　　(c) $\dfrac{235}{10,000}$

Solution

(a) $\dfrac{56}{100} = \dfrac{5 \cdot 10 + 6}{10^2} = \dfrac{5 \cdot 10}{10^2} + \dfrac{6}{10^2} = \dfrac{5}{10} + \dfrac{6}{10^2} = 0.56$

(b) $\dfrac{326}{10} = \dfrac{3 \cdot 10^2 + 2 \cdot 10 + 6}{10} = \dfrac{3 \cdot 10^2}{10} + \dfrac{2 \cdot 10}{10} + \dfrac{6}{10}$

$$= 3 \cdot 10 + 2 + \frac{6}{10} = 32.6$$

(c) $\dfrac{235}{10,000} = \dfrac{2 \cdot 10^2 + 3 \cdot 10 + 5}{10^4} = \dfrac{2 \cdot 10^2}{10^4} + \dfrac{3 \cdot 10}{10^4} + \dfrac{5}{10^4}$

$$= \frac{2}{10^2} + \frac{3}{10^3} + \frac{5}{10^4} = 0.0235$$

The ideas in Example 7-1 can be reinforced using a calculator. For example, in part (a), enter ⁵ ⁶ ÷ ¹ ⁰ ⁰ = and watch the display. Divide by 10 again and look at the new placement of the decimal point.

The fractions in Example 7-1 are easy to convert to decimals because the denominators are powers of ten. If the denominator of a fraction is not a power of 10, then the conversion to a decimal requires more work. For example, to write $\frac{3}{5}$ as a decimal, we use the problem-solving strategy of converting this problem to one we already know how to do. We know how to convert fractions in which the denominators are powers of ten to a decimal. Hence, we first change $\frac{3}{5}$ to a fraction in which the denominator is a power of 10, and then we convert it to a decimal.

$$\frac{3}{5} = \frac{3 \cdot 2}{5 \cdot 2} = \frac{6}{10} = 0.6$$

The reason for multiplying by 2 is apparent by observing that $10 = 2 \cdot 5$. Because $10^n = (2 \cdot 5)^n = 2^n \cdot 5^n$, the prime factorization of the denominator must be $2^n \cdot 5^n$, in order for the denominator of a rational number to be 10^n. We use these ideas to write each fraction in Example 7-2 as a fraction in which the denominator is a power of ten and then as a decimal.

Example 7-2

Express each of the following rational numbers as decimals.

(a) $\dfrac{7}{2^6}$ (b) $\dfrac{1}{2^3 \cdot 5^4}$ (c) $\dfrac{1}{125}$ (d) $\dfrac{7}{250}$

Solution

(a) $\dfrac{7}{2^6} = \dfrac{7 \cdot 5^6}{2^6 \cdot 5^6} = \dfrac{7 \cdot 15,625}{(2 \cdot 5)^6} = \dfrac{109,375}{10^6} = 0.109375$

(b) $\dfrac{1}{2^3 \cdot 5^4} = \dfrac{1 \cdot 2^1}{2^3 \cdot 5^4 \cdot 2^1} = \dfrac{2}{2^4 \cdot 5^4} = \dfrac{2}{(2 \cdot 5)^4} = \dfrac{2}{10^4} = 0.0002$

(c) $\dfrac{1}{125} = \dfrac{1}{5^3} = \dfrac{1 \cdot 2^3}{5^3 \cdot 2^3} = \dfrac{8}{(5 \cdot 2)^3} = \dfrac{8}{10^3} = 0.008$

(d) $\dfrac{7}{250} = \dfrac{7}{2 \cdot 5^3} = \dfrac{7 \cdot 2^2}{(2 \cdot 5^3)2^2} = \dfrac{28}{(2 \cdot 5)^3} = \dfrac{28}{10^3} = 0.028$

terminating decimals

The solutions in Example 7-2 are illustrations of **terminating decimals**, decimals that can be written with only a finite number of places to the right of the decimal point.

If we attempt to rewrite $\frac{2}{11}$ as a terminating decimal using the method just developed, we first try to find a number b such that the following holds.

$$\frac{2}{11} = \frac{2b}{11b}, \quad \text{where } 11b \text{ is a power of } 10$$

By the Fundamental Theorem of Arithmetic (discussed in Chapter 5), the only prime factors of a power of 10 are 2 and 5. Thus, we cannot write $11b$ as a power of 10. Therefore, there is no whole number b that will satisfy

$$\frac{2}{11} = \frac{2b}{11b}$$

where $11b$ is a power of 10. A similar argument using the Fundamental Theorem of Arithmetic holds in general, so we have the following result:

A *rational number* $\dfrac{a}{b}$ *in simplest form can be written as a terminating decimal if and only if the prime factorization of the denominator contains no primes other than* 2 *or* 5.

Example 7-3	Which of the following fractions can be written as terminating decimals?

(a) $\dfrac{7}{8}$ (b) $\dfrac{6}{125}$

(c) $\dfrac{21}{28}$ (d) $\dfrac{37}{768}$

Solution

(a) $\dfrac{7}{8} = \dfrac{7}{2^3}$. Because the denominator is 2^3, $\dfrac{7}{8}$ can be written as a terminating decimal, 0.875.

(b) $\dfrac{6}{125} = \dfrac{6}{5^3}$. The denominator is 5^3, so $\dfrac{6}{125}$ can be written as a terminating decimal, 0.048.

(c) $\dfrac{21}{28} = \dfrac{21}{(2^2 \cdot 7)} = \dfrac{3}{2^2}$. The denominator of the fraction in simplest form is 2^2, so $\dfrac{21}{28}$ can be written as a terminating decimal, 0.75.

(d) $\dfrac{37}{768} = \dfrac{37}{(2^8 \cdot 3)}$. This fraction is in simplest form and the denominator contains a factor of 3, so $\dfrac{37}{768}$ cannot be written as a terminating decimal.

Remark

To determine whether or not a rational number $\dfrac{a}{b}$ can be represented as a terminating decimal, consider the prime factorization of the denominator *only* if the fraction is in simplest form.

Decimal Operations

To develop an algorithm for decimal addition, consider the sum $3.26 + 14.7$. We can compute the sum by changing it to a problem we already know how to solve, that is, a sum involving fractions.

$$3.26 + 14.7 = \left(3 + \frac{2}{10} + \frac{6}{100}\right) + \left(14 + \frac{7}{10}\right)$$

$$= (3 + 14) + \left(\frac{2}{10} + \frac{7}{10}\right) + \left(\frac{6}{100}\right)$$

$$= 17 + \frac{9}{10} + \frac{6}{100}$$

$$= 17.96$$

This addition, using fractions, was accomplished by grouping the integers, the tenths, the hundredths and adding. Because $14.7 = 14 + \frac{7}{10} = 14 + \frac{7}{10} + \frac{0}{100} = 14.70$, the addition $3.26 + 14.7$ can be accomplished by lining up the decimal points and adding, as with whole numbers.

$$\begin{array}{r} 3.26 \\ + 14.70 \\ \hline 17.96 \end{array}$$

The algorithm for adding terminating decimals is a three-step process:

1. List the numbers vertically, lining up the decimal points. (Append zeros if necessary.)
2. Add the numbers as though they were whole numbers.
3. Insert the decimal point in the sum directly below the decimal points in the numbers being added.

Subtraction of terminating decimals also can be accomplished by lining up the decimal points. The argument that this is true is left as an exercise.

Example 7-4	Compute each of the following.

(a) $14.36 + 5.2 + 0.036$ (b) $17.013 - 2.98$
(c) $17.01 - 2.938$

Solution

(a) $\begin{array}{r} 14.360 \\ 5.200 \\ + 0.036 \\ \hline 19.596 \end{array}$ (b) $\begin{array}{r} 17.013 \\ - 2.980 \\ \hline 14.033 \end{array}$ (c) $\begin{array}{r} 17.010 \\ - 2.938 \\ \hline 14.072 \end{array}$

Algorithms for multiplication of terminating decimals can be found by multiplying the corresponding fractions, each in the form $\frac{a}{b}$. Consider the product $(4.62)(2.4)$.

$$(4.62)(2.4) = \frac{462}{100} \cdot \frac{24}{10} = \frac{462}{10^2} \cdot \frac{24}{10^1}$$

$$= \frac{462 \cdot 24}{10^2 \cdot 10^1}$$

$$= \frac{11,088}{10^3}$$

$$= 11.088$$

The answer is obtained by multiplying the whole numbers 462 and 24 and then dividing the result by 10^3.

The algorithm for multiplying decimals can be stated as follows:

> *If there are n digits to the right of the decimal point in one number and m digits to the right of the decimal point in a second number, multiply the two numbers, ignoring the decimals, and then place the decimal point so that there are m + n digits to the right of the decimal point in the product.*

There are $m + n$ digits to the right of the decimal point in the product because $10^n \cdot 10^m = 10^{n+m}$.

Example 7-5 | Compute each of the following.

(a) (6.2)(1.43)   (b) (0.02)(0.013)   (c) (1000)(3.6)

Solution | (a)   1.4 3   (2 digits after the decimal point)
　　　　　　　　× 6.2   (1 digit after the decimal point)
　　　　　　　　2 8 6
　　　　　　　　8 5 8
　　　　　　　　8.8 6 6   (3 digits after the decimal point)

(b)　　　0.0 1 3　　　　　　　　　(c)　　　　3.6
　　　　× 0.0 2　　　　　　　　　　　　× 1 0 0 0
　　　　0.0 0 0 2 6　　　　　　　　　3 6 0 0.0

Remark | Example 7-5(c) suggests that multiplication by 10^n, where n is a positive integer, results in moving the decimal point in the multiplicand n places to the right.

To develop an algorithm for dividing decimals, we first consider the case of dividing a terminating decimal by a whole number. Consider $0.96 \div 3$. This division can be approached by rewriting the decimal as a fraction and dividing.

$$0.96 \div 3 = \frac{96}{100} \div 3 = \frac{96}{100} \cdot \frac{1}{3} = \frac{96 \cdot 1}{100 \cdot 3} = \frac{32}{100} = 0.32$$

This problem and solution can be rewritten as follows.

$$
\begin{array}{r}
0.32 \\
3\overline{)0.96} \\
\underline{9} \\
6 \\
\underline{6} \\
\end{array}
$$

When the divisor is a whole number, we see that the division can be handled as with whole numbers and the decimal point placed directly over the decimal point in the dividend. To divide when the divisor is not a whole number, we use the strategy of changing the division problem to an equivalent division where the divisor is a whole number. For example, consider $1.2032 \div 0.32$. To obtain a whole number divisor in the problem, we use the Fundamental Law of Fractions and multiply the numerator and denominator of the fraction by 100.

$$
\frac{1.2032}{0.32} = \frac{1.2032 \cdot 100}{0.32 \cdot 100} = \frac{120.32}{32}
$$

This corresponds to rewriting the division problem in form (a) to an equivalent problem in form (b).

(a) $0.32\overline{)1.2032}$ (b) $32\overline{)120.32}$

In elementary texts, this process is usually described as "moving" the decimal point two places to the right in both the dividend and the divisor. This process is usually indicated with arrows, as shown below and on the student page taken from *Scott, Foresman Mathematics* 1980, Grade 6 (page 253). Notice from the student page that we sometimes need to write zeros in the dividend.

$$
\begin{array}{r}
3.7\,6 \\
0.3\,2\,)\overline{1.2\,0\,3\,2} \\
\underline{9\,6} \\
2\,4\,3 \\
\underline{2\,2\,4} \\
1\,9\,2 \\
\underline{1\,9\,2} \\
0 \\
\end{array}
$$

Example 7-6

Compute each of the following.

(a) $13.169 \div 0.13$ (b) $13.1 \div 1000$

Solution

(a)
$$
\begin{array}{r}
1\,0\,1.3 \\
0.1\,3\,)\overline{1\,3.1\,6\,9} \\
\underline{1\,3} \\
1\,6 \\
\underline{1\,3} \\
3\,9 \\
\underline{3\,9} \\
\end{array}
$$

(b)
$$
\begin{array}{r}
0.0\,1\,3\,1 \\
1\,0\,0\,0\,)\overline{1\,3.1\,0\,0\,0} \\
\underline{1\,0\,0\,0} \\
3\,1\,0\,0 \\
\underline{3\,0\,0\,0} \\
1\,0\,0\,0 \\
\underline{1\,0\,0\,0} \\
\end{array}
$$

Dividing Decimals: Zeros in the Dividend

In some cases when you divide by a decimal, you have to write zeros in the dividend before you start dividing.

A. Linda is making jewelry in a craft class. A pair of earring backs costs $0.75. How many pairs of earring backs can Linda buy with $9?

Find 9 ÷ 0.75.

$$0.75\overline{)9}$$

$$0.75\overline{)9.00}$$

Multiply the divisor and the dividend by 100. Place the decimal point in the quotient.

$$
\begin{array}{r}
12. \\
0.75\overline{)9.00} \\
-7\,5 \\
\hline
1\,50 \\
-1\,50 \\
\hline
0
\end{array}
$$

Divide 900 by 75.

Linda can buy 12 pairs of earring backs.

B. Find 9.4 ÷ 0.05.

$$0.05\overline{)9.40}$$

Multiply the divisor and the dividend by 100.

$$
\begin{array}{r}
1\,88. \\
0.05\overline{)9.40} \\
-5 \\
\hline
4\,4 \\
-4\,0 \\
\hline
40 \\
-40 \\
\hline
0
\end{array}
$$

Divide 940 by 5.

C. Find 95 ÷ 1.9.

$$
\begin{array}{r}
5\,0. \\
1.9\overline{)95.0} \\
-95 \\
\hline
0\,0
\end{array}
$$

Example 7-7	An owner of a gasoline station must collect a gasoline tax of $0.11 on each gallon of gasoline sold. One week the owner paid $1595 in gas taxes. The pump price of a gallon of gas that week was $1.35.

(a) How many gallons of gas were sold during the week?
(b) What was the revenue after taxes for the week?

Solution	(a) To find the number of gallons of gas sold during the week, we must divide the total gas tax bill by the amount of the tax.

$$\frac{1595}{0.11} = 14,500$$

Thus, 14,500 gallons were sold.

(b) To obtain the revenue after taxes, we must first determine the revenue before taxes by multiplying the number of gallons sold times the cost per gallon.

$$(14,500)(\$1.35) = \$19,575$$

We then subtract the cost remitted in gasoline taxes.

$$\$19,575 - \$1595 = \$17,980$$

Thus, the revenue after gasoline taxes is $17,980.

PROBLEM SET 7-1

1. Write each of the following in expanded form.
   (a) 0.023   (b) 206.06
   (c) 312.0103   (d) 0.000132

2. Rewrite each of the following as decimals.
   (a) $4 \cdot 10^3 + 3 \cdot 10^2 + 5 \cdot 10 + 6 + 7 \cdot 10^{-1} + 8 \cdot 10^{-2}$
   (b) $4 \cdot 10^3 + 6 \cdot 10^{-1} + 8 \cdot 10^{-3}$

3. Write each of the following as numerals.
   (a) Five hundred thirty-six and seventy-six ten-thousandths
   (b) Three and eight-thousandths
   (c) Four hundred thirty-six millionths
   (d) Five million and two-tenths

4. Write each of the following terminating decimals as fractions.
   (a) 0.436   (b) 25.16   (c) ⁻316.027
   (d) 28.1902   (e) ⁻4.3   (f) ⁻62.01

5. Determine which of the following represent terminating decimals, without performing the actual divisions.

(a) $\dfrac{4}{5}$ (b) $\dfrac{61}{2^2 \cdot 5}$ (c) $\dfrac{3}{6}$

(d) $\dfrac{1}{2^5}$ (e) $\dfrac{36}{5^5}$ (f) $\dfrac{133}{625}$

(g) $\dfrac{1}{3}$ (h) $\dfrac{2}{35}$ (i) $\dfrac{1}{13}$

6. Where possible, write each of the numbers in Problem 5 as terminating decimals.

7. Compute each of the following.
   (a) 36.812 + 0.43 + 1.96
   (b) 200.01 + 32.007 + ⁻1.32
   (c) 200.01 − 32.007   (d) ⁻4.612 − 386.0193
   (e) (3.61)(0.413)   (f) (0.0123)(4.681)
   (g) (⁻2.6)(4)   (h) 10.7663 ÷ 2.3
   (i) 0.006384 ÷ (⁻1.6)

8. Calculate the following by converting each decimal to a fraction, performing the computation and then converting the fraction answer to a decimal.
   (a) 13.62 + 4.082   (b) 12.62 − 4.082
   (c) (1.36)(0.02)   (d) (1.36) ÷ (0.02)

9. Multiply each of the following by: (i) 10; (ii) 1000; (iii) 10^8.

   (a) 4.63   (b) 0.04   (c) 46.3
   (d) 463.0   (e) 0.00463
   (f) 0.0000000463
   (g) 0.79   (h) 6.2

10. Explain why $10^3(0.abcd) = abc.d$.

11. Which of the following divisions are equivalent to $18 \div 2$?

   (a) $20\overline{)180}$ (b) $0.2\overline{)0.18}$
   (c) $0.002\overline{)0.018}$ (d) $20\overline{)1800}$
   (e) $0.0002\overline{)0.00018}$ (f) $0.2\overline{)1.8}$

12. Continue the decimal patterns shown below.

   (a) 0.9, 1.8, 2.7, 3.6, 4.5, ———, ———, ———
   (b) 0.3, 0.5, 0.7, 0.9, 0.11, ———, ———,

   ———
   (c) 1, 0.5, 0.25, 0.125, ———, ———, ———
   (d) 0.2, 1.5, 2.8, 4.1, 5.4, ———, ———, ———

13. The following are answers to various types of computations. Write an exercise for each answer.
   (a) 86.04 as an addition of two numbers
   (b) 353.76 as an addition of four numbers
   (c) 96.72 as a subtraction of two numbers
   (d) 0.0138 as a multiplication of two numbers
   (e) 0.12 as a subtraction of two numbers
   (f) 2.03 as a division of two numbers

14. Explain why subtraction of terminating decimals can be accomplished by lining up the decimal points and subtracting as if the numbers were whole numbers (or integers).

15. If 0.896 inch of rain fell during 7 hours, what was the average amount of rain per hour?

16. If the average for common stocks rose 8.395 points during 5 days of trading, what was the average gain per day?

17. If Moose went to the store and bought a chair for $17.95, a lawn rake for $13.59, a spade for $14.86, a lawn mower for $179.98, and two six-packs for $2.43 each, what was the bill?

18. If the rainfall was 1.9 inches in March and 2.7 inches in April, how much more rain was there in April than March?

19. At 60° Fahrenheit, 1 quart of water weighs 2.082 pounds. One cubic foot of water is 29.922 quarts. What is the weight of a cubic foot of water?

20. (a) Find the product of 0.22 and 0.35 on the calculator. How does the placement of the decimal point in the answer on the calculator compare with the placement of the decimal point using the rule in this chapter? Explain.
   (b) In a similar manner, investigate placement of the decimal point in the quotient obtained by performing the division $0.2436 \div 0.0006$.

21. At a local bank, two different systems are available for charging for checking accounts. System A is a "dime-a-time" plan, as there is no monthly service charge and the charge is 10¢ per check written. System B is a plan with a service charge of 75¢ per month plus 7¢ per check written during that month.
   (a) Which plan is the most economical if an average of 12 checks per month is written?
   (b) Which system is the most economical if an average of 52 checks per month is written?
   (c) What is the "break-even point" for the number of checks written (that is, the number of checks for which the costs of the two plans are as close as possible)?

22. A bank statement from a local bank shows that a checking account has a balance of $83.62. The balance recorded in the checkbook shows only $21.69. After checking the canceled checks against the record of these checks, the customer finds that the bank has not yet recorded six checks in the amounts of $3.21, $14.56, $12.44, $6.98, $9.51, $7.49. Is the bank record correct? (Assume the person's checkbook records *are* correct.)

23. The winner of the big sweepstakes has 15 minutes to decide whether to receive $1,000,000 cash immediately or to receive 1¢ on the first day of the month, 2¢ on the second day, 4¢ on the third, and so on, each day receiving double the previous day's amount, until the end of a 30-day month. However, only the amount received on that last day may be kept and all the rest of the month's "allowance" must be returned. Use a calculator to figure which of these two options is more profitable, and figure out how much more profitable one way is than the other.

★ 24. Given any reduced rational $\frac{a}{b}$ with $0 < a < b$, where b is of the form $2^m \cdot 5^n$ (m and n are whole numbers), determine a relationship between m and/or n and the number of digits in the terminating decimal.

BRAIN TEASER

Arrange four 7s using any
operations and decimal
points needed to obtain a
value of 100.

7-2 MORE ABOUT DECIMALS AND THEIR PROPERTIES

The division processes described in Section 7-1 can be used to develop a procedure for converting any rational number to a decimal. (Recall that $\frac{7}{8}$ can be written as a terminating decimal because it is in simplest form and the denominator contains only factors of 2.)

$$
\begin{array}{r}
0.875 \\
8\overline{)7.000} \\
\underline{6\ 4} \\
60 \\
\underline{56} \\
40 \\
\underline{40} \\
\end{array}
$$

In a similar way, nonterminating decimals can be obtained for other rational numbers. For example, to find a decimal representation for $\frac{2}{11}$, consider the following division.

$$
\begin{array}{r}
0.18 \\
11\overline{)2.00} \\
\underline{1\ 1} \\
90 \\
\underline{88} \\
2 \\
\end{array}
$$

repeating decimal
repetend

At this point if the division is continued, then the division pattern repeats. Thus, the quotient is $0.181818\ldots$. A decimal of this type is called a **repeating decimal,** and the repeating block of digits is called the **repetend.** The repeating decimal is written as $0.\overline{18}$, where the bar indicates that the block of digits underneath is repeated infinitely.

Example 7-8 | Convert $\frac{1}{7}$ to a decimal.

Solution

$$
\begin{array}{r}
0.142857 \\
7{\overline{\smash{\big)}\,1.000000}} \\
\underline{7} \\
30 \\
\underline{28} \\
20 \\
\underline{14} \\
60 \\
\underline{56} \\
40 \\
\underline{35} \\
50 \\
\underline{49} \\
1
\end{array}
$$

If the division process is continued at this point, the division pattern repeats; thus $\frac{1}{7} = 0.\overline{142857}$.

In Example 7-8, the remainders obtained in the division are 3, 2, 6, 4, 5, and 1. These are all the possible nonzero remainders that can be obtained when dividing by 7. (If the remainder of 0 had been obtained, the decimal would terminate.) If $\frac{a}{b}$ is any rational number in simplest form and it does not represent a terminating decimal, then the possible remainders upon division by b are 1, 2, 3, 4, . . . , $b - 1$. After b divisions, there are b remainders, which cannot *all* be different, because there are only $b - 1$ possible different remainders. Thus, after b divisions, at least one remainder appears twice. When this happens, a block of at most $b - 1$ digits in the quotient repeats. Therefore, a *rational number may always be represented either as a terminating decimal or as a repeating decimal.*

We have already considered how to write terminating decimals in the form $\frac{a}{b}$, where $a, b \in I$, $b \neq 0$. For example,

$$0.55 = \frac{55}{10^2} = \frac{55}{100}$$

To write $0.\overline{5}$ in a similar way, we naturally try the same method. However, the repeating decimal has infinitely many places, so there is no single power of 10 that can be placed in the denominator. To overcome this difficulty, we must somehow eliminate the infinite repeating part of the decimal. Suppose $n = 0.\overline{5}$. It can be shown that $10(0.555 . . .) = 5.555 . . . = 5.\overline{5}$. Hence, $10n = 5.\overline{5}$. Using this information, we subtract to obtain an equation whose solution is a fraction.

$$10n = 5.\overline{5}$$
$$\underline{-\,n = -0.\overline{5}}$$
$$9n = 5$$

$$n = \frac{5}{9}$$

Thus, $0.\overline{5} = \frac{5}{9}$. This result can be checked by performing the division $5 \div 9$. By performing the subtraction above, an equation containing only integers results. (The repeating blocks "cancel" each other.)

Suppose a decimal has a repetend of more than one digit, such as $0.\overline{235}$. In order to write it in the form $\frac{a}{b}$, it is reasonable to multiply by 10^3, since there is a three-digit repetend. Let $n = 0.\overline{235}$. Then,

$$1000n = 235.\overline{235}$$
$$\underline{-\,n = -0.\overline{235}}$$
$$999n = 235$$

$$n = \frac{235}{999}$$

Hence, $0.\overline{235} = \frac{235}{999}$.

Notice that $0.\overline{5}$ repeats in blocks of one digit, and to write it in the form $\frac{a}{b}$, we first multiply by 10^1; $0.\overline{235}$ repeats in blocks of three digits, and we first multiply by 10^3. In general, if the repetend is immediately to the right of the decimal point, first multiply by 10^n, where n is the number of digits in the repetend, and continue as above.

Now suppose the repeating block does *not* occur immediately after the decimal point. For example, let $n = 2.3\overline{45}$. A strategy for solving this problem is to change it to a problem we already know how to do, that is, change it to a problem where the repeating block immediately follows the decimal point. To do this, we multiply both sides by 10.

$$10n = 23.\overline{45}$$

We now proceed as with previous problems. Since $10n = 23.\overline{45}$, then $100(10n) = 2345.\overline{45}$. Thus,

$$1000n = 2345.\overline{45}$$
$$\underline{-\,10n = -\,23.\overline{45}}$$
$$990n = 2322$$

$$n = \frac{2322}{990}, \text{ or } \frac{387}{165}$$

Hence, $2.3\overline{45} = \frac{2322}{990}$, or $\frac{387}{165}$.

Since rational numbers can be written as either terminating or repeating decimals and vice versa, decimals of this type have all the properties of rational numbers. The properties of rational numbers that hold for all operations are summarized in Table 7-3. Because the denseness property holds for the set of rational numbers, it also holds for the set of all repeating or terminating decimals.

TABLE 7-3   Properties of Operations of Rational Numbers

Property	+	×	−	÷
Closure	Yes	Yes	Yes	Yes (except for division by 0)
Commutative	Yes	Yes	No	No
Associative	Yes	Yes	No	No
Identity	Yes	Yes	No	No
Inverse	Yes	Yes (except for 0)	No	No

The distributive properties of multiplication over addition and subtraction hold.

Ordering Decimals

Some students have trouble ordering decimals. They reason that $0.36 > 0.9$ because $36 > 9$. One way to see that this is not true is to convert both decimals to fractions and then compare the fractions. For example, because $0.36 = \frac{36}{100}$ and $0.9 = \frac{9}{10} = \frac{90}{100}$ and $\frac{36}{100} < \frac{90}{100}$, then $0.36 < 0.9$. Decimals can also be ordered without conversion to fractions. For example, because $0.9 = 0.90$, we can line up the decimal points as follows.

0.36
0.90

The digit in the tenths place of 0.90 is greater than the tenths digit in 0.36, so $0.36 < 0.90$. A similar procedure works for repeating decimals.

For example, to compare repeating decimals, such as $1.\overline{3478}$ and $1.347\overline{821}$, we write the decimals one under the other in their equivalent forms without the bars and line up the decimal points.

1.34783478 . . .
1.34782178 . . .

The digits to the left of the decimal points and the first four digits after the decimal points are the same in each of the numbers. Since the digit in the hundred-thousandths place of the top number is 3, which is greater than the digit 2 in the hundred-thousandths place of the bottom number, $1.\overline{3478}$ is greater than $1.347\overline{821}$.

It is easy to compare two fractions, such as $\frac{21}{43}$ and $\frac{37}{75}$, using a calculator. We convert each to a decimal and then compare the decimals.

$$\boxed{2}\ \boxed{1}\ \boxed{\div}\ \boxed{4}\ \boxed{3}\ \boxed{=} \longrightarrow 0.4883721$$
$$\boxed{3}\ \boxed{7}\ \boxed{\div}\ \boxed{7}\ \boxed{5}\ \boxed{=} \longrightarrow 0.4933333$$

Examining the digits in the hundredths place, we see that $\frac{37}{75} > \frac{21}{43}$.

Example 7-9

Find a rational number in decimal form between $0.\overline{35}$ and $0.\overline{351}$.

Solution

First line up the decimals.

0.353535 . . .
0.351351 . . .

To find a decimal between these two, observe that starting from the left, the first place that the two numbers differ is the thousandths place. Clearly, one decimal between these two is 0.352. Some others are 0.3514, 0.35$\overline{15}$, and 0.35136. In fact, there are infinitely many others.

Rounding

Frequently, it is not necessary to know the exact numerical answer to a question. For example, if we ask a person's age, we usually are not interested in an exact answer. Also, we do not know exactly how far it is to the moon or how many people live in New York City. However, we do know approximately how old we are, and we can find that it is approximately 239,000 miles to the moon and that there are approximately 7,772,000 people who live in New York City.

In order to approximate numbers, we adopt the following rules for rounding. Although the rounding rules given below are those used in the elementary school, these rules often vary at the high school and college level in the case when the digit to the right of the last digit to be retained is 5.

1. To round a whole number to a given place value, find the place value and then examine the digit to its right. If the digit to the right is 5 or greater, then replace all digits to the right by zeros and increase the given place values by 1. If the digit to the right is less than 5, then replace all digits to the right of the given place value by zeros.
2. To round a positive decimal less than 1 to a given place value or to a fixed number of decimal places, find the place value and then examine the digit to its right. If the digit to the right is 5 or greater, then drop all digits to the right and increase the given place value by 1. If the digit to the right is less than 5, then drop all the digits to the right of the given place value.

Remark | To symbolize approximations, we use $\doteq$. In some books, $\approx$ is used. To round a number like 216.38 to a place value greater than or equal to 1, use Rule 1. To round to a place value less than 1, use Rule 2.

Example 7-10 | Round each of the following numbers.

(a) 7.456 to the nearest hundredth
(b) 7.456 to the nearest tenth
(c) 7.456 to the nearest unit
(d) 7456 to the nearest thousand
(e) 745 to the nearest ten
(f) 74.56 to the nearest ten

Solution | (a) $7.456 \doteq 7.46$ (b) $7.456 \doteq 7.5$ (c) $7.456 \doteq 7$
(d) $7456 \doteq 7000$ (e) $745 \doteq 750$ (f) $74.56 \doteq 70$

Rounded numbers can be used for estimating answers to computations. For example, if we compute $(16.23)(4.08)$ and obtain an answer of 662.184, then by rounding 16.23 to 16 and 4.08 to 4, a quick check of $16 \cdot 4 = 64$ shows that there must be an error in the answer.

Scientific Notation

scientific notation | In disciplines such as chemistry, microbiology, and physics, where either very large or very small numbers are used, a special notation is used to help handle such numbers. In **scientific notation,** a number is written as the product of a number greater than or equal to 1 and less than 10, and a power of 10. For example, "the sun is 93,000,000 miles from Earth" is expressed as "the sun is $9.3 \cdot 10^7$ miles from Earth." A micrometer, a metric unit of measure that is 0.000001 m (meter), is written as $1 \cdot 10^{-6}$ m.

Example 7-11 | Write each of the following in scientific notation.

(a) 413,682,000   (b) 0.0000231

Solution | (a) $413,682,000 = 4.13682 \cdot 10^8$ (b) $0.0000231 = 2.31 \cdot 10^{-5}$

Example 7-12 | Convert each of the following to standard numerals.

(a) $6.84 \cdot 10^{-5}$ (b) $3.12 \cdot 10^7$

Solution | (a) $6.84 \cdot 10^{-5} = 6.84 \cdot \left(\dfrac{1}{10^5}\right) = 0.0000684$
(b) $3.12 \cdot 10^7 = 31,200,000$

To investigate how your calculator handles scientific notation, consider the computation $41,368,200 \times 1000$. The answer is 41,368,200,000, or $4.13682 \cdot 10^{10}$. On a calculator, perform the computation below.

On many calculators, the display will read

| 4.1368 10 |

The number to the right of the space is the power to which 10 is raised when the number is written in scientific notation.

PROBLEM SET 7-2

1. Find the decimal representation for each of the following.
   (a) $\dfrac{4}{9}$ (b) $\dfrac{2}{7}$ (c) $\dfrac{3}{11}$ (d) $\dfrac{1}{15}$
   (e) $\dfrac{2}{75}$ (f) $\dfrac{1}{99}$ (g) $\dfrac{5}{6}$ (h) $\dfrac{1}{13}$

2. Convert each of the following repeating decimals to fractions.
   (a) $2.4\overline{5}$ (b) $2.\overline{45}$ (c) $2.4\overline{54}$
   (d) $0.2\overline{45}$ (e) $0.02\overline{45}$ (f) $24.\overline{54}$
   (g) $0.\overline{4}$ (h) $0.\overline{6}$ (i) $0.\overline{55}$
   (j) $0.\overline{34}$ (k) $^-2.3\overline{4}$ (l) $^-0.0\overline{2}$

3. Order each of the following sets of decimals from greatest to least.
   (a) $\{3.2, 3.\overline{22}, 3.\overline{23}, 3.2\overline{3}, 3.23\}$
   (b) $\{^-1.454, ^-1.45\overline{4}, ^-1.45, ^-1.4\overline{54}, ^-1.\overline{454}\}$

4. Find a decimal between each of the following pairs of decimals.
   (a) 3.2 and 3.3   (b) 462.24 and 462.25
   (c) $462.2\overline{4}$ and $462.\overline{24}$ (d) 0.003 and 0.03

5. (a) Find a rational number in the form a/b for $0.\overline{9}$.
   (b) $0.\overline{9}$ is either less than 1, greater than 1, or equal to 1. Argue that both $0.\overline{9} < 1$ and $0.\overline{9} > 1$ are impossible.
   (c) Use the fact that $\frac{1}{3} = 0.\overline{3}$ and multiply both sides of the equation by 3 to show that $0.\overline{9} = 1$.
   * (d) Read "Persuasive Arguments: .9999 $\cdots$ = 1" by L. Hall, Jr., in *The Mathematics Teacher*, December 1971.

6. Suppose $a = 0.\overline{32}$ and $b = 0.\overline{123}$.
   (a) Find $a + b$ by adding from left to right. How many digits are in the repetend of the sum?
   (b) Find $a + b$ if $a = 1.2\overline{34}$ and $b = 0.\overline{1234}$. Is the answer a rational number? How many digits are in the repetend?

7. Find the decimal half-way between the two given decimals.
   (a) 3.2 and 3.3   (b) 462.24 and 462.25
   (c) 0.0003 and 0.03   ★ (d) $462.2\overline{4}$ and $462.\overline{24}$

8. Round each of the following numbers as specified.
   (a) 203.651 to the nearest hundred
   (b) 203.651 to the nearest ten
   (c) 203.651 to the nearest unit
   (d) 203.651 to the nearest tenth
   (e) 203.651 to the nearest hundredth

9. Express each of the following numbers in scientific notation.
   (a) 3325   (b) 46.32
   (c) 0.00013   (d) 930,146

10. Convert each of the following numbers to standard numerals.
    (a) $3.2 \cdot 10^{-9}$ (b) $3.2 \cdot 10^9$
    (c) $4.2 \cdot 10^{-1}$ (d) $6.2 \cdot 10^5$

11. Write the numerals in each of the following sentences in scientific notation.
    (a) The diameter of the earth is about 12,700,000 m.
    (b) The distance from Pluto to the sun is 5,797,000 km.
    (c) Each year about 50,000,000 cans are discarded in the United States.

12. Write the numerals in each sentence in decimal form.
    (a) A computer requires $4.4 \cdot 10^{-6}$ seconds to do an addition problem.

(b) There are about $1.99 \cdot 10^4$ km of coastline in the United States.

(c) The earth has existed approximately $3 \cdot 10^9$ years.

13. Audrey wants to buy some camera equipment to take pictures on her daughter's birthday. To estimate the total cost, she rounded each price to the nearest dollar and added the rounded prices. What is her estimate for the items listed below?

Camera $24.95

Film $3.50

Case $7.85

14. Continue the decimal patterns shown below.
    (a) $0, 0.\overline{3}, 0.\overline{6}, 1, 1.\overline{3},$ _____, _____, _____
    (b) $0, 0.5, 0.\overline{6}, 0.75, 0.8, 0.8\overline{3},$ _____, _____, _____

15. Some digits in the number shown below have been covered by squares. If each of the digits 1–9 is used exactly once in the number, what is the number in each of the following cases?

    4 ☐ ☐ 3 ☐ . ☐ ☐ 8 ☐

    (a) The number is as great as possible.
    (b) The number is as small as possible.

16. Sooner or later, most people are faced with the task of buying a number of items at the store, knowing that they have just barely enough money to cover the needed items. In order to avoid the embarrassment of coming up short and having to put some of the items back, they must use their estimating or rounding skills. For each of the following sets of items, estimate the cost. If you are short of funds, tell what must be returned to come just under the allotted amount to be spent. Use your calculator to check your answers.
    (a) Amount on hand—$2.98
        2 packs of gum at 24¢ each
        3 suckers at 10¢ each

        1 licorice at 4 for 20¢
        1 soft drink at 35¢
        1 pack dental floss at 99¢
    (b) Amount on hand—$20.00
        7 gal gas at $1.089 per gallon
        2 qt oil at $1.05 per quart
        a car wash at $1.99
        a new headlight at $3.39
        air in a tire at 0¢ per pound
        air freshener at 99¢
        starter fluid at 99¢
        parking ticket at $1.00
        windshield wiper at $1.59
        soft drink for your date at 35¢

17. This group of exercises concentrates on finding repeating decimals.
    (a) Use a calculator to find decimals for each of the following.

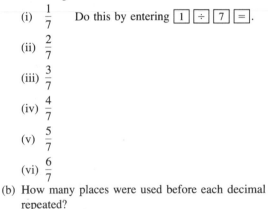

        (i) $\frac{1}{7}$ Do this by entering [1] [÷] [7] [=].
        (ii) $\frac{2}{7}$
        (iii) $\frac{3}{7}$
        (iv) $\frac{4}{7}$
        (v) $\frac{5}{7}$
        (vi) $\frac{6}{7}$

    (b) How many places were used before each decimal repeated?
    (c) Do you see any relationship among your answers in (i)–(vi)?

18. Use a calculator to find $\frac{26}{99}$ and $\frac{78}{99}$. Can you predict a decimal value for $\frac{51}{99}$? Will the technique used in your prediction always work? Why or why not?

* * * * * * * REVIEW PROBLEMS * * * * * * *

19. (a) Human bones make up 0.18 of a person's total body weight. How much do the bones of a 120-pound person weigh?
    (b) Muscles make up about 0.4 of a person's body weight. How much do the muscles of a 120-pound person weigh?

20. John is a payroll clerk for a small company. Last month the employees' gross earnings (earnings before deductions) totaled $27,849.50. He then deducted $1520.63 for social security, $723.30 for unemployment insurance, and $2843.62 for federal income tax. What was the employees' net pay (their earnings after deductions)?

21. How can you tell whether a fraction will represent a terminating decimal without performing the actual division?

22. Write each of the following decimals as fractions.
    (a) 16.72   (b) 0.003
    (c) ⁻5.07   (d) 0.123

COMPUTER   CORNER

The following BASIC program rounds decimals to a given number of places. See if it gives the same results as the rules given in this chapter.

```
 10 PRINT "THIS PROGRAM ROUNDS DECIMALS."
 20 PRINT
 30 PRINT "ENTER YOUR DECIMAL AND PRESS RETURN."
 40 INPUT D
 50 PRINT "HOW MANY DIGITS WOULD YOU LIKE TO THE "
 55 PRINT "RIGHT OF THE DECIMAL POINT?"
 60 INPUT N
 70 LET S = INT (D * 10 ** N + .5)
 80 LET R = S / (10** N)
 90 PRINT
100 PRINT D ; " ROUNDS TO "; R
110 PRINT
120 PRINT "TO ENTER ANOTHER DECIMAL: TYPE RUN."
130 END
```

7-3   PERCENTS

percent   Percents are very useful in conveying information. Many children become acquainted with percents before they study them in school. They hear that there is a 60 percent chance of rain or that their savings accounts are drawing 6 percent interest. Many become familiar with the sales tax when they make a purchase. The word **percent** comes from the Latin phrase *per centum,* which can be translated as per hundred. For example, a bank that pays 6 percent simple interest on a savings account pays $6 for each $100 in the account; that is, it pays $\frac{6}{100}$ of whatever amount is in the account. In general, *a percent is the numerator of a fraction in which the denominator is 100.* We use the symbol % to indicate percent and, for example, write 15% for $\frac{15}{100}$.

FIGURE 7-1

Percents can be illustrated by using a hundreds grid. For example, what percent of the squares are shaded in Figure 7-1?

Because 30 out of the 100, or $\frac{30}{100}$, of the squares are shaded, we say that 30% of the grid is shaded.

Percent is the numerator of a fraction whose denominator is 100, so we can convert any number to a percent by first writing the number as a fraction with denominator 100. For example,

$$0.4 = \frac{0.4 \cdot 100}{100} = \frac{40}{100}, \text{ or } 40\%$$

Example 7-13

Write each of the following as a percent.

(a) 0.03   (b) 0.0002   (c) $0.\overline{3}$ (d) 1.2

Solution

(a) $0.03 = \dfrac{0.03 \cdot 100}{100} = \dfrac{3}{100} = 3\%$

(b) $0.0002 = \dfrac{0.0002 \cdot 100}{100} = \dfrac{0.02}{100} = 0.02\%$

(c) $0.\overline{3} = \dfrac{0.\overline{3} \cdot 100}{100} = \dfrac{33.\overline{3}}{100} = 33.\overline{3}\%$

(d) $1.2 = \dfrac{1.2 \cdot 100}{100} = \dfrac{120}{100} = 120\%$

Because we know how to convert decimals to percents, we can convert fractions to percents by first writing them as decimals. For example, because $\frac{3}{5} = 0.6$ and $0.6 = 60\%$, we have $\frac{3}{5} = 60\%$. Another approach is to write $\frac{3}{5}$ as a fraction with denominator 100.

$$\frac{3}{5} = \frac{3 \cdot 20}{5 \cdot 20} = \frac{60}{100}, \quad \text{so} \quad \frac{3}{5} = 60\%$$

As we have seen, it is not always easy to find an equivalent fraction with denominator 100. For example, in the case of $\frac{2}{3}$, we must either write $\frac{2}{3}$ as a decimal and change the decimal to a percent or use a proportion to solve the equation $\frac{2}{3} = x\%$, as follows.

$$\frac{2}{3} = x\%$$

$$\frac{2}{3} = \frac{x}{100}$$

$$100 \cdot \frac{2}{3} = x$$

$$x = \frac{200}{3}, \text{ or } 66.\overline{6}$$

Hence, $\frac{2}{3} = 66.\overline{6}\%$. From this example we see that the problem of writing a fraction as a percent can be changed to one of finding the missing part of a proportion.

Example 7-14

Express each of the following as a percent.

(a) $\frac{4}{5}$ (b) $\frac{1}{11}$ (c) $2\frac{1}{7}$

Solution

(a) $\dfrac{4}{5} = \dfrac{x}{100}$

$100 \cdot \dfrac{4}{5} = x$

$80 = x$

Hence, $\dfrac{4}{5} = \dfrac{80}{100} = 80\%$

(b) $\dfrac{1}{11} = \dfrac{x}{100}$

$100\left(\dfrac{1}{11}\right) = x$

$x = \dfrac{100}{11}$, or $9\dfrac{1}{11}$

Hence, $\dfrac{1}{11} = \dfrac{9\frac{1}{11}}{100} = 9\dfrac{1}{11}\%$.

(c) $2\dfrac{1}{7} = \dfrac{x}{100}$

$\dfrac{15}{7} = \dfrac{x}{100}$

$100\left(\dfrac{15}{7}\right) = x$

$x = \dfrac{1500}{7} = 214\dfrac{2}{7}$

Hence, $2\dfrac{1}{7} = \dfrac{214\frac{2}{7}}{100} = 214\dfrac{2}{7}\%$.

From the above examples, we see that *to convert a given number to a percent, we need only to multiply that number by 100 and annex a percent sign.*

Many students feel that there is no such thing as 120% because "100% of something is all there is." Teachers should show the students examples of situations in which percents exceeding 100% occur. For example, a newspaper may report that a certain country has an annual inflation rate of 150%. To help students understand the concept of percent when the percent exceeds 100, the phrases "for every hundred" or "out of 100," rather than "per hundred," are helpful. For example, 120% can be thought of as 120 for every 100 and can be modeled as shown in Figure 7-2.

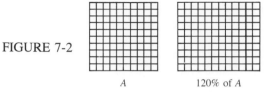

FIGURE 7-2

A 120% of A

In doing computations, it is sometimes useful to convert percents to decimals. This can be done by writing the percent as a fraction and then converting the fraction to a decimal.

Example 7-15 | Write each percent as a decimal.

(a) 5%   (b) 6.3%   (c) 100%

(d) 250%   (e) $\frac{1}{3}$%   (f) $33\frac{1}{3}$%

Solution | (a) $5\% = \frac{5}{100} = 0.05$

(b) $6.3\% = \frac{6.3}{100} = 0.063$

(c) $100\% = \frac{100}{100} = 1$

(d) $250\% = \frac{250}{100} = 2.50$

(e) $\frac{1}{3}\% = \frac{\frac{1}{3}}{100} = \frac{0.\overline{3}}{100} = 0.00\overline{3}$

(f) $33\frac{1}{3}\% = \frac{33\frac{1}{3}}{100} = \frac{33.\overline{3}}{100} = 0.\overline{3}$

Example 7-15 may be used to discover an algorithm for converting percents to decimals: *To change a percent to a decimal, drop the percent sign and divide by 100*. A percent key on a calculator may perform this algorithm. For example, if the buttons ③ ④ . ⑤ % are pushed in the order given, many calculators will display 0.345. You should investigate how your calculator handles percents.

We are now ready to solve word problems involving percents. Application problems usually involve finding a percent of a number, finding a number when a percent of that number is known, or finding what percent one number is of another. Before doing the examples illustrating these problems, recall what it means to find a fraction "of" a number. For example, $\frac{2}{3}$ of 70 means $\frac{2}{3} \cdot 70$. Similarly, to find 40% of 70, we have $\frac{40}{100}$ of 70, which means $\frac{40}{100} \cdot 70$, or $0.40 \cdot 70$.

Example 7-16 | A house that sells for $72,000 requires a 20% down payment. What is the amount of the down payment?

Solution | The down payment is 20% of $72,000 or $0.20 \cdot \$72,000 = \$14,400$. Hence, the amount of the down payment is $14,400.

Example 7-17

If Alberto has 45 correct answers on an 80-question test, what percent of his answers are correct?

Solution

Alberto has $\frac{45}{80}$ of the answers correct. To find the percent of correct answers, we need only to convert $\frac{45}{80}$ to a percent. This can be done by using a proportion:

$$\frac{45}{80} = \frac{n}{100}$$

$$\frac{45}{80} \cdot 100 = n$$

$$n = \frac{4500}{80} = 56.25$$

Thus, $\frac{56.25}{100}$, or 56.25%, of the answers are correct.

An alternate solution can be found by using the strategy of writing an equation. Let n be the percent of correct answers. Hence, we have the following.

$$45 = n\% \text{ of } 80$$

$$45 = \frac{n}{100} \cdot 80$$

$$45 = \frac{80}{100} \cdot n$$

$$45 = 0.80n$$

$$\frac{45}{0.80} = n$$

$$56.25 = n$$

Example 7-18

Forty-two percent of the parents of the school children in the Paxson School District are employed at Di Paloma University. If the number of parents employed by D.P.U. is 168, how many parents are in the school district?

Solution

If we let n be the number of parents in the school district, then we know that 42% of n is 168. We translate this information into an equation and solve for n.

$$42\% \text{ of } n = 168$$

$$\frac{42}{100} \cdot n = 168$$

$$0.42 \cdot n = 168$$

$$n = \frac{168}{0.42} = 400$$

Hence, there are 400 parents in the school district.

The problem can also be solved using proportion. We know that 42%, or $\frac{42}{100}$, of the parents are employed at D.P.U. If n is the total number of parents, then $\frac{168}{n}$ also represents the fraction of parents employed at D.P.U. Thus,

$$\frac{42}{100} = \frac{168}{n}$$

$$42n = 100 \cdot 168$$

$$n = \frac{16,800}{42} = 400$$

Example 7-19

A car that was bought for $8200 has a value 1 year later of $5740. What is the percent of depreciation?

Solution

From the problem, we find that the car has decreased in value by $8200 − $5740, or $2460, in 1 year. We are to determine what percent $2460 is of the original price, $8200. A ratio representing the depreciation is $\frac{2460}{8200}$. To find the percent of depreciation, we solve the following proportion.

$$\frac{2460}{8200} = \frac{x}{100}$$

$$100 \cdot \frac{2460}{8200} = x$$

$$x = \frac{246,000}{8200}$$

$$x = 30$$

Thus, the percent of depreciation is 30%.

Example 7-20

Mike bought a bicycle and then sold it for 20% more than he paid for it. If he sold the bike for $144, what did he pay for it?

Solution

We are looking for the original price, P, that Mike paid for the bike. We know that he sold the bike for $144 and that this included a 20% profit. Thus, we can write the following equation.

$144 = P +$ Mike's profit

Since Mike's profit is 20% of P, we proceed as follows.

$$\$144 = P + 20\% \cdot P$$

$$\$144 = P + 0.20 \cdot P$$

$$\$144 = (1 + 0.20) \cdot P$$

$$\$144 = 1.20P$$

$$\frac{\$144}{1.20} = P$$

$$\$120 = P$$

Thus, Mike originally paid $120 for the bike.

Example 7-21

Westerner's Clothing Store advertised a suit for 10% off, for a savings of $15. Later they marked the suit at 30% off the original price. What is the amount of the current discount?

Solution

A 10% discount amounts to a $15 savings. This information can be used to find the original price, P. Since 10% of P is $15, we have the following.

$$10\% \cdot P = \$15$$
$$0.10 \cdot P = \$15$$
$$P = \$150$$

We must now calculate 30% of $150 to find the current discount. Because $0.30 \cdot \$150 = \$45$, the amount of the 30% discount is $45.

In the Looking Back stage of problem solving, we check the answer and look for other ways to solve the problem. A different approach leads to a more efficient solution. If 10% of the price is $15, then 30% of the price is 3 times $15, or $45.

As a final example of an application of percent in this section, work through the student page on taxes from *Scott, Foresman Mathematics* 1980, Grade 7 (page 271).

Laboratory Activity

1. Complete the following percent activities.
   (a) Calculate what percent of your television-watching time is taken up by commercials.
   (b) Make a list of your classmates' first names. What percent of the class names begin with a vowel? What percent of the names begin with a consonant?
   (c) Look through the ads in a newspaper and list five items that have been marked down. Compute the discount from the marked price and the original price. Express this saving as a percent.
   (d) Look for newspaper advertisements that make claims such as "25% off." Use a calculator to see if the prices are as advertised.

2. The rectangle shown is 25% of a larger rectangle.
   (a) Draw 50% of the larger rectangle.
   (b) Draw 75% of the larger rectangle.
   (c) Draw 100% of the larger rectangle.
   (d) Draw 112.5% of the larger rectangle.
3. The hexagon shown is 120% of a smaller figure. Shade 100% of such a smaller figure.

SCHEDULE X—Single Taxpayers			
Taxable income		**Tax**	
Over—	But not over—		of the amount over—
$6,200	$8,200	$690 + 21%	$6,200
$8,200	$10,200	$1,110 + 24%	$8,200
$10,200	$12,200	$1,590 + 25%	$10,200
$12,200	$14,200	$2,090 + 27%	$12,200
$14,200	$16,200	$2,630 + 29%	$14,200
$16,200	$18,200	$3,210 + 31%	$16,200
$18,200	$20,200	$3,830 + 34%	$18,200
$20,200	$22,200	$4,510 + 36%	$20,200
$22,200	$24,200	$5,230 + 38%	$22,200
$24,200	$28,200	$5,990 + 40%	$24,200
$28,200	$34,200	$7,590 + 45%	$28,200

Find the income tax for each amount of taxable income.

1. $14,732   2. $24,608

3. $6575   4. $11,412

5. $15,781   6. $18,090

7. $10,402   8. $12,657

9. $13,577   10. $9739

11. $16,404   12. $19,000

13. $20,920   14. $21,200

15. $22,503   16. $13,964

17. Mr. Saxon's taxable income was $14,198. Ms. Brown's taxable income was $16,202. How much more tax did Ms. Brown have to pay than Mr. Saxon did?

PROBLEM SET 7-3

1. Express each of the following as percents.
   (a) 7.89   (b) 0.032   (c) 193.1
   (d) 0.2   (e) $\dfrac{5}{6}$ (f) $\dfrac{3}{20}$
   (g) $\dfrac{1}{75}$ (h) $\dfrac{40}{7}$

2. Convert each of the following percents to decimals.
   (a) 16%   (b) $4\dfrac{1}{2}\%$
   (c) $\dfrac{1}{5}\%$ (d) $\dfrac{2}{7}\%$

3. Answer each of the following.
   (a) Find 6% of 34.
   (b) 17 is what percent of 34?
   (c) 18 is 30% of what number?

4. Marc had 84 boxes of Cub Scout candy to sell. He sold 75% of the boxes. How many did he sell?

5. Gail made $16,000 last year and received a 6% raise. How much does she make now?

6. Gail received a 7% raise last year. If her salary is now $15,515, what was her salary last year?

7. Joe sold 180 newspapers out of 200. Bill sold 85% of his 260 newspapers. Ron sold 212 newspapers, 80% of those he had.
   (a) Who sold the most newspapers? How many?
   (b) Who sold the greatest percent of his newspapers? What percent?
   (c) Who started with the greatest number of newspapers? How many?

8. If a dress that normally sells for $35 is on sale for $28, what is the "percent off"? (This could be called a *percent of decrease,* or a discount.)

9. Mort bought his house in 1975 for $29,000. It was recently appraised at $55,000. What is the *percent of increase* in value?

10. Sally bought a dress marked at 20% off. If the regular price was $28.00, what was the sale price?

11. What is the sale price of a softball if the regular price is $6.80 and there is a 25% discount?

12. Xuan weighed 9 pounds when he was born. At 6 months, he weighed 18 pounds. What was the percent of increase in Xuan's weight?

13. In 1965, 728 eagles were counted in Glacier Park. Five years later, 594 were counted. What is the percent of decrease in the number of eagles counted?

14. A car originally cost $8000. One year later, it was worth $6800. What is the percent of depreciation?

15. Fill in the blanks to find other expressions for 4%.
    (a) _____ for every 100
    (b) _____ for every 50
    (c) 1 for every _____
    (d) 8 for every _____
    (e) 0.5 for every _____

16. If a $\frac{1}{4}$-cup serving of Crunchies breakfast food has 0.5% of the minimum daily requirement of Vitamin C, how many cups would you have to eat in order to obtain the minimum daily requirement of Vitamin C?

17. An airline ticket cost $320 without the tax. If the tax rate is 5%, what is the total bill for the airline ticket?

18. Bill got 52 correct answers on an 80-question test. What percent of the questions did he not answer correctly?

19. A real estate broker receives 4% of an $80,000 sale. How much does the broker receive?

20. A survey reported that $66\frac{2}{3}\%$ of 1800 employees favored a new insurance program. How many employees favored the new program?

21. A family has a monthly income of $2400 and makes a monthly house payment of $400. What percent of the income is the house payment?

22. A company bought a used typewriter for $350, which was 80% of the original cost. What was the original cost of the typewriter?

23. A plumber's wage one year was $19.80 an hour. This was a 110% increase over last year's hourly wage. What was the increase in the hourly wage over last year?

24. Ms. Price has received a 10% raise in salary in each of the last 2 years. If her annual salary this year is $100,000, what was her salary 2 years ago rounded to the nearest penny?

25. If we build a 10-by-10 model with blocks, as shown in the figure, and paint the entire model, what percent of the cubes will have each of the following?

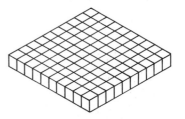

(a) Four faces painted   (b) Three faces painted
(c) Two faces painted

★ 26. Answer the questions in Problem 25 for models of the following sizes.
  (a) 9 by 9   (b) 8 by 8   (c) 7 by 7
  (d) 12 by 12   (e) *n* by *n*

27. Different calculators compute percents in various ways. To investigate this, consider 5 · 6%.
  (a) If the following sequence of buttons is pushed, is the correct answer of 0.3 displayed?

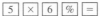

  (b) Push ⑥ ⑳ ⑳ ⑤ ⑳ . Is the answer 0.3?

28. The car Elsie bought 1 year ago has depreciated $1116.88, which is 12.13% of the price she paid for it. How much did she pay for the car to the nearest cent?

* * * * * * * REVIEW PROBLEMS * * * * * * *

29. A state charged a company $63.27 per day for overdue taxes. The total bill for the overdue taxes was $6137.19. How many days were the taxes overdue?

30. Write 33.21 as a fraction in simplest form.

31. Write $\frac{2}{9}$ as a decimal.

32. Write $31.0\overline{5}$ as a fraction in simplest form.

33. Write each of the following in scientific notation.
  (a) 3,250,000   (b) 0.00012

34. Round 32.015 to the indicated place.
  (a) The nearest tenth   (b) The nearest ten

BRAIN TEASER

The crust of a certain pumpkin pie is 25% of the pie. By what percent should the amount of crust be reduced in order to make it constitute 20% of the pie?

* 7-4 COMPUTING INTEREST

interest

principal

interest rate

simple interest

When a bank advertises a $5\frac{1}{2}$% interest rate on a savings account, this means that the bank is willing to pay for the privilege of using that money. The amount of money the bank will pay is called **interest.** If we borrow money from a bank, we must pay interest to the bank for using that money. The original amount deposited or borrowed is called the **principal.** The percent used to determine the interest is called the **interest rate.** Interest rates are given for specific periods of time, such as years, months, or days. Interest computed on the original principal is called **simple interest.** For example, suppose we borrow $5000 from a company at a simple interest rate of 12% for 1 year. The interest we owe on the loan for 1 year is 12% of $5000, or 12% · 5000. (This is usually computed as 5000 · 0.12.) In general, if a principal P is invested at an annual interest rate of r, then the simple interest after 1 year is $P · r$; after t years it is $P · r · t$, or Prt. If I represents simple interest, we have

$$I = Prt$$

The amount needed to pay off a $5000 loan at 12% simple interest is the $5000 borrowed plus the interest on the $5000, that is, $5000 + 5000 \cdot 0.12$, or $5600. In general, an amount (or balance) A is equal to the principal P plus the interest I; that is, $A = P + I$, or $A = P + Prt$. This formula can also be written as

$$A = P(1 + rt)$$

Example 7-22   Vera opens a savings account that pays simple interest at the rate of $5\frac{1}{4}\%$ per year. If she deposits $2000 and makes no other deposits, find the interest and the balance for the following periods of time.

(a) 1 year   (b) 90 days

Solution   (a) To find the interest for 1 year we proceed as follows.

$$I = \$2000 \cdot 5\tfrac{1}{4}\% \cdot 1 = \$2000 \cdot 0.0525 = \$105$$

Thus, her balance at the end of 1 year is

$$\$2000 + \$105 = \$2105$$

(b) When the interest rate is annual and the interest period is less than 1 year, we represent the time as a fractional part of a year by dividing the number of days by 365. Thus, to find the interest and the balance, we perform the following computations.

$$I = \$2000 \cdot 5\tfrac{1}{4}\% \cdot \frac{90}{365}$$

$$= \$2000 \cdot 0.0525 \cdot \frac{90}{365} \doteq \$25.89$$

Hence, $A = \$2000 + \$25.89 = \$2025.89$.

Example 7-23   A credit card company charges a customer 1.5% per month on the unpaid balance of charges. How much does a customer owe after 1 month on an unpaid balance of $185?

Solution   To find the interest, we multiply the principal by the monthly rate and then multiply this product by the time in months.

$$I = 185 \cdot 0.015 \cdot 1 \doteq \$2.78$$

Thus, the amount owed after 1 month is $187.78.

Example 7-24   Find the annual interest rate if a principal of $10,000 increased to $10,900 at the end of 1 year.

Solution   We use the strategy of writing an equation based on the relationship $I = Prt$. We need to solve for r, so we divide both sides of the equation by Pt, obtaining

$$r = \frac{I}{Pt}$$

To find the interest, we compute the difference between the balance and the principal. Thus, $I = \$10,900 - \$10,000 = \$900$. Substituting the values of I, P, and t in the above equation, we obtain

$$r = \frac{900}{(10,000) \cdot 1} = 0.09, \text{ or } 9\%$$

Thus, the interest rate is 9%.

compound interest   In all our discussions thus far, we have computed simple interest, which is based only on the original principal. This principal stayed fixed for the entire interest period. A second method of computing interest involves **compound interest.** Compound interest is different from simple interest because after the first interest calculation, the interest is added to the principal, so interest is earned on previous interest in addition to the principal. Compound interest rates are usually given as annual rates no matter how many times the interest is compounded per year.

The most common compounding periods are annual (1 time a year), semiannual (2 times a year), quarterly (4 times a year), monthly (12 times a year), and daily (365 times a year). Compound interest is evident when a bank advertises an account earning an annual rate of $5\frac{1}{2}\%$ compounded quarterly, with an effective yield of 5.65%. This means that $5\frac{1}{2}\%$ compounded quarterly yields the same interest as an amount earning 5.65% simple interest. Increasing the number of compounding periods increases the number of computations required to find the balance. In order to reduce the number of computations, a formula can be developed for computing compound interest. The procedure for computing interest is the same for each period; that is, the amount A at the end of each period is equal to the principal P at the beginning of the period plus the interest I for the period. If the interest rate per period is i, then we have the following.

$$A = P + I = P + P \cdot i = P(1 + i)$$

Table 7-4 shows that the amount at the end of the nth period is $P(1 + i)^n$.

TABLE 7-4

Period	Initial Amount	Final Amount
1	P	$P(1 + i)$
2	$P(1 + i)$	$P(1 + i)(1 + i)$, or $P(1 + i)^2$
3	$P(1 + i)^2$	$P(1 + i)^2(1 + i)$, or $P(1 + i)^3$
4	$P(1 + i)^3$	$P(1 + i)^3(1 + i)$, or $P(1 + i)^4$
.	.	.
.	.	.
.	.	.
n	$P(1 + i)^{n-1}$	$P(1 + i)^{n-1}(1 + i)$, or $P(1 + i)^n$

Therefore, the amount at the end of the nth period is $P(1 + i)^n$.

Example 7-25

Suppose we deposit $1000 in a savings account that pays 6% interest compounded quarterly.

(a) What is the balance at the end of 1 year?
(b) What is the effective annual yield on this investment?

Solution

(a) An annual interest rate of 6% earns $\frac{1}{4}$ of 6%, or an interest rate of $\frac{0.06}{4}$, in one quarter. Since there are four periods, we have the following.

$$A = 1000\left(1 + \frac{0.06}{4}\right)^4 \doteq \$1061.37$$

Thus, the balance at the end of one year is $1061.37.

(b) Because the interest earned is $1061.37 - \$1000.00 = \$61.37$, the effective annual yield can be computed using the simple interest formula, $I = Prt$.

$$61.37 = 1000 \cdot r \cdot 1$$

$$\frac{61.37}{1000} = r$$

$$0.06137 = r$$

$$6.137\% = r$$

Hence, the effective annual yield is 6.137%.

Finding compound interest using a calculator is demonstrated on the student page from *McGraw-Hill Mathematics,* 1981, Grade 8, p. 277. Try to work the problems at the bottom of the page.

Example 7-26

To save for their child's college education, a couple deposits $3000 into an account that pays 11% annual interest compounded daily. Find the amount in this account after 12 years.

Solution

The principal in the problem is $3000, the daily rate i is $\frac{0.11}{365}$, and the number of compounding periods is $12 \cdot 365$, or 4380. Thus, we have

$$A = \$3000\left(1 + \frac{0.11}{365}\right)^{4380} \doteq \$11,228$$

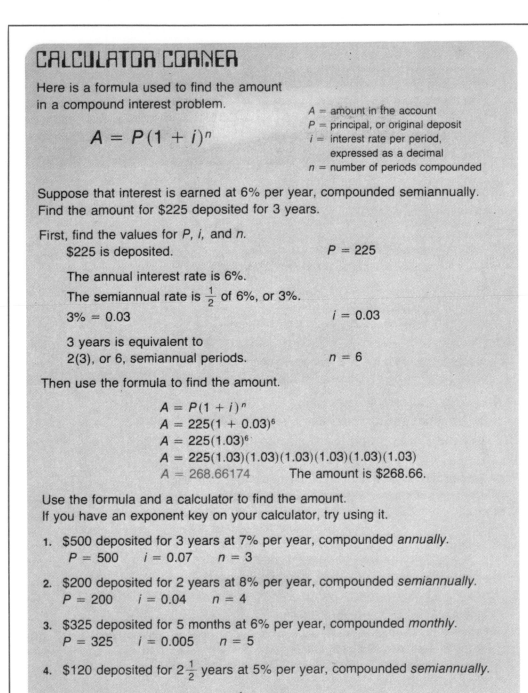

CALCULATOR CORNER

Here is a formula used to find the amount
in a compound interest problem.

$$A = P(1 + i)^n$$

A = amount in the account
P = principal, or original deposit
i = interest rate per period,
  expressed as a decimal
n = number of periods compounded

Suppose that interest is earned at 6% per year, compounded semiannually.
Find the amount for $225 deposited for 3 years.

First, find the values for P, i, and n.

$225 is deposited. $P = 225$

The annual interest rate is 6%.
The semiannual rate is $\frac{1}{2}$ of 6%, or 3%.
3% = 0.03 $i = 0.03$

3 years is equivalent to
2(3), or 6, semiannual periods. $n = 6$

Then use the formula to find the amount.

$$A = P(1 + i)^n$$
$$A = 225(1 + 0.03)^6$$
$$A = 225(1.03)^6$$
$$A = 225(1.03)(1.03)(1.03)(1.03)(1.03)(1.03)$$
$$A = 268.66174 \qquad \text{The amount is \$268.66.}$$

Use the formula and a calculator to find the amount.
If you have an exponent key on your calculator, try using it.

1. $500 deposited for 3 years at 7% per year, compounded *annually*.
   $P = 500 \qquad i = 0.07 \qquad n = 3$

2. $200 deposited for 2 years at 8% per year, compounded *semiannually*.
   $P = 200 \qquad i = 0.04 \qquad n = 4$

3. $325 deposited for 5 months at 6% per year, compounded *monthly*.
   $P = 325 \qquad i = 0.005 \qquad n = 5$

4. $120 deposited for $2\frac{1}{2}$ years at 5% per year, compounded *semiannually*.

5. $85 deposited for 1 year at $7\frac{1}{2}$% per year, compounded *quarterly*.

PROBLEM SET 7-4

A calculator is necessary in most of the following problems.
1. Complete the simple-interest chart.

	Interest	Principal	Rate	Time (Years)
(a)		2000	9%	3
(b)	42	700	6%	
(c)		8000	7.6%	2
(d)	70	1400		1
(e)	680		8.5%	2

2. Complete the following compound-interest chart.

	Compounding Period	Principal	Annual Rate	Length of Time (Years)	Interest Rate Per Period	Number of Periods	Amount of Interest Paid
(a)	Semi-annual	$1000	6%	2			
(b)	Quarterly	$1000	8%	3			
(c)	Monthly	$1000	10%	5			
(d)	Daily	$1000	12%	4			

3. Ms. Jackson borrowed $42,000 at 13% simple interest to buy her house. If she won the Irish Sweepstakes exactly 1 year later and was able to repay the loan without penalty, how much interest did she owe?

4. Carolyn went on a shopping spree with her Bank-amount card and made purchases totaling $125. If the interest rate is 1.5% per month on the unpaid balance and she does not pay this debt for 1 year, how much interest will she owe at the end of the year?

5. A man collected $28,500 on a loan of $25,000 he made 4 years ago. If he charged simple interest, what was the rate he charged?

6. Burger Queen will need $50,000 in 5 years for a new addition. To meet this goal, money is deposited today in an account that pays 9% annual interest compounded quarterly. What amount should be invested today to reach $50,000 in 5 years?

7. A company is expanding its line to include more products. To do so, it borrows $320,000 at 13.5% simple interest for a period of 18 months. How much interest must the company pay?

8. An amount of $3000 was deposited in a bank at a rate of 5% compounded quarterly for 3 years; the rate then increased to 8% and was compounded quarterly for the next 3 years. If no money was withdrawn, what was the balance at the end of this time period?

9. To save for their retirement, a couple deposits $4000 in an account that pays 9% interest compounded quarterly. What will be the value of their investment after 20 years?

10. A money-market fund pays 14% annual interest compounded daily. What is the value of $10,000 invested in this fund after 15 years?

11. A car company is offering car loans at a simple-interest rate of 9%. Find the interest charged to a customer who finances a car loan of $7200 for 3 years.

12. Linda deposits $200 at the end of the month in an account which pays 9% compounded monthly. If she does this each month, what will be the value of her account at the end of 6 months?

13. Johnny and Carolyn have three different savings plans, which accumulated the following amounts of interest for 1 year:
    (a) A passbook savings account that accumulated $53.90 on a principal of $980.
    (b) A certificate of deposit that accumulated $55.20 on a principal of $600.
    (c) A money market certificate that accumulated $158.40 on a principal of $1200.
    Which of these accounts paid the best interest rate for the year?

14. If a hamburger costs $1.35 and if the price continues to rise at a rate of 11% a year for the next 6 years, what will the price of a hamburger be at the end of 6 years?

15. If college tuition is $2500 this year, what will it be 10 years from now if we assume a constant inflation rate of 9% a year?

16. Sara invested money at a bank that paid 6.5% compounded quarterly. If she received $4650 at the end of 4 years, what was her initial investment?

17. A car is purchased for $15,000. If each year the car depreciates 10% of its value the preceding year, what will its value be at the end of 3 years?

COMPUTER CORNER

The following BASIC program will compute compound interest. Type it into the computer and compare the results with those obtained in this chapter.

```
 10 PRINT "COMPOUND INTEREST PROGRAM"
 20 PRINT
 30 PRINT "TYPE IN THE PRINCIPAL AND PRESS RETURN."
 40 INPUT P
 50 PRINT "TYPE IN THE RATE AS A DECIMAL AND PRESS RETURN."
 60 INPUT R
 70 PRINT "TYPE IN THE NUMBER OF YEARS AND PRESS RETURN."
 80 INPUT T
 90 PRINT "TYPE IN THE COMPOUNDING PERIOD AND PRESS RETURN."
100 PRINT "ENTER 2 FOR SEMIANNUALLY, 4 FOR QUARTERLY, "
110 PRINT "12 FOR MONTHLY, AND 365 FOR DAILY."
120 INPUT C
130 LET N = T * C
140 LET I = R/C
150 LET A = P * ((1 + I)**(N - 1))
160 PRINT
170 PRINT "PRINCIPAL"; TAB(11); "RATE"; TAB(16);
180 PRINT "TIME"; TAB(21); "COMPOUNDED"; TAB(32); "INTEREST"
190 PRINT P; TAB(11); R; TAB(16); T; TAB(21); C; TAB(32); A
200 PRINT
210 PRINT "TO ENTER ANOTHER PROBLEM TYPE RUN."
220 END
```

7-5   REAL NUMBERS

Are there any decimals that neither terminate nor repeat? Consider the characteristics that such decimals must have:

1. There must be an infinite number of nonzero digits to the right of the decimal point.
2. There cannot be a repeating block of digits (a repetend).

Does a decimal like 0.1432865 . . . have these characteristics? Because the decimal is infinite, the first characteristic is satisfied. However, without more information, there is no way to tell whether there is a repeating block of digits in the decimal.

There are several ways to construct a nonterminating, nonrepeating decimal. Perhaps the simplest is to devise a pattern of infinite digits in such a way that there will definitely be no repeated block. Consider the number 0.1010010001 . . . . If the pattern shown continues, the next groups of digits are four zeros followed by 1, five zeros followed by 1, and so on. It is possible to describe a pattern for this decimal, but there is no repeating block of digits. Because this decimal is nonterminating and nonrepeating, it cannot represent a rational number. Numbers

irrational numbers   that are not rational are called **irrational numbers.**

In the early twentieth century, it was proved that the number that is the ratio

π (pi)   of the circumference of a circle to its diameter, symbolized by π **(pi),** is irrational. In schools, we traditionally use $\frac{22}{7}$, 3.14, or 3.14159 for π. These are only rational approximations of π. The value of π has been computed to thousands of decimal places with no apparent pattern.

Other irrational numbers occur in the study of area. For example, to find the area of a square, we use the formula $A = s^2$, where A is the area and s is the length of a side of the square. If a side of a square is 3 cm long, then the area of the square is 9 cm^2 (square centimeters). Conversely, we can use the formula to find the length of a side, given the area. If the area of a square is 25 cm^2, then $s^2 = 25$, so

square root $s = 5$ or $^-5$. Each of these solutions is called a **square root** of 25. However, because lengths are always nonnegative, 5 is the only possible solution. The

principal square root   positive solution of $s^2 = 25$—namely, 5—is called the **principal square root** of 25 and is denoted by $\sqrt{25}$. Similarly, the principal square root of 2 is denoted by $\sqrt{2}$. Note that $\sqrt{16} \neq {}^-4$, because $^-4$ is not the principal square root of 16.

DEFINITION

> If a is any whole number, the **principal square root** of a is the nonnegative number b such that $b \cdot b = b^2 = a$.

The principal square root of a is denoted by $\sqrt{a}$, where the symbol $\sqrt{}$ is called a

radical sign   radicand   **radical sign** and a is called the **radicand.**

Example 7-27 | Find: (a) the square roots of 144;
                 (b) the principal square root of 144.

Solution | (a) The square roots of 144 are 12 and $^-$12.
      (b) The principal square root of 144 = 12.

Some square roots are rational. For example, $\sqrt{25}$ is 5, a rational number. Other square roots, like $\sqrt{2}$, are irrational. Since $1^2 = 1$ and $2^2 = 4$, there is no whole number s such that $s^2 = 2$. Is there a rational number $\dfrac{a}{b}$ such that $\left(\dfrac{a}{b}\right)^2 = 2$? If we assume there is such a rational number, then the following must be true.

$$\left(\frac{a}{b}\right)^2 = 2$$

$$\frac{a^2}{b^2} = 2$$

$$a^2 = 2b^2$$

Since $a^2 = 2b^2$, the Fundamental Theorem of Arithmetic says that the prime factorizations of a^2 and $2b^2$ are the same. In particular, the prime 2 appears the same number of times in the prime factorization of a^2 as it does in the factorization of $2b^2$. Since $b^2 = b \cdot b$, then no matter how many times 2 appears in the prime factorization of b, it appears twice as many times in $b \cdot b$. In $2b^2$, another factor of 2 is introduced, resulting in an odd number of 2s in the prime factorization of $2b^2$ and hence of a^2. But 2 cannot appear both an odd number of times and an even number of times in the same prime factorization. We have a contradiction. This contradiction could have been caused only by the assumption that $\sqrt{2}$ is a rational number. Consequently, $\sqrt{2}$ must be an irrational number. A similar argument can be used to show that $\sqrt{3}$ is irrational or $\sqrt{n}$ is irrational, where n is a whole number but not the square of another whole number.

Example 7-28 | Prove that $2 + \sqrt{2}$ is an irrational number.

Solution | Suppose $2 + \sqrt{2} = \dfrac{a}{b}$, where $\dfrac{a}{b}$ is a rational number. Then,

$$\sqrt{2} = \frac{a}{b} - 2$$

$$\sqrt{2} = \frac{a - 2b}{b}$$

But $\dfrac{(a - 2b)}{b}$ is a rational number (why?), and this is a contradiction because $\sqrt{2}$ is an irrational number. Thus, $2 + \sqrt{2}$ is an irrational number.

Remark | In a similar manner, we could prove $m + n\sqrt{2}$ is an irrational number for all rational numbers m and n except $n = 0$.

Pythagorean Theorem

Many irrational numbers can be interpreted geometrically. For example, a point can be found to represent $\sqrt{2}$ on a number line by using the **Pythagorean Theorem** (see Chapter 11). That is, if a and b are the lengths of the shorter sides (legs) of a right triangle and c the length of the longer side (hypotenuse), then $a^2 + b^2 = c^2$, as shown in Figure 7-3.

FIGURE 7-3

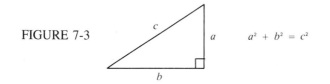

Figure 7-4 shows a segment one unit long constructed perpendicular to a number line at point P. Thus, two sides of the triangle shown are one unit long. By the Pythagorean Theorem, $1^2 + 1^2 = c^2$. Thus, $c^2 = 2$, and $c = \sqrt{2}$. The number $\sqrt{2}$ can also be thought of as the length of a diagonal of a square whose side is 1 unit long.

FIGURE 7-4

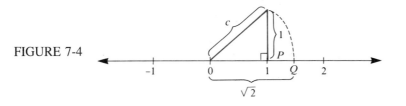

Because $\sqrt{2}$ is the length of the hypotenuse, there must be some point Q on the number line such that the distance from zero to Q is $\sqrt{2}$. Similarly, other square roots can be constructed, as shown in Figure 7-5.

FIGURE 7-5

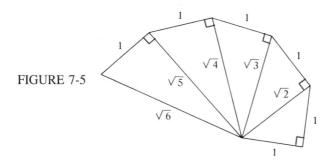

From Figure 7-4, we see that $\sqrt{2}$ must have a value between 1 and 2—that is, $1 < \sqrt{2} < 2$. To obtain a closer approximation of $\sqrt{2}$, we attempt to "squeeze" $\sqrt{2}$ between two numbers that are between 1 and 2. Because $(1.5)^2 = 2.25$ and $(1.4)^2 = 1.96$, it follows that $1.4 < \sqrt{2} < 1.5$, or $\sqrt{2} \doteq 1.4$. Because a^2 can be interpreted as the area of a square with side of length a, this discussion can be pictured geometrically, as in Figure 7-6.

FIGURE 7-6

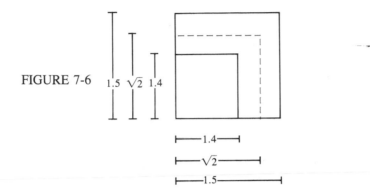

If a more accurate approximation for $\sqrt{2}$ is desired, then this squeezing process can be continued. We see that $(1.4)^2$, or 1.96, is closer to 2 than $(1.5)^2$, or 2.25, so we choose numbers closer to 1.4 in order to find the next approximation. We find the following.

$(1.42)^2 = 2.0164$

$(1.41)^2 = 1.9981$

Thus, $1.41 < \sqrt{2} < 1.42$, or $\sqrt{2} \doteq 1.41$. A calculator is a helpful aid in using this procedure. We can continue this process until we obtain the desired approximation.

Newton's method

A second algorithm for approximating square roots is called **Newton's method.** (It also is called the *guess-and-average* method.) If we make any guess G_1 (G_1 positive) for $\sqrt{2}$, it can be proved that $\sqrt{2}$ is always between G_1 and $\dfrac{2}{G_1}$. (The proof is left as an exercise.) Using G_1 and $\dfrac{2}{G_1}$, compute their average, $\dfrac{1}{2}\left(G_1 + \dfrac{2}{G_1}\right)$. Let this average be G_2, a second guess. The second guess G_2 is a more accurate approximation to $\sqrt{2}$ than is G_1. We continue the process until the desired number of decimal places is obtained. Suppose $G_1 = 1.4$; then $\dfrac{2}{G_1} = \dfrac{2}{1.4} \doteq 1.42$. Next, $\frac{1}{2}(1.4 + 1.42) = 1.41 = G_2$. Now, $\dfrac{2}{G_2} = \dfrac{2}{1.41} \doteq 1.418$. So, $G_3 = \frac{1}{2}(1.41 + 1.418) = 1.414$, and so on. In general, to approximate $\sqrt{n}$ for any number n, the following steps may be used:

1. Guess an approximate principal square root of n, that is, $G_1 \doteq \sqrt{n}$. It does not matter whether the guess is too large or too small, but the closer the guess, the fewer the steps it takes to reach a given accuracy.

2. Divide n by G_1 to obtain $\dfrac{n}{G_1}$.

3. Average G_1 and $\dfrac{n}{G_1}$ to determine G_2: $G_2 = \dfrac{1}{2}\left(G_1 + \dfrac{n}{G_1}\right)$.

4. Using G_2 as the new guess, repeat the process. Continue the process until the desired accuracy is reached.

It should be evident from this discussion and the next example that a calculator is a valuable aid in performing Newton's method for finding square roots. If your calculator has a square root button, use it to check your answers.

Example 7-29

(a) Find $\sqrt{30}$ correct to tenths using the squeezing method.
(b) Find $\sqrt{115}$ correct to tenths using Newton's method.

Solution

(a) $6^2 = 36$, $5^2 = 25$, and $25 < 30 < 36$, so $5 < \sqrt{30} < 6$.
$29.16 = (5.4)^2 < 30 < (5.5)^2 = 30.25$, so $5.4 < \sqrt{30} < 5.5$.
$29.9209 = (5.47)^2 < 30 < (5.48)^2 = 30.0304$, so $5.47 < \sqrt{30} < 5.48$.
Hence, $\sqrt{30} \doteq 5.4$. Notice that the answer rounded to the nearest tenth would be 5.5.

(b) Let $G_1 = 10$. Then

$$\frac{n}{G_1} = \frac{115}{10} = 11.5$$

$$\frac{1}{2} \cdot \left(G_1 + \frac{n}{G_1}\right) = \frac{10 + 11.5}{2} = 10.75$$

Let $G_2 = 10.75$. Then

$$\frac{n}{G_2} = \frac{115}{10.75} \doteq 10.698$$

$$\frac{1}{2} \cdot \left(G_2 + \frac{n}{G_2}\right) = \frac{10.75 + 10.698}{2} = 10.724$$

Let $G_3 = 10.724$. Because both G_2 and G_3 have the same digits in the tens, units, and tenths places, it can be shown that $\sqrt{15}$ correct to tenths is 10.7.

The System of Real Numbers

real numbers

The set of all decimals—terminating, repeating, and nonterminating non-repeating—comprises the set of **real numbers,** R. In other words, the set of real numbers is the union of both the set of rational numbers and the set of irrational numbers. The concept of fractions can now be extended to include all numbers of the form $\frac{a}{b}$, where a and b are real numbers with $b \neq 0$, such as $\frac{\sqrt{3}}{5}$. Addition, subtraction, multiplication, and division are defined on the set of real numbers in such a way that all the properties of these operations on rationals still hold. The properties are summarized below for addition and multiplication.

Properties

Closure Properties   For real numbers a and b, $a + b$ and $a \cdot b$ are unique real numbers.

Commutative Properties   For real numbers a and b, $a + b = b + a$ and $a \cdot b = b \cdot a$.

Associative Properties   For real numbers a, b, and c, $a + (b + c) = (a + b) + c$ and $a \cdot (b \cdot c) = (a \cdot b) \cdot c$.

Identity Properties   The number 0 is the unique additive identity and 1 is the unique multiplicative identity such that for any real number a, $0 + a = a = a + 0$ and $1 \cdot a = a = a \cdot 1$.

Inverse Properties   (1) For every real number a, ^-a is its unique additive inverse; that is, $a + {^-a} = 0 = {^-a} + a$. (2) For every nonzero real number, a, $\frac{1}{a}$ is its unique multiplicative inverse; that is, $a \cdot \left(\frac{1}{a}\right) = 1 = \left(\frac{1}{a}\right) \cdot a$.

Distributive Property of Multiplication over Addition   For real numbers a, b, and c, $a \cdot (b + c) = a \cdot b + a \cdot c$.

Denseness Property   For real numbers a and b, there exists a real number c such that $a < c < b$.

In addition, the properties of equality and inequality similar to those for rational numbers hold for real numbers. Using these properties, real-number equations and inequalities can be solved. The number line can be used to picture real numbers because every point on a number line corresponds to a real number and every real number corresponds to a point on the number line. Because such a one-to-one correspondence is possible, solution sets of real-number equations and inequalities can be graphed on a number line.

Example 7-30

Solve each of the following and show the solution on a number line.

(a) $x - 3 \leq \sqrt{2} + {^-2}$

(b) $\frac{3x^2}{2} - 4 = 5$

Solution

(a) $x - 3 \leq \sqrt{2} + {^-2}$

$\qquad x \leq \sqrt{2} + 1$

Thus, the solution set is $\{x \mid x \leq \sqrt{2} + 1$, where x is a real number$\}$ and it is shown in Figure 7-7.

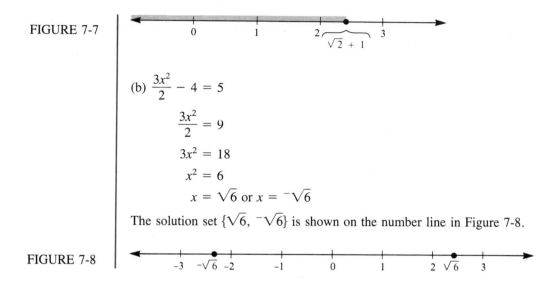

FIGURE 7-7

(b) $\dfrac{3x^2}{2} - 4 = 5$

$$\dfrac{3x^2}{2} = 9$$

$$3x^2 = 18$$

$$x^2 = 6$$

$$x = \sqrt{6} \text{ or } x = {}^{-}\sqrt{6}$$

The solution set $\{\sqrt{6},\ {}^{-}\sqrt{6}\}$ is shown on the number line in Figure 7-8.

FIGURE 7-8

PROBLEM SET 7-5

1. Without using a radical sign, write an irrational number all of whose digits are 2s and 3s.
2. Arrange the following real numbers in order from least to greatest.
   0.78, 0.$\overline{7}$, 0.$\overline{78}$, 0.788, 0.7$\overline{8}$, 0.7$\overline{88}$, 0.77, 0.787787778 . . .
3. Which of the following represent irrational numbers?
   (a) $\sqrt{51}$ (b) $\sqrt{64}$ (c) $\sqrt{324}$
   (d) $\sqrt{325}$ (e) $2 + 3\sqrt{2}$ (f) $\sqrt{2} \div 5$
4. Find the square roots correct to tenths for each of the following, if possible.
   (a) 225   (b) 251   (c) 169
   (d) 512   (e) ${}^{-}81$ (f) 625
5. Find the approximate square roots for each of the following correct to hundredths by (i) the squeezing method and (ii) Newton's method.
   (a) 17   (b) 7   (c) 21
   (d) 0.0120   (e) 20.3   (f) 1.64
6. Classify each of the following as true or false. If false, give a counterexample.
   (a) The sum of any rational number and any irrational number is a rational number.
   (b) The sum of any two irrational numbers is an irrational number.

(c) The product of any two irrational numbers is an irrational number.
(d) The difference of any two irrational numbers is an irrational number.

7. Is it true that $\sqrt{a + b} = \sqrt{a} + \sqrt{b}$? Either prove the statement or give a counterexample.
8. Solve each of the following for real numbers and graph the solution set on a number line.
   (a) $5x - 1 \le \dfrac{7}{2}x + 3$ (b) $4 + 3x \ge \sqrt{5} - 7x$
   (c) $\dfrac{2}{3}x + \sqrt{3} \le {}^{-}5x$ (d) $(2x - 1)^2 = 4$
   (e) $|x| \ge 7$ (f) $|x| \le 3$
9. Find three irrational numbers between 1 and 3.
10. Find an irrational number between $0.\overline{53}$ and $0.\overline{54}$.
11. Pi (π) is an irrational number. Could $\pi = \frac{22}{7}$? Why or why not?
12. Is it true that $\sqrt{13} = 3.60\overline{5}$? Why or why not?
13. For what real values of x is each statement true?
    (a) $\sqrt{x} = 8$ (b) $\sqrt{x} = {}^{-}8$
    (c) $\sqrt{{}^{-}x} = 8$ (d) $\sqrt{{}^{-}x} = {}^{-}8$
    (e) $\sqrt{x} > 0$ (f) $\sqrt{x} < 0$

14. If R is the set of real numbers, Q is the set of rational numbers, I is the set of integers, W is the set of whole numbers, and S is the set of irrational numbers, find each of the following.
    (a) $Q \cup S$ (b) $Q \cap S$ (c) $Q \cap R$
    (d) $S \cap W$ (e) $W \cup R$ (f) $Q \cup R$

15. If the letters below correspond to the sets listed in Problem 14, put a check mark under each set of numbers for which a solution to the problem exists.

	N	I	Q	R
(a) $x^2 + 1 = 5$				
(b) $2x - 1 = 32$				
(c) $x^2 = 3$				
(d) $x^2 = 4$				
(e) $\sqrt{x} = {}^-1$				
(f) $\frac{3}{4}x = 4$				

16. A diagonal brace is placed in a 4-foot by 5-foot rectangular gate. What is the length of the brace to the nearest tenth of a foot? (*Hint:* Use the Pythagorean Theorem.)

17. For a simple pendulum of length l, given in centimeters (cm), the time of the period T in seconds is given by $T = 2\pi\sqrt{\dfrac{l}{g}}$, where $g = 9.8$ cm/sec². Find the time T if:
    (a) $l = 20$ cm   (b) $l = 100$ cm

★ 18. Prove: $\sqrt{3}$ is irrational.

★ 19. Prove: If p is a prime number, then $\sqrt{p}$ is an irrational number.

★ 20. (a) For what whole numbers m is $\sqrt{m}$ a rational number?
    ★ (b) Prove your answer in part 20(a).

21. (a) Show that $0.5 + \dfrac{1}{0.5} \geq 2$.
    ★ (b) Prove that any positive real number x plus its reciprocal $\dfrac{1}{x}$ is greater than or equal to 2.

22. Recall that π is an irrational number that can be approximated by a decimal. One way to find an approximation for π is to use the sequence given by

$$\frac{\pi^2}{6} = 1 + \frac{1}{2^2} + \frac{1}{3^2} + \frac{1}{4^2} + \frac{1}{5^2} + \cdots$$

and then compute π as

$$\sqrt{6\left(1 + \frac{1}{2^2} + \frac{1}{3^2} + \frac{1}{4^2} + \frac{1}{5^2} + \cdots\right)}$$

(a) Find an approximation of π using the first 20 terms.
(b) Compare the answer in (a) to $\frac{22}{7}$, which is often used as a value for π.

$*$ $*$ $*$ $*$ $*$ $*$ $*$ REVIEW PROBLEMS $*$ $*$ $*$ $*$ $*$ $*$ $*$

23. Write 0.00024 as a fraction in simplest form.

24. Arrange the following from least to greatest.

   $4.09, 4.099, 4.0\overline{9}, 4.09\overline{1}$

25. Write $0.\overline{24}$ as a fraction in simplest form.

26. Write each of the following as a standard numeral.
    (a) $2.03 \cdot 10^5$ (b) $3.8 \cdot 10^{-4}$

27. Joan's salary this year is $18,600. If she receives a 9% raise, what is her salary next year?

28. If 800 of the 2000 students at the university are males, what percent of the university students are females?

$*$7-6   RADICALS AND RATIONAL EXPONENTS

The positive solution to $x^2 = 5$ is $\sqrt{5}$. Similarly, the positive solution to $x^3 = 5$ can be denoted as $\sqrt[3]{5}$. In general, the positive solution to $x^n = 5$ is $\sqrt[n]{5}$ and is

*n*th root   index

called the **nth root** of 5. The numeral n is called the **index.** Note that in the expression $\sqrt{5}$, the index 2 is understood and is not expressed.

In general, the positive solution to $x^n = b$, *where b is nonnegative*, is $\sqrt[n]{b}$. Substituting $\sqrt[n]{b}$ for x in the equation $x^n = b$ gives the following.

$$(\sqrt[n]{b})^n = b$$

If b is negative, $\sqrt[n]{b}$ cannot always be defined. For example, consider $\sqrt[4]{-16}$. If $\sqrt[4]{-16} = x$, then $x^4 = {}^-16$. Since any real number raised to the fourth power is positive, there is no real number solution to $x^4 = {}^-16$ and, therefore, $\sqrt[4]{-16}$ cannot be a real number. Similarly, it is not possible to find *any* even root of a negative number. However, the value $^-2$ satisfies the equation $x^3 = {}^-8$. Hence $\sqrt[3]{-8} = {}^-2$. In general, the odd root of a negative number is a negative number.

Now, consider an expression like $4^{1/2}$. What does it mean? By extending the properties of exponents previously developed for integer exponents, it must be that $4^{1/2} \cdot 4^{1/2} = 4^{1/2+1/2} = 4^1$. This implies that $(4^{1/2})^2 = 4$, or $4^{1/2}$ is a square root of 4. The number $4^{1/2}$ is assumed to be the principal square root of 4; that is, $4^{1/2} = \sqrt{4}$. In general, if x is a nonnegative real number, then $x^{1/2} = \sqrt{x}$. Similarly, $(x^{1/3})^3 = x^{(1/3)\cdot3} = x^1$, and $x^{1/3} = \sqrt[3]{x}$. This discussion leads to the following definition.

DEFINITION

> For any real number x and any positive integer n, $x^{1/n} = \sqrt[n]{x}$, where $\sqrt[n]{x}$ is meaningful.

Also, since $(x^m)^{1/n} = \sqrt[n]{x^m}$ and if $(x^m)^{1/n} = x^{m/n}$, it follows that $x^{m/n} = \sqrt[n]{x^m}$. If $x \geq 0$ then the fraction $\dfrac{m}{n}$ in $x^{m/n}$ can be replaced by an equivalent fraction. However, if $x < 0$, it is not always possible to replace $\dfrac{m}{n}$ by an equivalent fraction. For example, $(^-4)^{1/2}$ is not defined, but $(^-4)^{2/4} = \sqrt[4]{(^-4)^2} = \sqrt[4]{16} = 2$.

Example 7-31

Write each of the following in radical form.

(a) $16^{1/4}$
(c) $(^-8)^{1/3}$

(b) $32^{1/6}$
(d) $64^{3/2}$

Solution

(a) $16^{1/4} = \sqrt[4]{16}$
(c) $(^-8)^{1/3} = \sqrt[3]{-8}$

(b) $32^{1/6} = \sqrt[6]{32}$
(d) $64^{3/2} = \sqrt{64^3}$

The properties of integer exponents also hold for rational exponents. These properties are equivalent to the corresponding properties of radicals if the expressions involving radicals are meaningful.

Properties | Let r and s be any rational numbers, x and y be any real numbers, and n be any integer.

(a) $(xy)^r = x^r \cdot y^r$ implies $(xy)^{1/n} = x^{1/n}y^{1/n}$ and $\sqrt[n]{xy} = \sqrt[n]{x}\ \sqrt[n]{y}$.

(b) $\left(\dfrac{x}{y}\right)^r = \dfrac{x^r}{y^r}$ implies $\left(\dfrac{x}{y}\right)^{1/n} = \dfrac{x^{1/n}}{y^{1/n}}$ and $\sqrt[n]{\dfrac{x}{y}} = \dfrac{\sqrt[n]{x}}{\sqrt[n]{y}}$.

(c) $(x^r)^s = x^{rs}$ implies $(x^{1/n})^s = x^{s/n}$ and, hence, $(\sqrt[n]{x})^s = \sqrt[n]{x^s}$.

The preceding properties can be used to simplify the square roots of many numbers. For example, $\sqrt{96} = \sqrt{16 \cdot 6} = \sqrt{16}\ \sqrt{6} = 4\sqrt{6}$. When $\sqrt{96}$ is written as $4\sqrt{6}$, it is said to be in simplest form. In general, to simplify nth roots, factor out as many nth powers as possible. For example, $\sqrt{32} = \sqrt{4 \cdot 8} = 2\sqrt{8}$. Hence, $2\sqrt{8}$ is a simplified form, but not the simplest form. The simplest form of $\sqrt{32}$ is $4\sqrt{2}$.

Example 7-32 | Write each of the following in simplest form.

(a) $\sqrt{200}$ (b) $\sqrt{75}$ (c) $\sqrt[3]{240}$
(d) $\sqrt{3} \cdot \sqrt{15}$ (e) $\sqrt[3]{81} \cdot \sqrt[3]{32}$

Solution | (a) $\sqrt{200} = \sqrt{100 \cdot 2} = \sqrt{100}\ \sqrt{2} = 10\sqrt{2}$
(b) $\sqrt{75} = \sqrt{25 \cdot 3} = \sqrt{25}\ \sqrt{3} = 5\sqrt{3}$
(c) $\sqrt[3]{240} = \sqrt[3]{8 \cdot 30} = \sqrt[3]{8}\ \sqrt[3]{30} = 2\ \sqrt[3]{30}$
(d) $\sqrt{3} \cdot \sqrt{15} = \sqrt{3 \cdot 15} = \sqrt{45} = \sqrt{9 \cdot 5} = \sqrt{9} \cdot \sqrt{5} = 3\sqrt{5}$
(e) $\sqrt[3]{81} \cdot \sqrt[3]{32} = \sqrt[3]{81 \cdot 32} = \sqrt[3]{3^4 \cdot 2^5} = \sqrt[3]{3^3 \cdot 2^3 \cdot 3 \cdot 2^2}$
$= \sqrt[3]{3^3 \cdot 2^3} \cdot \sqrt[3]{3 \cdot 2^2} = 6\sqrt[3]{12}$

Some expressions in the form $\sqrt{x} + \sqrt{y}$ can be simplified. For example,

$$\sqrt{24} + \sqrt{54} = \sqrt{4 \cdot 6} + \sqrt{9 \cdot 6}$$
$$= \sqrt{4}\ \sqrt{6} + \sqrt{9}\ \sqrt{6}$$
$$= 2\sqrt{6} + 3\sqrt{6}$$
$$= (2 + 3)\sqrt{6}$$
$$= 5\sqrt{6}$$

Be careful! Notice that $\sqrt{9} + \sqrt{4} = 3 + 2 = 5$, but $\sqrt{9 + 4} = \sqrt{13}$. Thus, $\sqrt{9} + \sqrt{4} \neq \sqrt{9 + 4}$ and, in general, $\sqrt{x} + \sqrt{y} \neq \sqrt{x + y}$.

Example 7-33 | Write each expression in simplest form.

(a) $\sqrt{20} + \sqrt{45} - \sqrt{80}$ (b) $\sqrt{12} + \sqrt{13}$
(c) $\sqrt{49x} + \sqrt{4x}$

Solution | (a) $\sqrt{20} + \sqrt{45} - \sqrt{80} = 2\sqrt{5} + 3\sqrt{5} - 4\sqrt{5} = \sqrt{5}$
(b) $\sqrt{12} + \sqrt{13} = 2\sqrt{3} + \sqrt{13}$
(c) $\sqrt{49x} + \sqrt{4x} = 7\sqrt{x} + 2\sqrt{x} = 9\sqrt{x}$

PROBLEM SET 7-6

1. Write each of the following square roots in simplest form.
   (a) $\sqrt{180}$ (b) $\sqrt{529}$ (c) $\sqrt{363}$

   (d) $\sqrt{252}$ (e) $\sqrt{\dfrac{169}{196}}$ (f) $\sqrt{\dfrac{49}{196}}$

2. Write each of the following in simplest form.
   (a) $\sqrt[3]{-27}$ (b) $\sqrt[5]{96}$ (c) $\sqrt[5]{32}$

   (d) $\sqrt[3]{250}$ (e) $\sqrt[5]{-243}$ (f) $\sqrt[4]{64}$

3. Write each of the following expressions in simplest form.
   (a) $2\sqrt{3} + 3\sqrt{2} + \sqrt{180}$
   (b) $\sqrt[3]{4} \cdot \sqrt[3]{10}$
   (c) $(2\sqrt{3} + 3\sqrt{2})^2$
   (d) $\sqrt{6} \div \sqrt{12}$
   (e) $5\sqrt{72} + 2\sqrt{50} - \sqrt{288} - \sqrt{242}$
   (f) $\sqrt{\dfrac{8}{7}} \div \sqrt{\dfrac{4}{21}}$

4. Rewrite each of the following in simplest form.
   (a) $16^{1/2}$ (b) $16^{-1/2}$
   (c) $27^{2/3}$ (d) $27^{-2/3}$
   (e) $64^{5/6}$ (f) $32^{2/5}$
   (g) $3^{1/2} \cdot 3^{3/2}$ (h) $8^{3/2} \cdot 4^{1/4}$

   (i) $\dfrac{(32)^{-2/5}}{\left(\dfrac{1}{16}\right)^{-3/2}}$ (j) $(10^{1/3} \cdot 10^{-1/6})^6$

   (k) $9^{2/3} \cdot 27^{2/9}$

5. Is $\sqrt{x^2 + y^2} = x + y$ for all values of x and y?

6. The following exponential function approximates the number of bacteria after t hours: $E(t) = 2^{10} \cdot 16^t$.
   (a) What is the initial number of bacteria, that is, when $t = 0$?
   (b) After $\frac{1}{4}$ hour, how many bacteria are there?
   (c) After $\frac{1}{2}$ hour, how many bacteria are there?

7. Solve for x, where x is a rational number.
   (a) $3^x = 81$ (b) $4^x = 8$
   (c) $128^{-x} = 16$ (d) $\left(\dfrac{4}{9}\right)^{3x} = \dfrac{32}{243}$

★ 8. In the cartoon, Woodstock illustrates the technique for rationalizing fractions (removing the radical symbol from the denominator of a fraction). Use the technique demonstrated in the cartoon to rationalize the denominators for each of the following.
   (a) $\dfrac{2}{\sqrt{3}}$ (b) $\dfrac{7\sqrt{2}}{\sqrt{5}}$ (c) $\dfrac{5\sqrt{5}}{\sqrt{18}}$
   (d) $\dfrac{1}{\sqrt{3}}$ (e) $\dfrac{2}{\sqrt{2}}$ (f) $\dfrac{3}{\sqrt{8}}$

YOU'RE LUCKY, DO YOU KNOW THAT, BIRD? YOU'RE LUCKY BECAUSE YOU DON'T HAVE TO STUDY MATH!

YOU DON'T HAVE TO KNOW ABOUT RATIONALIZING THE DENOMINATOR AND DUMB THINGS LIKE THAT

YOU'RE REALLY LUCKY

$\dfrac{7\sqrt{2}}{\sqrt{6}} \cdot \dfrac{\sqrt{6}}{\sqrt{6}} = \dfrac{7\sqrt{2 \cdot 2 \cdot 3}}{6} = \dfrac{7}{3}\sqrt{3}$

2-20

© 1979 United Feature Syndicate, Inc.

SOLUTION TO THE PRELIMINARY PROBLEM

Understanding the Problem

Howard walked into the first store and the store owner gave him as much money as Howard had with him. Howard then spent 80% of his total amount of money. He left the first store with the remaining 20% of his money and walked into the second store. The second store owner gave Howard as much money as Howard had when he walked in, and Howard spent 80% of his total amount of money. Howard then went into the third store and repeated the same process, after which he has $12.00 left. We are to determine how much money Howard had when he entered the first store.

Devising a Plan

To determine a strategy for solving the problem, we draw a table to model the stores and the spending that occurred. We see from Table 7-5 that the only money entry we can make is the amount Howard had when he left the third store.

TABLE 7-5

Store	Amount With Which Howard Entered	Amount With Which Howard Left
First	?	
Second		
Third		$12

Because we know the amount of money Howard had when he left the third store, we can use the strategy of working backwards to find the amount he had when he entered that store. The amount he had when he entered the third store is the same as the amount with which he left the second store; hence, we can calculate the amount he had when he entered the second store. Similarly, we can calculate the amount he had when he entered the first store. The procedure is the same in each store and can be generalized. Let A be the amount of money he had when he entered a given store. Because he received the same amount, A, from the store owner, he then had $A + A$, or $2A$. When he spent 80% of $2A$, he was left with 20% of $2A$, or $0.20 \cdot (2A)$, or $0.4A$. Because this procedure works for every store, we start with the third store because we know Howard had $12 when he left that store.

Carrying Out the Plan

To complete Table 7-5, we first determine the other entry for the third store. To do this, we solve the following equation.

$$0.4A = \$12$$

$$A = \frac{\$12}{0.4} = \$30$$

Because the amount he had when he entered the third store is the same as the amount he had when he left the second store, we can make the entries shown in Table 7-6.

TABLE 7-6

Store	Amount With Which Howard Entered	Amount With Which Howard Left
First Second Third	 $30	 $30 $12

To determine the amount with which Howard entered the second store, we solve the following.

$$0.4A = \$30$$

$$A = \frac{\$30}{0.4} = \$75$$

Similarly, we can solve the following equation to find the amount A that Howard had when he entered the first store.

$$0.4A = \$75$$

$$A = \frac{\$75}{0.4} = \$187.50$$

Thus, Howard had $187.50 when he entered the first store.

Looking Back

The answer can now be checked by starting at the first store with $187.50 and following through the calculations to make sure that the amount Howard has when he leaves the third store is in reality $12.00.

An alternate solution to the problem can be found using the fact that the procedure for determining the amount of money that Howard had when he left each store is the same. If he entered the first store with amount A, we saw earlier that he left with $0.4A$. He then entered the second store with $0.4A$ and left with $0.4 \cdot (0.4A)$, or $(0.4)^2 \cdot A$. Similarly, he left the third store with $0.4 \cdot (0.4)^2 \cdot A$, or $(0.4)^3 \cdot A$. Thus, we need to solve the equation

$$(0.4)^3 \cdot A = 12$$

Hence, $A = \$187.50$.

Another related problem is the following: Suppose it is known that each store owner makes a 100% profit on all store sales. Is the scheme of agreeing to Howard's request profitable to each store owner? If not, what percent of profit would each store owner have to make in order to make it profitable?

QUESTIONS FROM THE CLASSROOM

1. A student argues that $0.\overline{9} \neq 1$. How do you respond?
2. A student says that $3\frac{1}{4}\% = 0.03 + 0.25 = 0.28$. What is the error, if any?
3. Why is $\sqrt{25} \neq {}^{-}5$?
4. A student says, "I know another way to express $\sqrt{n^2}$. It is $|n|$." Is the student correct?
5. A student claims that $\sqrt{({}^{-}5)^2} = {}^{-}5$ because $\sqrt{a^2} = a$. Is this correct?
6. Another student says that $\sqrt{({}^{-}5)^2} = [({}^{-}5)^2]^{1/2} = ({}^{-}5)^{2/2} = ({}^{-}5)^1 = {}^{-}5$. Is this correct?
7. A student claims that the equation $\sqrt{{}^{-}x} = 3$ has no solution since the square root of a negative number does not exist. Why is this argument wrong?
8. A student multiplies $(6.5)(8.5)$ to obtain the following

$$
\begin{array}{r}
8.5 \\
\times\ 6.5 \\
\hline
4\,2\,5 \\
5\,1\,0 \\
\hline
5\,5.2\,5
\end{array}
$$

However, when the student multiplies $8\frac{1}{2} \cdot 6\frac{1}{2}$, the following is obtained.

$$
\begin{array}{r}
8\frac{1}{2} \\
\times\ 6\frac{1}{2} \\
\hline
4\frac{1}{4} \qquad \left(\frac{1}{2} \cdot 8\frac{1}{2}\right) \\
48 \qquad (6 \cdot 8) \\
\hline
52\frac{1}{4}
\end{array}
$$

How is this possible?

9. On a test, a student wrote the following.

$$\frac{x^2}{7} - 2 \geq {}^{-}3$$

$$\frac{x^2}{7} > {}^{-}1$$

$$x^2 \geq {}^{-}7$$

Hence, there is no solution. What is the error?

10. A student reports that it is impossible to mark a product up 150% because 100% of something is all there is. What is your response?

CHAPTER OUTLINE

I. Decimals
   A. Every rational number can be represented as a terminating or repeating decimal.
   B. A rational number $\frac{a}{b}$, whose denominator is of the form $2^m \cdot 5^n$, where m and n are whole numbers, can be expressed as a **terminating decimal.**
   C. A **repeating decimal** is a decimal with a block of digits, called the **repetend,** repeated infinitely many times.
   D. A number is in **scientific notation** if it is written as the product of a number greater than or equal to 1 and less than 10 and a power of 10.
   E. An **irrational number** is represented by a nonterminating, nonrepeating decimal.
   F. **Percent** means *per hundred.* Percent is written using the % symbol; $x\% = \frac{x}{100}$.

* II. Interest
   A. **Simple interest** is computed using the formula $I = Prt$, where I is the interest, P is the principal, r is the annual interest rate, and t is the time in years.
   B. **Compound interest** is computed using the formula $A = P(1 + i)^n$, where A is the balance, P is the principal, i is the interest rate per period, and n is the number of periods.

III. Real numbers
   A. The set of **real numbers** is the set of all decimals, namely, the union of the set of rational and the set of irrational numbers.
   B. If a is any whole number, then the principal square root of a, denoted by $\sqrt{a}$, is the nonnegative number b such that $b \cdot b = b^2 = a$.
   C. Square roots can be found using the **squeezing method** or **Newton's method.**

* IV. Radicals and Rational Exponents
   A. $\sqrt[n]{x}$, or $x^{1/n}$, is called the **nth root** of x and n is called the **index.**
   B. The following properties hold for radicals if the expressions involving radicals are meaningful.
   (a) $\sqrt[n]{xy} = \sqrt[n]{x} \cdot \sqrt[n]{y}$
   (b) $\sqrt[n]{\dfrac{x}{y}} = \dfrac{\sqrt[n]{x}}{\sqrt[n]{y}}$
   (c) $(\sqrt[n]{x})^m = \sqrt[n]{x^m}$

CHAPTER TEST

1. Perform the following operations.
   (a) $3.6 + 2.007 - 6.3$ (b) $(5.2) \cdot (6.07)$
   (c) $(5.1 + 6.32) \cdot 0.02$ (d) $0.12032 \div 3.76$
   (e) $0.012 - 0.109$ (f) $(0.02)^4$
2. Write each of the following in expanded form.
   (a) 32.012 (b) 0.00103
3. Give a test to determine if a fraction can be written as a terminating decimal without actually performing the division.
4. A board is 442.4 cm long. How many shelves can be cut from it if each shelf is 55.3 cm long?
5. Write each of the following as a decimal.
   (a) $\dfrac{4}{7}$ (b) $\dfrac{1}{8}$
   (c) $\dfrac{2}{3}$ (d) $\dfrac{5}{8}$

6. Write each of the following as a fraction in simplest form.
   (a) 0.28 (b) $0.\overline{3}$ (c) $2.0\overline{8}$
7. Round each of the following numbers as specified.
   (a) 307.625 to the nearest hundredth
   (b) 307.625 to the nearest tenth
   (c) 307.625 to the nearest unit
   (d) 307.625 to the nearest hundred
8. Solve each of the following for x, where x is a real number.
   (a) $0.2x - 0.75 \geq \frac{1}{2}(x - 3.5)$
   (b) $0.\overline{9} + x = 1$
   (c) $23\%(x) = 4600$
   (d) 10 is x percent of 50
   (e) 17 is 50% of x
   (f) $0.\overline{3} + x = 1$

9. Answer each of the following.
   (a) 6 is what percent of 24?
   (b) What is 320% of 60?
   (c) 17 is 30% of what number?
   (d) 0.2 is what percent of 1?
10. Change each of the following to percents.

   (a) $\dfrac{1}{8}$ (b) $\dfrac{3}{40}$ (c) 6.27

   (d) 0.0123   (e) $\dfrac{3}{2}$

11. Change each of the following percents to decimals.

   (a) 60%   (b) $\left(\dfrac{2}{3}\right)\%$ (c) 100%

12. Answer each of the following and explain your answers.
   (a) Is the set of irrational numbers closed under addition?
   (b) Is the set of irrational numbers closed under subtraction?
   (c) Is the set of irrational numbers closed under multiplication?
   (d) Is the set of irrational numbers closed under division?
13. Find an approximation for $\sqrt{23}$ correct to three decimal places.
14. Rewrite each of the following in scientific notation.
   (a) 426,000   (b) 0.00000237
   (c) 32   (d) 0.325
15. Classify each of the following as rational or irrational. (Assume the patterns shown continue.)
   (a) 2.191199119991199991119 . . .

   (b) $\dfrac{1}{\sqrt{2}}$ (c) $\dfrac{4}{9}$

   (d) 0.0011001100110011 . . .
   (e) 0.001100011000011 . . .
* 16. Find the simplest form for each of the following.
   (a) $\sqrt{242}$ (b) $\sqrt{288}$
   (c) $\sqrt{360}$ (d) $\sqrt[3]{162}$
* 17. Write each of the following in simplest form with nonnegative exponents in the final answer.

   (a) $\left(\dfrac{1}{2}\right)^4\left(\dfrac{1}{2}\right)^7$ (b) $5^{-16} \div 5^4$

   (c) $\left[\left(\dfrac{2}{3}\right)^7\right]^{-4}$ (d) $3^{16} \cdot 3^2$

18. Sandy received a dividend that equals 11% of the value of her investment. If her dividend was $1020.80, how much was her investment?
19. Five computers in a shipment of 150 were found to be defective. What percent of the computers were defective?
20. On a mathematics examination, a student missed 8 of 70 questions. What percent of the questions, rounded to the nearest tenth, did the student do correctly?
21. A microcomputer system costs $3450 at present. This is 60% of the cost 4 years ago. What was the cost of the system 4 years ago?
* 22. A company was offered a $30,000 loan at a 12.5% annual interest rate for 4 years. Find the simple interest due on the loan at the end of 4 years.
* 23. A money-market fund pays 14% annual interest compounded quarterly. What is the value of a $10,000 investment after 3 years?

SELECTED BIBLIOGRAPHY

Allison, J. F. "A Picture of the Rational Numbers: Dense but Not Complete." *The Mathematics Teacher* 65 (January 1972): 87–89.

Carpenter, T., et. al. "Decimals: Results and Implications from National Assessment." *Arithmetic Teacher* 28 (April 1981): 34–37.

Chow, P., and T. Lin. "Extracting Square Root Made Easy." *Arithmetic Teacher* 29 (November 1981):48–50.

Cole, B. L., and H. S. Weissenfluh. "An Analysis of Teaching Percentages." *The Arithmetic Teacher* 21 (March 1974): 226–228.

Dana, M. E., and M. M. Lindquist. "Let's Do It: From Halves to Hundredths." *Arithmetic Teacher* 26 (November 1978):4–8.

deP. Soler, F., and R. Schuster. "Compound Growth and Related Situations: A Problem-Solving Approach." *The Mathematics Teacher* 75 (November 1982):640–643.

Firl, D. H. "Fractions, Decimals and Their Futures." *The Arithmetic Teacher* 24 (March 1977):238–240.

Harris, V. C. "On Proofs of the Irrationality of $\sqrt{2}$." *The Mathematics Teacher* 64 (January 1971):19–21.

Hilferty, M. R. "Some Convenient Fractions for Work with Repeating Decimals." *The Mathematics Teacher* 65 (March 1972):240–241.

Hutchinson, M. R. "Investigating the Nature of Periodic Decimals." *The Mathematics Teacher* 65 (April 1972):325–327.

Jacobs, J. E., and E. B. Herbert. "Making $\sqrt{2}$ Seem 'Real'." *The Arithmetic Teacher* 21 (February 1974):133–136.

Kidder, F. "Ditton's Dilemma, or What To Do About Decimals." *Arithmetic Teacher* 28 (October 1980):44–46.

Manchester, M. "Decimal Expansions of Rational Numbers." *The Mathematics Teacher* 65 (December 1972):698–702.

McGinty, R., and W. Mutch. "Repeating Decimals, Geometric Patterns, and Open-Ended Questions." *The Mathematics Teacher* 75 (October 1982):600–602.

Mielke, P. T. "Rational Points on the Number Line." *The Mathematics Teacher* 63 (October 1970):475–479.

Payne, J. N. "One Point of View: Sense and Nonsense about Fractions and Decimals." *Arithmetic Teacher* 27 (January 1980):4–7.

Prielipp, R. W. "Decimals." *The Arithmetic Teacher* 23 (April 1976):285–288.

Robidoux, D., and N. Montefusco. "An Easy Way to Change Repeating Decimals to Fractions—Nick's Method." *The Arithmetic Teacher* 24 (January 1977):81–82.

Schmalz, R. "A Visual Approach to Decimals." *Arithmetic Teacher* 25 (May 1978):22–25.

Shoemaker, R. "Please, My Dear Aunt Sally." *Arithmetic Teacher* 27 (May 1980):34–35.

Sullivan, K. "Money—A Key to Mathematical Success." *Arithmetic Teacher* 29 (November 1981):34–35.

Teahan, T. "How I Learned to Do Percents." *Arithmetic Teacher* 27 (January 1979):16–17.

Usiskin, Z. "The Future of Fractions." *Arithmetic Teacher* 27 (January 1979):18–20.

Wagner, S. "Fun with Repeating Decimals." *The Mathematics Teacher* 26 (March 1979):209–212.

Writt, E. " Mr. Manning's Money." *Arithmetic Teacher* 29 (September 1981):47.

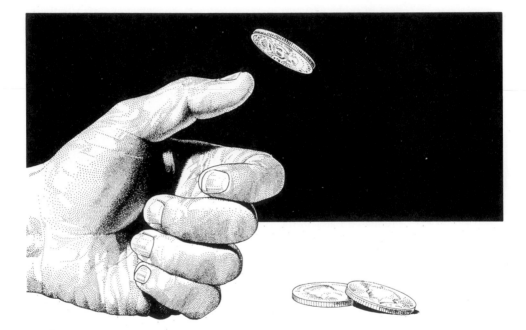

PRELIMINARY PROBLEM

Al and Betsy were playing a coin tossing game in which a fair coin was to be tossed five times. Al was to win when a total of three heads were obtained. Betsy was to win when a total of three tails were obtained. Each bet $50 on the game. The coin was lost when Al had two heads and Betsy had one tail. How should the stakes be fairly split if the game is not continued?

INTRODUCTION

Girolamo Cardano (1501–1576), a mathematician, physician, and astrologer, wrote one of the first books concerning probability and gambling. However, Blaise Pascal (1623–1662) and Pierre de Fermat (1601–1665) are generally recognized as the founders of probability theory. Their involvement in probability seems to have come as the result of questions asked of them by Chevalier de Meré in 1654. De Meré, a professional gambler, wanted to know how to divide the stakes if two players start, but fail to complete, a game in which the winner is the one who wins three matches out of five.

Today concepts of probability appear frequently in daily life. For example, uses of probability are found in ordinary conversations such as these:

"What is the *probability* the Braves will win the World Series?"

"The *odds* are 2 to 1 that Flea Bag will win the dog show."

"There is no *chance* I would marry you, even if you were the last person on earth."

"The pitcher's batting *average* is .173."

Children's interest in playing games can provide a high level of motivation to study probability, but there is no guarantee that the ideas of probability are a part of every child's background. In this chapter, we use tree diagrams to determine probabilities and to analyze games involving spinners, cards, and dice. Counting techniques are also introduced to aid in the solution of certain probability problems. Later in the chapter, we discuss descriptive statistics, the science of organizing and summarizing numerical data.

8-1 HOW PROBABILITIES ARE DETERMINED

experiments

Activities such as tossing a coin and throwing a die are called **experiments.** If we toss a fair coin—that is, one that is just as likely to land heads as it is to land tails—and if we assume that the coin cannot land on its edge, then there are only

outcomes

two distinct possible **outcomes,** heads (H) and tails (T).

Suppose a fair coin is tossed 40 times with the following result.

HTTHT HHHHH TTTHH HTTTH TTHTH TTHHT THTHT TTHTT

Observe the following.

$$\frac{\text{Number of heads}}{\text{Number of trials}} = \frac{18}{40}$$

Heads resulted in approximately $\frac{1}{2}$ of the tosses. The number of heads cannot be accurately predicted when a coin is tossed a few times. However, when the coin is tossed many times, heads appear in approximately $\frac{1}{2}$ of the tosses. For this reason, we say the probability of a head is $\frac{1}{2}$ and write $P(H) = \frac{1}{2}$. Another argument is that since a fair coin is symmetric and has two sides, each side should appear roughly half of the time in long strings of tosses, and hence,

$$P(H) = P(T) = \frac{1}{2}$$

sample space
outcome set

tree diagram

The set of all possible outcomes for an experiment is called a **sample space,** or **outcome set.** In the case of a single coin toss, the sample space S is given by $S = \{H,T\}$. Determining a sample space for an experiment is important in finding the probabilities of the various outcomes. The sample space S for the coin-tossing experiment can be modeled using a **tree diagram,** as shown in Figure 8-1.

FIGURE 8-1

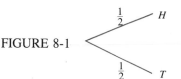

Each outcome of the experiment is designated by a separate branch in the tree diagram, with the probability of each outcome listed.

Example 8-1

(a) Write the sample space S for rolling a standard die.
(b) Use a tree diagram to develop the sample space for tossing a fair coin twice.
(c) Use a tree diagram to develop the sample space for an experiment consisting of tossing a fair coin and then rolling a die.

Solution

(a) The sample space is $S = \{1, 2, 3, 4, 5, 6\}$.
(b) The tree diagram is given in Figure 8-2.

FIGURE 8-2

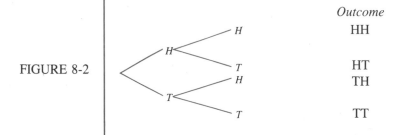

The sample space is $S = \{HH, HT, TH, TT\}$.

(c) The sample space for this experiment is taken from the tree diagram in Figure 8-3.

Outcome

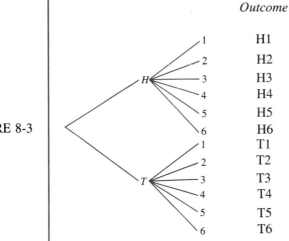

FIGURE 8-3

The sample space is

$S = \{$H1, H2, H3, H4, H5, H6, T1, T2, T3, T4, T5, T6$\}$

event   Any subset of a sample space is called an **event.** For example, the set of all even-numbered rolls of a die is a subset of all possible rolls of a die. The set of all even-numbered rolls is an event.

Example 8-2   Suppose an experiment is to draw one slip of paper from a jar containing 12 slips of paper, each with a month of the year written on it. Find each of the following.

(a) The sample space S for the experiment.
(b) The event A consisting of outcomes from drawing a slip having a month beginning with J.
(c) The event B consisting of outcomes from drawing a slip having the name of a month that has exactly four letters.
(d) The event C consisting of outcomes from drawing a slip having a month that begins with M or N.

Solution   (a) $S = \{$January, February, March, April, May, June, July, August, September, October, November, December$\}$
(b) $A = \{$January, June, July$\}$
(c) $B = \{$June, July$\}$
(d) $C = \{$March, May, November$\}$

Example 8-3

Two spinners are shown in Figure 8-4. Suppose an experiment is to spin X and then spin Y. Find each of the following.

(a) The sample space S for the experiment.
(b) The event A consisting of outcomes from spinning an even number followed by an even number.
(c) The event B consisting of outcomes from spinning at least one 2.
(d) The event C consisting of outcomes from spinning exactly one 2.

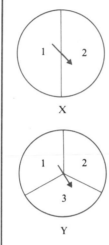

FIGURE 8-4

Solution

(a) The sample space for this experiment can be described using ordered pairs. The first component in each pair is the result of the first spin, and the second component is the result of the second spin.

$$S = \{(1,1),(1,2),(1,3),(2,1),(2,2),(2,3)\}$$

(b) $A = \{(2,2)\}$
(c) $B = \{(1,2),(2,1),(2,2),(2,3)\}$
(d) $C = \{(1,2),(2,1),(2,3)\}$

If a fair die with sample space given by $S = \{1, 2, 3, 4, 5, 6\}$ is rolled many times, each outcome will appear about $\frac{1}{6}$ of the time. Hence, we assign to each outcome a probability of $\frac{1}{6}$ and write, for example, $P(4) = \frac{1}{6}$ for the probability of tossing a 4. Because there are 6 sides to a die, the symmetry of the die suggests in a long string of tosses that any side will appear $\frac{1}{6}$ of the time.

Coin tossing and throwing a die are examples of experiments with **equally likely outcomes;** that is, one outcome is as likely to occur as another. The probability for tossing a 4 with a fair die, $\frac{1}{6}$, is the ratio of the number of elements in the event $A = \{4\}$ to the number of elements in the sample space S. In general, probability is defined in terms of equally likely events, as follows.

equally likely outcomes

DEFINITION

> If all outcomes of an experiment are equally likely, the probability of an event A from sample space S is given by $P(A) = \dfrac{n(A)}{n(S)}$.

Remark

> Recall that $n(A)$ means "the number of elements in A" and $n(S)$ means "the number of elements in S."

FIGURE 8-5

It is important to remember that the preceding definition applies *only to equally likely outcomes.* Applying the definition to outcomes that are not equally likely leads to incorrect conclusions. For example, the sample space for spinning the spinner in Figure 8-5 is given by $S = \{\text{Red, Blue}\}$. However, the outcome Blue is more likely to occur than the outcome Red, and hence $P(\text{Red})$ is not equal to $\frac{1}{2}$. Instead, if the spinner were spun 100 times, it would seem reasonable to expect that about $\frac{1}{4}$, or 25, of the outcomes would be Red, while about $\frac{3}{4}$, or 75, of the outcomes would be Blue. Similarly, one might incorrectly reason that if a die is tossed, then either a 6 appears or it does not. Thus, there are two possible outcomes, and the probability of rolling a 6 is $\frac{1}{2}$. It is correct to say that "6" and "no 6" are two possible outcomes, but these outcomes are not equally likely. There are five numbers on the die that are not equal to 6. Thus, the probability that a 6 appears is $\frac{1}{6}$, whereas the probability that no 6 appears is $\frac{5}{6}$.

impossible event

An event such as rolling a 7 on a single roll of a normal die is called an **impossible event.** Since no face has 7 spots, there are 0 elements in the event, and therefore $P(7) = \frac{0}{6} = 0$. *An event is an impossible event if and only if it has a probability of* 0.

certain event

Consider the event consisting of rolling a number less than 7 on a single roll of a die. Since every face of the die has less than 7 spots, $P(\text{number less than 7}) = \frac{6}{6} = 1$. *An event that has probability* 1 *is called a* **certain event.**

No event has a probability greater than 1 because the number of ways the outcome of an event occurs cannot be greater than the total number of outcomes in the sample space. Likewise, no event has a probability less than 0. Consequently, if A is any event, then the following inequality holds:

$$0 \le P(A) \le 1$$

Example 8-4

at random

A golf bag contains 2 red tees, 4 blue tees, and 5 white tees.

(a) What is the probability of the event A that a tee drawn **at random** is red? The phrase *at random* means that each tee has an equal chance of being drawn.

(b) What is the probability of the event not A, that is, a tee drawn at random is not red?

Solution

(a) Because the bag contains a total of $2 + 4 + 5$, or 11, tees and 2 tees are red, $P(A) = \frac{2}{11}$.

(b) The bag contains 11 tees and 9 are not red, so the probability of "not A" is $\frac{9}{11}$.

complements

The notation $\bar{A}$ designates the event "not A." Events A and $\bar{A}$ are said to be **complements** of each other since $A \cup \bar{A} = S$ and $A \cap \bar{A} = \varnothing$. In the golf bag example, $\bar{A}$ is the set of all possible outcomes for *not* drawing a red tee. Thus, $P(\bar{A}) = \frac{9}{11}$ and $P(A) + P(\bar{A}) = 1$. This is true for complements in general and, therefore,

$$P(A) = 1 - P(\bar{A})$$

This formula enables us to find the probability of an event if the probability of its complement is known. Sometimes it is easier to calculate $P(\bar{A})$ than it is to calculate $P(A)$.

Example 8-5

One number is selected at random from the numbers in the set S given by $S = \{1, 2, 3, 4, \ldots, 24, 25\}$. List the elements in each event given below and calculate each probability.

(a) The event A, consisting of outcomes from drawing an even number.
(b) The event B, consisting of outcomes from drawing a number less than 10 and greater than 20.
(c) The event C, consisting of outcomes from drawing a prime number.
(d) The event D, consisting of outcomes from drawing a number that is not prime.
(e) The event E, consisting of outcomes from drawing a number that is both even and prime.

Solution

In this experiment, $n(S) = 25$.

(a) $A = \{2, 4, 6, 8, 10, 12, 14, 16, 18, 20, 22, 24\}$, so $n(A) = 12$. Thus,

$$P(A) = \frac{n(A)}{n(S)} = \frac{12}{25}$$

(b) $B = \varnothing$, so $n(B) = 0$. Thus, $P(B) = \frac{0}{25} = 0$.

(c) $C = \{2, 3, 5, 7, 11, 13, 17, 19, 23\}$, so $n(C) = 9$. Thus,

$$P(C) = \frac{n(C)}{n(S)} = \frac{9}{25}$$

(d) $D = \{1, 4, 6, 8, 9, 10, 12, 14, 15, 16, 18, 20, 21, 22, 24, 25\}$, so $n(D) = 16$. Thus, $P(D) = \frac{16}{25}$. Notice that D is the same as "not C." Thus, $P(D) = 1 - P(C) = 1 - \frac{9}{25} = \frac{16}{25}$.

(e) $E = \{2\}$, so $n(E) = 1$. Thus,

$$P(E) = \frac{n(E)}{n(S)} = \frac{1}{25}$$

PROBLEM 1

A butcher wrapped three 1-pound packages of meat in butcher paper while having a conversation with a customer. The packages contained round steak, ground beef, and sausage and were to be labeled R, G, and S, respectively. During the conversation, the butcher forgot which package was which, but labeled them anyway. What is the probability that each of the packages is labeled correctly?

Understanding the Problem

The packages of round steak, ground beef, and sausage were labeled R, G, and S. The problem of determining the probability that each of the three packages of meat is labeled correctly depends upon determining the sample space, or at least how many elements are in the sample space.

Devising a Plan

To aid in the solution, we represent the contents—round steak, ground beef, and sausage—as r, g, and s, respectively. To construct the sample space, we use the strategy of making a table. The table should show all the possibilities of what could be in each package, that is, the table should show all the one-to-one correspondences between the set of labels $\{R, G, S\}$ and the set of contents $\{r, g, s\}$. Once the table is completed, the probability that each package is labeled correctly can be determined.

Carrying Out the Plan

Table 8-1 is constructed using the package labels R, G, and S as headings and listing all possibilities of contents, r, g, and s, underneath the headings.

TABLE 8-1   Labels

		R	G	S
C	1	r	g	s
a	2	r	s	g
s	3	g	r	s
e	4	g	s	r
s	5	s	r	g
	6	s	g	r

Case 1 is the only case out of six in which each of the packages is labeled correctly, so the probability that each package is labeled correctly is $\frac{1}{6}$.

Looking Back

Another question to consider is whether or not the probability of having each package labeled incorrectly is the same as the probability of having each package labeled correctly. A first guess might be that the probabilities are the same, but that is not true. Can you determine why?

PROBLEM SET 8-1

1. Write the sample space for each of the following experiments.
   (a) Draw one letter from a jar containing single letters *m, a, t, h.*
   (b) Spin the spinner once.
   (c) Spin the spinner once.

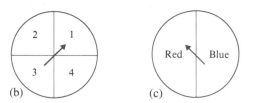

(b)   (c)

   (d) Spin the spinner in (b) once. Then spin the spinner in (c) once.
   (e) Toss a penny, a nickel, and a quarter.
   (f) Spin the spinner in (c) once. Then roll a die.
   (g) Spin the spinner in (b) twice.
2. An experiment consists of selecting the last digit of various telephone numbers. Assume that each of the ten digits is equally likely to appear as a last digit. List each of the following.
   (a) The sample space.
   (b) The event consisting of outcomes that the digit is less than 5.
   (c) The event consisting of outcomes that the digit is odd.
   (d) The event consisting of outcomes that the digit is not 2.
3. Find the probability of each of the events (b)–(d) in Problem 2.
4. A card is selected from an ordinary bridge deck consisting of 52 cards. Find the probabilities for each of the following.

(a) A red card
(b) A face card
(c) A red card or a ten
(d) A queen
(e) Not a queen
(f) A face card or a club
(g) A face card and a club
(h) Not a face card and not a club

5. A drawer contains six black socks, four brown socks, and two green socks. Suppose one sock is drawn from the drawer, and it is equally likely that any one of the socks is drawn. Find the probabilities for each of the following.
   (a) The sock is brown.
   (b) The sock is either black or green.
   (c) The sock is red.
   (d) The sock is not black.
6. When two events, A and B, are disjoint, the events are called *mutually exclusive* events. For such events, $P(A \cup B) = P(A) + P(B)$. Use the formula for probabilities of mutually exclusive events to find the probability that a ball drawn at random from a bag containing two red, three blue, and five white balls is either red or white.
7. What, if anything, is wrong with each of the following statements?
   (a) If the probability that a person drinks is $\frac{54}{100}$ and the probability that a person smokes is $\frac{45}{100}$, then the probability that a person drinks or smokes is $\frac{54}{100} + \frac{45}{100}$ or $\frac{99}{100}$.
   (b) The probability that the Steelers will win the Superbowl is $\frac{3}{4}$ and the probability that they will lose is $\frac{1}{5}$.
   (c) Since there are 50 states, the probability of being born in Montana is $\frac{1}{50}$.

8. If each letter of the alphabet is written on a separate piece of paper and placed in a box and then one piece of paper is drawn at random, what is the probability that the paper has a vowel written on it? What is the probability that the paper has a consonant written on it?

9. The questions below refer to a very popular dice game, craps, in which a player rolls two dice.
    (a) Rolling a sum of 7 or 11 on the first roll of the dice is a win. What is the probability of winning on the first roll?
    (b) Rolling a sum of 2, 3, or 12 on the first roll of the dice is a loss. What is the probability of losing on the first roll?
    (c) Rolling a sum of 4, 5, 6, 8, 9, or 10 on the first roll is neither a win nor a loss. What is the probability of neither winning nor losing on the first roll?
    (d) After rolling a sum of 4, 5, 6, 8, 9, or 10, a player must roll the same sum again before rolling a sum of 7. Which sum 4, 5, 6, 8, 9, or 10 has the highest probability of occurring again?
    (e) What is the probability of rolling a sum of 1 on any roll of the dice?
    (f) What is the probability of rolling a sum less than 13 on any roll of the dice?
    (g) If the two dice are rolled 60 times, approximately how many sums of 7 can be expected?

10. The probability of spinning an odd number on a spinner is $\frac{7}{8}$. Out of 240 spins, how many outcomes can be expected to be odd numbers?

11. A roulette wheel has 38 slots around the rim. The first 36 slots are numbered from 1 to 36. Half of these 36 slots are red and the other half are black. The remaining 2 slots are numbered 0 and 00 and are colored green. As the roulette wheel is spun in one direction, a small ivory ball is rolled along the rim in the opposite direction. The ball has an equally likely chance of falling into any one of the 38 slots. Find each of the following.
    (a) The probability the ball lands in a black slot.
    (b) The probability the ball lands on 0 or 00.
    (c) The probability the ball does not land on a number from 1 through 12.
    (d) The probability the ball lands on an odd number or a green slot.

12. If the roulette wheel in Problem 11 is spun 190 times, about how many times can we expect the ball to land on 0 or 00?

13. The manager of the Good Food Kitchen anticipates that about 80% of the patrons order baked potatoes. What is the anticipated number of baked potatoes necessary to serve 50 patrons?

14. According to a weather report there is a 30% chance that it will rain tomorrow. What is the probability that it will not rain tomorrow?

Laboratory Activity

1. Suppose a paper cup is tossed in the air. The different ways it can land are shown below.

Top   Bottom   Side

Toss a cup 100 times and record each result. From this information, calculate the experimental probability of each outcome. Do the outcomes appear to be equally likely? Based on experimental probabilities, how many times would you predict the cup will land on its side if tossed 200 times?

2. Toss a coin 100 times and record the results. From this information, calculate the experimental probability of tossing a head. Does the experimental result agree with the expected theoretical probability of $\frac{1}{2}$?

BRAIN TEASER

A game called WIN is played with a set of nonstandard dice whose faces are shown flattened out. The game is played with two players. Each player chooses one die and the players roll the dice at the same time. The player with the greater number showing on his die wins the game.

If you were to play WIN, would you choose your die first or second? Why? Can you find a strategy for maximizing your chances of winning the game? (The game of WIN was suggested by Joseph Smyth of Santa Rosa Junior College.)

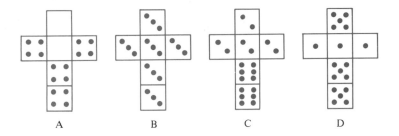

A   B   C   D

8-2 MULTISTAGE EXPERIMENTS

In Section 8-1 we considered one-stage experiments—that is, experiments that are over after one step. For example, the box in Figure 8-6 has one black ball and three white balls. Suppose one ball is drawn at random from the box; that is, no one of the four balls is preferred. Thus, the probability of any one particular ball being drawn is $\frac{1}{4}$. Since there are three indistinguishable white balls and one black ball, the probability of drawing a white ball is $\frac{3}{4}$, and the probability of drawing a black ball is $\frac{1}{4}$. The sample space for the experiment is $\{\bigcirc, \bullet\}$. A tree diagram for this experiment is given in Figure 8-7. Notice that the sum of the probabilities of the branches coming from a single point equals one.

FIGURE 8-6

FIGURE 8-7

two-stage experiments
multistage experiments

Next, we consider several **two-stage experiments** and then other **multistage experiments**. The box in Figure 8-8 contains one black and two white balls. A ball is drawn at random and its color recorded. The ball is then *replaced* and a second ball is drawn and its color recorded. The sample space for this experiment is given by $S = \{\bullet\bullet, \bullet\circ, \circ\bullet, \circ\circ\}$. Figure 8-9 shows a tree diagram for this two-stage experiment.

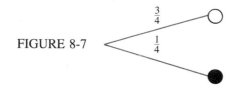

FIGURE 8-8

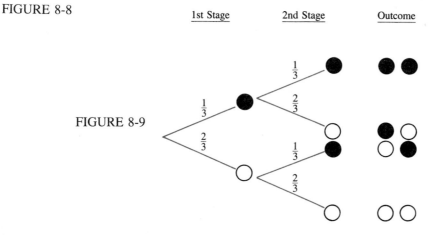

FIGURE 8-9

One path along the tree corresponds to each outcome. What probability should be assigned to each outcome? Consider the path for the outcome $\bullet\circ$. In the first stage, the probability of obtaining a black ball is $\frac{1}{3}$. Then the probability of obtaining a white ball in the second stage (second draw) is $\frac{2}{3}$. Thus, we expect to obtain a black ball on the first draw $\frac{1}{3}$ of the time and then to draw a white ball $\frac{2}{3}$ of those times that we obtained a black ball; that is, $\frac{2}{3}$ of $\frac{1}{3}$ or $\frac{2}{3} \cdot \frac{1}{3}$. Observe that this product may be obtained by multiplying the probabilities along the branches used for the path leading to $\bullet\circ$; that is, $\frac{1}{3} \cdot \frac{2}{3}$, or $\frac{2}{9}$. The probabilities shown in Table 8-2 are obtained by following the paths leading to each of the four outcomes and by multiplying the probabilities along the paths.

TABLE 8-2

Outcome	$\bullet$ $\bullet$	$\bullet$ $\circ$	$\circ$ $\bullet$	$\circ$ $\circ$
Probability	$\frac{1}{3} \cdot \frac{1}{3}$ or $\frac{1}{9}$	$\frac{1}{3} \cdot \frac{2}{3}$ or $\frac{2}{9}$	$\frac{2}{3} \cdot \frac{1}{3}$ or $\frac{2}{9}$	$\frac{2}{3} \cdot \frac{2}{3}$ or $\frac{4}{9}$

For all multistage experiments, the probability of the outcome along any path is equal to the product of all the probabilities along the branches of the path. The sum of the probabilities on branches from any point always equals one. (Why?)

Look at the box pictured in Figure 8-8 again. This time, suppose two balls are drawn one by one without replacement. A tree diagram for this experiment, along with the set of possible outcomes, is shown in Figure 8-10. Notice that the denominators of the fractions along the second branch are all two. Since the draws are made without replacement, there are only two balls remaining for the second draw.

FIGURE 8-10

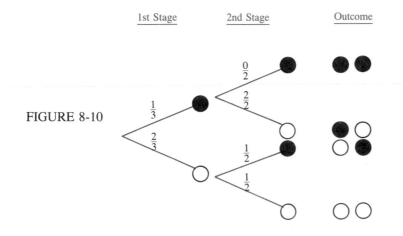

The probabilities for each outcome of the experiment are given in Table 8-3.

TABLE 8-3

Outcome	●●	●○	○●	○○
Probability	$\frac{1}{3} \cdot \frac{0}{2}$ or 0	$\frac{1}{3} \cdot \frac{2}{2}$ or $\frac{2}{6}$	$\frac{2}{3} \cdot \frac{1}{2}$ or $\frac{2}{6}$	$\frac{2}{3} \cdot \frac{1}{2}$ or $\frac{2}{6}$

Table 8-3 can be used to find the probabilities of various events. Consider the event, A, consisting of the outcomes for drawing exactly one black ball in the two draws without replacement. This event is given by $A = \{●○, ○●\}$. Since the outcome ●○ appears $\frac{2}{6}$ of the time, and the outcome ○● appears $\frac{2}{6}$ of the time, then either ●○ or ○● will appear $\frac{4}{6}$ of the time. Thus, $P(A) = \frac{2}{6} + \frac{2}{6} = \frac{4}{6}$.

The event B, consisting of outcomes for drawing *at least* one black ball, could be recorded as $B = \{●○, ○●, ●●\}$. Because $P(●○) = \frac{2}{6}$, $P(○●) = \frac{2}{6}$, and $P(●●) = 0$, then $P(B) = \frac{2}{6} + \frac{2}{6} + 0 = \frac{4}{6}$. Since $\bar{B} = \{○○\}$ and $P(\bar{B}) = \frac{2}{6}$, the probability of B could have been computed as follows: $P(B) = 1 - P(\bar{B}) = 1 - \frac{2}{6} = \frac{4}{6}$.

FIGURE 8-11

> PROBABILITY

Figure 8-11 shows a box with 11 letters. An example of a four-stage experiment is to draw four letters at random from the box one by one *without replacement*. The probability of the outcome BABY may be found by using just one branch of a much larger tree diagram. Because the entire tree is not needed to find this probability, only the portion required to complete the problem is pictured in Figure 8-12. Notice that, because the experiment is performed without replacement, each successive denominator decreases by one.

FIGURE 8-12

$$\frac{2}{11} \quad \frac{1}{10} \quad \frac{1}{9} \quad \frac{1}{8}$$
$$\longrightarrow B \longrightarrow A \longrightarrow B \longrightarrow Y$$

Thus, $P(\text{BABY}) = \left(\frac{2}{11}\right) \cdot \left(\frac{1}{10}\right) \cdot \left(\frac{1}{9}\right) \cdot \left(\frac{1}{8}\right)$, or $\frac{2}{7920}$.

Suppose four letters are drawn one by one from the box in Figure 8-11, and the letters replaced after each drawing. In this case the branch needed to find $P(\text{BABY})$ is pictured in Figure 8-13.

FIGURE 8-13

$$\frac{2}{11} \quad \frac{1}{11} \quad \frac{2}{11} \quad \frac{1}{11}$$
$$\longrightarrow B \longrightarrow A \longrightarrow B \longrightarrow Y$$

Thus, $P(\text{BABY}) = \left(\frac{2}{11}\right) \cdot \left(\frac{1}{11}\right) \cdot \left(\frac{2}{11}\right) \cdot \left(\frac{1}{11}\right)$, or $\frac{4}{14,641}$.

Example 8-6

Consider the three boxes in Figure 8-14.

FIGURE 8-14

> AAB   AB   ABBB
>   1   2   3

A letter is drawn from box 1 and placed in box 2. Then a letter is drawn from box 2 and placed in box 3. Finally, a letter is drawn from box 3. What is the probability that the letter drawn from box 3 is B?

Solution | A tree diagram and outcomes for this experiment follow.

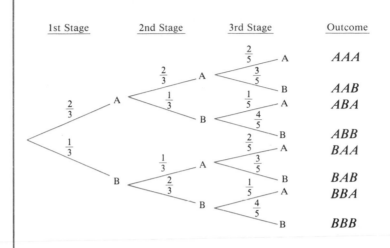

To find the probability that a B is drawn from box 3, add the probabilities for *AAB* and *ABB* and *BAB* and *BBB*.

$$P(AAB) = \frac{2}{3} \cdot \frac{2}{3} \cdot \frac{3}{5} = \frac{12}{45}$$

$$P(ABB) = \frac{2}{3} \cdot \frac{1}{3} \cdot \frac{4}{5} = \frac{8}{45}$$

$$P(BAB) = \frac{1}{3} \cdot \frac{1}{3} \cdot \frac{3}{5} = \frac{3}{45}$$

$$P(BBB) = \frac{1}{3} \cdot \frac{2}{3} \cdot \frac{4}{5} = \frac{8}{45}$$

Thus, the probability of obtaining a B in this experiment is $\frac{12}{45} + \frac{8}{45} + \frac{3}{45} + \frac{8}{45} = \frac{31}{45}$.

We now summarize the ideas in this section for a general case. Suppose an experiment has a sample space given by $S = \{s_1, s_2, s_3, \ldots, s_n\}$ and suppose the probability of each outcome is given in Table 8-4.

TABLE 8-4

Outcome	s_1	s_2	s_3	. . .	s_n
Probability	p_1	p_2	p_3	. . .	p_n

By definition, the probabilities are nonnegative and each is greater than or equal to zero and less than or equal to one. The sum of the probabilities, $p_1 + p_2 + p_3 + \cdots + p_n$, equals one. If A is some event, say $A = \{s_2, s_3\}$, then $P(A)$ equals the sum of the probabilities of all the outcomes in A, that is, $P(A) = p_2 + p_3$. Also, $P(A) = 1 - P(\bar{A})$. A tree diagram for the general experiment is given in Figure 8-15.

FIGURE 8-15

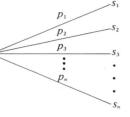

PROBLEM 2

A woman in a small foreign town applies for a marriage permit when she is 18. To obtain the permit, she is handed six strings that she must hold in her hand so that the ends of the strings are exposed. On one side, the ends (top or bottom) are picked randomly, two at a time, and tied forming three separate knots. The same procedure is then repeated for the other set of string ends forming three more knots. If the tied strings form one closed ring, the woman obtains the permit. If not, she must wait until her next birthday to reapply for a permit. What is the probability that she will obtain a marriage permit on her first try?

Understanding the Problem

The problem is to determine the probability that one closed ring will be formed. One closed ring means that all six pieces are joined end-to-end to form one and only one ring.

Devising a Plan

Figure 8-16(a) shows what happens when the ends of the strings of one set are tied in pairs. Notice that no matter in what order those ends are tied, the result appears as in the figure.

Then the other ends are tied in a three-stage experiment. If we pick any string in the first stage, then there are five choices for its mate. Four of these choices are favorable choices for forming a ring. Thus, the probability of forming a favorable first tie is $\frac{4}{5}$. Figure 8-16(b) shows a favorable tie at the first stage.

For any one of the remaining four strings, there are three choices for its mate. Two of these choices are favorable ones. Thus, the probability of forming a favorable second tie is $\frac{2}{3}$. Figure 8-16(c) shows a favorable tie at the second stage.

FIGURE 8-16

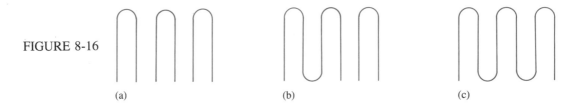

(a)   (b)   (c)

Now two ends remain. Since nothing can go wrong at the third stage, the probability of making a favorable tie is 1. If we use the probabilities completed at each stage and a single branch of a tree diagram, we can calculate the probability for performing three successful ties in a row and hence the probability of forming one closed ring.

Carrying Out the Plan

If we let S represent a successful tie at each stage, then the branch of the tree with which we are concerned is shown in Figure 8-17.

FIGURE 8-17

Thus, the probability of forming one ring is

$$P(\text{ring}) = \frac{4}{5} \cdot \frac{2}{3} \cdot \frac{1}{1} = \frac{8}{15} = 0.5\overline{3}$$

Looking Back

The probability of a woman obtaining a marriage permit in any given year is $\frac{8}{15}$. The fact that this result is larger than $\frac{1}{2}$ is surprising to most people. A class might simulate this problem with strings to see how the experimental probability compares with the theoretical probability of $\frac{8}{15}$.

Related problems that could be attempted are the following:

1. If a woman fails to get a ring 10 years in a row, she must remain single. What is the probability of such a streak of bad (good) luck?
2. If the number of strings were reduced to three and the rule was that an upper end must be tied to a lower end, what is the probability of a single ring?
3. If the number of strings were three, but an upper end could be tied to either an upper or lower end, what is the probability of a single ring?
4. What is the probability of forming three rings in the original problem?
5. What is the probability of forming two rings in the original problem?

Scientists, business consultants, engineers, and biologists use what is called the *Monte Carlo method* for many probability problems. It is a method for simulating problems through the use of coin tossing, rolling dice, drawing cards, or using tables of random digits. The sample student page (page 315) from *Scott, Foresman Mathematics*, 1980, Grade 8, shows the use of a table of random digits.

COMPUTER CORNER

An event such as tossing a fair coin can be simulated on a computer by means of the random digit function **RND**. (This function is explored in a Laboratory Activity in Chapter 13.) Run the following BASIC program to simulate tossing a coin 100 times.

```
10   PRINT "THIS PROGRAM SIMULATES TOSSING A FAIR COIN."
20   PRINT "A RECORD OF THE NUMBER OF HEADS AND TAILS IS"
25   PRINT "RECORDED."
30   FOR C = 1 TO 100
40   LET N = INT(10*RND(X))
50   IF N / 2 = INT(N/ 2) THEN 90
60   LET T = T + 1
70   NEXT C
80   GOTO 110
90   LET H = H + 1
100  GOTO 70
110  PRINT "THE NUMBER OF HEADS IS "; H
120  PRINT "THE NUMBER OF TAILS IS "; T
130  END
```

Career

Simulation Consultant

You know there are ten digits:
0, 1, 2, 3, 4, 5, 6, 7, 8, and 9.
Suppose ten cards are placed in a hat with a different digit written on each card. If you were to draw a card, record its digit, replace it, scramble the cards, draw again, and so on, you would get a **table of random digits.** Here is such a table.

```
1 9 1 0 3 8 8 3 4 4 3 7 2 1 3 9 0 2 3 5 5 3 2 2
7 9 5 1 6 7 8 8 3 5 3 1 4 3 6 5 0 2 6 1 7 1 3 3
5 2 8 4 3 3 7 3 1 0 5 2 6 9 2 0 1 0 5 4 7 0 7 1
3 1 2 3 9 1 6 3 5 8 1 6 8 3 5 5 3 4 7 9 5 5 2 8
2 0 0 4 6 3 9 0 2 2 4 4 0 7 6 1 3 5 8 2 3 8 8 4
4 3 0 0 1 9 9 0 7 4 3 7 1 8 0 1 9 5 7 0 2 3 0 0
2 2 7 6 3 9 6 8 5 3 6 4 2 2 2 5 6 2 9 8 8 6 3 5
9 5 6 6 7 5 0 6 4 8 8 6 7 5 4 2 0 7 0 8 3 5 2 8
4 1 2 0 2 4 5 9 1 1 0 1 1 1 3 6 6 8 6 5 8 9 9 8
7 5 4 7 5 6 8 8 7 9 6 5 5 9 6 3 9 2 6 8 8 2 6 3
1 0 1 4 5 7 0 0 8 6 9 1 2 8 2 9 8 3 3 0 2 3 6 5
3 9 2 3 3 5 8 1 9 0 9 9 5 0 5 0 7 3 5 0 3 7 7 5
3 1 5 9 5 7 6 5 8 3 3 3 7 4 1 8 8 5 2 7 1 5 4 2
6 4 7 0 4 8 7 9 9 5 6 9 7 9 3 9 7 9 5 6 8 5 1 2
9 2 3 4 7 9 7 6 9 9 0 5 3 1 1 6 5 8 2 8 4 8 0 5
```

Nick Caruso uses tables of random digits in his job as a simulation consultant. Simulate means imitate.

A baseball coach asks Mr. Caruso how likely it is for a player who hits 0.400, or 40%, to get a hit three or more times in a row.

Since there are ten digits, Mr. Caruso picks the first four digits (0, 1, 2, and 3) to represent "hits." This mimics the 0.400, or 40%. Then he circles the "hits" in the table.

For the first 120 digits, the following hits are circled.

```
①9①0③8 8③4 4③7②①③9①②③5 5③②②
7 9 5①6 7 8 8③5③①4③6 5①②6①7①③③
5②8 4③③7③①①5②6 9②①①①5 4 7①7①
③①②③9①6③5 8①6 8③5 5③4 7 9 5 5②8
②①①4 6③9①②②4 4①7 6①③5 8②③8 8 4
```

This simulation of 120 times at bat shows that the coach can expect the player to get three or more hits in sequence about 10 times. A better estimate would use more numbers from the table.

1. What is the longest string of hits that seems likely in 120 times at bat?

2. Did the "player" ever go four times to bat without a hit?

3. Use the entire table of random digits. Now what is the longest string of hits that seems likely?

4. Use the columns of the entire table instead of the rows. What is the longest string of hits that seems likely?

5. For a player who hits 0.250, or 25%, Mr. Caruso ignores the digits 0 and 1 so that he can work with eight digits. He calls 2 and 3 "hits" to simulate 25%. Refer to all the rows of the table of random digits and use simulation. What is the longest string of hits that seems likely?

PROBLEM SET 8-2

1. A box contains six letters shown below. What is the probability of the outcome DAN if three letters are drawn one by one (a) with replacement and (b) without replacement?

RANDOM

2. Three boxes with letters are shown below.

MATH	AND	HISTORY
1	2	3

Answer each of the following questions about the boxes.

(a) From box 1, three letters are drawn one by one without replacement and recorded in order. What is the probability that the outcome is HAT?

(b) From box 1, three letters are drawn one by one with replacement and recorded in order. What is the probability the outcome is HAT?

(c) One letter is drawn at random from each box and the results are recorded in order. What is the probability that the outcome is HAT?

(d) If a box is chosen at random and then a letter is drawn at random from the box, what is the probability the outcome is A?

3. An executive committee consisted of ten members—four women and six men. Three members were selected at random to be sent to a meeting in Hawaii. A blindfolded woman drew three of the ten names from a hat. All three names drawn were women. If the woman who drew the names was honest, what was the probability of such luck?

4. Two boxes with letters follow. Choose a box and draw three letters at random, one by one, without replacement. If the outcome is SOS, you win a prize.

(a) Which box should you choose?

(b) Which box would you choose if the letters are drawn with replacement?

SOS	SOSSOS
1	2

5. Three boxes containing balls are shown below. Draw a ball from box 1 and place it in box 2. Then draw a ball from box 2 and put it in box 3. Finally, draw a ball from box 3.

(a) What is the probability that the last ball, drawn from box 3, is white?

(b) What is the probability that the last ball drawn is black?

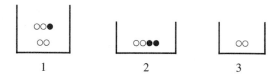

1	2	3

6. Carolyn will win a large prize if she wins two tennis games in a row out of three games. She is to play alternately against Billie and Bobby. She may choose to play Billie-Bobby-Billie or Bobby-Billie-Bobby. She wins against Billie 50% of the time and against Bobby 80% of the time. Which alternative should she choose and why?

7. Two boxes with black and white balls are shown below. A ball is drawn at random from box 1, and then a ball is drawn at random from box 2 and the colors recorded in order.

1	2

Find each of the following.

(a) The probability of two white balls

(b) The probability of at least one black ball

(c) The probability of at most one black ball

(d) The probability of ●○ or ○●

8. A penny, nickel, dime, and quarter are tossed. What is the probability of at least three heads?

9. Assume the probability that a child born is a boy is $\frac{1}{2}$. What is the probability that if a family is going to have four children that they will have all boys?

10. The number of symbols on each of the three dials of a standard slot machine is shown in the table.

Symbol	Dial 1	Dial 2	Dial 3
Bar	1	3	1
Bell	1	3	3
Plum	5	1	5
Orange	3	6	7
Cherry	7	7	0
Lemon	3	0	4
Total	20	20	20

Find the probability for each of the following.

(a) Three plums   (b) Three oranges

(c) Three lemons   (d) No plums

11. If a person takes a five-question true-or-false test, what is the probability that the score is 100% if the person guesses on every question?

12. In a drawer there are 10 blue socks and 12 black socks. Suppose it is dark and you choose 3 socks. What is the probability that you will choose a matching pair?

13. Consider the events A, drawing an ace from an ordinary bridge deck, and C, drawing a club from an ordinary bridge deck.

(a) Show that $P(A \cap C) = P(A) \cdot P(C)$.

(b) Show that we could find the probability of drawing an ace or a club with the following formula.

$$P(A \cup C) = P(A) + P(C) - P(A \cap C).$$

14. Rattlesnake and Paxson Elementary Schools play four games against each other in a chess tournament. Rob Fisher, the chess whiz from Paxson, withdrew from the tournament, so the probabilities of Rattlesnake and Paxson winning each game are $\frac{2}{3}$ and $\frac{1}{3}$, respectively. What are the following probabilities?

(a) Paxson loses all four games.

(b) The match is a draw with each school winning two games.

15. The combinations on the lockers at Russell High School consist of three numbers each ranging from 0 to 39. If a combination is chosen at random, what is the probability that the first two numbers are multiples of nine and the third number is a multiple of four?

16. Use the table of random digits from the sample student page of this section to simulate tossing a coin 100 times. Let an odd number represent heads and an even number represent tails.

(a) What is the probability of obtaining heads in the 100-toss simulation if you start in the upper left-hand corner and use rows of the random digits?

(b) Answer the question in (a) starting in the upper left-hand corner but using columns of the random digits to simulate the coin toss.

17. A box contains the 11 letters shown. The letters are drawn one by one without replacement and the results recorded in order. Find the probability of the outcome MISSISSIPPI.

MIIIIPPSSSS

* * * * * * * REVIEW PROBLEMS * * * * * * * *

18. Match the phrase to the probability that describes it.

(a) A certain event

(b) An impossible event

(c) A very likely event

(d) An unlikely event

(e) A 50% chance

(i) $\dfrac{1}{1000}$

(ii) $\dfrac{999}{1000}$

(iii) 0

(iv) $\dfrac{1}{2}$

(v) 1

19. A date in the month of April is chosen at random. Find the probabilities of the date being each of the following.

(a) April 7

(b) April 31

(c) Before April 20

BRAIN TEASER

Suppose *n* people are in a room. Two people bet that at least two of the people in the room have a birthday on the same date during the year (for example, October 14). Assume that a person is as likely to be born on one day as another and ignore leap years. How many people must be in the room before the bet is even? (If *n* = 366, it is a sure bet.) Poll your class to see if two people have the same birthday. Use this information to find an experimental answer. Then find a theoretical solution. A calculator is very helpful for the computations.

Laboratory Activity

Reese's Peanut Butter Pieces became very popular after release of the movie *E.T.* Suppose we are making brownies and have enough dough to make exactly 100 brownies with exactly 100 Reese's Pieces mixed into the brownies. What is the probability that a brownie chosen at random contains exactly 1 Reese's Piece? A Monte Carlo method can be used to simulate this cookie experiment and to estimate this probability.

1. Construct a 10 × 10 grid and label it with coordinates as shown in Figure 8-18 to represent the brownies.

FIGURE 8-18

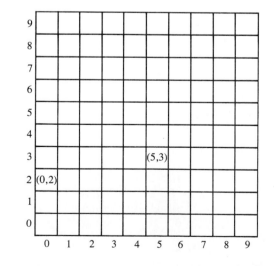

2. Associate each small square with an ordered pair, where the first component is for the horizontal scale and the second component is for the vertical scale. For example, (0, 2) and (5, 3) are pictured in Figure 8-18.

3. Using the table of random digits on page 315, close your eyes, take a pencil, and point to one number to start. Look at that number and the number after it. Consider these two numbers as an ordered pair. Group the next two numbers as an ordered pair. Continue this process until 100 pairs are obtained. Use each pair of numbers as the coordinates for a square and place a tally mark on your grid to represent each Reese's Piece.

4. Estimate the probability that a brownie chosen at random has exactly one Reese's Piece in it by counting the number of squares with exactly one tally mark and dividing by 100.

* 8-3 ODDS AND MATHEMATICAL EXPECTATION

odds

People often speak about the *odds in favor of* or the *odds against* a particular team in an athletic contest. For example, when we say that the **odds** in favor of the Falcons' winning a particular football game are 4 to 1, we are speaking of how likely the Falcons are to win relative to how likely they are to lose. In other words, in this example the probability of their winning is four times the probability of their losing. Thus, if W represents the event Falcons win and L represents the event Falcons lose, then $P(W) = 4P(L)$; as a proportion, we have

$$\frac{P(W)}{P(L)} = \frac{4}{1}$$

Furthermore, because W and L are complements of each other, we have

$$\frac{P(W)}{P(\overline{W})} = \frac{P(W)}{1 - P(W)} = \frac{4}{1}$$

Formally, odds are defined as follows.

DEFINITION

> The **odds in favor** of an event A, where $P(A)$ is the probability that A occurs and $P(\overline{A})$ is the probability that A does not occur, are given by the following.
>
> $$\frac{P(A)}{P(\overline{A})} \quad \text{or} \quad \frac{P(A)}{1 - P(A)}$$
>
> The **odds against** an event A are given by the following.
>
> $$\frac{P(\overline{A})}{P(A)} \quad \text{or} \quad \frac{1 - P(A)}{P(A)}$$

Thus, the odds against tossing a 4 on one throw of a die are $(\frac{5}{6})/(\frac{1}{6}) = \frac{5}{1}$, or 5 to 1.

Notice that in calculating odds, the denominators of the probabilities divide out. Thus, alternate definitions for odds in case of equally likely outcomes are as follows.

$$\text{Odds in favor} = \frac{\text{number of favorable outcomes}}{\text{number of unfavorable outcomes}}$$

$$\text{Odds against} = \frac{\text{number of unfavorable outcomes}}{\text{number of favorable outcomes}}$$

When rolling a die, the number of favorable ways of rolling a four in one throw of a die is 1, and the number of unfavorable ways is 5. Thus, the odds in favor of rolling a four are 1 to 5.

Example 8-7

For each of the following, find the odds in favor of the event occurring.

(a) Rolling a number less than 5 on a die.
(b) Tossing a head on a fair coin.
(c) Drawing an ace from an ordinary 52-card deck.
(d) Drawing a heart from an ordinary 52-card deck.

Solution

(a) Because the probability of rolling a number less than 5 is $\frac{4}{6}$ and the probability of rolling a number not less than 5 is $\frac{2}{6}$, the odds in favor of rolling a number less than 5 are $(\frac{4}{6}) \div (\frac{2}{6})$, or 4 to 2.
(b) Because $P(\text{H}) = \frac{1}{2}$ and $P(\overline{\text{H}}) = \frac{1}{2}$, the odds in favor of getting a head are $(\frac{1}{2}) \div (\frac{1}{2})$, or 1 to 1.
(c) Because the probability of drawing an ace is $\frac{4}{52}$ and the probability of not drawing an ace is $\frac{48}{52}$, the odds in favor of drawing an ace are $(\frac{4}{52}) \div (\frac{48}{52})$, or 4 to 48. The odds 4 to 48 are the same as the odds 1 to 12.
(d) Because the probability of drawing a heart is $\frac{13}{52}$, or $\frac{1}{4}$, and the probability of not drawing a heart is $\frac{39}{52}$, or $\frac{3}{4}$, the odds in favor of drawing a heart are $(\frac{13}{52}) \div (\frac{39}{52}) = \frac{13}{39}$, or 13 to 39. This can be expressed as 1 to 3.

Given the probability of an event, it is possible to find the odds in favor of (or against) the event. Conversely, given the odds in favor of (or against) an event, it is possible to find the probability of the event. For example, if the odds in favor of an event A are 5 to 1, then the following proportion holds.

$$\frac{P(A)}{1 - P(A)} = \frac{5}{1}$$

$$P(A) = 5(1 - P(A))$$

$$6P(A) = 5$$

$$P(A) = \frac{5}{6}$$

Remark

Note that the probability $\frac{5}{6}$ is a ratio. The exact number of favorable outcomes and the exact total of all outcomes is not necessarily known.

Example 8-8 | In the cartoon, Snoopy is told that the odds are 1000 to 1 that he will end up with a broken arm if he touches Linus' blanket. What is the probability of this event E?

© 1974 United Feature Syndicate, Inc.

Solution | $\dfrac{P(E)}{1 - P(E)} = \dfrac{1000}{1}$, which implies $P(E) = \dfrac{1000}{1001}$

An important concept related to probability is *mathematical expectation*. Suppose Jane has won an $800 oven on a television game show. She has a choice of keeping the oven or trading it for a prize behind one of three doors. Behind one of the doors is a $2400 vacation prize, behind another is a $1200 living room set, and behind the third is $90 worth of peanuts. Should she trade her $800 for what is behind one of the doors? If each door has a probability of $\frac{1}{3}$ of being chosen, then to determine how much Jane could expect to win if the experiment were repeated a large number of times, we multiply the probability of choosing a door by the payoff behind the door, as shown in Table 8-5.

TABLE 8-5

Probability	Payoff	Product
$\frac{1}{3}$	$2400	$ 800
$\frac{1}{3}$	$1200	$ 400
$\frac{1}{3}$	$ 90	$ 30
		$1230

mathematical expectation, expected value

The total value of the products, $1230, is called the **mathematical expectation, or expected value**, of the experiment. The expected value is a kind of average of winnings for the long run. If Jane were allowed to repeat the game a large number of times, she could expect to win an average of $1230 per game. Because $1230 is greater than $800, the value of the oven, Jane should probably try her luck with the doors. Of course, Jane has only one try, so she may lose. Mathematical expectation can be used to predict the average result of an experiment when it is repeated many times, but expectation cannot be used to determine the outcome of any single experiment.

DEFINITION

If, in an experiment, the possible outcomes are numbers $a_1, a_2, \ldots, a_n$, occurring with probabilities $p_1, p_2, \ldots, p_n$, respectively, then the **mathematical expectation** (expected value), E, is given by the equation

$$E = a_1 \cdot p_1 + a_2 \cdot p_2 + a_3 \cdot p_3 + \cdots + a_n \cdot p_n$$

Suppose Mega-Mouth Toothpaste Company is giving away $20,000 in a contest. To win the contest, a person must send in a postcard with his or her name on it (no purchase of toothpaste is necessary). Suppose the company expects to receive 1 million postcards. Is it worth the time and expense of a postcard and postage to enter the contest? The expected value is one-millionth of $20,000, that is, $E = (\frac{1}{1,000,000}) \cdot (\frac{20,000}{1}) = \frac{2}{100} = 0.02$. The game is worthwhile if the expected value equals the cost of playing the game. Because the cost of the postcard and postage exceeds $0.02, the contest is not worthwhile.

Example 8-9

Consider the spinner in Figure 8-19 with the payoff for each region written on the spinner. Should the owner of this spinner expect to make money over an extended period of time if the charge is $2.00 per spin?

Solution

If the spinner is fair, then the following probabilities can be assigned to each region.

$$P(\$1.00) = \frac{1}{2} \qquad P(\$2.00) = \frac{1}{4} \qquad P(\$3.00) = \frac{1}{8} \qquad P(\$4.00) = \frac{1}{8}$$

The expected value is given by $E = (\frac{1}{2})1 + (\frac{1}{4})2 + (\frac{1}{8})3 + (\frac{1}{8})4 = 1.875$ or about 1.88. The owner can expect to pay out about $1.88 per spin, and $1.88 is less than the $2.00 charge, so the owner should make a profit on the spinner if it is used many times.

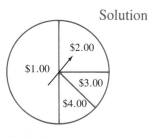

FIGURE 8-19

fair game

The game in Example 8-9 is not a **fair game.** A game is considered fair if the net winnings are $0; that is, the expected value of the game equals the price of playing the game.

Example 8-10

Lori spends $1.00 for one ticket in a raffle with a $100 prize. If 200 tickets are sold, is $1.00 a fair price to pay for the ticket?

Solution

The probability of winning $100 is $\frac{1}{200}$. Thus, $E = (\frac{1}{200})100$, or 0.50. Because $1.00 is greater than $0.50, $1.00 is not a fair price. If the raffle is repeated many times, Lori can expect to lose $0.50 per raffle on the average.

PROBLEM SET 8-3

1. What are the odds in favor of drawing a face card from an ordinary deck of playing cards? What are the odds against drawing a face card?
2. On a single roll of a pair of dice, what are the odds against rolling a sum of 7?
3. Assume the probability of a boy being born is $\frac{1}{2}$. If a family plans to have four children what are the odds against having all boys?
4. Diane tossed a coin nine times and got nine tails. Assume Diane's coin is fair, and answer each of the following questions.
   (a) What is the probability of tossing a tail on the tenth toss?
   (b) What is the probability of tossing ten more tails in a row?
   (c) What are the odds against tossing ten more tails in a row?
5. If the odds against Sam winning his first prize fight are 3 to 5, what is the probability he will win the fight?
6. What are the odds in favor of tossing at least two heads if a fair coin is tossed three times?
7. A game involves tossing two coins. A player wins $1.00 if both tosses result in heads. What should you pay to play this game in order to make it a fair game?
8. Suppose a player rolls a fair die and receives the number of dollars equal to the number of spots showing on the die. What is the expected value?

9. A punchout card contains 500 spaces. One particular space pays $1000, five other spaces each pay $100, and the other spaces pay nothing. If a player chooses one space, what is the expected value of the game?
10. The following chart shows the probabilities assigned by Stu to the number of hours spent on homework on a given night.

Hours	Probability
1	0.15
2	0.20
3	0.40
4	0.10
5	0.05
6	0.10

If Stu's friend Stella calls and asks how long his homework will take, what would you expect his answer to be based on this table?
11. Suppose 5 quarters, 5 dimes, 5 nickels, and 10 pennies are in a box. One coin is selected at random. What is the expected value of this experiment?
12. If the odds in favor of Fast Leg winning a horse race are 5 to 2 and the first prize is $14,000, what is the expected value of Fast Leg winning?

8-4 METHODS OF COUNTING

Tree diagrams can be used to list possible outcomes of experiments. For example, the tree diagram in Figure 8-20 lists the different ways three different flavors of ice cream, chocolate (c), vanilla (v), and strawberry (s), can be arranged on a cone.

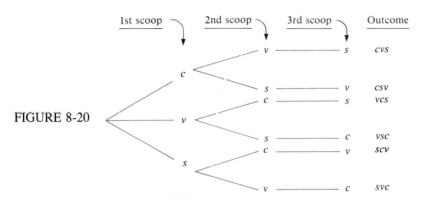

FIGURE 8-20

The tree starts out with three branches in the first stage, representing the three possibilities for the first scoop. For each outcome in the first stage, there are two possibilities at the second stage. Hence, there are $3 \cdot 2$ possibilities at the second stage. Then, for each outcome in the second stage, there is only one possibility at the third stage. Consequently, there are $3 \cdot 2 \cdot 1$ or 6 different arrangements.

Now, consider a double-dip ice cream cone for which there are ten flavors of ice cream and six flavors of sherbet. How many different double-dip cones can be made with ice cream on the bottom and sherbet on the top? Since for each of the ten ice cream flavors there are six flavors of sherbet, the number of all possible double dip cones is

$$\underbrace{6 + 6 + 6 + \cdots + 6}_{10 \text{ terms}} \quad \text{or} \quad 10 \cdot 6 = 60$$

A tree diagram can be used to verify the result. The counting argument used to find the number of possible double-dip cones is an example of the Fundamental Counting Principle.

Property | **Fundamental Counting Principle** If event M can occur in m ways and, after it has occurred, event N can occur in n ways, then event M followed by event N can occur in $m \cdot n$ ways.

Remark | The Fundamental Counting Principle can be extended to any number of events.

Example 8-11 | Solve each of the following.

(a) If a man owns seven shirts and six pairs of pants, how many different shirt-pant combinations are possible?
(b) Sally is taking a five-item true-or-false test. If she guesses at every item, how many different patterns of answers are possible?
(c) Suppose eight horses are entered in a race. In how many different ways can the winning horses finish? Count win, place, and show.

(d) If automobile license plates consist of two letters followed by four digits, what is the total number of different license plates possible if numbers and letters may be repeated?

Solution

(a) Because a shirt can be chosen in seven ways and a pair of pants can be chosen in six ways, there are 7 · 6, or 42, shirt-pant combinations.
(b) Because there are two ways to answer question 1 on the test, two ways to answer question 2, and so on, there are 2 · 2 · 2 · 2 · 2, or 32, different possible patterns of answers.
(c) There are eight possible winners, leaving seven possible places, and six possible shows. Thus, there are 8 · 7 · 6, or 336, ways in which the win, place, and show horses can finish the race.
(d) There are 26 · 26 · 10 · 10 · 10 · 10, or 6,760,000, different license plates possible.

Now consider how many ways the owner of an ice cream parlor can display ten ice cream flavors in a row along the front of the display case. The first position can be filled in ten ways, the second position in nine ways, the third position in eight ways and so on. Thus, by the Fundamental Counting Principle there are $10 \cdot 9 \cdot 8 \cdot 7 \cdot 6 \cdot 5 \cdot 4 \cdot 3 \cdot 2 \cdot 1$ or 3,628,800 ways to display the flavors. If there were 16 flavors, there would be $16 \cdot 15 \cdot 14 \cdot 13 \cdot \ldots \cdot 3 \cdot 2 \cdot 1$ ways to arrange them. In general, *if there are n containers with n positions, then the number of ways to arrange the containers in a row is the product of all the natural numbers less than or equal to n.* This expression is called **n factorial** and is denoted by **n!**, as shown below.

n factorial

$$n! = n \cdot (n - 1) \cdot (n - 2) \cdot \ldots \cdot 3 \cdot 2 \cdot 1$$

Using factorial notation is helpful in counting and probability problems. A calculator is also very useful for finding the products in such problems. Practice problems with factorials are included in Problem Set 8-4.

The ice cream cone arrangements discussed previously were in a definite order. A scoop of chocolate ice cream on top of a scoop of vanilla is a different arrangement than a scoop of vanilla on top of chocolate. An arrangement of things in a definite order is called a **permutation.**

permutation

Consider the set of people in a small club, {Al, Betty, Carl, Dan}. In how many ways can they elect a president and a secretary? Order is important for counting the possibilities. Thus, this is a permutation problem. Since there are four ways of choosing a president and then three ways of choosing a secretary, by the Fundamental Counting Principle, there are 4 · 3 or 12 ways of choosing a president and secretary. Note that an Al-Betty choice is different from a Betty-Al choice. Choosing two officers from a club of four is a permutation of four people chosen two at a time. The number of possible permutations of four objects taken two at a time is denoted by $_4P_2$. Hence, $_4P_2 = 4 \cdot 3$, or 12. In general, if n objects are chosen r at a time, then the number of possible permutations is denoted by $_nP_r$. Because there are n choices for the first object, $n - 1$ choices for the second object, $n - 2$ choices for the third object, and so on, then by the Fundamental Counting Principle, we have

$$_nP_r = n \cdot (n - 1) \cdot (n - 2) \cdot \ldots \cdot [n - (r - 1)]$$

or

$$_nP_r = n \cdot (n - 1) \cdot (n - 2) \cdot \ldots \cdot (n - r + 1)$$

This formula can also be written in terms of factorials. Because

$$n! = n \cdot (n - 1) \cdot (n - 2) \cdot \ldots \cdot (n - r + 1) \cdot (n - r) \cdot (n - r - 1) \cdot \ldots \cdot 3 \cdot 2 \cdot 1$$

we can write $_nP_r$ as

$$_nP_r = n \cdot (n - 1) \cdot (n - 2) \cdot \ldots \cdot (n - r + 1)$$

$$= \frac{n \cdot (n - 1) \cdot (n - 2) \cdot \ldots \cdot (n - r + 1) \cdot [(n - r) \cdot (n - r - 1) \cdot \ldots \cdot 3 \cdot 2 \cdot 1]}{[(n - r) \cdot (n - r - 1) \cdot \ldots \cdot 3 \cdot 2 \cdot 1]}$$

$$= \frac{n!}{(n - r)!}$$

Hence

$$_nP_r = \frac{n!}{(n - r)!}$$

Example 8-12

(a) A baseball team has nine players. Find the number of ways a baseball coach can arrange the batting order.

(b) Find the number of ways of choosing three initials from the alphabet if none of the letters can be repeated.

Solution

(a) Here order is important, and this is a permutation problem. Because there are nine ways to choose the first batter, eight ways to choose the second batter, and so on, there are $9 \cdot 8 \cdot 7 \cdot \ldots \cdot 2 \cdot 1 = 9!$, or 362,880, ways of arranging the batting order. Hence, $_9P_9 = 9! = 362,880$.

(b) Because order is important, this is a permutation problem. There are 26 ways of choosing the first letter, 25 ways of choosing the second letter, and 24 ways of choosing the third letter; hence, there are $26 \cdot 25 \cdot 24$, or 15,600, ways of choosing the three letters. Hence, $_{26}P_3 = 26 \cdot 25 \cdot 24 = 15,600$.

combination

Reconsider the club, {Al, Betty, Carl, Dan}. Suppose a two-person committee is selected with no chair. In this case, order is not important. In other words, an Al-Betty choice is the same as a Betty-Al choice. An arrangement of things in which the order does not make any difference is called a **combination.** A comparison of the results of electing a president and secretary for the club and the results of simply selecting a two-person committee are shown in Figure 8-21. From Figure 8-21, the number of permutations divided by 2 is the number of combinations, $\frac{(4 \cdot 3)}{2}$, or 6.

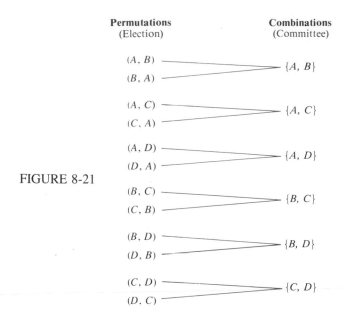

FIGURE 8-21

In how many ways can a committee of three people be selected from the club {Al, Betty, Carl, Dan}? To solve this problem, first we solve the simpler problem of finding the number of three-person committees assuming that a president, vice president and secretary are chosen. A partial list of possibilities for both problems is shown in Figure 8-22.

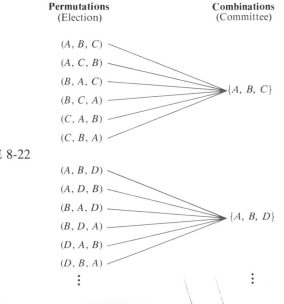

FIGURE 8-22

There are 3!, or 6, times as many permutations as there are combinations. By the Fundamental Counting Principle, the number of permutations is $4 \cdot 3 \cdot 2$, or 24. The number of combinations is

$$\frac{(4 \cdot 3 \cdot 2)}{3!} = 4$$

The number of permutations is divided by 3! since each committee choice can be arranged 3! ways. In general, use the following rule to count combinations: *To find the number of combinations possible in a counting problem, first use the Fundamental Counting Principle to find the number of permutations and then divide by the number of ways in which each choice can be arranged.*

Symbolically, the number of combinations of n objects taken r at a time is denoted by $_nC_r$. Based upon the above rule, the following formula can be developed.

$$_nC_r = \frac{_nP_r}{_rP_r} = \frac{\dfrac{n!}{(n-r)!}}{r!} = \frac{n!}{r!(n-r)!}$$

Example 8-13

A book-of-the-month club offers 3 free books from a list of 42 books. How many combinations are possible?

Solution

By the Fundamental Counting Principle, there are $42 \cdot 41 \cdot 40$ ways to choose the three free books in order. The number of ways the three choices of books can be arranged is 3!, or 6. Therefore, the number of combinations possible for three books is

$$\frac{42 \cdot 41 \cdot 40}{3!} = 11{,}480$$

Example 8-14

At the beginning of the second quarter of a mathematics class for elementary teachers, each of the 25 students shook hands with each of the other students exactly once. How many handshakes took place?

Solution

Since the handshake between persons A and B is the same as between persons B and A, order is not important in this problem. This is a problem of choosing combinations of 25 people two at a time. Thus, there are

$$\frac{25 \cdot 24}{2!} = 300$$

different handshakes.

PROBLEM 3

In the cartoon, Peppermint Patty took a ten-question, true-false test. If she answered each question true or false at random, what is the probability that she answered 50% of the questions correctly?

Understanding the Problem

A score of 50% indicates that Peppermint Patty got $\frac{1}{2}$ of the ten questions, or five questions, correct. Also, if she answered questions true or false at random, then this means that the probability she answers a given question correctly is $\frac{1}{2}$. We are asked to determine the probability that Patty answered exactly five of the questions correctly.

Devising a Plan

We do not know which five questions Patty missed. She could have missed any five questions out of ten on the test. Suppose she answered Questions 2, 4, 5, 6, and 8 incorrectly. In this case, she would have answered Questions 1, 3, 7, 9, and 10 correctly. We can compute the probability of this set of answers by using Figure 8-23, where C represents a correct answer and I represents an incorrect answer.

FIGURE 8-23

Questions: 1   2   3   4   5   6   7   8   9   10
$\xrightarrow{\frac{1}{2}} C \xrightarrow{\frac{1}{2}} I \xrightarrow{\frac{1}{2}} C \xrightarrow{\frac{1}{2}} I \xrightarrow{\frac{1}{2}} I \xrightarrow{\frac{1}{2}} I \xrightarrow{\frac{1}{2}} C \xrightarrow{\frac{1}{2}} I \xrightarrow{\frac{1}{2}} C \xrightarrow{\frac{1}{2}} C$

To find the probability for the set of answers in Figure 8-23, we multiply the probabilities along the branches. Hence, $(\frac{1}{2})^{10}$ is the probability of answering Questions 1–10 in the following way: C I C I I I C I C C. However, there are other ways to answer exactly five questions correctly: for example, C C C C C I I I I I. The probability of answering Questions 1–10 in this way is also $(\frac{1}{2})^{10}$. How many such ways are possible to answer the questions? The number of such ways is simply the number of ways of arranging five C's and 5 I's in a row, which is also the number of ways of choosing five correct questions out of ten, that is, $_{10}C_5$. Because all these arrangements give Patty a score of 50%, then the desired probability is the sum of the probabilities for each arrangement.

Carrying Out the Plan

There are $_{10}C_5$, or 252, ways that the C's and I's can be arranged. Hence, there are 252 sets of answers similar to the one in Figure 8-23 with five correct and five incorrect answers. The product of the probabilities for each of these sets of answers is $(\frac{1}{2})^{10}$, so the sum of the probabilities for all 252 sets is $252 \cdot (\frac{1}{2})^{10}$, or approximately 0.246. Thus, Peppermint Patty has a probability of 0.246 of obtaining a score of 50% on the test.

Looking Back

It seems paradoxical to learn that the probability of obtaining a score of 50% on a ten-question, true-false test is not close to 1. As an extension of the problem, suppose that passing is a score of 70%. Now what is the probability that Peppermint Patty will pass?

PROBLEM SET 8-4

1. The eighth-grade class at a grade school has 16 girls and 14 boys. How many different possible boy-girl dates can be arranged?
2. How many different three-digit numbers can be formed from the digits 1, 2, 3, 4, 5, 6, 7? Each digit can be used only once.
3. If a coin is tossed five times, in how many different ways can the sequence of heads and tails appear?
4. The telephone prefix for a university is 243. The prefix is followed by four digits. How many telephones are possible before a new prefix is needed?
5. Radio stations in the United States have call letters that begin with either K or W. Some have a total of three letters, while others have four letters. How many sets of three-letter call letters are possible? How many sets of four-letter call letters are possible?
6. Carlin's Pizza House offers 3 kinds of salads, 15 kinds of pizza, and 4 kinds of desserts. How many different three-course meals can be ordered?
7. Decide whether each of the following is true or false.
   (a) $6! = 6 \cdot 5!$ (b) $3! + 3! = 6!$
   (c) $\dfrac{6!}{3!} = 2!$ (d) $\dfrac{6!}{3} = 2!$
   (e) $\dfrac{6!}{5!} = 6$ (f) $\dfrac{6!}{4!2!} = 15$
   (g) $n!(n + 1) = (n + 1)!$
8. How many ways can the letters in the word SCRAMBLE be rearranged?
9. How many two-person committees can be formed from a group of six people?
10. Explain the difference between a permutation and a combination.
11. Assume a class has 30 members.
    (a) In how many ways can a president, vice president, and secretary be selected?
    (b) How many committees of three persons can be chosen?
12. A basketball coach was criticized in the newspaper for not trying out every combination of players. If the team roster has twelve players, how many five-player combinations are possible?
13. Solve the problem posed by the following cartoon. (AAUGHH! is not an acceptable answer.)

© 1979 United Feature Syndicate, Inc.

14. A five-volume numbered set of books is placed randomly on a shelf. What is the probability that the books will be numbered in the correct order from left to right?

15. Take ten points in a plane, no three on a line. How many straight lines can be drawn if each line is drawn through a pair of points?

16. A committee of three people is selected at random from a set consisting of seven Americans, five French people, and three English people.
    (a) What is the probability that the committee consists of all Americans?
    (b) What is the probability that the committee has no Americans?

17. The triangular array of numbers pictured is called **Pascal's triangle.** Notice that the first and last number in each row is 1. Every other number is the sum of the two numbers immediately above it. The rows are counted starting at 0.

								Row
			1					(0)
		1		1				(1)
		1	2	1				(2)
	1	3		3	1			(3)
1		4	6	4		1		(4)
1	5	10	10	5	1			(5)
1	6	15	20	15	6	1		(6)

It can be shown that the entries in Pascal's triangle are the numbers of combinations of n objects taken r at a time where n is the number of the row and r is the number of the item in the row. (Note that r could be 0.) For example, the number of combinations of six objects taken three at a time is 20, the fourth number in the sixth row. Use the triangle to determine the following.
    (a) $_5C_3$ (b) $_5C_5$ (c) $_6C_0$ (d) $_3C_2$

18. The probability of a basketball player making a free throw at any time in a game is $\frac{2}{3}$. If the player attempts ten free throws in a game, what is the probability that exactly six free throws are made?

★ 19. In a word such as LOOP, the O's are indistinguishable. To determine how many ways the letters of the word LOOP can be arranged, consider four empty slots. Where can the O's be placed in these four slots? The choice of slots is a combination of four slots taken two at a time. Thus, there are $_4C_2$, or 6, ways the O's can fit in the slots. Once the O's are placed, there are two slots left to place the L and then one slot left for the P. Thus there are $6 \cdot 2 \cdot 1$, or 12, arrangements altogether. Find the number of ways to rearrange the letters in the following words.
    (a) OHIO   (b) ALABAMA
    (c) ILLINOIS   (d) MISSISSIPPI
    (e) TENNESSEE

★ 20. In how many ways can five couples be seated in a row of ten chairs if no couple is separated?

★ 21. From a group of six girls and nine boys, how many five-member committees can be formed involving three boys and two girls?

22. Which is greater, 10! or 2^{10}?

★ 23. Solve the problem for Peppermint Patty.

© 1974 United Feature Syndicate, Inc.

* * * * * * * REVIEW PROBLEMS * * * * * * *

24. A single card is drawn from an ordinary bridge deck. What is the probability of obtaining each of the following?
    (a) A club
    (b) A queen and a spade
    (c) Not a queen
    (d) Not a heart
    (e) A spade or a heart
    (f) The six of diamonds
    (g) A queen or a spade
    (h) Either red or black

25. From a sack containing seven red marbles, eight blue marbles, and four white marbles, marbles are drawn at random for several experiments. What is the probability of each of the following events?
    (a) One marble drawn at random is either red or blue.
    (b) The first draw is red and the second is blue if one marble is drawn at random, the color recorded, the marble is replaced, and another marble drawn.
    (c) The event in (b) if the first marble is not replaced.

BRAIN TEASER

Jane has two tennis serves, a hard serve and a soft serve. Her hard serve has a 50% chance of being good. If her hard serve is good, then she has an 80% chance of winning the point. Her soft serve has a 90% chance of being good. If her soft serve is good, she has a 50% chance of winning the point.

(a) What is the probability that Jane wins the point if she serves hard and then, if necessary, soft?
(b) What is the probability that Jane wins the point if she serves her first serve hard and then, if necessary, her second serve hard?

8-5 STATISTICAL GRAPHS

For a long time the word *statistics* referred to numerical information about state or political territories. The word itself comes from the Latin *statisticus* meaning "of the state." Statistics as we know it today took several centuries and many great minds to develop. John Graunt (1620–1674) was one of the first people to record his work in the area of statistics. He studied birth and death records in various cities and discovered that more boys were born than girls. He also found that since men were more subject to death from occupational accidents, diseases, and war, the number of men and women at the age of marriage was about equal. Graunt's work on the predictability of deaths via mortality tables led to the development of ideas used by life insurance companies today.

descriptive statistics   **Descriptive statistics** is the science of organizing and summarizing numerical data. Newspapers, magazines, radio, and television all use descriptive statistics to inform and persuade us on certain courses of action. Governments and organizations use statistics to make decisions that directly affect our lives. Statistics are both used and abused. Do you know when or how, or are you like Charlie Brown?

Visual illustrations are an important part of statistics. Such illustrations take many forms—histograms, bar graphs, frequency polygons, line graphs, or circle graphs. For example, suppose that Dan offers the following deal. He rolls a die. If any number other than 6 appears, he pays $5. If a 6 appears, you pay him $5. With a fair die, the probability of Dan's winning is $\frac{1}{6}$. Thus, it is not likely that Dan will win unless the die is loaded, or 6 appears more often than normally expected. The following data show the results of 60 rolls with Dan's die.

```
1   6   6   2   6   3   6   6   4   6
6   2   6   6   4   5   6   6   1   6
1   6   6   5   6   6   4   6   5   6
6   5   6   2   4   2   5   6   3   4
3   6   1   6   3   6   6   1   6   6
6   4   6   3   6   3   6   4   6   5
```

raw data

frequency table

These numbers are referred to as **raw data** and are arranged in order of occurrence. The raw data become more meaningful when they are summarized in a **frequency table,** as shown in Table 8-6.

TABLE 8-6

Number	Tally	Frequency
1	⅂⅂⅂⅂⅂	5
2	⅃⅃⅃⅃	4
3	⅂⅂⅂⅂⅂ ⅃	6
4	⅂⅂⅂⅂⅂ ⅃⅃	7
5	⅂⅂⅂⅂⅂ ⅃	6
6	⅂⅂⅂⅂⅂ ⅂⅂⅂⅂⅂ ⅂⅂⅂⅂⅂ ⅂⅂⅂⅂⅂ ⅂⅂⅂⅂⅂ ⅂⅂⅂⅂⅂ ⅃⅃	32
	Total	60

According to the frequency table, 6 appears many more times than could be expected from a fair die. (If the die were fair, the number of 6s should be close to $\frac{1}{6} \cdot 60$, or 10.)

histogram

Figure 8-24 shows a **histogram** which gives a good picture of the results from throwing Dan's die. A histogram is made up of contiguous (touching) rectangles comparing various frequencies. The numbers on the die are shown on the horizontal axis. The numbers along the vertical axis give the scale for the frequency. The frequencies of the numbers on the die are shown by vertical bars. The bars are all the same width. The higher the bar, the greater the frequency.

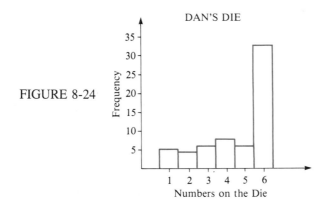

FIGURE 8-24

bar graph

A histogram is a particular kind of **bar graph.** A typical bar graph showing the height in centimeters of five students is given in Figure 8-25. This bar graph is not a histogram because of the spaces between the bars.

The break in the vertical axis, denoted by a squiggle, indicates that part of the scale has been omitted. Therefore, the scale is not accurate from 0 to 130. The height of each bar represents the height in centimeters of each student named on the horizontal axis. Each space between the bars is usually one-half the width of the bars.

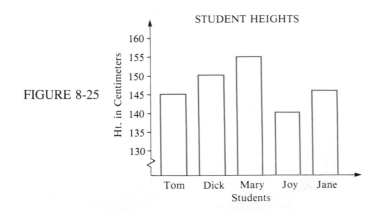

FIGURE 8-25

Another graphic form for presenting the data from a frequency table is a **frequency polygon,** or **line graph.** A frequency polygon can be plotted from a frequency table, or it can be constructed from a histogram by connecting the midpoints of the top of each of the bars with line segments. Figure 8-26(a) shows the frequency polygon (line graph) for the data from Table 8-6. Figure 8-26(b) shows how to obtain the same frequency polygon from the histogram of Figure 8-24.

frequency polygon
line graph

FIGURE 8-26

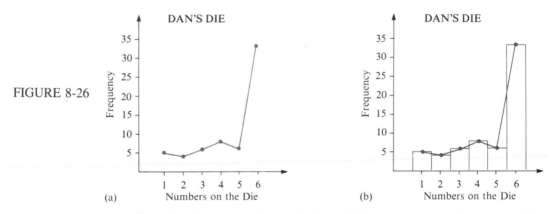

From the frequency polygons in Figure 8-26, it may appear that it is possible to find the frequency of any number between 1 and 6. For example, a frequency corresponding to 2.5 is approximately 6, but 2.5 does not appear on a roll of a die. Thus, for this particular case, a frequency polygon is misleading, and the histogram is a more meaningful graph.

Table 8-7 shows the temperatures recorded during a 9-hour period from 8:00 A.M. to 5:00 P.M. at 1-hour intervals. Figure 8-27 contains a line graph showing the data. All temperature values are meaningful, because there is a temperature at all times. The graph shows that temperatures increased from 8 A.M. to 12 P.M. and decreased from 12 P.M. to 5 P.M. The graph can be used to estimate temperatures at other times. For example, at 11:30 A.M., the temperature might have been 6°C.

TABLE 8-7

Time	Temperature (°C)
8:00 A.M.	0
9:00	2
10:00	4
11:00	5
12:00	8
1:00	7
2:00	6
3:00	6
4:00	5
5:00 P.M.	5

FIGURE 8-27

pictograph

Examples of a bar graph and a type of graph called a **pictograph** are illustrated in a page from *Scott, Foresman Mathematics,* 1980, Grade 4, p. 337.

The greater the amount of data, the more difficult it becomes to construct a frequency table for individual items. In such cases the data may be grouped. For example, consider the following 50 grades.

52	56	25	56	68	73	66	64	56	100
20	39	9	50	98	54	54	40	50	96
36	44	18	97	100	65	21	60	44	54
92	49	37	94	72	88	89	35	59	34
48	32	15	53	84	72	88	16	52	60

classes

grouped frequency table

A frequency table for these data would represent 39 difference scores. A better "quick" picture of the data can be obtained by grouping the data into **classes.** For example, the classes can be arranged in intervals of ten: 1–10, 11–20, 21–30, 31–40, and so on. Each class is assigned two class limits. For the first class, the lower limit is 1 and the upper limit is 10. The **grouped frequency table** for intervals of length ten is given in Table 8-8.

TABLE 8-8

Classes	Tally	Frequency
1–10			1
11–20	||||	4
21–30	||	2
31–40	||| ||	7
41–50	|||		6
51–60	||| ||| ||	12
61–70	||||	4
71–80	|||	3
81–90	||||	4
91–100	||| ||	7

FIGURE 8-28

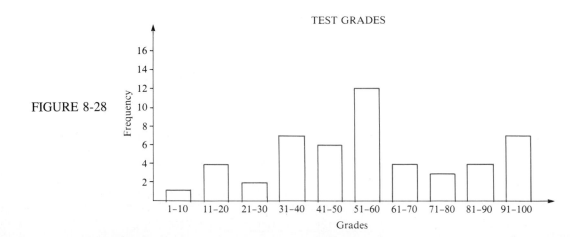

TEST GRADES

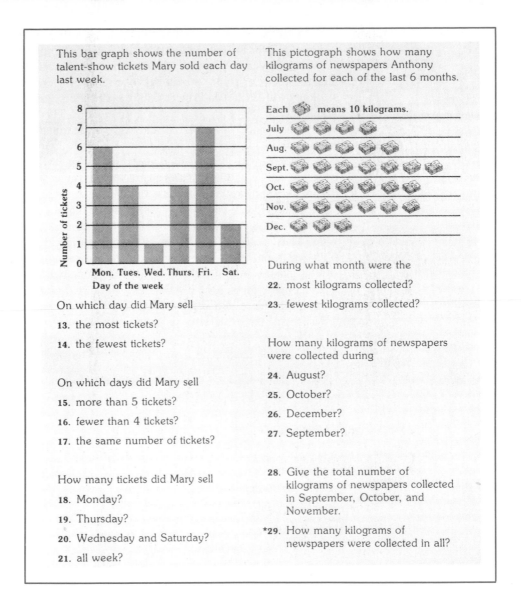

This bar graph shows the number of talent-show tickets Mary sold each day last week.

On which day did Mary sell

13. the most tickets?

14. the fewest tickets?

On which days did Mary sell

15. more than 5 tickets?

16. fewer than 4 tickets?

17. the same number of tickets?

How many tickets did Mary sell

18. Monday?

19. Thursday?

20. Wednesday and Saturday?

21. all week?

This pictograph shows how many kilograms of newspapers Anthony collected for each of the last 6 months.

During what month were the

22. most kilograms collected?

23. fewest kilograms collected?

How many kilograms of newspapers were collected during

24. August?

25. October?

26. December?

27. September?

28. Give the total number of kilograms of newspapers collected in September, October, and November.

*29. How many kilograms of newspapers were collected in all?

The grouped frequency table is concise, but some information is lost by the grouping. For example, although the table shows that 12 scores fall in the interval 51–60, it does not show the particular scores in the interval. The greater the size of the interval, the greater the amount of information lost (possibly beyond the usable point). The choice of the interval size may vary, but as a general rule, the number of intervals should be between 6 and 15. No matter what interval size is used, the same interval size must be used for each class throughout the table. Classes should be chosen to accommodate *all* the data, and each item should fit into only one class; that is, the classes should not overlap.

circle graph
pie chart

A bar graph can be used to display the data from a grouped frequency table. A bar graph for the data in Table 8-8 is shown in Figure 8-28.

Another type of graph used to represent data is the **circle graph,** or **pie chart.** A circle graph consists of a circular region partitioned into disjoint sections, with each section representing a part or percentage of the whole. A circle graph shows how parts are related to the whole. This type of picture usually is used when money is involved and various distributions of dollars are to be displayed.

Suppose two college roommates, Larry and Moe, kept a record of their expenses and at the end of the quarter made Table 8-9 based on their records. Figure 8-29 shows a circle graph with the data. A circle has a total of 360 degrees, written 360°. Thus, 360° represents the total expenses for the month, or 100% of the expenses. Since food is 30% of the total expenses, 30% of 360° is devoted to food. Thus, 0.30(360°), or 108°, is devoted to food expense. In the same way, 0.25(360°), or 90°, is devoted to rent. The remaining sections are computed in a similar manner. A protractor is used to construct circle graphs, and a calculator is useful in determining the percentages. The circle graph is usually marked with section identification and the percent of the circle represented by the section.

TABLE 8-9

Item	Percent of Total
Food	30
Rent	25
Clothing	10
Books	10
Entertainment	15
Other	10

Expenses Last Quarter

FIGURE 8-29

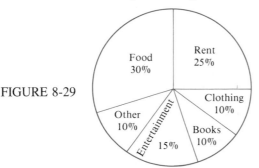

Example 8-15

Construct a circle graph for the following data obtained by tossing Dan's loaded die 60 times.

Number	Frequency
1	5
2	4
3	6
4	7
5	6
6	$\frac{32}{60}$

Solution

There are two computation steps necessary to prepare the data for a circle graph. We need to determine the number of degrees in each section to draw the graph and to determine what percent of the circle is pictured in each section. Table 8-10 shows this information. A circle graph depicting the information is given in Figure 8-30.

TABLE 8-10

Item	Degrees	Percent
1	$\frac{5}{60} \cdot 360°$, or $30°$	$\frac{5}{60} \doteq 8.3\%$
2	$\frac{4}{60} \cdot 360°$, or $24°$	$\frac{4}{60} \doteq 6.7\%$
3	$\frac{6}{60} \cdot 360°$, or $36°$	$\frac{6}{60} \doteq 10\%$
4	$\frac{7}{60} \cdot 360°$, or $42°$	$\frac{7}{60} \doteq 11.7\%$
5	$\frac{6}{60} \cdot 360°$, or $36°$	$\frac{6}{60} = 10\%$
6	$\frac{32}{60} \cdot 360°$, or $192°$	$\frac{32}{60} \doteq 53.3\%$

FIGURE 8-30

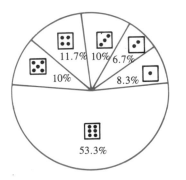

An example of a circle graph from *Houghton-Mifflin Mathematics*, 1981, Grade 7, is given below. Find the angle measures for each percent.

Just as graphs can be used to accurately display data, they can also be used to distort data or exaggerate certain pieces of information. A frequency polygon, histogram, or bar graph can be altered by changing the scale of the graph. For example, consider the data for the number of graduates from a community college for the years 1979 to 1983.

Year	1979	1980	1981	1982	1983
Number of of graduates	140	180	200	210	160

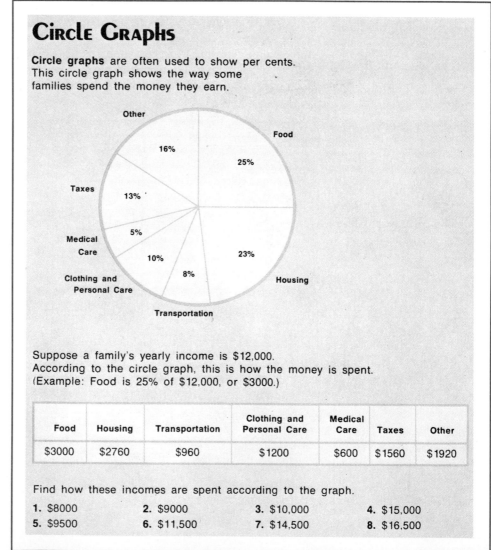

Circle Graphs

Circle graphs are often used to show per cents. This circle graph shows the way some families spend the money they earn.

Suppose a family's yearly income is $12,000.
According to the circle graph, this is how the money is spent.
(Example: Food is 25% of $12,000, or $3000.)

Food	Housing	Transportation	Clothing and Personal Care	Medical Care	Taxes	Other
$3000	$2760	$960	$1200	$600	$1560	$1920

Find how these incomes are spent according to the graph.

1. $8000
2. $9000
3. $10,000
4. $15,000
5. $9500
6. $11,500
7. $14,500
8. $16,500

The two graphs in Figure 8-31 represent the same data, but different scales are used in each. The statistics presented are the same, but these two graphs do not convey the same psychological message. Notice that the years on the horizontal axis of the graph are spread out and the numbers on the vertical axis are condensed. Both of these changes minimize the variability of the data. A college administrator probably would use the graph in (b) to convince people that the college was not in serious enrollment trouble.

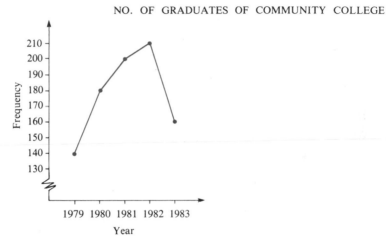

FIGURE 8-31   (a)

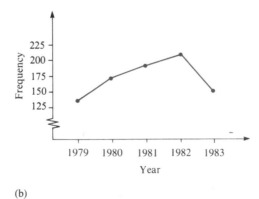

(b)

Bar graphs can also be misleading. Suppose, for example, the number of boxes of cereal sold by Sugar Plops last year was 2 million and the number of boxes of cereal sold by Korn Krisp was 8 million. The Korn Krisp executives prepared the bar graph in Figure 8-32 to demonstrate the data. The Sugar Plop people objected. Do you see why?

The graph in Figure 8-32 clearly distorts the data, since the bar for Korn Krisps is four times as high and four times as wide as the bar for Sugar Plops. Thus, the area representing Korn Krisp is sixteen times the area representing Sugar Plops, rather than four times the area, as indicated by the original data. Other examples of distorted data are given in the problem set.

FIGURE 8-32

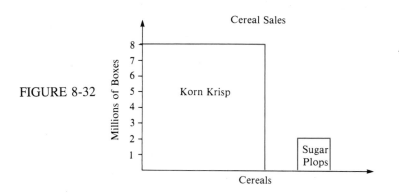

PROBLEM SET 8-5 #1,2,5,7-16

1. The figure shows a bar graph for the rainfall in centimeters during the last school year. Answer each of the following questions.
   (a) Which month had the greatest rainfall and how much did it have?
   (b) What were the amounts of rainfall in October, December, and January?

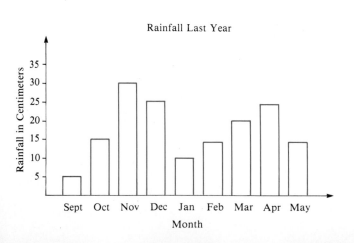

2. A list of presidents with the number of children for each follows.

   1. Washington, 0   2. J. Adams, 5
   3. Jefferson, 6   4. Madison, 0
   5. Monroe, 2   6. J. Q. Adams, 4
   7. Jackson, 0   8. Van Buren, 4
   9. W. H. Harrison, 10   10. Tyler, 14
   11. Polk, 0   12. Taylor, 6
   13. Fillmore, 2   14. Pierce, 3
   15. Buchanan, 0   16. Lincoln, 4
   17. A. Johnson, 5   18. Grant, 4
   19. Hayes, 8   20. Garfield, 7
   21. Arthur, 3   22. Cleveland, 5
   23. B. Harrison, 3   24. McKinley, 2
   25. T. Roosevelt, 6   26. Taft, 3
   27. Wilson, 3   28. Harding, 0
   29. Coolidge, 2   30. Hoover, 2
   31. F. D. Roosevelt, 6   32. Truman, 1
   33. Eisenhower, 2   34. Kennedy, 3
   35. L. B. Johnson, 2   36. Nixon, 2
   37. Ford, 4   38. Carter, 3
   39. Reagan, 4
   (a) Make a frequency table for these data.
   (b) What is the most frequent number of children?

3. The given data represent total car sales for Johnson's car lot from January through June. Draw a bar graph for this data.

Month	Jan.	Feb.	March	April	May	June
Number of Cars Sold	90	86	92	96	90	100

4. Five coins are tossed 64 times. A distribution for the number of heads obtained is shown.

Number of Heads	0	1	2	3	4	5
Frequency		2	10	20	20	10	2

(a) Draw a histogram for these data.
(b) Draw a frequency polygon for these data.

5. The grade distribution for the final examination for the mathematics course for elementary teachers is shown.

Grade	Frequency
A	4
B	10
C	37
D	8
F	1

(a) Draw a bar graph for these data.
(b) Draw a circle graph for these data.

6. The following are the amounts (rounded to the nearest dollar) paid by 25 students for textbooks during the fall term.

```
35  42  33  48  45  42  50  39  41  37
37  16  23  49  62  60  58  53  62  30
50  39  51  40  23
```

(a) Construct a grouped frequency table for these data, starting the first class at $15.00 with intervals of $5.00 each.
(b) Draw a histogram for the data.
(c) Draw a frequency polygon for the data.

7. Make a pictograph to represent the data, using 🥤 to represent 10 glasses of lemonade sold.

GLASSES OF LEMONADE SOLD

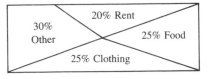

	Tally	Frequency
Monday	ЖЖЖ	15
Tuesday	ЖЖЖЖ	20
Wednesday	ЖЖЖЖЖЖ	30
Thursday	Ж	5
Friday	ЖЖ	10

8. Suppose the following circle graphs are used to illustrate the fact that the number of elementary teaching majors at teachers' colleges has doubled from 1973 to 1983, while the percentage of male elementary teaching majors has stayed the same. What is misleading about the way the graphs are constructed?

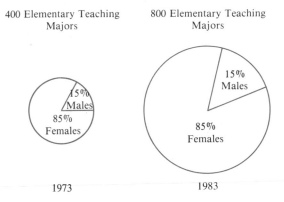

9. What is wrong with the line graph shown?

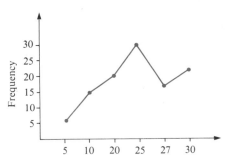

10. Give an example of a situation in which a circle graph would be preferable to a bar graph or line graph.

11. Give an example of a situation in which a line graph would be preferable to a bar graph.

12. Discuss the problems with a rectangular pie chart, such as the one pictured.

13. The following graphs give the temperatures for a certain day. Which graph is more helpful for guessing the temperature at 10:00 A.M.? Why?

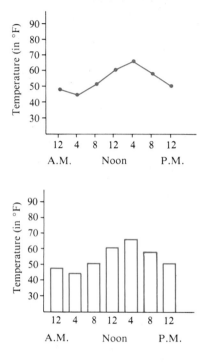

14. The circle graph below is from *Economic Road Maps*, Nos. 1898–1899, March, 1981. Use it to answer the following.
    (a) Find the number of degrees in the sections representing Italy and Japan.
    (b) Which country had the most investments?

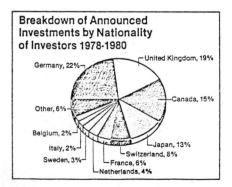

15. The line graph, from *Economic Road Maps*, Nos. 1894–1895, January, 1981, pictures trends in international tourist receipts based upon annual percent change. (International tourist receipts are monies spent by foreign tourists in a country or group of countries.)

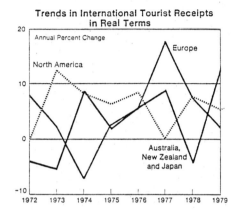

In what year did North America experience the greatest change?

16. The circle graph shows how an average family spent $500 last month on groceries. Find out how much they spent on each item.

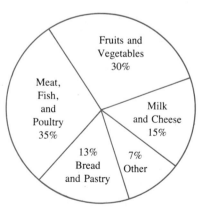

* * * * * * *   REVIEW PROBLEMS   * * * * * * *

17. The Venn diagram shows the number of members of a club who drink ale, beer, and cola, denoted by A, B, and C, respectively. Each member of the club drinks at least one of the three beverages. One of the members of the club is chosen at random. Find the probability that the chosen member drinks the following.

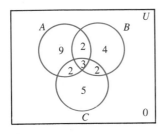

(a) Ale

(b) Beer, but not cola

(c) Both ale and cola, but not beer

(d) If a member who drinks cola is chosen at random, what is the probability that the member also drinks ale?

18. A pair of ordinary dice is thrown. Classify the following statements as true or false.

(a) Rolling two fives is less likely than rolling two ones.

(b) The probability that the numbers on both dice in a single roll is the same is $\frac{1}{6}$.

(c) Rolling an even sum and rolling an odd sum are equally likely events.

(d) The most likely sum is 7.

19. How many distinct ways can the digits of the given phone numbers be rearranged?

(a) 728-3594   (b) 243-2493

8-6   ON THE AVERAGE—MEASURES OF CENTRAL TENDENCY AND VARIATION

average

It is often easier to look at tables or graphs than to study large quantities of raw data. Another way to study raw data is to determine a single number that represents the data. This single number is called an **average.** The word *average* is often used loosely, and in many cases, it is not clear what is meant.

Consider the following set of data for three teachers, each of whom claims that, "on the average," his or her class scored better than the other two classes.

Mr. Smith: 62, 94, 95, 98, 98

Mr. Jones: 62, 62, 98, 99, 100

Ms. Leed: 40, 62, 85, 99, 99

All these teachers are correct in their assertions. Each one has used a different average. There are five different averages in general use: the arithmetic mean, the median, the mode, the geometric mean, and the harmonic mean. We discuss only the arithmetic mean, the median, and the mode. *A calculator is a definite aid in this section.*

arithmetic mean

mean

The most commonly used average is the **arithmetic mean,** which we simply call the **mean.** To find the mean of scores for each of the three teachers given above, find the sum of the scores in each case and divide by 5, the number of scores.

Mean (Smith): $\dfrac{62 + 94 + 95 + 98 + 98}{5} = \dfrac{447}{5} = 89.4$

Mean (Jones): $\dfrac{62 + 62 + 98 + 99 + 100}{5} = \dfrac{421}{5} = 84.2$

Mean (Leed): $\dfrac{40 + 62 + 85 + 99 + 99}{5} = \dfrac{385}{5} = 77$

Thus, using the mean as the average, Mr. Smith's class scored better "on the average" than the other two classes. In general, the mean is defined as follows.

DEFINITION

> The **mean** of the numbers $x_1, x_2, \ldots, x_n$, denoted by $\bar{x}$, is given by
>
> $$\bar{x} = \frac{x_1 + x_2 + x_3 + \cdots + x_n}{n}$$

median

The value exactly in the middle of an ordered distribution is called the **median.** To find the median for the teachers' scores, arrange each of their scores in increasing order and pick the middle score. Intuitively, half the scores are greater than the median and half are less.

Median (Smith): 62, 94, ⟨95,⟩ 98, 98   median = 95

Median (Jones): 62, 62, ⟨98,⟩ 99, 100   median = 98

Median (Leed):   40, 62, ⟨85,⟩ 99, 99   median = 85

Thus, using the median, Mr. Jones' class scored better "on the average" than the other two classes.

With an odd number of scores, as in the preceding case, the median is the middle score. With an even number of scores, the median is defined as the mean of the middle two scores; that is, to find the median, add the middle two scores and divide by 2. For example, the median of the scores 64, 68, 70, 74, 82, 90 is

$\dfrac{(70 + 74)}{2}$, or 72

In general, to find the median for a set of n numbers, proceed as follows.

1. Arrange the numbers in order from least to greatest.
2. (a) If n is odd, the median is the middle number.
   (b) If n is even, the median is the arithmetic mean of the two middle numbers.

mode

The **mode** of a set of data is the number that appears most frequently, if there is one. In some distributions, no number appears more than once, and some distributions may have more than one mode. For example, the set of scores 64, 79, 80, 82, 90 has no mode (or five modes). The set of scores 64, 75, 75, 82, 90, 90, 98 is **bimodal** (two modes), because both 75 and 90 are modes. It is possible for a set of data to have too many modes to be useful.

bimodal

For the three classes listed earlier, if the mode is used, then Ms. Leed's class has the best average.

Mode (Smith):   62, 94, 95, 98, 98   mode = 98

Mode (Jones):   62, 62, 98, 99, 100   mode = 62

Mode (Leed):   40, 62, 85, 99, 99   mode = 99

Example 8-16

Find the (a) mean, (b) median, and (c) mode for the following collection of data:

60, 60, 70, 95, 95, 100

Solution

(a) $\bar{x} = \dfrac{60 + 60 + 70 + 95 + 95 + 100}{6} = \dfrac{480}{6} = 80$

(b) The median is $\dfrac{(70 + 95)}{2}$, or 82.5.

(c) The set of data is bimodal and has both 60 and 95 as modes.

Although the mean is the average most commonly used, it may not always be the best average to use. Suppose, for example, a company employs twenty people. The president of the company earns $200,000, the vice president earns $75,000, and eighteen employees earn $10,000 each. The mean salary for this company is

$$\frac{\$200,000 + \$75,000 + 18(\$10,000)}{20} = \frac{\$455,000}{20} = \$22,750$$

In this case, the mean salary of $22,750 is not representative, and either the median or mode, which are both $10,000, would better describe the typical salary. Notice that the value of the mean is affected by extreme values.

In most cases, the value of the median is not affected by extreme values. The median, however, can be misleading. For example, suppose nine students make the following scores on a test: 30, 35, 40, 40, 92, 92, 93, 98, 99. From the median score of 92, one might possibly infer that the individuals all scored very well, yet 92 is certainly not a typical score.

The mode can be misleading in describing a set of data with very few items or many frequently occurring items. For example, the scores 40, 42, 50, 62, 63, 65, 98, 98 have a mode of 98, which is not a typical value.

PROBLEM 4

Lacking time to record his students' homework grades, Mr. Van Gruff asked them to keep track of their own grades. A few days later, Mr. Van Gruff asked the students to report their grades. One of the students, Eddy, had lost his papers but remembered the grades on four of six assignments—100, 82, 74, and 60. Also, according to Eddy, the mean of all six papers was 69, and the other two papers had identical grades. What were the grades on Eddy's other two homework papers?

Understanding the Problem

Eddy reported that he had scores of 100, 82, 74, and 60 on four of his six papers. He also reported that the mean average of all six papers was 69 and that he had identical scores on the missing two grades. The problem is to determine the two missing grades from this information.

Devising a Plan

Because the mean is obtained by finding the sum of the scores and then dividing by the number of scores, which is six, if we let x stand for each of the two missing grades, we have

$$69 = \frac{100 + 82 + 74 + 60 + x + x}{6}$$

To find the missing grades we solve this equation for x.

Carrying Out the Plan

We now solve this equation as follows:

$$69 = \frac{100 + 82 + 74 + 60 + x + x}{6}$$

$$69 = \frac{316 + 2x}{6}$$

$$49 = x$$

Since the solution to the equation is $x = 49$, we conclude that each of the two missing scores was 49.

Looking Back

The answer of 49 seems reasonable since the mean of 69 is below three of the four given scores. This can be easily checked by computing the mean of the scores 100, 82, 74, 60, 49, 49 and showing that it is indeed 69.

The choice of which average to use for a particular set of data is not always easy. In the example involving the three teachers, each teacher chose the average that best suited his or her needs. For clarity and honesty, the average that is used should always be specified. However, in many cases no average gives adequate information about a set of data. The need for other numbers to describe data will be apparent in the following discussion.

Suppose Professors Abel and Babel both taught a section of a statistics course and each professor had six students. Both professors gave the same final exam. The results, along with the means for each group of scores, are given in Table 8-11.

TABLE 8-11

Abel	Babel
100	70
80	70
70	60
50	60
50	60
10	40

$$\bar{x} = \frac{360}{6} = 60 \qquad \bar{x} = \frac{360}{6} = 60$$

Each set of scores has the same mean. Each median also equals 60. Although the mean and median for these two groups are the same, the two distributions of scores are very different. The first set of scores is more spread out, or varies more, than the second.

There are several ways to measure the spread (variation) of data. The simplest way is to subtract the least number from the greatest number. This difference is called the **range.** The range for Professor Abel's class is $100 - 10$, or 90. The range for Professor Babel's class is $70 - 40$, or 30. Although the range is easy to calculate, it has the disadvantage of being affected by one extremely high or one extremely low score. For example, the sets of scores 10, 20, 25, 30, 100 and 10, 80, 85, 90, 90, 100 both have a range of 90.

There are several ways to measure the spread of data that are more useful than the range. We consider the two most commonly used measures of variation: variance and standard deviation. The two measures are essentially equivalent, but the standard deviation has the same units as the original data and is particularly useful in making precise statements about the spread of data.

The steps for calculating the **variance,** v, and **standard deviation,** s, of n numbers are as follows:

range

variance
standard deviation

1. Find the mean of the numbers.
2. Subtract the mean from each number.
3. Square each difference found in Step 2.
4. Find the sum of the squares in Step 3.
5. Divide by n to obtain the variance.
6. Find the square root of v to obtain the standard deviation, s.

These six steps can be summarized for the numbers $x_1, x_2, x_3, \ldots, x_n$ as follows, where $\bar{x}$ is the mean of these numbers.

$$s = \sqrt{v} = \sqrt{\frac{(x_1 - \bar{x})^2 + (x_2 - \bar{x})^2 + (x_3 - \bar{x})^2 + \cdots + (x_n - \bar{x})^2}{n}}$$

Remark | In some textbooks, the formula just given involves division by $n - 1$ instead of n. Division by $n - 1$ is more useful for advanced work in statistics.

The variances and standard deviations for the final exam data for the classes of Professors Abel and Babel are calculated using Tables 8-12 and 8-13, respectively.

TABLE 8-12   Abel

x	$x - \bar{x}$	$(x - \bar{x})^2$
100	40	1600
80	20	400
70	10	100
50	$^-10$	100
50	$^-10$	100
10	$^-50$	2500
Totals 360	0	4800

$\bar{x} = \dfrac{360}{6} = 60$

$v = \dfrac{4800}{6} = 800$

$s = \sqrt{800} \doteq 28.3$

TABLE 8-13   Babel

x	$x - \bar{x}$	$(x - \bar{x})^2$
70	10	100
70	10	100
60	0	0
60	0	0
60	0	0
40	$^-20$	400
Totals 360	0	600

$\bar{x} = \dfrac{360}{6} = 60$

$v = \dfrac{600}{6} = 100$

$s = \sqrt{100} = 10$

The standard deviation is a large number when the values from a set of data are widely spread. The standard deviation is a small number (close to 0) when the data values are close together.

Example 8-17

Given the data 32, 41, 47, 53, 57, find each of the following.

(a) The range   (b) The variance
(c) The standard deviation

Solution

(a) The range is $57 - 32$, or 25.
(b) The variance, v, is computed using the information in the table.

x	$x - \bar{x}$	$(x - \bar{x})^2$
32	⁻14	196
41	⁻5	25
47	1	1
53	7	49
57	11	121
Totals 230	0	392

$$\bar{x} = \frac{230}{5} = 46$$

$$v = \frac{392}{5} = 78.4$$

(c) $s = \sqrt{78.4} \doteq 8.9$

normal curve

Standard deviations are especially useful when working with a **normal curve.** A normal curve is a smooth, bell-shaped curve, which depicts the frequencies of many different sets of data in the real world. In a normal curve, frequency values are distributed symmetrically about the mean. (Also, the mean, median, and mode all have the same value.) On a normal curve, 68% of the values lie within one standard deviation of the mean, 95% lie within two standard deviations, and 99% are within three standard deviations. This is illustrated in Figure 8-33.

FIGURE 8-33

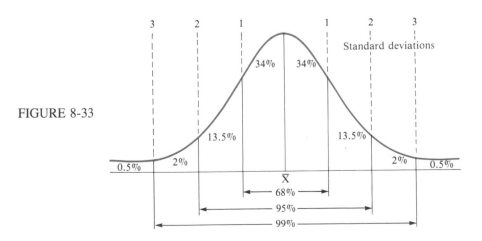

Example 8-18 | A standarized test was scored, and there was a mean of 500 and a standard deviation of 100. Suppose 10,000 students took the test and their scores approximated a normal curve.

(a) How many scored between 400 and 600?
(b) How many scored between 300 and 700?
(c) How many scored between 200 and 800?

Solution | (a) Since one standard deviation on either side of the mean is from 400 to 600, about 68% of the scores fall in this interval. Thus, 0.68(10,000), or 6800, students scored between 400 and 600.
(b) About 95% of 10,000, or 9500, students scored between 300 and 700.
(c) About 99% of 10,000, or 9900, students scored between 200 and 800.

Remark | About 1% or 100 students' scores in Example 8-18 fall outside three standard deviations. About 50 of these students did very well on the test and about 50 students did very poorly.

BRAIN TEASER

The speeds of racing cars were timed after 3 miles, $4\frac{1}{2}$ miles, and 6 miles. Freddy averaged 140 miles per hour (mph) for the first 3 miles, 168 mph for the next $1\frac{1}{2}$ miles, and 210 mph for the last $1\frac{1}{2}$ miles. What was his mean speed for the total 6-mile run?

PROBLEM SET 8-6

1. Calculate the mean, median, and mode for each of the following collections of data.
   (a) 2, 8, 7, 8, 5, 8, 10, 5
   (b) 10, 12, 12, 14, 20, 16, 12, 14, 11
   (c) 18, 22, 22, 17, 30, 18, 12
   (d) 82, 80, 63, 75, 92, 80, 92, 90, 80, 80
   (e) 5, 5, 5, 5, 5, 10
2. Suppose each of ten students scored 50 on a test. Find the mean, median, and mode of the test scores.
3. The mean score on a set of 20 tests is 75. What is the sum of the 20 test scores?
4. The tram at a ski area has a capacity of 50 people with a load limit of 7500 pounds. What is the mean weight of the passengers if the tram is loaded to capacity?
5. The mean for a set of 28 scores is 80. Suppose two more students take the test and score 60 and 50. What is the new mean?

6. The names and ages for each person in a family of five follow.

Name	Age
Dick	40
Jane	36
Kirk	8
Jean	6
Scott	2

(a) What is the mean age?
(b) Find the mean of the ages 5 years from now.
(c) Find the mean 10 years from now.
(d) Describe the relationships between the means found in parts (a), (b), and (c).

7. Ten alumni of a state college are chosen at random and asked their annual incomes, which are $15,000, $20,000, $18,000, $28,000, $12,000, $30,000,

$20,000, $14,000, $20,000, $50,000. Find the mean, median, and mode for these incomes.

8. Suppose you own a hat shop and decide to order hats in only *one* size for the coming season. To decide which size to order, you look at last year's sales figures, which are itemized according to size. Should you find the mean, median, or mode for the data?

9. A temperature of 25°C is considered ideal. In the city of Podunk, the mean temperature is 25°C. Does this mean that the temperature in Podunk is ideal? Explain.

10. Jenny averaged 70 on her quizzes during the first part of the quarter and 80 on her quizzes the second part of the quarter, yet her average for the quarter was not 75. How can this be?

11. The results of Jon's fall quarter grades follow. Find his grade point average for the term (A = 4, B = 3, C = 2, D = 1, F = 0).

Course	Credits	Grades
Math	5	B
English	3	A
Physics	5	C
German	3	D
Handball	1	A

12. If the mean weight of seven linemen on a football team is 230 pounds and the mean weight of the four backfield members is 190 pounds, what is the mean weight of the eleven-man team?

13. A total of 210 people stayed at the Rancho Costa Plenty over the weekend for a total cost of $67,200. What was the mean cost per person?

14. If 99 people had a mean income of $12,000, how much is the mean income increased by the addition of a single income of $200,000?

15. The following table gives the annual salaries for the 40 players of a certain professional football team. Find the mean annual salary for the team.

Salary	Number of Players
$18,000	2
22,000	4
26,000	4
35,000	3
38,000	12
44,000	8
50,000	4
80,000	2
150,000	1

16. Write a list of scores for which the mean and median are not equal and such that half the values are above the mean and half are below.

17. For each of the following sets, find the range, the variance, and the standard deviation.
   (a) 5, 7, 8, 9, 1
   (b) 18, 32, 17, 43, 63, 10, 35, 90, 80, 72

18. What is the standard deviation of the heights of seven trapeze artists if their heights are 175 cm, 182 cm, 190 cm, 180 cm, 192 cm, 172 cm, 190 cm?

19. For certain workers, the mean wage is $5.00 per hour with standard deviation $0.50. If a worker is chosen at random, what is the probability that the worker's wage is between $4.50 and $5.50? Assume a normal distribution of wages.

20. What happens to the mean and standard deviation of a set of data when the same number is added to each value in the data?

21. The mean IQ score for 1500 students is 100, with a standard deviation of 15. Assuming the scores have a normal curve:
   (a) How many have an IQ between 85 and 115?
   (b) How many have an IQ between 70 and 130?
   (c) How many have an IQ under 55 or over 145?
   (d) How many have an IQ over 145?

22. Sugar Plops boxes say they hold 16 ounces. To make sure, the manufacturer fills the box to a mean weight of 16.1 ounces with a standard deviation of 0.05 ounce. If the weights have a normal curve, what percent of the boxes actually contain 16 ounces or more?

23. (a) If all the numbers in a set are equal, what is the standard deviation?
   (b) If the standard deviation of a set of numbers is zero, must all the numbers in the set be equal?

★ 24. Show that the following formula for variance is equivalent to the one given in the text.

$$v = \frac{x_1^2 + x_2^2 + \cdots + x_n^2}{n} - \bar{x}^2$$

25. In a Math 131 class at DiPaloma University, the grades on the first exam were as follows.

96	71	43	77	75	76	61
83	71	58	97	76	74	91
74	71	77	83	87	93	79

   (a) Find the mean average.
   (b) Find the median score.
   (c) Find the mode.
   (d) Find the variance of the scores.
   (e) Find the standard deviation of the scores.

* * * * * * REVIEW PROBLEMS * * * * * * *

26. Five horses, Deadbeat, Applefarm, Bandy, Cash, and Egglegs, run in a race.
    (a) How many elements are in the sample space for the win, place, and show horses?
    (b) Find the probability that Deadbeat finished first and Bandy finished second in the race.
    (c) Find the probability that the win, place, and show horses are Deadbeat, Egglegs, and Cash in that order.

27. Charles and Rudy each roll an ordinary die once. What is the probability that the number on Rudy's roll is greater than the number on Charles' roll?

28. Amy has a quiz on which she is to answer any three of the five questions. If she is equally versed on all questions and chooses three questions at random, what is the probability that Question 1 is not chosen?

29. What are the odds in favor of choosing the correct answer to a five-part multiple-choice question if the choice is made at random?

30. Raw test scores from a history test are given below.

86	85	87	96	55
90	94	82	68	77
88	89	85	74	90
72	80	76	88	73
64	79	73	85	93

(a) Construct a grouped frequency table for these scores with intervals of 5 starting the first class at 55.
(b) Draw a histogram for the data.
(c) Draw a frequency polygon for the data.
(d) If a circle graph were drawn for the grouped data in (a), how many degrees would be in the section representing the 85–89 interval?

SOLUTION TO THE PRELIMINARY PROBLEM

Understanding the Problem

Al and Betsy each bet $50 on a coin-tossing game in which a fair coin was to be tossed five times. Al was to win when a total of three heads was obtained; Betsy was to win when a total of three tails was obtained. When Al had two heads and Betsy had one tail, the coin was lost. The problem is how to split the stakes fairly.

If the stakes of the game are to be split fairly, then we should agree on what this means. There could be many interpretations, but possibly the best is to agree that the pot will be split in proportion to the probabilities of each player winning the game when play was halted.

Devising a Plan

A tree diagram that simulates the completion of the game allows us to find the probability of each player winning the game. Once the probabilities are found, all that is necessary is to multiply the probabilities times the amount of the pot, $100, to determine each player's fair share.

Carrying Out the Plan

The tree diagram in Figure 8-34 shows the possibilities for game winners.

FIGURE 8-34

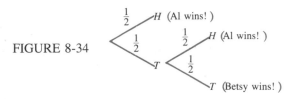

We can find the probabilities of each player's winning as follows:

$$P \text{ (Betsy wins)} = \frac{1}{2} \cdot \frac{1}{2} = \frac{1}{4}$$

$$P \text{ (Al wins)} \quad = 1 - \frac{1}{4} = \frac{3}{4}$$

Hence, the fair way to split the stakes is for Al to receive $\frac{3}{4}$ of $100, or $75, while Betsy should receive $\frac{1}{4}$ of $100, or $25.

Looking Back

The problem could be made even more interesting by assuming that the coin is not fair, so that the probability is not $\frac{1}{2}$ for each branch in the tree diagram. Other possibilities arise if the players have unequal amounts of money in the pot or more tosses are required to win. (This problem is a version of the one mentioned in the chapter introduction that de Meré asked Pascal and Fermat to solve.)

QUESTIONS FROM THE CLASSROOM

1. A student claims that if a fair coin is tossed and a head appears five times in a row, then according to the law of averages, the probability of a tail on the next toss is greater than the probability of a head. What is your reply?

2. A student observes the spinner below and claims that the color red has the highest probability of appearing since there are two red areas on the spinner. What is your reply?

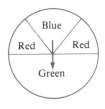

3. A student tosses a coin three times and tails appears each time. The student concludes that the coin is not fair. What is your response?

4. An experiment consists of tossing a coin twice. The student reasons that there are three possible outcomes: two heads, one head and one tail, or two tails. Thus, $P(\text{HH}) = \frac{1}{3}$. What is your reply?

5. A student asks if the average income of each of ten people is $10,000 and one person gets a raise of $10,000, is the median, the mean, or the mode changed and, if so, by how much?

6. A student asks for an example of when the mode is the best average. What is your response?

7. Suppose the class takes a test and the following averages are obtained: mean, 80; median, 90; mode, 70. Tom, who scored 80, would like to know if he did better than half the class. What is your response?

8. A student asks for the advantages of presenting data in graphical form rather than in tabular form. What is your response? What are the disadvantages?

9. A student asks if it is possible to find the mode for data in a grouped frequency table. What is your response?

10. A student asks if she can make any conclusions about a set of data knowing that the mean for the data is less than the median. How do you answer?

11. A student asks if it is possible to have a standard deviation of zero. What is your answer?

12. A student reports that the average life of a pickup is around 10 years, since she read that nine out of ten pickup trucks sold in the last 10 years are still on the road. Is she correct?

CHAPTER OUTLINE

I. Probability
   A. If all outcomes of an experiment are equally likely, the **probability** of an event, A, from sample space, S, is given by

   $$P(A) = \frac{n(A)}{n(S)}$$

   B. A **sample space** is the set of all possible outcomes of an experiment.
   C. An **event** is a subset of a sample space.
   D. Outcomes are **equally likely** if each outcome is as likely to occur as another.
   E. An **impossible event** is an event with a probability of zero. An impossible event can never occur.
   F. A **certain event** is an event with a probability of one. A certain event is sure to happen.
   G. The probability of the **complement of an event** is given by $P(\overline{A}) = 1 - P(A)$, where A is the event and $\overline{A}$ is its complement.

* II. Odds and expectation
   A. The **odds in favor** of an event A are given by

   $$\frac{P(A)}{1 - P(A)}$$

   B. The **odds against** an event A are given by

   $$\frac{1 - P(A)}{P(A)}$$

   C. If, in an experiment, the possible outcomes are numbers $a_1, a_2, \ldots, a_n$, occurring with probabilities $p_1, p_2, \ldots, p_n$, respectively, then

the **mathematical expectation,** E, is defined as

$$E = a_1 \cdot p_1 + a_2 \cdot p_2 + a_3 \cdot p_3 + \cdots + a_n \cdot p_n$$

III. Counting principles
   A. **Fundamental Counting Principle**   If an event M can occur in m ways and, after it has occurred, event N can occur in n ways, then event M followed by event N can occur in $m \cdot n$ ways.
   B. **Permutations** are arrangements in which order is important.
   C. **Combinations** are arrangements in which order is *not* important.
   D. To find the number of combinations possible, first use the Fundamental Counting Principle to find the number of permutations and then divide by the number of ways in which each choice can be arranged.
   E. The expression **$n!$,** called **n factorial,** represents the product of all the natural numbers less than or equal to n.

IV. Descriptive statistics
   A. **Descriptive statistics** is the science of organizing and summarizing numerical data.
   B. Information can be summarized in **frequency tables.**
   C. Data can be pictured on different graphs.
      1. **Histograms** or **bar graphs**
      2. **Frequency polygons** or **line graphs**
      3. **Circle graphs**
      4. **Pictographs**

V. Averages
   A. An **average** is a single numerical figure used to represent data.
   B. The **mean** of n given numbers is the sum of the numbers divided by n.
   C. The **median** of a set of numbers is the middle number if the numbers are arranged in numerical order or, if there is no middle number, it is the mean of the two middle numbers.
   D. The **mode** of a set of numbers is the number or numbers that occur most frequently in the set.
VI. Measures of variation
   A. The **range** is the difference between the greatest and least numbers in the set.

   B. The **variance** is found by subtracting the mean from each value, squaring each of these differences, finding the sum of these squares, and dividing by n, when n is the number of observations.
   C. The **standard deviation** is equal to the square root of the variance.
   D. In a **normal curve,** 68% of the numbers are within one standard deviation of the mean, 95% are within two standard deviations of the mean, and 99% are within three standard deviations of the mean.

CHAPTER TEST

1. Suppose the names of the days of the week are placed in a box and one name is drawn at random.
   (a) List the sample space for this experiment.
   (b) List the event consisting of outcomes that the day drawn starts with the letter T. .
   (c) What is the probability of drawing a day that starts with T?

2. Complete each of the following.
   (a) If A is an impossible event, then $P(A) =$ _____.
   (b) If A is a certain event, then $P(A) =$ _____.
   (c) If A is any event, then _____ $\leq P(A) \leq$ _____.
   (d) If A is any event, then $P(\bar{A}) =$ _____.

3. A box contains three red balls, five black balls, and four white balls. Suppose one ball is drawn at random. Find the probability for each of the following events.
   (a) A black ball is drawn.
   (b) A black or a white ball is drawn.
   (c) Neither a red nor a white ball is drawn.
   (d) A red ball is not drawn.
   (e) A black ball and a white ball are drawn.
   (f) A black or white or red ball is drawn.

4. One card is selected at random from an ordinary set of 52 cards. Find the probability for each of the following events.
   (a) A club is drawn.
   (b) A spade and a 5 are drawn.
   (c) A heart or a face card are drawn.
   (d) A jack is not drawn.

5. A box contains five black balls and four white balls. If three balls are drawn one by one, find the probability that they are all white if the draws are made as follows.
   (a) With replacement
   (b) Without replacement

6. Suppose a three-stage rocket is launched into orbit. The probability for failure at stage one is $\frac{1}{10}$, at stage two is $\frac{1}{5}$, and at stage three is $\frac{1}{3}$. What is the probability for a successful flight?

7. Consider the two boxes pictured below. If a letter is drawn from box 1 and placed in box 2, and then a letter is drawn from box 2, what is the probability that the letter is an L?

      1   2

8. Consider the following two-stage experiment using the boxes below. First, select a box at random and then select a letter at random from the box. What is the probability of drawing an A?

    1   2   3   4

9. Consider the boxes below. Draw a ball from box 1 and put it in box 2. Then draw a ball from box 2 and put it into box 3. Finally, draw a ball from box 3. Construct a tree diagram for this experiment and calculate the probability that the last ball chosen is black.

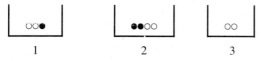

    1   2   3

* 10. What are the odds in favor of drawing a jack when one card is drawn from an ordinary deck of playing cards?
* 11. A die is rolled once. What are the odds against rolling a prime number?
* 12. If the odds in favor of a certain event are 3 to 5, what is the probability the event will occur?
* 13. A game consists of rolling two dice. Rolling double 1's pays $7.20. Rolling double 6's pays $3.60. Any other roll pays nothing. What is the expected value for this game?
* 14. A total of 3000 tickets have been sold for a drawing. If one ticket is drawn for a single prize of $1000, what is a fair price for a ticket?
15. How many four-digit numbers can be formed if the first digit cannot be zero and the last digit must be two?
16. A club consists of ten members. In how many different ways can a group of three people be selected to go on a European trip?
17. In how many ways can the names of four candidates be listed on a ballot for an election?
18. Compute 100!/98!. (Look for shortcuts!)
19. Find the number of different ways that four flags can be displayed on flag pole, one above the other, if ten different flags are available.
20. Five women live together in an apartment. Two of the women have blue eyes. If two of the women are chosen at random, what is the probability that they both have blue eyes?
21. Suppose you read that "the average family in Rattlesnake Gulch has 2.41 children." What average is being used? Explain your answer. Suppose the sentence said 2.5. Then what are the possibilities?
22. At Bug's Bar-B-Q restuarant, the average weekly wage for full-time workers is $150. If there are ten part-time employees whose average weekly salary is $50 and the total weekly payroll is $3950, how many full-time employees are there?
23. Find the mean, median, and mode for each of the following groups of data.

(a) 10, 50, 30, 40, 10, 60, 10
(b) 5, 8, 6, 3, 5, 4, 3, 6, 1, 9

24. Find the range, variance, and standard deviation for each set of scores in Problem 23.
25. The masses, in kilograms, of children in a certain class follow.

40	49	43	48
42	41	42	39
46	42	49	39
47	49	44	42
41	40	45	43

(a) Make a frequency table for this data.
(b) Draw a bar graph for the data.

26. The grades on a test for 30 students follow.

96	73	61	76	77	84
78	98	98	80	67	82
61	75	79	90	73	80
85	63	86	100	94	77
86	84	91	62	77	64

(a) Make a grouped frequency table for these scores using four classes, starting the first class at 61.
(b) Draw a histogram for the grouped data.
(c) Draw a line graph for the data.

27. The budget for the Wegetem Crime Company is $2,000,000. If $600,000 is spent on bribes, $400,000 is spent for legal fees, $300,000 for bail money, $300,000 for contracts, and $400,000 for public relations, draw a circle graph to indicate how the company spent its money.
28. What, if anything, is wrong with the following bar graph?

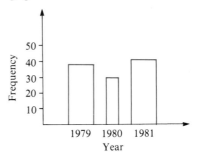

29. The mean salary of 24 people is $9000. How much will one additional salary of $80,000 increase the mean salary?
30. A standardized test has a mean of 600 and a standard deviation of 75. If 1000 students took the test and their scores approximated a normal curve, how many scored between 600 and 750?

SELECTED BIBLIOGRAPHY

Austin, J. "Overbooking Airline Flights." *The Mathematics Teacher* 75 (March 1982):221–223.

Bestgen, B. "Making and Interpreting Graphs and Tables: Results and Implications from National Assessment." *Arithmetic Teacher* 28 (December 1980):26–29.

Billstein, R. "A Fun Way to Introduce Probability." *The Arithmetic Teacher* 24 (January 1977):39–42.

Boas, R. "Snowfalls, and Elephants, Pop Bottles and π." *The Mathematics Teacher* 74 (January 1981):49–55.

Bruni, J., and H. Silverman. "Graphing as a Communication Skill." *The Arithmetic Teacher* 22 (May 1975):354–366.

Buzitis, B., and J. Kella. *The News Math*. Seattle: The Seattle Times, 1974.

Carpenter, T., M. Corbitt, H. Kepner, Jr., M. Lindquist, and R. Reys. "What Are the Chances of Your Students Knowing Probability?" *The Mathematics Teacher* 74 (May 1981):342–344.

Choate, S. "Activities in Applying Probability Ideas." *Arithmetic Teacher* 26 (February 1979):40–42.

Christopher, L. "Graphs Can Jazz Up the Mathematics Curriculum." *Arithmetic Teacher* 30 (September 1982):28–30.

Corbet, J., and J. Milton. "Who Killed the Cook?" *Arithmetic Teacher* 71 (April 1978):263–266.

Curlette, W. "The Randomized Response Technique: Using Probability to Ask Sensitive Questions." *The Mathematics Teacher* 73 (November 1980):618–621, 627.

Duncan, D., and B. Litwiller. "Randomness, Normality, and Hypothesis Testing: Experiences for the Statistics Class." *The Mathematics Teacher* 74 (May 1981):368–374.

Enman, V. "Probability in the Intermediate Grades." *Arithmetic Teacher* 26 (February 1979):38–39.

Fennell, F., L. Houser, D. McPartland, and S. Parker. "Ideas." *Arithmetic Teacher* 29 (March 1982):27–32.

Fennell, F., L. Houser, D. McPartland, and S. Parker. "Ideas." *Arithmetic Teacher* 29 (May 1982):19–24.

Fielker, D. *Topics from Mathematics, Statistics*. New York: Cambridge University Press, 1967.

Heiny, R. "Gambling, Casinos and Game Simulation." *The Mathematics Teacher* 74 (February 1981):139–143.

Higgins, J. "Probability with Marbles and a Juice Container." *The Arithmetic Teacher* 20 (March 1973):165–166.

Hinders, D. "Monte Carlo, Probability, Algebra, and Pi." *The Mathematics Teacher* 74 (May 1981):335–339.

Horak, V., and W. Horak. "Collecting and Displaying the Data Around Us." *Arithmetic Teacher* 30 (September 1982):16–20.

Houser, L. "Baseball Monte Carlo Style." *The Mathematics Teacher* 74 (May 1981):340–341.

Hutcheson, J. "Computer-Assisted Instruction Is Not Always Drill." *The Mathematics Teacher* 73 (December 1980):689–691, 715.

Hyatt, D. "M and M's Candy: A Statistical Approach." *The Arithmetic Teacher* 24 (January 1977):34.

Jacobson, M. "Graphing in the Primary Grades: Our Pets." *Arithmetic Teacher* 26 (February 1979):25–26.

Jacobson, M., and M. Tabler. "Ideas." *Arithmetic Teacher* 28 (February 1981):31–36.

Jamski, W. "Introducing Standard Deviation." *The Mathematics Teacher* 74 (March 1981):197–198.

Jensen, R., and D. O'Neil. "We've Got You Pegged!" *Arithmetic Teacher* 29 (October 1981):10–16.

Johnson, E. "Bar Graphs for First Graders." *Arithmetic Teacher* 29 (December 1981):30–31.

Joiner, B., and C. Campbell. "Some Interesting Examples for Teaching Statistics." *The Mathematics Teacher* 68 (May 1975):364–369.

Jones, G. "A Case For Probability." *Arithmetic Teacher* 26 (February 1979):37, 57.

Klitz, R., and J. Hofmeister. "Statistics in the Middle School." *Arithmetic Teacher* 26 (February 1979):35–36.

Lai, T. "Bingo and the Law of Equal Ignorance." *The Arithmetic Teacher* 24 (January 1977):83–84.

Lappan, G., and M. Winter. "Probability Simulation in Middle School." *The Mathematics Teacher* 73 (September 1980):446–449.

MacDonald, A. "A Stem-Leaf Plot: An Approach to Statistics." *The Mathematics Teacher* 75 (January 1982):27, 28, 25.

Mullet, G. "Watch the Red, Not the Black." *The Mathematics Teacher* 73 (May 1980):349–353.

Niman, J., and R. Postman. "Probability on the Geoboard." *The Arithmetic Teacher* 20 (March 1973):167–170.

Noether, G. "The Nonparametric Approach in Elementary Statistics." *The Mathematics Teacher* 67 (February 1974):123–126.

O'Neil, D., and R. Jensen. "Looking at Facts." *Arithmetic Teacher* 29 (April 1982):12–15.

Piaget, J., and B. Inhelder. *The Origin of the Idea of Chance in Children*. London: Routledge and Kegan, 1975.

Reeves, C. "Volleyball and Probability." *The Mathematics Teacher* 71 (October 1978):595–596.

Richbart, L. "Probability and Statistics for Grades 9–11." *The Mathematics Teacher* 74 (May 1981):346–348.

Rudd, D. "A Problem in Probability." *The Mathematics Teacher* 67 (February 1974):180–181.

Schell, V. "Out of Thin Air." *The Mathematics Teacher* 75 (April 1982):313–317.

Shulte, A. "A Case for Statistics," *Arithmetic Teacher* 26 (February 1979):24.

Smith, R. "Bar Graphs for Five Year Olds." *Arithmetic Teacher* 27 (October 1979):38–41.

Sterba, D. "Probability and Basketball." *The Mathematics Teacher* 74 (November 1981):624–627, 656.

Stone, J. "Place Value and Probability (with Promptings from Pascal)," *Arithmetic Teacher* 27 (March 1980):47–49.

Sullivan, D., and M. O'Neil. "THIS IS US! Great Graphs for Kids." *Arithmetic Teacher* 28 (September 1980):14–18.

Travers, K., and K. Gray. "The Monte Carlo Method: A Fresh Approach to Teaching Probabilistic Concepts." *The Mathematics Teacher* 74 (May 1981):327–334.

Watson, J. "A Current Event for the Mathematics Classroom." *The Mathematics Teacher* 71 (November 1978):658–663.

Webb, L., and J. McKay. "Making Inferences from Marbles and Coffee Cans." *Arithmetic Teacher* 26 (September 1978):33–35.

Introductory Geometry 9

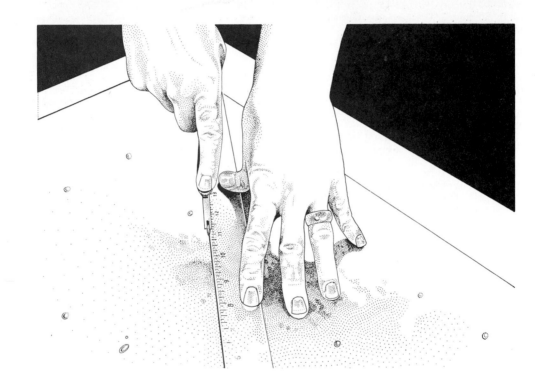

PRELIMINARY PROBLEM

Tiff A. Nee, a noted stained glass window maker, needed assorted triangular pieces of glass for a project. One rectangular plate of glass that she planned to cut contained ten air bubbles, no three in a line, as shown in the figure. To avoid having an air bubble showing in her finished project, she decided to cut triangular pieces by making the air bubbles and the corners of the plate the vertices of the triangles. How many triangular pieces did she cut?

INTRODUCTION

In Greek, the word *geometry* means "earth measure," which suggests the practical origins of geometry. A different side of geometry emerged in the first half of the sixth century B.C. Thales (640–550 B.C.), a Greek philosopher and mathematician, insisted that geometric facts be demonstrated by logical reasoning, rather than by observation and experimentation. Along with Euclid, Eudoxus, and others, Thales helped to establish geometry on an abstract, deductive level. In *The Elements*, a treatise on geometry, Euclid was probably the first to represent geometry in an organized logical fashion. He started with a few basic assumptions called **axioms** and logically deduced other geometric information. Euclid's work so influenced the teaching of geometry that many people describe it as the subject in which "you prove theorems."

axioms

A rigorous approach to Euclidean geometry requires many axioms and proofs and is inappropriate for the majority of students in elementary school. In this chapter and following chapters, geometry is presented from an experimental, constructive point of view. Many geometric properties are accepted on the basis of intuition. These properties then are used to deduce other geometric facts.

9-1 BASIC NOTIONS

points   lines

Points and **lines** are mathematical abstractions and are undefined terms in geometry. We represent a point by a dot and usually name the point with a capital letter. A point has no dimensions, but can be used to describe a location. A line is a collection of points. Figure 9-1 shows a line and names two points on the line, A and B. The arrowheads on the line in Figure 9-1 indicate that the line extends indefinitely. Lines have no thickness or width. The line through the points A and B can be designated as $\overleftrightarrow{AB}$ or $\overleftrightarrow{BA}$ or by any lowercase letter. (In Figure 9-1, $\overleftrightarrow{AB} = \ell$.) Many lines can be drawn through a given point, but only one line exists through two points.

FIGURE 9-1

As shown in Figure 9-1, line ℓ goes through points A and B. Any other collection of points going through A and B is not a line. (In our discussions, a "line" always means "a straight line.")

A line contains infinitely many points. We say that the points A and B belong to $\overleftrightarrow{AB}$ or are contained in $\overleftrightarrow{AB}$, and write $A \in \overleftrightarrow{AB}$ and $B \in \overleftrightarrow{AB}$. Points that belong to the same line are called **collinear points.** Thus, points A, B, and C in Figure 9-2 are collinear. Points B, D, and C are not collinear. If three collinear points A, B, and C are arranged as in Figure 9-2, we say that B is **between** A and C. Point D is not between B and C, since B, D, and C are not collinear.

collinear points

between

FIGURE 9-2

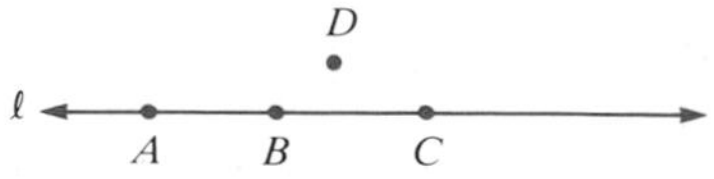

Certain subsets of a line are given separate names and symbols. A **line**
line segment   **segment** is a subset of a line that contains two points and all the points between
them. The line segment in Figure 9-3(a) is denoted by $\overline{AB}$ or $\overline{BA}$.

FIGURE 9-3

(a)   (b)

Any point on a line separates the line into three disjoint subsets, the point
half-lines   itself and two **half-lines.** The point itself in union with either of the half-lines is
ray   called a **ray.** The ray in Figure 9-3(b) can be denoted by $\overrightarrow{AB}$, where A is the
endpoint and B is any point on the ray different from A. In $\overrightarrow{AB}$ the arrowhead
indicates that the direction of the ray is from A toward B. The notation for a ray
with endpoint B and containing A is $\overrightarrow{BA}$. Thus, $\overrightarrow{AB} \neq \overrightarrow{BA}$. A half-line, denoted by
$\overset{\leftharpoondown}{AB}$, consists of all the points of $\overrightarrow{AB}$ except the starting point A.

Example 9-1   Find each of the following in Figure 9-4.

(a) $\overleftrightarrow{AD} \cap \overleftrightarrow{EC}$ (b) $\overrightarrow{AB} \cap \overrightarrow{BA}$ (c) $\overrightarrow{AB} \cup \overrightarrow{BD}$

(d) $\overrightarrow{AB} \cap \overleftrightarrow{BC} \cap \overleftrightarrow{AC}$ (e) $\overrightarrow{AB} \cap \overset{\leftharpoondown}{BC}$

FIGURE 9-4

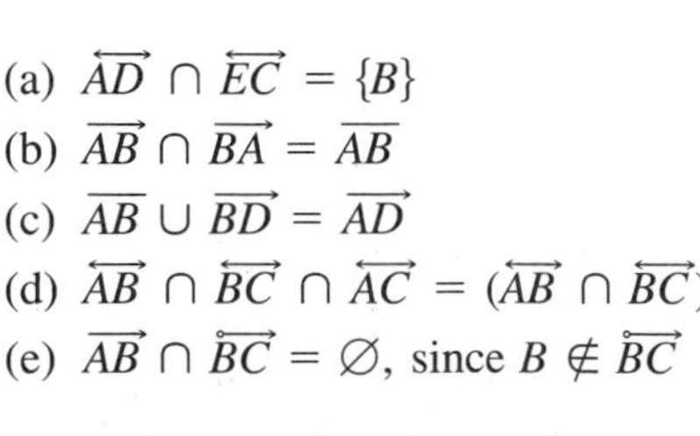

Solution   (a) $\overleftrightarrow{AD} \cap \overleftrightarrow{EC} = \{B\}$

(b) $\overrightarrow{AB} \cap \overrightarrow{BA} = \overline{AB}$

(c) $\overrightarrow{AB} \cup \overrightarrow{BD} = \overrightarrow{AD}$

(d) $\overrightarrow{AB} \cap \overleftrightarrow{BC} \cap \overleftrightarrow{AC} = (\overrightarrow{AB} \cap \overleftrightarrow{BC}) \cap \overleftrightarrow{AC} = \{B\} \cap \overleftrightarrow{AC} = \varnothing$

(e) $\overrightarrow{AB} \cap \overset{\leftharpoondown}{BC} = \varnothing$, since $B \notin \overset{\leftharpoondown}{BC}$

plane   Another collection of points is called a **plane.** *Plane* is another undefined
term in geometry. To picture a plane, think of a flat tabletop extending horizon-
tally in all directions, as shown in Figure 9-5(a). A plane is a flat surface that
extends indefinitely in all directions and has no thickness. A plane contains
infinitely many points, as well as infinitely many lines. A plane is usually denoted

by a lowercase Greek letter, such as alpha (α), beta (β), or gamma (γ), and may be pictured as in Figure 9-5(b). Another notation used is plane ABC, where A, B, and C are three noncollinear points in the plane. (We see later that three noncollinear points determine a plane.) Points (or lines) in the same plane are called **coplanar points** (or **lines**). Points A, B, and C in Figure 9-5(b) are coplanar.

coplanar points
coplanar lines

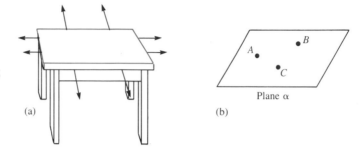

FIGURE 9-5

(a)   (b)

Plane α

intersecting lines

Two lines m and n, as in Figure 9-6(a), are called **intersecting lines** if the intersection point P is the only point that belongs to both lines. This can be written as $m \cap n = \{P\}$. Distinct coplanar lines that do not intersect are called **parallel lines.** The lines r and s in Figure 9-6(b) are parallel. We write $r \parallel s$.

parallel lines

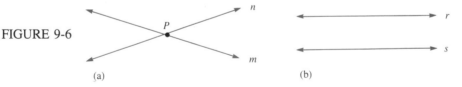

FIGURE 9-6

(a)   (b)

The number of points of intersection determined by different numbers of lines is investigated in the next problem.

PROBLEM 1

What is the greatest number of points of intersection determined by n distinct lines?

Understanding the Problem

Because the greatest number of intersection points for n distinct lines is required, the lines cannot be parallel. As shown in Figure 9-7, the greatest number of points of intersection for two, three, and four lines is one, three, and six, respectively. We are to determine the greatest number of points of intersection for n lines.

FIGURE 9-7

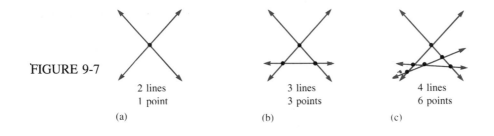

2 lines 1 point	3 lines 3 points	4 lines 6 points
(a)	(b)	(c)

Devising a Plan

In order to discover a pattern for the maximum number of intersection points of n distinct lines, we reason as follows. Because no two lines are parallel, when one new line is added to a drawing containing a given number of lines, the new line must intersect each of the existing lines. Thus, when a new line is added to the two lines in Figure 9-7(a), we obtain Figure 9-7(b) with 1 existing point of intersection and 2 new ones, for a total of $1 + 2$ points of intersection. Next, when a new line is added to Figure 9-7(b), we obtain Figure 9-7(c), with $1 + 2$ existing points of intersection and 3 new points of intersection created by the fourth line. Thus, the maximum number of intersection points for four lines is $1 + 2 + 3$. Similarly, for five lines we have all the existing intersection points for four lines, plus four new ones created by the fifth line, giving a total of $1 + 2 + 3 + 4$. We summarize this in Table 9-1.

TABLE 9-1

Number of Lines	Greatest Number of Points of Intersection
2	1
3	$3 = 1 + 2$
4	$6 = (1 + 2) + 3$
5	$10 = (1 + 2 + 3) + 4$
$\vdots$	$\vdots$
n	$? = 1 + 2 + 3 +, 4 + \cdots + (n - 1)$

Carrying Out the Plan

From the previous discussion, it follows that for n lines we have all the intersection points created by $n - 1$ lines plus $n - 1$ new points created by the nth line. Thus, the number of intersection points for n distinct lines is given by $1 + 2 + 3 + 4 + \cdots + (n - 1)$. Recalling Gauss' formula from Chapter 1, we can write this sum as follows.

$$1 + 2 + 3 + 4 + \cdots + (n - 1) = \frac{(n - 1)[(n - 1) + 1]}{2} = \frac{(n - 1) \cdot n}{2}$$

Looking Back

The formula $\frac{(n - 1) \cdot n}{2}$ works for the first four cases in Table 9-1. We also notice that this is the same formula as the one derived in the solution to the problem in Chapter 1 on page 12. How are the two problems related?

The solution to this problem can also be approached as follows. No two lines are parallel, so each line intersects all the lines except itself. Thus, using n lines, each line must intersect $n - 1$ lines. Hence, on each line there are $n - 1$ points of intersection. Because there are n lines, we can count a total of $n \cdot (n - 1)$ intersection points. However, in this counting process each intersection point is counted twice since it is on two lines. Thus, the actual number of intersection points is $\frac{1}{2}$ of $n(n - 1)$, or $\frac{n(n - 1)}{2}$.

It is possible for two lines not to intersect and yet not be parallel. This occurs when lines are in different planes. Two distinct lines that cannot be contained in skew lines   any single plane are called **skew lines.** Only intersecting lines and parallel lines are coplanar. Skew lines are noncoplanar. For example, the lines p and q in Figure 9-8 are skew lines.

FIGURE 9-8

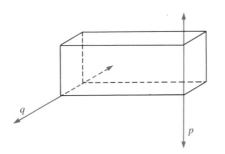

Many planes can be drawn through a given point. Similarly, many planes can be drawn through any two given points, as shown in Figure 9-9(a). However, exactly one plane can be drawn through three noncollinear points, as illustrated by the sheet of glass resting on the three pencil points in Figure 9-9(b).

FIGURE 9-9

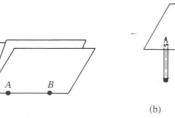

(a)   (b)

There are several ways to determine a plane. The most important are the following:

1. Three noncollinear points determine a plane.
2. A line and a point not on the line determine a plane.
3. Two parallel lines determine a plane.
4. Two intersecting lines determine a plane.

Two distinct planes either intersect in a line or are parallel. In Figure 9-10(a), the planes are parallel, that is, $\alpha \cap \beta = \varnothing$. In Figure 9-10(b), the planes intersect in a line, $\overleftrightarrow{AB}$, that is, $\alpha \cap \beta = \overleftrightarrow{AB}$.

FIGURE 9-10

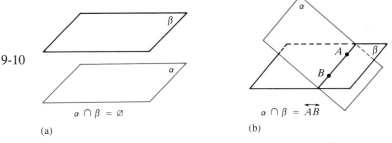

$\alpha \cap \beta = \varnothing$

(a)

$\alpha \cap \beta = \overleftrightarrow{AB}$

(b)

The floor and ceiling of a typical room together represent parallel planes. The floor and a wall together represent intersecting planes. The edge between the floor and wall represents the **line of intersection.**

line of intersection

parallel to the plane

A line and a plane can be related in one of three possible ways. If a line and a plane have no points in common, we say that the line is **parallel to the plane.** If two points of a line are in the plane, then the entire line containing the points is contained in the plane. If a line shares all its points with a plane, we say the line is in the plane. If a line intersects a plane, but is not contained in the plane, it intersects the plane in only one point. The three relative positions between a line ℓ and a plane α are shown in Figure 9-11.

FIGURE 9-11

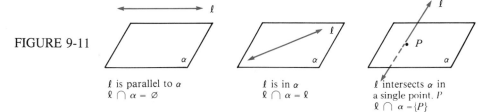

ℓ is parallel to α
$\ell \cap \alpha = \varnothing$

ℓ is in α
$\ell \cap \alpha = \ell$

ℓ intersects α in
a single point. P
$\ell \cap \alpha = \{P\}$

Example 9-2 | Given Figure 9-12, answer each of the questions.

FIGURE 9-12 |

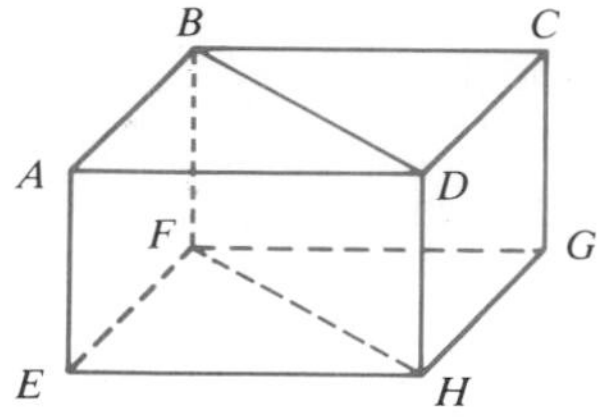

(a) Name two pairs of skew lines.
(b) Are $\overleftrightarrow{BD}$ and $\overleftrightarrow{FH}$ parallel, skew, or intersecting lines?
(c) Are $\overleftrightarrow{BD}$ and $\overleftrightarrow{GH}$ parallel?
(d) Find the intersection of $\overleftrightarrow{BD}$ and plane EFG.
(e) Find the intersection of $\overleftrightarrow{BH}$ and the plane DCG.

Solution |

(a) $\overleftrightarrow{BC}$ and $\overleftrightarrow{DH}$, and $\overleftrightarrow{AE}$ and $\overleftrightarrow{BD}$. Others are possible.
(b) $\overleftrightarrow{BD}$ and $\overleftrightarrow{FH}$ are parallel.
(c) No, $\overleftrightarrow{BD}$ and $\overleftrightarrow{GH}$ are skew lines.
(d) The intersection is the empty set since $\overleftrightarrow{BD}$ and the plane EFG have no points in common.
(e) The intersection of $\overleftrightarrow{BH}$ and the plane DCG is $\{H\}$.

space

half-planes
half-spaces

Points, lines, and planes are all subsets of **space.** Space is the set of all points. A point separates a line into two half-lines and the point itself. Similarly, a line separates a plane into two **half-planes** and the line itself and a plane separates space into two **half-spaces** and the plane itself. In Figure 9-13, ℓ separates the plane α into two half-planes. Point A is in one half-plane determined by ℓ and point B is in the other half-plane. The line separating the plane does not belong to either half-plane. A line and the two half-planes determined by the line are three disjoint subsets of a plane. Likewise, a plane and the two half-spaces determined by the plane are three disjoint subsets of space.

FIGURE 9-13

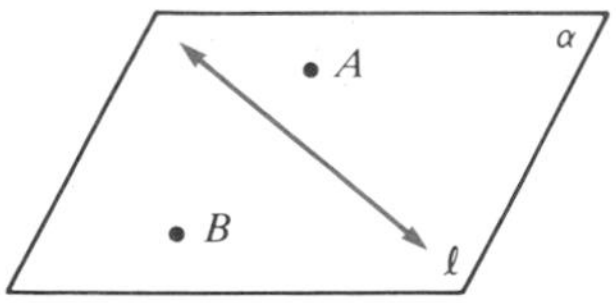

term:
collinear pts
ray, half-line
skew line

notation:
$\overleftrightarrow{AB}$
$\overline{AB}$
$\overrightarrow{AB}$
$\overrightarrow{BA}$

PROBLEM SET 9-1

class 1. Given the figure below, find each of the following.

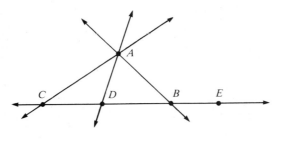

(a) $\overleftrightarrow{AC} \cap \overrightarrow{BE}$
(b) $\overline{AC} \cap \overline{BE}$
(c) $\overrightarrow{CA} \cap \overrightarrow{EB}$
(d) $\overrightarrow{CA} \cap \overrightarrow{BC}$
(e) $\overline{CB} \cup \overline{BE}$
(f) $\overline{AB} \cup \overrightarrow{AB}$
(g) $\overrightarrow{AB} \cup \overrightarrow{BA}$
(h) $\overrightarrow{AD} \cup \overrightarrow{DA}$

Hmwk 2. Given the line ℓ, answer the following.

$$\overset{A}{\bullet} \quad \overset{B}{\bullet} \quad \overset{C}{\bullet} \quad \overset{D}{\bullet}$$

(a) How many different ways can you name line ℓ using the points labeled on the line?
(b) How many different line segments are determined using the points labeled on the line?

class 3. Consider the following figure and answer each of the following questions. Point D is neither in plane α nor plane β.

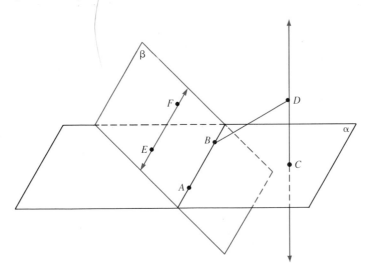

(a) Name a pair of skew lines.
(b) If $\overleftrightarrow{EF}$ and $\overleftrightarrow{AB}$ are parallel, what can be said about $\overleftrightarrow{EF}$ and α?

(c) Find and name the intersections for each of the following pairs of planes.
  (i) α and β (ii) *BDC* and α (iii) *ABD* and *BDC*
(d) Is there a single plane containing the points *E, F, B,* and *D*? Explain your answer.

4. Indicate whether each of the following statements is true or false. If false, explain why.
  (a) Two distinct planes either intersect in a line or are parallel.
  (b) If there are two points common to a line and a plane, then the entire line is in the plane.
  (c) It is always possible to find a plane through four given points in space.
  (d) If two distinct lines do not intersect, they are parallel.
  (e) The intersection of three planes may be a single point.
  (f) If two distinct lines intersect, there is one and only one plane containing the lines.
  (g) There are infinitely many planes containing two skew lines.
  (h) If each of two parallel lines is parallel to a plane, α, then the plane determined by the two parallel lines is parallel to α.
  (i) If three points are coplanar, then they must be collinear.
  (j) If two distinct lines are parallel to a third line in space, then the two lines are parallel to each other.
  (k) If a plane, α, contains one line, ℓ, but not another line, *m*, and ℓ is parallel to *m*, then α is parallel to *m*.
  (l) A line parallel to each of two intersecting planes is parallel to the line of intersection of these planes.

5. Suppose ℓ is a line and *A* is a point not on ℓ.
  (a) How many lines intersecting ℓ may be drawn through *A*?
  (b) How many planes contain ℓ and *A*?

6. Suppose ℓ is a line and two points, *A* and *B*, are not on ℓ. For each of the following, how many planes contain *A* and *B* and at least one point on ℓ?
  (a) $\overleftrightarrow{AB}$ and ℓ are skew lines   (b) $\overleftrightarrow{AB}$ and ℓ are not skew lines

7. (a) If two parallel planes, α and β, intersect a third plane, γ, in two lines, ℓ and *m*, are ℓ and *m* necessarily parallel? Explain your answer.
  (b) If two planes, α and β, intersect a third plane in two parallel lines, are α and β always parallel? Why?
  (c) Suppose two intersecting lines are both parallel to a plane, α. Is the plane determined by these intersecting lines parallel to α? Why?

8. How many rays are determined by each of the following?
  (a) Three collinear points   (b) Four collinear points
  (c) Five collinear points   (d) *n* collinear points

9. (a) How many lines are determined by three noncollinear points?
  (b) How many lines are determined by four points, no three of which are collinear?
  (c) How many lines are determined by five points, no three of which are collinear?
  (d) How many lines are determined by *n* points, no three of which are collinear?

10. Give a mathematical explanation of why a three-legged stool is always stable and a four-legged stool sometimes rocks.

★ 11. Use the statement, "There is one and only one plane containing three distinct noncollinear points," to prove each of the following.
  (a) A line and a point not on the line determine a plane.
  (b) Two intersecting lines determine a plane.

★ 12. Prove that if two parallel planes are intersected by a third plane, the lines of intersection are parallel.

Laboratory Activity

Assign

If a sheet of paper is creased and unfolded, then two regions are formed. If the paper is creased again, how many regions are formed? Could there be more than one answer? How should the second crease be made in order to obtain the maximum number of regions? What is the least number of creases needed in order to obtain: (a) 11 regions; (b) 23 regions?

9-2   PLANE FIGURES

angle

In a plane, an **angle** is the union of two distinct rays that have a common endpoint. Figure 9-14(a) illustrates an angle.

FIGURE 9-14

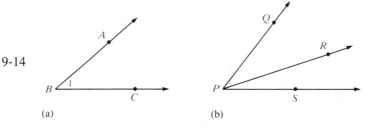

(a)   (b)

sides
vertex

    The rays of an angle are called the **sides** of the angle, and the common endpoint is called the **vertex** of the angle. An angle can be named by three different points: the vertex and a point on each ray, with the vertex always listed between the other two points. Thus, the angle in Figure 9-14(a) can be named as ∡*CBA* or ∡*ABC*. The latter is read "angle *ABC*." When there is no confusion, it is also customary to name an angle either by its vertex or by a number. Thus, the angle in Figure 9-14(a) can be named as ∡*B* or ∡1. However, in Figure 9-14(b), there is more than one angle with vertex *P*, namely, ∡*QPR*, ∡*RPS*, and ∡*QPS*. Thus, the notation ∡*P* is inadequate for naming any one of the angles.

    An angle separates the plane into three distinct sets of points: the angle itself, the interior, and the exterior. The interior of angle *A* is shaded in Figure 9-15(a). In Figure 9-15(b), the two rays forming the angle are collinear. This angle also separates the plane into three disjoint sets. However, there is no interior or exterior of this angle. Such an angle is called a **straight angle.**

straight angle

FIGURE 9-15

(a)   (b)

adjacent angles

Two intersecting lines form four nonstraight angles in the plane. In Figure 9-16, the four angles are ∡1, ∡2, ∡3, and ∡4. Angles 1 and 2 are called **adjacent angles.** Adjacent angles are angles that have a common vertex, a common side, and nonoverlapping interiors. Can you name three more pairs of adjacent angles in Figure 9-16?

FIGURE 9-16

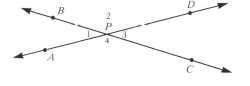

vertical angles

Nonadjacent angles formed by two intersecting lines, such as ∡1 and ∡3 in Figure 9-16, are called **vertical angles.** Another pair of vertical angles in Figure 9-16 is ∡2 and ∡4.

plane curve

Other subsets of the plane that are studied in geometry are curves. A careful definition of a curve requires advanced mathematical concepts. Therefore, we intuitively describe a plane curve. A **plane curve** is a set of points in a plane that can be traced without lifting a pencil from the paper and without retracing any portion of the drawing other than single points. We use the terms *plane curve* and *curve* interchangeably. Figure 9-17(a), (b), (d), and (e) are examples of curves. Figure 9-17(c) is not a curve because it cannot be traced without lifting the pencil.

FIGURE 9-17

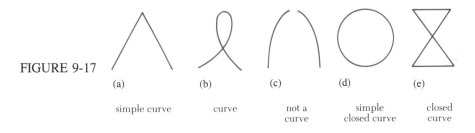

(a)　　　　　(b)　　　　(c)　　　(d)　　　(e)

simple curve　　　curve　　　not a　　simple　　closed
　　　　　　　　　　　　　　　curve　closed curve　curve

simple curve

Figure 9-17(a) and (d) are examples of simple curves. A **simple curve** is a curve that can be traced in such a way that no point is traced more than once except the tracing may stop at the same point where it started. Figure 9-17(d) and (e) are examples of **closed curves.** A closed curve is a curve that can be traced so that the starting and stopping points are the same. Notice that Figure 9-17(d) is a **simple closed curve.**

closed curve

simple closed curve

Example 9-3

Which of the figures in Figure 9-18 represent the following?

(a) Curves
(b) Simple curves
(c) Closed curves
(d) Simple closed curves

FIGURE 9-18

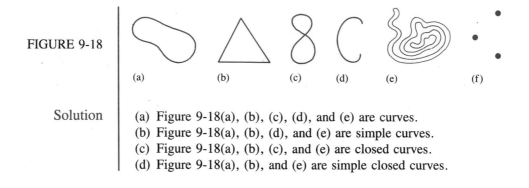

(a)   (b)   (c)   (d)   (e)   (f)

Solution

(a) Figure 9-18(a), (b), (c), (d), and (e) are curves.
(b) Figure 9-18(a), (b), (d), and (e) are simple curves.
(c) Figure 9-18(a), (b), (c), and (e) are closed curves.
(d) Figure 9-18(a), (b), and (e) are simple closed curves.

As shown in Figure 9-19, any simple closed curve partitions the plane into three mutually disjoint sets of points—the curve itself, the interior, and the exterior of the curve. This property of simple closed curves is known as the **Jordan curve theorem.**

Jordan curve theorem

FIGURE 9-19

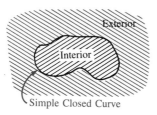

polygonal curve

Any plane curve that is the union of line segments only is called a **polygonal curve.** All the curves in Figure 9-20 are examples of polygonal curves.

FIGURE 9-20

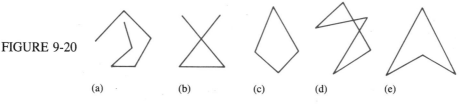

(a)   (b)   (c)   (d)   (e)

polygon

Polygonal curves, such as in Figure 9-20(c) and (e), which are simple and closed, are called polygons. A **polygon** is a simple, closed polygonal curve such that no two segments with a common endpoint are collinear. The line segments forming a polygon are called **sides** of the polygon. A point where the two sides meet is called a **vertex.** Together, a polygon and its interior are called a **polygonal region.**

sides
vertex
polygonal region

Strictly speaking, there are no angles in a polygon since an angle is composed of two rays, whereas the sides of a polygon are line segments. However, there are angles associated with a polygon. For example, in Figure 9-21, $\angle ABC$, $\angle BCA$, and $\angle CAB$ are called the three angles of polygon ABC.

FIGURE 9-21

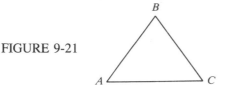

A polygon has three or more sides and is classified by the number of sides (or angles) it has. The names for many polygons have prefixes indicating the number of sides (angles), as shown in Table 9-2. A polygon having n sides is *n*-gon referred to as an ***n*-gon.**

TABLE 9-2

Number of Sides	Name
3	Triangle
4	Quadrilateral
5	Pentagon
6	Hexagon
7	Heptagon
8	Octagon
9	Nonagon
10	Decagon
12	Dodecagon

diagonal

Any line segment connecting nonconsecutive vertices of a polygon is called a **diagonal.** Thus, in Figure 9-22(a), the segments $\overline{AC}$, $\overline{AD}$, $\overline{BE}$, $\overline{BD}$, and $\overline{CE}$ are diagonals of the given pentagon. In Figure 9-22(b), the segments $\overline{QS}$ and $\overline{PR}$ are the diagonals of the quadrilateral *PQRS*.

FIGURE 9-22

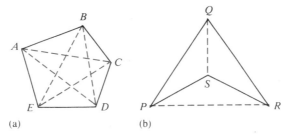

(a)   (b)

convex polygon
concave polygon

Notice that, except for their endpoints, all the diagonals of the pentagon in Figure 9-22(a) lie in the interior of the pentagon. The quadrilateral in Figure 9-22(b) has a diagonal that, except for its endpoints, lies in the exterior of the quadrilateral. A polygon having no diagonals in its exterior is called a **convex polygon,** whereas a polygon having at least one diagonal in its exterior is called a **concave polygon.**

The pentagon in Figure 9-22(a) is convex, while the quadrilateral in Figure 9-22(b) is concave. Because a triangle has no diagonals, it has no diagonals in its exterior and hence is convex. (A definition of a convex region is given in Problem 17 of Problem Set 9-2.)

Example 9-4   Which of the polygons in Figure 9-23 are convex and which are concave?

FIGURE 9-23

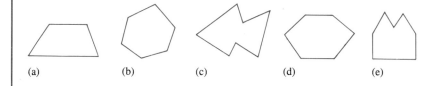

(a)   (b)   (c)   (d)   (e)

Solution   Polygons in parts (a), (b), and (d) are convex because they have no diagonals in their exteriors. Polygons in (c) and (e) are concave because in each case at least one diagonal can be drawn in the exterior.

In the following problem, we investigate a relationship between the number of sides of a polygon and the number of diagonals it has.

PROBLEM 2

How many diagonals does a convex n-gon have?

Understanding the Problem

We are given a polygon with n sides and we are to determine how many different diagonals can be drawn by connecting the n vertices of the polygon in all possible ways.

Devising a Plan

We use the strategy of examining related simple cases of the problem in order to develop a pattern for the original problem. Figure 9-24 shows that a triangle has no diagonals, a square has two diagonals, a pentagon has five diagonals, and a hexagon has nine diagonals.

FIGURE 9-24

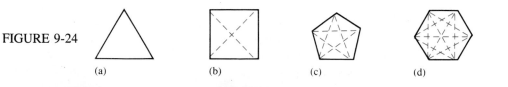

(a)   (b)   (c)   (d)

Examining Figure 9-24(c), we see that if we choose any vertex, then we can draw only two diagonals from that vertex. In general, we cannot draw a diagonal from a chosen vertex to itself or from a chosen vertex to its adjacent vertices. Thus, in Figure 9-24(d), the number of diagonals that can be drawn from any vertex is three less than the number of vertices, that is, $6 - 3$, or 3. In a polygon with n sides, the number of diagonals that can be drawn from any vertex is three less than the number of vertices, that is, $n - 3$. From each of the n vertices of an n-gon, $n - 3$ diagonals can be drawn, and hence it appears that there are $n \cdot (n - 3)$ diagonals in the n-gon.

Based upon this formula, the number of diagonals for the hexagon in Figure 9-24(d) is 18. This result does not agree with the actual answer of 9. Because each diagonal is determined by two vertices, when the number of diagonals from each vertex was counted, we counted each diagonal twice. In general, to obtain the number of diagonals of a given n-gon, we must divide the number $n(n - 3)$ by 2.

Carrying Out the Plan

From the above discussion, we have the following formula for determining the number of diagonals of a convex n-gon:

$$\frac{n \cdot (n - 3)}{2}$$

Looking Back

The formula developed in Carrying Out the Plan gives results consistent with the number of diagonals pictured in Figure 9-24. An alternate solution to this problem uses the notion of combinations developed in Chapter 8. The number of ways that all the vertices in an n-gon can be connected two at a time is the number of combinations of n vertices chosen two at a time, that is, $_nC_2$, or $\frac{n(n - 1)}{2}$. This number of segments includes both the number of diagonals and the number of sides. Hence, the number of diagonals is $\frac{n \cdot (n - 1)}{2} - n$.

It can be shown that

$$\frac{n \cdot (n - 1)}{2} - n = \frac{n \cdot (n - 3)}{2}$$

congruence
congruent segments

The next concept that we investigate is **congruence.** Two line segments are described as **congruent** if a tracing of one line segment can be fitted exactly on top of the other. If $\overline{AB}$ is congruent to $\overline{CD}$, we write $\overline{AB} \cong \overline{CD}$. The symbol $\cong$ is read "is congruent to."

Triangles can be classified according to congruent sides as follows:

isosceles triangle
equilateral triangle
scalene triangle

1. An **isosceles triangle** is a triangle with at least two congruent sides.
2. An **equilateral triangle** is a triangle with all sides congruent.
3. A **scalene triangle** is a triangle having no two sides congruent.

Two angles are said to be congruent if the two angles can be fitted exactly one on top of the other. For example, in Figure 9-25, $\angle XYZ$ is congruent to $\angle RST$ if a tracing of $\angle XYZ$ can be placed so that $\overrightarrow{YZ}$ is on top of $\overrightarrow{ST}$, and $\overrightarrow{YX}$ can be made to coincide with $\overrightarrow{SR}$. We write $\angle XYZ \cong \angle RST$.

regular polygons

Polygons in which all the angles are congruent and all the sides are congruent are called **regular polygons.** We say that a regular polygon is both *equiangular* and *equilateral*. A regular triangle is an equilateral triangle. A regular pentagon and a regular hexagon are illustrated in Figure 9-26. The congruent sides and congruent angles are marked.

FIGURE 9-25

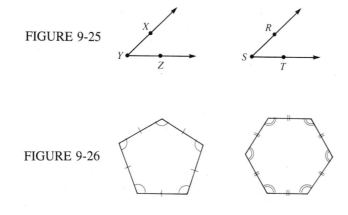

FIGURE 9-26

perpendicular lines
right angles

When two lines intersect so that all the nonstraight angles formed are congruent to one another, we say that the lines are **perpendicular lines.** The four angles formed are called **right angles.** In Figure 9-27, the two lines, m and n, are perpendicular and we write $m \perp n$. The symbol ⌐ is used to indicate right angles. Two intersecting segments, two intersecting rays, or a segment and a ray that intersect are called perpendicular if they lie on perpendicular lines. For example, in Figure 9-27, $\overline{AB} \perp \overline{BC}$, $\overrightarrow{BA} \perp \overrightarrow{BC}$, and $\overline{AB} \perp \overrightarrow{BC}$.

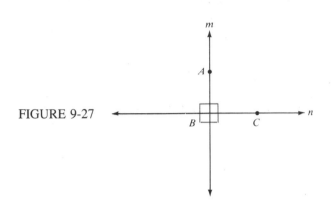

FIGURE 9-27

Quadrilaterals may be classified using angles and sides as follows:

parallelogram   1. A **parallelogram** is a quadrilateral in which each pair of opposite sides (nonintersecting) is parallel.

rectangle   2. A **rectangle** is a parallelogram with a right angle.

square   3. A **square** is a rectangle with all sides congruent. (A square is a regular quadrilateral.)

rhombus   4. A **rhombus** is a parallelogram with all sides congruent.

trapezoid   5. A **trapezoid** is a quadrilateral with exactly two sides parallel.

Remark | The following section presents information needed to show that if a parallelogram has one right angle, then it has four right angles. Thus, all angles in a rectangle are right angles.

The types of quadrilaterals listed above are pictured in Figure 9-28. In how many different ways can each of the quadrilaterals in Figure 9-28 be named?

Parallelogram   Rectangle

FIGURE 9-28

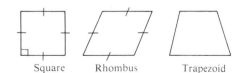

Square   Rhombus   Trapezoid

PROBLEM SET 9-2

class

1. Use the accompanying figure to solve each of the following.

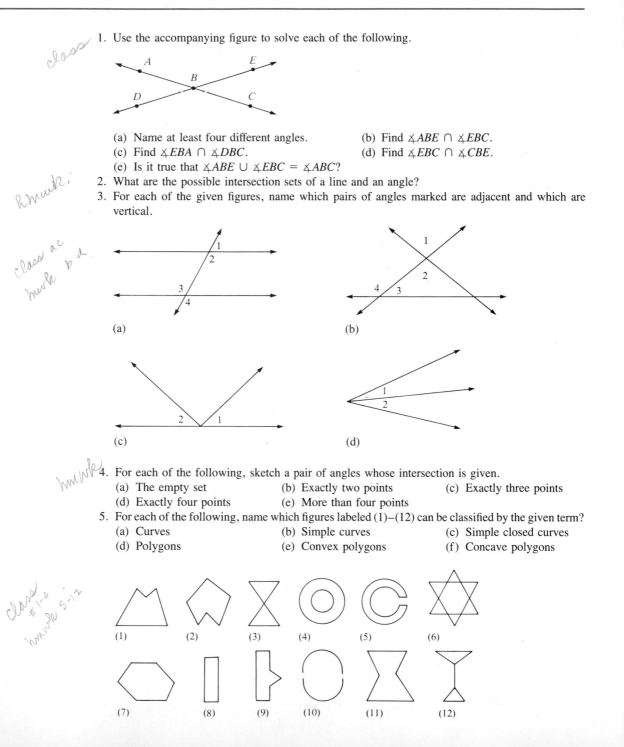

(a) Name at least four different angles.
(b) Find $\angle ABE \cap \angle EBC$.
(c) Find $\angle EBA \cap \angle DBC$.
(d) Find $\angle EBC \cap \angle CBE$.
(e) Is it true that $\angle ABE \cup \angle EBC = \angle ABC$?

hmwk;

2. What are the possible intersection sets of a line and an angle?
3. For each of the given figures, name which pairs of angles marked are adjacent and which are vertical.

class ac
hwk b d

(a)

(b)

(c)

(d)

hmwk

4. For each of the following, sketch a pair of angles whose intersection is given.
   (a) The empty set
   (b) Exactly two points
   (c) Exactly three points
   (d) Exactly four points
   (e) More than four points
5. For each of the following, name which figures labeled (1)–(12) can be classified by the given term?
   (a) Curves
   (b) Simple curves
   (c) Simple closed curves
   (d) Polygons
   (e) Convex polygons
   (f) Concave polygons

class #1-4
hmwk 5-12

(1)   (2)   (3)   (4)   (5)   (6)

(7)   (8)   (9)   (10)   (11)   (12)

p369 9cd

*9-2 Plane Figures p37**379** Cab*

P378

homework

6. Which of the printed capital letters of the English alphabet can be classified as follows? #2, 3bd)
   (a) Simple curves   (b) Closed curves   (c) Simple closed curves
   (d) Polygons

7. Is it possible for a polygon to have fewer than three sides? Why or why not?

8. How many diagonals does each of the following have?
   (a) Decagon   (b) 20-gon   (c) 100-gon

9. Use the given drawing to find each of the following.
   (a) $\ell \cap$ (polygon $ABCD$)   (b) $\ell \cap$ (interior of polygon $ABCD$)
   (c) $\ell \cap$ (exterior of polygon $ABCD$) (d) $\ell \cap \overrightarrow{AC}$

#5 a–f
figs 5–12
6) 10, 12
15, 16
20–22

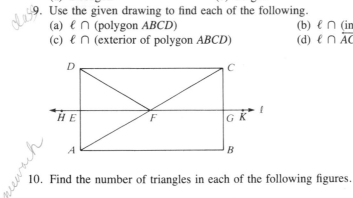

10. Find the number of triangles in each of the following figures.

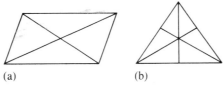

   (a)   (b)

11. Identify each of the following triangles as scalene, isosceles, or equilateral.

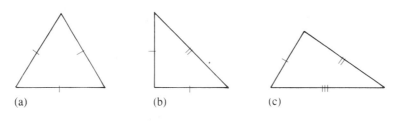

   (a)   (b)   (c)

12. Tell whether each of the following is true or false. If the statement is false, explain why.
   (a) Every isosceles triangle is equilateral.   (b) All equilateral triangles are isosceles.
   (c) All squares are rectangles.   (d) Some rectangles are rhombi.
   (e) All parallelograms are quadrilaterals.   (f) Every rhombus is a regular quadrilateral.

13. How many pairs of adjacent angles are there in the figure?

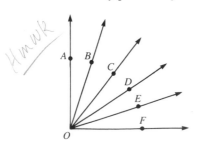

14. If three distinct rays with the same vertex are drawn as shown, then three different angles are formed: $\angle AOB$, $\angle AOC$, and $\angle BOC$.
    (a) How many different angles are formed using ten distinct noncollinear rays with the same vertex?
    (b) How many different angles are formed using n distinct noncollinear rays with the same vertex?

15. If five lines all meet in a single point, how many pairs of vertical angles are formed?

16. Use Venn diagrams to describe the relationships among the sets of all quadrilaterals (Q), parallelograms (P), trapezoids (T), rhombi (R), rectangles (F), and squares (S).

17. A region is called convex if, for every two points in the region, a segment joining them lies completely within the region. Otherwise, the region is called concave. Which of the following regions are convex and which are concave?

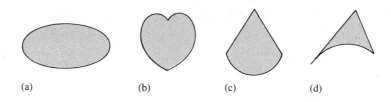

(a)   (b)   (c)   (d)

★ 18. The maximum number of intersection points for a square and a triangle in which no two sides lie on the same straight line is six, as shown in the figure. If we have two polygons with m and n sides, respectively, what is the maximum number of intersection points where no two sides lie on the same straight line?

* * * * * * * REVIEW PROBLEMS * * * * * * *

19. Find each of the following in the given figure.
    (a) $\overleftrightarrow{AC} \cap \overline{BC}$
    (b) $\overline{BD} \cup \overline{CD}$
    (c) List three line segments containing point A using the letters in the figure.
    (d) $\overrightarrow{DC} \cap \overrightarrow{DA}$

20. Classify the following as true or false. If false, tell why.
    (a) A ray has two endpoints.
    (b) For any points M and N, $\overleftrightarrow{MN} = \overleftrightarrow{NM}$.
    (c) Skew lines are coplanar.
    (d) $\overrightarrow{MN} = \overrightarrow{NM}$
    (e) A line segment contains an infinite number of points.
    (f) If two distinct planes intersect, their intersection is a line segment.

21. How many distinct lines are determined by four noncollinear points?

22. Draw two line segments $\overline{AB}$ and $\overline{CD}$ such that $\overline{AB} \cap \overline{CD} = \varnothing$ and $\overleftrightarrow{AB} \cup \overleftrightarrow{CD}$ is a single line.

BRAIN TEASER

Given three factories, A, B, and C, as shown in the figure on the right, and three utility centers, electricity (E), gas (G), and water (W), is it possible to connect each of the three factories to each of the three utility centers without crossing lines?

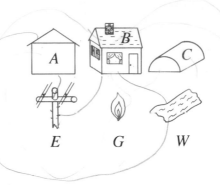

Laboratory Activity

A geoboard consists of a square array of nails driven into a board at equally spaced intervals. Students form various geometric shapes by stretching rubber bands around the nails. Geoboard exercises can be simulated by connecting dots on paper.

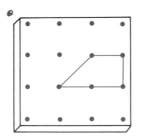

Form each of the following using either geoboards or dotted paper.

(a) Scalene triangle
(b) Isosceles triangle
(c) Square
(d) Parallelogram
(e) Trapezoid
(f) Pentagon
(g) Convex hexagon
(h) Concave hexagon

9-3   MORE ABOUT ANGLES

degree

A unit commonly used for measuring angles is the **degree.** Figure 9-29 shows that $\angle BAC$ has a measure of 30 degrees, written $m(\angle BAC) = 30°$. The measuring device pictured is called a **protractor.**

protractor

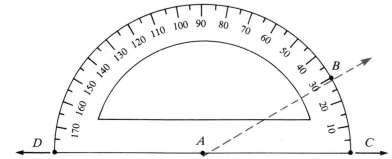

FIGURE 9-29

minutes
seconds

A degree is subdivided into 60 equal parts called **minutes,** and each minute is further subdivided into 60 equal parts called **seconds.** The measurement 29 degrees, 47 minutes, 13 seconds is written 29°47′13″.

Example 9-5

(a) In Figure 9-30, find the measure of ∢*BAC* if $m(\angle 1) = 27°58′$ and $m(\angle 2) = 19°47′$.

FIGURE 9-30

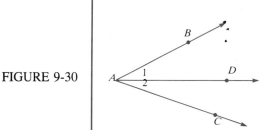

(b) Express 21.8° in degrees and minutes without decimals.

Solution

(a) $m(\angle BAC) = 27°58′ + 19°47′$
$= (27° + 19°) + (58′ + 47′)$
$= 46° + 105′$
$= 46° + 1° + 45′$
$= 47°45′$

(b) $21.8° = 21° + 0.8°$. There are 60 minutes in 1 degree. Thus, $0.8° = 0.8(60′) = 48′$ and, therefore, $21.8° = 21°48′$.

Remark

In the solution of Example 9-5(a) we used the fact that $m(\angle BAC) = m(\angle 1) + m(\angle 2)$. In general, if D is in the interior of ∢*BAC*, then $m(\angle BAC) = m(\angle BAD) + m(\angle DAC)$. Also $m(\angle BAC) - m(\angle BAD) = m(\angle DAC)$.

Angles can be classified according to their measure:

1. If the degree measure of an angle is greater than 0° and less than 90°, the angle is called an **acute angle.**

acute angle

obtuse angle
right angle
straight angle

2. If the degree measure of an angle is greater than 90° but less than 180°, the angle is called an **obtuse angle.**
3. If the degree measure of an angle is 90°, the angle is called a **right angle.**
4. If the degree measure of an angle is 180°, the angle is called a **straight angle.**

Remark | Angles with measure greater than 180° or with negative measure are important in mathematics but are not discussed in this text.

supplementary angles

complementary angles

FIGURE 9-31

Two angles are called **supplementary angles** if the sum of their measures is 180°. Each is said to be a supplement of the other. Two angles are called **complementary angles** if the sum of their measures is 90°. Each is said to be a complement of the other. Figure 9-31 shows examples of supplementary and complementary angles.

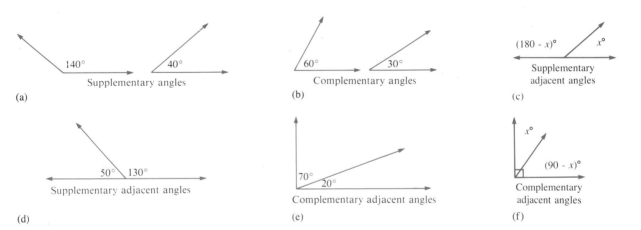

congruent angles

Intuitively, two angles are congruent if they can be fitted exactly one atop the other. More precisely, two angles are **congruent angles** if and only if they have the same measure. Using the notion of congruence, we can derive the following properties of supplementary and complementary angles.

Properties | 1. Supplements of the same angle, or congruent angles, are congruent.
2. Complements of the same angle, or congruent angles, are congruent.

Using Property 1, it is easy to prove that vertical angles are congruent. Look at Figure 9-32. Because ℓ is a straight line, $\angle 1$ is a supplement of $\angle 4$. Because m is a straight line, $\angle 2$ is a supplement of $\angle 4$. As $\angle 1$ and $\angle 2$ are the supplements of the same angle, $\angle 4$, they are congruent and equal in measure. Similarly, $\angle 3$ and $\angle 4$ are supplements of $\angle 1$ and, therefore, are congruent. Thus, vertical angles are congruent.

FIGURE 9-32

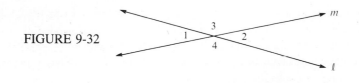

The property of complementary angles can also be used to deduce congruence relationships among certain angles as shown in Example 9-6.

Example 9-6

In Figure 9-33, suppose that $\angle APC$ and $\angle BPD$ are right angles. Prove that $\angle 1$ and $\angle 3$ are congruent.

FIGURE 9-33

Solution

Because $\angle APC$ is a right angle, $\angle 1$ is a complement of $\angle 2$. Because $\angle BPD$ is a right angle, $\angle 3$ is also a complement of $\angle 2$. Thus, $\angle 1$ and $\angle 3$ are complements of the same angle and hence are congruent.

transversal

corresponding angles
interior angles
exterior angles
alternate interior angles
alternate exterior angles

Angles are formed when a line intersects two distinct lines. Any line that intersects a pair of lines is called a **transversal** of these lines. In Figure 9-34(a), line p is a transversal of lines m and n. Two lines and a transversal form four pairs of **corresponding angles:** $\angle 1$ and $\angle 2$; $\angle 3$ and $\angle 4$; $\angle 5$ and $\angle 7$; $\angle 6$ and $\angle 8$. Angles 2, 4, 5, and 6 are called **interior angles** and angles 1, 3, 7, and 8 are called **exterior angles.** There are two pairs of **alternate interior angles,** namely $\angle 2$ and $\angle 5$, and $\angle 4$ and $\angle 6$. Angles 1 and 7 and angles 3 and 8 are pairs of **alternate exterior angles.**

FIGURE 9-34

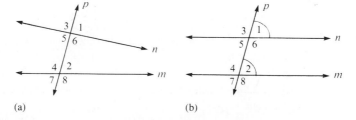

(a)　　　　　　　　　　　　(b)

If corresponding angles, such as ∡1 and ∡2, are congruent, as in Figure 9-34(b), it can be shown that members of each pair of corresponding angles are congruent. Also, in Figure 9-34(b), it appears that n and m are parallel. This is true. We leave it as an exercise to show that if a transversal intersecting two lines forms congruent corresponding angles, then the alternate interior or alternate exterior angles also are congruent. A summary of this discussion follows.

Property | If any two distinct lines are cut by a transversal, a pair of corresponding angles, or alternate interior angles, or alternate exterior angles are congruent if and only if the lines are parallel.

The proof that parallel lines determine congruent corresponding angles depends upon what is known in geometry as the *Parallel Postulate*.

Parallel Postulate | Given a line and a point, P, not on the line, there exists exactly one line through P parallel to the given line.

Remark | This postulate was assumed to be true by Euclid. The denial of this postulate led to the development of non-Euclidean geometries by Karl Gauss (1777–1855), Nikolai Lobachevsky (1792–1856), and János Bolyai (1802–1860).

The sum of the measures of the angles in a triangle can intuitively be shown to be 180° using paper folding, as demonstrated on the student page on page 386 taken from *Scott, Foresman Mathematics*, Grade 6, 1980. This result will be proved using the Parallel Postulate and the properties of parallel lines just discussed.

To prove that the sum of the measures of the angles of a triangle is 180°, consider triangle ABC in Figure 9-35(a). We want to show that $m(\angle 1) + m(\angle 2) + m(\angle 3) = 180°$. To prove this assertion, we show that the sum of the measures of the three angles of the triangle is the same as the measure of a straight angle. This can be accomplished by drawing line ℓ parallel to $\overrightarrow{BC}$ through vertex A, as shown in Figure 9-35(b). Because ℓ and $\overrightarrow{BC}$ are parallel with transversals $\overrightarrow{AB}$ and $\overrightarrow{AC}$, it follows that alternate interior angles are congruent. Consequently, $m(\angle 1) = m(\angle 4)$ and $m(\angle 3) = m(\angle 5)$. Thus, $m(\angle 1) + m(\angle 2) + m(\angle 3) = m(\angle 4) + m(\angle 2) + m(\angle 5) = 180°$. Consequently, $m(\angle 1) + m(\angle 2) + m(\angle 3) = 180°$.

FIGURE 9-35

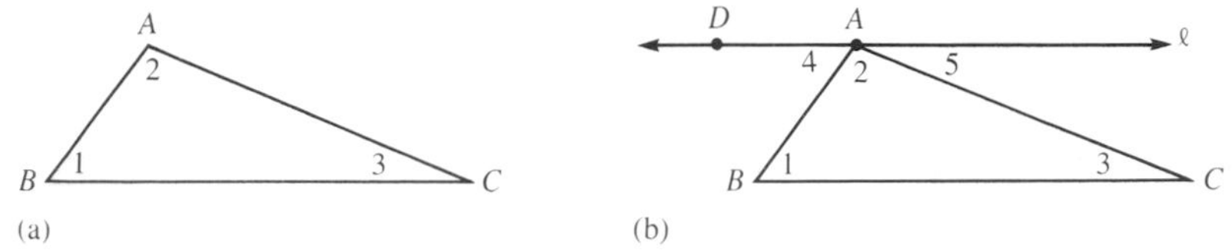

(a)   (b)

The Sum of the Angle Measures in a Triangle

A. This triangle was folded so that point B is on side AC. The fold is parallel to side AC. Then the corners at A and C were folded over to B.

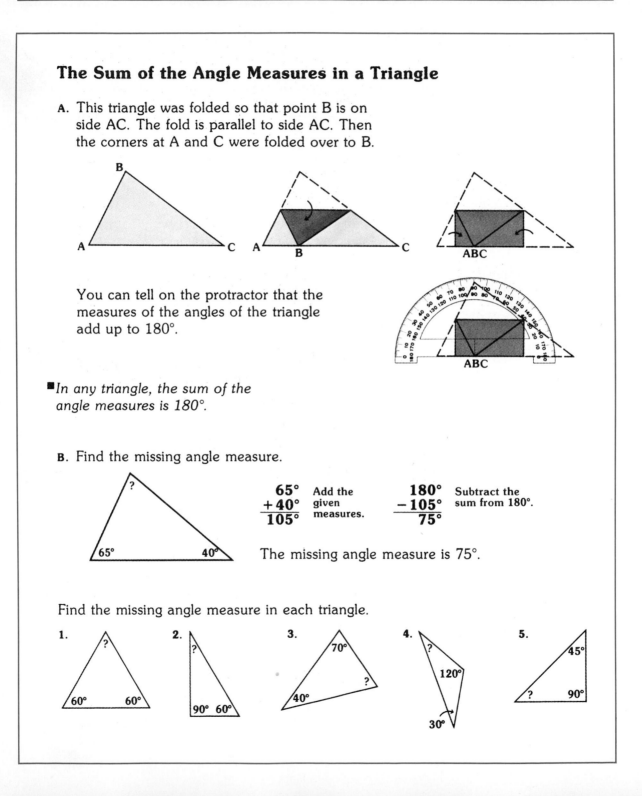

You can tell on the protractor that the measures of the angles of the triangle add up to 180°.

■*In any triangle, the sum of the angle measures is 180°.*

B. Find the missing angle measure.

$$\begin{array}{r} 65° \\ +40° \\ \hline 105° \end{array}$$ Add the given measures.

$$\begin{array}{r} 180° \\ -105° \\ \hline 75° \end{array}$$ Subtract the sum from 180°.

The missing angle measure is 75°.

Find the missing angle measure in each triangle.

1.

2.

3.

4.

5.

Based upon the proof, we have the following theorem.

THEOREM 9-1

The sum of the measures of the angles of a triangle is 180°.

Example 9-7

(a) In Figure 9-36(a), $m(\angle D) = 90°$ and $m(\angle E) = 25°$. Find $m(\angle A)$.
(b) In Figure 9.36(b), the measures of $\angle A$ and $\angle B$ are twice the measure of $\angle C$. Find the measures of each of the angles in the triangle.

FIGURE 9-36

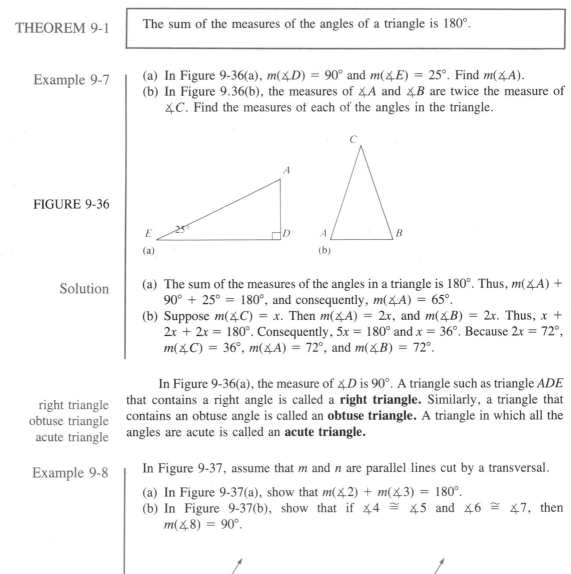

(a)   (b)

Solution

(a) The sum of the measures of the angles in a triangle is 180°. Thus, $m(\angle A) + 90° + 25° = 180°$, and consequently, $m(\angle A) = 65°$.
(b) Suppose $m(\angle C) = x$. Then $m(\angle A) = 2x$, and $m(\angle B) = 2x$. Thus, $x + 2x + 2x = 180°$. Consequently, $5x = 180°$ and $x = 36°$. Because $2x = 72°$, $m(\angle C) = 36°$, $m(\angle A) = 72°$, and $m(\angle B) = 72°$.

In Figure 9-36(a), the measure of $\angle D$ is 90°. A triangle such as triangle ADE that contains a right angle is called a **right triangle.** Similarly, a triangle that contains an obtuse angle is called an **obtuse triangle.** A triangle in which all the angles are acute is called an **acute triangle.**

right triangle
obtuse triangle
acute triangle

Example 9-8

In Figure 9-37, assume that m and n are parallel lines cut by a transversal.

(a) In Figure 9-37(a), show that $m(\angle 2) + m(\angle 3) = 180°$.
(b) In Figure 9-37(b), show that if $\angle 4 \cong \angle 5$ and $\angle 6 \cong \angle 7$, then $m(\angle 8) = 90°$.

FIGURE 9-37

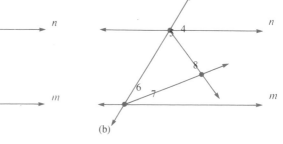

(a)   (b)

Solution | (a) $m(\angle 2) + m(\angle 1) = 180°$. Because $\angle 1$ and $\angle 3$ are corresponding angles formed by a transversal cutting parallel lines, $m(\angle 1) = m(\angle 3)$. Consequently, $m(\angle 2) + m(\angle 3) = 180°$.
(b) Let $m(\angle 4) = m(\angle 5) = x$ and $m(\angle 6) = m(\angle 7) = y$. Then by part (a), it follows that $2x + 2y = 180°$. Dividing both sides of this equation by 2, we obtain $x + y = 90°$. The sum of the measures of angles of a triangle is $180°$, so we have $x + y + m(\angle 8) = 180°$, which implies $m(\angle 8) = 90°$.

PROBLEM 3

Find the sum of the measures of the interior angles in any convex n-gon.

Understanding the Problem

Given a polygon with n sides, we are to find a formula that will give the sum of the measures of the angles. We know that the sum of the measures of the angles in any triangle is $180°$. Any formula that we develop for an n-gon must hold for a triangle.

Devising a Plan

Consider several simple cases before trying to generalize the result. From any vertex of a polygon, diagonals can be drawn to form adjacent nonoverlapping triangles. For example, in the quadrilateral in Figure 9-38(a), the diagonal from B partitions the quadrilateral into two triangles.

FIGURE 9-38

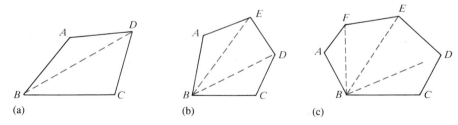

(a)   (b)   (c)

In the pentagon in Figure 9-38(b), the diagonals from B partition the pentagon into three triangles. In the hexagon in Figure 9-38(c), the diagonals from B partition the hexagon into four triangles. In general, the diagonals from a single vertex in any n-gon partition the n-gon into $(n - 2)$ triangles. This fact and the fact that the sum of the measures of the angles of a triangle is $180°$ can be used to solve the problem.

Carrying Out the Plan

Since the sum of the measures of the angles in any triangle is 180°, the sum of the measures of the angles in $(n - 2)$ triangles is $(n - 2)180°$.

Looking Back

An interesting exercise is to determine whether the formula developed holds for concave polygons. Other Looking Back activities using these ideas are given in Example 9-9 and in Problem 13(b) of the Problem Set.

THEOREM 9-2

The sum of the measures of the angles of any convex n-gon is $(n - 2)180°$.

Example 9-9

(a) Find the measure of each angle of a regular decagon.
(b) Find the number of sides of a regular polygon, each of whose angles has a measure of 175°.

Solution

(a) The sum of the measures of the angles in any n-gon is $(n - 2)180°$, and a decagon has ten sides. Thus, the sum of the measures of the angles of a decagon is $(10 - 2)180°$ or 1440°. A regular decagon has ten angles, all of which are congruent, so each one has a measure of $\dfrac{1440°}{10}$, or 144°.

(b) The sum of the measures of the angles is $(n - 2)180°$ and there are n congruent angles, so each angle has a measure of

$$\frac{(n - 2)180}{n}$$

The measure of each angle is 175°, and therefore,

$$\frac{(n - 2)180}{n} = 175$$

To obtain the value of n, we solve this equation as follows.

$$\frac{(n - 2)180}{n} = 175$$
$$(n - 2)180 = 175n$$
$$180n - 360 = 175n$$
$$180n - 175n = 360$$
$$5n = 360$$
$$n = 72$$

Thus, the polygon has 72 sides.

BRAIN TEASER

Find the sum of the measure of the angles ∢1, ∢2, ∢3, ∢4, and ∢5, in any five-pointed star like the one in the accompanying figure. What is the sum of the measures of the angles in any seven-pointed star?

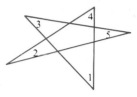

PROBLEM SET 9-3

1. Use a protractor to find the measures of each of the pictured angles.

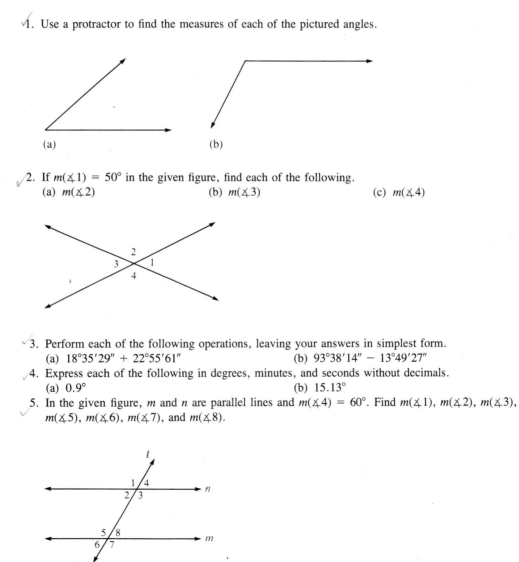

   (a)   (b)

2. If $m(\angle 1) = 50°$ in the given figure, find each of the following.
   (a) $m(\angle 2)$ (b) $m(\angle 3)$ (c) $m(\angle 4)$

3. Perform each of the following operations, leaving your answers in simplest form.
   (a) $18°35'29'' + 22°55'61''$ (b) $93°38'14'' - 13°49'27''$
4. Express each of the following in degrees, minutes, and seconds without decimals.
   (a) $0.9°$ (b) $15.13°$
5. In the given figure, m and n are parallel lines and $m(\angle 4) = 60°$. Find $m(\angle 1)$, $m(\angle 2)$, $m(\angle 3)$, $m(\angle 5)$, $m(\angle 6)$, $m(\angle 7)$, and $m(\angle 8)$.

6. In the following figure, $\overleftrightarrow{DE} \parallel \overleftrightarrow{BC}$, $\overleftrightarrow{EF} \parallel \overleftrightarrow{AB}$ and $\overleftrightarrow{DF} \parallel \overleftrightarrow{AC}$. Also $m(\measuredangle 1) = 45°$ and $m(\measuredangle 2) = 65°$. Find each value.

(a) $m(\measuredangle 3)$ (b) $m(\measuredangle D)$ (c) $m(\measuredangle E)$ (d) $m(\measuredangle F)$

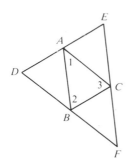

7. In each of the pictured cases, are m and n parallel lines? Justify your answer.

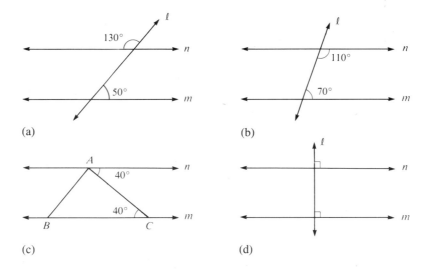

(a)   (b)

(c)   (d)

8. (a) If one of the angles in a triangle is obtuse, can another angle be obtuse? Why?
   (b) If one of the angles in a triangle is acute, can the other two angles be acute? Why?
   (c) Can a triangle have two right angles? Why?
   (d) If a triangle has one acute angle, is it necessarily an acute triangle? Why?

9. Find the measure of the third angle in each of the following triangles.

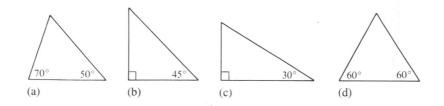

(a)   (b)   (c)   (d)

10. In each figure, find the measures of the angles marked x and y.

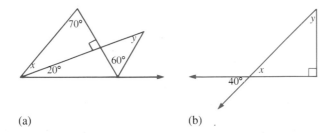

(a)   (b)

11. (a) Find the sum of the measures of the angles of any convex pentagon.
    (b) Find the sum of the measures of the angles of any convex hexagon.
    (c) How many sides does a convex polygon have if the sum of the measures of its angles is 2880°?
12. (a) In a regular polygon, the measure of each angle is 162°. How many sides does the polygon have?
    (b) Find the measure of each of the angles of a regular dodecagon.
13. (a) Show how to find the sum of the measures of the angles of any convex pentagon by choosing any point, P, in the interior and constructing triangles as shown below.

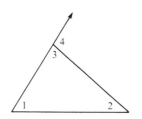

    (b) Using the method suggested by the diagram in part (a), find the sum of the measures of the angles of any convex n-gon. Is your answer the same as the one already obtained in this section, that is, $(n - 2)180$?
14. For the given figure, prove that $m(\angle 4) = m(\angle 1) + m(\angle 2)$.

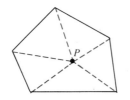

15. Calculate the measure of each angle of a pentagon if the measures of the angles form an arithmetic sequence and the least measure is 60°.
16. What is the measure of an angle whose measure is twice the measure of its complement?
17. If two angles of a triangle are complementary, what is the measure of the third angle?
18. If the measures of the three angles of a triangle are $(3x + 15)°$, $(5x - 15)°$, and $(2x + 30)°$, what is the measure of each angle?
19. In the figure, A is a point not on line ℓ. Why is it impossible to have two distinct perpendicular segments from A to ℓ?

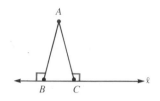

20. Prove that two distinct coplanar lines perpendicular to the same line are parallel.
21. Suppose that the polygon $ABCD$ shown is a parallelogram. Prove each of the following.
   (a) $m(\angle A) + m(\angle B) = 180°$　　　　　　　(b) $m(\angle A) = m(\angle C)$ and $m(\angle B) = m(\angle D)$

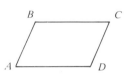

22. Use the definition of a rectangle and properties of parallel lines to show that all the angles in a rectangle are right angles.
★ 23. Prove that if the opposite angles in a quadrilateral are congruent, then the quadrilateral is a parallelogram.
★ 24. In the given figure, prove that $\overrightarrow{AD}$ and $\overrightarrow{CE}$ are parallel. (*Hint:* Draw $\overleftrightarrow{EC}$ and $\overleftrightarrow{AB}$.)

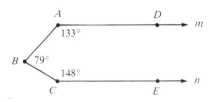

★ 25. For triangle ABC, $m(\angle C) = 102°$, $m(\angle 1) = m(\angle 2)$, and $m(\angle 3) = m(\angle 4)$. Find $m(\angle BPA)$.

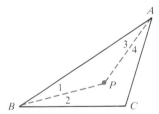

★ 26. What is the measure of the angle between the hands of the clock at exactly 4:37?

* * * * * * * REVIEW PROBLEMS * * * * * * *

27. If four distinct lines lie in a plane, what is the maximum number of intersection points of the four lines?
28. Is it possible for the union of two rays to be a line segment? Explain your answer.
29. Draw a polygonal curve that is closed but not simple.
30. Sketch two angles whose intersection is exactly one line segment.
31. Can two adjacent angles be vertical? Why or why not?

COMPUTER   CORNER

An intuitive justification that the sum of the measures of the angles in a triangle is 180° uses ideas from the computer language Logo and the Logo turtle.

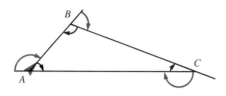

Suppose the turtle represented by the arrowhead is initially positioned at vertex A heading toward vertex B. When the turtle walks along the boundary of the triangle, it turns through each of the exterior colored angles shown until it returns to its initial position and heading. When the turtle has returned to its starting point, it has turned through one complete turn, or 360°. Each interior angle marked in black is the supplement of each exterior angle marked with a colored arrow. Therefore, the sum of measures of the three black interior angles plus the sum of the measures of the three colored exterior angles equals $3 \cdot 180°$. Hence,

$$\text{the sum of the measures of the three black interior angles} = 3 \cdot 180° - \text{the sum of the measures}$$
$$\text{of the three colored exterior angles}$$
$$= 3 \cdot 180° - 360°$$
$$= 180°$$

Thus, the sum of the measures of the angles in a triangle is 180°. Use this idea of Turtle Geometry to find the sum of the measures of the angles in: (a) a pentagon; and (b) an n-gon.

9-4   GEOMETRY IN THREE DIMENSIONS

Most of the concepts developed so far in this chapter have dealt with figures in a plane. Many concepts can be extended to three-dimensional space. In a plane, an angle is the union of two distinct noncollinear rays with a common endpoint. A *dihedral angle* is a plane angle's three-dimensional counterpart. The **dihedral angle** shown in Figure 9-39 consists of all the points on $\overleftrightarrow{AB}$, all the points of the half-plane containing C, and all the points of the half-plane containing D.

dihedral angle

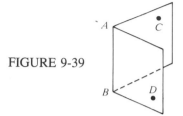

FIGURE 9-39

Perpendicularity also can be extended to three dimensions. For example, in Figure 9-40, planes β and γ represent two walls of the room intersecting along line $\overleftrightarrow{AB}$. The edge, $\overleftrightarrow{AB}$, is perpendicular to the floor. Every line in the plane of the floor (plane α) passing through point A is perpendicular to $\overleftrightarrow{AB}$.

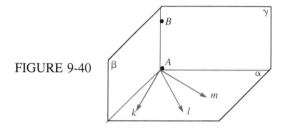

FIGURE 9-40

DEFINITION

> **A line and a plane are perpendicular** if and only if they intersect and the line is perpendicular to every line in the plane that passes through the point of intersection.

The plane containing one wall and the plane containing the floor of a typical room, such as α and β in Figure 9-40, are perpendicular planes. Notice that β and γ contain $\overleftrightarrow{AB}$, which is perpendicular to α. In fact, any plane containing $\overleftrightarrow{AB}$ is perpendicular to plane α.

DEFINITION

> **Two planes are perpendicular** if and only if one plane contains a line perpendicular to the other plane.

simple closed surface

A concept analogous to a simple closed curve in a plane is a **simple closed surface** in space. A simple closed surface partitions space into three sets—points outside the surface, points belonging to the surface, and points inside the surface. Simple closed surfaces have no holes and are hollow. (Simple closed surfaces can be thought of as figures that can be distorted into spheres.) For example, in Figure 9-41, parts (a), (b), and (c) are simple closed surfaces; (d) and (e) are not. A **polyhedron** is a simple closed surface formed entirely by polygonal regions. Parts (a) and (b) of Figure 9-41 are examples of polyhedra, but (c), (d), and (e) are not. The union of the points on a simple closed surface and the interior points is referred to as a **solid.**

polyhedron

solid

FIGURE 9-41

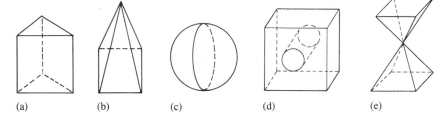

(a)　　　(b)　　　(c)　　　(d)　　　(e)

face
vertices
edges
prism

bases

Each of the polygonal regions of a polyhedron is called a **face.** The vertices of the polygonal regions are called the **vertices** of the polyhedron, and the sides of each polygonal region are called the **edges** of the polyhedron.

A **prism** is a polyhedron in which two congruent polygonal faces lie in parallel planes, and the other faces are bounded by parallelograms. Figure 9-42 shows four different prisms. The parallel faces of a prism, like the faces *ABC* and *DEF* on top and bottom of the prism in Figure 9-42(a), are called the **bases** of the prism. A prism usually is named after its bases. Thus, the prism in Figure 9-42(a) is called a triangular prism, the one in Figure 9-42(b) is a quadrilateral prism, and the prisms in Figure 9-42(c) and (d) are hexagonal prisms.

FIGURE 9-42

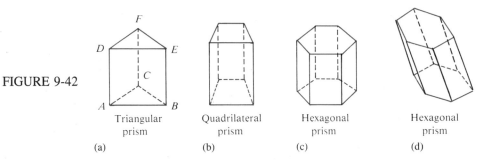

| Triangular prism | Quadrilateral prism | Hexagonal prism | Hexagonal prism |
| (a) | (b) | (c) | (d) |

lateral faces

right prism
oblique prism

pyramid

The **lateral faces** of a prism, the faces other than the bases, are bounded by parallelograms. If the lateral faces of a prism are all bounded by rectangles, the prism is called a **right prism.** The first three prisms in Figure 9-42 are right prisms. Figure 9-42(d) is called an **oblique prism** because its lateral edges are *not* perpendicular to the bases, and, therefore, its faces are *not* bounded by rectangles.

A **pyramid** is a polyhedron determined by a simple closed polygonal region, a point not in the plane of the region, and triangular regions determined by the point and each pair of consecutive vertices of the polygonal region. The polygonal region is called the **base** of the pyramid, and the point is called the **apex.** The faces other than the base are called **lateral faces.** Pyramids are classified according to their bases, as shown in Figure 9-43.

base   apex
lateral faces

FIGURE 9-43

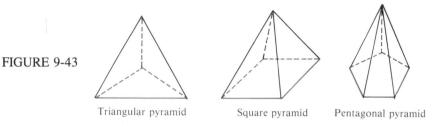

Triangular pyramid   Square pyramid   Pentagonal pyramid

convex polyhedron

A polyhedron is **convex** if and only if a segment connecting any two points in the interior of the polyhedron is itself in the interior. Figure 9-44 shows a polyhedron that is not convex.

FIGURE 9-44

regular polyhedron

A **regular polyhedron** is a polyhedron whose faces are congruent regular polygonal regions such that the number of edges that meet at each vertex is the same for all the vertices of the polyhedron. The ancient Greeks discovered the five regular polyhedra shown in Figure 9-45. A **tetrahedron** is formed by 4 congruent triangular regions; a **cube** is formed by 6 congruent square regions; an **octahedron** is formed by 8 congruent triangular regions; a **dodecahedron** is formed by 12 congruent pentagonal regions; and an **icosahedron** is formed by 20 congruent triangular regions.

tetrahedron
cube   octahedron
dodecahedron
icosahedron

FIGURE 9-45

Regular   Cube   Regular   Regular   Regular
tetrahedron   octahedron   dodecahedron   icosahedron

Platonic solids

These regular, solid polyhedra are also called the **Platonic solids,** after the Greek philosopher Plato (fourth century B.C.). Plato attached a mystical significance to the five regular polyhedra, associating them with what he believed were the four elements—earth, air, fire, water—and the universe. Plato suggested that the smallest particles of earth have the form of a cube, those of air look like an octahedron, those of fire have a tetrahedron shape, those of water are shaped like the icosahedron, and those of the universe have the shape of a dodecahedron.

A simple relationship between the number of faces, edges, and vertices of any polyhedron was discovered by the French mathematician and philosopher René Descartes (1596–1650) and rediscovered by the Swiss mathematician Leonhard Euler (1707–1783). Table 9-3 suggests the relationship for the number of vertices (V), edges (E), and faces (F).

TABLE 9-3

Name	V	F	E	$V + F - E$
Tetrahedron	4	4	6	2
Cube	8	6	12	2
Octahedron	6	8	12	2
Dodecahedron	20	12	30	2
Icosahedron	12	20	30	2

Euler's formula

In each case, $V + F - E = 2$. This result is known as **Euler's formula.**

A cylinder is an example of a simple closed surface that is not a polyhedron. Consider a line segment, $\overline{AB}$, and a line, ℓ, as shown in Figure 9-46. When $\overline{AB}$ moves so that it is always parallel to a given line ℓ and points A and B trace simple closed curves other than polygons, the surface generated by $\overline{AB}$ along with the simple closed curves and their interiors form a **cylinder.** The simple closed curves along with their interiors are called the **bases** of the cylinder and the remaining points constitute the *lateral surface of the cylinder*. Three different cylinders are pictured in Figure 9-46.

cylinder

bases

FIGURE 9-46

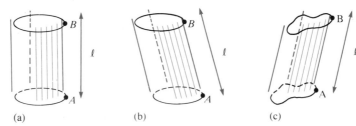

(a)   (b)   (c)

circular cylinder

right cylinder
oblique cylinders

If a base of a cylinder is a circular region, the cylinder is called a **circular cylinder.** If the line segment forming a cylinder is perpendicular to a base, the cylinder is called a **right cylinder.** Cylinders that are not right cylinders are called **oblique cylinders.** The cylinder in Figure 9-46(a) is a right cylinder; those in Figure 9-46(b) and (c) are oblique cylinders.

Suppose we have a simple closed curve, other than a polygon, in a plane and a point, *P*, not in the plane of the curve. The union of the set of line segments connecting point *P* to each point of a simple closed curve and the simple closed curve and its interior is called a **cone.** Cones are pictured in Figure 9-47. Point *P* is called the **vertex** of the cone. The points of the cone that are not in the base constitute the *lateral surface of the cone.* A line segment from the vertex, *P*, perpendicular to the base is called the **altitude.** A **right circular cone,** such as the one in Figure 9-47(a), is a cone whose altitude intersects the base (a circular region) at the center of the circle. Figure 9-47(b) illustrates an oblique cone and Figure 9-47(c) illustrates an **oblique circular cone.**

cone
vertex

altitude
right circular cone

oblique circular cone

FIGURE 9-47

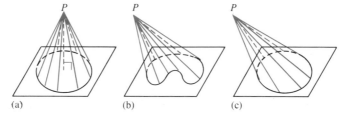

(a)   (b)   (c)

Laboratory Activity

1. The following are patterns for constructing the five regular polyhedra. Enlarge these patterns and fold them appropriately to construct the corresponding polyhedra.

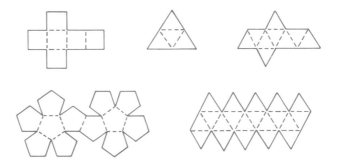

2. (a) Construct a pattern for making a square pyramid.
   (b) Construct a pattern for making a right pentagonal prism. (*Hint:* Imagine a pentagonal prism cut along one of the lateral edges.)
   (c) Construct a pattern for making a right circular cone.

PROBLEM SET 9-4

1. In the given figure, m is a line perpendicular to a plane, α. The intersection of m with α is C. Points A and B are in the plane α. $D \in m$, but $D \notin \alpha$.

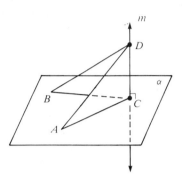

(a) Are triangle BDC and triangle ADC right triangles? Explain your answer.

(b) Is it is possible to find a point, P, in the plane α so that the $\angle DPC$ is obtuse? Justify your answer.

(c) Is the plane determined by the points A, D, and C perpendicular to plane α? Why?

2. (a) Is it possible that a line is perpendicular to one line in a plane but is not perpendicular to the plane?

(b) Can a line be perpendicular to two distinct lines in a plane and not be perpendicular to the plane?

(c) If a line not in a given plane is perpendicular to two distinct lines in the plane, is the line necessarily perpendicular to the plane?

3. Identify each of the following polyhedra. If a polyhedron can be described in more than one way, give as many names as possible.

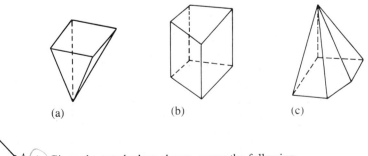

(a)   (b)   (c)

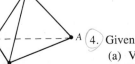

4. Given the tetrahedron shown, name the following.

(a) Vertices   (b) Edges   (c) Faces

(d) Intersection of face DRW and edge $\overline{RA}$.

5. What type of polygon is each face of the following polyhedra?
   (a) Dodecahedron   (b) Icosahedron
6. For each of the following, what is the minimum number of faces possible?
   (a) Prism   (b) Pyramid   (c) Polyhedron
7. Classify each of the following as true or false.
   (a) If the lateral faces of a prism are rectangles, it is a right prism.
   (b) Every pyramid is a prism.
   (c) Every pyramid is a polyhedron.
   (d) The bases of a prism lie in perpendicular planes.
   (e) The bases of all cones are circles.
   (f) A cylinder has only one base.
   (g) All lateral faces of an oblique prism are rectangular regions.
   (h) All regular polyhedra are convex.
8. Given a rectangular prism, how many possible pairs of bases does it have? Explain.
9. For each of the following, draw a prism and a pyramid having the given region as a base.
   (a) Triangle   (b) Pentagon   (c) Regular hexagon
10. Verify Euler's formula for each of the polyhedra in Problem 3.
11. Answer each of the following concerning a pyramid and a prism, each having an n-gon as a base.
    (a) How many faces does it have?
    (b) How many vertices does it have?
    (c) How many edges does it have?
    (d) Use your answers to parts (a), (b), and (c) to verify Euler's formula for all pyramids and all prisms.
12. Complete the table for each of the polyhedra listed below.

Polyhedron	Vertices	Faces	Edges
(a)		8	12
(b)	20	30	
(c)	6		15

13. Check whether Euler's formula holds for each figure.

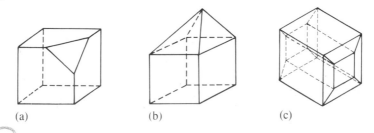

(a)   (b)   (c)

14. Could the congruent faces of the square pyramid be isosceles triangles?

★ 15. In the cube, $\overline{BF}$ and $\overline{AE}$ are diagonals of the upper and lower faces, respectively.

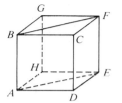

(a) Is quadrilateral ABFE a parallelogram? Is it a rectangle? Explain.
(b) Find six planes perpendicular to the plane containing square ADEH.
(c) Is $\overleftrightarrow{CD}$ parallel to the plane containing the quadrilateral ABFE? Why?

* * * * * * * REVIEW PROBLEMS * * * * * * *

16. Draw a line and label four distinct points, A, B, C, D, in order from left to right. Using your figure, find each of the following.
    (a) $\overline{AB} \cup \overline{BC}$ (b) $\overrightarrow{BC} \cap \overrightarrow{BA}$ (c) $\overleftrightarrow{AD} \cap \overline{BC}$ (d) $\overrightarrow{BA} \cap \overrightarrow{DA}$
17. Is $\overrightarrow{AB} = \overrightarrow{BA}$ for any two points A and B?
18. Why is it not possible to have a polygon with fewer than three sides?
19. How many diagonals does a decagon have?
20. Write 3.14° in terms of degrees, minutes, and seconds without decimals.
21. Is it possible for two planes to intersect in a single point? Why or why not?
22. In the figure, $\overline{AB}$ and $\overline{DE}$ are perpendicular to $\overline{AC}$. Which sets of labeled angles are congruent to each other?

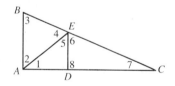

23. Triangles ABC and CDE are equilateral triangles. Find the measure of ∢BCD.

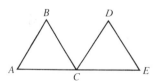

24. What is the measure of each angle in a regular nonagon?
25. Classify the following as true or false. If false, tell why.
    (a) Every rhombus is a parallelogram.
    (b) Every polygon has at least three sides.
    (c) Triangles can have at most two acute angles.
    (d) An angle is a polygon.
    (e) Two vertical angles can be supplementary.
    (f) If ∢ABC ≅ ∢XYZ, then $\overline{AB} \cong \overline{XY}$.

BRAIN TEASER

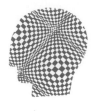

A rectangular region can be rolled to form the lateral surface of a right circular cylinder. What shape of paper is needed to make an oblique circular cylinder? (See "Making a Better Beer Glass" by A. Hoffer.)

*9-5 NETWORKS

A famous problem introduced by Leonhard Euler in 1735 is known as the *Königsberg bridge problem.* The old German city of Königsberg contained a river, two islands, and seven bridges, as shown is Figure 9-48. The problem is to determine if a person can take a walk around the city in such a way that each bridge is crossed exactly once. A person can start at any land area and end at the same or a different land area. The person may visit any part of the city more than once. We designate the land areas A, B, C, and D by points and a path between land areas by a curve connecting the appropriate points.

network
vertices arcs

The diagram in Figure 9-48 is an example of a **network.** The points are called **vertices,** and the curves are called **arcs.** Using a network diagram, the Königsberg bridge problem can be restated as follows: Is there a path through the network beginning at some vertex and ending at the same or another vertex such that each arc is traversed exactly once? A network having such a path is called **traversable,** that is, each arc is passed through exactly once.

traversable

FIGURE 9-48

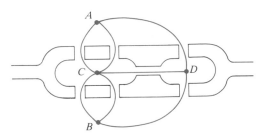

Consider the networks in Figure 9-49. The first three networks, (a), (b), and (c), are traversable; the fourth network, (d), is not. Notice that the number of arcs meeting at each vertex in networks (a) and (c) is even. Any such vertex is called an **even vertex.** If the number of arcs meeting at a vertex is odd, it is called an **odd vertex.** In network (b), only the odd vertices are possible starting or stopping

even vertex
odd vertex

points. In network (d), which is not traversable, all the vertices are odd. If a network is traversable, each arrival at a vertex other than a starting or a stopping point requries a departure. Thus, each vertex that is not a starting or stopping point must be even. The starting and stopping vertices in a traversable network may be even or odd, as seen in Figure 9-49(a) and (b), respectively.

FIGURE 9-49

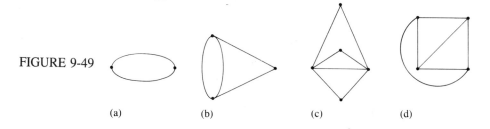

(a) (b) (c) (d)

In general, networks have the following properties:

1. If a network has all even vertices, it is traversable. Any vertex can be a starting point, and the same vertex must be the stopping point.
2. If a network has two odd vertices, it is traversable. One odd vertex must be the starting point, and the other odd vertex must be the stopping point.
3. If a network has more than two odd vertices, it is not traversable.
4. There is no network with exactly one odd vertex.

Example 9-10

Which of the networks in Figure 9-50 are traversable?

(a) (b) (c)

FIGURE 9-50

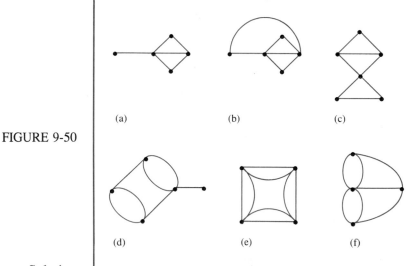

(d) (e) (f)

Solution

Networks in (b) and (e) have all even vertices and therefore are traversable. Networks in (a) and (c) have exactly two odd vertices and are traversable. Networks in (d) and (f) have four odd vertices and are not traversable.

The network of Figure 9-50(f) represents the Königsberg bridge problem. The network has four odd vertices, and consequently, the network is not traversable, and hence, no walk is possible to complete the problem.

Example 9-11

Look at the floor plan of the house shown in Figure 9-51. Is it possible to go through all the rooms of the house and pass through each door only once?

FIGURE 9-51

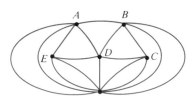

Solution

Represent the floor plan as a network. Designate the rooms and the outside as vertices and the paths through the doors as arcs.

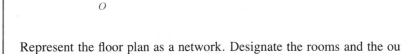

The network has more than two odd vertices, namely, A, B, D, and O. Thus, the network is not traversable, and it is impossible to go through all the rooms and pass through each door only once.

Network problems are useful in determining the most efficient routes for such tasks as mail delivery and garbage collection where it is desirable to travel along a street only once.

PROBLEM SET 9-5

1. Which of the following networks are traversable? If the network is traversable, draw an appropriate path labeling the starting and stopping vertices.

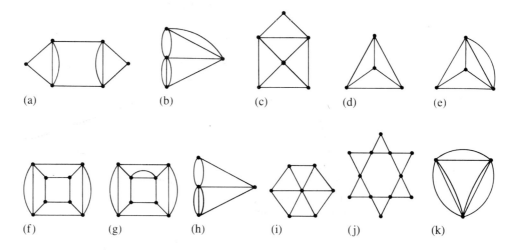

(a)   (b)   (c)   (d)   (e)

(f)   (g)   (h)   (i)   (j)   (k)

2. A city contains a river, three islands, and ten bridges as shown in the accompanying figure. Is it possible to take a walk around the city by starting at any land area and returning after visiting every part of the city and crossing each bridge exactly once? If so, show such a path both on the original figure and on the corresponding network.

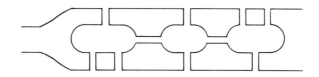

3. Use the accompanying floor plans for each of the following.
   (a) Draw a network that corresponds to each floor plan.
   (b) Determine if it is possible to pass through each room of each house by passing through each door exactly once. If possible, draw such a trip.

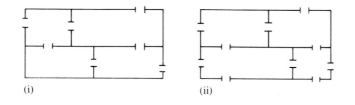

(i)   (ii)

4. Can a person walk through each door once and only once and, also, go through both of the following houses in a single path? If possible, draw such a path.

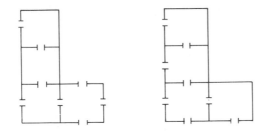

5. At a party, some people shake hands with each other. No person shakes hands more than once with the same person. A person who shakes hands with an odd number of people is called an odd fellow and a person who shakes hands with an even number of people is called an even fellow. Someone makes the statement, "At every party, regardless of how many handshakes take place, the number of odd fellows is even."
   (a) Check the validity of the above statement for at least four different cases by drawing appropriate networks.
   (b) Is a similar statement regarding even fellows true? Why?

6. Euler's formula for polyhedra can be interpreted for networks by designating F as the number of regions in the plane, V as the number of vertices, and E as the number of arcs. For example, network (a) in the figure separates the plane into three regions and network (b) forms only one region, the outside. For network (a), $V - E + F = 2 - 3 + 3 = 2$, and for network (b), $V - E + F = 6 - 5 + 1 = 2$. Verify Euler's formula for each of the networks in Problem 1.

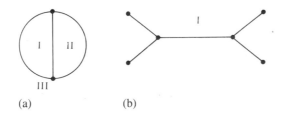

(a)   (b)

7. Molly is making her first trip to the United States and would like to tour the eight states pictured. She would like to plan her trip so that she can cross each border between neighboring states exactly once, that is, the Washington-Oregon border, the Washington-Idaho border, and so on. Is such a trip possible? If so, does it make any difference in which state she starts her trip?

Laboratory Activity

1. Take a strip of paper like the one shown below. Give one end a half-twist and join the ends by taping them. The surface obtained is called a Moebius strip.

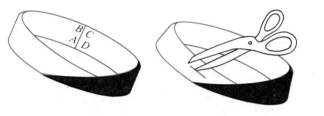

   (a) Use a pencil to shade one side of a Moebius strip. What do you discover?

   (b) Imagine cutting a Moebius strip all around midway between the edges. What do you predict will happen? Now, do the actual cutting. What is the result?

   (c) Imagine cutting a Moebius strip one-third of the way from an edge and parallel to the edge all the way through until you return to the starting point. Predict the result. Then, actually do the cutting. Was your prediction correct?

   (d) Imagine cutting around a Moebius strip one-fourth of the way from an edge. Predict the result. Then, actually do the cutting. How does the result compare to the result of experiment (c)?

2. (a) Take a strip of paper and give it two half-twists (one full twist). Then, join the ends together. Answer the questions in Problem 1.

   (b) Repeat the experiment in (a) using three half-twists.

   (c) Repeat the experiment in (a) using four half-twists. What do you find for odd-numbered twists? Even-numbered twists?

SOLUTION TO THE PRELIMINARY PROBLEM

Understanding the Problem

Tiff A. Nee has to cut assorted triangular pieces from a rectangular plate of glass for a project. The plate contained ten air bubbles, no three in a line. To aid in visualizing the plate, we draw a model as in Figure 9-52 and label the corners of the plate X, Y, Z, and W and the bubbles A through J. One of the many possible ways to cut the glass is illustrated with dotted lines. Observe that in this particular model, there are 22 triangular regions. There are many different ways that the bubbles and corners of the plate could be connected to produce the triangular regions. For example, instead of connecting *B* with *W* and *X*, we could have connected *A* with *W* and *X* to obtain a triangular region. Hence, in devising a solution to the problem, we must determine whether a different configuration yields a different number of triangles or whether the given constraints will always yield twenty-two triangular pieces.

FIGURE 9-52

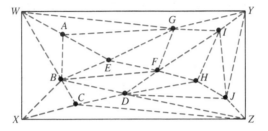

Devising a Plan

The sum of the measures of the angles of all the triangles formed is 180 times the number of triangles. If we knew that sum, we could divide by 180 to find the number of triangles. What is the sum of the measures of all the angles in the triangles? Observe that in Figure 9-52 the angles of the triangles are either angles around the air bubbles or are in the corners of the rectangular plate. No matter how the triangles are drawn, the sum of the measures of the angles of the rectangle is always the same. The sum of the measures of the angles around each bubble is $360°$. Since there are ten bubbles, the sum of the measures of the angles around the bubbles is $10 \cdot 360° = 3600°$. The sum of the measures of the four angles at the corners of the rectangular plate is $360°$; thus, we can find the sum of the measures of the angles in the triangles.

Carrying Out the Plan

The sum of the measures of the angles in all the triangles is $3600° + 360° = 3960°$. Consequently, the number of triangles is $\frac{3960}{180} = 22$, and our model gave us an accurate number.

Looking Back

The problem can be generalized to a plate of glass that is in the shape of a convex *n*-gon with *m* air bubbles. The procedure for solving the problem is similar to the one used in the original problem. The sum of the measures of the angles of the

n-gon is $(n - 2)180$. The sum of the measures of the angles about the air bubbles is $360m$. Hence, the number of the triangles formed is

$$\frac{(n - 2)180 + 360m}{180} = n - 2 + 2m$$

QUESTIONS FROM THE CLASSROOM

1. A student claims that if any two planes that do not intersect are parallel, then any two lines that do not intersect should also be parallel. How do you respond?
2. A student says that it is actually impossible to measure an angle, since each angle is the union of two rays that extend infinitely and, therefore, continue forever. What is your response?
3. A student asks, if every rhombus is a parallelogram, why is a special name for a rhombus necessary? What is your reply?
4. A student asks whether a polygon whose sides are congruent is necessarily a regular polygon and whether a polygon with all angles congruent is necessarily a regu-

lar polygon. How do you answer?
5. A student thinks that a square is the only regular polygon with all right angles. The student asks if this is true and if so, why. How do you answer?
6. A student says that a line is parallel to itself. How do you reply?
7. A student says that a line in the plane of the classroom ceiling cannot be parallel to a line in the plane of the classroom floor since the lines are not in the same plane. Is this student correct? Why?
8. A student says that she heard the shortest distance between any two points is a straight line. Therefore straight lines should have endpoints. What is your reply?

CHAPTER OUTLINE

I. Basic geometrical notions
  A. Properties of points, lines, and planes
    1. **Points, lines,** and **planes** are basic, but undefined, terms.
    2. Through any two points there is one and only one line.
    3. **Collinear points** are points that belong to the same line.
    4. A **line segment** is a subset of a line that contains two distinct points of the line and all the points between them.
    5. **Coplanar points** are points that lie in the same plane.
    6. **Parallel lines** are distinct lines in the same plane that do not intersect.
    7. **Skew lines** are two lines that do not intersect and are not contained in any single plane.
    8. A line that has no points in common with a plane is parallel to the plane.
    9. **Parallel planes** are planes that have no points in common.
    10. **Space** is the set of all points.
    11. **Perpendicular lines** are two lines that intersect to form a right angle.
    12. A line and a plane are perpendicular if and only if they intersect and the line is perpendicular to every line in the plane that passes through the point of intersection.
    13. Two planes are perpendicular if and only if one plane contains a line that is perpendicular to the other plane.
  B. Plane figures
    1. A **plane curve** is a set of points in a plane that can be traced without lifting a pencil from the paper or retracing any portion of the drawing other than single points.
    2. A **simple closed curve** is a plane curve that can be traced so that the starting and stopping points are the same and no point other than the endpoint is traced more than once.
    3. A **polygon** is a simple closed curve that is the union of line segments such that no two

segments with a common endpoint are collinear.

  (a) A **convex polygon** is a polygon with no diagonals in the exterior.

  (b) A **concave polygon** is a polygon with at least one diagonal in the exterior.

  (c) A **regular polygon** is a polygon in which all the angles are congruent and all the sides are congruent.

  (d) A **diagonal** is any line segment connecting two nonconsecutive vertices of a polygon.

II. Angles

  A. An **angle** is the union of two distinct rays with a common endpoint. The rays are called the **sides** and the common endpoint the **vertex.**

    1. **Adjacent angles** are angles with a common vertex, a common side, and whose interiors do not overlap.

    2. **Vertical angles** are nonadjacent angles formed by two intersecting lines.

    3. A **right angle** has a measure of 90°.

    4. An **acute angle** is an angle whose measure is greater than 0° and less than 90°.

    5. An **obtuse angle** is an angle whose measure is greater than 90° and less than 180°.

    6. A **straight angle** has a measure of 180°.

    7. **Supplementary angles** are two angles, the sum of whose measures is 180°.

    8. **Complementary angles** are two angles, the sum of whose measures is 90°.

  B. Two lines cut by a transversal are **parallel** if and only if either congruent corresponding angles, congruent alternate interior angles or congruent alternate exterior angles are formed.

  C. The sum of the measures of the angles in a triangle is 180°.

  D. The sum of the measures of the angles in a convex n-gon is $(n - 2)180°$.

III. Three dimensional figures

  A. A **polyhedron** is a simple closed surface formed by polygonal regions.

  B. **Euler's formula,** $V + F - E = 2$, holds for polyhedra, where V, E, and F represent the number of vertices, the number of edges, and the number of faces of a polyhedron, respectively.

* IV. Networks

  A. A **network** is a collection of points called **vertices** and a collection of curves called **arcs.**

  B. A vertex of a network is called an **even vertex** if the number of arcs meeting at the vertex is even. A vertex is called an **odd vertex** if the number of arcs meeting at a vertex is odd.

  C. A network is called **traversable** if there is a path through the network such that each arc is passed through exactly once.

    1. If all the vertices of a network are even, then the network is traversable. Any vertex can be a starting point and the same vertex must be the stopping point.

    2. If a network has two odd vertices, it is traversable. One odd vertex must be the starting point and the other odd vertex must be the stopping point.

    3. If a network has more than two odd vertices, it is not traversable.

    4. No network has exactly one odd vertex.

CHAPTER TEST

1. (a) List three different names for line m.

  (b) Name two different rays on m with endpoint B.

  (c) Find a simpler name for $\overrightarrow{AB} \cap \overrightarrow{BA}$.

  (d) Find a simpler name for $\overrightarrow{AB} \cap \overrightarrow{BC}$.

  (e) Find a simpler name for $\overrightarrow{BA} \cap \overrightarrow{AC}$.

2. In the figure, $\overleftrightarrow{PQ}$ is perpendicular to α.

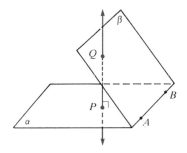

   (a) Name a pair of skew lines.

   (b) Using only the letters in the figure, name as many planes as possible each perpendicular to α.

   (c) What is the intersection of the planes APQ and β.

   (d) Is there a single plane containing A, B, P, and Q? Explain your answer.

3. List at least three ways to determine a plane.

4. For each of the following sketch two parallelograms, if possible, that satisfy the given conditions.

   (a) Their intersection is a single point.

   (b) Their intersection is exactly two points.

   (c) Their intersection is exactly three points.

   (d) Their intersection is exactly one line segment.

5. Draw each of the following curves:

   (a) A simple closed curve   (b) A closed curve that is not simple

   (c) A concave hexagon   (d) A convex decagon

6. Prove that the measure of $\measuredangle 4$ equals the sum of the measures of $\measuredangle 2$ and $\measuredangle 3$.

7. (a) Can a triangle have two obtuse angles? Justify your answer.

   (b) Can a parallelogram have four acute angles? Justify your answer.

8. In a certain triangle, the measure of one angle is twice the measure of the smallest angle. The measure of the third angle is seven times greater than the measure of the smallest angle. Find the measures of each of the angles in the triangle.

9. (a) Explain how to derive an expression for the sum of the measures of the angles in a convex n-gon.

   (b) In a certain regular polygon, the measure of each angle is $176°$. How many sides does the polygon have?

10. (a) Sketch a convex polyhedron with at least ten vertices.

   (b) Count the number of vertices, edges, and faces for the polyhedron in part (a) and determine if Euler's formula holds for this polyhedron.

11. If $3x°$ and $(6x - 18)°$ are measures of corresponding angles formed by two parallel lines and a transversal, what is the value of x?

12. Find $6°48'59'' + 28°19'36''$. Write your answer in simplest terms.

13. In the figure, ℓ is parallel to m, and $m(\measuredangle 1) = 60°$. Find each of the following.

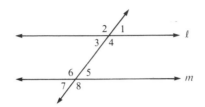

    (a) $m(\measuredangle 3)$ (b) $m(\measuredangle 6)$ (c) $m(\measuredangle 8)$

14. If a pyramid has an octagon for a base, how many lateral faces does it have?

15. If ABC is a right triangle and $m(\measuredangle)A = 42°$, what is the measure of the other acute angle?

* 16. (a) Which of the following networks are traversable?

    (b) Find a corresponding path for those networks that are traversable.

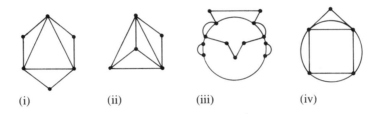

    (i)   (ii)   (iii)   (iv)

SELECTED BIBLIOGRAPHY

Alexick, H., and F. Kidder. "Why Is a Rectangle Not a Square?" *Arithmetic Teacher* 27 (December 1979):26–27.

Anderson, H. "Griefless Graphing for the Novice." *The Mathematics Teacher* 66 (October 1973):519–522.

Barr, S. *Experiments in Topology*. New York: Thomas Y. Crowell, 1964.

Beard, R. *Patterns in Space*. Palo Alto, Calif.: Creative Publications, 1973.

Bright, G. "Using Tables to Solve Some Geometry Problems." *Arithmetic Teacher* 25 (May 1978), 39–43.

Brydegaard, M., and J. Inskeep, Jr. *Readings in Geometry from the Arithmetic Teacher*. Washington, D.C.: National Council of Teachers of Mathematics, 1970.

Charles, R. "Some Guidelines for Teaching Geometry Concepts." *Arithmetic Teacher* 27 (April 1980):18–20.

Cohen, D. *Inquiry in Mathematics via the Geoboard, Teacher Guide*. New York: Walker Educational Book Corp., 1967.

Cundy, H., and A. Rollett. *Mathematical Models*. London: Oxford University Press, 1961.

Damarin, S. "What Makes a Triangle." *Arithmetic Teacher* 29 (September 1981):39–41.

Gilbert, E. "The Ways to Build a Box." *The Mathematics Teacher* 64 (December 1971):689–695.

Golomb, S. *Polyominoes*. New York: Charles Scribner's Sons, 1965.

Henderson, G., and C. Collier. "Geometric Activities for Later Childhood Education." *The Arithmetic Teacher* 20 (October 1973):444–453.

Hoffer, A. "Making a Better Beer Glass." *The Mathematics Teacher* 75 (May 1982):378–379.

Immerzeel, G. "Geometric Activities for Early Childhood Education." *The Arithmetic Teacher* 20 (October 1973):438–443.

Laycock, M. *Straw Polyhedra*. Palo Alto, Calif.: Creative Publications, 1970.

Lietzmann, W. *Visual Topology*. London: Chatto and Windus, 1969.

Morrell, L. "GE-O-ME-TR-Y." *Arithmetic Teacher* 27 (March 1980):52.

O'Daffer, P., and S. Clemens. *Geometry: an Investigative Approach*. Reading, Mass.: Addison-Wesley, 1976.

Ore, O. *Graphs and Their Uses*. New York: Random House, L. W. Singer, 1963.

Phillips, J. "The History of the Dodecahedron." *The Mathematics Teacher* 58 (March 1965): 248–250.

Ryan, Sister M., S.S.N.D. "Probability and the Platonic Solids." *The Mathematics Teacher* 64 (November 1971):621–624.

Shengle, C. "A Look at Regular and Semi-Regular Polyhedra." *The Mathematics Teacher* 65 (December 1972):713–718.

Toth, L. *Regular Figures.* Oxford: Pergamon Press, 1964.

Trigg, C. "Collapsible Models of Regular Octahedrons." *The Mathematics Teacher* 65 (October 1972):530–533.

Wahl, M. "Marshmallows, Toothpicks, and Geodesic Domes." *Arithmetic Teacher* 25 (December 1977):39–42.

Walter, M. "Frame Geometry: An Example in Posing and Solving Problems." *Arithmetic Teacher* 28 (October 1980):16–18.

Wenninger, M. *Polyhedron Models.* New York: Cambridge University Press, 1970.

Wenninger, M. *Polyhedron Models for the Classroom.* Washington, D.C.: National Council of Teachers of Mathematics, 1966.

Young, J. "Improving Spatial Abilities with Geometric Activities." *Arithmetic Teacher* 30 (September 1982):38–43.

Zaslavsky, C. "Networks—New York Subways, A Piece of String, and African Traditions." *Arithmetic Teacher* 29 (October 1981):42–47.

PRELIMINARY PROBLEM

At the site of an ancient settlement, archaeologists found a fragment of a saucer as shown. To restore the saucer, the archaeologists had to determine the radius of the original saucer. How can they find the radius?

INTRODUCTION

In this chapter we introduce the concepts of congruence and similarity. Properties of congruent triangles are investigated through compass and straightedge constructions. Construction problems have always been a favorite topic in geometry. The restriction to ruler and compass goes back to antiquity. The straight line and circle were considered the basic geometrical figures by the Greeks and the straightedge and compass are their physical analogues. It is also believed that the Greek philosopher Plato (427–347 B.C.) rejected the use of other mechanical devices because they emphasized practicality rather than "ideas," which he regarded as more important. Many important mathematical results were discovered as by-products of efforts to solve various challenging construction problems. In teaching geometry, compass-and-ruler constructions are important because they reinforce the learning of geometrical concepts. The basic constructions, which are introduced and explained in this chapter, are summarized in a step-by-step approach in Appendix III. Constructions are also done using paperfolding and a Mira, a plastic device that acts as a reflector.

Throughout the chapter we use linear metric measurement and the notion of length, although a formal discussion of measurement is postponed until Chapter 11.

10-1   CONGRUENCE THROUGH CONSTRUCTIONS

In mathematics, the word *congruence* is used to describe objects that have exactly the same size and shape. For example, the two squares in Figure 10-1 are congruent because each has a side of measure 2 cm (centimeters). We say that *ABCD* is congruent to *EFGH* and write *ABCD* ≅ *EFGH*.

Tracing is a method for determining congruence in elementary schools. For example, the squares in Figure 10-1 are congruent because a tracing of one square can be made to match the other.

Any two line segments have the same shape, so *two line segments are congruent if they have the same size (length). Two angles are congruent if their measures are the same.* Also, any segment is congruent to itself and any angle is congruent to itself.

FIGURE 10-1

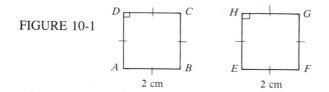

Ancient Greek mathematicians constructed geometric figures with a straight-edge (no markings on it) and a collapsible compass. Figure 10-2(a) shows a modern compass. It is used to mark off and duplicate lengths but not to measure them. The compass is also used to draw arcs or circles as in Figure 10-2(b). To draw a circle or an arc, open the compass to some width; hold the pointer in place, marking the center of the circle or arc; then, move the pencil. The figure formed is a circle or an arc.

FIGURE 10-2

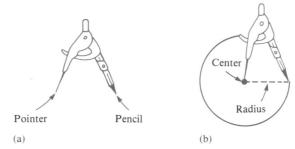

Pointer   Pencil

(a)

Center

Radius

(b)

circle
radius
center

The construction of a circle with a compass shows that a **circle** can be defined as the set of all points in a plane at a given distance, the **radius,** from a given point, the **center.** The notation used in this text for a circle with center C is circle C.

arc

An **arc** of a circle can be thought of as any part of the circle that can be drawn without lifting a pencil. An arc is either a part of a circle or the entire circle. Two points on a circle determine two different arcs. To avoid this ambiguity, an arc is normally named by three letters, such as arc ACB as in Figure 10-3. Arc ACB is denoted by $\overset{\frown}{ACB}$. In this notation, the first and last letters indicate the endpoints of the arc, while the middle letter indicates which of two possible arcs is intended. If there is no danger of ambiguity in a discussion, we use two letters to name the smaller arc formed. For example, in Figure 10-3, the smaller arc is

minor arc
major arc
semicircle

named either $\overset{\frown}{ACB}$ or $\overset{\frown}{AB}$. The smaller arc is called the **minor arc.** The larger arc, called the **major arc,** is always named by three letters, such as $\overset{\frown}{ADB}$. If the major arc and the minor arc of a circle are the same size, each is called a **semicircle.**

There are many ways to construct a segment congruent to a given segment, $\overline{AB}$. A natural approach is to use a ruler, measure $\overline{AB}$, and then draw the congruent segment. A different way is to trace $\overline{AB}$ onto another piece of paper. A third method is to use a straightedge and compass. To copy $\overline{AB}$ on any line, ℓ, using a compass, first fix the compass so that the pointer is on A and the pencil is on B, as in Figure 10-4(a). The compass opening represents the length of $\overline{AB}$. Then, on ℓ, we choose a point C. Next, without changing the compass setting, place the point of the compass at C and strike an arc that intersects the line, as in Figure 10-4(b). Label the point of intersection of the arc and the line as D. Then, $\overline{AB} \cong \overline{CD}$. (A summary of each boxed construction in this chapter is given in Appendix III.)

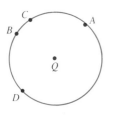

FIGURE 10-3

FIGURE 10-4
reproduce a line segment

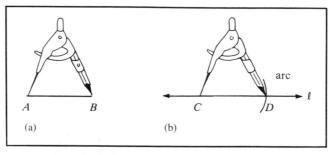

(a)   (b)

In Figure 10-5(a), circle C is given. By placing the compass point at an arbitrary point Q and opening the compass to a width equal to CR, circle Q can be constructed congruent to circle C. Thus, *two circles are congruent if their radii have the same length.*

FIGURE 10-5
construct a circle

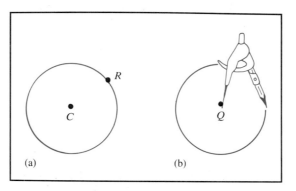

(a)   (b)

We use the concept of congruence for segments and angles as the basis for determining whether polygons, specifically triangles, are congruent. Attempting to construct congruent triangles provides motivation for necessary and sufficient conditions for determining congruent triangles.

Consider the two triangles shown in Figure 10-6. If triangle ABC is congruent to triangle $A'B'C'$, written $\triangle ABC \cong \triangle A'B'C'$, then the congruency establishes a one-to-one correspondence between vertices A and A', B and B', C and C' such that $\overline{AB} \cong \overline{A'B'}$, $\overline{AC} \cong \overline{A'C'}$, $\overline{BC} \cong \overline{B'C'}$, $\angle A \cong \angle A'$, $\angle B \cong \angle B'$, and $\angle C \cong \angle C'$.

FIGURE 10-6

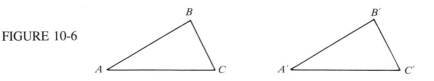

The order of the letters in the symbolic congruence is important. For example, in Figure 10-7, if $\triangle ABC \cong \triangle DEF$, then vertex A corresponds to vertex D, B corresponds to E, and C corresponds to F. This correspondence also identifies the congruent angles and sides of the triangles, as listed.

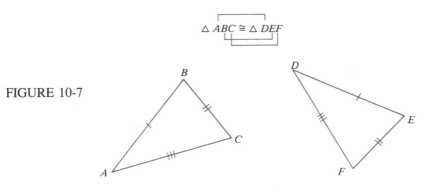

FIGURE 10-7

$$\angle A \cong \angle D, \ \angle B \cong \angle E, \text{ and } \angle C \cong \angle F$$

$$\overline{AB} \cong \overline{DE}, \ \overline{BC} \cong \overline{EF}, \text{ and } \overline{AC} \cong \overline{DF}$$

If △*ABC* ≅ △*DEF*, as in Figure 10-7, then any rearrangement of the letters *ABC* and a corresponding rearrangement of *DEF* results in another symbolic representation of the same congruence. For example, △*BAC* ≅ △*EDF*. There are 3 · 2 · 1, or 6, ways to rearrange the letters *ABC*, so each pair of congruent triangles can be symbolized in six ways. However, each of the six symbolic representations gives the same information about the triangles.

Example 10-1 | Assume that each of the pairs of triangles in Figure 10-8 is congruent and write an appropriate symbolic congruence in each case.

FIGURE 10-8

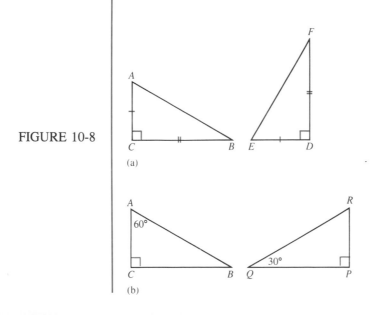

(a)

(b)

Solution

(a) Vertex C corresponds to D because the angles at C and D are right angles. Also, $\overline{CB} \cong \overline{DF}$ and C corresponds to D, so B corresponds to F. Consequently, the remaining vertices must correspond; that is, A corresponds to E. Thus, one possible symbolic congruence is $\triangle ABC \cong \triangle EFD$.

(b) Vertex C corresponds to P because the angles at C and D are both right angles. To establish the other correspondences, we first find the missing angles in the triangles. We see that $m(\angle B) = 90° − 60° = 30°$ and $m(\angle R) = 90° − 30° = 60°$. Consequently, A corresponds to R because $m(\angle A) = m(\angle R) = 60°$ and B corresponds to Q because $m(\angle B) = m(\angle Q) = 30°$. Thus, one possible symbolic congruence is $\triangle ABC \cong \triangle RQP$.

Is it necessary to use all three sides and all three angles of a $\triangle ABC$ to construct another triangle congruent to it? Actually, $\triangle ABC$ can be duplicated by copying fewer parts of the triangle. For example, using only segments of lengths AB, BC, and AC, as shown in Figure 10-9(a), we can construct $\triangle A'B'C'$ congruent to $\triangle ABC$.

FIGURE 10-9

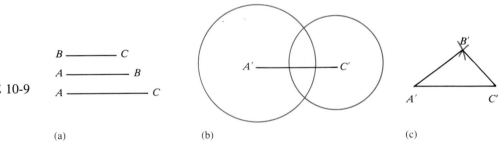

(a)   (b)   (c)

First, we construct $\overline{A'C'}$ so that it is congruent to $\overline{AC}$. To complete the triangle construction, the other vertex, B', must be located. The distance from A' to B' is AB. All points at a distance AB from A' are on a circle with center at A' and radius AB. Similarly, B' must be on a circle with center C' and radius of length BC. Figure 10-9(b) shows the two circles. Because B' is on both circles, the only possible locations for B' are at the points where the two circles intersect. Either point is acceptable. Usually a picture of the construction shows only one possibility, and the construction uses only arcs as pictured in Figure 10-9(c).

From the above construction, it may seem that given any three segments it is possible to construct a triangle whose sides are congruent to the given segments. However, this is not the case. For example, consider the segments in Figure 10-10(a), whose measures are p, q, and r. If we choose the base of the triangle to be a side of length p and attempt to find the third vertex by intersecting arcs, as in Figure 10-10(b), we find that the arcs do not intersect. Because no intersection occurs, a triangle is not determined.

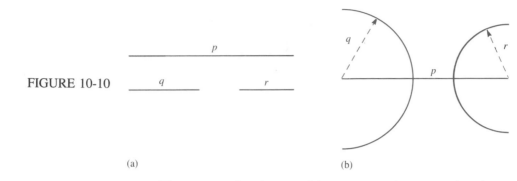

FIGURE 10-10

(a)   (b)

Thus, we see that *the sum of the measures of any two sides of a triangle must be greater than the measure of the third side*. For example, segments of length 3 cm, 5 cm, and 9 cm do not determine a triangle because $3 + 5$ is not greater than 9.

The construction in Figure 10-10 suggests that the size and shape of a triangle is determined by its three sides. In other words, if three sides of one triangle are congruent, respectively, to three sides of another triangle, then the triangles are congruent. This property is called **Side, Side, Side** and is abbreviated **SSS.**

Side, Side, Side (SSS)

Property | **Side, Side, Side (SSS)** If the three sides of one triangle are congruent, respectively, to the three sides of a second triangle, then the triangles are congruent.

Example 10-2 | For each of the parts in Figure 10-11, use SSS to explain why the given pair of triangles is congruent.

FIGURE 10-11

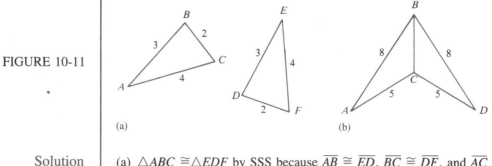

(a)   (b)

Solution | (a) $\triangle ABC \cong \triangle EDF$ by SSS because $\overline{AB} \cong \overline{ED}$, $\overline{BC} \cong \overline{DF}$, and $\overline{AC} \cong \overline{EF}$.
(a) $\triangle ABC \cong \triangle DBC$ by SSS because $\overline{AB} \cong \overline{DB}$, $\overline{AC} \cong \overline{DC}$, and $\overline{BC} \cong \overline{BC}$.

We use the SSS notion of congruent triangles to construct an angle congruent to a given angle ∡*B* by making ∡*B* a part of a triangle and then by reproducing this triangle. For example, given ∡B in Figure 10-12(a), we draw a segment having endpoints A and C on the sides of ∡B to determine △ABC. Then construct △A'B'C' congruent to △ABC using SSS, as shown in Figure 10-12(b). Because congruent triangles have corresponding congruent parts, ∡B ≅ ∡B'.

FIGURE 10-12

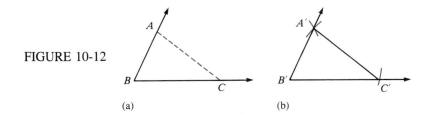

(a)   (b)

A more efficient way to copy ∡B is as follows. First, construct an isosceles triangle, △ABC, with $\overline{AB} \cong \overline{BC}$ by marking off any arc $\overset{\frown}{AC}$ with center B. Then, duplicate the triangle. Figure 10-13 shows the construction.

FIGURE 10-13
copy an angle

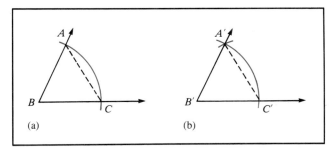

(a)   (b)

We have seen that three sides of a triangle determine the triangle. Are two sides sufficient to determine a triangle; that is, are two sides sufficient to construct a triangle congruent to a given triangle? Two line segments are given in Figure 10-14(a). Figure 10-14(b) shows three different triangles with sides congruent to the given segments. The length of the third side depends on the measure of the angle between the other two sides. Hence, congruent triangles are not determined by two segments; we must also specify the angle included between the segments. Figure 10-15 shows the construction of a triangle congruent to △ABC using two sides $\overline{AB}$ and $\overline{AC}$ and the *included angle,* ∡A, formed by these sides. First, a ray with an arbitrary endpoint A' is drawn, and $\overline{A'C'}$ is constructed congruent to $\overline{AC}$. Then, ∡A' is constructed so that ∡A' ≅ ∡A, and B' is marked on the side of ∡A' not containing C' so that $\overline{A'B'} \cong \overline{AB}$. Connecting B' and C' completes △A'B'C' so that △A'B'C' ≅ △ABC.

FIGURE 10-14

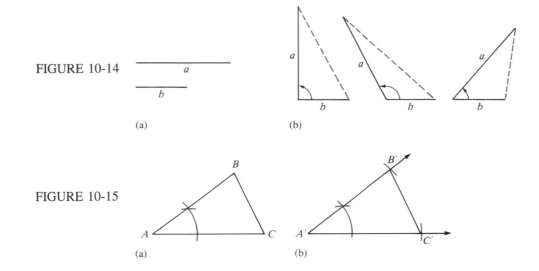

(a)   (b)

FIGURE 10-15

(a)   (b)

Side, Angle, Side (SAS)

Thus, two triangles are congruent if two corresponding sides and the included angle of each triangle are congruent. This property is called **Side, Angle, Side** and is abbreviated **SAS.**

Property

Side, Angle, Side (SAS)   If two sides and the included angle of one triangle are congruent to two sides and the included angle of another triangle, respectively, then the two triangles are congruent.

Remark

When A is written between S and S, as in SAS, it is assumed to be the included angle.

Example 10-3

For each part of Figure 10-16, use SAS to prove that the given pair of triangles is congruent.

FIGURE 10-16

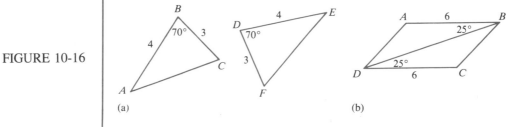

(a)   (b)

Solution

(a) $\triangle ABC \cong \triangle EDF$ by SAS because $\overline{AB} \cong \overline{ED}$, $\measuredangle B \cong \measuredangle D$, and $\overline{BC} \cong \overline{DF}$.
(b) $\triangle ABC \cong \triangle CDB$ by SAS because $\overline{AB} \cong \overline{CD}$, $\measuredangle ABD \cong \measuredangle CDB$, and $\overline{DB} \cong \overline{DB}$.

Example 10-4

Given isosceles triangle ABC with $\overline{AB} \cong \overline{AC}$ and $\overrightarrow{AD}$ the bisector of $\angle A$, as shown in Figure 10-17, use SAS to prove that $\angle B \cong \angle C$.

FIGURE 10-17

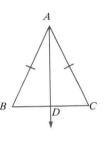

Solution

Because $\overrightarrow{AD}$ is the bisector of $\angle A$, then $\angle BAD \cong \angle CAD$. Also, $\overline{AD} \cong \overline{AD}$ and $\overline{AB} \cong \overline{AC}$, so $\triangle BAD \cong \triangle CAD$ by SAS. Therefore, $\angle B \cong \angle C$ because the angles are corresponding parts of congruent triangles.

Remark

Example 10-4 proves that the *base angles of an isosceles triangle are congruent*.

If, in two triangles, two sides and an angle not included between these sides are respectively congruent, the information is not sufficient to guarantee congruent triangles. For example, use $\overline{AB}$, $\overline{AC}$, and $\angle C$ of Figure 10-18(a). By making $\overline{A'C'} \cong \overline{AC}$, reproducing $\angle C$ as $\angle C'$, and finding the set of all points at a distance AB from A', it is possible to construct two noncongruent triangles, as shown in Figure 10-18(b) and (c). In certain special cases, if the arc formed by the circle with center A' and radius AB intersects the side of $\angle C$ in exactly one point, only one triangle can be formed. (For what kind of triangles does this happen? For what cases is no triangle formed?)

FIGURE 10-18

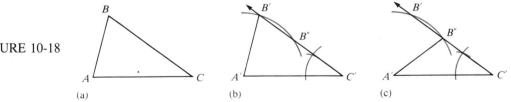

(a)   (b)   (c)

PROBLEM SET 10-1

1. For each of the following, determine whether the given conditions are sufficient to prove that $\triangle PQR \cong \triangle MNO$. Justify your answer.
   (a) $\overline{PQ} \cong \overline{MN}$, $\overline{PR} \cong \overline{MO}$, $\angle P \cong \angle M$
   (b) $\overline{PQ} \cong \overline{MN}$, $\overline{PR} \cong \overline{MO}$, $\overline{QR} \cong \overline{NO}$
   (c) $\overline{PQ} \cong \overline{MN}$, $\overline{PR} \cong \overline{MO}$, $\angle Q \cong \angle N$

2. For each of the following, determine whether the two triangles, (1) and (2), are congruent. Justify your answer.

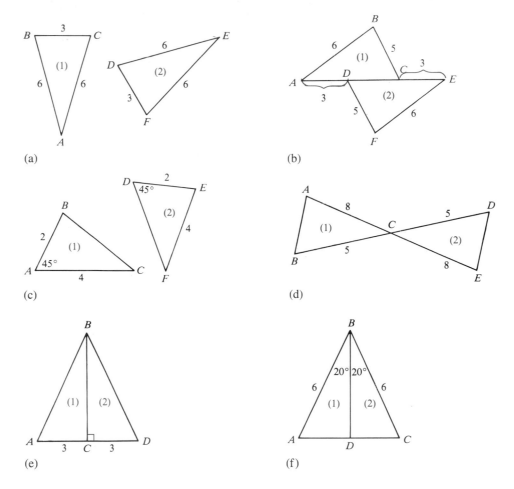

(a)   (b)

(c)   (d)

(e)   (f)

3. Using a ruler, protractor, compass, or tracing paper, construct each of the following, if possible.
   (a) A segment congruent to $\overline{AB}$ and an angle congruent to $\angle CAB$

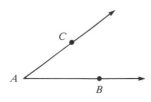

   (b) A triangle with sides of lengths 2 cm, 3 cm, and 4 cm
   (c) A triangle with sides of lengths 4 cm, 3 cm, and 5 cm (What kind of triangle is it?)
   (d) A triangle with sides 4 cm, 5 cm, and 10 cm
   (e) An equilateral triangle with sides 5 cm

(f) A triangle with sides 6 cm and 7 cm and an included angle of measure 75°

(g) A triangle with sides 6 cm and 7 cm and a nonincluded angle of measure 40°

(h) A right triangle with legs 4 cm and 8 cm (The legs include the right angle.)

4. For each of the conditions in Problem 3(b)–(h), does the given information determine a unique triangle? Explain why or why not.

5. Using only a compass and straightedge, perform each of the following.

(a) Reproduce ∡A.   (b) Construct an equilateral triangle with side $\overline{AB}$.

(c) Construct a 60° angle.

(d) Construct an isosceles triangle with ∡A as the angle included between the two congruent sides.

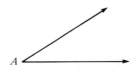

6. Prove that an equilateral triangle is also equiangular.

7. In the accompanying drawing, $\overrightarrow{BD}$ bisects ∡ABC of isosceles triangle ABC with $\overline{AB} \cong \overline{CB}$. Prove each of the following.

(a) $\overline{AD} \cong \overline{CD}$ (the angle bisector bisects the base).

(b) ∡ADB and ∡CDB are right angles (the angle bisector is perpendicular to the base).

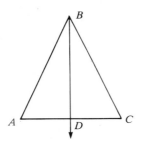

8. In the following figure, find all congruent triangles. Justify your answer. Circle O has radius OA. Circle A has radius AC. Circle B has radius BC. $\overline{BC} \cong \overline{AC}$.

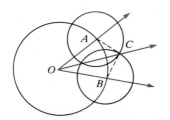

9. Suppose polygon *ABCD* is any square. Prove that the diagonals of the square bisect each other.

10. Prove that a quadrilateral in which the diagonals bisect each other is a parallelogram.

11. A group of students on a hiking trip wants to find the distance *AB* across a pond. One student suggests choosing any point *C*, connecting it with *B* and then finding point *D* such that ∢*DCB* ≅ ∢*ACB* and $\overline{DC} \cong \overline{AC}$. How and why does this help in finding the distance *AB*?

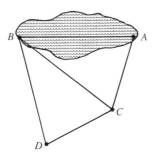

COMPUTER CORNER

Logo programs can be used to construct triangles using parts of a triangle. Type the program below into your computer and then run the following.
(a) SAS 50 75 83
(b) SAS 60 120 60

```
TO SAS :SIDE1 :ANGLE :SIDE2
FORWARD :SIDE1
RIGHT 180 - :ANGLE
FORWARD :SIDE2
HOME
END
```

10-2   OTHER CONGRUENCE THEOREMS

We have seen that triangles can be determined to be congruent by SSS and SAS. Can a triangle be constructed congruent to a given triangle using two angles and a side? There are two possibilities, one with the side included between the angles and one with the side not between the angles. Figure 10-19 shows the construction of a triangle congruent to $\triangle ABC$ using $\measuredangle A$ and $\measuredangle C$ and the included side $\overline{AC}$. Hence, $\triangle A'B'C'$ can be constructed congruent to $\triangle ABC$. This property of congruence is called **Angle, Side, Angle** and is abbreviated **ASA.**

Angle, Side, Angle (ASA)

FIGURE 10-19

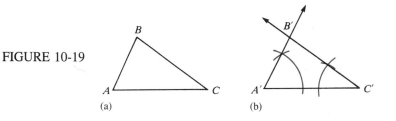

(a)   (b)

Property | **Angle, Side, Angle (ASA)** If two angles and the included side of one triangle are congruent to two angles and the included side of another triangle, respectively, then the triangles are congruent.

Angle, Angle, Side (AAS)

Angle, Angle, Side (abbreviated **AAS**) follows directly from ASA. Because the sum of the measures of the angles in any triangle is 180°, if two angles in one triangle are congruent to two angles in another triangle, then the third angle must also be congruent. Consequently, the triangles are congruent by ASA.

Property | **Angle, Angle, Side (AAS)** If two angles and a side of one triangle are congruent to two angles and a side of another triangle, respectively, then the triangles are congruent.

Example 10-5 | Use ASA to prove that each of the given pairs of triangles in Figure 10-20 are congruent.

FIGURE 10-20

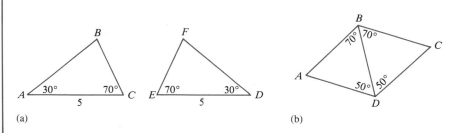

(a)   (b)

Solution | (a) $\angle A \cong \angle D$, $\overline{AC} \cong \overline{DE}$, and $\angle C \cong \angle E$. Consequently, by ASA, $\triangle ABC \cong \triangle DFE$.
(b) $\angle ABD \cong \angle CBD$, $\overline{BD} \cong \overline{BD}$, and $\angle ADB \cong \angle CDB$. Consequently, by ASA, $\triangle ABD \cong \triangle CBD$.

Example 10-6 | Use AAS to prove that each of the given pairs of triangles in Figure 10-21 are congruent.

FIGURE 10-21

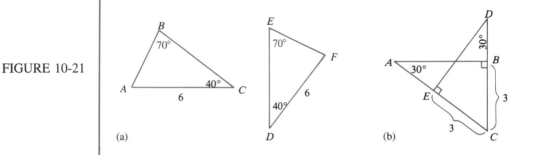

(a)   (b)

Solution | (a) $\angle B \cong \angle E$, $\angle C \cong \angle D$, and $\overline{AC} \cong \overline{FD}$. Consequently, by AAS, $\triangle ABC \cong \triangle FED$.
(b) $\angle A \cong \angle D$, $\angle ABC \cong \angle DEC$, and $\overline{BC} \cong \overline{EC}$. Consequently, by AAS, $\triangle ABC \cong \triangle DEC$.

In Figure 10-22, the angles of one triangle are congruent to corresponding angles in another triangle, and the triangles are not congruent. Thus, an AAA property for congruency does not exist. (The triangles are *similar,* a concept discussed later in this chapter.)

FIGURE 10-22

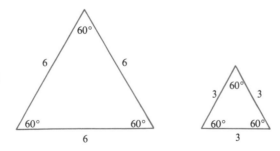

The properties of congruent triangles can be used in a variety of ways. One common use is to show that angles or segments of a given figure are congruent.

Example 10-7 | Given square $ABCD$ in Figure 10-23, use congruent triangles to prove that the diagonals $\overline{AC}$ and $\overline{BD}$ are congruent.

FIGURE 10-23

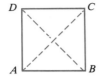

Solution

We need to show that the diagonals $\overline{AC}$ and $\overline{BD}$ are congruent. These diagonals are sides in different triangles. Diagonal $\overline{AC}$ is in right triangle ABC and $\overline{BD}$ is a side in right triangle BAD. If it is true that $\triangle ABC \cong \triangle BAD$, then because corresponding parts in congruent triangles are congruent, $\overline{AC} \cong \overline{BD}$. Because $\overline{BC} \cong \overline{AD}$, $\overline{AB} \cong \overline{BA}$, and $\angle A \cong \angle B$ (using the definition of a square), it follows by SAS that $\triangle ABC \cong \triangle BAD$. From this congruence, we conclude that $\overline{AC} \cong \overline{BD}$.

PROBLEM 1

Prove that a quadrilateral in which all sides are congruent is a rhombus.

Understanding the Problem

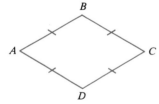

A quadrilateral is a four-sided figure, as shown in Figure 10-24. We are told that all the sides of the quadrilateral are congruent and we have to show that the figure is a rhombus. Recall that a rhombus is a parallelogram in which all sides are congruent. Thus, we must show that the given quadrilateral is a parallelogram.

FIGURE 10-24

Devising a Plan

To show that a quadrilateral is a parallelogram, it is sufficient to show that its opposite sides are parallel. Thus, we need to show that $\overleftrightarrow{AB} \parallel \overleftrightarrow{DC}$ and $\overleftrightarrow{AD} \parallel \overleftrightarrow{BC}$. This can be done by showing that a pair of alternate interior angles, alternate exterior angles or corresponding angles formed by a transversal are congruent.

Carrying Out the Plan

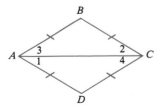

FIGURE 10-25

To show that $\overleftrightarrow{BC}$ and $\overleftrightarrow{AD}$ are parallel, a transversal, such as the diagonal $\overline{AC}$ in Figure 10-25, is needed. The diagonal forms $\angle 1$ and $\angle 2$, which are alternate interior angles of the lines $\overleftrightarrow{BC}$ and $\overleftrightarrow{AD}$. Are these angles congruent? Using SSS, we see that $\triangle ABC \cong \triangle CDA$; hence, the corresponding parts of the triangles—specifically, the desired angles—are congruent. It follows that $\overleftrightarrow{BC} \parallel \overleftrightarrow{AD}$. From the congruence of triangles ABC and CDA, it follows that $\angle 3 \cong \angle 4$ and hence that $\overleftrightarrow{AB} \parallel \overleftrightarrow{DC}$. (Why?) Thus, $ABCD$ is a parallelogram and hence a rhombus.

Looking Back

One possible Looking Back activity is to investigate if a quadrilateral in which all angles are congruent must also be a rhombus.

Determining congruency conditions for polygons other than triangles is not an easy task. For example, the SSS property for congruent triangles has no analogy for quadrilaterals. The quadrilaterals in Figure 10-26 are not the same shape. *One way to be sure that two polygons are congruent is to know that all corresponding sides and angles of the polygons are congruent.* This may be done by "moving" one figure to see if it "fits" exactly on top of the other figure. The moving process is discussed in more detail in Sections 10-4 and 10-5.

FIGURE 10-26

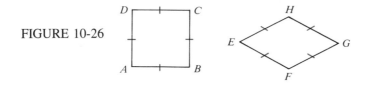

PROBLEM SET 10-2

1. For each of the following, determine whether the given conditions are sufficient to prove that $\triangle PQR \cong \triangle MNO$. Justify your answer.
   (a) $\angle Q \cong \angle N$, $\angle P \cong \angle M$, $\overline{PQ} \cong \overline{MN}$
   (b) $\angle R \cong \angle O$, $\angle P \cong \angle M$, $\overline{QR} \cong \overline{NO}$
   (c) $\overline{PQ} \cong \overline{MN}$, $\overline{PR} \cong \overline{MO}$, $\angle N \cong \angle Q$
   (d) $\angle P \cong \angle M$, $\angle Q \cong \angle N$, $\angle R \cong \angle O$
2. Determine whether each of the following pairs of triangles, (1) and (2), is congruent. Justify your answer.

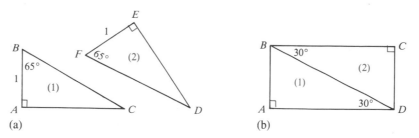

(a)   (b)

3. Use a ruler, protractor, compass, or tracing paper to construct each of the following, if possible.
   (a) A triangle with angles 60° and 70° and an included side of 8 inches.
   (b) A triangle with angles 60° and 70° and nonincluded side of 8 cm on a side of the 60° angle.

(c) A right triangle with one acute angle of 75° and a leg of 5 cm on a side of the 75° angle.

(d) A triangle with angles of 30°, 70°, and 80°.

4. For each of the conditions in Problem 3(a)–(d), is it possible to construct two noncongruent triangles? Explain why or why not.

5. Using only a compass and straightedge, perform each of the following.

   (a) Construct $\measuredangle C$ so that $m(\measuredangle C) = m(\measuredangle A) + m(\measuredangle B)$.

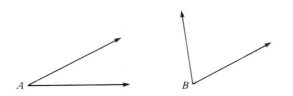

   (b) Using the angles in part (a), construct $\measuredangle C$ so that $m(\measuredangle C) = m(\measuredangle B) - m(\measuredangle A)$.

6. What information is necessary to determine congruency for each of the following?

   (a) Two squares   (b) Two rectangles

7. Suppose polygon $ABCD$ is any parallelogram. Use congruent triangles to·prove each of the following.

   (a) $\measuredangle A \cong \measuredangle C$ and $\measuredangle B \cong \measuredangle D$ (opposite angles are congruent).

   (b) $\overline{BC} \cong \overline{AD}$ and $\overline{AB} \cong \overline{CD}$ (opposite sides are congruent).

   (c) $\overline{BF} \cong \overline{DF}$ and $\overline{AF} \cong \overline{CF}$ (the diagonals bisect each other).

   (d) Prove that $\measuredangle DAB$ and $\measuredangle ABC$ are supplementary.

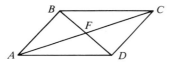

8. Suppose polygon $ABCD$ is any rectangle. Use congruent triangles to prove each of the following.

   (a) $\overline{AC}$ and $\overline{BD}$ bisect each other (the diagonals bisect each other).

   (b) $\overline{BD} \cong \overline{AC}$ (the diagonals are congruent).

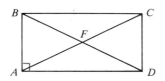

9. (a) Construct quadrilaterals having exactly one, two, and four right angles.

   (b) Why can a convex quadrilateral not have exactly three right angles?

   (c) Can a parallelogram have exactly two right angles?

10. In parallelogram $ABCD$ below, suppose $\overline{PQ}$ is any segment with endpoints on the parallelogram containing the intersection point, O, of the diagonals. Prove $\overline{OP} \cong \overline{OQ}$.

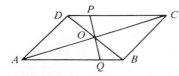

11. If $\overline{AB}$ is perpendicular to plane α, $\measuredangle C \cong \measuredangle D$ and points C, B, D are in plane α, prove that $\overline{AC} \cong \overline{AD}$.

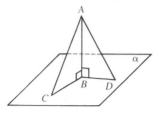

12. If $\overline{AD}$ is perpendicular to plane α and $\overline{AO} \cong \overline{OD}$, prove each of the following.
 (a) $\overline{AB} \cong \overline{BD}$ (b) $\overline{AC} \cong \overline{CD}$ (c) $\measuredangle CAB \cong \measuredangle CDB$

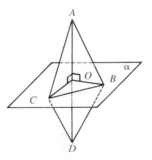

13. If $ABCDE$ is a regular pentagon, prove that $\overline{AC} \cong \overline{CE} \cong \overline{BE} \cong \overline{BD} \cong \overline{DA}$.

* * * * * * * REVIEW PROBLEMS * * * * * * *

14. If possible, construct a triangle having the following three segments, a, b, c, as its sides.

        a b c
   ├──────────────┤   ├────────┤   ├────────────────┤

15. Construct an equilateral triangle whose sides are congruent to the following segment.

   ├────────────────┤

16. For each pair of triangles shown, determine whether the given conditions are sufficient to show that the triangles are congruent. If the triangles are congruent, tell which property can be used to verify this fact.

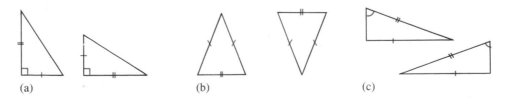

   (a)   (b)   (c)

COMPUTER  CORNER

Logo programs can be used to construct triangles using parts of a triangle. Type the given programs into your computer and then run the following.

(a) ASA 60 50 70
(b) ASA 80 50 60
(c) AAS 60 50 70
(d) AAS 130 20 50

```
TO ASA :ANGLE1 :SIDE :ANGLE2
RIGHT 90
FORWARD 120
BACK 120
LEFT :ANGLE1
FORWARD :SIDE
RIGHT (180 - :ANGLE2)
FORWARD 120
END

TO AAS :ANGLE1 :ANGLE2 :SIDE
ASA :ANGLE1 :SIDE 180 - (:ANGLE1 + :ANGLE2)
END
```

BRAIN TEASER

A treasure map, shown in the accompanying figure, floated ashore in a bottle. It showed Shipwreck Island, where a treasure was buried. According to the directions on the map, the treasure is equidistant from two roads, one joining Bluebeard's Cove with Bottle O'Rum Inn and the other joining Long John's Bay with Bottle O'Rum Inn. Also, the treasure is equidistant from Long John's Bay and the Bottle O'Rum Inn. Can you find the treasure?

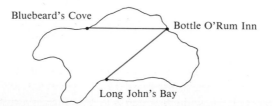

Bluebeard's Cove

Bottle O'Rum Inn

Long John's Bay

10-3 OTHER CONSTRUCTIONS

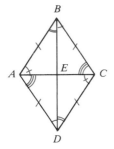

FIGURE 10-27

In the previous chapter, we defined a rhombus as a parallelogram with all sides congruent. In this section, we investigate properties of a rhombus and use these properties to do basic compass and straightedge constructions.

In the rhombus $ABCD$ in Figure 10-27, diagonals $\overline{AC}$ and $\overline{BD}$ intersect at E. By the definition of a rhombus, $\overline{AB} \cong \overline{BC} \cong \overline{CD} \cong \overline{DA}$. In addition, because a rhombus is a parallelogram, its opposite sides are parallel and hence alternate interior angles formed along the diagonals are congruent.

It appears in Figure 10-27 that BD and AC are perpendicular to each other. One way to prove that $\overline{AC} \perp \overline{BD}$ is to show that $\angle AEB$ and $\angle CEB$ are congruent and supplementary. We leave this as an exercise. It can also be proved that diagonals $\overline{AC}$ and $\overline{BD}$ bisect each other. (Bisecting a segment results in separating the segment into two congruent parts.) In addition, it can be shown that $\overline{BD}$ bisects the angles of the rhombus at vertices B and D, and $\overline{AC}$ bisects the angles at A and C. The proofs of these properties are left as exercises.

A summary of the properties of a rhombus follows:

Properties

1. The diagonals of a rhombus are perpendicular to each other.
2. The diagonals of a rhombus bisect each other.
3. The diagonals of a rhombus bisect the vertex angles of the rhombus.

The properties of a rhombus can be used for a variety of constructions. For example, to construct a line parallel to a given line ℓ through a point P not on ℓ, consider the following. In Figure 10-28(a), in constructing a line parallel to ℓ through point P, our strategy is to construct a rhombus with one of its vertices at P and one of its sides on line ℓ. Because the opposite sides of a rhombus are parallel, one of the sides through P will be parallel to ℓ. Through P we draw any line interesecting ℓ, as shown in Figure 10-28(b). We then construct a rhombus, as shown in Figure 10-28(c); $\overrightarrow{PY}$ is the required line parallel to ℓ.

FIGURE 10-28
construct parallel lines
(rhombus method)

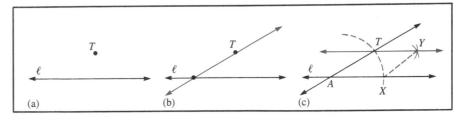

Figure 10-29 shows another way to do the construction. If congruent corresponding angles are formed by a transversal cutting two lines, then the lines are parallel. Thus, the first step is to draw a transversal through P that intersects ℓ.

The angle marked α is formed by the transversal and line ℓ. By constructing an angle with a vertex at P congruent to α, as shown in Figure 10-29(b), congruent corresponding angles are formed; therefore, $m \parallel \ell$. Two more ways to construct parallel lines use congruent alternate interior or alternate exterior angles. (These constructions are left as exercises.)

FIGURE 10-29
construct parallel lines
(corresponding angle
method)

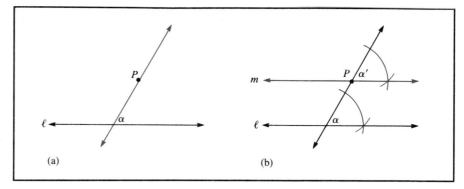

(a)

(b)

angle bisector

Another construction that is based upon a property of a rhombus is that of constucting an **angle bisector.** In Figure 10-30(a), given $\angle A$, a rhombus having A as a vertex and sides on the rays is constructed. The diagonal of the rhombus through A bisects $\angle A$, as shown in Figure 10-30(b). In other words, $\overrightarrow{AC}$ bisects $\angle A$.

FIGURE 10-30
bisect an angle

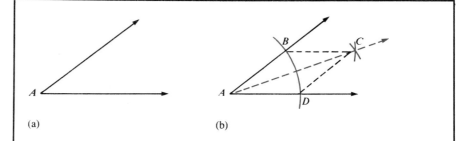

(a)

(b)

In order to construct a line through p perpendicular to line ℓ, where P is not a point on ℓ, as shown in Figure 10-31(a), again use properties of the diagonals of a rhombus. Recall that the diagonals of a rhombus are perpendicular to each other. By constructing a rhombus with a vertex at P and two vertices A and B on ℓ, as in Figure 10-31(b), the segment connecting the fourth vertex Q to P is perpendicular to ℓ because $\overline{AB}$ and $\overline{PQ}$ are diagonals. To obtain A and B, we choose any length longer than the distance between P and ℓ and draw an arc with center P that intersects ℓ. Then, the rhombus with vertices P, A, and B can be completed and the perpendicular determined.

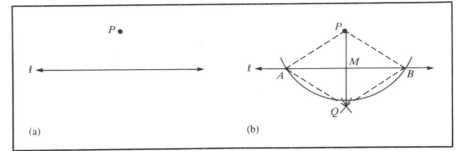

(a)   (b)

To construct the perpendicular bisector of a line segment $\overline{AB}$, as shown in Figure 10-32(a), we use the fact that the diagonals of a rhombus are perpendicular bisectors of each other. The construction yields a rhombus such that $\overline{AB}$ is one of its diagonals. The other diagonal of the rhombus is the perpendicular bisector. Arcs with the same radius and with centers at A and B are drawn. The points P and Q where the arcs intersect are the other vertices of the rhombus since $\overline{AP} \cong \overline{PB} \cong \overline{AQ} \cong \overline{BQ}$. Connecting P and Q gives the perpendicular bisector of $\overline{AB}$ at M.

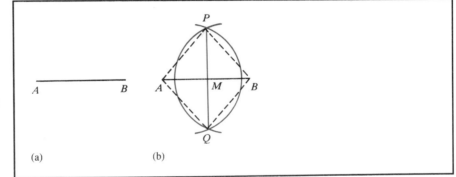

(a)   (b)

Determining a perpendicular to a line ℓ at a point P on ℓ, as shown in Figure 10-33(a), is also based on a property of a rhombus. We determine points A and B on ℓ so that P is the midpoint of $\overline{AB}$. Then, we construct any rhombus with two vertices at A and B. In Figure 10-33(b), $ADBC$ is such a rhombus, and $\overleftrightarrow{CD}$ is the required perpendicular. Notice that since point P is given, the required perpendicular could have been determined by connecting C with P.

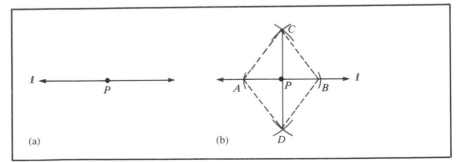

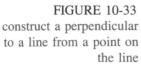

(a)   (b)

Angles and intersecting lines

Try these constructions. Check the results by measuring the angles with a protractor.

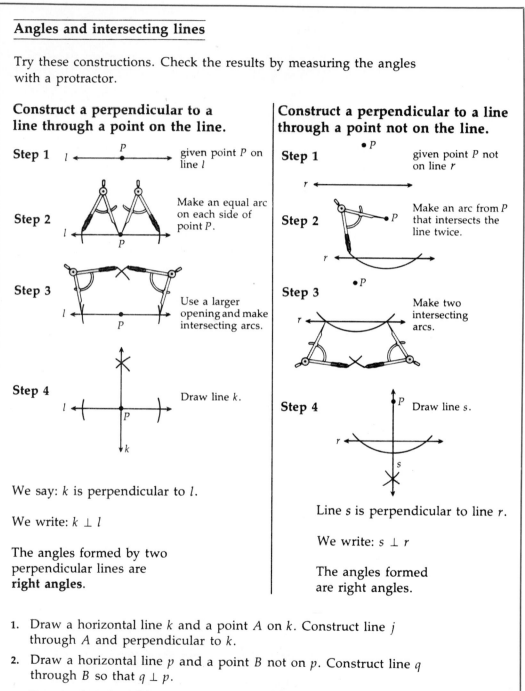

Construct a perpendicular to a line through a point on the line.

Step 1   given point P on line l

Step 2   Make an equal arc on each side of point P.

Step 3   Use a larger opening and make intersecting arcs.

Step 4   Draw line k.

We say: k is perpendicular to l.

We write: $k \perp l$

The angles formed by two perpendicular lines are **right angles**.

Construct a perpendicular to a line through a point not on the line.

Step 1   given point P not on line r

Step 2   Make an arc from P that intersects the line twice.

Step 3   Make two intersecting arcs.

Step 4   Draw line s.

Line s is perpendicular to line r.

We write: $s \perp r$

The angles formed are right angles.

1. Draw a horizontal line k and a point A on k. Construct line j through A and perpendicular to k.

2. Draw a horizontal line p and a point B not on p. Construct line q through B so that $q \perp p$.

3. Do exercises 1 and 2 with lines k and p drawn vertically.

This construction is shown in the sample on page 438 from *Mathematics in Our World,* 1979, Grade 8, by Addison-Wesley.

The perpendicularity constructions can also be completed by paper folding or by using a Mira. A Mira is a plastic device that acts as a reflector so that the image of an object can be seen behind the Mira. The drawing edge of the Mira acts as a folding line on paper. In fact, any construction demonstrated in this text that uses paper folding can be done using a Mira.

To construct a perpendicular to a given line ℓ at a point P on the line using paper folding, we fold the line onto itself as in Figure 10-34(a). The fold line is perpendicular to ℓ. To perform the construction with a Mira, we place the Mira with the drawing edge on P, as in Figure 10-34(b), so that ℓ is reflected onto itself. The line along the drawing edge is the required perpendicular.

FIGURE 10-34

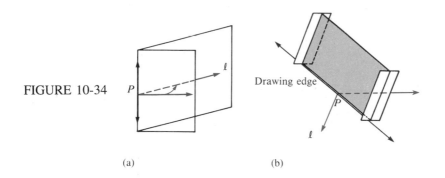

(a)   (b)

Using this same procedure, it is possible to construct any number of lines perpendicular to ℓ. In Figure 10-35, m and n are both perpendicular to ℓ. Since two lines perpendicular to the same line are parallel, $m \parallel n$. Thus, perpendicularity constructions can be used to construct parallel lines.

FIGURE 10-35

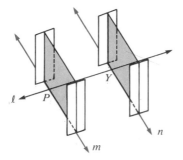

A Mira can also be used to construct the bisector of an angle by placing the Mira on the vertex of the angle and reflecting one side of the angle onto the other.

Consider the angle bisector in Figure 10-36. It seems that any point P on the angle bisector is equidistant from the sides of the angle; that is, $\overline{PD} \cong \overline{PE}$. (The distance from a point to a line is the length of the perpendicular from the point to the line.)

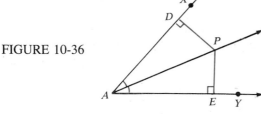

FIGURE 10-36

To prove this, find two congruent triangles that have these segments as corresponding sides. The only triangles pictured are $\triangle ADP$ and $\triangle AEP$. What do we know about these triangles? Since $\overrightarrow{AP}$ is the angle bisector, $\measuredangle DAP \cong \measuredangle EAP$. Also, $\measuredangle PDA$ and $\measuredangle PEA$ are right angles and are thus congruent. Since $\overline{AP}$ is congruent to itself, $\triangle PDA \cong \triangle PEA$ by AAS. Thus, $\overline{PD} \cong \overline{PE}$ because they are corresponding parts of congruent triangles PDA and PEA. Consequently, *any point P on an angle bisector is equidistant from the sides of the angle*. It can also be proved that if a point is equidistant from the sides of an angle, it must be on the angle bisector of that angle.

perpendicular bisector

A different type of bisector is the **perpendicular bisector** of a segment, that is, a line perpendicular to the segment through the midpoint of the segment. In Figure 10-37(a), ℓ is the perpendicular bisector of $\overline{AB}$. Consider some point P on ℓ. It appears that P is equidistant from points A and B; that is, $\overline{PA} \cong \overline{PB}$. To prove this, we find two congruent triangles with sides $\overline{PA}$ and $\overline{PB}$. Triangles PCA and PCB, as shown in Figure 10-37(b), are such triangles.

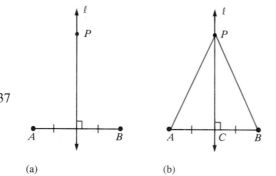

FIGURE 10-37

(a)   (b)

Because ℓ is the perpendicular bisector of $\overline{AB}$, $\overline{AC} \cong \overline{BC}$ and $\measuredangle PCA$ and $\measuredangle PCB$ are congruent right angles. Also, $\overline{PC} \cong \overline{PC}$ so that $\triangle PCA \cong \triangle PCB$ by SAS. Hence, $\overline{PA} \cong \overline{PB}$ since the line segments are corresponding sides of congruent triangles. Since P is an arbitrary point, it follows that *any point on the perpendicular bisector of a line segment is equidistant from the endpoints of the segment*. It can also be proved that a point equidistant from the endpoints of a segment must be on a perpendicular bisector of the segment.

PROBLEM SET 10-3

1. Given a rhombus *ABCD*, prove the following.
   (a) The diagonals bisect each other.
   (b) The diagonals bisect the vertex angles of the rhombus.
   (c) The diagonals are perpendicular to each other.

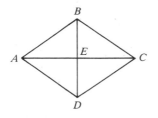

2. Determine which properties of a rhombus listed in Problem 1 are true for any parallelogram.
3. Use a compass and straightedge to construct a line *m* through *P* parallel to ℓ using each of the following.
   (a) Alternate interior angles
   (b) Alternate exterior angles

4. Construct each of the following using (i) a compass and straightedge, (ii) paper folding, and (iii) a Mira, if available.
   (a) Bisector of $\measuredangle A$ (b) Perpendicular bisector of $\overline{AB}$

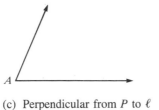

   (c) Perpendicular from *P* to ℓ

5. An **altitude** of a triangle is the perpendicular from a vertex to the opposite side or extended side of the triangle. Construct the three altitudes of each of the following triangles using any method.

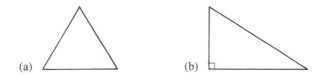

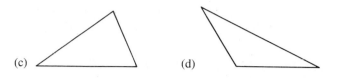

(c)   (d)

6. Construct the perpendicular bisectors of each of the sides of the triangles in Problem 5.
7. A **median** of a triangle is a segment from a vertex of the triangle to the midpoint of the opposite side. Construct the three medians of each triangle in Problem 5.
8. Prove that the medians of an equilateral triangle are congruent.
9. If two opposite sides of a quadrilateral are parallel and congruent, prove that the quadrilateral is a parallelogram.
10. If both pairs of opposite sides of a quadrilateral are congruent, prove that the quadrilateral is a parallelogram.
11. Prove that the figure formed by joining the midpoints of the sides of a rectangle is a rhombus.

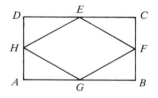

12. Prove that the figure formed by joining the midpoints of the sides of a parallelogram is a parallelogram.
13. Construct a square with $\overline{AB}$ as a side.

14. Using a compass and straightedge, construct a parallelogram with A, B, and C as vertices.

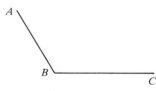

15. Using only a compass and a straightedge, construct angles with each of the following measures.
    (a) 30°   (b) 15°   (c) 45°
    (d) 75°   (e) 105°
16. In the accompanying figure, show that $\overrightarrow{PQ}$ is the perpendicular bisector of $\overline{AB}$.

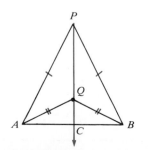

17. A planning committee for a new tri-city airport wants to build the airport so that it will be the same distance from each city. A map of the three cities is shown. How can the location of the airport be found?

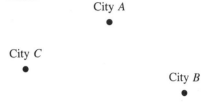

City A

City C

City B

18. Construct each of the following, if possible. If not possible, explain why.
    (a) A square given its side.
    (b) A square given its diagonal.
    (c) A rectangle given its diagonal.
    (d) A parallelogram given two of its adjacent sides.
    (e) A rhombus given two of its diagonals.
  ★ (f) An isosceles triangle given its base and the angle opposite the base.
  ★ (g) A trapezoid given four of its sides.
★ 19. Prove that the figure formed by joining the midpoints of the sides of a rhombus is a rectangle.

* * * * * * *   REVIEW PROBLEMS   * * * * * * *

20. For each of the following, determine whether the two triangles (1) and (2) are congruent. Justify your answers.

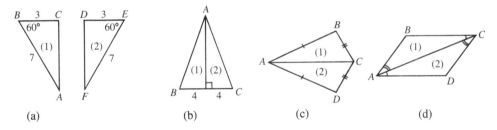

(a)   (b)   (c)   (d)

21. Given $\overrightarrow{AB} \parallel \overrightarrow{ED}$ and $\overline{BC} \cong \overline{CE}$, why is $\overline{AC} \cong \overline{CD}$?

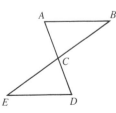

22. Draw △ABC; then, construct △PQR congruent to △ABC by each method.
    (a) Using two sides of △ABC and an angle included between these sides.
    (b) Using the three sides of △ABC.
    (c) Using two angles and a side included between these angles.

BRAIN TEASER

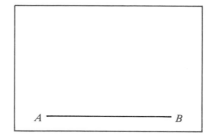

Given $\overline{AB}$ in the accompanying figure, use a compass and a straightedge to construct the perpendicular bisector of $\overline{AB}$. You are not allowed to put any marks outside the border.

A ——————————— B

10-4   CONGRUENCE VIA SLIDES AND FLIPS

In the first three sections of this chapter, we developed congruence using tracings. Euclid seems to have envisioned moving one geometric figure and placing it on top of another to determine if the two figures were congruent. The results of two simple types of motion, slides and flips, are illustrated in Figure 10-38(a) and (b), respectively.

FIGURE 10-38

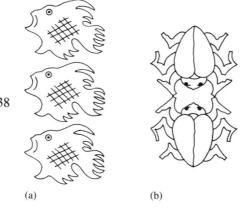

(a)   (b)

slide
translation

slide arrow

In Figure 10-39 a child gliding down a slide has moved a certain distance, d, in a certain direction along a line. This type of motion is called a **slide,** or **translation.** *A slide (translation) is a motion of a specified distance and direction along a straight line without any accompanying twisting or turning.* Distance and direction of a slide are both indicated by a **slide arrow.** Figure 10-40 shows a slide of $\triangle ABC$ to $\triangle A'B'C'$. The arrow indicates a slide of d units to the right. The drawing on the piece of paper labeled X is traced upon the tracing paper labeled Y.

When the tracing paper is slid along the slide line, $\overrightarrow{MN}$, until M matches N, the slide images of A, B, and C are A', B', and C'. The physical motion of sliding tracing paper establishes a one-to-one correspondence between the points of plane X and itself such that $AA' = BB' = CC' = d$ and such that $\overline{AA'} \parallel \overline{BB'} \parallel \overline{CC'}$. Notice that any point of plane X has exactly one image point and, moreover, that each point is the image of some point.

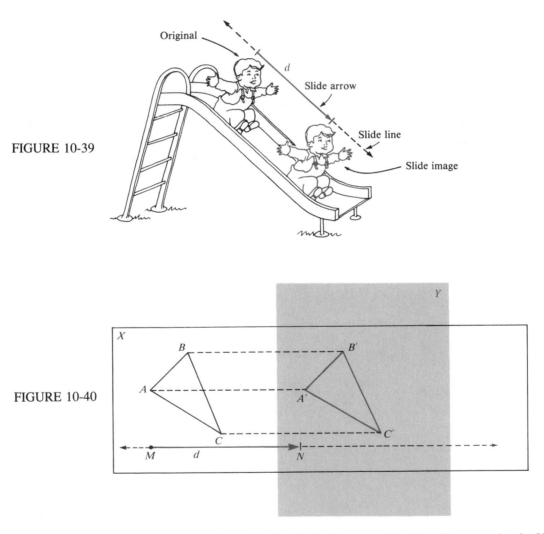

FIGURE 10-39

FIGURE 10-40

flip, reflection

Another transformation is called a **flip,** or a **reflection.** One example of a flip often encountered in our daily lives is a mirror image. Figure 10-41 shows a figure with its mirror image.

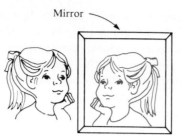

Mirror

FIGURE 10-41

In a plane, we can simulate reflections in various ways. Consider the half

flip line

flip image

tree shown in Figure 10-42(a). Folding the paper along the **flip line** ℓ and drawing the image gives the **flip image** of the tree. In Figure 10-42(b), the paper is unfolded. The figure obtained is symmetric about the fold line in much the same way that a mirror gives symmetry in space. Another way to simulate a reflection or flip in a line uses a Mira and is illustrated in Figure 10-43.

FIGURE 10-42
(left)

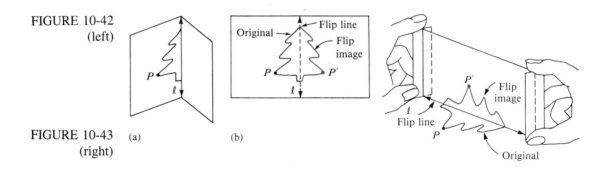

FIGURE 10-43   (a)   (b)
(right)

In Figure 10-44(a), the image of P under a flip in line ℓ is P'. In Figure 10-44(b), P is its own image under the flip in line ℓ.

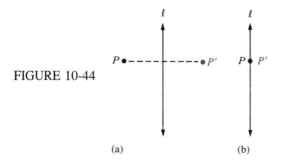

FIGURE 10-44

(a)   (b)

In general, *a flip (or reflection) in a line ℓ is a motion that pairs each point P of the plane with a point P' in such a way that ℓ is the perpendicular bisector of $\overline{PP'}$ as long as $P \notin \ell$. If $P \in \ell$, then $P = P'$.*

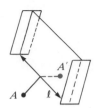

FIGURE 10-45

Given any point A and its flip image A', the flip line ℓ can be found as long as $A \notin \ell$ because ℓ is the perpendicular bisector of $\overline{AA'}$. This can be done by placing a Mira so that A is reflected onto A' and drawing the flip line, ℓ, along the drawing edge, as shown in Figure 10-46(a). With paper folding, we simply fold A onto A', as shown in Figure 10-46(b). The folding line is the required flip line. With a compass and straightedge, we construct the perpendicular bisector of $\overline{AA'}$ using the methods of the previous section. This is illustrated in Figure 10-46(c).

FIGURE 10-46

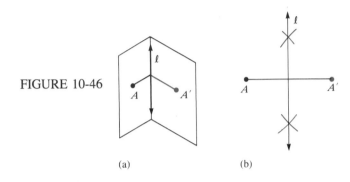

(a)   (b)

The concept of a flip, or reflection, can be used to solve a variety of geometrical problems, as the following problem illustrates.

PROBLEM 2

The hiker in Figure 10-47 sees that his tent is on fire. To what point on the bank of the river should the hiker run to fill his bucket and to make his trip to the tent as short as possible?

FIGURE 10-47

Understanding the Problem

To better understand the problem, we first draw a diagram, as seen in Figure 10-48. We label the hiker H, the tent T, and the river r. The hiker needs to find point P on the bank of the river so that the distance $HP + PT$ is as short as possible.

FIGURE 10-48

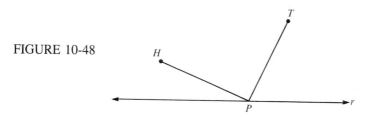

Devising a Plan

From the properties of reflections, we know that if T' is the reflection of the tent T in line r, then r is the perpendicular bisector of $\overline{TT'}$ as shown in Figure 10-49(a). Hence, any point on r is equidistant from T and T'. Thus, $PT = PT'$. Therefore, the hiker may solve the problem by finding a point, P, on r such that the path from H to P and then to T' is as short as possible. The shortest path connecting H and T' is a segment. The intersection of $\overline{HT'}$ and r determines the point on the river toward which the hiker should run.

FIGURE 10-49
(left)

FIGURE 10-50
(right)

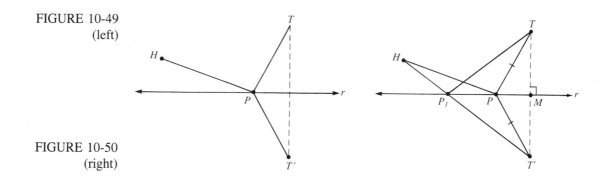

Carrying Out the Plan

Connect H with T', as shown in Figure 10-50. The point of intersection, P_1, is the required point. The hiker should run to P_1 and then from P_1 to T.

Looking Back

To prove that the path $H - P_1 - T$ is the shortest possible, we need to prove that $HP_1 + P_1T < HP + PT$ where P is any point on r different from P_1. Because any point P on the perpendicular bisector r of the segment $\overline{TT'}$ is equidistant from T and T', then $HP_1 + P_1T = HP_1 + P_1T' = HT'$. Because $\overline{HT'}$ is a side of $\triangle HPT'$, it follows that $HT' < HP + PT'$. Because $HT' = HP_1 + P_1T$ and $PT' = PT$, we have $HP_1 + P_1T < HP + PT$.

PROBLEM SET 10-4

1. What type of motion is involved in each of the following?
   (a) A skier skiing straight down a slope.
   (b) A leaf floating down a stream.
   (c) A page turning in a book.
2. For each of the following, find the image of the given quadrilateral.

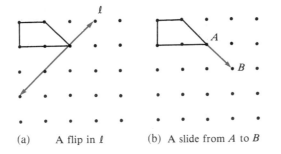

(a)   A flip in ℓ (b) A slide from A to B

3. Use (a) tracing paper and (b) compass and straightedge to construct the images for each of the following:

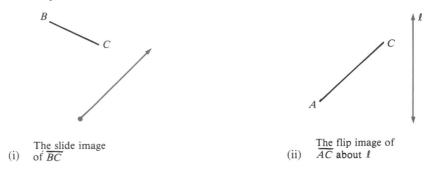

(i)   The slide image of $\overline{BC}$

(ii) The flip image of $\overline{AC}$ about ℓ

4. Use any construction method to find the image of △ABC if it is flipped about ℓ to obtain △A'B'C' and then △A'B'C' is flipped about m to obtain △A"B"C". (The lines ℓ and m are parallel.)

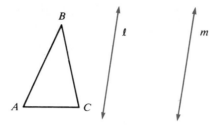

★ 5. Can the result in Problem 4 be accomplished using a single motion? Explain why or why not.

6. What is the result of performing two successive flips about line ℓ in the figure?

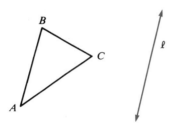

★ 7. Suppose ℓ and m are parallel and △ABC is flipped about ℓ and then m. How does the final image compare to the final image after flipping about m then ℓ? Are the images ever the same?

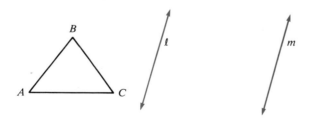

★ 8. A **glide reflection** is defined as the result of a successive slide and flip. Find the image of the footprint in the glide reflection that is the result of a slide from M to N followed by a flip about ℓ.

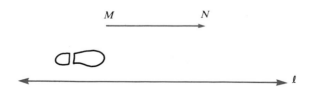

★ 9. If a Mira is available, use it to investigate Problems 4 and 6–8.

★ 10. Two cities, represented by points A and B, are located near two perpendicular roads, as shown. The cities' mayors found it necessary to build another road connecting A with a point P on road 1, then connecting P with a point Q on road 2, and finally connecting Q with B. How should the road $APQB$ be constructed if it is to be as short as possible? Copy the figure shown and use a straightedge and compass to construct the shortest possible path.

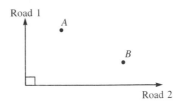

Road 1

A

B

Road 2

*　*　*　*　*　*　* REVIEW PROBLEMS *　*　*　*　*　*　*

11. Use a compass and a straightedge to construct each of the following.
    (a) A parallelogram in which one of the angles is 60°.
    (b) A right triangle in which the longest side is twice as long as the shortest side.
    (c) A 165° angle.
12. Divide $\overline{AB}$ into four congruent segments.

$A \vdash\!\!\!-\!\!\!-\!\!\!-\!\!\!-\!\!\!-\!\!\!-\!\!\!-\!\!\!-\!\!\!\dashv B$

13. Prove that a quadrilateral whose diagonals are perpendicular bisectors of each other is a rhombus.

BRAIN TEASER

Two cities are on opposite sides of a river, as shown. The cities' engineers want to build a bridge across the river that is perpendicular to the banks of the river and access roads to the bridge, so that the total distance between the cities is as short as possible. Where should the bridge and the roads be built?

A

B

COMPUTER CORNER

Slides may be explored in Logo using a figure called an EE. Type the given programs into your computer and then run the following.

(a) SLIDE 40 45
(b) SLIDE 200 57
(c) SLIDE (−50) (−75)

```
TO SLIDE :DIRECTION :DISTANCE
EE
PENUP
SETHEADING :DIRECTION
FORWARD :DISTANCE
PENDOWN
SETHEADING 0
EE
END
```

```
TO EE
FORWARD 50
RIGHT 90
FORWARD 25
BACK 25
LEFT 90
BACK 25
RIGHT 90
FORWARD 10
BACK 10
LEFT 90
BACK 25
RIGHT 90
FORWARD 25
BACK 25
LEFT 90
END
```

10-5 TURNS AND SYMMETRY

turn   rotation   A **turn,** or **rotation,** is another kind of motion that can be used to establish congruence. Figure 10-51 illustrates congruent figures resulting from a turn.

FIGURE 10-51

turn image
center of the turn
angle of the turn

In Figure 10-52(a), $\triangle ABC$ and point O are traced on tracing paper. Holding point O fixed, the tracing paper can be turned to obtain a **turn image,** $\triangle A'B'C'$, as shown in Figure 10-52(b). Point O is called the **center of the turn,** and $\angle COC'$ is called the **angle of the turn.**

FIGURE 10-52

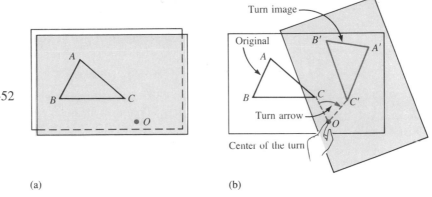

(a)   (b)

In order to determine a turn, three things must be given: (1) the center of the turn; (2) the direction of the turn—either clockwise or counterclockwise; and (3) the amount of the turn. The amount and the direction of the turn can be illus-

turn arrow

trated by a **turn arrow,** as shown with $\angle COC'$ in Figure 10-52(b), or specified as a number of degrees. A counterclockwise turn is indicated by a positive number of degrees; and a negative number of degrees indicates a clockwise turn. In general, *a turn (rotation) is a motion determined by holding one point, the center, fixed and rotating the plane about this point a certain amount in a certain direction.*

turn symmetry
rotational symmetry

A figure has **turn symmetry** or **rotational symmetry** when the traced figure can be turned less than 360° about its turn center so that it matches the original figure. In Figure 10-53, the tracing of the fan blade matches after a turn of 120°. Hence, we say that the blade has 120° turn symmetry.

FIGURE 10-53

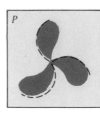

Other examples of figures that have turn symmetry are shown in Figure 10-54. In Figure 10-54, (a), (b), (c), and (d) have 72°, 90°, 180°, and 180° turn symmetry, respectively. (Parts (a) and (b) also have other turn symmetries.)

FIGURE 10-54

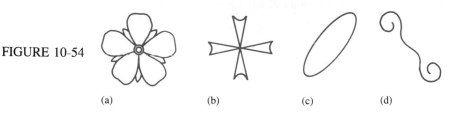

(a)   (b)   (c)   (d)

point symmetry

Any figure that has 180° turn symmetry is said to have **point symmetry** about the center of the turn. Figures with point symmetry are shown in Figure 10-55.

FIGURE 10-55

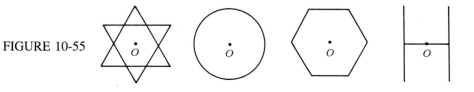

Suppose P is any point of a figure with point symmetry such as in Figure 10-56(a). If the figure is turned 180° about its center, point O, there is a corresponding point P', as shown in part (b) of the figure. Points P, O, and P' are collinear, and O is the midpoint of $\overline{PP'}$.

FIGURE 10-56

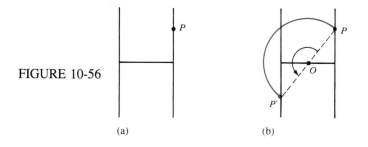

(a)   (b)

line of symmetry

Turns are related to both rotational and point symmetry. Flips are related to line symmetry. A figure has a **line of symmetry** if it is its own image under a flip. The flip line is the line of symmetry. Examples of figures with line symmetry are shown in Figure 10-57. There are three, one, and seven lines of symmetry, respectively, in parts (a), (b), and (c) of Figure 10-57.

FIGURE 10-57

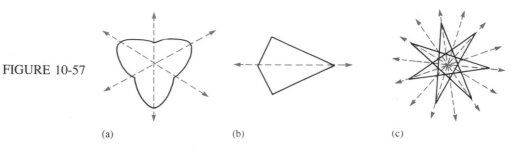

(a)   (b)   (c)

plane of symmetry

A three-dimensional figure has a **plane of symmetry** when every point of the figure on one side of the plane has a mirror image on the other side of the plane. Examples of figures with plane symmetry are shown in Figure 10-58. Solids can also have point symmetry, line symmetry, and turn symmetry. These symmetries are analogous to the two-dimensional symmetries and will be investigated in the exercises.

FIGURE 10-58

BRAIN TEASER

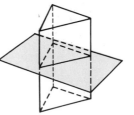

Simon and Susan decided to repair a hole in their living room shag carpet. The hole was in the shape of a scalene triangle as shown below. In order to cut a patch, Simon placed his only remnant of the carpet upside down over the hole so that he could cut the triangular shape through the jute backing. When he had cut the patch, he was astonished that it did not fit unless the jute side was up. How can he recut the patch using the minimum number of cuts and piece it together so that it will fit the hole?

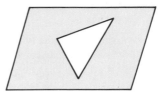

PROBLEM SET 10-5

1. Name three "everyday" examples of turns.
2. Which types of symmetry—point, line, or turn—does each of the following have? If a figure is three dimensional, determine if it has plane symmetry.
   - (a) A ball
   - (b) An equilateral triangle
   - (c) A regular polygon
   - (d) A basketball court
   - (e) A football
   - (f) A cube
3. For each of the following, name the printed capital letters of the English alphabet having the given property.
   - (a) Line symmetry
   - (b) Turn symmetry
   - (c) Point symmetry
4. (a) Determine the number of lines of symmetry of each flag below.
   (b) Sketch the lines of symmetry for each flag.

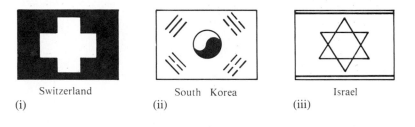

Switzerland   South Korea   Israel

(i)   (ii)   (iii)

5. Find the lines of symmetry, if any, for each of the following trademarks.

(a) The Bell System   (b) The Yellow Pages   (c) Chevrolet

(d) Volkswagen of America   (e) Chrysler Corporation   (f) International Harvester

6. Answer each of the following. If your answer is no, provide a counterexample.
   - (a) If a figure has point symmetry, must it have turn symmetry? Why?
   - (b) If a figure has turn symmetry, must it have point symmetry? Why?
   - (c) Can a figure have point, line, and turn symmetry? If so, sketch a figure with these properties.
   - (d) If a figure has point symmetry, must it have line symmetry? Is the converse true?
   - (e) If a figure has both point and line symmetry, must it have turn symmetry? Why?

7. Find the image of the given quadrilateral for a 90° counterclockwise turn about O.

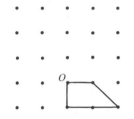

A 90° counterclockwise
turn about O

8. How many lines of symmetry does each of the following figures have?
   (a) Equilateral triangle   (b) Square
   (c) Rectangle   (d) Rhombus
   (e) Circle

9. In each of the following, complete the sketches so that they have the indicated symmetry.

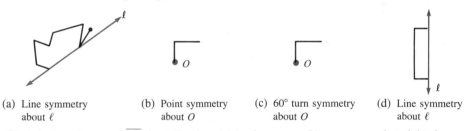

(a) Line symmetry   (b) Point symmetry   (c) 60° turn symmetry   (d) Line symmetry
   about ℓ about O about O about ℓ

10. Find the turn image of $\overline{AB}$ about O using: (a) tracing paper; (b) compass and straightedge.

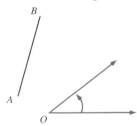

11. For the following, use any construction methods to find the image of $\triangle ABC$ if $\triangle ABC$ is flipped about ℓ to obtain $\triangle A'B'C'$ and then $\triangle A'B'C'$ is flipped about m to obtain $\triangle A''B''C''$ (ℓ and m intersect at O).

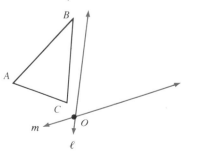

★ 12. Can the result in Problem 11 be accomplished using a single motion? Explain why or why not.

★ 13. Suppose lines ℓ and m intersect and triangle ABC is flipped first about ℓ and then about m. How does the final image compare to the final image after flipping first about m and then about ℓ?

★ 14. (a) In succession, perform the two turns, each with center O, in the figure.
   (b) What is the result of the two turns?
   (c) Is the order of the turns important?
   (d) Could the result have been accomplished in one turn?

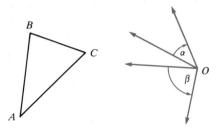

★ 15. If a Mira is available, use it to investigate Problems 11, 13, and 14.

* * * * * * * REVIEW PROBLEMS * * * * * * *

16. If $\overline{BC} \cong \overline{ED}$, $\overline{AB} \cong \overline{FE}$ and $\angle B \cong \angle E$, prove that $\overline{AD} \cong \overline{FC}$.

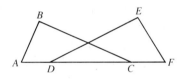

17. Using a compass and a straightedge, construct each of the following.
   (a) A rectangle with one side three times as long as the other.
   (b) An angle whose measure is the sum of the measures of the two angles given below.

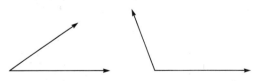

   (c) A triangle with angles of 90°, 60°, and 30°.

18. For each case, find the image of the given figure.

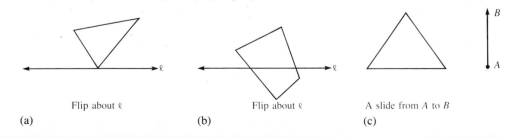

Flip about ℓ	Flip about ℓ	A slide from A to B
(a)	(b)	(c)

COMPUTER CORNER

With Logo it is possible to draw figures with many different symmetries. Type the given procedures into your computer and tell the types of symmetries that the figures have when POLYROLL is run for: (a) POLYROLL 75 90 30; (b) POLYROLL 55 60 45.

```
TO POLYSTOP :SIDE :ANGLE :START
FD :SIDE
RT :ANGLE
IF HEADING = :START STOP
POLYSTOP :SIDE :ANGLE :START
END
TO POLYROLL :SIDE :ANGLE1 :ANGLE2
FULLSCREEN
POLYSTOP :SIDE :ANGLE1 HEADING
RT :ANGLE2
IF HEADING = Ø STOP
POLYROLL :SIDE :ANGLE1 :ANGLE2
END
```

(Note: In Apple Logo, STOP is in brackets.)

10-6   SIMILAR TRIANGLES AND SIMILAR FIGURES

If an 8-inch by 10-inch reprint is made of an 8-inch by 10-inch picture, then the two photographs are congruent; that is, they have the same size and shape. However, if an 8-inch by 10-inch picture is blown up to obtain a 16-inch by 20-inch picture, as shown in Figure 10-59, the resulting photographs are not congruent. They have the same shape, but not the same size. When a germ is examined through a microscope, when a slide is projected on a screen, or when a wet wool sweater shrinks when dried in a clothes dryer, the shapes in each case remain the same, but the sizes are altered. In mathematics we say that *two figures that have the same shape but not necessarily the same size are **similar.***

similar

For example, if we project an equilateral triangle onto a screen without distortion (so that the same shape is kept), the image on the screen is an equilateral scale factor   triangle, as shown in Figure 10-60. In this figure, $\triangle ABC$ is enlarged by a **scale factor** of 2, so that the following proportion holds.

$$\frac{A'B'}{AB} = \frac{B'C'}{BC} = \frac{A'C'}{AC} = \frac{2}{1}$$

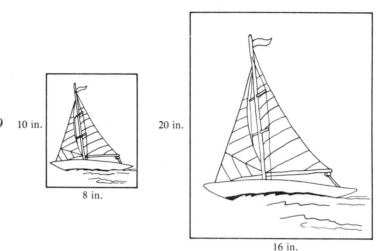

FIGURE 10-59   10 in.   20 in.

8 in.

16 in.

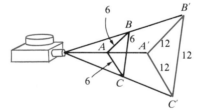

FIGURE 10-60

The ratio of the sides is 2 to 1. However, the angle sizes pictured do not change because both triangles are equilateral and hence equiangular. It is reasonable to assume that *any* triangle projected in this manner has an image triangle similar to the original. The angle measures remain the same, and the sides are proportional. In general, we have the following definition of similar triangles.

DEFINITION
> $\triangle ABC$ is similar to $\triangle DEF$, written $\triangle ABC \sim \triangle DEF$, if and only if $\angle A \cong \angle D$, $\angle B \cong \angle E$, $\angle C \cong \angle F$, and $\dfrac{AB}{DE} = \dfrac{AC}{DF} = \dfrac{BC}{EF}$.

Remark
> Note that the one-to-one correspondence in similar triangles is analogous to that in congruent triangles.

Example 10-8

Given the pairs of similar triangles in Figure 10-61, find a one-to-one correspondence among the vertices of the triangles such that the corresponding angles are congruent. Then write the proportion for the corresponding sides that follows from the definition.

FIGURE 10-61

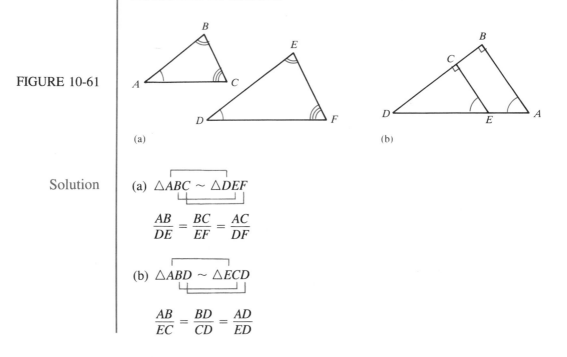

(a)   (b)

Solution

(a) $\triangle ABC \sim \triangle DEF$

$$\frac{AB}{DE} = \frac{BC}{EF} = \frac{AC}{DF}$$

(b) $\triangle ABD \sim \triangle ECD$

$$\frac{AB}{EC} = \frac{BD}{CD} = \frac{AD}{ED}$$

As with congruent triangles, minimal conditions may be used to determine when two triangles are similar. For example, suppose two triangles each have angles with measures of 50°, 30°, and 100°, but the side opposite the 100° angle is 5 units long in one of the triangles and 1 unit long in the other. The triangles appear to have the same shape, as shown in Figure 10-62. The figure suggests that if the angles of the two triangles are congruent, then the sides are proportional and the triangles are similar. There is no easy proof of this statement, but it is true in general. It is called the **Angle, Angle, Angle** property of similarity for triangles and is abbreviated as **AAA.**

Angle, Angle, Angle (AAA)

FIGURE 10-62

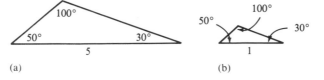

(a)   (b)

Property

Angle, Angle, Angle (AAA)   If three angles of one triangle are congruent to the three angles of a second triangle, respectively, then the triangles are similar.

Remark

Angle, Angle (AA)

Given the measures of any two angles of a triangle, the measure of the third angle can be found. Hence, if two angles in one triangle are congruent to two angles in another triangle, respectively, then the third angles must also be congruent. Consequently, the AAA condition may be reduced to **Angle, Angle (AA).**

Example 10-9

For each part of Figure 10-63, determine if the pairs of triangles are similar.

FIGURE 10-63

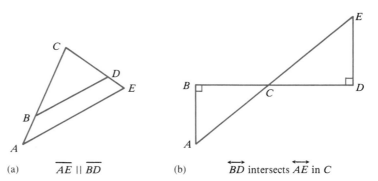

(a) $\overline{AE} \parallel \overline{BD}$ (b) $\overleftrightarrow{BD}$ intersects $\overleftrightarrow{AE}$ in C

Solution

(a) Because $\overline{AE} \parallel \overline{BD}$, congruent corresponding angles are formed by a transversal cutting the parallel segments. Thus, $\angle CBD \cong \angle CAE$, and $\angle CDB \cong \angle CEA$. Also, $\angle C \cong \angle C$, so that $\triangle CBD \sim \triangle CAE$ by AAA.

(b) $\angle B \cong \angle D$ since both are right triangles. Also, $\angle ACB \cong \angle ECD$ since they are vertical angles. Thus, $\triangle ACB \sim \triangle ECD$ by AA.

In general, knowing that the corresponding angles are congruent is not sufficient to determine similarity for any two polygons. For example, in a square of side 4 cm and a rectangle 2 cm by 4 cm, all the angles are congruent, but the two figures are not similar. In fact, *two polygons are similar if and only if the corresponding angles are congruent and the corresponding sides are proportional.*

Example 10-10

In each pair of similar triangles in Figure 10-64, find x.

FIGURE 10-64

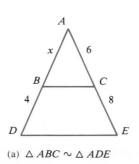

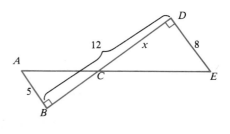

(a) $\triangle ABC \sim \triangle ADE$ (b) $\triangle ABC \sim \triangle EDC$

Solution

(a) $\triangle ABC \sim \triangle ADE$, so

$$\frac{AB}{AD} = \frac{AC}{AE} = \frac{BC}{DE}$$

Now, $AB = x$, $AD = x + 4$, $AC = 6$, $AE = 6 + 8 = 14$. Thus,

$$\frac{x}{x + 4} = \frac{6}{14}$$

$$14x = 6(x + 4)$$

$$14x = 6x + 24$$

$$8x = 24$$

$$x = 3$$

(b) $\triangle ABC \sim \triangle EDC$, so

$$\frac{AB}{ED} = \frac{AC}{EC} = \frac{BC}{DC}$$

Now, $AB = 5$, $ED = 8$, and $CD = x$, so that $BC = 12 - x$. Thus,

$$\frac{5}{8} = \frac{12 - x}{x}$$

$$5x = 8(12 - x)$$

$$5x = 96 - 8x$$

$$13x = 96$$

$$x = \frac{96}{13}$$

Similar triangles give rise to various properties involving proportions. For example, in Figure 10-65, if $\overline{BC} \parallel \overline{DE}$, then $\frac{AB}{BD} = \frac{AC}{CE}$. This can be justified as follows: $\overline{BC} \parallel \overline{DE}$, so $\triangle ADE \sim \triangle ABC$. (Why?) Consequently, $\frac{AD}{AB} = \frac{AE}{AC}$, which may be written as shown below.

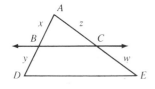

FIGURE 10-65

$$\frac{x + y}{x} = \frac{z + w}{z}$$

$$\frac{x}{x} + \frac{y}{x} = \frac{z}{z} + \frac{w}{z}$$

$$1 + \frac{y}{x} = 1 + \frac{w}{z}$$

$$\frac{y}{x} = \frac{w}{z}$$

$$\frac{x}{y} = \frac{z}{w}$$

This result is summarized in the following property.

Property | If a line parallel to one side of a triangle intersects the other sides, then it divides those sides into proportional segments.

In Figure 10-65, if B is the midpoint of $\overline{AD}$, then $x = y$. Consequently, $\frac{x}{y} = 1$. Because $\frac{x}{y} = \frac{z}{w}$, it follows that $\frac{z}{w} = 1$ and, hence, that $z = w$. That is, if B is the midpoint of $\overline{AD}$ and $\overline{BC} \parallel \overline{DE}$, then C is the midpoint of $\overline{AE}$. Similarly, if parallel lines intersect $\triangle ADE$, as shown in Figure 10-66, so that $a = b = c = d$, it can be shown that $e = f = g = h$. This result is summarized in the following property.

FIGURE 10-66

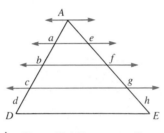

Property | If parallel lines cut off congruent segments on one transversal, then they cut off congruent segments on any transversal.

The preceding property is the basis for separating a line segment into any number of congruent parts. Consider dividing the segment $\overline{AB}$ in Figure 10-67(a) into three congruent parts. To obtain a figure similar to the one in Figure 10-66, we proceed as follows:

1. Through A draw any ray $\overrightarrow{AC}$ such that A, B, and C are not collinear.
2. Mark off any three congruent segments on $\overrightarrow{AC}$, as shown in Figure 10-67(b).
3. Connect B with A_3.
4. Construct parallels to $\overline{BA_3}$ through A_1 and A_2, as shown in Figure 10-67(c).
5. The intersection points of the parallels with $\overline{AB}$, P and Q, determine the three congruent parts of $\overline{AB}$.

FIGURE 10-67
Separate a line segment
into congruent parts

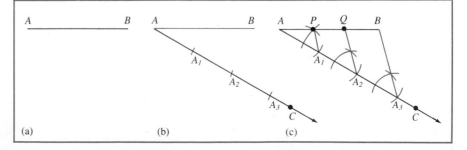

Similar triangles have also been used to make indirect measurements since the time of Thales of Miletus (ca 600 B.C.), who is believed to have determined the height of the Great Pyramid of Egypt. Most likely he used ratios involving shadows, similar to those in Figure 10-68. The sun is so far away it should make approximately congruent angles at B and B'. Because the angles at C and C' are right angles, $\triangle ABC \sim \triangle A'B'C'$. Hence,

$$\frac{AC}{A'C'} = \frac{BC}{B'C'}$$

and because $AC = AE + EC$, the following proportion is obtained.

$$\frac{AE + EC}{A'C'} = \frac{BC}{B'C'}$$

FIGURE 10-68

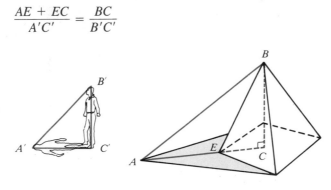

The person's height and shadow can be measured. Also, the length of the shadow of the pyramid AE, can be measured, and EC can be found since the base of the pyramid is a square. Each term of the proportion except the height of the pyramid is known. Thus, the height of the pyramid can be found by solving the proportion.

Example 10-11

On a sunny day, a tall tree casts a 40 m (meter) shadow. At the same time, a meter stick held vertically casts a 2.5 m shadow. How tall is the tree?

Solution

Look at Figure 10-69. The pictured triangles are similar by AA since the tree and the stick both meet the ground at right angles, and the angles formed by the sun's rays are congruent (because the shadows are measured at the same time).

FIGURE 10-69

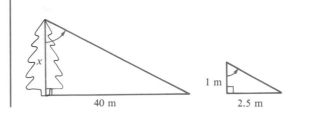

$$\frac{x}{40} = \frac{1}{2.5}$$

$$2.5x = 40$$

$$x = 16$$

The tree is 16 m tall.

PROBLEM 3

A brick with dimensions as shown in Figure 10-70 is leaning against a wall at point A. The point D where the edge of the brick rests on the ground is 20 cm away from the wall. How high above the ground is point C?

FIGURE 10-70

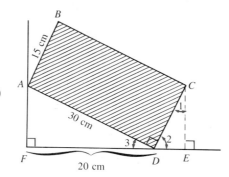

Understanding the Problem

Given the data in Figure 10-70, we are to find the length of $\overline{CE}$, which is perpendicular to $\overline{FE}$.

Devising a Plan

$\overline{CE}$ is a side in the right triangle EDC. If we could find a triangle with some known sides that is similar to $\triangle EDC$, we could set up a proportion and find CE. Triangle FAD is a right triangle in which two sides are known. Are the two triangles similar? The triangles have right angles at F and E, respectively. Also, $m(\angle 1) = 90° - m(\angle 2)$. Because $\triangle ADC$ is an angle in a rectangle, it is a right angle and $m(\angle 3) + 90° + m(\angle 2) = 180°$ or $m(\angle 3) = 90° - m(\angle 2)$. Now $m(\angle 1) = m(\angle 3)$ and $\triangle EDC$ is similar to $\triangle FAD$ by AA.

Carrying Out the Plan

Because $\triangle EDC \sim \triangle FAD$, we have the following proportions.

$$\frac{EC}{FD} = \frac{DC}{AD} = \frac{ED}{FA}$$

Because $AD = 30$ cm, $FD = 20$ cm, and $DC = AB = 15$ cm, it follows that

$$\frac{EC}{20} = \frac{15}{30}$$

$$EC = 10 \text{ cm}$$

Looking Back

Given the data in the problem, it seems that we should be able to find how high above the ground the other corners of the brick are. However, this requires the use of the Pythagorean Theorem, which is introduced in Chapter 11.

PROBLEM SET 10-6

1. Which of the following triangles is not similar to the other three?

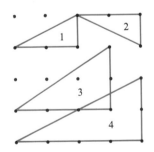

2. Which of the following are always similar? Why?
   (a) Any two equilateral triangles
   (b) Any two squares
   (c) Any two rectangles
   (d) Any two rhombi
   (e) Any two circles
   (f) Any two regular polygons
   (g) Any two regular polygons with the same number of sides

3. Use a grid like the following one to draw a figure that has sides three times as large as the given figure.

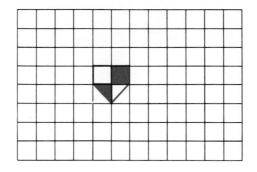

4. (a) Which pairs of the following triangles are similar? If they are similar, explain why.
   (b) For each pair of similar triangles, find the ratio of the sides of the triangles.

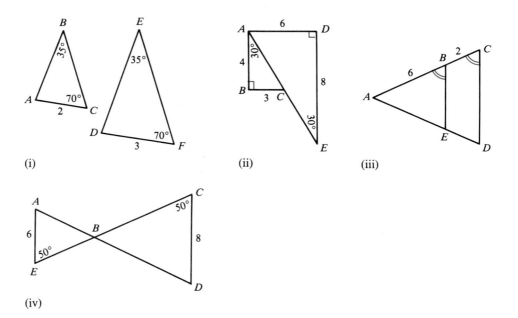

(i) (ii) (iii)

(iv)

5. Assume that the triangles in each part are similar and find the measures of the unknown sides.

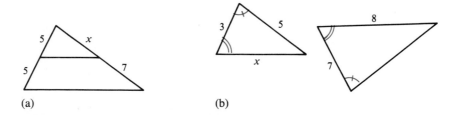

(a) (b)

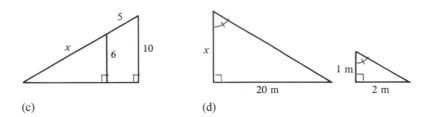

(c)   (d)

6. Polly claims that each of the following pairs of triangles are similar. In each part, determine if Polly is right or wrong. Explain why.

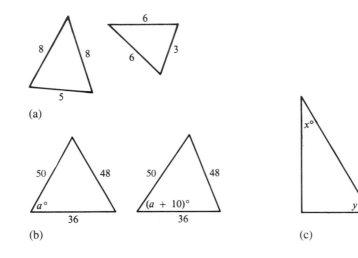

(a)

(b)   (c)

7. For each of the following, find x.

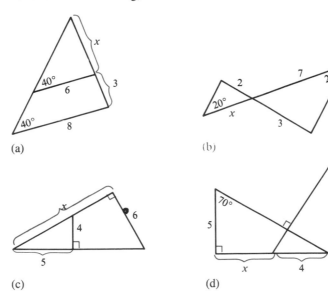

(a)   (b)

(c)   (d)

8. In right triangle ABC, we have $\overline{CD} \perp \overline{AB}$.

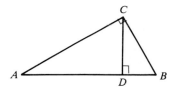

(a) Find three pairs of similar triangles. Justify your answers.

(b) Write the corresponding proportions for each set of similar triangles.

9. Are congruent triangles similar? Why?

10. (a) Construct a triangle with lengths of sides 4 cm, 6 cm, and 8 cm.

(b) Construct another triangle with lengths of sides 2 cm, 3 cm, and 4 cm.

(c) Make a conjecture about the similarity of triangles having proportional sides only.

11. (a) Construct a triangle with sides of lengths 4 cm and 6 cm and an included angle of 60°.

(b) Construct a triangle with sides of lengths 2 cm and 3 cm and an included angle of 60°.

(c) Make a conjecture about the similarity of triangles having two sides proportional and the included angles congruent.

12. (a) Sketch two nonsimilar polygons for which corresponding angles are congruent.

(b) Sketch two nonsimilar polygons for which corresponding sides are proportional.

13. Examine several examples of similar polygons to make a conjecture concerning the ratio of their perimeters.

14. Use a compass and straightedge to separate $\overline{AB}$ into five congruent pieces.

15. Construct a square with a side two-thirds the length of the square below.

16. Find the distance AB across the pond using the following similar triangles.

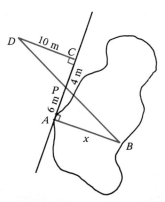

17. In the isosceles triangle, $\triangle ABC$, $m(\sphericalangle A) = 36°$, $\overrightarrow{BD}$ bisects $\sphericalangle ABC$, and $\overline{AB} \cong \overline{AC}$. Find two similar triangles in the figure and prove that they are similar.

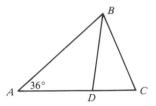

18. To find the height of a tall building, we can place a mirror on the ground and then walk an appropriate distance away from the mirror so that we can see the top of the building in the mirror. Find the height of the building if a person 6 feet tall sees the top of the building when the mirror is 45 feet from the building and the person is 2 feet from the mirror. Assume that $\sphericalangle ECD$, the angle of incidence, is congruent to $\sphericalangle ACB$, the angle of reflection.

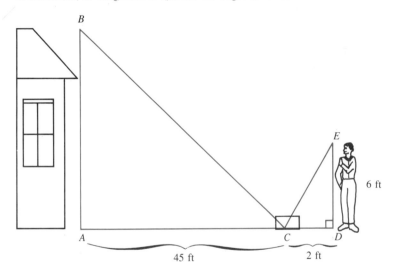

19. To find the height of a tree, a group of Girl Scouts devised the following method. A girl walks away from the tree along its shadow until the shadow of the top of her head coincides with the shadow of the top of the tree. If the girl is 150 cm tall, her distance to the foot of the tree is 1500 cm, and the length of her shadow is 300 cm, how tall is the tree?

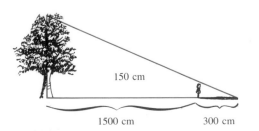

20. If *ABCD* is a parallelogram, *BF* = 6, *FC* = 3, and *BD* = 7.5, find *BE* and *ED*.

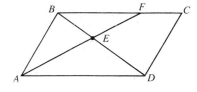

* * * * * * * REVIEW PROBLEMS * * * * * * *

21. What type of motion is involved in each of the following?
    (a) A circular radio knob turned from "off" to "on."
    (b) A child swinging.
    (c) Two children on a teeter-totter.
22. Find the image of △*ABC* when it is flipped about side $\overline{AC}$.

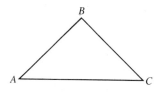

23. Draw any triangle *ABC* and then find its image when it is turned counterclockwise by ∡*A* about each of the following.
    (a) Vertex *A*
    (b) Vertex *B*
24. For each of the following, draw a figure other than a circle which has the given symmetry.
    (a) Turn symmetry
    (b) Point symmetry
    (c) Four lines of symmetry
25. Triangle *ABC* is equilateral. Each side of the triangle has been extended by its own length, that is, *BD* = *AB*, *CE* = *BC*, *AF* = *AC*, as shown in the figure below. Prove that the new triangle *DEF* is also equilateral.

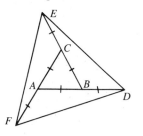

26. Use a straightedge and compass to construct a right triangle if *a* is one of the sides and *c* is the side opposite the right angle.

_____   _____

       a   *c*

BRAIN TEASER

Two neighbors, Smith and Wesson, planned to erect flagpoles in their yards. Smith wanted a 10-ft pole, while Wesson wanted a 15-ft pole. In order to keep the poles straight while the concrete bases hardened, they agreed to tie guy wires from the tops of the flagpoles to a 6-ft fencepost on the property lines and to the bases of the flagpoles as shown. How far apart should they erect flagpoles for this scheme to work?

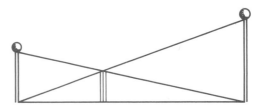

10-7   PROPERTIES OF CIRCLES AND SPHERES

Recall that a circle is a set of points in a plane equidistant from a given point called the center, as shown in Figure 10-71. The radius is the length of any segment connecting the center with a point of the circle. Any segment with both endpoints on the circle is called a **chord.** A line that contains a chord is called a **secant.** A chord that passes through the center of the circle is called a **diameter.** A diameter is the longest chord of the circle, and its length equals twice the length of the radius.

chord   secant
diameter

FIGURE 10-71

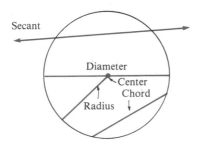

Given a circle, it is easy to find many chords of the circle. If we pick any two points on the circle and connect them, we obtain a chord. However, suppose that $\overline{AB}$ is given and we want to find a circle in which $\overline{AB}$ is a chord. Because a diameter is also a chord, we could find a circle whose diameter is $\overline{AB}$. This is done in Figure 10-72(a) by finding the midpoint O of $\overline{AB}$ and drawing a circle with center O and radius $\overline{OA}$.

There are circles in which $\overline{AB}$ is a chord but not a diameter. To construct such a circle, consider Figure 10-72(b). What do we know about the center M? Because $\overline{AM}$ and $\overline{MB}$ are radii, M must be equidistant from the endpoints of $\overline{AB}$. In Section 10-3, we saw that such a point must be on the perpendicular bisector of $\overline{AB}$. In fact, any point on the perpendicular bisector of $\overline{AB}$ can be the center of a circle in which $\overline{AB}$ is a chord. Different circles containing $\overline{AB}$ as a chord are shown in Figure 10-72(c).

FIGURE 10-72

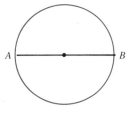

(a)

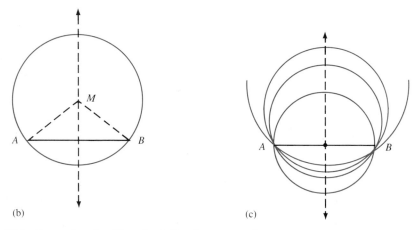

(b)   (c)

This discussion justifies the following property.

Property | If $\overline{AB}$ is a chord of a circle, then the center of the circle lies on the perpendicular bisector of $\overline{AB}$.

Congruent chords in a circle seem to intersect the circle to form congruent arcs. For example, in Figure 10-73, chords $\overline{AB}$ and $\overline{CD}$ are congruent. The chords or their corresponding arcs determine two angles, $\angle AOB$ and $\angle COD$. These

central angles

angles are called **central angles** because their vertices are the center of the circle. By performing a turn about O, one chord can be placed on top of the other. The arrows show which way to turn. One outcome of the turn is that $\overset{\frown}{AB}$ matches $\overset{\frown}{CD}$. Thus, congruent chords have congruent arcs. Also, the turn suggests that $\angle AOB$ is congruent to $\angle COD$. This also follows from the congruence of triangles OAB and OCD. Thus, *congruent chords determine congruent central angles and congruent arcs of the circle.* Conversely, it can be shown that *congruent central angles determine congruent chords and congruent arcs of a circle.*

FIGURE 10-73

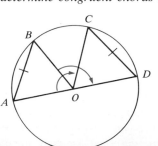

inscribed polygon

When all the vertices of a polygon are points of a given circle, the polygon is called an **inscribed polygon.** A regular hexagon inscribed in a circle is shown in Figure 10-74. All sides of a regular hexagon are congruent, so the corresponding arcs are congruent and the six corresponding central angles are congruent. Because the sum of the measures of these angles is 360°, the measure of each central angle is 60°. This fact is sufficient to inscribe a hexagon in a given circle using a protractor. A compass and straightedge construction can also be accomplished. Look at $\triangle AOB$. Because $\overline{OA} \cong \overline{OB}$, the triangle is isosceles. Hence, the base angles $\angle BAO$ and $\angle ABO$ are congruent. The central angle is 60°, so $m(\angle BAO) + m(\angle ABO) = 120°$. Consequently, $m(\angle BAO) = m(\angle ABO) = 60°$, and the triangle is equiangular and equilateral. Thus, $\overline{AB}$ is congruent to a radius of the circle. As a result, to inscribe a regular hexagon in a circle, we pick any point P on the circle and mark off chords congruent to the radius. Figure 10-75 shows such a construction.

FIGURE 10-74
(left)

FIGURE 10-75
(right)

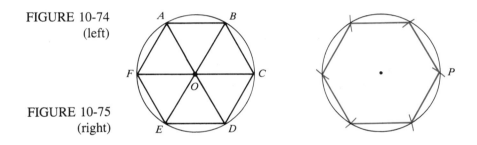

In a similar manner, to inscribe a regular dodecagon (12 sides) in a circle, we construct either twelve congruent chords of the circle appropriately placed or twelve congruent central angles. To find the twelve congruent central angles, we bisect the central angles of a regular hexagon, as shown in Figure 10-76.

FIGURE 10-76

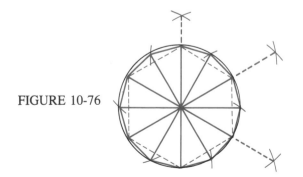

To inscribe a square in a circle, we determine four congruent central angles. The central angles must be right angles because the sum of their measures is 360°. Hence, we need only to construct two perpendicular diameters of the circle. Figure 10-77 shows the construction. First, we draw any diameter $\overline{PQ}$. Then we construct a perpendicular to $\overline{PQ}$ at O and thus determine points R and S. Quadrilateral $PRQS$ is the required square.

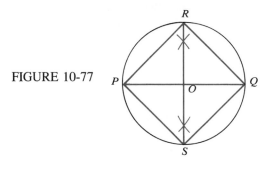

FIGURE 10-77

Determining which polygons can and cannot be inscribed in a circle using only a compass and straightedge has intrigued mathematicians for centuries. In fact, Gauss considered one of his master achievements to be the inscription of a regular 17-gon in a circle, and he wanted a replica of his construction placed on his tombstone. Gauss also proved that a regular n-gon can be inscribed in a circle if all the odd factors of n are distinct and of the form $2^{2^k} + 1$. (It is beyond the scope of this text to prove this result.) Thus, a regular heptagon cannot be inscribed in a circle with a compass and straightedge since 7 is not of the form $2^{2^k} + 1$.

circumscribing

A triangle is inscribed in a circle by connecting any three points of the circle with line segments. Conversely, given three vertices of any triangle, a circle that contains the vertices can be drawn. This process is called **circumscribing** a circle about a triangle. For example, in Figure 10-78, circle O is circumscribed about $\triangle ABC$. Such a circle must contain $\overline{AB}$, $\overline{BC}$, and $\overline{AC}$ as chords. Also, it must have $\overline{OA} \cong \overline{OB} \cong \overline{OC}$, since they are all radii. Hence, O must be equidistant from A and B and, consequently O must be on the perpendicular bisector of $\overline{AB}$. Similarly, O is on the perpendicular bisectors of $\overline{BC}$ and $\overline{AC}$. Hence, to find the center of the circle, construct perpendicular bisectors of any two chords. The point of intersection of the chords is the center of the circle. Segments connecting O with A, B, and C are the radii of the circle.

FIGURE 10-78

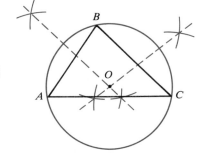

FIGURE 10-79

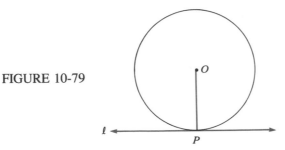

tangent

point of contact

inscribed

A line that intersects a circle in exactly one point is called a **tangent.** In Figure 10-79, it appears that tangent ℓ and the radius pictured form right angles at their point of intersection or **point of contact.** In fact, this is true in general and can be proved. However, we will assume this property of a tangent without proof. Thus, to construct a tangent to a given circle at any point on the circle, we construct a perpendicular to the radius at that point.

A circle is **inscribed** in a triangle if it is tangent to the three sides of the triangle. For example, in Figure 10-80(a), circle O is inscribed in $\triangle DEF$ and A, B, and C are the points of contact. Since $\overline{OA}$, $\overline{OB}$, and $\overline{OC}$ are radii, they all have the same length, and they are perpendicular to the three sides of the triangle they each intersect. Thus, O is equidistant from the sides, so it lies on the bisectors of $\angle 1$, $\angle 2$, and $\angle 3$ (see Section 10-3).

To inscribe a circle in a triangle, we first construct the bisectors of two of the angles. Their intersection point O is the center of the inscribed circle. The radius of the circle can be determined by constructing a perpendicular from O to a side of the triangle. Figure 10-80(b) shows the construction. The circle with center O and radius $\overline{OC}$ is the required circle.

FIGURE 10-80

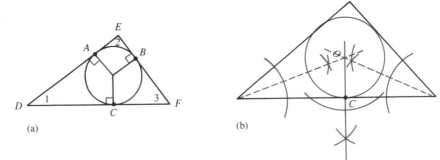

(a)

(b)

sphere

A **sphere** is the three-dimensional analog of a circle. It is defined as the set of all points in space that are the same distance from a given point (called the center). The definitions of chord, secant, and tangent apply to spheres as well as to circles. A plane is tangent to a sphere if it intersects the sphere in exactly one point.

If a plane intersects a sphere in more than one point, then the intersection is a circle, as shown in Figure 10-81.

FIGURE 10-81

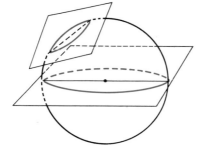

great circle

The largest of all such circles, a circle that contains a diameter of a sphere, is called a **great circle.** Any plane containing the center of the sphere intersects the sphere in a great circle. As with circles, spheres have point, line, and turn symmetry. In addition, a sphere has plane symmetry with respect to any plane that passes through its center.

PROBLEM SET 10-7

1. What is the relation between a diameter of a circle and any chord that is not a diameter?
2. If a triangle is drawn in a circle so that one vertex is at the center and the other two vertices are on the circle, what type of triangle must it be? Why?
3. If one side of a triangle is a diameter of a circle and the third vertex is also a point on the circle, what type of triangle must it be? Measure the angles of several such triangles to decide.
4. Use paper folding (or a Mira) to determine the center of the given circle.

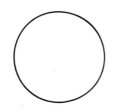

5. **Concentric circles** are circles with the same center. Can you construct a common tangent to two distinct concentric circles? Why?
6. Inscribe an equilateral triangle in a given circle.
7. Inscribe a regular octagon in a given circle.
8. Draw a circle.
   (a) Inscribe several quadrilaterals.
   (b) Measure the angles of the quadrilaterals from part (a) and find the sums of the measures of pairs of opposite angles.
   (c) What seems to be true about the relationship among the angles?

9. Inscribe a circle in the given square.

10. Is it possible to inscribe a circle in every quadrilateral? Explain.
11. Construct a circle with center O which is tangent to ℓ.

12. Construct a circle that is tangent to lines ℓ, m, and n, where $\ell \parallel m$.

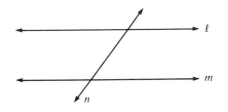

13. In the accompanying figure, $\overline{AC}$ is a diameter of circle O, and $\overline{CB}$ is a chord of the circle.
    (a) What type of triangle is $\triangle OCB$?
    (b) Prove that $m(\angle 1) + m(\angle 2) = m(\angle 3)$.
    (c) Prove that $m(\angle 1) = \frac{1}{2}[m(\angle 3)]$.

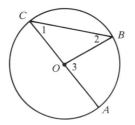

14. (a) In how many points can a line intersect a sphere?
    (b) In how many points can a plane intersect a sphere?

★ 15. Construct a circle that contains point P and that is tangent to the two given parallel lines ℓ and m.

★ 16. Prove that congruent chords in a circle are the same distance from the center.

★ 17. Prove that if a triangle is inscribed in a circle and one of its sides is a diameter, then the angle opposite that side must be a right angle. That is, show that if O is the center of the circle shown, than $\angle C$ must be a right angle. (*Hint:* Connect C with O and use the fact that the sum of the measures of the angles in a triangle is 180°.)

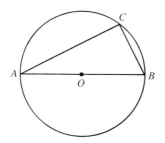

* * * * * * * REVIEW PROBLEMS * * * * * * *

18. For each of the following, prove that appropriate triangles are similar and find x and y.

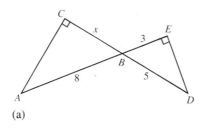

(a)

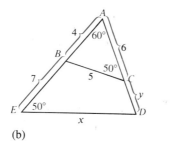

(b)

19. If *ABCD* is a parallelogram, prove that △*BFE* ~ △*CDE*.

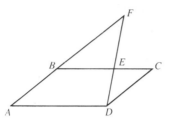

20. If $\overrightarrow{BC} \parallel \overrightarrow{DE}$, find *x*.

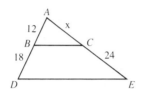

21. In the figure, *ABCD* is a square and $\overline{DE} \cong \overline{BF}$. Prove that *AECF* is a parallelogram.

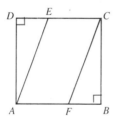

22. In the figure, *DEFG* is a square and $m(\angle ACB) = 90°$.
    (a) Prove that △*ADG* ~ △*GCF*.
    (b) Is it also true that △*ADG* ≅ △*GCF*? Justify your answer.

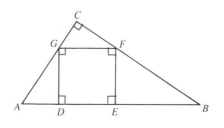

SOLUTION TO THE PRELIMINARY PROBLEM

Understanding the Problem

A shard of a fragile pottery saucer was found by archaeologists at a dig in Virginia. The border of the shard (shown in Figure 10-82) was part of a circle. In order to reconstruct the saucer, the archaeologists must determine the radius of the circle.

Devising a Plan

A mathematical model can be used to determine the radius. Trace an outline of the three-dimensional shard on a piece of paper. The result is an arc of a two-dimensional circle, as shown in Figure 10-83. To determine the radius, find the center, O. A circle has infinitely many lines of symmetry, and each line passes through the center of the circle, where all the lines of symmetry intersect.

FIGURE 10-82

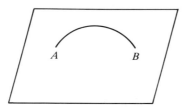

FIGURE 10-83

Carrying Out the Plan

To find a line of symmetry, fold the paper containing $\overset{\frown}{AB}$ so that a portion of the arc is folded onto itself. Then unfold the paper and draw the line of symmetry on the fold mark, as shown in Figure 10-84(a). By refolding the paper in Figure 10-84(a) so that a different portion of the arc $\overset{\frown}{AB}$ is folded onto itself, determine a second line of symmetry as shown in Figure 10-84(b). The two dotted lines of symmetry intersect in O, the center of the circle of which $\overset{\frown}{AB}$ is an arc. To complete the problem, measure the length of either $\overline{OB}$ or $\overline{OA}$. (They should be the same.)

FIGURE 10-84

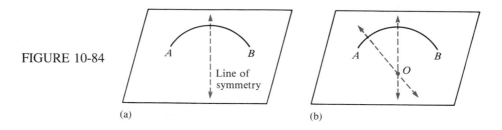

(a)   (b)

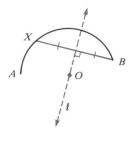

FIGURE 10-85

Looking Back

In the first fold, endpoint B of the arc was folded onto another point of the arc. Label this other point X. The result is shown in Figure 10-85. Because the fold line ℓ is a line of symmetry of the circle containing $\overset{\frown}{AB}$, it must be the perpendicular bisector of $\overline{XB}$ and contain the center of the circle. This is the property proved in Section 10-7 which states that the center of the circle lies on the perpendicular bisector of a chord. This property could have been used to determine the center of the circle by choosing two chords on the arc and finding the point where the perpendicular bisectors of the chords intersect.

A related problem is: What would happen if the piece of pottery had been part of a sphere? Would the same ideas still work?

QUESTIONS FROM THE CLASSROOM

1. On a test, a student wrote $AB \cong CD$ instead of $\overline{AB} \cong \overline{CD}$. Is this answer correct?
2. A student asks if there are any constructions that cannot be done using a compass and straightedge. How do you answer?
3. A student asks for a mathematical definition of congruence that holds for all figures. How do you respond? Is your response the same for similarity?
4. One student claims that by trisecting $\overline{AB}$ and drawing $\overset{\rightarrow}{CD}$ and $\overset{\rightarrow}{CE}$ as shown, she has trisected $\angle ACB$. How do you convince her that her construction is wrong?

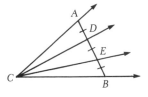

5. In the following drawing, a student claims that polygon $ABCD$ is a parallelogram if $\angle 1 \cong \angle 2$. Is he correct?

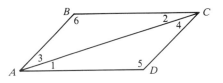

6. A student claims that by connecting the midpoints of the sides of any polygon, a polygon similar to the original results. Is this true?
7. A student asks if the only transformations are flips, slides, turns, or glide reflections. How do you respond?
8. A student asks why $\cong$ rather than $=$ is used to discuss triangles that have the same size and shape. What do you say?
9. A student draws the following figure and claims that since every triangle is congruent to itself, then we can write $\triangle ABC \cong \triangle BCA$. What is your response?

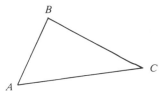

CHAPTER OUTLINE

I. Congruence
   A. Two geometric figures are **congruent** if and only if they have the same size and shape.
   B. Two triangles are congruent if they satisfy any of the following conditions.
      1. Side, Side, Side (SSS)
      2. Side, Angle, Side (SAS)
      3. Angle, Side, Angle (ASA)
      4. Angle, Angle, Side (AAS)
   C. The simple motions are slides, flips, and turns.
      1. A **slide** (or **translation**) is a motion of a specified distance and direction along a straight line without any accompanying turning and twisting.
      2. A **flip** (or **reflection**) in a line ℓ is a motion that pairs each point P of the plane with a point P' in such a way that ℓ is the perpendicular bisector of $\overline{PP'}$ if $P \notin \ell$, and $P = P'$ if $P \in \ell$.
      3. A **turn** (or **rotation**) is a motion determined by holding one point, the center, fixed and rotating the plane about this point a certain amount in a certain direction.
II. Types of symmetry
   A. A figure has **line symmetry** if it is its own image under a flip.
   B. A figure has **turn symmetry** when it is its own image under a turn of less than 360° about its center.
   C. A figure that has 180° turn symmetry is said to have **point symmetry.**
   D. A figure has **plane symmetry** when every point of the figure on one side of a plane has a mirror image on the other side of the plane so that the point and its mirror image are equidistant from the plane.
III. Similar figures
   A. Two polygons are **similar** if and only if their

corresponding angles are congruent and their corresponding sides are proportional.
   B. AAA or AA: If three (two) angles of one triangle are congruent to three (two) angles of a second triangle, respectively, the triangles are similar.
IV. Proportion
   A. If a line parallel to one side of a triangle intersects the other sides, then it divides those sides into proportional segments.
   B. If parallel lines cut off congruent segments on one transversal, then they cut off congruent segments on any transversal.
V. Circles and spheres
   A. A **circle** is a set of points in a plane that are the same distance (radius) from a given point (center).
   B. A **chord** is a segment with endpoints on a circle.
   C. A **secant** is a line that contains a chord of a circle.
   D. A **tangent** is a line that intersects a circle in exactly one point.
   E. A **sphere** is a set of points in space that are the same distance (radius) from a given point (center).
VI. Constructions using compass and straightedge
   A. Copy a line segment.
   B. Copy an angle.
   C. Bisect a segment.
   D. Bisect an angle.
   E. Construct a perpendicular from a point to a line.
   F. Construct a perpendicular through a point on a line.
   G. Construct a parallel to a line through a point not on the line.
   H. Divide a segment into congruent parts.
   I. Inscribe regular polygons in a circle.
   J. Circumscribe a circle about a triangle.
   K. Inscribe a circle in a triangle.

CHAPTER TEST

1. In each of the following figures there is at least one pair of congruent triangles. Identify them and tell why they are congruent.

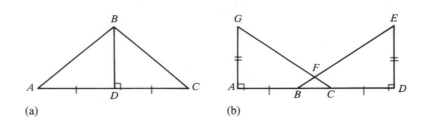

(a)   (b)

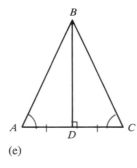   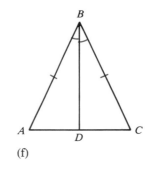

(c)   (d)

(e)   (f)

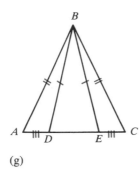   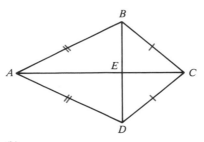

(g)   (h)

2. How many lines of symmetry, if any, does each of the following figures have?

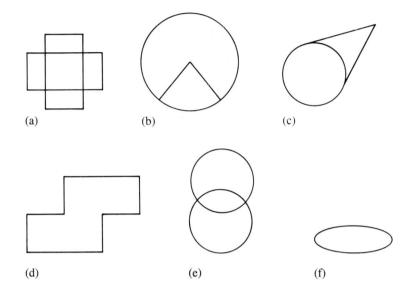

(a)   (b)   (c)

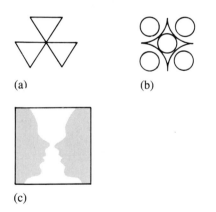

(d)   (e)   (f)

3. For each of the following, identify the types of symmetry (line, turn, or point) of the given figure.

(a)   (b)

(c)

4. For each of the following, describe the locations of all the planes of symmetry.

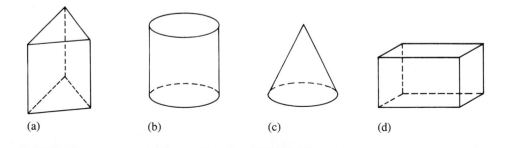

(a)   (b)   (c)   (d)

5. Complete each of the following motions.

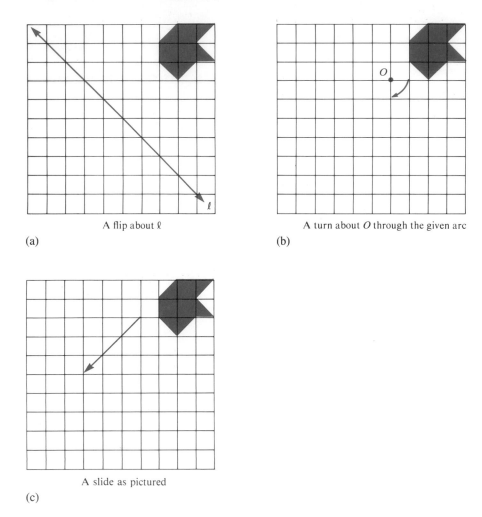

A flip about ℓ

(a)

A turn about O through the given arc

(b)

A slide as pictured

(c)

6. For each of the following, construct the image of △ABC.

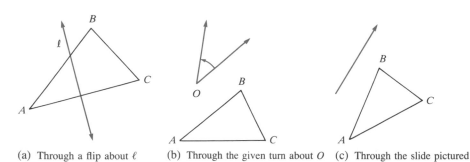

(a) Through a flip about ℓ   (b) Through the given turn about O   (c) Through the slide pictured

7. Construct each of the following using (i) compass and straightedge, (ii) paper folding.

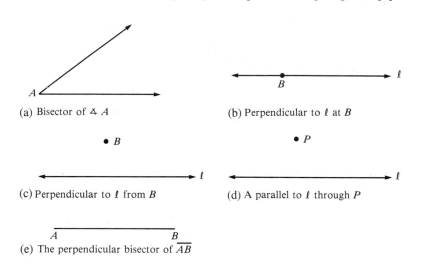

(a) Bisector of ∡ A

(b) Perpendicular to ℓ at B

(c) Perpendicular to ℓ from B

(d) A parallel to ℓ through P

(e) The perpendicular bisector of $\overline{AB}$

8. For each of the following pairs of similar triangles, find the missing measures.

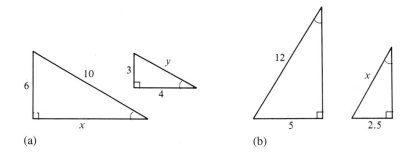

(a)   (b)

9. Divide the segment below into five congruent parts.

10. If ABCD is a trapezoid, $\overline{EF} \parallel \overline{AD}$, and $\overline{AC}$ is a diagonal, prove that $\dfrac{a}{b} = \dfrac{c}{d}$.

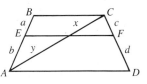

11. Construct a circle containing A and B whose center is on ℓ.

A •

• B

ℓ

12. Determine whether each of the following is true or false. If false, explain why.
    (a) A radius of a circle is a chord of the circle.
    (b) A diameter of a circle may be a tangent of the circle.
    (c) If a radius bisects a chord of a circle, then it is perpendicular to the chord.
    (d) Two spheres may intersect in exactly one point.
    (e) Two spheres may intersect in a circle.

13. $\overline{AC}$ and $\overline{BD}$ are diameters of the circle with center P given below.
    (a) Prove that $\overline{AD} \parallel \overline{BC}$.
    (b) Prove that polygon $ABCD$ is a rectangle.

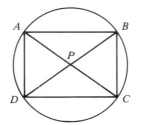

14. A person 2 m tall casts a shadow 1 m long when a building has a 6 m shadow. How high is the building?

15. (a) Which of the following polygons can be inscribed in a circle? Assume all sides of each polygon are congruent and all the angles of polygons (iii) and (iv) are congruent.
    (b) Based on the answer to part (a), make a conjecture about what kinds of polygons can be inscribed in a circle.

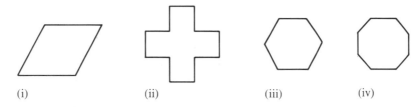

(i)   (ii)   (iii)   (iv)

16. Explain how to circumscribe a circle about a regular heptagon using only a compass and straightedge.

17. Explain how to inscribe a circle in a square using only a compass and straightedge.

18. In the circle with center O, $\overrightarrow{AB}$ is tangent to the circle. If $\angle CBA \cong \angle BDA$, prove that $(AB)^2 = (AC)(AD)$.

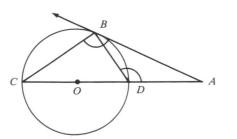

SELECTED BIBLIOGRAPHY

Brown, R. "Making Geometry a Personal and Inventive Experience." *The Mathematics Teacher* 75 (September 1982): 442–446.

Burton, G. "Metrification of Elementary Mathematics Textbooks in the Seventies—the 1870's, That Is." *Arithmetic Teacher* 27 (December 1979):28–31.

Edwards, R. "Discoveries in Geometry by Folding and Cutting." *The Arithmetic Teacher* 24 (March 1977):196–198.

Graening, J. "The Geometry of Tennis." *The Mathematics Teacher* 75 (November 1982):658–663.

Hiatt, A. "Problem Solving in Geometry." *The Mathematics Teacher* 65 (November 1972):595–600.

Immerzeel, G. "Geometric Activities for Early Childhood Education." *The Arithmetic Teacher* 20 (October 1973):438–443.

Johnson, M. "Generating Patterns for Transformations." *The Arithmetic Teacher* 24 (March 1977):191–195.

Juraschek, W., and G. McGlathery. "Funny Letters: A Discrepant Event." *Arithmetic Teacher* 27 (April 1980):43–47.

Kerr, D. "A Case for Geometry: Geometry Is Important, It Is There, Teach It." *Arithmetic Teacher* 26 (February 1979):14.

Kerr, D. "The Study of Space Experiences: A Framework for Geometry for Elementary Teachers." *The Arithmetic Teacher* 23 (March 1976):169–174.

Kidder, R. "Euclidean Transformations: Elementary School Spaceometry." *The Arithmetic Teacher* 24 (March 1977):201–207.

Krause, M. "Wind Rose, the Beautiful Circle." *The Arithmetic Teacher* 20 (May 1973):375–379.

Lindquist, M., and M. Dana. "The Surprising Circle!" *Arithmetic Teacher* 25 (January 1978):4–10.

Lindquist, M., and M. Dana. "Wallpaper Capers." *Arithmetic Teacher* 26 (February 1979):4–9.

Lott, J. and I. Dayoub. "What Can Be Done with a Mira?" *The Mathematics Teacher* 70 (May 1977):394–399.

Maletsky, E. "Activities: Fun with Flips." *The Mathematics Teacher* 66 (October 1973):531–534.

Moulton, J. "Some Geometry Experiences for Elementary School Children." *The Arithmetic Teacher* 21 (February 1974): 114–116.

Reid, J. "Cutting Across a Circle." *Arithmetic Teacher* 26 (April 1979):27.

Sanok, G. "Living in a World of Transformations." *Arithmetic Teacher* 25 (April 1978):36–40.

Silverman, H. "Geometry in the Primary Grades: Exploring Geometric Ideas in the Primary Grades." *Arithmetic Teacher* 26 (February 1979):15–16.

Thomas, D. "Geometry in the Middle School: Problem Solving with Trapezoids." *Arithmetic Teacher* 26 (February 1979): 20–21.

Van de Walle, J., and C. Thomson. "A Triangle Treasury." *Arithmetic Teacher* 28 (February 1981):6–11.

Van de Walle, J., and C. Thomson. "Concepts, Art, and Fun from Simple Tiling Patterns." *Arithmetic Teacher* 28 (November 1980):4–8.

Woodward, E. "Geometry with a Mira." *The Arithmetic Teacher* 24 (February 1977):117–118.

Zweng, M. "A Geometry Course for Elementary Teachers." *The Arithmetic Teacher* 20 (October 1973):457–467.

Concepts of Measurement

PRELIMINARY PROBLEM

Rancher Larry purchased a plot of land surrounded by a fence. The former owner had marked off nine squares of equal size to subdivide the land, as shown. Larry wants to divide the land into two plots of equal area. To divide the property, he wishes to build a single, straight fence beginning at the far left corner (point P on the drawing). Is such a fence possible? If so, where should it be?

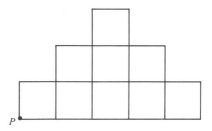

INTRODUCTION

In this chapter we develop the metric system of measurement for length, area, volume, mass and temperature with the philosophy that students should learn to think within a measurement system. Consequently, conversions among units of measure in the metric and the English systems are not considered.

In addition, we develop formulas for the areas of plane figures and for surface areas and volumes of solids. We also use the concept of area to discuss the Pythagorean Theorem.

11-1   THE METRIC SYSTEM: UNITS OF LENGTH

Early attempts at measurement used hands, arms, and feet as units of measure. These early crude measurements were eventually refined and standardized by the English into a very complicated system, including three types of weights: troy, avoirdupois, and apothecary. The English system of weights and measures has been used in many countries, including the United States. However, when faced with problems using English measures, many people feel like Peppermint Patty does in the cartoon.

© 1974 United Feature Syndicate, Inc.

meter

The metric system was first proposed by Gabriel Mouton in France in 1670. However, not until the French Revolution in 1790 did the French Academy of Sciences bring various groups together to develop the new system. The academy recognized the need for a standard base unit of linear measurement. The members chose $\frac{1}{10,000,000}$ of the distance from the equator to the North Pole, on a meridian through Paris, as the base unit of length and called it the **meter.** Later, the meter was redefined in terms of krypton 86 wavelengths. The name *meter* was derived from the Greek word *metron*, meaning "a measure." Base units of volume and mass were derived from the meter. For ease in computation, larger and smaller units were created by multiplying or dividing the base units by powers of ten. Thus, the metric system is a decimal system, just as our monetary system is a decimal system.

The krypton 86 definition of meter is important for accuracy but not very meaningful in everyday life. If you turn your head away from your outstretched arm, then the distance from your nose to your fingertip is about 1 meter. Also, 1 meter is about the distance from a door knob to the floor; 1 meter is about 39 inches, slightly longer than 1 yard. Most educators strongly recommend that the metric system be taught independently and not taught as conversions to and from the English system.

Different units of length in the metric system are obtained by combining an appropriate prefix with the base unit. The prefixes, the multiplication factors they indicate, and their symbols are given in Table 11-1.

TABLE 11-1

Prefix	Factor		Symbol
kilo	1000	(one thousand)	k
hecto	100	(one hundred)	h
deka	10	(ten)	da
deci	0.1	(one tenth)	d
centi	0.01	(one hundredth)	c
milli	0.001	(one thousandth)	m

Remark

Hecto, deka, and deci are not common prefixes and have limited use. These should not be stressed when teaching the metric system. Kilo, hecto, and deka are Greek prefixes, whereas deci, centi, and milli are Latin prefixes.

Using the metric prefixes along with meter gives the names for different units of length. Table 11-2 gives these units along with their relationship to the meter and the symbol for each. The symbol m stands for meter. Notice that there is no period after the m; it is a symbol rather than an abbreviation.

TABLE 11-2

Unit	Symbol	Relationship to Basic Unit	
kilometer	km	1000	meters
*hectometer	hm	100	meters
*dekameter	dam	10	meters
meter	**m**	**base unit**	
*decimeter	dm	0.1	meter
centimeter	cm	0.01	meter
millimeter	mm	0.001	meter

*Not commonly used.

The relationships among metric units of length are based on powers of ten, as reflected by the prefixes in the names of the units. For example, 1 centimeter is

0.01 of a meter, because "centi" means one-hundredth. We write this as 1 cm = 0.01 m. Consequently, when 1 m is divided into 100 congruent parts, each part is 1 cm long. Hence, 1 m = 100 cm. One centimeter is about the width of your little finger, the diameter of the head of a thumbtack, or the width of a white Cuisenaire rod. A unit smaller than a centimeter is found by dividing 1 m into 1000 congruent parts or by dividing 1 cm into ten congruent parts. Thus, 1 mm = 0.1 cm = 0.001 m, or 1000 mm = 100 cm = 1 m. One millimeter is about the thickness of a paper clip or a dime. Some estimations for a meter, a centimeter and a millimeter are shown in Figure 11-1.

FIGURE 11-1

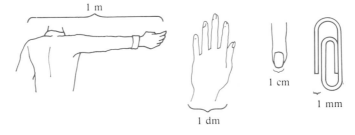

The units decimeter, dekameter, and hectometer represent 0.1 m, 10 m, and 100 m, respectively, but, as indicated in Table 11-2, they are not commonly used. The kilometer is commonly used for measuring long distances. Because "kilo" stands for 1000, 1 km = 1000 m. Nine football fields, including end zones, laid end-to-end are approximately 1 km long.

Because metric units of length are based on powers of ten, the conversion from one metric unit to another is easy. As with money, we simply move the decimal point to the left or right, depending on the units. For example,

$$0.123 \, \text{km} = 1.23 \, \text{hm} = 12.3 \, \text{dam} = 123 \, \text{m} = 1230 \, \text{dm} = 12{,}300 \, \text{cm} = 123{,}000 \, \text{mm}$$

It is possible to convert units using the chart in Figure 11-2. We count the number of steps from one unit to the other and move the decimal point that many steps in the same direction.

FIGURE 11-2

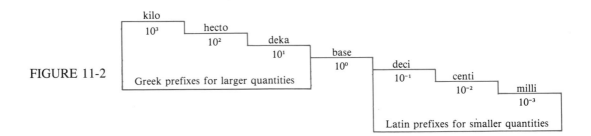

Example 11-1 | Convert each of the following.

(a) 1.4 km = _____ m   (b) 285 mm = _____ m

Solution | (a) 1 km = 1000 m, so to change from kilometers to meters we multiply by 1000. Therefore, we move the decimal point three places to the right. Hence, 1.4 km = 1400 m.

(b) 1 mm = 0.001 m, so to change from millimeters to meters we multiply by 0.001. In other words, we move the decimal point three places to the left. Thus, 285 mm = 0.285 m.

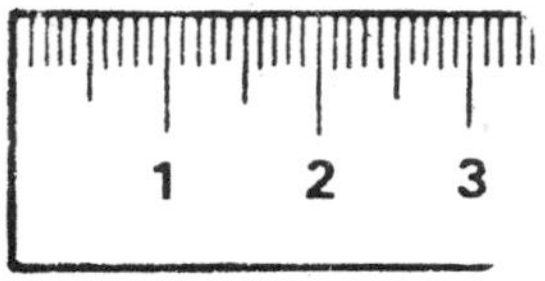

FIGURE 11-3

In geometry, units of length are usually used to measure distances along lines and thus are called linear measure. Recall that in the development of the number line (Chapter 3), we chose a point on the line to represent 0 and a second point to represent 1. If we select the points so that the distance between 0 and 1 is 1 centimeter and develop the number line accordingly, then the number line can be used to measure lengths of segments in terms of centimeters. Similarly, by making the distance between 0 and 1 an inch, a meter, a foot, and so on, we can develop other rulers for measuring lengths. Figure 11-3 shows part of a centimeter ruler.

The following are three basic properties of distance:

1. The distance between any two points A and B is greater than or equal to 0, written $AB \geq 0$.
2. The distance between any two points A and B is the same as the distance between B and A, written $AB = BA$.
3. For any three points, A, B, and C, the distance between A and B plus the distance between B and C is greater than or equal to the distance between A and C, written $AB + BC \geq AC$.

Remark | The third property is called the **triangle inequality.** As noted in Section 10-1, in a triangle inequality | triangle the sum of the lengths of two sides is always greater than the length of the third side. Notice that as in Figure 11-4, $AB + BC = AC$ if and only if $A, B,$ and C are collinear and B is between A and C.

FIGURE 11-4

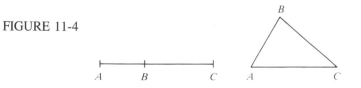

perimeter

The **perimeter** of a simple closed curve is the length of the curve, that is, the distance around the figure. If a figure is a polygon, its perimeter is the sum of the lengths of the sides. Perimeter is always expressed using linear measure.

Example 11-2

Find the perimeter of each of the shapes in Figure 11-5.

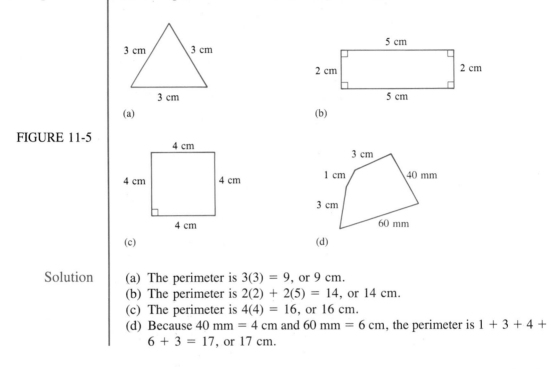

FIGURE 11-5

Solution

(a) The perimeter is 3(3) = 9, or 9 cm.
(b) The perimeter is 2(2) + 2(5) = 14, or 14 cm.
(c) The perimeter is 4(4) = 16, or 16 cm.
(d) Because 40 mm = 4 cm and 60 mm = 6 cm, the perimeter is 1 + 3 + 4 + 6 + 3 = 17, or 17 cm.

circumference

The distance around a circle is called its **circumference.** The ancient Greeks discovered that if they divided the circumference of a circle by the length of a diameter, they always obtained approximately the same number, regardless of the size of the circle. The value of the number is approximately 3.14. Today, the ratio

pi

of circumference C to diameter d is symbolized as π **(pi).** In the early twentieth century, mathematicians proved that this ratio $\dfrac{C}{d}$, or π, is not a terminating or repeating decimal but an irrational number.

The relationship $\dfrac{C}{d} = \pi$ gives a formula for finding the circumference of a circle. Usually, it is written as $C = \pi d$ or $C = 2\pi r$ since the length of a diameter d is twice the radius of the circle. For most practical purposes, π is approximated by $\frac{22}{7}$, $3\frac{1}{7}$, or 3.14. These values are only approximations and are not exact values of π. If you are asked for the exact circumference of a circle with diameter 6 cm, the answer is 6π cm. Circumference is always expressed in linear measure.

Example 11-3 | Find each of the following.

(a) The circumference of a circle if the radius is 2 m.
(b) The radius of a circle if the circumference is 15π m.

Solution | (a) $C = 2\pi(2) = 4\pi$. Thus, the circumference is 4π m.
(b) $C = 2\pi r$ implies $15\pi = 2\pi r$. Hence, $r = \frac{15}{2}$. Thus, the radius is $\frac{15}{2}$ m.

PROBLEM SET 11-1

1. A millimeter is the smallest distance pictured on the metric ruler in the following figure. Starting from the left end of the ruler, the distance from the end to A is 1 mm, and the distance from the end to B is 10 mm, or 1 cm. The distance from the end to J is 100 mm, 10 cm, or 1 dm.

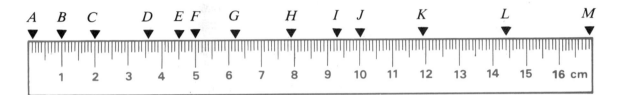

Use the ruler to answer each of the following.
(a) C points to _____ mm or _____ cm
(b) D points to _____ mm or _____ cm
(c) E points to _____ mm or _____ cm
(d) F points to _____ cm or _____ mm
(e) G points to _____ cm or _____ mm
(f) H points to _____ cm or _____ mm
(g) I points to _____ mm or _____ cm
(h) K points to _____ cm or _____ mm
(i) L points to _____ mm or _____ cm
(j) M points to _____ mm or _____ cm

2. Draw segments that you estimate to be of the following lengths. Then, using a metric ruler, check the estimates.
   (a) 10 mm   (b) 100 mm   (c) 1 cm   (d) 10 cm
   (e) 0.01 m   (f) 15 cm   (g) 0.1 m   (h) 27 mm
   (i) 23 cm   (j) 5 cm

3. Estimate and then measure the following segment. Express the measurement in each of the following units.

$$\vdash\!\!\!-\!\!\!-\!\!\!-\!\!\!-\!\!\!-\!\!\!-\!\!\!-\!\!\!-\!\!\!-\!\!\!-\!\!\!\dashv$$

(a) millimeters   (b) centimeters   (c) meters

4. Choose an appropriate metric unit and estimate each of the following. Measure, if possible, to check the estimate.
   (a) The length of a pencil
   (b) The diameter of a nickel
   (c) The width of the top of a desk
   (d) The thickness of the top of a desk
   (e) The length of this sheet of paper
   (f) The height of a door
   (g) Your height
   (h) Your handspan

5. Complete the following table.

Item	m	cm	mm
(a) Length of a piece of paper		350	
(b) Height of a woman	1.63		
(c) Width of a film			35
(d) Length of a cigarette			100
(e) Length of two meter sticks laid end-to-end	2		

6. For each of the following, place a decimal point in the number to make the sentence reasonable.
   (a) A stack of ten dimes is 1000 mm high.
   (b) The desk is 770 m high.
   (c) It is 100 m across the street.
   (d) A dollar bill is 155 cm long.
   (e) The basketball player is 1950 cm tall.
   (f) A new piece of chalk is about 8100 cm long.
   (g) The speed limit in town was 400 km/hour.

7. List the following in decreasing order:

   8 cm, 38 dm, 5218 mm, 245 cm, 91 mm, 6 m, 700 mm, 52 dm

8. Complete each of the following:
   (a) 17 m + 24 cm = _____ cm
   (b) 1 m + 40 mm + 2 cm = _____ cm
   (c) 3 m + 130 mm + 3 cm = _____ cm

9. Guess the perimeter of each figure in centimeters and then check the estimates using a ruler.

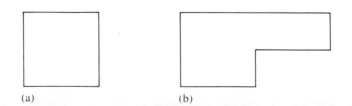

(a)   (b)

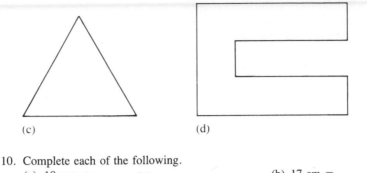

(c)   (d)

10. Complete each of the following.
    (a) 10 mm = _____ cm
    (b) 17 cm = _____ m
    (c) 262 m = _____ km
    (d) 3 km = _____ m
    (e) 30 mm = _____ m
    (f) 0.17 km = _____ m
    (g) 35 m = _____ cm
    (h) 26,418 m = _____ km
    (i) 359 mm = _____ m
    (j) 1 mm = _____ cm
    (k) 647 mm = _____ cm
    (l) 0.1 cm = _____ mm
    (m) 5 km = _____ m
    (n) 51.3 m = _____ cm

11. Find the perimeter of each of the following.

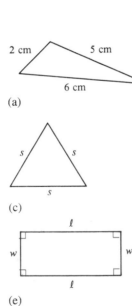

2 cm   5 cm

6 cm

(a)

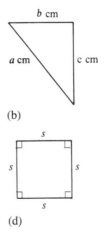

b cm

a cm c cm

(b)

s s

s

(c)

s

s s

s

(d)

ℓ

w w

ℓ

(e)

(f) A regular polygon with n sides, each of whose length is s.

12. For each of the following circumferences, find the exact length of the radius of the circle.
    (a) 12π cm   (b) 6 m   (c) 0.67 m   (d) 92π cm

13. For each of the following, if a circle has the dimensions given, what is its circumference?
    (a) 6 cm diameter   (b) 3 cm radius
    (c) $\frac{2}{\pi}$ cm radius   (d) 6π cm diameter

14. What happens to the circumference of a circle if the length of the radius is doubled?

15. The following figure is a circle whose radius is r units. The diameters of the two semicircular regions inside the large circle are both r units, too. Compute the length of the curve that separates the black and white regions.

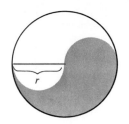

16. Draw a triangle ABC. Measure the length of each of its sides in millimeters. For each of the following, tell which is greater and by how much.
    (a) $AB + BC$ or AC (b) $BC + CA$ or AB (c) $AB + CA$ or BC

BRAIN TEASER

Suppose a wire is stretched tightly around the earth. (The radius of the earth is approximately 6400 km.) If the wire is cut, its circumference is increased by 20 m, and the wire is placed back around the earth so that the wire is the same distance from the earth at every point, could you walk under the wire?

11-2 AREAS OF POLYGONS AND CIRCLES

area The term **area** refers to an amount of surface. By the area of a figure we mean the area of the interior region determined by the figure. For example, by the area of a rectangle we mean the area of the rectangular region determined by the rectangle. The most commonly used region for measuring area is the square. For example, a square measuring 1 inch on each side has area of 1 square inch, denoted by 1 sq in. A square measuring 1 cm on each side has an area of 1 square centimeter, denoted by 1 cm^2. A square measuring 1 m on each side has an area of 1 square meter, denoted by 1 m^2. Recall that perimeters and circumferences are measured using linear units. The measure of area is always in square units.

To determine how many square centimeters are in a square meter, look at Figure 11-6(a). There are 100 cm in 1 m, so each side of the square meter has a measure of 100 cm. Thus, it takes 100 rows of 100 square centimeters each to fill a square meter—that is $100 \cdot 100$ or $10,000$ cm^2. In general, the area, A, of a square that is s units on a side is s^2, as given in Figure 11-6(b).

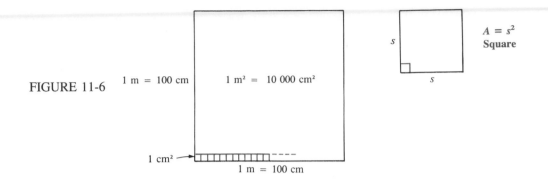

FIGURE 11-6

Other metric conversions of area measure can be developed using the formula for the area of a square. For example, Figure 11-7 shows that $1 \text{ m}^2 = 10,000 \text{ cm}^2 = 1,000,000 \text{ mm}^2$. Likewise, Figure 11-8 shows that $1 \text{ m}^2 = 0.000001 \text{ km}^2$. Similarly, $1 \text{ cm}^2 = 100 \text{ mm}^2$ and $1 \text{ km}^2 = 1,000,000 \text{ m}^2$.

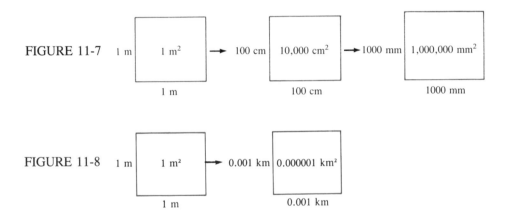

FIGURE 11-7

FIGURE 11-8

Table 11-3 shows the symbols for metric units of area and their relationship to the square meter.

TABLE 11-3

Unit	Symbol	Relationship to square meter
square kilometer	km^2	$1,000,000 \ \ m^2$
*square hectometer	hm^2	$10,000 \ \ m^2$
*square dekameter	dam^2	$100 \ \ m^2$
square meter	m^2	$1 \ \ m^2$
*square decimeter	dm^2	$0.01 \ \ m^2$
square centimeter	cm^2	$0.0001 \ \ m^2$
square millimeter	mm^2	$0.000001 \ \ m^2$

*Not commonly used.

Example 11-4

Convert each of the following.

(a) $5 \text{ cm}^2 = $ _____ mm^2 (b) $1240 \text{ m}^2 = $ _____ km^2

Solution

(a) $1 \text{ cm}^2 = 100 \text{ mm}^2$ implies $5 \text{ cm}^2 = 5 \cdot 1 \text{ cm}^2 = 5 \cdot 100 \text{ mm}^2 = 500 \text{ mm}^2$.
(b) $1 \text{ m}^2 = 0.000001 \text{ km}^2$ implies $1240 \text{ m}^2 = 1240 \cdot 1 \text{ m}^2 = $
    $1240 \cdot 0.000001 \text{ km}^2 = 0.001240 \text{ km}^2$.

One of the most common applications of area today is in land measure. Old deeds in the United States include land measures in terms of chains, poles, rods, acres, sections, lots, and townships. In the metric system, small land areas are
are measured in terms of a square unit 10 m on a side, called an **are** (pronounced "air") and denoted by a. Larger land areas, currently measured in acres, are
hectares measured in **hectares.** A hectare is 100 a. A hectare, denoted by ha, is the amount of land whose area is $10{,}000 \text{ m}^2$, about $2\frac{1}{2}$ acres. One hectare is the area of a
square kilometer square 100 m on a side. For very large land measures, the **square kilometer,** denoted by km^2, is used. One square kilometer is the area of a square with a side 1 km, or 1000 m, long.

Example 11-5

A square field has a side of 400 m. Find the area of the field in hectares.

Solution

$A = (400 \text{ m})^2 = 160{,}000 \text{ m}^2 = 16 \text{ ha}$

One way to measure area is to count the number of units of area contained in any given region. For example, suppose the square in Figure 11-9(a) represents one square unit. Then, the rectangle $ABCD$ in Figure 11-9(b) contains $3 \cdot 4$, or 12, nonoverlapping square units, since there are three rows of squares with four squares in a row.

FIGURE 11-9

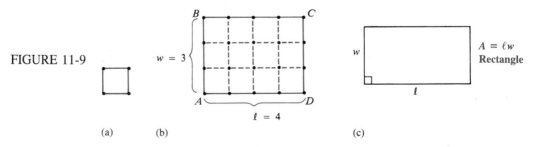

(a)   (b)   (c)

Hence, the area of rectangle $ABCD$ is 12 square units. If the unit is 1 cm^2, then the area of rectangle $ABCD$ is 12 cm^2. As with rectangle $ABCD$, the area of any rectangle may be found by multiplying the lengths of two adjacent sides. In general, if A represents the area of any rectangle whose adjacent sides have lengths ℓ and w (each in the same unit length), then $A = \ell w$, as given in Figure 11-9(c).

Example 11-6   Find the area of each rectangle in Figure 11-10.

FIGURE 11-10

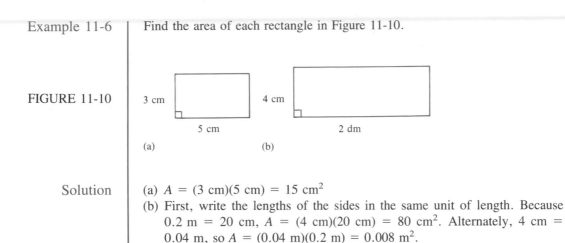

3 cm

5 cm

(a)

4 cm

2 dm

(b)

Solution

(a) $A = (3 \text{ cm})(5 \text{ cm}) = 15 \text{ cm}^2$
(b) First, write the lengths of the sides in the same unit of length. Because $0.2 \text{ m} = 20 \text{ cm}$, $A = (4 \text{ cm})(20 \text{ cm}) = 80 \text{ cm}^2$. Alternately, $4 \text{ cm} = 0.04 \text{ m}$, so $A = (0.04 \text{ m})(0.2 \text{ m}) = 0.008 \text{ m}^2$.

Formulas for areas of various polygons follow from the formula for the area of a rectangle. Consider, for example, the parallelogram $ABCD$ in Figure 11-11(a). The parallelogram can be separated into two parts. The shaded triangle can be placed on the right of the parallelogram, as in Figure 11-11(b), to obtain a rectangle with length b and width h. The parallelogram and the rectangle have the same area. (Why?) Since the area of the rectangle is bh, the area of the original parallelogram $ABCD$ is also bh. In general, any side of a parallelogram can be designated as a **base** with measure b. We will use b to represent either the base or its measure, depending on the context. The **height,** h, is always the length of a segment from the opposite side, to the base and perpendicular to the base. Thus, the area of a parallelogram with base b and height h to that base is $A = b \cdot h$, as given in Figure 11-11(b).

base

height

FIGURE 11-11

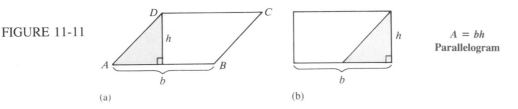

D C

h

A B

b

(a)

h

b

(b)

$A = bh$
Parallelogram

A formula for the area of a triangle follows from the formula for the area of a parallelogram. In Figure 11-12(a), $\triangle ABC$ has base b and altitude h. If $\triangle ABD$ is constructed congruent to $\triangle ABC$ and placed as shown in Figure 11-12(b), it can be proved that quadrilateral $BCAD$ is a parallelogram. The area of parallelogram $BCAD$ is bh, so the area of $\triangle ABC$ is $\frac{1}{2}bh$. That is, the area of a triangle is equal to one-half the product of the length of a side and the altitude to that side or to the line containing that side.

FIGURE 11-12

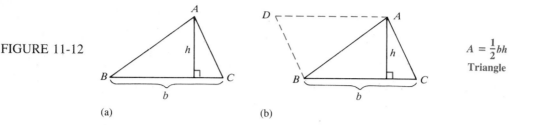

(a)   (b)

$$A = \frac{1}{2}bh$$
Triangle

Example 11-7 | Find the area of each drawing in Figure 11-13. Assume that the quadrilaterals in (a) and (b) are parallelograms.

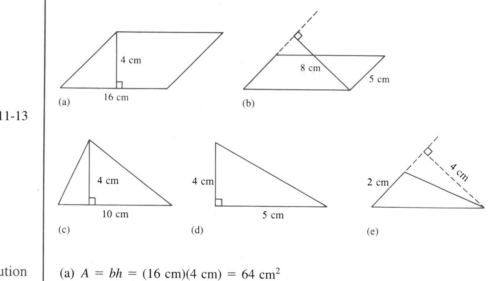

FIGURE 11-13

Solution | (a) $A = bh = (16 \text{ cm})(4 \text{ cm}) = 64 \text{ cm}^2$
(b) $A = bh = (5 \text{ cm})(8 \text{ cm}) = 40 \text{ cm}^2$
(c) $A = \frac{1}{2}bh = \frac{1}{2}(10 \text{ cm})(4 \text{ cm}) = 20 \text{ cm}^2$
(d) $A = \frac{1}{2}bh = \frac{1}{2}(5 \text{ cm})(4 \text{ cm}) = 10 \text{ cm}^2$
(e) $A = \frac{1}{2}bh = \frac{1}{2}(2 \text{ cm})(4 \text{ cm}) = 4 \text{ cm}^2$

Areas of other polygons can be found by partitioning the polygons into triangles. Trapezoid $ABCD$ in Figure 11-14(a), has bases b_1 and b_2 and height h. By drawing diagonal $\overline{BD}$ (or $\overline{AC}$), as in Figure 11-14(b), two triangles are formed, one with base $\overline{AB}$ and height $\overline{DE}$ and the other with base $\overline{CD}$ and height $\overline{BF}$. Since $\overline{DE} \cong \overline{BF}$, each has height h. Thus, the areas of triangles ADB and DCB are $\frac{1}{2}(b_1h)$ and $\frac{1}{2}(b_2h)$, respectively. Hence, the area of trapezoid $ABCD$ is $\frac{1}{2}(b_1h) + \frac{1}{2}(b_2h)$ or $\frac{1}{2}h(b_1 + b_2)$. That is, the area of a trapezoid is equal to one-half the length of the height times the sum of the lengths of the bases.

FIGURE 11-14

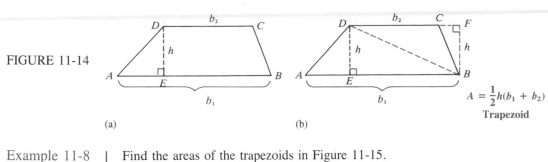

(a)   (b)

$$A = \frac{1}{2}h(b_1 + b_2)$$
Trapezoid

Example 11-8

Find the areas of the trapezoids in Figure 11-15.

FIGURE 11-15

(a)   (b)

Solution

(a) $A = \frac{1}{2}h(b_1 + b_2) = \frac{1}{2}(4 \text{ cm})(12 \text{ cm} + 16 \text{ cm}) = 56 \text{ cm}^2$

(b) To find the area, we need to find h, the height of the trapezoid. In Figure 11-15(b), $BE = CF = h$. Also, $\overline{BE}$ is a side of $\triangle ABE$, which has angles with measures of 45° and 90°. Consequently, the third angle in triangle ABE is $180 - (45 + 90)$, or 45°. Therefore, $\triangle ABE$ is isosceles and $AE = BE = h$. Similarly, it follows that $FD = h$. Because $BCFE$ is a rectangle, $EF = 2$ cm and we have the following equation for h:

$$AD = AE + EF + FD = h + 2 + h = 6$$

Thus, $h = 2$ cm and the area of the trapezoid is $A = \frac{1}{2}(2 \text{ cm})(2 \text{ cm} + 6 \text{ cm})$, or 8 cm².

apothem

Just as the area of a triangle was used to find the area of a trapezoid, it can be used to find the area of any regular polygon. For example, consider the regular hexagon pictured in Figure 11-16(a). The hexagon can be separated into six congruent triangles, each with a vertex at the center, with side s, and height a. (The height of such a triangle of a regular polygon is called the **apothem** and is denoted by a.) The area of each triangle is $\frac{1}{2}as$. Since there are six triangles that make up the hexagon, the area of the hexagon is $6(\frac{1}{2}as)$ or $\frac{1}{2}a(6s)$. However, $6s$ is the perimeter p of the hexagon, so the area of the hexagon is $\frac{1}{2}ap$. The same process can be used to develop the formula for the area of any regular polygon. That is, the area of any regular polygon is $\frac{1}{2}ap$, where a is the height of one of the triangles involved and p is the perimeter of the polygon.

FIGURE 11-16

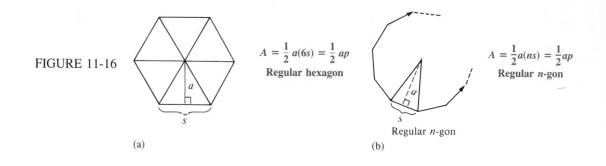

$$A = \frac{1}{2} a(6s) = \frac{1}{2} ap$$

Regular hexagon

(a)

$$A = \frac{1}{2} a(ns) = \frac{1}{2} ap$$

Regular n-gon

Regular n-gon

(b)

The formula for the area of a regular polygon can be used to develop the formula for the area of a circle. Consider, for example, the circle in Figure 11-17(a). The area of a regular polygon inscribed in the circle as in Figure 11-17(b) approximates the area of the circle. The area of any inscribed regular n-gon is $\frac{1}{2}ap$, where a is the height of a triangle of the n-gon and p is the perimeter. If the number of sides, n, is made very large, then the perimeter and the area of the n-gon are close to those of the circle. Also, a is approximately equal to the radius r of the circle and the perimeter approximates the circumference, $2\pi r$. Because the area of the circle is approximately equal to the area of the n-gon, then $\frac{1}{2}ap \doteq \frac{1}{2}r \cdot 2\pi r = \pi r^2$, as given in Figure 11-17(b). In fact, the area of the circle is exactly πr^2.

FIGURE 11-17

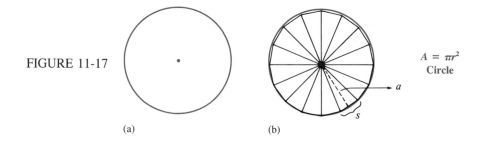

$$A = \pi r^2$$

Circle

(a)   (b)

sector
central angle

A **sector** of a circle is a pie-shaped region of the circle determined by a **central angle** of the circle, that is, an angle whose vertex is at the center of the circle. The area of a sector depends upon the radius of the circle and the central angle determining the sector. If the angle has a measure of 90°, as in Figure 11-18(a), the area of the sector is one-fourth the area of the circle or $\frac{90}{360}\pi r^2$. In any circle there are 360 sectors, each of whose central angle has measure of 1°, so the area of each such sector is $\frac{1}{360}(\pi r^2)$. A sector whose central angle has measure θ degrees has area

$$\theta\left(\frac{1}{360}\right)(\pi r^2) \quad \text{or} \quad \frac{\theta}{360}(\pi r^2)$$

as shown in Figure 11-18(b).

FIGURE 11-18

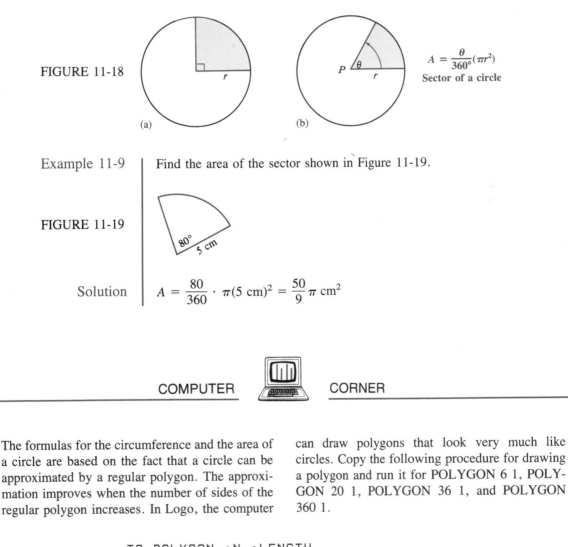

$$A = \frac{\theta}{360°}(\pi r^2)$$
Sector of a circle

(a)　　　(b)

Example 11-9 | Find the area of the sector shown in Figure 11-19.

FIGURE 11-19

80° 5 cm

Solution | $A = \dfrac{80}{360} \cdot \pi(5 \text{ cm})^2 = \dfrac{50}{9}\pi \text{ cm}^2$

COMPUTER ▯ CORNER

The formulas for the circumference and the area of a circle are based on the fact that a circle can be approximated by a regular polygon. The approximation improves when the number of sides of the regular polygon increases. In Logo, the computer can draw polygons that look very much like circles. Copy the following procedure for drawing a polygon and run it for POLYGON 6 1, POLYGON 20 1, POLYGON 36 1, and POLYGON 360 1.

```
TO POLYGON :N :LENGTH
REPEAT :N[FD :LENGTH RT 360/:N]
END
```

PROBLEM SET 11-2

1. Choose the most appropriate metric units (cm^2, m^2, or km^2) for measuring each of the following.
   (a) Area of a sheet of notebook paper
   (b) Area of a quarter
   (c) Area of a desk top
   (d) Area of a classroom floor
   (e) Area of a parallel parking space
   (f) Area of an airport runway
2. Complete the following conversion table.

Item	m^2	cm^2	mm^2
Area of a sheet of paper		588	
Area of a cross section of a crayon			192
Area of a desk top	1.5		
Area of a dollar bill		100	
Area of a postage stamp		5	

3. Estimate, then measure, each of the following using either cm^2, m^2, or km^2.
   (a) Area of door   (b) Area of chair seat
   (c) Area of desk top   (d) Area of chalkboard
4. Explain the difference between a 2-m square and 2 m^2.
5. Find the area of each of the following triangles.

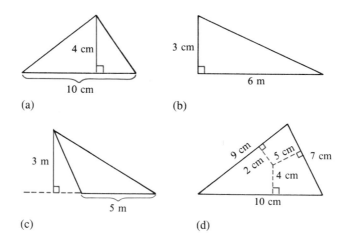

(a)   (b)

(c)   (d)

6. Find the area of each of the following quadrilaterals.

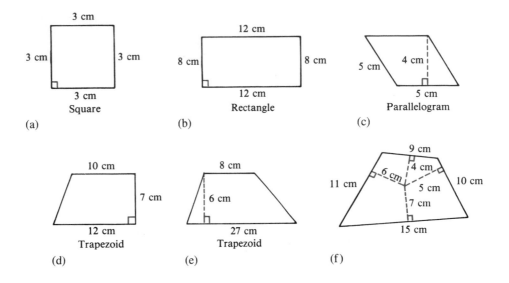

(a) Square

(b) Rectangle

(c) Parallelogram

(d) Trapezoid

(e) Trapezoid

(f)

7. In the figure, $\ell \parallel \overleftrightarrow{AB}$. If the area of $\triangle ABP$ is 10 cm², what are the areas of $\triangle ABQ$, $\triangle ABR$, $\triangle ABS$, $\triangle ABT$, and $\triangle ABU$? Explain your answers.

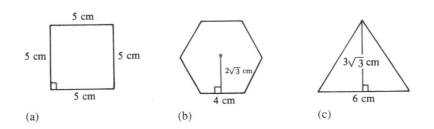

8. Find the area of each regular polygon.

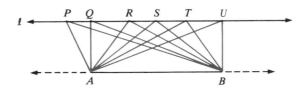

(a)

(b)

(c)

9. Find the area of each of the following. Leave your answers in terms of π.

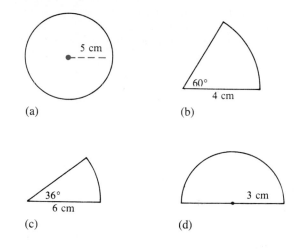

(a)   (b)

(c)   (d)

10. (a) If a circle has a circumference of 8π cm, what is its area?
    (b) If a circle with radius r and a square with a side of length s have the same area, express r in terms of s.

11. Find the area of each of the following shaded parts. Assume all arcs are circular.

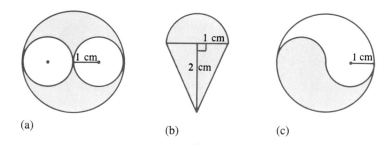

(a)   (b)   (c)

12. Solve each of the following for x.

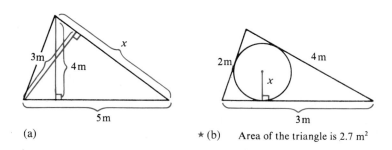

(a)   ★ (b)   Area of the triangle is 2.7 m²

13. Find the area of rhombus $ABCD$ if $AC = 6$ m and $BD = 8$ m.

14. Complete each of the following:
    (a) A football field is about 49 m by 100 m or _____ m².
    (b) About _____ ares are in two football fields.
    (c) About _____ hectares are in two football fields.

15. A circular flower bed is 6 m in diameter and has a circular sidewalk around it 1 m wide. Find the area of the sidewalk in square meters.

16. (a) A rectangular piece of land is 1300 m by 1500 m. What is the area in square kilometers? What is the area in hectares?
    (b) A rectangular piece of land is 1300 yards by 1500 yards. What is the area in square miles? What is the area in acres? Compare this problem to part (a).

17. Joe uses stick-on square carpet tiles to cover his 3-m by 4-m bathroom. If each tile is 10 cm on a side, how many tiles does he need?

18. A rectangular plot of land is to be seeded with grass. If the plot is 22 m by 28 m and if a 1-kg bag of seed is needed for 85 m² of land, how many bags of seed will it take?

19. (a) Find the area of each polygon in the figure if the area of the figure in the upper right hand corner is one square unit.

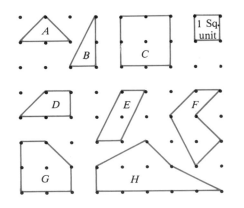

(b) If all vertices of a polygon are points on dot paper, it is called a **lattice polygon.** In 1899, G. Pick discovered a surprising theorem involving I, the number of dots *inside* the polygon, and B, the number of dots that lie *on* the polygon. The theorem states that the area of any lattice polygon is $I + \frac{1}{2}B - 1$. Check that this is true for the polygons in (a).

20. The area of a trapezoid can be found by constructing trapezoid (2) congruent to another trapezoid, (1), and placing them to form a parallelogram as follows. Explain how the drawing can be used to determine the formula $A = \frac{1}{2}h(b_1 + b_2)$ for the area of a trapezoid.

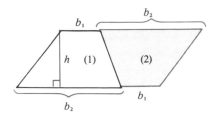

21. Explain how the drawing can be used to determine a formula for the area of △*ABC*.

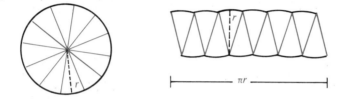

22. A different method for approximating the area of a circle is to separate the circle into congruent sectors and place them as pictured below. Explain how these drawings can be used to approximate the area of the circle.

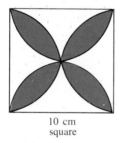

23. Find the area of the shaded region.

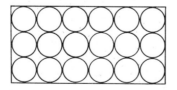

10 cm
square

⋆ 24. Congruent circles are cut out of a rectangular piece of tin, as shown, to make lids. Find what percent of the tin is wasted.

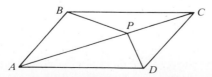

⋆ 25. In the drawing, quadrilateral *ABCD* is a parallelogram and *P* is any point on $\overline{AC}$. Prove that the area of △*BCP* is equal to the area of △*DPC*.

* * * * * * * REVIEW PROBLEMS * * * * * * *

26. Complete each of the following.
    (a) 100 mm = _____ cm
    (b) 10.4 cm = _____ mm
    (c) 350 mm = _____ m
    (d) 0.04 m = _____ mm
    (e) 8 km = _____ m
    (f) 6504 m = _____ km

27. Find the perimeters for each of the following if all arcs shown are semicircles.

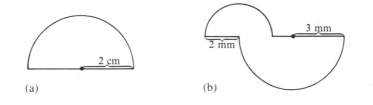

(a)   (b)

BRAIN TEASER

The accompanying rectangle was apparently formed by cutting the square shown along the dotted lines and reassembling the pieces as pictured.

1. What is the area of the square?
2. What is the area of the rectangle?
3. How do you explain the discrepancy?

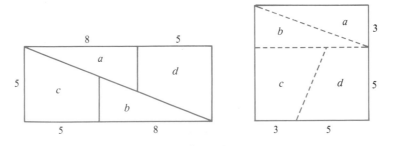

11-3   THE PYTHAGOREAN RELATIONSHIP

Pythagoras is one of the two most famous geometers of Greek antiquity (the other being Euclid). Exactly how much geometry Pythagoras himself either discovered or invented is not known, since he was the head of a group known as the Pythagoreans who attributed all of their discoveries to him. One of the most famous and useful discoveries is known as the Pythagorean Theorem, which involves a right triangle.

In Figure 11-20, the side of the triangle opposite the right angle c is called the **hypotenuse** of the triangle. The other two sides are called **legs.** The hypotenuse is always the longest side of a right triangle.

hypotenuse, legs

FIGURE 11-20

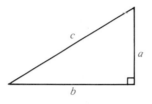

THEOREM 11.1

> **The Pythagorean Theorem**   If a right triangle has legs of lengths a and b and hypotenuse of length c, then $c^2 = a^2 + b^2$.

FIGURE 11-21

Interpreted in terms of area, the Pythagorean Theorem says that the area of a square with the hypotenuse of a right triangle as a side is equal to the sum of the areas of the squares with the legs as sides. This relationship was illustrated on a Greek stamp in 1955, shown in Figure 11-21, to honor the 2500th anniversary of the founding of the Pythagorean School.

The Pythagoreans affirmed geometric results on the basis of special cases. As a result, mathematical historians believe that they did not have a proof of the Pythagorean Theorem. It is possible that the Pythagoreans discovered the theorem by looking at a floor tiling consisting of squares like the ones shown in Figure 11-22. Each square can be divided by its diagonal into two congruent isosceles right triangles, so we see that the shaded square constructed with $\overline{AB}$ as a side consists of four triangles each congruent to $\triangle ABC$. Similarly, each of the shaded squares with legs $\overline{BC}$ and $\overline{AC}$ as sides consists of two triangles congruent to $\triangle ABC$. Thus, the area of the larger square is equal to the sum of the areas of the two smaller squares.

FIGURE 11-22

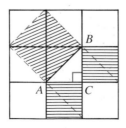

The above argument does not constitute a proof of the Pythagorean Theorem because it holds only for a right isosceles triangle but not for a right triangle in general. There are hundreds of known proofs for the Pythagorean Theorem today. The classic book, *The Pythagorean Proposition*, contains many of these proofs.

Many proofs of the Pythagorean Theorem involve constructing a square with area c^2 from squares of area a^2 and b^2.

FIGURE 11-23

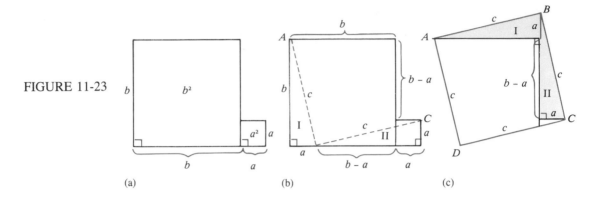

(a)   (b)   (c)

Figure 11-23(a) shows two squares with areas a^2 and b^2 side by side. Dissect Figure 11-23(b) along the dotted lines. Then, rotate triangle I counterclockwise 90° about point A to its new position in Figure 11-23(c). Similarly, rotate triangle II 90° clockwise about point C to its new position in Figure 11-23(c). As quadrilateral $ABCD$, in Figure 11-23(c), is composed of pieces of the squares in Figure 11-23(a), it must have the same area—that is, $a^2 + b^2$. However, it can be shown that quadrilateral $ABCD$ is a square with side c, and hence it has area c^2. Consequently, $a^2 + b^2 = c^2$.

A proof of the Pythagorean Theorem using similar triangles is discussed in Problem 7 of Problem Set 11-3. Other proofs of the Pythagorean Theorem are discussed in Problems 8 and 9 of Problem Set 11-3.

Example 11-10

For Figures 11-24 and 11-25 find x by using the Pythagorean Theorem.

FIGURE 11-24
(left)

FIGURE 11-25
(right)

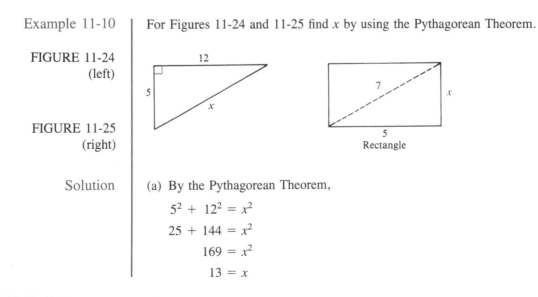

Rectangle

Solution

(a) By the Pythagorean Theorem,

$$5^2 + 12^2 = x^2$$

$$25 + 144 = x^2$$

$$169 = x^2$$

$$13 = x$$

(b) In the rectangle, the diagonal partitions the rectangle into two right triangles with length 5 units and width x units. Thus, we have the following.

$$5^2 + x^2 = 7^2$$
$$25 + x^2 = 49$$
$$x^2 = 24$$
$$x = \sqrt{24}, \quad \text{or approximately } 4.9$$

The student page from *Heath Mathematics*, Grade 8, 1981, on page 517 contains examples of the Pythagorean Theorem and the method for approximating square roots discussed in Chapter 7.

Given a triangle with sides of lengths a, b, and c such that $a^2 + b^2 = c^2$, must the triangle be a right triangle? This is the case and we state the following without proof.

THEOREM 11.2

Converse of the Pythagorean Theorem   If $\triangle ABC$ is a triangle with sides of lengths a, b, and c such that $a^2 + b^2 = c^2$, then $\triangle ABC$ is a right triangle with the right angle opposite the side of length c.

Example 11-11

Determine whether or not the following can be the lengths of the sides of a right triangle.

(a) 51, 68, 85   (b) 2, 3, $\sqrt{13}$ (c) 3, 4, 7

Solution

(a) $51^2 + 68^2 = 7225 = 85^2$, so 51, 68, and 85 can be the lengths of the sides of a right triangle.
(b) $2^2 + 3^2 = 4 + 9 = 13 = (\sqrt{13})^2$, so 2, 3, and $\sqrt{13}$ can be the lengths of the sides of a right triangle.
(c) $3^2 + 4^2 \neq 7^2$, so the measures cannot be the lengths of the sides of a right triangle.

PROBLEM SET 11-3

1. Use the Pythagorean Theorem to find x in each of the following.

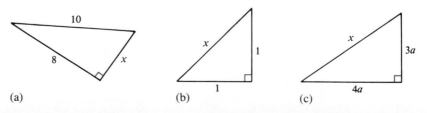

(a)   (b)   (c)

The Rule of Pythagoras

Ancient mathematicians discovered this remarkable fact about right triangles:

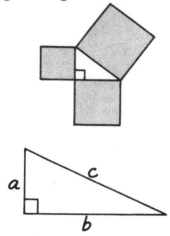

The square drawn on the hypotenuse is equal in area to the sum of the areas of the squares drawn on the legs.

This fact is called the Rule of Pythagoras. It is often stated like this:

In a right triangle the square of the hypotenuse is equal to the sum of the squares of the legs:

$$a^2 + b^2 = c^2$$

We can use the Rule of Pythagoras to compute the length of a side of a right triangle when we know the lengths of the other two sides.

EXAMPLE 1.

$$a^2 + b^2 = c^2$$
$$7^2 + 9^2 = c^2$$
$$49 + 81 = c^2$$
$$130 = c^2$$
$$\sqrt{130} = c$$

EXAMPLE 2.

$$a^2 + b^2 = c^2$$
$$6^2 + b^2 = 15^2$$
$$36 + b^2 = 225$$
$$b^2 = 189$$
$$b = \sqrt{189}$$

In Example 1 we have found that the length of the hypotenuse is exactly $\sqrt{130}$ cm. When we need a decimal approximation, we can use the divide-and-average method.

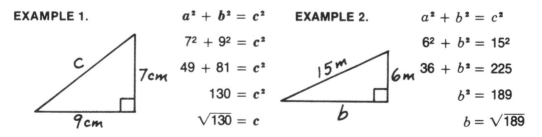

Guess and divide.

$$\begin{array}{r} 11.8 \\ 11\overline{)130} \end{array}$$

Average divisor and quotient.

$$\frac{11 + 11.8}{2} = 11.4$$

Divide.

$$\begin{array}{r} 1\ 1.40 \\ 11.4\overline{)130.0\ 0} \end{array}$$

The answer to the nearest tenth is 11.4.

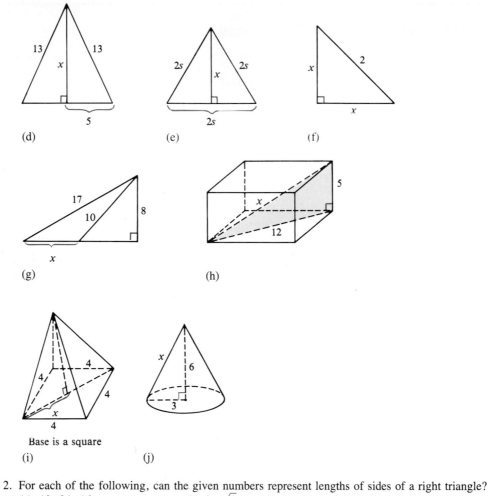

(d)   (e)   (f)

(g)   (h)

Base is a square

(i)   (j)

2. For each of the following, can the given numbers represent lengths of sides of a right triangle?
   - (a) 10, 24, 16
   - (b) 2, $\sqrt{3}$, 1
   - (c) 16, 34, 30
   - (d) $\sqrt{2}$, $\sqrt{3}$, $\sqrt{5}$
   - (e) $\sqrt{2}$, $\sqrt{2}$, 2
   - (f) $\dfrac{3}{2}, \dfrac{4}{2}, \dfrac{5}{2}$

3. For each of the following, solve for the unknowns.

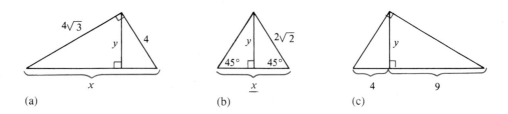

(a)   (b)   (c)

4. What is the longest line segment that can be drawn in a right rectangular prism that is 12 cm wide, 15 cm long, and 9 cm high?

5. Two cars leave a house at the same time. One car travels 60 km/hour north, while the other car travels 40 km/h east. After 1 hour, how far apart are the cars?

6. On a square baseball field, 90 ft on each side, a baseball is thrown by the shortstop, who is on the baseline 10 ft from second base, to home plate. How far did he throw the ball?

7. Use the following drawing to prove the Pythagorean Theorem by using corresponding parts of similar triangles, $\triangle ACD$, $\triangle CBD$, and $\triangle ABC$. Lengths of sides are indicated by a, b, c, x, and y. (*Hint:* Show that $b^2 = cx$ and $a^2 = cy$.)

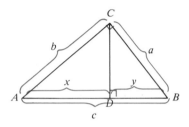

8. Before he was elected President of the United States, James Garfield discovered a proof of the Pythagorean Theorem. He formed a trapezoid like the one that follows and found the area of the trapezoid in two different ways. Can you discover his proof?

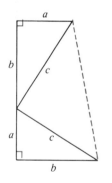

9. Use the given figure to prove the Pythagorean Theorem by first proving that the quadrilateral with side c is a square; then compute the area of the square with side $a + b$ in two different ways: (1) as $(a + b)^2$; and (2) as the sum of the areas of the four triangles and the square with side c.

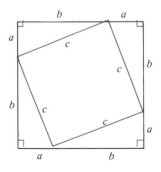

10. Find the area of each of the following.

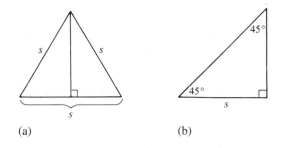

(a)   (b)

11. Construct semicircles on right triangle *ABC* with $\overline{AB}$, $\overline{BC}$, and $\overline{AC}$ as diameters. Is the area of the semicircle on the hypotenuse equal to the sum of the areas of the semicircles on the legs?

12. If the hypotenuse and a leg of one right triangle are congruent to the hypotenuse and a leg of the other right triangle, respectively, must the triangles be congruent?

13. What is the length of the diagonal of the cube? (*Hint:* Draw a diagonal of a base.)

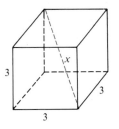

14. A 15-foot ladder is leaning against a wall. The base of the ladder is 3 feet from the wall. How high above the ground is the top of the ladder?

15. (a) Prove that the side opposite the 30° angle in a 30°-60°-90° triangle is half as long as the hypotenuse. (*Hint:* Two such triangles can be placed to make an equilateral triangle.)
    (b) If the hypotenuse in a 30°-60°-90° triangle is *c* units long, what is the length of the side opposite the 60° angle?

16. If the length of the hypotenuse in a 45°-45°-90° triangle is *c*, find the length of a leg.

17. Find *x* in the given figure.

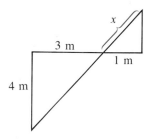

18. Given any four congruent right triangles with legs *a* and *b* and hypotenuse *c*, it is possible to arrange them to form a square with sides *a* + *b*, as shown in the figure. The shaded figure, a square whose area is c^2, also has area equal to the area of the large square minus the sum of the areas of the four congruent triangles.

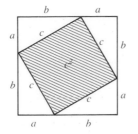

In the next figure, the shaded area also equals the area of the large square minus the areas of the four congruent triangles. Use this discussion and both figures to prove the Pythagorean Theorem.

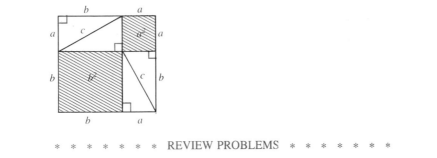

* * * * * * * REVIEW PROBLEMS * * * * * * *

19. Arrange the following in decreasing order: 3.2 m, 322 cm, 0.032 km, 3.020 mm.
20. Find the area of each figure.

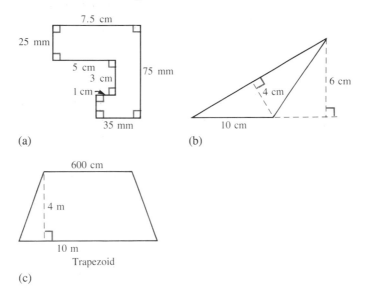

(a)

(b)

(c)

21. A 10-m-long wire is wrapped around a circular region. If the wire fits exactly, what is the area of the region?

22. Complete the following table concerning circles.

	Radius	Diameter	Circumference	Area
(a)	5 cm			
(b)		24 cm		
(c)				17π m^2

BRAIN TEASER

A spider sitting at A, the midpoint of the edge of the ceiling in the room shown, spies a fly on the floor at C, the midpoint of the edge of the floor. If the spider must walk along the wall, ceiling, or floor, what is the length of the shortest path the spider can travel to reach the fly?

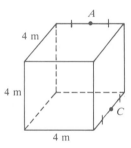

11-4   SURFACE AREAS OF THREE-DIMENSIONAL FIGURES

The surface area of a polyhedron is the sum of the areas of the faces of the polyhedron. Cubes are the simplest polyhedra. The surface area of the cube in Figure 11-26 is the sum of the areas of the faces of the cube. Since each of the six faces is a square of area 16 cm^2, the surface area is 6 · (16 cm^2) or 96 cm^2.

In general, if the edges of a cube are e units, as in Figure 11-27, then each face is a square with area e^2 units. Because there are six faces, the surface area of the cube is given by $S.A. = 6e^2$, where e is the length of a side and $S.A.$ is the surface area.

FIGURE 11-26
(left)

FIGURE 11-27
(right)

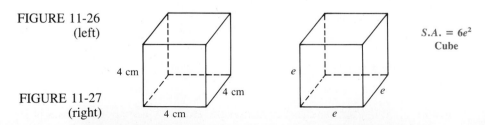

$S.A. = 6e^2$
Cube

To find the surface area of other right prisms, we find the sum of the areas of the rectangles that comprise the lateral faces and the areas of the top and bottom. The sum of the areas of the lateral faces is called the **lateral surface area.** Thus, the **surface area** is the sum of the lateral surface area and the area of the bases.

lateral surface area

surface area

FIGURE 11-28
(left)

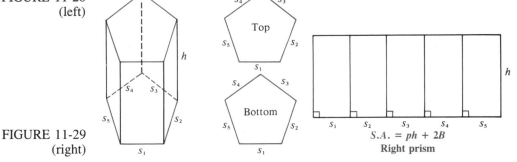

FIGURE 11-29
(right)

Figure 11-28 shows a right pentagonal prism and Figure 11-29 shows the figure cut into three pieces. The cuts show the top, the bottom, and the lateral faces. The section formed by the lateral faces is stretched out flat. It forms a rectangle whose length is $s_1 + s_2 + s_3 + s_4 + s_5$ and whose width is h. Because $s_1 + s_2 + s_3 + s_4 + s_5$ is the perimeter p of the base of the prism, the lateral surface area is $(s_1 + s_2 + s_3 + s_4 + s_5) \cdot h$ or ph. If B stands for the area of each of the prism's bases, then the surface area ($S.A.$) of the right prism is given by the following formula.

$$S.A. = ph + 2B$$

This formula holds for any right prism regardless of the shape of its bases.

Example 11-12

Find the surface area of each of the right prisms in Figure 11-30.

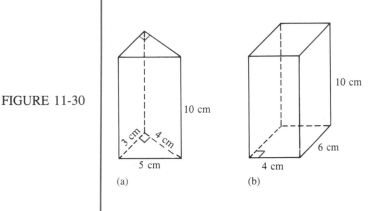

FIGURE 11-30

(a)   (b)

Solution

(a) Each base is a right triangle. Hence, the area of the bases is $2(\frac{1}{2} \cdot 3 \text{ cm} \cdot 4 \text{ cm})$, or 12 cm^2. The perimeter of a base is $3 \text{ cm} + 4 \text{ cm} + 5 \text{ cm}$, or

12 cm. Hence, the lateral surface area is (12 cm)(10 cm) or 120 cm², and the surface area is 132 cm².

(b) The area of the bases is 2(4 cm)(6 cm) or 48 cm². The lateral surface area is 2(4 cm + 6 cm) · 10 cm or 200 cm², so the surface area of the right prism is 248 cm².

To find the surface area of the right circular cylinder shown in Figure 11-31(a), cut it into a top and a bottom and the lateral surface shown in Figure 11-31(b).

FIGURE 11-31

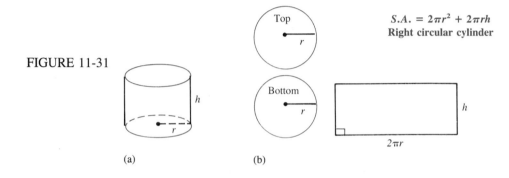

(a) (b)

The lateral surface stretched out is a rectangle whose length is the circumference of the circular base, $2\pi r$, and whose width is the height of the cylinder, h. Hence, the surface area is the sum of the areas of the two circular bases and the lateral surface areas.

$$S.A. = 2\pi r^2 + 2\pi rh$$

slant height   Similarly, the surface area of a right circular cone can be determined by cutting the cone along a **slant height** ℓ, removing the base, and flattening the lateral surface, as shown in Figure 11-32.

FIGURE 11-32

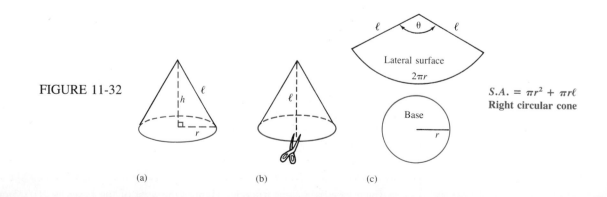

(a) (b) (c)

The area of the base is the area of a circle with radius r, namely, πr^2. The lateral surface area is the sector of a circle whose radius is ℓ shown in Figure 11-32(c). Since the area of a sector with radius ℓ and central angle θ degrees is $\frac{\theta}{360} \cdot \pi \ell^2$, the area of the sector could be found if the measure of the central angle θ was known. Thus, our goal is to find θ in terms of the given quantities r and ℓ. An equation involving θ, r, and ℓ can be obtained by finding the given arc length in two different ways. The length of the arc corresponding to θ is $\frac{\theta}{360} \cdot 2\pi \ell$. Also, the length of this arc is $2\pi r$, because it is the circumference of the circular base of the cone. Hence, $\frac{\theta}{360} \cdot 2\pi \ell = 2\pi r$. Therefore, $\frac{\theta}{360} = \frac{r}{\ell}$. Consequently, the area of the sector is $A = \frac{\theta}{360} \cdot \pi \ell^2 = \frac{r}{\ell} \cdot \pi \ell^2 = \pi r \ell$. Thus, the surface area of a cone is given by

$$S.A. = \pi r^2 + \pi r \ell$$

Example 11-13 Find the surface area of each of the figures in Figure 11-33.

FIGURE 11-33

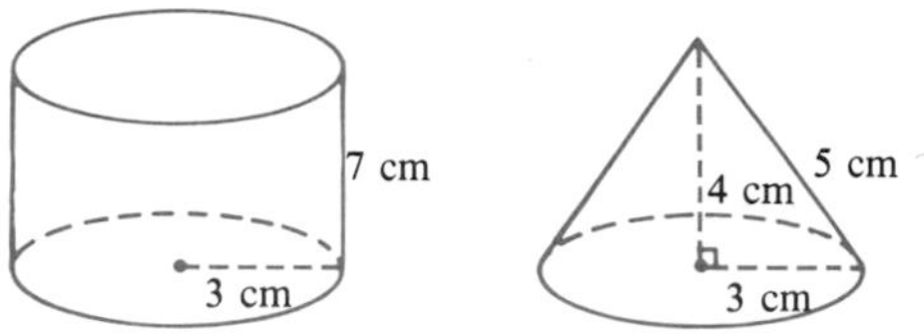

(a) Right circular cylinder   (b) Right circular cone

Solution

(a) $S.A. = 2\pi r^2 + 2\pi rh$
$= 2\pi(3 \text{ cm})^2 + 2\pi(3 \text{ cm})(7 \text{ cm})$
$= 18\pi \text{ cm}^2 + 42\pi \text{ cm}^2$
$= 60\pi \text{ cm}^2$

(b) $S.A. = \pi r^2 + \pi r \ell$
$= \pi(3 \text{ cm})^2 + \pi(3 \text{ cm})(5 \text{ cm})$
$= 9\pi \text{ cm}^2 + 15\pi \text{ cm}^2$
$= 24\pi \text{ cm}^2$

right regular pyramid

The surface area of a pyramid is the sum of the lateral surface area of the pyramid and the area of the base. A **right regular pyramid** is a pyramid such that the segments connecting the apex to each vertex of the base are congruent and the base is a regular polygon. The lateral faces of the right regular pyramid pictured in Figure 11-34 are congruent triangles. Each triangle has an altitude of length ℓ called the slant height. Since the pyramid is right regular, each side of the base has the same length, b. Hence, the lateral surface area of the right regular pyramid pictured is $4\left(\frac{1}{2}b\ell\right)$. Adding the lateral surface area to the area of the base B gives the surface area.

FIGURE 11-34

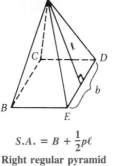

$$S.A. = B + \frac{1}{2}p\ell$$

Right regular pyramid

In general, for any right regular pyramid, the surface area is found by adding the area B of the base and the area of the n congruent triangular faces, each with side b and slant height ℓ. The surface area is given by the following formula.

$$S.A. = B + n\left(\frac{1}{2}b\ell\right)$$

Since nb is the perimeter of the base, the formula reduces to the following.

$$S.A. = B + \frac{1}{2}p\ell$$

Example 11-14

Find the surface area of the right regular pyramid in Figure 11-35.

FIGURE 11-35

Solution

$$S.A. = B + \frac{1}{2}p\ell$$

$$= (4 \text{ cm})(4 \text{ cm}) + \frac{1}{2}[4(4 \text{ cm})](5 \text{ cm})$$

$$= 16 \text{ cm}^2 + 40 \text{ cm}^2$$

$$= 56 \text{ cm}^2$$

Finding a formula for the surface area of a sphere is not a simple task using elementary mathematics. The formula for the surface area of a sphere is $S.A. = 4\pi r^2$. That is, the surface area of a sphere is four times the area of the great circle pictured in Figure 11-36.

FIGURE 11-36

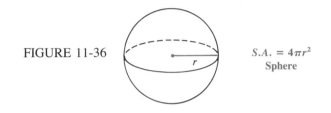

$$S.A. = 4\pi r^2$$
Sphere

PROBLEM 1

A toymaker decides to design a wooden cube with square holes in each of the cube's faces. The holes extend all the way through the cube, as shown in Figure 11-37. The toymaker wants the length of each side of the square holes to be one-third the length of a side of the cube. If the total surface area of the toy is to be 2 m², how long should the sides of the cube be?

FIGURE 11-37

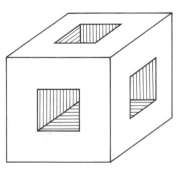

BRAIN TEASER

How can a stack of fourteen cubes, each having sides of length 1 cm, be arranged so that each touches at least two others and the arrangement has the maximum possible total surface area?

Understanding the Problem

We know that the total surface area of the toy in Figure 11-37 is 2 m². The space formed by the cutting may be thought of as seven congruent cubes, six corresponding to the faces and one to the hole in the middle. The hole in the middle has no surface area. The length of a side of each hole is to be one-third of the length of a side of the cube. We are asked to find the length of a side of the cube.

Devising a Plan

We designate the length of the side of the cube by x, so that the length of a side of one of the holes is $\frac{x}{3}$. If we can find the total surface area of the toy in terms of x, then by setting this expression equal to 2, solving for x, we will have the required length of a side of the cube.

Carrying Out the Plan

Since a hole is to be cut through each face of the cube, the area of each face excluding the area of the hole is

$$x^2 - \left(\frac{x}{3}\right)^2 \quad \text{or} \quad x^2 - \frac{x^2}{9} \quad \text{or} \quad \frac{8}{9}x^2$$

Since the cube has six faces, the area of these six faces with the areas of the holes excluded is $6 \cdot \frac{8}{9}x^2$, or $\frac{16}{3}x^2$. Due to cutting, there is an "inside cube," which corresponds to each of the six faces, cut away. Cutting away an inside cube leaves only four faces to be considered for the total surface area. The surface area of the four faces is $4 \cdot \frac{x^2}{9}$. Now the surface area of these six inside cubes is

$$6 \cdot 4 \cdot \frac{x^2}{9}, \quad \text{or} \quad \frac{8}{3}x^2$$

The space in the center of the original cube is empty and has no surface area. Therefore, the total surface area of the toy is $\frac{16}{3}x^2 + \frac{8}{3}x^2$, or $\frac{24}{3}x^2$ or $8x^2$. Consequently,

$$8x^2 = 2$$

$$x^2 = \frac{1}{4}$$

$$x = \frac{1}{2}$$

Thus, the side of the cube should be $\frac{1}{2}$ m, or 50 cm, long.

Looking Back

A related problem is to find the total surface area if cylindrical holes were drilled through each face of a cube.

PROBLEM SET 11-4

1. Find the surface area of each of the following right prisms.

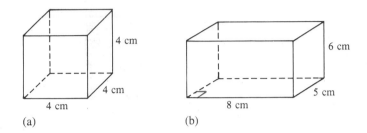

4 cm   4 cm   4 cm

(a)

8 cm   6 cm   5 cm

(b)

2. Find the surface area of each of the following.

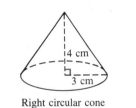

4 cm
3 cm

Right circular cone

(a)

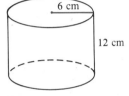

6 cm
12 cm

Right circular cylinder

(b)

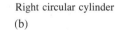

4 cm

Sphere

(c)

6.5 cm
2.5 cm
2.5 cm

Right square pyramid

(d)

3. Find the surface area of each of the following.

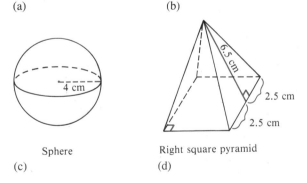

8 ft
15 ft
40 ft
30 ft

(a)

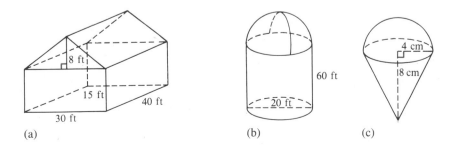

60 ft
20 ft

(b)

4 cm
18 cm

(c)

4. How many liters of paint are needed to paint the walls of a room 6 m long, 4 m wide, and 2.5 m tall if 1 L (liter) of paint covers 20 m²? (Assume there are no doors or windows.)

5. The napkin ring pictured below is to be resilvered. How many square millimeters of surface area must be covered?

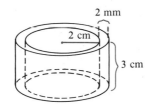

6. Assume that the radius of the earth is 6370 km and the earth is a sphere. What is its surface area?

7. Two cubes have sides of length 4 cm and 6 cm, respectively. What is the ratio of their surface areas?

8. (a) What happens to the surface area of a cube if each side is tripled?
   (b) What is the effect on the lateral surface area of a cylinder if the height is doubled?

9. A sphere is inscribed in a right cylinder, as shown below. Prove that the surface area of the sphere equals the lateral surface area of the cylinder.

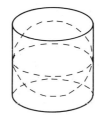

10. Suppose one cylinder has radius 2 m and height 6 m and another has radius 6 m and height 2 m.
    (a) Which cylinder has the greater lateral surface area?
    (b) Which cylinder has the greater total surface area?

★ 11. Find the total surface area of the following stand, which was cut from a right circular cone.

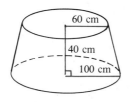

 12. The total surface area of a cube is 10,648 cm³. What is the length of each of the following?
    (a) One of the sides.
    (b) A diagonal that is not a diagonal of a face.

* * * * * * * REVIEW PROBLEMS * * * * * * *

13. Complete each of the following.
    (a) $10 \text{ m}^2 =$ _____ cm^2
    (b) $13,680 \text{ cm}^2 =$ _____ m^2
    (c) $5 \text{ cm}^2 =$ _____ mm^2
    (d) $2 \text{ km}^2 =$ _____ m^2
    (e) $10^6 \text{ m}^2 =$ _____ km^2
    (f) $10^{12} \text{ mm}^2 =$ _____ m^2
14. The sides of a rectangle are 10 cm and 20 cm. Find the length of a diagonal of the rectangle.
15. The length of the side of a rhombus is 30 cm. If the length of one of the diagonals is 40 cm, find the length of the other diagonal.
16. Find the perimeters and the areas of the following figures.

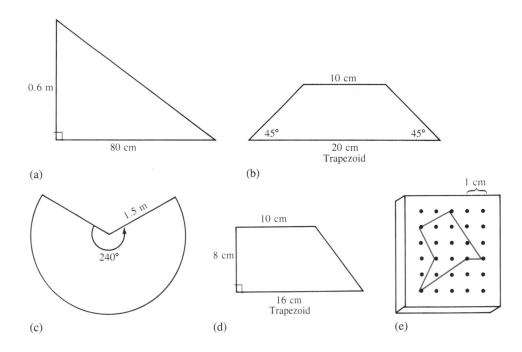

(a)

(b)

(c)

(d)

(e)

★ 17. The length of the longer diagonal of a rhombus is 40 cm. The altitude is 24 cm long. Find the length of the side of the rhombus and the length of the other diagonal.

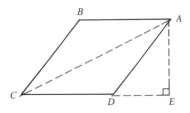

11-5   VOLUME MEASURE AND VOLUMES

As area measure is used to describe the interior region of a geometric figure, volume measure is associated with three-dimensional figures. Volume is concerned with how much space a figure occupies. The unit of measure for volume must be a shape that will "fill space." Cubes can be closely stacked with no gaps and fill space. Standard units of volume are based on cubes and are called cubic units. The volume of a rectangular right prism can be measured, for example, by determining how many cubes are needed to build it. One way is to count how many cubes cover the base and then count how many layers of these cubes are used to reach the height of the prism, as shown in Figure 11-38(a). There are $8 \cdot 4$ or 32 cubes in the base and there are five such layers. Hence, the volume of the rectangular prism is $8 \cdot 4 \cdot 5$ cubic units. For any rectangular right prism with dimensions ℓ, w, and h measured in the same linear units, the volume of the prism is given by $V = \ell wh$, as shown in Figure 11-38(b).

FIGURE 11-38

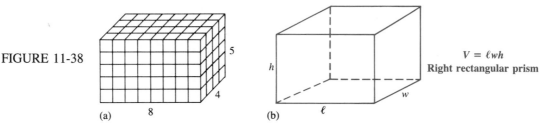

In the English system of measurement, a commonly used unit of volume is the cubic foot. The most commonly used metric units are the cubic centimeter and the cubic meter. A cubic centimeter is the volume of a cube whose length, width, and height are each one centimeter. One cubic centimeter is denoted by 1 cm^3. Similarly, a cubic meter is the volume of a cube whose length, width, and height are each 1 m. One cubic meter is denoted by 1 m^3. Other metric units of volume are also symbolized with a raised 3 next to the standard symbol.

Figure 11-39 shows that since 1 dm = 10 cm, $1 \text{ dm}^3 = (10 \text{ cm}) \cdot (10 \text{ cm}) \cdot (10 \text{ cm}) = 1000 \text{ cm}^3$.

FIGURE 11-39

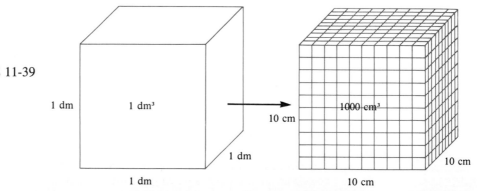

Similarly, Figure 11-40 shows that $1 \text{ m}^3 = 1{,}000{,}000 \text{ cm}^3$ and $1 \text{ dm}^3 = 0.001 \text{ m}^3$.

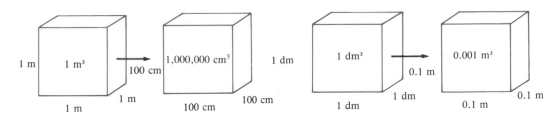

FIGURE 11-40

Each metric unit of length is 10 times as great as the next smaller unit. Each metric unit of area is 100 times as great as the next smaller unit. Each metric unit of volume is 1000 times as great as the next smaller unit. Hence to convert from cubic decimeters to cubic centimeters, multiply by 1000, that is, move the decimal point three places to the right. Also, since $1 \text{ cm} = 0.01 \text{ m}$, then $1 \text{ cm}^3 = (0.01 \times 0.01 \times 0.01) \text{ m}^3$ or 0.000001 m^3. Thus, to convert from cubic centimeters to cubic meters, all that is required is to move the decimal point six places to the left.

Example 11-15

Convert each of the following.

(a) $5 \text{ m}^3 = \underline{\hspace{1cm}} \text{ cm}^3$ (b) $12{,}300 \text{ mm}^3 = \underline{\hspace{1cm}} \text{ cm}^3$

Solution

(a) $1 \text{ m} = 100 \text{ cm}$, so $1 \text{ m}^3 = (100 \text{ cm})(100 \text{ cm})(100 \text{ cm})$ or $1{,}000{,}000 \text{ cm}^3$. Thus, $5 \text{ m}^3 = (5)(1{,}000{,}000 \text{ cm}^3) = 5{,}000{,}000 \text{ cm}^3$.

(b) $1 \text{ mm} = 0.1 \text{ cm}$, so $1 \text{ mm}^3 = (0.1 \text{ cm})(0.1 \text{ cm})(0.1 \text{ cm})$ or 0.001 cm^3. Thus, $12{,}300 \text{ mm}^3 = 12{,}300(0.001 \text{ cm}^3) = 12.3 \text{ cm}^3$.

1 cm³ = 1 mL   liter

In the metric system, cubic units may be used for either dry or liquid measure, although units such as liters and milliliters are usually used for capacity measures, that is, for liquids. By definition, one **liter,** symbolized by L, equals one cubic decimeter, that is $1 \text{ L} = 1 \text{ dm}^3$. Note that L is not a universally accepted symbol for liter. However, since the liter is not a standard international unit but derived from other units, there is no proper standard international symbol. In the United States, L is preferred to either ℓ or l.

Since $1 \text{ L} = 1 \text{ dm}^3$ and $1 \text{ dm}^3 = 1000 \text{ cm}^3$, then $1 \text{ L} = 1000 \text{ cm}^3$ and $1 \text{ cm}^3 = 0.001 \text{ L}$. Prefixes can be used with all base units in the metric system, so $0.001 \text{ L} = 1 \text{ milliliter} = 1 \text{ mL}$. Hence, $1 \text{ cm}^3 = 1 \text{ mL}$. These relationships are summarized in Figure 11-41.

The metric prefixes used with linear measure can also be used with the liter. Both symbols and conversions work the same as they did for length. Table 11-4 shows how metric units involving the liter are related.

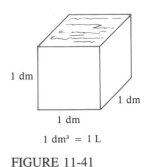

1 dm³ = 1 L

FIGURE 11-41

TABLE 11-4

Unit	Symbol	Relation to liter	
kiloliter	kL	1000	liters
*hectoliter	hL	100	liters
*dekaliter	daL	10	liters
liter	**L**	**1**	**liter**
*deciliter	dL	0.1	liter
centiliter	cL	0.01	liter
milliliter	mL	0.001	liter

*Not commonly used.

Example 11-16

Convert each of the following as indicated.

(a) 27 L = _____ mL   (b) 362 mL = _____ L
(c) 3 mL = _____ cm^3 (d) 3 m^3 = _____ L

Solution

(a) 1 L = 1000 mL, so 27 L = 27 · 1000 mL = 27,000 mL.
(b) 1 mL = 0.001 L, so 362 mL = 362(0.001 L) = 0.362 L.
(c) 1 mL = 1 cm^3, so 3 mL = 3 cm^3.
(d) 1 m^3 = 1000 dm^3 and 1 dm^3 = 1 L, so 1 m^3 = 1000 L and 3 m^3 = 3000 L.

Volume of Other Three-Dimensional Figures

The volume of a right rectangular prism is given by $V = \ell wh$, where ℓ and w are the length and width of a base, respectively, and h is the height of the prism. Notice that ℓw is the area of a base of the prism. Hence, using B for the area of the base the formula can be written as $V = Bh$. The same formula holds for any three-dimensional figure *if* all cross sections parallel to the base are congruent to the base. The formulas for volumes of right prisms and right circular cylinders are given in Figure 11-42.

FIGURE 11-42

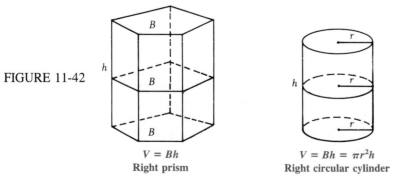

$V = Bh$
Right prism

$V = Bh = \pi r^2 h$
Right circular cylinder

Example 11-17 | Find the volume of each of the figures in Figure 11-43.

FIGURE 11-43

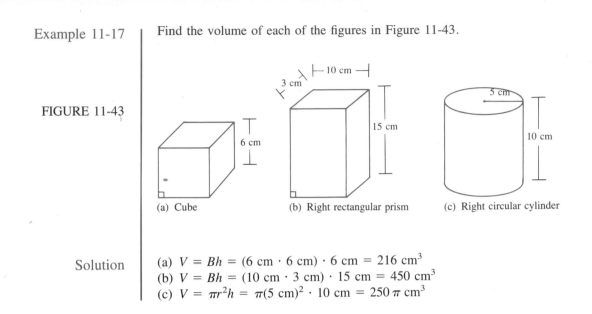

(a) Cube   (b) Right rectangular prism   (c) Right circular cylinder

Solution | (a) $V = Bh = (6 \text{ cm} \cdot 6 \text{ cm}) \cdot 6 \text{ cm} = 216 \text{ cm}^3$
(b) $V = Bh = (10 \text{ cm} \cdot 3 \text{ cm}) \cdot 15 \text{ cm} = 450 \text{ cm}^3$
(c) $V = \pi r^2 h = \pi (5 \text{ cm})^2 \cdot 10 \text{ cm} = 250\,\pi \text{ cm}^3$

Figure 11-44 shows a right triangular prism with an equilateral triangle as a base. This prism can be separated into three pyramids that have bases with the same area and height the same as that of the prism. In this special case, the volume of the right triangular pyramid is one-third the volume of the triangular prism; that is $V = \frac{1}{3}Bh$. In fact, it can be shown that the volume of any pyramid is $\frac{1}{3}Bh$, where B is the area of its base and h is its height.

FIGURE 11-44

(a)   (b)   (c)

$$V = \frac{1}{3}Bh$$
Pyramid

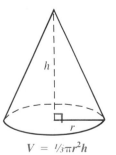

$V = \frac{1}{3}\pi r^2 h$
Right circular cone

FIGURE 11-45

To find the volume of a right cone with a circular base, shown in Figure 11-45, consider the polygonal base of a pyramid with many sides. The base approximates a circle and the volume of the pyramid is approximately the volume of the cone with the circle as a base and the same height as the pyramid. The area of the base is approximately πr^2, where r is the apothem of the polygon. Hence, the formula for the volume of a right circular cone with a circular base is $V = \frac{1}{3}\pi r^2 h$ or $V = \frac{1}{3}Bh$.

Example 11-18   Find the volume of each of the figures in Figure 11-46.

FIGURE 11-46

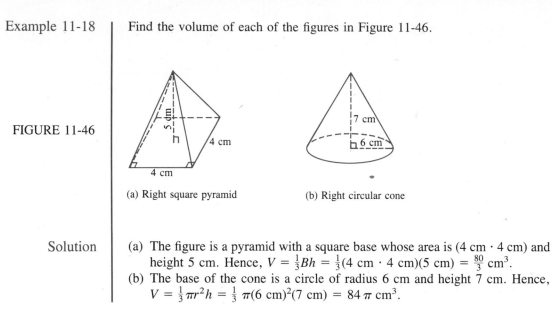

(a) Right square pyramid   (b) Right circular cone

Solution   (a) The figure is a pyramid with a square base whose area is (4 cm · 4 cm) and height 5 cm. Hence, $V = \frac{1}{3}Bh = \frac{1}{3}(4 \text{ cm} \cdot 4 \text{ cm})(5 \text{ cm}) = \frac{80}{3}$ cm³.

(b) The base of the cone is a circle of radius 6 cm and height 7 cm. Hence, $V = \frac{1}{3}\pi r^2 h = \frac{1}{3}\pi(6 \text{ cm})^2(7 \text{ cm}) = 84\pi$ cm³.

To find the volume of a sphere, imagine that a sphere is composed of a great number of congruent pyramids with apexes at the center of the sphere and that the vertices of the base touch the sphere, as shown in Figure 11-47.

FIGURE 11-47

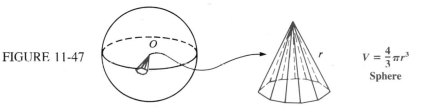

$$V = \frac{4}{3}\pi r^3$$
Sphere

If the pyramids have very small bases, then the height of each pyramid is nearly the radius, r. Hence, the volume of each pyramid is $\frac{1}{3}Bh$ or $\frac{1}{3}Br$, where B is the area of the base. If there are n pyramids each with base area B, then the total volume of the pyramids is $V = \frac{1}{3}nBr$. Because nB is the total surface area of all the bases of the pyramids and the sum of the areas of all the bases of the pyramids is very close to the surface area of the sphere, $4\pi r^2$, the volume of the sphere is given by $V = \frac{1}{3}(4\pi r^2)r = \frac{4}{3}\pi r^3$.

Example 11-19   Find the volume of a sphere whose radius is 6 cm.

Solution $V = \frac{4}{3}\pi(6 \text{ cm})^3 = \frac{4}{3}\pi(216 \text{ cm}^3) = 288\pi$ cm³

PROBLEM SET 11-5

1. Complete each of the following.
   (a) $8 \text{ m}^3 =$ _____ dm^3
   (b) $500 \text{ cm}^3 =$ _____ m^3
   (c) $675,000 \text{ m}^3 =$ _____ km^3
   (d) $3 \text{ m}^3 =$ _____ cm^3
   (e) $7000 \text{ mm}^3 =$ _____ cm^3
   (f) $0.002 \text{ m}^3 =$ _____ cm^3

2. Why is a unit sphere, a sphere with radius 1 cm, not a "good" unit of volume measure, even for measuring the volume of another sphere?

3. Find the volume of each of the following.

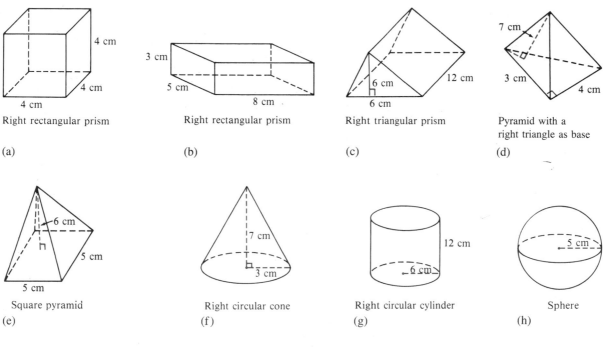

Right rectangular prism

(a)

Right rectangular prism

(b)

Right triangular prism

(c)

Pyramid with a
right triangle as base

(d)

Square pyramid
(e)

Right circular cone
(f)

Right circular cylinder
(g)

Sphere
(h)

4. Find the volume of each of the following.

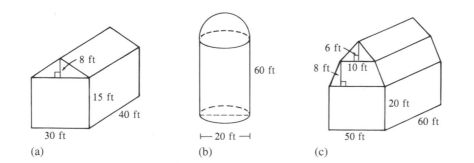

(a)

(b)

(c)

(d)

5. What volume of silver is needed to make the napkin ring out of solid silver? Give your answer in cubic millimeters.

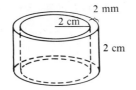

6. Two cubes have sides of lengths 4 cm and 6 cm, respectively. What is the ratio of their volumes?
7. What happens to the volume of a sphere if the radius is doubled?
8. Complete the following.

	(a)	(b)	(c)	(d)	(e)	(f)
cm^3		500			750	4800
dm^3	2					
L			1.5			
mL				5000		

9. Complete the chart for right rectangular prisms with the given dimensions.

	(a)	(b)	(c)	(d)
Length	20 cm	10 cm	2 dm	15 cm
Width	10 cm	2 dm	1 dm	2 dm
Height	10 cm	3 dm		
Volume in cm^3				
Volume in dm^3				7.5
Volume in L			4	

10. Place a decimal point in each of the following to make it an accurate sentence.
    (a) A paper cup holds about 2000 mL.
    (b) A regular soft drink bottle holds about 320 L.
    (c) A quart milk container holds about 10 L.
    (d) A teaspoonful of cough syrup would be about 500 mL.
11. A right cylindrical tank holds how many liters if it is 6 m long and 13 m in diameter?
12. If the length of the diameter of the earth is approximately four times the length of the diameter of the moon and both are spheres, what is the ratio of their volumes?
13. A bread pan is 18 cm × 18 cm × 5 cm. How many liters does it hold?

14. An Olympic pool in the shape of a right rectangular prism is 50 m long and 25 m wide. If it is 2 m deep throughout, how many liters of water does it hold?

15. If a faucet is dripping at the rate of 15 drops per minute and there are 20 drops per milliliter, how many liters of water are wasted in a 30-day month?

16. A standard straw is 25 cm long and 4 mm in diameter. How much liquid can be held in the straw at one time?

17. In the drawing, a marble 12 cm in diameter is resting in a can whose circular base has a radius of 6 cm. If water just covers the marble and then the marble is removed from the can, how far does the water drop?

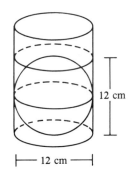

18. A theater decides to change the shape of its popcorn container from their regular box to a right regular pyramid and charge only half as much. If the containers are the same height and the tops are the same size, is this a bargain for the customer?

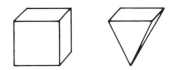

19. Which is the better buy, a grapefruit 5 cm in radius that costs 22¢ or a grapefruit 6 cm in radius that costs 31¢?

20. A right rectangular prism with base $ABCD$ as the bottom is shown below. Suppose X is drawn so that $AX = 3 \cdot AP$, where AP is the height of the prism, and X is connected to A, B, C, and D, forming a pyramid. How do the volumes of the pyramid and the prism compare?

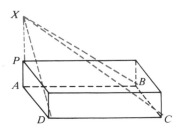

21. A right cylindrical can is to hold exactly 1 L of water. What should the height of the can be if the radius is 12 cm?

22. A box is packed with six pop cans as shown below. What percent of the volume of the interior of the box is not occupied by the pop cans?

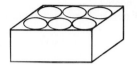

* * * * * * * REVIEW PROBLEMS * * * * * * *

23. Find the surface areas of the following.

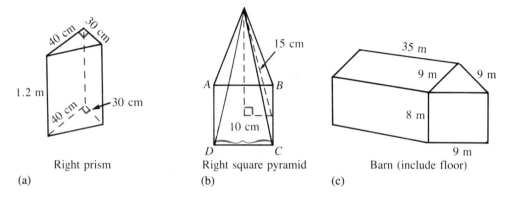

Right prism	Right square pyramid	Barn (include floor)
(a)	(b)	(c)

24. The diagonal of a rectangle has measure 1.3 m and a side has measure 120 cm. Find each of the following.
    (a) Perimeter of the rectangle
    (b) Area of the rectangle
25. A ladder 13 m long is leaning against a wall. The top of the ladder is 12 m above the ground. How far away from the wall is the bottom of the ladder?

11-6   MASS AND TEMPERATURE

Three centuries ago, Isaac Newton pointed out that in everyday life, the term "weight" is used for what is really mass. He called *mass* a quantity of matter as opposed to *weight*, which is a force exerted by gravitational pull. When an astronaut is in orbit above the earth, his weight has changed even though his mass remains the same. For common use on the earth, weight and mass are still used interchangeably.

gram

In the metric system, the base unit for mass is the **gram,** denoted by g. A gram is the mass of 1 cm^3 of water. An ordinary paper clip or a thumbtack each has a mass of about 1 g.

As with other base metric units, prefixes are added to gram to obtain other units. For example, a kilogram (kg) is 1000 g. Since 1 cm^3 of water has a mass of 1 g, the mass of 1 L of water is 1 kg. A person's mass is measured in kilograms. Two standard loaves of bread have a mass of about 1 kg. A newborn baby has a

metric ton

mass of about 4 kg. Another unit of mass in the metric system is the **metric ton** (t), which is equal to 1000 kg. The metric ton is used to record the masses of objects such as cars and trucks. A small foreign car has a mass of about 1 t.

Table 11-5 lists metric units of mass. Conversions involving metric units of mass are handled in the same way as units of length.

TABLE 11-5

Unit	Symbol	Relationship to gram
ton	t	1,000,000 grams
kilogram	kg	1000 grams
*hectogram	hg	100 grams
*dekagram	dag	10 grams
gram	**g**	**1 gram**
*decigram	dg	0.1 gram
*centigram	cg	0.01 gram
milligram	mg	0.001 gram

*Not commonly used.

Example 11-20

Complete each of the following.

(a) 34 g = _____ kg   (b) 6836 kg = _____ t

Solution

(a) 34 g = 34(0.001 kg) = 0.034 kg
(b) 6836 kg = 6836(0.001 t) = 6.836 t

The relationship among the units of volume and mass in the metric system is illustrated in Figure 11-48.

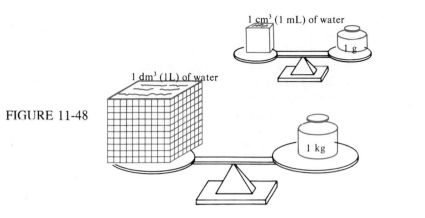

FIGURE 11-48

Example 11-21

A waterbed is 180 cm wide, 210 cm long, and 20 cm thick.

(a) How many liters of water can it hold?
(b) What is its mass in kilograms when it is full of water?

Solution

(a) The volume of the waterbed is found by multiplying the length times the width times the height.

$$V = \ell wh$$
$$= 180 \text{ cm} \cdot 210 \text{ cm} \cdot 20 \text{ cm}$$
$$= 756{,}000 \text{ cm}^3 \text{ or } 756{,}000 \text{ mL}$$

Since 1 mL = 0.001 L, the volume is 756 L.

(b) Since 1 L of water has a mass of 1 kg, 756 L of water has a mass of 756 kg.

Remark

To see one advantage of the metric system, suppose the bed is 6 ft by 7 ft by 9 in. Try to find the volume in gallons and the weight of the water in pounds.

Temperature

degree Kelvin

The base unit of temperature for the metric system is the **degree Kelvin.** However, it is used only for scientific measurements and not for everyday measurements of temperature. For normal temperature measurements in the metric

degree Celsius

system, the base unit is **degree Celsius,** named for Anders Celsius, the Swedish scientist who invented the system. The Celsius scale has 100 equal divisions between zero degrees Celsius (0°C), the freezing point of water, and one hundred degrees Celsius (100°C), the boiling point of water. In the English system, the Fahrenheit scale has 180 equal divisions between 32°F, the freezing point of water, and 212°F, the boiling point of water. Because the Celsius scale has 100 divisions between the freezing point and boiling point of water whereas the Fahrenheit scale has 180 divisions, the relationship between the two scales is 100 to 180 or 5 to 9. Hence, for every 5 degrees on the Celsius scale, there are 9 degrees on the Fahrenheit scale, and for each degree on the Fahrenheit scale, there is $\frac{5}{9}$ degree on the Celsius scale. Figure 11-49 gives some temperature comparisons on the two scales and further illustrates the relationship between them.

FIGURE 11-49

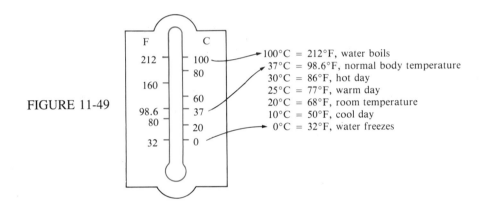

100°C = 212°F, water boils
37°C = 98.6°F, normal body temperature
30°C = 86°F, hot day
25°C = 77°F, warm day
20°C = 68°F, room temperature
10°C = 50°F, cool day
0°C = 32°F, water freezes

A simple relationship can be developed for converting temperatures between the two scales. Because 50°F is (50 − 32)°F or 18°F above freezing, in degrees Celsius it is $[\frac{5}{9}(50 - 32)]$°C or 10°C above freezing. In general, $C = \frac{5}{9}(F - 32)$. Solving for F in terms of C, we have $F = \frac{9}{5}C + 32$.

Example 11-22

Convert 20°C to degrees Fahrenheit.

Solution

$$F = \frac{9}{5}C + 32$$

$$= \frac{9}{5} \cdot 20 + 32$$

$$= 36 + 32$$

$$= 68$$

Thus, 20°C is 68°F.

PROBLEM SET 11-6

1. For each of the following, select the appropriate metric unit of measure (gram, kilogram, or metric ton).
   - (a) Car
   - (b) Woman
   - (c) Can of frozen orange juice
   - (d) Elephant
   - (e) Jar of mustard
   - (f) Bag of peanuts
   - (g) Army tank
   - (h) Cat
   - (i) Dictionary

2. For each of the following, choose the correct unit (milligram, gram, or kilogram) to make each sentence reasonable.
   - (a) A staple has a mass of about 340 _____.
   - (b) A professional football player has a mass of about 110 _____.
   - (c) A vitamin tablet has a mass of 1100 _____.
   - (d) A dime has a mass of 2 _____.
   - (e) The recipe said to add 4 _____ of salt.
   - (f) One strand of hair has a mass of 2 _____.

3. Complete each of the following.
   - (a) 15,000 g = _____ kg
   - (b) 8000 kg = _____ t
   - (c) 0.036 kg = _____ g
   - (d) 72 g = _____ kg
   - (e) 4230 mg = _____ g
   - (f) 3 g 7 mg = _____ g
   - (g) 5 kg 750 g = _____ g
   - (h) 5 kg 750 g = _____ kg
   - (i) 0.03 t = _____ kg
   - (j) 0.03 t = _____ g

4. If a paper dollar has a mass of approximately 1 g, is it possible to lift $1,000,000 in the following denominations?
   - (a) $1 bills
   - (b) $10 bills
   - (c) $100 bills
   - (d) $1000 bills
   - (e) $10,000 bills

5. A fish tank, which is a right rectangular prism, is 40 cm by 20 cm by 20 cm. If it is filled with water, what is the mass of the water?

6. In a grocery store, one kind of meat costs $5.80 per kilogram. How much does 400 g of this meat cost?

7. If a certain spice costs $20 per kilogram, how much does 1 g cost?

8. Abel bought a kilogram of Moxwill coffee for $9 and Babel bought 400 g of the same brand of coffee for $4.60. Who made the better buy?

9. Answer each of the following.
   - (a) The thermometer reads 20°C. Can you go snow skiing?
   - (b) The thermometer reads 26°C. Will the outdoor ice rink be open?
   - (c) Your temperature is 37°C. Do you have a fever?
   - (d) If your body temperature is 39°C, are you ill?
   - (e) It is 40°C. Will you need a sweater at the outdoor concert?
   - (f) The temperature reads 35°C. Should you go water skiing?
   - (g) The temperature reads ⁻10°C. Is it appropriate to go ice fishing?
   - (h) Your bath water is 16°C. Will you have a hot, warm, or chilly bath?
   - (i) It's 30°C in the room. Are you uncomfortably hot or cold?

10. Convert each of the following from degrees Fahrenheit to the nearest integer degree Celsius.
    - (a) 10°F
    - (b) 0°F
    - (c) 30°F
    - (d) 100°F
    - (e) 212°F
    - (f) ⁻40°F

11. Convert each of the following from degrees Celsius to the nearest integer degree Fahrenheit.
    - (a) 10°C
    - (b) 0°C
    - (c) 30°C
    - (d) 100°C
    - (e) 212°C
    - (f) ⁻40°C

* * * * * * *   REVIEW PROBLEMS   * * * * * * *

12. Find the perimeter and the area of the following.

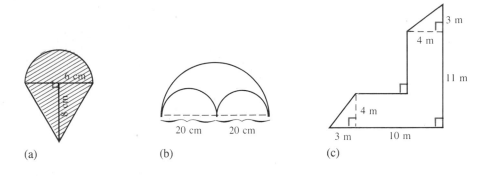

(a)   (b)   (c)

13. Complete the following.
    (a) 350 mm = _____ cm
    (b) 1600 cm^2 = _____ m^2
    (c) 0.4 m^2 = _____ mm^2
    (d) 5.2 m^3 = _____ cm^3
    (e) 5.2 m^3 = _____ L
    (f) 3500 cm^3 = _____ m^3

14. Determine whether each of the following is a right triangle.

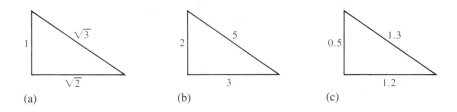

(a)   (b)   (c)

15. A person walks 5 km North, 3 km East, 1 km North, and then 2 km East. How far is the person from the starting point?

16. Find the volume and the surface area of each of the solids.

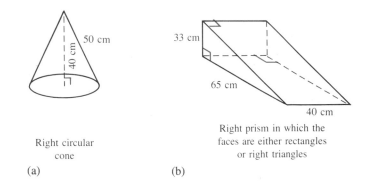

Right circular cone

Right prism in which the faces are either rectangles or right triangles

(a)   (b)

Laboratory Activity

1. Record the mass of each U.S. coin. Which coin has the greatest mass? Which of the following sets have the same mass?
   (a) A half-dollar vs. two quarters
   (b) A quarter vs. two dimes and a nickel
   (c) A dime vs. two nickels
   (d) A dime vs. ten pennies
   (e) A nickel vs. five pennies
2. Record the temperature of the room on a Celsius thermometer. Pour 200 mL of water into a liter container. Record the temperature of the water. Add 100 mL of ice to the water. Wait one minute and record the temperature of the ice water.

SOLUTION TO THE PRELIMINARY PROBLEM

Understanding the Problem

Rancher Larry wants to divide his land, shown in Figure 11-50(a), into two plots of equal area with a straight fence starting at point P. Because the area of the entire plot is 9 square units, the area of each part formed by the fence must be $4\frac{1}{2}$ square units.

FIGURE 11-50

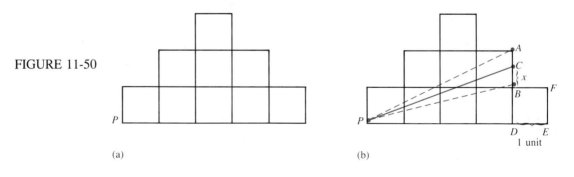

(a)　　　　　　　　　　　　(b)

Devising a Plan

In order to find an approximate location for the fence, consider a fence connecting P with point A shown in Figure 11-50(b). If we denote the length of the side of each square by one unit, then the area of the land below the fence $\overline{PA}$ can be found as the sum of the areas of $\triangle APD$ and the square $DBFE$. The area of $\triangle APD$ is $\dfrac{PD \cdot DA}{2}$ and the area of square $DBFE$ is 1. Hence, the desired area below the fence PA is

$$\frac{PD \cdot DA}{2} + 1 = \frac{4 \cdot 2}{2} + 1 = 5 \text{ square units}$$

Because the area of each plot is supposed to be $4\frac{1}{2}$ square units, this allows too much area below the fence. Consequently, the other end of the fence should be closer to D.

   A similar argument shows that the area below $\overline{PB}$ is 3 square units and the end of the fence should be closer to A. It follows that the other end of the fence should be at a point C between A and B, as shown in Figure 11-50(b). To find the exact location of the fence, we need to find CB. To do this, we designate CB by x, write an equation for x by finding the area below $\overline{PC}$ in terms of x, make it equal to $\frac{9}{2}$, and solve for x.

Carrying Out the Plan

The area below $\overline{PC}$ equals the area of $\triangle PCD$ plus the area of the square $DBFE$. The area of $\triangle PCD$ is

$$\frac{PD \cdot DC}{2} = \frac{4(1 + x)}{2} = 2(1 + x)$$

Thus, the total area below $\overline{PC}$ is $2(1 + x) + 1$. This area should equal half the area of the plot, that is, $\frac{9}{2}$. Consequently, we have the following.

$$2(1 + x) + 1 = \frac{9}{2}$$

$$2 + 2x + 1 = \frac{9}{2}$$

$$2x = \frac{3}{2}$$

$$x = \frac{3}{4}$$

Therefore, the fence should be built along the line connecting point P to the point C, which is $\frac{3}{4}$ units directly above point B.

Looking Back

The point C can be found by dividing $\overline{AB}$ into four equal parts. We can also check that the solution is correct by finding the area above $\overline{PC}$. To find the area above $\overline{PC}$, we consider the areas of the trapezoids $PQRS$ and $STAC$, and square $UVWY$, as shown in Figure 11-51(a). The areas of the trapezoids are not easy to find because the length of RS is not known. However, if square $UVWY$ is moved to the shaded space shown in Figure 11-51(b), then the desired area above $\overline{PC}$ is the area of trapezoid $PCAO$, that is, $\frac{1}{2}(OP + AC) \cdot OA = \frac{1}{2} \cdot (2 + \frac{1}{4}) \cdot 4$, or $4\frac{1}{2}$.

FIGURE 11-51

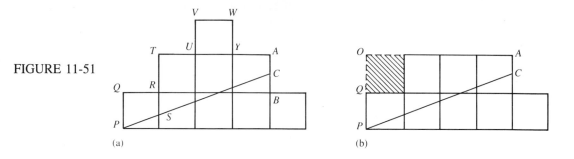

(a)

(b)

An alternate approach for solving the problem utilizes trapezoid $PCAO$ in Figure 11-51(b). Let $AC = y$; we find the area of trapezoid $PCAO$ in terms of y and set that area equal to $\frac{9}{2}$. Then we have $\frac{1}{2}(2 + y) \, 4 = \frac{9}{2}$, or $y = \frac{1}{4}$. That is, point C is $\frac{1}{4}$ unit below point A.

QUESTIONS FROM THE CLASSROOM

1. A student asks if the units of measure must be the same for each term to use the formulas for volumes. How do you respond?
2. In the discussion of the Pythagorean Theorem, squares were constructed on each side of a right triangle. A student asks if different similar figures are constructed on each side of the triangle, does the same type relationship still hold? How do you reply?
3. A student asks, "Can I find the area of an angle?" How do you respond?
4. A student argues that a square has no area since its interior can be thought of as the union of infinitely many line segments, each of which has no area. How do you react?
5. A student asks if the volume of a prism is always a lesser number than its surface area. How do you answer?
6. A students asks, "Why should the United States switch to the metric system?" How do you reply?
7. A student claims that in a triangle with 20° and 40° angles, the side opposite the 40° angle is twice as long as the side opposite the 20° angle. How do you reply?
8. A student interpreted 5 cm^3 using the drawing at left. What is wrong with this interpretation?
9. A student has a can containing three tennis balls. To the student's surprise, the perimeter of the top of the can is longer than the height of the can. The student wants to know if this fact can be explained without performing any measurements. Can you help?

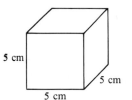

5 cm
5 cm
5 cm

10. A student argues that because 8 ounces $= \frac{1}{2}$ pound, 32 ounces $= 2$ pounds, and equals multiplied times equals gives equals, we should conclude that 256 ounces $= 1$ pound. What is your reply?

CHAPTER OUTLINE

I. The metric system
  A. A summary of relationships among prefixes and the base unit of linear measure follows.

Prefix	Unit	Relationship to Base Unit	Symbol
kilo	kilometer	1000 meters	km
*hecto	hectometer	100 meters	hm
*deka	dekameter	10 meters	dam
meter		**1 meter**	**m**
*deci	decimeter	0.1 meter	dm
centi	centimeter	0.01 meter	cm
milli	millimeter	0.001 meter	mm

*Not commonly used.

  B. Area measure
    1. Units commonly used are the square kilometer (km^2), square meter (m^2), square centimeter (cm^2), and square millimeter (mm^2).
    2. Land can be measured using the **are** (100 m^2) and the **hectare** (10,000 m^2).
  C. Volume measure
    1. Units commonly used are the cubic meter (m^3), cubic decimeter (dm^3), and cubic centimeter (cm^3).
    2. 1 dm^3 = 1 L and 1 cm^3 = 1 mL.
  D. Mass
    1. Units of mass commonly used are the milligram (mg), gram (g), kilogram (kg), and metric ton (t).
    2. 1 L and 1 mL of water have masses of approximately 1 kg and 1 g, respectively.
  E. Temperature
    1. The official unit of metric temperature is the **degree Kelvin,** but the unit commonly used is the **degree Celsius.**
    2. Basic temperature reference points are the following:

100°C—boiling point of water
37°C—normal body temperature
20°C—comfortable room temperature
0°C—freezing point of water

    3. $C = \frac{5}{9}(F - 32)$ and $F = \frac{9}{5}C + 32$

II. Distance
  A. **Distance,** or length, has the following properties: Given points A, B, and C.
    1. $AB \geqq O$
    2. $AB = BA$
    3. Triangular inequality: $AB + BC \geqq AC$
  B. The distance around a two-dimensional figure is called the **perimeter.** The distance C around a circle is called the **circumference.** $C = 2\pi r = \pi d$, where r is the radius of the circle and d is the diameter.

III. Areas
  A. Formulas for areas
    1. **Square:** $A = s^2$, where s is a side.
    2. **Rectangle:** $A = \ell w$, where ℓ is the length and w is the width.
    3. **Parallelogram:** $A = bh$, where b is the base and h is the height.
    4. **Triangle:** $A = \frac{1}{2}bh$, where b is the base and h is the altitude to that base.
    5. **Trapezoid:** $A = \frac{1}{2}h(b_1 + b_2)$, where b_1 and b_2 are the bases and h is the height.
    6. **Regular polygon:** $A = \frac{1}{2}ap$, where a is the apothem and p is the perimeter.
    7. **Circle:** $A = \pi r^2$, where r is the radius.
    8. **Sector:** $A = \theta \pi r^2/360$, where θ is the measure of the central angle forming the sector and r is the radius of the circle containing the sector.
  B. **The Pythagorean Theorem:** In any right triangle, the square of the length of the hypotenuse is equal to the sum of the squares of the lengths of the legs.
  C. **Converse of the Pythagorean Theorem:** In any triangle, $\triangle ABC$, with sides of lengths a, b, and c such that $a^2 + b^2 = c^2$, $\triangle ABC$ is a right triangle with the right angle opposite the side of length c.

IV. Surface areas and volumes
   A. Formulas for areas
      1. **Right prism:** $S.A. = 2B + ph$, where B is the area of a base, p is the perimeter of the base, and h is the height of the prism.
      2. **Right regular pyramid:** $S.A. = B + \frac{1}{2}p\ell$, where B is the area of the base, p is the perimeter of the base, and ℓ is the slant height.
      3. **Right circular cylinder:** $S.A. = 2\pi r^2 + 2\pi rh$, where r is the radius of the circular base and h is the height of the cylinder.
      4. **Right circular cone:** $S.A. = \pi r^2 + \pi r\ell$, where r is the radius of the circular base and ℓ is the slant height.
      5. **Sphere:** $S.A. = 4\pi r^2$, where r is the radius of the sphere.
   B. Formulas for volumes
      1. **Right prism:** $V = Bh$, where B is the area of the base and h is the height.
         (a) **Right rectangular prism:** $V = \ell wh$, where ℓ is the length, w is the width, and h is the height.
         (b) **Cube:** $V = e^3$, where e is an edge.
      2. **Right circular cylinder:** $V = \pi r^2 h$, where r is the radius of the base and h is the height of the cylinder.
      3. **Pyramid:** $V = \frac{1}{3}Bh$, where B is the area of the base and h is the height of the pyramid.
      4. **Circular cone:** $V = \frac{1}{3}\pi r^2 h$, where r is the radius of the circular base and h is the height.
      5. **Sphere:** $V = \frac{4}{3}\pi r^3$, where r is the radius of the sphere.

CHAPTER TEST

1. Complete the following chart converting metric measures.

	mm	cm	m	km
(a)				0.05
(b)		320		
(c)	260,000,000			
(d)			190	

2. For each of the following choose an appropriate metric unit—millimeter, centimeter, meter, or kilometer.
   (a) The thickness of a penny
   (b) The length of a new lead pencil
   (c) The diameter of a dime
   (d) The distance the winner travels in the Indianapolis 500
   (e) The height of a doorknob
   (f) The length of a soccer field
3. For each of the following, describe how you can find the area of the parallelogram.
   (a) Using *DE*.   (b) Using *BF*.

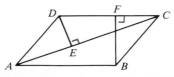

4. What is the area of the shaded region in the figure?

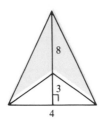

5. What is the area of the shaded region on the geoboard if the unit of measure is 1 cm^2?

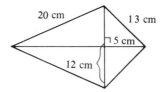

6. Find the area of the kite.

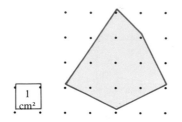

7. Explain how the formula for the area of a trapezoid can be found using the given pictures.

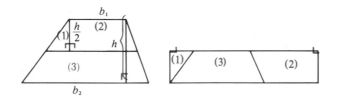

8. Use the figure to find each of the following.
   (a) The area of the hexagon
   (b) The area of the circle.

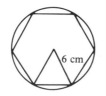

9. Find the area of each shaded region.

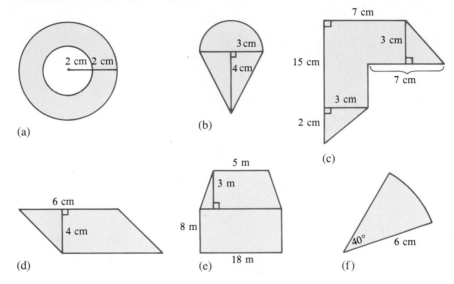

10. For each of the following, can the measures represent sides of a right triangle? Explain your answers.
    (a) 5 cm, 12 cm, 13 cm   (b) 40 cm, 60 cm, 104 cm

11. Find the surface area and volume of each of the following.

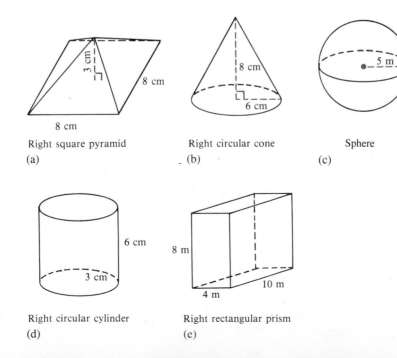

12. Complete each of the following.
    (a) Very heavy objects have mass which is measured in _____ .
    (b) A cube whose length, width, and height are each 1 cm has a volume of _____ .
    (c) If the cube in part (b) is filled with water, the mass of the water is _____ .
    (d) Which has a larger volume, 1 L or 1 dm^3? _____
    (e) If a car used 1 L of gas to go 12 km, the amount of gas needed to go 300 km is _____ L.
    (f) 20 ha = _____ a
    (g) 51.8 L = _____ cm^3
    (h) 10 km^2 = _____ m^2
    (i) 50 L = _____ mL
    (j) 5830 mL = _____ L
    (k) 25 m^3 = _____ dm^3
    (l) 75 dm^3 = _____ mL
    (m) 52,813 g = _____ kg
    (n) 4800 kg = _____ t

13. For each of the following, fill in the correct unit to make the sentence reasonable.
    (a) Anna filled the gas tank with 80 _____ .
    (b) A man has a mass of about 82 _____ .
    (c) The textbook has a mass of 978 _____ .
    (d) A nickel has a mass of 5 _____ .
    (e) A typical adult cat has a mass of about 4 _____ .
    (f) A compact car has a mass of about 1.5 _____ .
    (g) The amount of coffee in the cup is 180 _____ .

14. For each of the following, decide if the situation is likely or unlikely.
    (a) Carrie's bath water has a temperature of 15°C.
    (b) She found 26°C too warm and lowered the thermostat to 21°C.
    (c) Jim was drinking water with a temperature of ⁻5°C.
    (d) The water in the teakettle has a temperature of 120°C.
    (e) The outside temperature dropped to 5°C, and ice appeared on the lake.

15. Complete each of the following.
    (a) 2 dm^3 of water has a mass of _____ g.
    (b) 1 L of water has a mass of _____ g.
    (c) 3 cm^3 of water has a mass of _____ g.
    (d) 4.2 mL of water has a mass of _____ kg.
    (e) 0.2 L of water has a volume of _____ m^3.

SELECTED BIBLIOGRAPHY

Brougher, J. "Discovery Activities with Area and Perimeter." *The Arithmetic Teacher* 20 (May 1973):382–385.

Bruni, J. "Geometry for the Intermediate Grades." *Arithmetic Teacher* 26 (February 1979):17–19.

Donegan, J., and J. Pricken. "Putting an Old Puzzle to Work." *Arithmetic Teacher* 28 (May 1981):15–16.

Ewbank, W. "If Pythagoras Had a Geoboard . . ." *The Mathematics Teacher* 66 (March 1973):215–221.

Hildreth, D. "The Use of Strategies in Estimating Measurements." *Arithmetic Teacher* 30 (January 1983):50–54.

Hirstein, J., C. Lamb, and A. Osborne. "Student Misconceptions About Area Measure." *Arithmetic Teacher* 25 (March 1978):10–16.

Hoffer, A. "Making a Better Beer Glass." *The Mathematics Teacher* 75 (May 1982):378–379.

Hunt, J. "How High Is a Flagpole?" *Arithmetic Teacher* 25 (February 1978):42–43.

Jamski, W. "So Your Students Know About Area?" *Arithmetic Teacher* 26 (December 1978):37.

Jencks, S., and D. Peck. "Thought Starters for the Circular Geoboard." *The Mathematics Teacher* 67 (March 1974):228–233.

Jensen, R., and D. O'Neil. "Meaningful Linear Measurement." *Arithmetic Teacher* 29 (September 1981):6–12.

Jensen, R., and D. O'Neil. "Informal Geometry Through Geometric Blocks." *Arithmetic Teacher* 29 (May 1982):4–8.

Juraschek, W., and G. McGlathery. "Funny Letters: A Discrepant Event." *Arithmetic Teacher* 27 (April 1980):43–47.

Leffin, W. *Going Metric Grades K–6: Guidelines for the Mathematics Teacher*. Reston, Va; National Council of Teachers of Mathematics, 1975.

Leutzinger, L., and G. Nelson. "Let's Do It: Meaningful Measurements, *Arithmetic Teacher* 27 (March 1980):6–11.

Lichtenberg, D. "More About Triangles with the Same Area and the Same Perimeter." *The Mathematics Teacher* 67 (November 1974):659–660.

Lindquist, M., and M. Dana. "Let's Do It: Measurement for the Times." *Arithmetic Teacher* 26 (April 1979):4–9.

Loomis, E. *The Pythagorean Propositions*. Washington, D.C.: National Council of Teachers of Mathematics, 1972.

Lott, J., and H. Nguyen. "Extremal Problems on a Geoboard." *The Mathematics Teacher* 72 (January 1979):28–29.

Mercaldi, R. "An Application of Volume and Surface Area." *The Mathematics Teacher* 66 (January 1974):71–73.

NCTM Metric Implementation Committee. "Metric, not IF, but HOW." *The Arithmetic Teacher* 22 (February 1975):103–109.

NCTM Metric Implementation Committee. "Metric Competency Goals." *The Arithmetic Teacher* 23 (January 1976):70–71.

Prielipp, R. "Are Triangles That Have the Same Area and the Same Perimeter Congruent?" *The Mathematics Teacher* 67 (February 1974):157–159.

Russell, D., and E. Bologna. "Teaching Geometry with Tangrams." *Arithmetic Teacher* 30 (October 1982):34–38.

Sherman, H. "Take the Metric System Personally—Play 'Merrily Metric.'" *Arithmetic Teacher* 29 (October 1981):19–20.

Splitler, G. "The Shear Joy of Area." *Arithmetic Teacher* 29 (April 1982):36–38.

Thomas, D. "Geometry in the Middle School: Problem Solving with Trapezoids." *Arithmetic Teacher* 26 (February 1979): 20–21.

Tolman, M. "The 'Steps' of Metric Conversion." *Arithmetic Teacher* 30 (November 1982):32–33.

Urion, D. "Using the Cuisenaire Rods to Discover Approximations of Pi." *Arithmetic Teacher* 27 (December 1979):17.

Walter, M. "Frame Geometry: An Example in Posing and Solving Problems." *Arithmetic Teacher* 28 (October 1980):16–18.

Warburton, J. "A 'Friend' in Need." *Arithmetic Teacher* 27 (January 1980):42–43.

PRELIMINARY PROBLEM

One day, Linda left home, H, for school, S. Rather than stopping at school, she went on to the corner, A, which is twice as far from home as the school and on the same street as her home and the school. Then she headed for the ice cream parlor, I. Passing the ice cream parlor, she headed straight for the next corner, B, which is on the same street as A and I and twice as far from A as I. Walking toward the park, P, she continued beyond it to the next corner, C, so that C, P, and B are on the same street, and C is twice as far from B as P. At this point, she again headed for the school, but continued walking in a straight line twice as far, reaching point D. Then, she headed for the ice cream parlor, but continued in a straight line twice as far to point E. From E, Linda headed for the park but continued in a straight line twice as far to F where she stopped. The figure shows the first part of Linda's walk. What is the location of Linda's final stop?

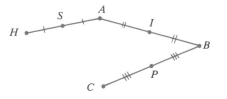

INTRODUCTION

In 1637 René Descartes, a French philosopher and mathematician, revolutionized mathematics by successfully combining geometry with algebra. He described the location of a point in a plane using a pair of real numbers and was able to characterize geometric figures with algebraic equations. Today the area of mathematics that Descartes developed is known as **analytic geometry,** or **coordinate geometry.**

analytic geometry
coordinate geometry

12-1   COORDINATE SYSTEM IN A PLANE

To set up a Cartesian coordinate system (named for Descartes), two number lines are placed perpendicular to each other at the point where both have coordinate 0. The intersection point of the two lines is called the **origin.** The two lines are usually drawn as shown in Figure 12-1, with the horizontal line called the **x-axis** and the vertical line called the **y-axis.**

origin
x-axis
y-axis

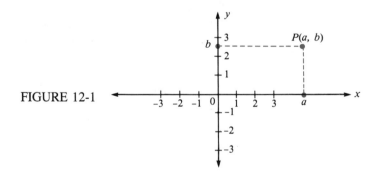

FIGURE 12-1

The location of any point P can be described by an ordered pair of numbers as shown in Figure 12-1. If a perpendicular from P to the x-axis intersects the x-axis at a and a perpendicular from P to the y-axis intersects the y-axis at b, then we say that point P has coordinates (a, b). The first component in the ordered pair (a, b) is called the **abscissa,** or the **x-coordinate,** of P. The second component is called the **ordinate,** or **y-coordinate,** of P. For example, on the student page from *McGraw-Hill Mathematics,* 1981, Grade 3, p. 557, the Firehouse has coordinates $(2, 1)$.

abscissa   x-coordinate
ordinate   y-coordinate

In Figure 12-2, the x-coordinate of P is $^-3$ and the y-coordinate of P is 2, so that P has coordinates $(^-3, 2)$. Similarly, R has an x-coordinate of $^-4$ and a y-coordinate of $^-3$, which can be written as $R(^-4, ^-3)$. The first number in the parentheses is always the x-coordinate, and the second number is always the y-coordinate.

Points on a Graph

This graph is like a map. It shows the location of different places in Parkville.

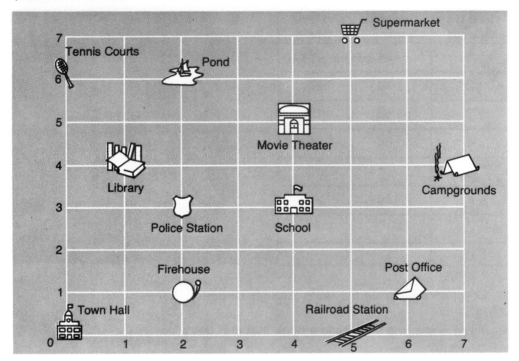

Follow the directions. Always start at the Town Hall.

To find the Firehouse, go over 2 and up 1.
You write this as (2, 1).

over, up

To find the Movie Theater, go over 4 and up 5.
You write this as (4, 5).

To find the Railroad Station, go over 5.
There you are. You do not have to go up.
You write this as (5, 0).

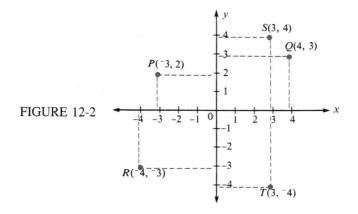

FIGURE 12-2

To each point in the plane, there corresponds an ordered pair (a, b). Conversely, to every ordered pair of real numbers, there corresponds a point in the plane. Hence, there is a one-to-one correspondence between all the points in the plane and all the ordered pairs of real numbers. Such a one-to-one correspondence is called a **coordinate system** for the plane.

coordinate system

Together, the x-axis and y-axis separate the plane into four parts called **quadrants.** Figure 12-3 shows the four quadrants. The first quadrant can be described as the set of all ordered pairs (x, y), whose x-coordinate and y-coordinate are positive. The other quadrants can be described in a similar manner.

quadrants

Quadrant I $= \{(x, y) \mid x > 0 \text{ and } y > 0\}$

Quadrant II $= \{(x, y) \mid x < 0 \text{ and } y > 0\}$

Quadrant III $= \{(x, y) \mid x < 0 \text{ and } y < 0\}$

Quadrant IV $= \{(x, y) \mid x > 0 \text{ and } y < 0\}$

FIGURE 12-3

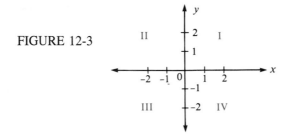

Notice that the quadrants do not include points on the axes. Every point on the x-axis has a y-coordinate of zero. Thus, the x-axis can be described as the set of all points (x, y) such that $y = 0$. The set of points on the x-axis is usually denoted by the equation $y = 0$, and we say that the equation of the x-axis is $y = 0$. Similarly, the y-axis can be described as a set of points in the plane, (x, y), for which $x = 0$ and y is an arbitrary real number. Thus, $x = 0$ is the equation of the y-axis. If we plot the set of all points that satisfy a given condition, the resulting picture on the Cartesian coordinate system is called the **graph** of the set.

graph

Example 12-1

Sketch the graph for each of the following.

(a) $x = 2$ (b) $y = 3$
(c) $x < 2$ and $y = 3$ (d) $x < 2$

Solution

(a) The equation $x = 2$ represents the set of all points (x, y) for which $x = 2$ and y is any real number. This set represents a line perpendicular to the x-axis at $(2, 0)$ (Figure 12-4). Note that the set does not consist of a single point only.

FIGURE 12-4

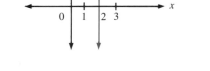

(b) The equation $y = 3$ represents the set of all points (x, y) for which $y = 3$ and x is any real number. This set represents a line perpendicular to the y-axis at $(0, 3)$ (Figure 12-5). Note that the set does not consist of a single point only.

FIGURE 12-5

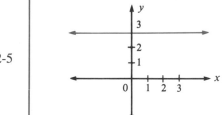

(c) Together, the statements represent the set of all points (x, y) for which $x < 2$, but y is always 3. The set describes a half-line, as shown in Figure 12-6.

FIGURE 12-6

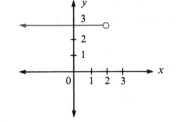

(d) The statement represents $\{(x, y) \mid x < 2 \text{ and } y \in R\}$. Because there are no restrictions on the y-coordinates, the coordinates of any point to the left of the line with equation $x = 2$, but not on the line, satisfy the condition. The half-plane in Figure 12-7 is the graph.

FIGURE 12-7

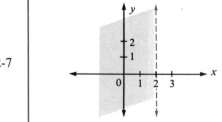

Remark | Had the inequality in the graph of Example 12-1(d) been $x \le 2$, then the line $x = 2$ would have been a part of the set and would have been shown as a solid line. The fact that the line is not included is indicated by using the dotted line.

PROBLEM SET 12-1

1. (a) Give the coordinates of each of the points $A, B, C, D, E, F, G,$ and H of the accompanying figure.

   (b) Find the coordinates of another point (not drawn) that is collinear with $E, D,$ and C.

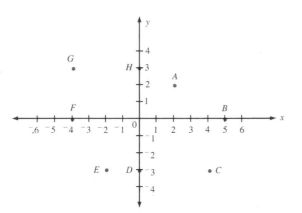

2. Name the quadrant in which each ordered pair is located.
   (a) (3, 7)   (b) ($^-$5, $^-$8)
   (c) ($^-$10, 32)   (d) (10, $^-$40)
   (e) (0, 7)

3. Find the coordinates of two other points collinear with each pair of given points.
   (a) $P(2, 2)$, $Q(4, 2)$ (b) $P(^-1, 0)$, $Q(^-1, 2)$
   (c) $P(^-3, 0)$, $Q(3, 0)$ (d) $P(0, ^-2)$, $Q(0, 3)$
   (e) $P(0, 0)$, $Q(0, 1)$ (f) $P(0, 0)$, $Q(1, 1)$

4. Complete each of the following sentences.
   (a) The y-coordinate of every point on the x-axis is _____.

   (b) The x-coordinate of every point on the y-axis is _____.

5. For each of the following, give as much information as possible about x and y.
   (a) The ordered pairs ($^-$2, 0), ($^-$2, 1) and (x, y) represent collinear points.
   (b) The ordered pairs ($^-$2, 1), (0, 1) and (x, y) represent collinear points.
   (c) The ordered pair (x, y) is in the fourth quadrant.

6. Consider the lines through $P(2, 4)$ and perpendicular to the x- and y-axes, respectively. Find both the area and the perimeter of the rectangle formed by these lines and the axes.

7. Plot each of the points $A(^-3, ^-2)$, $B(^-3, 6)$, $C(4, 6)$ and then find the coordinates of a point D such that quadrilateral $ABCD$ is a rectangle.

8. Plot at least six points each having the sum of its coordinates equal to 4.

9. Sketch the graphs for each of the following.
   (a) $x = ^-3$ (b) $y = ^-1$
   (c) $x > ^-3$ (d) $y > ^-1$
   (e) $x > ^-3$ and $y = 2$ (f) $y \geq ^-1$ and $x = 0$

10. Find the equations for each of the following.
    (a) The line containing $P(3, 0)$ and perpendicular to the x-axis
    (b) The line containing $P(0, ^-2)$ and parallel to the x-axis
    (c) The line containing $P(^-4, 5)$ and parallel to the x-axis
    (d) The line containing $P(^-4, 5)$ and parallel to the y-axis

11. Use the figure to answer the following questions.

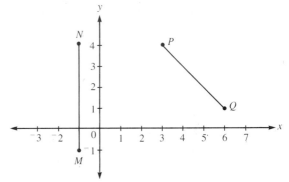

    (a) Give the coordinates of the endpoints of $\overline{PQ}$.
    (b) Give the coordinates of the endpoints of $\overline{MN}$.
    (c) Write the equation of the line parallel to $\overline{MN}$ and containing point P.
    (d) Write the equation of the line perpendicular to $\overline{MN}$ and containing point Q.

12. Use the graph to answer the following questions.

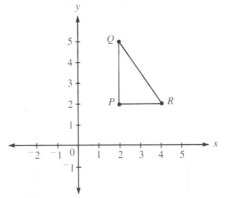

    (a) Give the coordinates of the images of points P, Q, and R if $\triangle PQR$ is reflected about the x-axis.
    (b) Give the coordinates of the images of points P, Q, and R if $\triangle PQR$ is rotated 90° counterclockwise with the origin as the center of the rotation.

12-2   EQUATIONS OF LINES

The graph of the equation $x = a$, where a is some real number, is a line perpendicular to the x-axis through the point with coordinates $(a, 0)$ as shown in Figure 12-8. Similarly, the graph of the equation $y = b$ is a line perpendicular to the y-axis through the point with coordinates $(0, b)$.

FIGURE 12-8

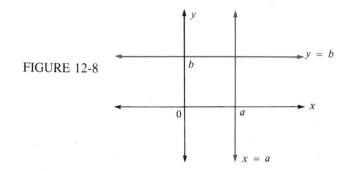

To graph the equation $y = x$, we plot all points whose x- and y-coordinates are equal. For example, $(0, 0)$, $(1, 1)$, $(1.3, 1.3)$, $(4, 4)$, $(4.5, 4.5)$, $(10, 10)$ $(^-3, \ ^-3)$ all belong to the graph. However, $(1, \ ^-1)$ and $(2, 4)$ do not belong to the graph. Plotting some of the points shows that the points lie on a line ℓ, as shown in Figure 12-9. In fact, all points represented by the equation $y = x$ lie on line ℓ.

FIGURE 12-9

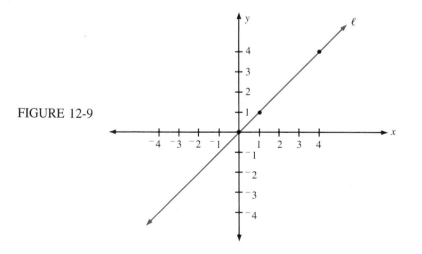

Next, consider the equation $y = 2x$. For any value of x, there is a corresponding value of y. Table 12-1 shows several values of x with corresponding values of y.

TABLE 12-1

x	$y = 2x$
0	0
1	2
2	4
$^-1$	$^-2$
$^-2$	$^-4$

These five coordinate pairs are plotted in Figure 12-10, along with the graph of $y = x$. The five points appear to be on a straight line. In fact, all points whose coordinates satisfy the equation $y = 2x$ lie on the same straight line.

FIGURE 12-10

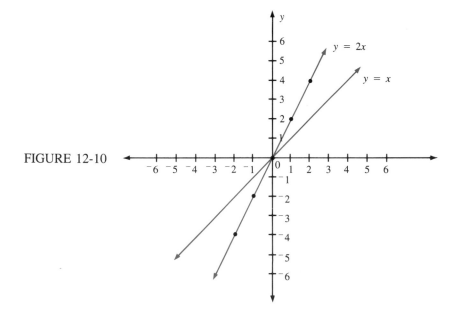

As Figure 12-10 shows, the graph of $y = 2x$ is *steeper* than the graph of $y = x$. We further explore the notion of steepness by examining the graphs in Figure 12-11.

All six lines in Figure 12-11 have equations of the form $y = mx$, where m takes the values 2, 1, $\frac{1}{2}$, $^-\frac{1}{2}$, $^-1$, and $^-2$. The number m is a measure of steepness and is called the **slope** of the line whose equation is $y = mx$. The graph goes up from left to right (increases) if m is positive and goes down from left to right (decreases) if m is negative.

slope

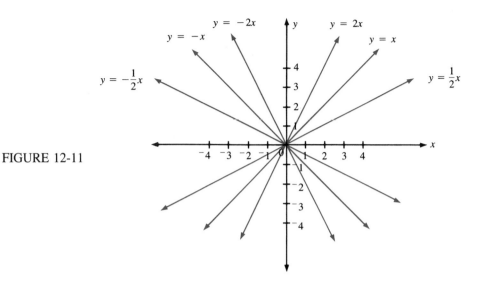

FIGURE 12-11

Observe that all six lines in Figure 12-11 pass through the origin. This is true for any line whose equation is $y = mx$. If $x = 0$, then $y = m \cdot 0 = 0$, and $(0, 0)$ is a point on the graph of $y = mx$. Conversely, it is possible to show that any nonvertical line passing through the origin has an equation of the form $y = mx$, for some value of m.

Example 12-2   Find the equation of the line that contains $(0, 0)$ and $(2, 3)$.

Solution   The line goes through the origin; its equation has the form $y = mx$. To find the equation of the line, we must find the value of m. The line contains $(2, 3)$, so substitute 2 for x and 3 for y into the equation $y = mx$ to obtain $3 = m \cdot 2$ and thus $m = \frac{3}{2}$. Hence, the required equation is $y = \frac{3}{2}x$.

Next, we consider equations of the form $y = mx + b$, where b is a real number. To do this, we examine the graphs of $y = x + 2$ and $y = x$. Given the graph of $y = x$, the graph of $y = x + 2$ can be obtained by "raising" each point on the first graph by two units because, for a certain value of x, the corresponding y value is two units greater. This is shown in Figure 12-12(a). Similarly, to sketch the graph of $y = x - 2$, we first draw the graph of $y = x$ and then lower each point vertically by two units as shown in Figure 12-12(b).

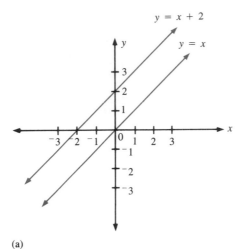

(a)

FIGURE 12-12

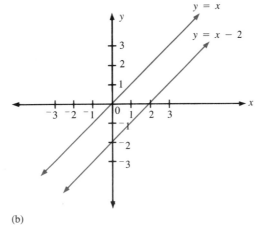

(b)

The graphs of $y = x + 2$ and $y = x - 2$ are straight lines. Moreover, the lines whose equations are $y = x$, $y = x + 2$, and $y = x - 2$ are parallel. In general, for a given value of m, the graph of $y = mx + b$ is a straight line through $(0, b)$ and parallel to the line whose equation is $y = mx$. Hence, *two nonvertical lines are parallel if their slopes are equal.*

The graph of the line $y = mx + b$, where $b > 0$, can be obtained from the graph of $y = mx$ by sliding $y = mx$ up b units, as shown in Figure 12-13. If $b < 0$, $y = mx$ must be slid down $|b|$ units.

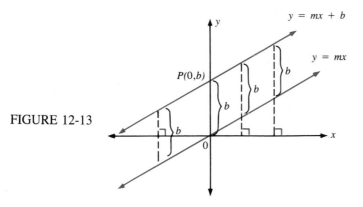

FIGURE 12-13

The graph of $y = mx + b$ in Figure 12-13 crosses the y-axis at the point $P(0, b)$. The value of y at the point of intersection of any line with the y-axis is *y*-intercept called the **y-intercept.** Thus, b is the y-intercept of $y = mx + b$, and this form of slope-intercept form the equation of a straight line is called the **slope-intercept form.** Similarly, the value of x at the point of intersection of a line with the x-axis is called the *x*-intercept **x-intercept.**

Example 12-3 | Given the equation $y - 3x = {}^{-}6$, find each of the following.

    (a) The slope of the line.
    (b) The y-intercept.
    (c) The x-intercept.
    (d) Sketch the graph of the equation.

Solution | (a) To write the equation in the form $y = mx + b$, we add $3x$ to both sides of the given equation to obtain $y = 3x + ({}^{-}6)$. Hence, the slope is 3.
    (b) The form $y = 3x + ({}^{-}6)$ shows that $b = {}^{-}6$, which is the y-intercept. (The y-intercept can also be found directly by substituting $x = 0$ in the equation and finding the corresponding value of y.)
    (c) The x-intercept is the x-coordinate of the point where the graph intersects the x-axis. At that point, $y = 0$. Substituting 0 for y in $y = 3x - 6$ gives 2 as the x-intercept.
    (d) The y-intercept and x-intercept are located at $(0, {}^{-}6)$ and $(2, 0)$ on the line. Plot these points and draw the line through them to obtain the desired graph, as shown in Figure 12-14. Note that any two points of the line can be used to sketch the graph because any two points determine a line.

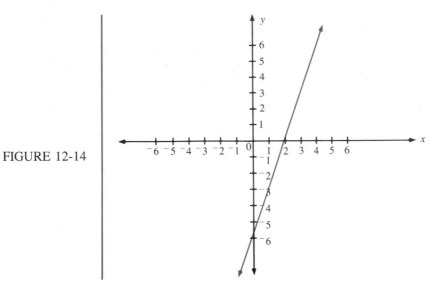

FIGURE 12-14

The equation $y = b$ can be written in slope-intercept form as $y = 0 \cdot x + b$. Consequently, its slope is 0 and its y-intercept is b. This should not be surprising as the line is parallel to the x-axis; consequently, its steepness, or slope, should be 0. Any vertical line parallel to the y-axis has equation $x = a$ for some real number a. This equation cannot be written in slope-intercept form. The slope of a vertical line is undefined and will be discussed later in the chapter. In general, *every straight line has an equation of either the form $y = mx + b$ or $x = a$*. Any equation that can be put in one of these forms is called a **linear equation.**

linear equation

EQUATION
OF A LINE

> Every straight line has an equation either of the form $y = mx + b$ or $x = a$.

Because a line is determined by any two of its points, then given the coordinates of two points on a line, it is possible to find the equation of the line. For example, given $A(4, 2)$ and $B(1, 6)$, we can find the equation of $\overleftrightarrow{AB}$. Because the line is not perpendicular to the x-axis (why?), it must be of the form $y = mx + b$. Substituting the coordinates of A and B in $y = mx + b$ results in the following equations.

$$2 = m \cdot 4 + b, \quad \text{or} \quad 2 = 4m + b$$
$$6 = m \cdot 1 + b, \quad \text{or} \quad 6 = m + b$$

To find the equation of the line, we must find the values of m and b. If we solve for b in each of these equations, we obtain $b = 2 - 4m$ and $b = 6 - m$, respectively. Consequently, $2 - 4m = 6 - m$, so $m = {}^-\frac{4}{3}$. Substituting this value of m in either one of the equations gives $b = \frac{22}{3}$. Consequently, the equation of the line through A and B is $y = {}^-\frac{4}{3}x + \frac{22}{3}$. The correctness of this equation can be checked by substituting the coordinates of the two given points, $A(4, 2)$ and $B(1, 6)$, in the equation.

Using an analogous approach, it is possible to find a general formula for the slope of a line given two points on the line, $A(x_1, y_1)$ and $B(x_2, y_2)$. If the line is not a vertical line, its equation is given by $y = mx + b$. Substituting the coordinates of A and B into this equation gives the following.

$$y_1 = mx_1 + b \quad \text{and, therefore,} \quad y_1 - mx_1 = b$$

$$y_2 = mx_2 + b \quad \text{and, therefore,} \quad y_2 - mx_2 = b$$

By equating these two values for b and solving for m, the formula for slope results.

$$y_1 - mx_1 = y_2 - mx_2$$

$$mx_2 - mx_1 = y_2 - y_1$$

$$m(x_2 - x_1) = y_2 - y_1$$

$$m = \frac{y_2 - y_1}{x_2 - x_1}$$

SLOPE
FORMULA

Given two points $A(x_1, y_1)$ and $B(x_2, y_2)$ with $x_1 \neq x_2$, the slope m of the line $\overleftrightarrow{AB}$ is given by $m = \dfrac{y_2 - y_1}{x_2 - x_1}$.

By multiplying both the numerator and denominator on the right side of the slope formula by $^-1$, we obtain

$$m = \frac{y_2 - y_1}{x_2 - x_1} = \frac{(y_2 - y_1)(^-1)}{(x_2 - x_1)(^-1)} = \frac{y_1 - y_2}{x_1 - x_2}$$

This shows that it is irrelevant which point is named (x_1, y_1) and which is named (x_2, y_2), but *the order of the coordinates in the subtraction must be consistent.* The slope of the line $\overleftrightarrow{AB}$ is the change in y-coordinates divided by the corresponding change in x-coordinates of any two points on $\overleftrightarrow{AB}$. The difference $x_2 - x_1$ is often called the **run,** while the difference $y_2 - y_1$ is called the **rise.** Thus, the slope is often defined as "rise over run," or $\dfrac{\text{rise}}{\text{run}}$.

run   rise

Example 12-4 | Find the slope of $\overleftrightarrow{AB}$ given $A(3, 1)$ and $B(5, 4)$.

Solution | $m = \dfrac{4 - 1}{5 - 3} = \dfrac{3}{2}$ or $\dfrac{1 - 4}{3 - 5} = \dfrac{^-3}{^-2} = \dfrac{3}{2}$

Example 12-5 | Find the slope and the equation of the line passing through the points $A(^-3, 4)$ and $B(^-1, 0)$.

Solution | $m = \dfrac{4 - 0}{^-3 - (^-1)} = \dfrac{4}{^-2} = ^-2$

The equation of the line must be of the form $y = mx + b$. Because $m = ^-2$, $y = ^-2x + b$ and now the value of b must be found. The required line contains each of the given points, so the coordinates of each point must satisfy the equation. We substitute the coordinates of $B(^-1, 0)$ into $y = ^-2x + b$ and proceed as follows.

$y = ^-2x + b$

$0 = ^-2(^-1) + b$

$0 = 2 + b$

$^-2 = b$

The required equation is $y = ^-2x + ^-2$, or $y = ^-2x - 2$. To check that $y = ^-2x - 2$ is the required equation, we must verify that the coordinates of both A and B satisfy the equation. The verification is left for you.

Using the slope formula, it is possible to find the equation of a line given any point on the line and the slope of the line. In Figure 12-15, line ℓ has slope m and contains a given point (x_1, y_1). Point (x, y) represents any other point on line ℓ if and only if the slope determined by points (x_1, y_1) and (x, y) is m. We use the slope formula and proceed as follows.

$\dfrac{y - y_1}{x - x_1} = m$

$y - y_1 = m(x - x_1)$

point-slope form | The result is called the **point-slope form** of a line.

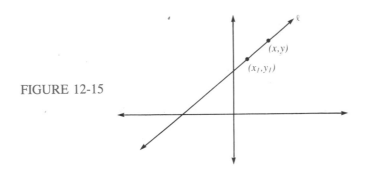

FIGURE 12-15

<table>
<tr>
<td>POINT-SLOPE
FORM OF LINE</td>
<td>The equation of a line with slope m through a given point (x_1, y_1) is

$y - y_1 = m(x - x_1)$</td>
</tr>
</table>

Example 12-6

(a) Find the equation of a line through point $P(3, 4)$ with slope $^-2$.

(b) Find the equation of a line through points $A(2, 4)$ and $B(^-6, 3)$.

Solution

(a) $\dfrac{y - 4}{x - 3} = {}^-2$

$y - 4 = {}^-2(x - 3)$

$y = {}^-2x + 10$

(b) $m = \dfrac{3 - 4}{{}^-6 - 2} = \dfrac{{}^-1}{{}^-8}$, or $\dfrac{1}{8}$

Now we use point $A(2, 4)$ and the slope to find the equation of the line. (Point B may be used instead.)

$\dfrac{y - 4}{x - 2} = \dfrac{1}{8}$

$y - 4 = \dfrac{1}{8}(x - 2)$

$y = \dfrac{1}{8}x + \dfrac{15}{4}$

To examine the slope of a vertical line, pick any two points on the line, (x_1, y_1) and (x_2, y_2). Since the line is vertical, $x_1 = x_2$. Consequently,

$m = \dfrac{y_2 - y_1}{x_2 - x_1} = \dfrac{y_2 - y_1}{0}$

which is not meaningful. Thus, *the slope of a vertical line is undefined.* Consequently, we can also state that *any two lines are parallel if they both have the same slope or both lines have undefined slope.*

In applications of mathematics, we often need to graph inequalities as well as equations. Consider, for example, the inequality $y - 3x > {}^-6$. This inequality is equivalent to $y > 3x + ({}^-6)$. A point whose coordinates satisfy $y > 3x + ({}^-6)$ is above the line represented by $y = 3x + ({}^-6)$. Consequently, the graph of the inequality is the half-plane above the line given by $y = 3x + ({}^-6)$. The graph is sketched in Figure 12-16. To indicate that the line itself is not included in the graph, the line is dotted.

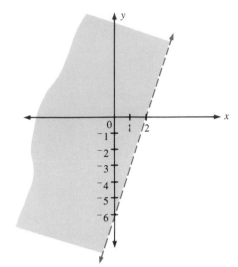

FIGURE 12-16

The graph of any inequality in one of the forms $y > mx + b$ or $y < mx + b$ is a half-plane either above or below the line $y = mx + b$. Thus, in order to graph an inequality like $y - 3x > {}^-6$, first we graph the corresponding straight line. Then, we check some point not on the line to see if it satisfies the inequality. If it does, the half-plane containing the point is the graph, and if not, the half-plane not including the point is the graph. For example, checking $(0,0)$ in $y - 3x > {}^-6$ gives $0 - 3 \cdot 0 > {}^-6$, which is a true statement. Thus, the half-plane determined by $y - 3x = {}^-6$ and containing the origin is the graph of the inequality as pictured in Figure 12-16.

Example 12-7

Graph the following inequalities on the same coordinate system to determine all points that satisfy both inequalities.

(1) $2x + 3y > 6$
(2) $x - y \le 0$

Solution

First we graph the lines represented by the equations $2x + 3y = 6$ and $x - y = 0$. Next we must determine the half-planes to be shaded. Substituting $x = 0$ and $y = 0$ in inequality (1) gives $0 > 6$, a false statement, so the required half-plane determined by the first inequality does not contain the point $(0, 0)$. In Figure 12-17, the graph of this inequality is marked with vertical colored lines. Substituting $x = 0$ and $y = 0$ in inequality (2) gives $0 \le 0$, a true statement. Thus, $(0, 0)$ is part of the required solution. However, $(0, 0)$ is on the line $x - y = 0$, so it is in neither of the half-planes determined by this line. Another point must be checked. Consider, for example, $(1, 2)$. Substituting $x = 1$ and $y = 2$ in inequality (2) gives ${}^-1 \le 0$, a true statement; hence, $(1, 2)$ is in the half-plane determined by equation (2). In Figure 12-17, the graph of this inequality is marked with horizontal black lines. Hence, the set of common points is the crosshatched shaded portion of Figure 12-17.

FIGURE 12-17

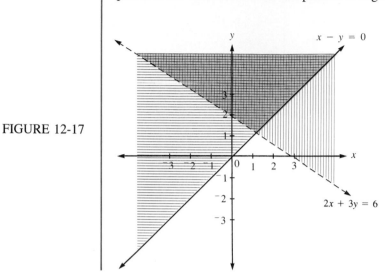

PROBLEM SET 12-2

1. Sketch the graphs of the equations $y = {}^-x$ and $y = {}^-x + 3$ on the same coordinate system.

2. The graph of $y = mx$ is given in the accompanying figure. Sketch the graphs for each of the following on the same figure.

   (a) $y = mx + 3$ (b) $y = mx - 3$

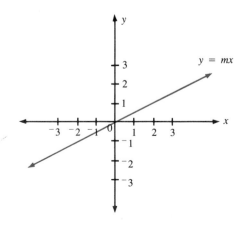

3. Sketch the graphs for each of the following equations or inequalities.

   (a) $y = \dfrac{{}^-3}{4}x + 3$ (b) $y = 3x - 1$

   (c) $y = {}^-3$ (d) $x = {}^-2$

   (e) $y \geq 15x - 30$ (f) $y \leq \dfrac{1}{20}x$

4. Find the x-intercept and y-intercept for the equations in Problem 3, if they exist.

5. Write each of the equations in slope-intercept form.

   (a) $3y - x = 0$ (b) $x + y = 3$

   (c) $3x - 4y + 7 = 0$ (d) $x = 3y$

   (e) $x - y = 4(x - y)$

6. For each of the following, find the slope, if it exists, of the line determined by the given pair of points.

   (a) $(4, 3)$ and $({}^-5, 0)$

   (b) $({}^-4, 1)$ and $(5, 2)$

   (c) $(\sqrt{5}, 2)$ and $(1, 2)$

   (d) $({}^-3, 81)$ and $({}^-3, 198)$

   (e) $(1.0001, 12)$ and $(1, 10)$

   (f) (a, a) and (b, b)

7. For each of the following, write the equation of the line determined by the given pair of points in slope-intercept form or in the form $x = a$.
   (a) $(^-4, 3)$ and $(1, ^-2)$ (b) $(0, 0)$ and $(2, 1)$
   (c) $(0, 1)$ and $(2, 1)$ (d) $(2, 1)$ and $(2, ^-1)$
   (e) $\left(0, \dfrac{^-1}{2}\right)$ and $\left(\dfrac{1}{2}, 0\right)$ (f) $(^-a, 0)$ and $(a, 0)$, $a \neq 0$

8. Use slopes to determine which of the following pairs of lines are parallel.
   (a) $y = 2x - 1$ and $y = 2x + 7$
   (b) $4y - 3x + 4 = 0$ and $8y - 6x + 1 = 0$
   (c) $y - 2x = 0$ and $4x - 2y = 3$
   (d) $\dfrac{x}{3} + \dfrac{y}{4} = 1$ and $y = \dfrac{4}{3}x$

9. For each of the following, find the equation of a line through $P(^-2, 3)$ and parallel to the line represented by the given equation.
   (a) $y = ^-2x$ (b) $3y + 2x + 1 = 0$
   (c) $x = 3$ (d) $y = ^-4$

10. Determine the slope of each of the following lines.

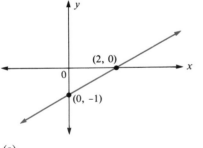

(a)

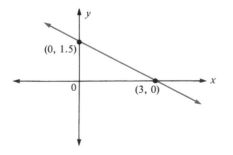

(b)

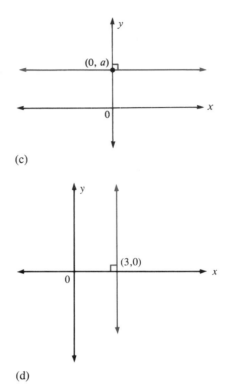

(c)

(d)

11. The door on a house was 4 feet above ground level. To allow handicap access, a ramp with a slope of $\dfrac{1}{10}$ was placed from the ground to the door. How long was the ramp?

12. (a) Let ℓ be a nonvertical line through the origin. Let n be a vertical line through $(1, 0)$. Show that P, the point of intersection of ℓ and n, has coordinates $(1, m)$, where m is the slope of ℓ.
    (b) Let b be a real number and ℓ be a nonvertical line through $(0, b)$. Let P be the point where ℓ intersects the vertical line n through $(1, 0)$. Show that the y-coordinate of P is the sum of b and the slope of ℓ.

13. The vertices of quadrilateral $ABCD$ are $A(2, 1)$, $B(3, 5)$, $C(^-5, 1)$, $D(^-6, ^-3)$. Prove that quadrilateral $ABCD$ is a parallelogram.

14. Prove that the points represented by $(0, ^-1)$, $(1, 2)$, and $(^-1, ^-4)$ are collinear.

15. For each of the following, find the equation of the line which passes through the given point and has the given slope.
    (a) $(^-3, 0)$ with slope $\dfrac{^-1}{2}$

(b) $(1, {}^-3)$ with slope $\dfrac{2}{3}$

(c) $({}^-1, {}^-5)$ with slope $\dfrac{{}^-5}{7}$

16. Find the x-intercept and y-intercept of the line whose equation is $\dfrac{x}{a} + \dfrac{y}{b} = 1$, where $a \neq 0$ and $b \neq 0$.

17. Find the equation of the flip image of the line $y = 3x + 1$ in each of the following.
   (a) The x-axis   (b) The y-axis

18. Assuming that the relationship between temperature in degrees Celsius and temperature in degrees Fahrenheit is a linear relationship, develop a formula that will convert temperature in Fahrenheit into temperature in Celsius if $0°C = 32°F$ and $100°C = 212°F$.

19. Graph each of the following inequalities.
   (a) $x - y + 3 > 0$ (b) $2x > 3y$
   (c) $x - 2y + 1 \leq 0$ (d) $x - 2y + 1 \geq 0$

20. The number of chirps made by a cricket is linearly related to the temperature. If a cricket chirped 40 times a minute when it was $10°C$ and 112 times a minute when it was $20°C$, find an equation to describe this relationship.

21. (a) Use the given drawing and properties of similar triangles to prove that the slopes m_1 and m_2 of two perpendicular lines ℓ_1 and ℓ_2 satisfy the relationship $m_1 m_2 = {}^-1$.
   (b) Prove that if $CD = 1$, then $m_1 = AD$ and $m_2 = {}^-DB$.

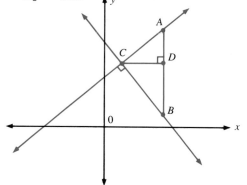

★ 22. Graph each of the following equations.
   (a) $y = |x|$ (b) $|y| = x$
   (c) $|y| = |x|$ (d) $|x + y| = 1$
   (e) $|x| + |y| = 1$

* * * * * * * REVIEW PROBLEMS * * * * * * *

23. Find the equation for each of the following.
   (a) The line containing $({}^-7, {}^-8)$ and parallel to the x-axis.
   (b) The line containing $({}^-7, {}^-8)$ and perpendicular to the x-axis.

24. Find the coordinates of two other points collinear with the given points.
   (a) $P({}^-2, {}^-2)$, $Q({}^-4, {}^-2)$
   (b) $P({}^-7, {}^-8)$, $Q(3, 4)$

25. Plot each of the points $A(2, 2)$, $B(6, 6)$, and $C(8, {}^-4)$ and then find the coordinates of a point D such that quadrilateral $ABCD$ is a parallelogam.

COMPUTER CORNER

The following BASIC program finds the coordinates of the point of intersection of two lines with equations in slope-intercept form. Type the program into your computer. Find the coordinates of the point of intersection of the lines $y = 3x + 4$ and $y = 2x - 6$. Check your work by running the program.

```
 10 PRINT "THIS PROGRAM FIND THE"
 15 PRINT "SOLUTION TO TWO EQUATIONS"
 20 PRINT "IN TWO UNKNOWNS,"
 25 PRINT
 30 PRINT "ARE YOUR EQUATIONS IN POINT-"
 35 PRINT "SLOPE FORM?"
 40 INPUT A$
 45 IF A$ = "YES" THEN 65
 50 PRINT "START OVER WHEN THE"
 55 PRINT "EQUATIONS ARE IN THIS FORMAT,"
 60 STOP
 65 PRINT "PRINT TYPE IN THE SLOPE AND"
 70 PRINT "Y-INTERCEPT OF THE FIRST"
 75 PRINT "EQUATION SEPARATED BY A COMMA,"
 80 INPUT M1, B1
 85 PRINT "TYPE IN THE SLOPE AND"
 90 PRINT "Y-INTERCEPT OF THE SECOND"
 95 PRINT "EQUATION SEPARATED BY A COMMA,"
100 INPUT M2, B2
105 IF M1 - M2 = 0 THEN 155
110 LET X = (B2 - B1)/(M1 - M2)
115 LET Y = M1 * X + B1
120 PRINT "THE SOLUTION IS X = "; X
125 PRINT "AND Y = "; Y
130 PRINT
135 PRINT "DO YOU WANT TO SOLVE OTHERS?"
140 INPUT B$
145 IF B$ = "YES" THEN 30
150 STOP
155 IF B1 = B2 THEN 165
160 GOTO 175
165 PRINT "ANY POINT ON EITHER LINE IS A SOLUTION,"
170 GOTO 135
175 PRINT "YOUR EQUATIONS HAVE NO SOLUTIONS,"
180 GOTO 135
185 END
```

12-3 SYSTEMS OF LINEAR EQUATIONS

The mathematical descriptions of many problems involve more than one equation, each involving more than one unknown. To solve such problems, a common solution to the equations must be found if it exists. For example, finding the solution to a problem may involve finding all x and y values that satisfy both $y = x + 3$ and $y = 2x - 1$. Together, $y = x + 3$ and $y - 2x - 1$ are an example of a

system of linear equations **system of linear equations.** Any solution to the system is an ordered pair (x, y) that satisfies both equations.

Geometrically, an ordered pair satisfying both equations is a point that belongs to each of the lines. Figure 12-18 shows the graphs of $y = x + 3$ and $y = 2x - 1$. The two lines appear to intersect at $(4, 7)$. Thus, $(4, 7)$ appears to be the solution of the given system of equations. This solution can be checked by substituting 4 for x and 7 for y into each equation. Since $7 = 4 + 3$ and $7 = 2 \cdot 4 - 1$, the ordered pair $(4, 7)$ is a solution. The lines intersect in only one point. Thus, $(4, 7)$ is the only solution to the system.

FIGURE 12-18

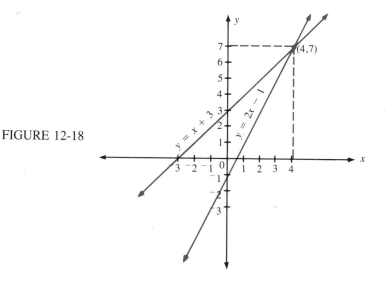

In the upper elementary grades, students learn to graph linear equations. Often, they also learn the relationship between a pair of linear equations and the intersection of two lines, as the excerpt on page 577 from the Addison-Wesley text, *Mathematics in Our World*, Grade 8, 1979, shows.

There are certain drawbacks to estimating a solution to a system of equations graphically. The sketch of a graph is often inaccurate, especially if noninteger, real numbers are involved in the solution. Moreover, the graphic approach is impractical in solving linear equations with three variables and impossible when more than three variables are involved. There are various algebraic methods for

✪ Graphing pairs of equations

Graph on the same coordinate grid
the pair of equations

$$y = x - 2$$

$$y = 4 - x$$

where x and y are rational numbers.

Find the point of intersection
of the graphs.

$y = x - 2$

x	5	4	3	2	1	0	-1
y	3	2	1	0	-1	-2	-3

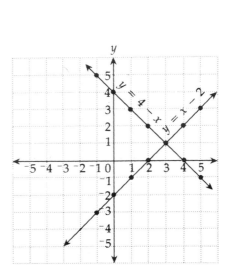

$y = 4 - x$

x	5	4	3	2	1	0	-1
y	-1	0	1	2	3	4	5

Notice that the ordered pair (3, 1)
appears in both tables. The point
(3, 1) is the point of intersection
of the graphs.

1. The graphs of $y = x + 3$ and
   $y = {}^-2x$ intersect at point P.
   What are the coordinates of
   point P?

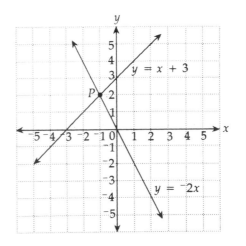

2. Substitute the x and y coordinates
   of point P in the equation
   $y = x + 3$. Do you get a true
   statement?

3. Substitute the x and y coordinates
   of point P in the equation
   $y = {}^-2x$. Do you get a true
   statement?

solving systems of linear equations. Consider, for example, the system $y = x + 3$ and $y = 2x - 1$. Because the solution (x, y) must satisfy each equation, we want x and y in each equation to be the same. Consequently, the expressions $x + 3$ and $2x - 1$ can be equated. The equation $x + 3 = 2x - 1$ has one unknown, x. Solving for x gives $3 + 1 = 2x - x$, and hence, $4 = x$. Substituting 4 for x in either equation gives $y = 7$. Thus, $(4, 7)$ is the solution to the given system. As before, this solution can be checked by substitution. This method for solving a system of

substitution method   linear equations is called the **substitution method.**

Example 12-8   Solve the following system.

$$3x - 4y = 5$$
$$2x + 5y = 1$$

Solution   First, rewrite each equation, expressing y in terms of x.

$$y = \frac{3x - 5}{4} \quad \text{and} \quad y = \frac{1 - 2x}{5}$$

Then, equate the expressions for y and solve the resulting equation for x.

$$\frac{3x - 5}{4} = \frac{1 - 2x}{5}$$
$$5(3x - 5) = 4(1 - 2x)$$
$$15x - 25 = 4 - 8x$$
$$23x = 29$$
$$x = \frac{29}{23}$$

Substituting $\frac{29}{23}$ for x in $y = \frac{3x - 5}{4}$ gives $y = \frac{^-7}{23}$.

Hence, $x = \frac{29}{23}$ and $y = \frac{^-7}{23}$. This can be checked by substituting the values for x and y in the original equations.

Remark   Sometimes it is more convenient to solve a system of equations by expressing x in terms of y in one of the equations and substituting the obtained expression for x in the other equation.

elimination method   The **elimination method** for solving two equations with two unknowns is based on eliminating one of the variables by adding or subtracting the original or equivalent equations. For example, consider the system

$$x - y = {^-3}$$
$$x + y = 7$$

By adding the two equations, the variable y is eliminated. The resulting equation can be solved for x.

$$
\begin{array}{rl}
x - y = & {}^-3 \\
\underline{x + y = } & \underline{7} \\
2x \quad\;\; = & 4 \\
x \quad\;\; = & 2
\end{array}
$$

Substituting 2 for x in the first equation (either equation may be used) gives $2 - y = {}^-3$ and, hence, $y = 5$. Checking this result shows that $x = 2$ and $y = 5$, or $(2, 5)$, is the solution to the system.

Often another operation is required before equations are added so that an unknown can be eliminated. For example, consider the following system.

$$3x + 2y = 5$$

$$5x - 4y = 3$$

Adding the equations does not eliminate either unknown. If the first equation contained $4y$ rather than $2y$, the variable y could be eliminated by adding. To obtain $4y$ in the first equation, multiply both sides of the equation by 2 to obtain the equivalent equation $6x + 4y = 10$. Adding the equations in the equivalent system gives the following.

$$
\begin{array}{rl}
6x + 4y = & 10 \\
\underline{5x - 4y = } & \underline{3} \\
11x \quad\;\; = & 13 \\
x \quad\;\; = & \dfrac{13}{11}
\end{array}
$$

To find the corresponding value of y, substitute $\frac{13}{11}$ for x in either of the original equations and solve for y, or use the elimination method again and solve for y.

To eliminate the x-values from the original system, multiply the first equation by 5 and the second by $^-3$ (or the first by $^-5$ and the second by 3). Then, add and solve for y.

$$
\begin{array}{rl}
15x + 10y = & 25 \\
\underline{{}^-15x + 12y = } & \underline{{}^-9} \\
22y = & 16 \\
y = & \dfrac{16}{22} \quad \text{or} \quad \dfrac{8}{11}
\end{array}
$$

Consequently, $(\frac{13}{11}, \frac{8}{11})$ is the solution of the original system. This solution, as always, should be checked by substitution in the *original* equations.

All examples thus far have had unique solutions. However, other situations may arise. Geometrically, a system of two linear equations has a unique solution if and only if the graphs of the equations intersect in a single point. If the equations represent parallel lines, the system has no solution. If the equations have graphs that are on the same line, the system has infinitely many solutions.

Consider the following system.

$$2x - 3y = 1$$
$$^-4x + 6y = 5$$

In an attempt to solve for x, we multiply the first equation by 2 and then add as follows.

$$
\begin{array}{r}
4x - 6y = 2 \\
^-4x + 6y = 5 \\
\hline
0 = 7
\end{array}
$$

A false statement results. The equation $0 = 7$ actually is $0 \cdot x + 0 \cdot y = 7$. Since there are no x and y values for which $0 \cdot x + 0 \cdot y = 7$, there are no values of x and y that satisfy the original system. In other words, the solution set is $\varnothing$. This situation arises if and only if the corresponding lines are parallel.

Next, consider the following system.

$$2x - 3y = 1$$
$$^-4x + 6y = ^-2$$

To solve this system, we multiply the first equation by 2 and add as follows.

$$
\begin{array}{r}
4x - 6y = 2 \\
^-4x + 6y = ^-2 \\
\hline
0 = 0
\end{array}
$$

The resulting statement, $0 = 0$, is always true. Rewriting the equation as $0 \cdot x + 0 \cdot y = 0$ shows that all values of x and y satisfy this equation. The values of x and y that satisfy both $0 \cdot x + 0 \cdot y = 0$ and $2x - 3y = 1$ are those that satisfy $2x - 3y = 1$. There are infinitely many such pairs x and y that correspond to points on the line $2x - 3y = 1$ and hence to $^-4x + 6y = ^-2$.

One way to check that a system has infinitely many solutions is by observing whether each of the original equations represents the same line. In the preceding system, both equations may be written as $y = \frac{2}{3}x - \frac{1}{3}$. Another way to check that a system has infinitely many solutions is to observe whether one equation can be multiplied by some number to obtain the second equation. For example, multiplying the equation $2x - 3y = 1$ by $^-2$ yields the second equation, $-4x + 6y = -2$.

Example 12-9	Identify each of the following systems as having a unique solution, no solutions, or infinitely many solutions.

(a) $2x - 3y = 5$ (b) $\dfrac{x}{3} - \dfrac{y}{4} = 1$ (c) $6x - 9y = 5$

$\ \dfrac{1}{2}x - y = 1$ $\ 3y - 4x + 12 = 0$ $\ ^-8x + 12y = 7$

Solution | One approach is to attempt to solve each system. Another approach is to write each equation in the slope-intercept form and interpret the system geometrically.

(a) *First method.* To eliminate x, multiply the second equation by $^-4$ and add the equations.

$$\begin{aligned} 2x - 3y &= 5 \\ ^-2x + 4y &= ^-4 \\ \hline y &= 1 \end{aligned}$$

Substituting 1 for y in either equation gives $x = 4$. Thus, $(4, 1)$ is the unique solution of the system.

Second method. In slope-intercept form, the first equation is $y = \frac{2}{3}x - \frac{5}{3}$. The second equation is $y = \frac{1}{2}x - 1$. The slopes of the corresponding lines are $\frac{2}{3}$ and $\frac{1}{2}$, respectively. Consequently, the lines are distinct and are not parallel and, therefore, intersect in a single point whose coordinates are the unique solution to the original system.

(b) *First method.* Multiply the first equation by 12 and rewrite the second equation as $^-4x + 3y = ^-12$. Then, adding the resulting equations gives the following.

$$\begin{aligned} 4x - 3y &= 12 \\ ^-4x + 3y &= ^-12 \\ \hline 0 &= 0 \end{aligned}$$

Since every pair (x, y) satisfies $0 \cdot x + 0 \cdot y = 0$, the original system has infinitely many solutions.

Second method. In slope-intercept form, both equations have the form

$$y = \frac{4}{3}x - 4$$

Thus, the two lines are identical, so the system has infinitely many solutions.

(c) *First method.* To eliminate y, multiply the first equation by 4 and the second by 3; then, add the resulting equations.

$$\begin{aligned} 24x - 36y &= 20 \\ ^-24x + 36y &= 21 \\ \hline 0 &= 41 \end{aligned}$$

No pair of numbers satisfies $0 \cdot x + 0 \cdot y = 41$, so this equation has no solutions, and consequently, the original system has no solutions.

Second method. In slope-intercept form, the first equation is $y = \frac{2}{3}x - \frac{5}{9}$. The second equation is $y = \frac{2}{3}x + \frac{7}{12}$. The corresponding lines have the same slope $\frac{2}{3}$, but different y-intercepts. Consequently, the lines are parallel and the original system has no solutions.

Example 12-10	At the Parkins Restaurant, one can get two eggs with sausage for \$1.80, or one egg with sausage for \$1.35. If there is no break in price for quantity, what is the cost of one egg?
Solution	Let x be the cost of one egg and y be the cost of the sausage. The cost of two eggs and sausage is $2x + y$, or \$1.80. The cost of one egg and sausage is $x + y$, or \$1.35. Thus, the following system is obtained.

$$2x + y = 1.80$$
$$x + y = 1.35$$

Subtracting the equations gives $x = 0.45$. Thus, the cost of one egg is \$0.45.

PROBLEM SET 12-3

1. Use the equation $2x - 3y = 5$ for each of the following.
   (a) Find four solutions of the equation.
   (b) Graph all the solutions for which $^-2 \le x \le 2$.
   (c) Graph all the solutions for which $0 \le y \le 2$.
2. Solve each of the following systems, if possible. Indicate whether the system has a unique solution, infinitely many solutions, or no solutions.
   (a) $y = 3x - 1$
       $y = x + 3$
   (b) $2x + 3y = 1$
       $3x - y = 1$
   (c) $3x + 4y = ^-17$
       $2x + 3y = ^-13$
   (d) $5x - 18y = 0$
       $x - 24y = 0$
   (e) $2x - 6y = 7$
       $3x - 9y = 10$
   (f) $8y - 6x = ^-8$
       $9x - 12y = 12$
3. Solve each of the following systems, if possible.
   (a) $y = x + 3$
       $3x - 4y + 1 = 0$
   (b) $\dfrac{x}{3} - \dfrac{y}{4} = 1$
       $\dfrac{x}{5} - \dfrac{y}{3} = 2$
   (c) $3x - 4y = ^-x + 3$
       $x - 2 = 4(y - 3)$
   (d) $x - y = \dfrac{x}{3}$
       $y - x = \dfrac{3}{4}y + 1$
   (e) $x - y = \dfrac{2}{3}(x + y)$
       $x + y = \dfrac{2}{3}(x - y)$
   (f) $\sqrt{2}x - y = 3$
       $x - \sqrt{2}y = 1$

4. Using the concept of slope, identify whether each of the following systems has a unique solution, infinitely many solutions, or no solutions.
   (a) $3x - 4y = 5$
       $\dfrac{x}{3} - \dfrac{y}{5} = 1$
   (b) $4y - 3x + 4 = 0$
       $8y - 6x + 40 = 0$
   (c) $3y - 2x = 15$
       $\dfrac{2}{3}x - y + 5 = 0$
5. The vertices of a triangle are given by $(0, 0)$, $(10, 0)$, and $(6, 8)$. Show that the segments connecting $(5, 0)$ and $(6, 8)$, $(10, 0)$ and $(3, 4)$, and $(0, 0)$ and $(8, 4)$ intersect at a common point.
6. Two adjacent sides of a parallelogram are on lines with equations $x - 3y + 3 = 0$ and $x + 2y - 2 = 0$. One vertex is at $(0, ^-4)$. Write the equations of the lines containing the other two sides.
7. The sum of two numbers is $\frac{3}{4}$ and their difference is $\frac{7}{9}$. Find the numbers.
8. The owner of a 5000-gallon oil truck loads the truck with gasoline and kerosene. The profit on each gallon of gasoline is 13¢ and on each gallon of kerosene is 12¢. Find how many gallons of each kind the owner loaded if the profit was \$640.
9. A health food store has two different kinds of granola—cashew nut granola selling for \$1.80 a pound and golden granola selling at \$1.20 a pound. How much of each kind should be mixed to produce a 200-pound mixture selling at \$1.60 a pound?
10. A laboratory carries two different solutions of the same acid, a 60% solution and a 90% solution. How many liters of each solution should be mixed in order to produce 150 L of 80% solution?

11. A physician invests $80,000 in two stocks. At the end of the year, the physician sells the stocks, the first at a 15% profit and the second at a 20% profit. How much did the physician invest in each stock if the total profit was $15,000?

★ 12. (a) Solve each of the following systems of equations. What do you notice about the answers?

(i) $x + 2y = 3$
    $4x + 5y = 6$

(ii) $2x + 3y = 4$
     $5x + 6y = 7$

(iii) $31x + 32y = 33$
      $34x + 35y = 36$

(b) Write another system similar to those in part (a). What solution did you expect? Check your guess.

(c) Write a general system similar to those in part (a). What solution does this system have? Why?

13. At the end of 10 months, the balance of an account earning simple interest is $2100.

(a) If, at the end of 18 months, the balance is $2180, how much money was originally in the account?

(b) What is the rate of interest?

14. If five times the width of a water bed equals four times its length and its perimeter is 270 inches, what are the length and width of the bed?

15. Josephine's bank contains 27 coins. If all the coins are either dimes or quarters and the value of the coins is $5.25, how many of each kind of coin are there?

* * * * * * * REVIEW PROBLEMS * * * * * * * *

16. Which of the following are not equations of lines?

(a) $x + y = 3$

(b) $xy = 7$

(c) $2x + 3y \le 4$

(d) $y = 5$

17. Find the slope and y-intercept of each of the following.

(a) $6y + 5x = 7$

(b) $\frac{2}{3}x + \frac{1}{2}y = \frac{1}{5}$

(c) $0.2y - 0.75x - 0.37 = 0$

(d) $y = 4$

18. Write the equation of each of the following.

(a) A line through (4, 7) and ($^-6$, $^-2$).

(b) A line through (4, 7) parallel to the line $y = \frac{5}{3}x + 6$.

(c) A line through ($^-6$, $^-8$) perpendicular to the y-axis.

19. Graph each of the following.

(a) $3x + 2y = 14$

(b) $^-x - y = ^-8$

(c) $2x + 3y \le 4$

(d) $x - 16 \ge ^-8y$

BRAIN TEASER

A school committee meeting began between 3:00 and 4:00 P.M. and ended between 6:00 and 7:00 P.M. The positions of the minute hand and the hour hand of the clock were reversed at the end of the meeting from what they were at the beginning of the meeting. When did the meeting start and end?

12-4 THE DISTANCE AND MIDPOINT FORMULAS

One way to *approximate* the distance between two points in a coordinate plane is to measure it with a ruler that has the same scale as the coordinate axes. Using algebraic techniques, we can calculate the *exact distance* between two points in the plane. First, suppose the two points are on one of the axes. For example, in Figure 12-19(a), $A(2, 0)$ and $B(5, 0)$ are on the x-axis. The distance between these two points is three units.

$$AB = OB - OA = 5 - 2 = 3$$

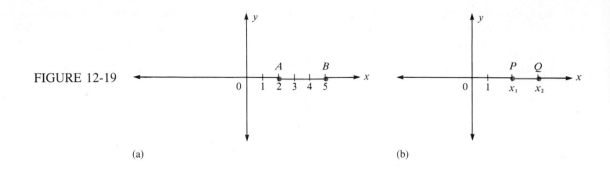

FIGURE 12-19

(a)   (b)

In general, if two points P and Q are on the x-axis, as in Figure 12-19(b), with x-coordinates x_1 and x_2, respectively, and $x_2 > x_1$, then $PQ = x_2 - x_1$. In fact, the distance between two points on the x-axis is the absolute value of the difference between the x coordinates of the points. (Why?)

DEFINITION

> Given two points, $P(x_1, 0)$ and $Q(x_2, 0)$, the distance between them is given by $PQ = |x_2 - x_1| = |x_1 - x_2|$.

A similar definition is given for any two points on the y-axis.

DEFINITION

> Given two points, $P(0, y_1)$ and $Q(0, y_2)$, the distance between them is given by $PQ = |y_2 - y_1| = |y_1 - y_2|$.

Figure 12-20 shows two points in the plane, $C(2, 5)$ and $D(6, 8)$. The distance between C and D can be found by drawing perpendiculars from the points to the x-axis and y-axis, respectively, which determines right triangle CDE. The lengths of the legs are found using horizontal and vertical distances and properties of rectangles.

$CE = |6 - 2| = 4$

$DE = |5 - 8| = 3$

The distance between C and D can be found by applying the Pythagorean Theorem.

$$CD^2 = DE^2 + CE^2$$
$$= 3^2 + 4^2$$
$$= 25$$
$$CD = \sqrt{25}, \text{ or } 5$$

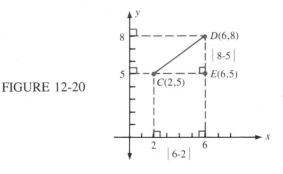

FIGURE 12-20

The method just described can be used to find a formula for the distance between any two points $A(x_1, y_1)$ and $B(x_2, y_2)$. Construct a right triangle with $\overline{AB}$ as one of its sides by drawing a line through A parallel to the x-axis and a line through B parallel to the y-axis as shown in Figure 12-21. These lines intersect in point C forming right triangle ABC. Now apply the Pythagorean Theorem.

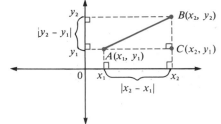

FIGURE 12-21

Figure 12-21 shows that $AC = |x_2 - x_1|$ and $BC = |y_2 - y_1|$. By the Pythagorean Theorem, $(AB)^2 = |x_2 - x_1|^2 + |y_2 - y_1|^2$, and, consequently, $AB = \sqrt{|x_2 - x_1|^2 + |y_2 - y_1|^2}$. Because $|x_2 - x_1|^2 = (x_2 - x_1)^2$ and $|y_2 - y_1|^2 = (y_2 - y_1)^2$, $AB = \sqrt{(x_2 - x_1)^2 + (y_2 - y_1)^2}$. This result is known as the distance formula   **distance formula.**

DISTANCE
FORMULA

The distance between the points $A(x_1, y_1)$ and $B(x_2, y_2)$ is given by

$$AB = \sqrt{(x_2 - x_1)^2 + (y_2 - y_1)^2}$$

Remark

In using the distance formula, it is important to remember that it does not make any difference whether $x_2 - x_1$ or $x_1 - x_2$ is used, because $(x_2 - x_1)^2 = (x_1 - x_2)^2$. The same is true for the y-values.

Example 12-11

For each of the following, find the distance between P and Q.

(a) $P(2, 7)$, $Q(3, 5)$ (b) $P(0, {}^-3)$, $Q(4, {}^-7)$
(c) $P(0, 0)$, $Q(3, {}^-4)$

Solution

(a) $PQ = \sqrt{(3 - 2)^2 + (5 - 7)^2} = \sqrt{1 + 4} = \sqrt{5}$

(b) $PQ = \sqrt{(4 - 0)^2 + [{}^-7 - ({}^-3)]^2} = \sqrt{16 + 16} = \sqrt{32}$

(c) $PQ = \sqrt{(0 - 3)^2 + [0 - ({}^-4)]^2} = \sqrt{9 + 16} = \sqrt{25} = 5$

Example 12-12

(a) Show that $A(7, 4)$, $B({}^-2, 1)$, and $C(10, {}^-5)$ are the vertices of an isosceles triangle.

(b) Show that $\triangle ABC$ is a right triangle.

Solution

(a) Using the distance formula, find the length of the sides.

$$AB = \sqrt{({}^-2 - 7)^2 + (1 - 4)^2} = \sqrt{({}^-9)^2 + ({}^-3)^2} = \sqrt{90}$$

$$BC = \sqrt{[10 - ({}^-2)]^2 + ({}^-5 - 1)^2} = \sqrt{12^2 + ({}^-6)^2} = \sqrt{180}$$

$$AC = \sqrt{(10 - 7)^2 + ({}^-5 - 4)^2} = \sqrt{3^2 + ({}^-9)^2} = \sqrt{90}$$

$AB = AC$, so the triangle is isosceles.

(b) Because $(\sqrt{90})^2 + (\sqrt{90})^2 = (\sqrt{180})^2$, $\triangle ABC$ is a right triangle with $\overline{BC}$ as hypotenuse and $\overline{AB}$ and $\overline{AC}$ as legs.

Using the distance formula, we can find the equation of a circle. A circle can be described by knowing the location of the center and the length of the radius. Figure 12-22 shows the circle with center $C(5, 4)$ and radius 3 units long. To find the equation of this circle, consider a point $P(x, y)$ on the circle. The distance from P to the center of the circle is 3 units—that is, $CP = 3$. By the distance formula, $\sqrt{(x - 5)^2 + (y - 4)^2} = 3$. Squaring both sides of the equation, we obtain $(x - 5)^2 + (y - 4)^2 = 9$. Thus, the coordinates of any point on the circle satisfy the equation $(x - 5)^2 + (y - 4)^2 = 9$.

FIGURE 12-22

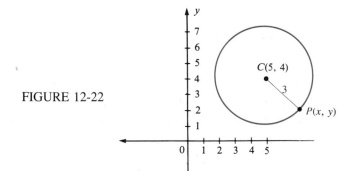

To find the equation of any circle with center $C(a, b)$ and radius r, proceed in a similar way. Figure 12-23 shows that any point $P(x, y)$ is on the circle if and only if $PC = r$, that is, if and only if $\sqrt{(x - a)^2 + (y - b)^2} = r$. Squaring both sides results in the *equation of a circle*.

EQUATION OF A CIRCLE

The equation of a circle with center (a, b) and radius r is

$$(x - a)^2 + (y - b)^2 = r^2$$

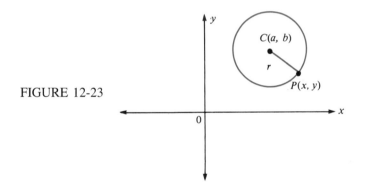

FIGURE 12-23

Example 12-13

(a) Find the equation of the circle with the center at the origin and radius 4.
(b) Find the equation of the circle with center at $C(^-4, 3)$ and radius 5.
(c) Sketch the graph of $(x + 2)^2 + (y - 3)^2 = 9$.
(d) Write a condition for the set of points in the interior of the circle given in part (c).

Solution

(a) The center is at $(0, 0)$ and $r = 4$, so the equation $(x - a)^2 + (y - b)^2 = r^2$ becomes $(x - 0)^2 + (y - 0)^2 = 4^2$ or $x^2 + y^2 = 16$.
(b) The equation is $[x - (^-4)]^2 + (y - 3)^2 = 5^2$, or $(x + 4)^2 + (y - 3)^2 = 25$.
(c) The equation $(x + 2)^2 + (y - 3)^2 = 9$ is in the form $(x - a)^2 + (y - b)^2 = r^2$ if and only if $x - a = x + 2$, $y - b = y - 3$, and $r^2 = 9$. Thus, $a = ^-2$, $b = 3$, and $r = 3$. Hence, the center of the circle is at $(^-2, 3)$, $r = 3$, and Figure 12-24 shows the graph of the circle.
(d) A point (x, y) is in the interior of the circle if and only if the distance between the point and the center of the circle is less than the radius. In this case $\sqrt{[x - (^-2)]^2 + (y - 3)^2} < 3$ or $(x + 2)^2 + (y - 3)^2 < 9$.

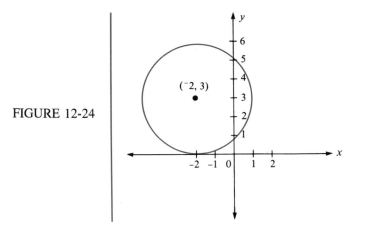

FIGURE 12-24

Example 12-14

Find all points on the y-axis that are 10 units away from $C(8, 3)$.

Solution

Suppose P is a point on the y-axis satisfying the given requirements. Then P has 0 as its x-coordinate. Thus, the coordinates of P are $(0, y)$. Find y so that $PC = 10$.

$$\sqrt{(0 - 8)^2 + (y - 3)^2} = 10$$

Square both sides of the equation and solve for y.

$$(0 - 8)^2 + (y - 3)^2 = 100$$
$$64 + (y - 3)^2 = 100$$
$$(y - 3)^2 = 36$$

Thus, $y - 3 = 6$ or $y - 3 = {}^-6$, so $y = 9$ or $y = {}^-3$.
Hence, two points, $P_1(0, 9)$ and $P_2(0, {}^-3)$, satisfy the condition.

Using the distance formula, it is possible to find the length of a segment if the coordinates of its endpoints are known. In addition, the notion of distance can be used to find the coordinates of the midpoint of a segment. Given two points $A(x_1, y_1)$ and $B(x_2, y_2)$, the coordinates of the midpoint M of the segment $\overline{AB}$ can be found as follows. First, consider a simpler problem. Let $y_1 = y_2 = 0$. Then, the two points $A(x_1, 0)$ and $B(x_2, 0)$ lie on the x-axis as shown in Figure 12-25 with $x_1 < x_2$. To find the x coordinate of the midpoint M, use the given information to write an equation for x in terms of x_1 and x_2 and then solve for x. Because M is the midpoint of $\overline{AB}$, $AM = MB$, which implies that $x - x_1 = x_2 - x$; therefore,

$$2x - x_1 = x_2$$
$$2x = x_1 + x_2$$
$$x = \frac{x_1 + x_2}{2}$$

FIGURE 12-25

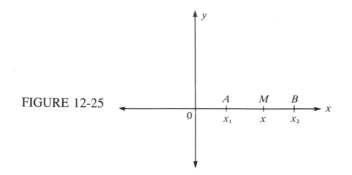

Similarly, for the case where two points lie on the y-axis, the two points are $A(0, y_1)$ and $B(0, y_2)$ and the y-coordinate of the midpoint is $\dfrac{y_1 + y_2}{2}$.

Now, consider the general case. Let $A(x_1, y_1)$ and $B(x_2, y_2)$ be the endpoints of segment $\overline{AB}$ whose midpoint $M(x, y)$ is shown in Figure 12-26. Since $\overline{AA_1}$, $\overline{MM_1}$, and $\overline{BB_1}$ are parallel, and M is the midpoint of $\overline{AB}$, M_1 is the midpoint of $\overline{A_1B_1}$. (Why?) Hence, $x = \dfrac{x_1 + x_2}{2}$. By an analogous argument, $y = \dfrac{y_1 + y_2}{2}$.

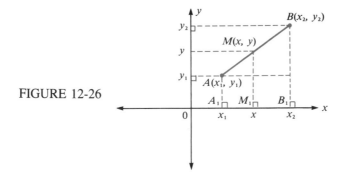

FIGURE 12-26

MIDPOINT FORMULA	Given $A(x_1, y_1)$ and $B(x_2, y_2)$, the midpoint M of $\overline{AB}$ is $$M\left(\frac{x_1 + x_2}{2}, \frac{y_1 + y_2}{2}\right)$$

Remark   To find the midpoint of a line segment, simply find the mean of the respective coordinates of the two endpoints.

Example 12-15

(a) Find the coordinates of the midpoint of $\overline{AB}$ if A has coordinates $(^-3, 2)$ and B has coordinates $(3, ^-5)$.

(b) Suppose M is the midpoint of $\overline{AB}$, A has coordinates $(2, ^-3)$, and M has coordinates $(^-2, 1)$. Find the coordinates of B.

Solution

(a) Let (x, y) be the coordinates of the midpoint of $\overline{AB}$. Then, use the midpoint formula.

$$x = \frac{x_1 + x_2}{2} = \frac{^-3 + 3}{2} = 0$$

$$y = \frac{y_1 + y_2}{2} = \frac{2 + (^-5)}{2} = \frac{^-3}{2}$$

Hence, the midpoint has coordinates $(0, \frac{^-3}{2})$.

(b) Let the coordinates of B be (x, y) as shown in Figure 12-27. The coordinates of the midpoint M are the average of the respective coordinates of the endpoints of $\overline{AB}$.

FIGURE 12-27

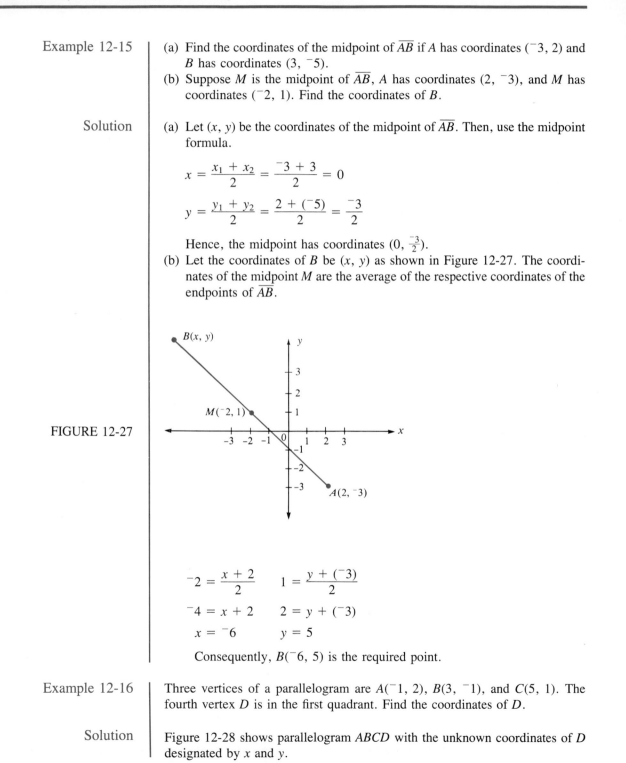

$$^-2 = \frac{x + 2}{2} \qquad 1 = \frac{y + (^-3)}{2}$$

$$^-4 = x + 2 \qquad 2 = y + (^-3)$$

$$x = ^-6 \qquad y = 5$$

Consequently, $B(^-6, 5)$ is the required point.

Example 12-16

Three vertices of a parallelogram are $A(^-1, 2)$, $B(3, ^-1)$, and $C(5, 1)$. The fourth vertex D is in the first quadrant. Find the coordinates of D.

Solution

Figure 12-28 shows parallelogram $ABCD$ with the unknown coordinates of D designated by x and y.

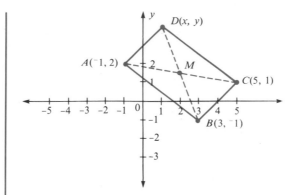

FIGURE 12-28

The strategy is to use the properties of parallelograms to write equations for x and y and then solve the equations. Since the diagonals of a parallelogram bisect each other, the midpoint formula should be useful. In Figure 12-28, M is the intersection point of the diagonals and, hence, the midpoint of each diagonal. If the coordinates of M were known, the midpoint formula could be used to find the coordinates of D.

M is the midpoint of $\overline{AC}$. Thus, M has coordinates

$$\left(\frac{^-1 + 5}{2}, \frac{2 + 1}{2}\right), \quad \text{or} \quad \left(2, \frac{3}{2}\right)$$

Also, M is the midpoint of $\overline{DB}$. Thus, $2 = \frac{x + 3}{2}$, or $4 = x + 3$, and, consequently, $x = 1$. Similarly, $\frac{3}{2} = \frac{y + (^-1)}{2}$, or $3 = y + (^-1)$, and $y = 4$. Hence, D has coordinates $(1, 4)$.

PROBLEM SET 12-4

1. For each of the following find the length of $\overline{AB}$.
   (a) $A(0, 3), B(0, 7)$
   (b) $A(0, ^-3), B(0, ^-7)$
   (c) $A(0, 3), B(4, 0)$
   (d) $A(0, ^-3), B(^-4, 0)$
   (e) $A(^-1, 2), B(3, ^-4)$
   (f) $A(4, 0), B(5.2, ^-3.7)$
   (g) $A(5, 3), B(5, ^-2)$
   (h) $A(0, 0), B(^-4, 3)$
   (i) $A(5, 2), B(^-3, 4)$
   (j) $A(4, ^-5), B\left(\frac{1}{2}, \frac{^-7}{4}\right)$

2. Find the perimeter of the triangle with vertices at $A(0, 0), B(^-4, ^-3)$, and $C(^-5, 0)$.

3. Show that $(0, 6), (^-3, 0)$ and $(9, ^-6)$ are the vertices of a right triangle.

4. Show that the triangle whose vertices are $A(^-2, ^-5)$, $B(1, ^-1), C(5, 2)$ is isosceles.

5. Find x if the distance between $P(1, 3)$ and $Q(x, 9)$ is 10 units.

6. For each of the following, find the midpoint of the line segment whose endpoints have the given coordinates.
   (a) $(^-3, 1)$ and $(3, 9)$
   (b) $(4, ^-3)$ and $(5, ^-1)$
   (c) $(1.8, ^-3.7)$ and $(2.2, 1.3)$
   (d) $(1 + a, a - b)$ and $(1 - a, b - a)$

7. One endpoint of a diameter of a circle with center $C(^-2, 5)$ is given by $(3, ^-1)$. Find the coordinates of the other endpoint.

8. Find the lengths of the medians of the triangle whose

vertices are given by $(0, 0)$, $(^-4, 6)$, and $(4, 2)$. (A **median** is a segment connecting a vertex of a triangle to the midpoint of the opposite side.)

9. For each of the following, write the equations of the circle given the center C and radius r.
   (a) $C(3, ^-2)$ and $r = 2$
   (b) $C(^-3, ^-4)$ and $r = 5$
   (c) $C(^-1, 0)$ and $r = 2$
   (d) $C(0, 0)$ and $r = 3$

10. Given the circle whose equation is $x^2 + y^2 = 9$, which of the following points are in its interior, which are in the exterior, and which are on the circle?
    (a) $(3, ^-3)$ (b) $(2, ^-2)$
    (c) $(1, 8)$ (d) $(3, 1982)$
    (e) $(5.1234, ^-3.7894)$ (f) $\left(\dfrac{1}{387}, \dfrac{1}{1983}\right)$
    (g) $\left(\dfrac{^-1}{2}, \dfrac{35}{2}\right)$

11. Find the equation of the circle whose center is at the origin and that contains the point with coordinates $(^-3, 5)$.

12. For each of the following, find the equation of the circle whose center is at $C(4, ^-3)$ and that passes through the point indicated.
    (a) The origin   (b) $(5, ^-2)$

13. Find the equation of the circle with a diameter having endpoints at $(^-8, 2)$ and $(4, ^-6)$.

14. Graph each of the following equations, if possible.
    (a) $x^2 + y^2 > 4$ (b) $x^2 + y^2 \leq 4$
    (c) $x^2 + y^2 - 4 = 0$ (d) $x^2 + y^2 + 4 = 0$

15. Find the equation of the circle that passes through the origin and the point $(5, 2)$ and has its center on the x-axis.

16. Is $2x^2 + 2y^2 = 1$ an equation of a circle? If it is, find its center and radius; if not, explain why not.

★ 17. Find the area enclosed between the curves $x^2 + y^2 = 1$ and $|x| + |y| = 1$.

★ 18. Find the area of the region defined by $y \geq |x|$ and $x^2 + y^2 \leq 1$.

★ 19. Three vertices of a parallelogram are given by $(^-1, 4)$, $(3, 8)$, and $(5, 0)$. For each of the following, find the coordinates of the fourth vertex if it is in the specified quadrant.
    (a) Quadrant I   (b) Quadrant II
    (c) Quadrant IV

★ 20. Use the distance formula to show that the points with coordinates $(^-1, 5)$, $(0, 2)$, and $(1, ^-1)$ are collinear.

★ 21. Use coordinates to prove that the midpoint M of the hypotenuse of a right triangle is equidistant from the vertices. (*Hint:* Use the coordinate system shown in the accompanying figure.)

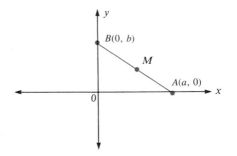

* * * * * * * REVIEW PROBLEMS * * * * * * *

22. Find the equation for each of the following.
    (a) The line containing $P(5, 0)$ and parallel to the y-axis.
    (b) The line containing $P(5, 0)$ and perpendicular to the y-axis.
    (c) The line containing $P(5, 0)$ and parallel to the line $y = \frac{3}{5}x - 7$.
    (d) The line through $P(5, ^-6)$ and $Q(^-7, 8)$.

23. Find the inequality representing each of the following.
    (a) The half-plane determined by $y = \frac{2}{3}x + 7$ and containing the origin.
    (b) The half-plane determined by $y = \frac{^-3}{5}x - 10$ and not containing the origin.

24. Graph each of the following.
    (a) $y = 3x + 7$ (b) $y = \dfrac{^-2}{3}x - 4$
    (c) $x \geq 5$ (d) $y < 2x - 5$

25. Solve each of the following systems, if possible.
    (a) $y = x + 3$ (b) $2x - y = 7$
        $3x - 5y = 4$ $8x - 4y = 12$

26. Graph the solution sets of each of the following systems.
    (a) $2x + y \leq 3$ (b) $x > 4$
        $y - 4 \geq 5x$ $y \leq 3$
                                        $3x - 4y \leq 6$

BRAIN TEASER

Among his great-grandfather's papers, José found a parchment describing the location of a hidden treasure. The treasure was buried by a band of pirates on a deserted island that contained an oak tree, a pine tree, and a gallows where the pirates hanged traitors. The map looked like the figure below and gave the following directions.

Count the steps from the gallows to the oak tree. At the oak, turn 90° to the right. Take the same number of steps and then put a spike in the ground. Next, return to the gallows and walk to the pine tree, counting the number of steps. At the pine tree, turn 90° to the left, take the same number of steps, and then put another spike in the ground. The treasure is buried halfway between the spikes.

José found the island and the two trees but could not find the gallows or the spikes, which had long since rotted. José dug all over the island, but since the island was large, he gave up. Devise a plan to help José find the treasure.

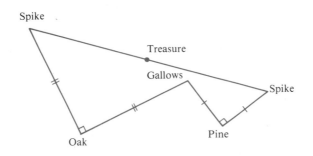

SOLUTION TO THE PRELIMINARY PROBLEM

Understanding the Problem

Linda went for a walk, as shown in Figure 12-29. She started at H and walked to A, then to B, from B to C, and from C to D in such a way that S, I, P, and S were the midpoints of $\overline{HA}$, $\overline{AB}$, $\overline{BC}$, and $\overline{CD}$, respectively. From D, Linda continued her walk to E and then to F so that I and P were the midpoints of $\overline{DE}$ and $\overline{EF}$, respectively. We are to find the exact location of Linda's final stop, F.

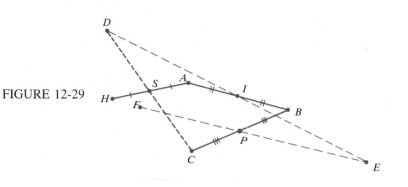

FIGURE 12-29

Devising a Plan

Because the entire problem is based on midpoints, one strategy is to use the midpoint formula. For convenience, we consider a coordinate system with H at the origin; that is, H has coordinates $(0, 0)$. We let the coordinates of the points S, I, and P be (x_1, y_1), (x_2, y_2) and (x_3, y_3), respectively. Applying the midpoint formula to the midpoint S of $\overline{HA}$, we can find the coordinates of A. Then applying the midpoint formula to the midpoint I of $\overline{AB}$, we can express the coordinates of B using the coordinates of S and I. Continuing in this way, we can express the coordinates of F in terms of the coordinates of S, I, and P.

Carrying Out the Plan

We have to apply the midpoint formula six times and then each time solve the corresponding equation for the coordinates of an endpoint. To reduce the amount of work, we develop a formula to find the coordinates of an endpoint of a segment if we are given its midpoint and the other endpoint. Let M be the midpoint of some segment $\overline{RQ}$ with (x_R, y_R), (x_M, y_M) and (x, y) the coordinates of R, M, and Q as shown in Figure 12-30.

FIGURE 12-30

$Q (x, y)$

$M (x_M, y_M)$

$R (x_R, y_R)$

endpoint formula

Using the midpoint formula, we have $x_M = \dfrac{x_R + x}{2}$, which implies $x = 2x_M - x_R$. Similarly, $y = 2y_M - y_R$. We refer to this result as the **endpoint formula.** We now apply the endpoint formula to the six segments $\overline{HA}$, $\overline{AB}$, $\overline{BC}$, $\overline{CD}$, $\overline{DE}$, and $\overline{EF}$, where $x_A, x_B, x_C, x_D, x_E,$ and x_F are the x-coordinates of A, B, C, D, E, and F, respectively.

$$x_A = 2x_1 - 0 = 2x_1$$
$$x_B = 2x_2 - x_A = 2x_2 - 2x_1$$
$$x_C = 2x_3 - x_B = 2x_3 - (2x_2 - 2x_1) = 2x_1 - 2x_2 + 2x_3$$
$$x_D = 2x_1 - x_C = 2x_1 - (2x_1 - 2x_2 + 2x_3) = 2x_2 - 2x_3$$
$$x_E = 2x_2 - x_D = 2x_2 - (2x_2 - 2x_3) = 2x_3$$
$$x_F = 2x_3 - x_E = 2x_3 - 2x_3 = 0$$

Thus, $x_F = 0$; similarly, $y_F = 0$, where y_F is the y-coordinate of F. Consequently, F has coordinates $(0, 0)$ and thus Linda stops where she started, at home.

Looking Back

Regardless of the values of (x_1, y_1), (x_2, y_2) (x_3, y_3), the coordinates of F are always $(0, 0)$. Consequently, no matter where S, I, and P are located, Linda's final stop will be at home.

The problem can be extended in different ways. For example, would Linda's final stop be at home if four locations were used rather than three (S, I, and P)? If not, how many other locations can be used if Linda's final stop is at home?

QUESTIONS FROM THE CLASSROOM

1. A student asks, "If slope is such an important concept, why is slope of a vertical line undefined?" What is your response?

2. A student argues, "Since 0 is nothing and a horizontal line has slope 0, a horizontal line also has no slope." How do you reply?

3. Trying to find the midpoint, M, of $\overline{AB}$, where A and B have coordinates $(x_1, 0)$ and $(x_2, 0)$ and $x_2 > x_1$, a student argues as follows. "Since $AB = x_2 - x_1$, half that distance is $\frac{x_2 - x_1}{2}$ and, since the midpoint M is halfway between A and B, the x-coordinate of M is $\frac{x_2 - x_1}{2}$." How do you respond?

4. A student does not understand why, when solving a system of linear equations, it is necessary to check the solution in the original equations rather than in some simpler equivalent equations. How do you respond?

5. A student claims that the graph of every inequality of the form $ax + by + c > 0$ is the half-plane above the line $ax + by + c = 0$, while the graph of $ax + by + c < 0$ is always below the line. How do you respond?

6. A student claims that the distance formula can be further simplified as follows.
$$d = \sqrt{(x_1 - x_2)^2 + (y_1 - y_2)^2}$$
$$= \sqrt{(x_1 - x_2)^2} + \sqrt{(y_1 - y_2)^2}$$
$$= |x_1 - x_2| + |y_1 - y_2|$$
How do you respond?

7. A student wishes to know how to check the solution of a system of inequalities. How do you respond?

CHAPTER OUTLINE

I. Coordinate system in the plane
   A. Any point in the plane can be described by an ordered pair of real numbers, the first of which is the **x-coordinate** and the second the **y-coordinate.**
   B. Together the x-axis and y-axis divide the plane into four **quadrants.**
II. Equations of sets of points and notions of slope
   A. The **slope** of a line is a measure of its steepness.
      1. Given (x_1, y_1) and (x_2, y_2) with $x_2 \neq x_1$, the slope m of the line through the two points is given by $m = \dfrac{(y_2 - y_1)}{(x_2 - x_1)}$.
      2. The slope of a vertical line is not defined.
   B. The equation of any nonvertical line can be written in the form $y = mx + b$, where m is the slope and b is the y-intercept.
   C. The equation of any vertical line can be written in the form $x = a$.
III. Systems of linear equations
   A. A system of linear equations can be solved graphically by drawing the graphs of the equations.

1. If the equations represent two intersecting lines, the system has a unique solution; that is, the ordered pair corresponding to the point of intersection.
2. If the equations represent two different parallel lines, the system has no solutions.
3. If the two equations represent the same line, the system has infinitely many solutions.
   B. A system of linear equations can be solved algebraically either by the substitution method or the elimination method.
IV. Distance concepts
   A. The **distance** between the points (x_1, y_1) and (x_2, y_2) is given by $d = \sqrt{(x_2 - x_1)^2 + (y_2 - y_1)^2}$.
   B. Given $A(x_1, y_1)$ and $B(x_2, y_2)$, the coordinates of the **midpoint** M of $\overline{AB}$ are

$$\left(\frac{x_1 + x_2}{2}, \frac{y_1 + y_2}{2} \right)$$

   C. The equation of the circle with center at (a, b) and radius r is $(x - a)^2 + (y - b)^2 = r^2$.

CHAPTER TEST

1. Find the perimeter of the triangle with vertices at $A(0, 0)$, $B(^-4, 3)$, and $C(0, 6)$.
2. Show algebraically in at least two different ways that $(4, 2)$, $(0, ^-1)$, and $(^-4, ^-4)$ are collinear points.
3. Sketch the graph for each of the following.
   (a) $3x - y = 1$ (b) $3x - y \leq 1$
   (c) $2x + 3y + 1 = 0$
4. For each of the following, write the equation of the line determined by the given pair of points.
   (a) $(2, ^-3)$ and $(^-1, 1)$ (b) $(^-3, 0)$ and $(^-3, 2)$
   (c) $(^-2, 3)$ and $(2, 3)$
5. The vertices of $\triangle ABC$ are $A(^-3, 0)$, $B(0, 4)$, and $C(2, 5)$. Find each of the following.
   (a) The equation of the line through C and parallel to $\overline{AB}$.
   (b) The equation of the line through C and parallel to the x-axis.
   (c) The point where the line found in part (b) intersects $\overline{AB}$.

6. Solve each of the following systems, if possible. Indicate whether the system has a unique solution, infinitely many solutions, or no solution.
   (a) $x + 2y = 3$ (b) $\dfrac{x}{2} + \dfrac{y}{3} = 1$
   $\quad\ 2x - y = 9$ $\quad\ 4y - 3x = 2$
   (c) $x - 2y = 1$
   $\quad 4y - 2x = 0$
7. A store sells nuts in two types of containers, regular and deluxe. Each regular container contains 1 lb of cashews and 2 lb of peanuts. Each deluxe container contains 3 lb of cashews and 1.5 lb of peanuts. The store used 170 lb of cashews and 205 lb of peanuts. How many containers of each kind were used?
8. (a) Find the midpoint of the line segment whose endpoints are given by $(^-4, 2)$ and $(6, ^-3)$.
   (b) The midpoint of a segment is given by $(^-5, 4)$ and one of its endpoints is given by $(^-3, 5)$. Find the coordinates of the other endpoint.

9. Graph each of the following.
    (a) $x^2 + y^2 = 16$
    (b) $(x + 1)^2 + (y - 2)^2 = 9$
    (c) $x^2 + y^2 \leq 16$
10. Find the equation of the circle whose center is at $C(^-3, 4)$ and that passes through the origin.
11. Graph each of the following systems.
    (a) $x \geq\ ^-7$ (b) $y \leq 2x + 3$
        $y \leq 4$ $y \geq x +\ ^-7$
12. The sum of the numbers of red and black jellybeans on Ronnie's desk is 12. Also, the sum is twice the difference of the numbers of the two colors. How many jellybeans of each color does he have if there are more red than black jellybeans?
13. The freshman class at the university has 225 fewer enrolled than the sophomore class. The number in the sophomore class is only 50 students short of being twice as great as the number in the freshman class. How many students are in each class?
14. In the presidential election of 1932, Franklin D. Roosevelt received 6,563,988 more votes than Herbert Hoover. If one-fifth of Roosevelt's votes had been won by Herbert Hoover, then Hoover would have won the election by 2,444,622 votes. How many votes did each receive?

SELECTED BIBLIOGRAPHY

Arnsdorf, E. "Orienteering, New Ideas for Outdoor Mathematics." *Arithmetic Teacher* 25 (April 1978):14–17.

Battista, M. "Distortions: An Activity for Practice and Exploration." *Arithmetic Teacher* 29 (January 1982):34–36.

Bell, W. "Cartesian Coordinates and Battleship." *The Arithmetic Teacher* 21 (May 1974):421–422.

Bergen, S. "A Discovery Approach for the *y*-Intercept." *The Mathematics Teacher* 70 (November 1977):675–676.

Bruni, J., and H. Silverman. "Using a Pegboard to Develop Mathematical Concepts." *The Arithmetic Teacher* 22 (October 1975):452–458.

Burns, M. "Ideas." *The Arithmetic Teacher* 22 (April 1975):296–304.

Dossey, J. "Do All Graphs Have Points with Integral Coordinates?" *The Mathematics Teacher* 74 (September 1981):455–457.

Dugdale, S. "Green Globs: A Micro-computer Application for Graphing of Equations." *The Mathematics Teacher* 75 (March 1982):208–214.

Eicholz, R., P. O'Daffer, and C. Fleenor, *Mathematics in Our World*. Reading, Mass.: Addison-Wesley, 1979.

Giles, D. "Graphing Inequalities Directly." *The Arithmetic Teacher* 18 (March 1971):185–186.

Good, R. "Two Mathematical Games with Dice." *The Arithmetic Teacher* 21 (January 1974):45–47.

Lappan, G., and M. Winter. "A Unit on Slope Functions—Using a Computer in Mathematics Class." *The Mathematics Teacher* 75 (February 1982):118–122.

Liedtke, W. "Geoboard Mathematics." *The Arithmetic Teacher* 21 (April 1974):273–277.

Miller, W. "Graphs Alive." *The Mathematics Teacher* 71 (December 1978):756–758.

Nicolai, M. "A Discovery in Linear Algebra." *The Mathematics Teacher* 67 (May 1974):403–404.

Pereira-Mendoza, L. "Graphing and Prediction in Elementary School." *The Arithmetic Teacher* 24 (February 1977):112–113.

Rainsbury, R. "Where is Droopy?" *The Arithmetic Teacher* 19 (April 1972):271–272.

Ruppel, E. "Business Formulas As Cartesian Curves." *The Mathematics Teacher* 75 (May 1982):398–403.

Vance, I. "The Content of the Elementary School Geometry Program." *The Arithmetic Teacher* 20 (October 1973):470.

Wallace, E. "Unifying Slopes, Proportions, and Graphing." *The Mathematics Teacher* 73 (November 1980):597–600.

Zweng, M. "A Geometry Course for Elementary Teachers." *The Arithmetic Teacher* 20 (October 1973):457–467.

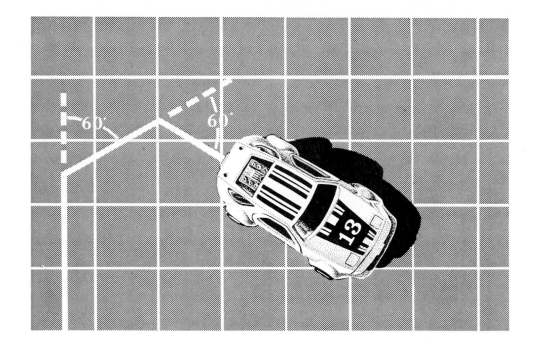

PRELIMINARY PROBLEM

A turn-about robot toy car is designed so that after it travels some distance straight ahead, it turns 60° to the right and then travels straight ahead four-fifths of the previous distance. It continues in this way as long as the length of the segment to be traveled is greater than or equal to 1 cm. When the length of the segment to be traveled is less than 1 cm, the car stops. How can the distance between the starting position of the car and the place where it stops be determined?

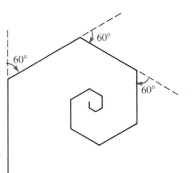

INTRODUCTION

A computer is a machine capable of doing a large number of arithmetic calculations in a very short time and at the same time of storing a great amount of information, which can be made readily available to the user. Unlike most simple calculators, the computer is capable of storing instructions necessary to process information and of interacting with the user.

Rapid advances in computer technology have been responsible for continuous reductions in the size and price of computers. The microcomputer was developed when advances in computer chips were made in the mid-seventies. Microcomputer chips, less than a centimeter on a side, have the calculating capability of a computer that would have filled a complete room about 25 years ago. Mass production has made it possible to sell these chips for under $10. A small number of chips contain most of the circuitry necessary for a computer. Because of the relatively low price and small size, and the potential use, microcomputers are becoming very popular in education. The National Council of Teachers of Mathematics (NCTM) in *An Agenda for Action: Recommendations for School Mathematics of the 1980s* states that "calculators and computers should be used in imaginative ways for exploring, discovering and developing mathematical concepts. . . ." NCTM recommends that:

> Teacher education programs for all levels of mathematics should include computer literacy, experience with computer programming, and the study of ways to make the most effective use of computers and calculators in instruction.

With the availability of inexpensive microcomputers, this NCTM recommendation can be realistically implemented.

Many people feel that computers are creatures of superior intelligence possessing giant electronic brains. However, such machines exist only in cartoons, science fiction books, movies, and imaginations. In reality, a computer must be told in precise detail how to solve a given problem or how to perform a given task. A set of instructions for solving a problem written in a way that a program computer can follow is called a **program.** Computer programs are referred to as software **software.** If a certain calculation needs to be done only once, it may be much more efficient to do it with a pencil and paper or a calculator. Computers are especially useful when the same type of calculation has to be performed many times or when the problem involves very long and complicated calculations.

The Parts of a Computer

Many people are overwhelmed by computer vocabulary when they are first introduced to it, as illustrated in the cartoon on page 600.

hardware

Some computer terminology is useful in reading journal articles and understanding the basics of computer literacy. A minimum of terminology is introduced here. A computer system, known as **hardware,** consists of three major groups of components: the INPUT/OUTPUT group, the COMPUTING group, and the AUXILIARY STORAGE group. Computers generally used in school classrooms are called microcomputers. A schematic picture of such a computer system is shown in Figure 13-1.

FIGURE 13-1

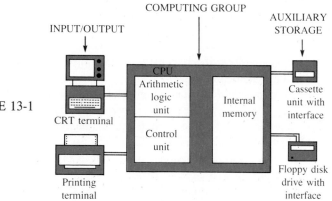

input unit

The **input unit** is used to get information into the computer. Modes of input include special punched cards, magnetic tapes or disks, and computer keyboards on which users type their data and instructions.

output unit
Cathode-Ray Tube
Central Processing
Unit (CPU)
Internal Memory

The **output unit** sends the obtained information to the user. The information may be seen on punched cards, a televisionlike screen called a **Cathode-Ray Tube (CRT),** or on a lineprinter, which prints the computer's responses on paper.

The computing group consists of a **Central Processing Unit (CPU)** and an **Internal Memory.** The central processing unit contains an arithmetic logic unit consisting of electronic circuits that perform arithmetic and logical operations, and a control unit which coordinates all the computer's activities. The internal memory unit is used for temporary storage of programs, input data, intermediate results, and output results.

The microcomputer has an auxiliary storage unit, which usually consists of either a cassette recorder, where programs are stored on tapes, or a "floppy disk" system, where programs are stored magnetically on something that resembles a flexible phonograph record. The complete understanding of these electronic parts of a computer is not necessary for most users.

Computer Languages

machine language

A computer understands instructions coded in **machine language,** that is, the fundamental language understood by the particular computer. Machine language consists of numeric codes in the form of binary numbers, which are sequences of 0s and 1s (base two) that instruct the computer to perform its basic functions. Because machine language is hard for people to use, computer scientists have developed easier languages. Such computer languages include the following:

BASIC	**B**eginner's **A**ll-purpose **S**ymbolic **I**nstruction **C**ode
COBOL	**CO**mmon **B**usiness **O**riented **L**anguage
FORTRAN	**FOR**mula **TRAN**slation
ALGOL	**ALGO**rithmic Language
Pascal	Named after the French mathematician Blaise Pascal
Logo	Recently developed at MIT

One of the most widespread and easiest to learn languages is BASIC. BASIC was originally developed in the mid-sixties at Dartmouth College by two mathematics professors, John Kemeny and Thomas Kurtz. Because of its simplicity and common use, we use BASIC as one of the programming languages for this text?

Another language that is gaining in popularity and recognition is Logo. Logo was developed at the Massachusetts Institute of Technology for educational use and became commercially available in 1982. Logo is being used by students of all ages. We use Logo in the second part of this chapter and emphasize its graphical capabilities, known as *turtle graphics*.

Writing Computer Programs

The four-step, Polya-type approach introduced in Chapter 1 is very useful in writing computer programs to solve problems. In the first step—Understanding the Problem—we should be sure of what the program is to accomplish, that is, what the output is to be. We must identify what information is input data. We must determine if we have enough input data to obtain the desired output. In the second step—Devising a Plan—we must decide how to organize the sequence to produce the desired output. Sometimes flowcharts are used in this step to help devise the program. The strategy used in this step will depend on the programmer's experience and the difficulty of the problem. In the third step—Carrying Out the Plan—we run the program and make any necessary corrections—that is, we debug the program. In the fourth step—Looking Back—we analyze the program to see if it accomplished the goal. In this step we can revise the program to become more efficient, to improve the format, or to perform different tasks. These four steps will be helpful when writing computer programs.

Once a program has been written, it can often be used on many different types of computers. A few minor differences may exist from one version of BASIC or Logo to another, which may necessitate program revision. The execution of a program is done by the computer in several steps. After the program has been entered, the translator converts the statements to the computer's own machine language. Then the machine language program is executed, and the output data are displayed.

13-1 BASIC: VARIABLES AND OPERATIONS

BASIC is a language consisting of words, punctuation, and syntax used in combination to form statements. Some BASIC words are system commands, such as RUN and LIST; other BASIC key words are programming commands such as PRINT, LET, INPUT, REM, END, GOTO, IF-THEN, and FOR-NEXT. Statements are put together using programming commands to form a program. Figure 13-2 illustrates two examples of very simple BASIC programs: the first for printing a message and the second for calculating the value of Y for a given value of X, where

$$Y = 5X^4 + \frac{4}{X} - 3$$

```
10 PRINT "HERE WE GO"
20 PRINT "LET'S LEARN TO PROGRAM"
30 END
```

FIGURE 13-2   (a)

```
10 INPUT X
20 LET Y = 5*X**4 + 4/X - 3
30 PRINT Y
40 END
```

(b)

In Figure 13-2(b) the variables X and Y are used. In most versions of BASIC, a variable is named by any single letter from the alphabet or a letter followed by a single digit, such as A1, A2, B5, Q7, or Z9. Examples of invalid variables are 7A or A*. (Other types of variables, called string variables, are not discussed here.)

Some of the symbols in Figure 13-2(b) that are used in BASIC to represent arithmetic operations are different from usual symbols. Multiplication is indicated by an asterisk (*); two asterisks (**) or a vertical arrow (↑) or (∧) are used to raise a quantity to a power; addition is represented by a plus sign (+); subtraction by a minus sign (−); and division by a slash (/). Examples are given in Table 13-1.

TABLE 13-1

Operation	Math Symbol	Math Example	BASIC Symbol	BASIC Example
Addition	+	$2 + 3$	+	$2+3$
Subtraction	−	$5 - 2$	−	$5-2$
Multiplication	× or ·	5×3 or $5 \cdot 3$	*	$5*3$
Division	÷	$16 \div 4$	/	$16/4$
Exponentiation		2^3	** or ↑ or ∧	$2**3$ or $2 \uparrow 3$ or $2 \wedge 3$

System Commands

line number

RUN

LIST

Each line in the programs in Figure 13-2 is a statement, which gives the computer an instruction. Notice that each statement begins with a **line number.** A system command such as RUN does not require a line number. When **RUN** is entered with a program in the internal memory, the computer executes the instructions in the program by using the order of the line numbers. In most cases, the numbers 10, 20, 30, . . . or 100, 200, 300, . . . are used for line numbers in order to leave room for forgotten statements which may be added later. For example, suppose that after typing line 30 in Figure 13-2(b) (PRINT Y) you realize that you should have had a statement between lines 10 and 20. All that is necessary is to type the new statement preceded by a line number which is between 10 and 20, such as 15. The new line can be typed at any time when the program is still active. The computer will rearrange all the lines in the correct order and will execute the program in the correct order. To correct errors in a given line, retype the line correctly. When the system command **LIST** is entered, the program will be displayed with all the line numbers in correct numerical order and all corrections included.

Programming Commands

INPUT

LET

PRINT

END

The four BASIC key words that were used in Figure 13-2(b) are INPUT, LET, PRINT, and END. These are called programming commands. In line 10 the key word **INPUT** is followed by the variable X. The INPUT statement causes the computer to stop during the run and print "?". The user must assign a specific numerical value for X in this particular program by typing in that value and pressing the Return key. After the value is entered, the program will continue. An INPUT statement always consists of the word INPUT and a variable or a list of variables separated by commas.

In line 20 we see a statement that contains the key word **LET.** A LET statement is used to assign a value to a variable. The LET statement places data in a memory location. In Figure 13-2(b) the variable Y is assigned the value

```
5*X**4+4/X-3
```

and this value is stored in the memory location labeled Y. The statement is composed of a line number followed by the word LET followed by a variable that equals a mathematical expression. The command LET is frequently optional. For example, LET X = 17 is often simply written as X = 17 on many machines.

In line 30 we see the key word **PRINT.** PRINT Y is a direction to the computer to print the value of the variable Y when the program is run. (Other uses of the key word PRINT will be discussed later.)

The **END** statement indicates the end of a program, and it must have the greatest line number. Some systems do not require an END statement.

When the program in Figure 13-2(b) is run, the computer acts like the function machine (see Chapter 2), shown in Figure 13-3. When the value of the variable X is input, the machine assigns a value for Y according to the rule $Y = 5X^4 + \dfrac{4}{X} - 3$. Thus, if the input is 2 (that is, X = 2), the output will be

$Y = 5 \cdot 2^4 + \dfrac{4}{2} - 3 = 79.$

To use the program in Figure 13-2(b) to find the value of Y for a given X, such as X = 2, type RUN and then depress the Return key. Pressing the Return key will be denoted hereafter by Ⓡ.

FIGURE 13-3

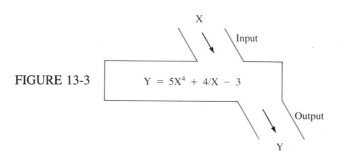

X

Input

$Y = 5X^4 + 4/X - 3$

Output

Y

The computer will print a question mark which indicates that the user should input a value, in our case 2. The computer then prints the corresponding value of Y, which is 79. The interaction with the computer will look like this (the boldface characters are typed by the computer):

RUN Ⓡ
? 2
79
READY

READY   On many computers the word **READY** is printed when the run is completed. Other machines may indicate this by the word OK or a flashing cursor or some other device. These are the computer's ways of saying that it is ready for your next instruction. If you wish to input a new number for X into the program, type RUN again and press the Return key. Another question mark will appear and the new number may be input. If we input 180 for X and run the program, the printout appears as follows:

RUN Ⓡ
? 180
5.2488E+09
READY

E-notation   The answer, 5.2488E+09, is represented using an **E-notation.** This notation is like scientific notation in that the letter E means exponent and indicates the power or exponent on the base ten. The number of places before a machine reports E-notation may vary from one brand of computer to another.

1.876E+07 means $1.876 \cdot 10^7$, or 18,760,000

7.9325E−04 means $7.9325 \cdot 10^{-4}$, or 0.00079325

The order of operations that a computer uses is the same as those discussed in previous chapters; that is, exponentiations (if any) are done first, multiplications and divisions are done next in order from left to right, and additions and subtractions are done last, also in order from left to right. *When you are in doubt as to how the computer will execute the operations, use parentheses.*

Example 13-1 | Write (a) through (c) in BASIC notation, and (d) and (e) in base ten notation.

(a) $b^2 - 4ac$ (b) $\dfrac{3(4 + b)}{c}$

(c) $3 + 4c^3$ (d) 3.47985E+08

(e) 4.5935E−05

Solution | (a) B**2 − 4*A*C   (b) 3*(4 + B)/C
(c) 3 + 4*C**3   (d) $3.47985 \cdot 10^8 = 347,985,000$
(e) $4.5935 \cdot 10^{-5} = 0.000045935$

Example 13-2 | Evaluate each of the following.

(a) (5+6)*9−2   (b) 5+6*9−2   (c) 5+6*(9−2)

Solution | (a) 11 · 9 − 2 = 97   (b) 5 + 54 − 2 = 57   (c) 5 + 42 = 47

Several BASIC programming commands are used in the solution to the following problem.

PROBLEM 1

A surveyor often needs to compute the length of the hypotenuse of a right triangle, given the length of its legs. Write a program that will compute the length of the hypotenuse of any right triangle given the length of its legs. Run the program for legs of length 50 m and 37 m.

Solution

If c is the length of the hypotenuse and a and b are the lengths of the legs, then it follows from the Pythagorean Theorem (Chapter 11) that $c^2 = a^2 + b^2$ and hence that $c = \sqrt{a^2 + b^2}$.

SQR   To write this program, we use the INPUT statement to give the computer values for a and b. We then use the square root function, **SQR** (called SQRT on some computers), to tell the computer to compute the value of c. A PRINT statement causes the computer to output the length of the hypotenuse. The program can be written as shown in Figure 13-4.

FIGURE 13-4

```
10 INPUT A, B
20 LET C = SQR (A**2 + B**2)
30 PRINT C
40 END
```

A run of the program follows.

RUN Ⓡ

? 50, 37 Ⓡ

62.201286

READY

So that other people may use a program, it is always wise to tell what a program does. Programs containing such information are known as *user friendly*.

FIGURE 13-5

To accomplish this, appropriate PRINT statements may be used. For example, the program in Figure 13-4 may be changed to that shown in Figure 13-5.

```
 6 PRINT "THIS PROGRAM FINDS THE LENGTH OF THE HYPOTENUSE ";
 7 PRINT "OF A RIGHT TRIANGLE."
 8 PRINT "ENTER THE LENGTHS OF THE LEGS OF THE TRIANGLE ";
 9 PRINT "SEPARATED BY A COMMA".
10 INPUT A, B
20 LET C = SQR (A**2 + B**2)
30 PRINT "THE LENGTH OF THE HYPOTENUSE IS "; C
40 END
```

In lines 6, 7, 8, and 9, we have used the programming command PRINT. When the program is run, the computer prints everything inside the quotation marks. When a semicolon is ·placed at the end of a PRINT statement, the computer continues the next PRINT statement on the same line, one space to the right of the last printed character. In line 30, PRINT is used with a phrase in quotation marks followed by a semicolon and the letter C. When the semicolon is used, the value of C is printed immediately following the phrase. (You should investigate what happens when a comma is used in place of a semi-colon.) When the program in Figure 13-5 is run, the printout will appear as follows:

RUN Ⓡ
THIS PROGRAM FINDS THE LENGTH OF THE HYPOTENUSE OF A RIGHT TRIANGLE.
ENTER THE LENGTHS OF THE LEGS OF THE TRIANGLE SEPARATED BY A COMMA.
? 50, 37 Ⓡ
THE LENGTH OF THE HYPOTENUSE IS 62.201286
READY

Because the computer prints exactly what is in the quotation marks, if C were inside the quotation marks in line 30 of Figure 13-5, the last line of the executed program would appear as follows:

THE LENGTH OF THE HYPOTENUSE IS C

Other uses of the key word PRINT will be investigated in the exercises.

REM

A programmer may wish to make a remark or title the program on the very first line. This can be done using the programming command PRINT or a new programming command REM (for REMARK). If a **REM** statement is used, the computer will save the line as an explanation of the program for anybody who desires to list the program. The REM statement is ignored during execution and is not printed during a run. To title the program in Figure 13-5, the REM statement below may be added:

5 REM THE HYPOTENUSE PROBLEM

Example 13-3   Fair State University is increasing the salaries of its faculty based upon performance. A departmental secretary needs a computer program to check the controller's figures. The program must calculate the next year's salary for each faculty member given the present salary and the percent of increase of the salary of that faculty member. Write a program for the secretary to calculate each new salary. Try your program if the old salary is $38,479 and the percent of increase is 17%.

Solution   If the old salary and the percent of increase are denoted by S and P, respectively, then the new salary, N, is given by $N = S + S \cdot \dfrac{P}{100}$, or $N = S \cdot \left(1 + \dfrac{P}{100}\right)$. A program for this computation is given in Figure 13-6.

FIGURE 13-6

```
10 REM UNIVERSITY SALARY INCREASE
20 PRINT "ENTER THE OLD SALARY AND THE PERCENT ";
30 PRINT "OF INCREASE SEPARATED BY A COMMA."
40 INPUT S, P
50 LET N = S*(1 + P/100)
60 PRINT "THE NEW SALARY IS $"; N
```

When the program in Figure 13-6 is run for the given salary and percent of increase, the printout follows:

RUN Ⓡ

ENTER THE OLD SALARY AND PERCENT OF INCREASE SEPARATED BY A COMMA.

?38479, 17 Ⓡ

THE NEW SALARY IS $45020.43

READY

PROBLEM SET 13-1

1. Which of the following are valid variables in BASIC?
   (a) P   (b) M4   (c) 3Z   (d) M**2
2. Write each of the following using BASIC notation.

   (a) $X^2 + Y^2 - 3Z$ (b) $\left(\dfrac{24 \cdot 34}{2}\right)^3$

   (c) $a + b - \dfrac{c^2}{d}$ (d) $\dfrac{a + b}{c + d}$

   (e) $\dfrac{15}{a(2b^2 + 5)}$

3. Perform the following calculations in the same order as a computer would.
   (a) 3*5 - 2*6 + 4   (b) 7*(6 - 2)/4
   (c) 3*(5 + 7)/(3 + 3) (d) 3**3/9
   (e) (2*(3 - 5))**2   (f) 9**2 - 5**3
4. Write each of the following as a base ten number in standard form.
   (a) 3.52E+07   (b) 1.93E−05
   (c) −1.233E−06

5. Predict the output, if any, for each of the following programs.

(a) ```
10 A = 5
20 B = 10
30 PRINT A,B
40 END
```

(b) ```
10 A = 5
20 B = 10
30 PRINT "A,B"
40 END
```

(c) ```
10 A = 5
20 B = 10
30 PRINT A,,B
40 END
```

(d) ```
10 A = 5
20 B = 10
30 PRINT A;B
40 END
```

(e) ```
10 A = 5
20 B = 10
   PRINT A,B
40 END
```

(f) ```
10 A = 5
20 B = 10
30 PRINT A
40 PRINT B
50 END
```

(g) ```
10 A = 5
20 B = 10
30 PRINT A;
40 PRINT B
50 END
```

(h) ```
10 A = 5
20 B = 10
30 PRINT "THE VALUE OF A "
35 PRINT "IS ";A;".";
40 PRINT "THE VALUE OF B "
45 PRINT "IS ";B;"."
50 END
```

(i) ```
10 A = 5
20 B = 10
30 PRINT "THE VALUE OF A "
35 PRINT "IS",A,".";
40 PRINT "THE VALUE OF B "
45 PRINT "IS ";B;"."
50 END
```

6. (a) Write a computer program for calculating the value of $Y$ for a given $X$, where $Y = 13X^5 - \dfrac{27}{X} + 3$.

(b) Use the program in part (a) to find the value of $Y$ for: (i) $X = 1.873$; (ii) $X = 7$.

7. Most computers can be used as calculators by using a PRINT statement with no line number. For example, typing PRINT $5+3$ ⓡ causes the computer to print 8. Write a single PRINT statement to compute $25 \cdot (0.97)^{365}$.

8. (a) Write a program (including a title and directions) for converting degrees Fahrenheit into degrees Celsius using the formula $C = \frac{5}{9}(F - 32)$.

(b) Use the program from part (a) to convert the following Fahrenheit temperatures to Celsius.

(i) 212°F  (ii) 98.6°F  (iii) 68°F
(iv) 32°F  (v) ⁻40°F

9. Write a program for computing the perimeter, $P$, of a rectangle given its length, $L$, and width, $W$, where $P = 2L + 2W$. Try your program for $L = 16$ cm and $W = 5$ cm.

10. Write a program for computing the volume of a box given its three dimensions, $L$, $W$, and $H$, where $V = LWH$. (Assume the box is a right rectangular prism.) Try your program for $L = 8$, $W = 5$, and $H = 3$.

In Problems 11–14, use the formula for compound interest developed in Chapter 7.

11. $100 is invested in a bank for 25 years at 18% compounded annually. (a) Find the balance by using a single PRINT statement. (b) Find the balance by writing a program with an input $N$, where $N$ is the number of years the money is invested.

12. (a) A certain bank pays 7% interest rate compounded annually. Write a program to calculate the balance after a given number of years for a given initial investment. Make the program give directions to the user, and utilize an INPUT statement.

(b) Use the program in part (a) to find the balance if $800 is invested in the bank for 8 years.

13. (a) A $30,000 property depreciates after one year by 3% of its value. Write a program for finding the value of the property after $N$ years, assuming this rate of depreciation stays constant.

(b) Find the value of the property after 30 years.
```

14. In 1626, Peter Minuit, a Dutch settler, bought Manhattan Island for $24 worth of trinkets. If this money had been invested in 1626 in a bank at 5% interest compounded annually, what would it be worth 359 years later in 1985? How much more would it be worth in 1985 if the $24 had been compounded: (a) by the month; (b) by the day; (c) by the second?

13-2 BRANCHING

IF-THEN Statements

One possible use of the computer in education is in computer-assisted instruction—for example, in designing programs to create drill problems. Suppose John, a second-grade elementary school teacher, wants to design a program that can be used repeatedly to allow students to practice adding two numbers. He wants the students to keep working on a problem until they get it correct; then they will receive a new problem. The repeated use of drill examples can be conveniently accomplished through **branching.** One way that branching occurs is when decisions are made in a program through the use of the new programming command **IF-THEN.** The general form of an IF-THEN statement is IF (condition) THEN (line number). For example,

branching

IF-THEN

```
30 IF X<2 THEN 60
```

When the computer executes line 30, it evaluates the condition, $X < 2$. If the value of X is less than 2, then the computer branches to the line number following the word THEN, in this case, line 60. If the value of X is not less than 2, the computer executes the next statement listed in numerical order. The condition following the IF part always includes an equality or inequality symbol. However, in BASIC, some of these symbols differ from their mathematical counterparts. The symbols are compared in Table 13-2.

TABLE 13-2

Mathematical Symbol	BASIC Symbol	Meaning
$=$	$=$	Equal
$<$	$<$	Is less than
$\leq$	$<=$	Is less than or equal to
$>$	$>$	Is greater than
$\geq$	$>=$	Is greater than or equal to
$\neq$	$<>$	Is not equal to

We now attempt to write the two-number drill program mentioned above. In order for a program to be meaningful to another user, it should contain instructions telling exactly what to do. These instructions can be given by using PRINT statements. The numbers to be added must either be input by the user or generated by the computer's random number generator. We choose the first option and use an INPUT statement to accomplish this. Once the numbers are input and added, we must inform the user whether the sum is correct. We must also determine if the user wishes to continue the practice. IF-THEN and GOTO statements are used to accomplish this. **GOTO** statements allow the program to branch to another statement instead of following the statements in the order given by the line numbers. These ideas are incorporated in the program in Figure 13-7.

GOTO

FIGURE 13-7

```
10 PRINT "THIS PROGRAM PROVIDES ADDITION PRACTICE."
20 PRINT "TYPE THE TWO NUMBERS TO BE ADDED SEPARATED BY A COMMA."
30 INPUT A,B
40 PRINT "AFTER THE QUESTION MARK, TYPE THE SUM."
50 PRINT A;"+";B;"=";
60 INPUT C
70 IF A + B = C THEN 100
80 PRINT "SORRY, TRY AGAIN."
90 GOTO 40
100 PRINT "VERY GOOD. DO YOU WANT TO ADD OTHER NUMBERS?"
110 PRINT "IF YES, TYPE 1. IF NO, TYPE 2.";
120 INPUT D
130 IF D = 1 THEN 20
140 END
```

Note that there are two IF-THEN statements in Figure 13-7. When the program is run and line 70 is reached and if $A + B = C$ is true, then the computer branches to line 100 and continues the run. In line 70, if $A + B = C$ is not true, the computer automatically goes to the next line, line 80, and continues the run. What happens in line 130 if the user types a 1? What happens in line 130 if the user types a 2?

When the program is run and the computer reaches line 90, the program automatically loops back to line 40 and the run continues. It should be noted that if a student running the computer continually misses the addition, the run will never get past line 90. On different machines, the procedure to get out of such a loop varies. On many machines the keys STOP or BREAK are used. On some other machines, the user should depress the control key and the "C" key at the same time (called a control C). This may have to be done several times to stop the run, at which time the computer types READY or the equivalent indicator.

Counters

Suppose we want to keep a record of how many drill exercises an individual attempts. This can be done by using a *counter*, which uses either IF-THEN or

GOTO statements along with a LET statement. A LET statement allows us to set the value of a variable; for example, LET X = 10. BASIC also allows a variable to be defined in terms of itself; for example, LET X = X + 1.

The computer does not interpret X = X + 1 as an equation, but rather replaces X with X + 1. This is useful in a program that counts how many exercises were correctly answered or, in general, how many times a certain section of a program has been executed. Consider the program in Figure 13-8.

FIGURE 13-8

```
10 LET X = 0
20 LET X = X + 1
30 PRINT X
40 IF X < 10 THEN 20
50 END
```

In line 10, X is *initialized*, or set to 0. Line 20 is the counter. When the program is run, the printout appears as follows.

RUN ®
1
2
3
.
.
.
10
READY

To understand this, notice in line 10 that X equals 0; then the new value of X in line 20 becomes 0 + 1, or 1. Hence, at line 30 the value 1 is printed. Next, the computer executes the instructions in line 40. Because 1 < 10, it branches to line 20. As X now has value 1, the new value of X in line 20 becomes 1 + 1, or 2. Thus, 2 is printed, and so on. After 9 is printed, we are again at line 40. Because 9 < 10, the computer again branches to line 20 and the new value of X becomes 9 + 1, or 10. This value is printed; because 10 < 10 is false, the program continues to line 50 and ends.

We now return to our original program in Figure 13-7. A counter needs to be initiated between lines 30 and 40 to keep a record of how many exercises are attempted. A PRINT statement between lines 130 and 140 outputs the desired record. The revised program is given in Figure 13-9.

FIGURE 13-9

```
10 PRINT "THIS PROGRAM PROVIDES ADDITION PRACTICE."
20 PRINT "TYPE THE TWO NUMBERS TO BE ADDED SEPARATED BY A COMMA."
30 INPUT A,B
```

```
31 LET X = 0
35 LET X = X + 1
40 PRINT "AFTER THE QUESTION MARK, TYPE THE SUM."
50 PRINT A;"+";B;"=";
60 INPUT C
70 IF A + B = C THEN 100
80 PRINT "SORRY, TRY AGAIN."
90 GOTO 40
100 PRINT "VERY GOOD, DO YOU WANT TO ADD OTHER NUMBERS?"
110 PRINT "IF YES, TYPE 1. IF NO, TYPE 2.";
120 INPUT D
130 IF D = 1 THEN 20
135 PRINT "THE NUMBER OF ATTEMPTED EXERCISES WAS ";X
140 END
```

FOR-NEXT Statements

FOR-NEXT

Another method for having the computer count is through the use of the key words **FOR-NEXT.** In a BASIC program, FOR-NEXT statements always occur in pairs with the FOR statement preceding the associated NEXT statement. For example, we could utilize FOR-NEXT statements as shown in Figure 13-10

```
20 FOR X = 1 TO 10
    .
    .
    .
120 NEXT X
```

FIGURE 13-10

If a program containing the lines in Figure 13-10 is run and line 20 is reached, the computer initializes a counter by assigning the value of 1 to X. At line 120, the computer loops back to line 20, assigns the value 2 to X, again continues to line 120, loops back, and so on until X = 10. When X is 10 and line 120 is reached, the computer continues on to the next line of the program following line 120. With no other directions in line 20, the computer automatically increments X by 1 each time the loop is passed through. X can be incremented for other values by using the word **STEP** and the desired value. For example, replace line 20 with the following:

STEP

```
20 FOR X = 1 TO 10 STEP 0.5
```

The above line will initialize X with a value of 1 and increase this value by 0.5 each time line 20 is reached. For example, the values of X will be 1, 1.5, 2, 2.5, 3, . . . , 9, 9.5, 10.

STEP can also be used to decrement, rather than increment, the FOR-NEXT loop. For example, consider the following line.

```
20 FOR X = 10 TO 1 STEP -0.5
```

Here the value of X will be initialized at 10 and decrease in steps of 0.5 until it reaches $X = 1$. Thus, the values of X will be 10, 9.5, 9, 8.5, 8, . . . , 1.

FOR-NEXT commands are very useful when you know how many times to go through the loop. The counter and the IF-THEN loop are useful when you are not sure of the number of iterations. A further use of the FOR-NEXT command is given in the following problem.

Example 13-4

Doña Alvarez was asked to create a table of squares of the integers from 1 to 100 for her math class. Help her by writing a program to generate such a table.

Solution

A FOR-NEXT loop can easily generate all the integers from 1 through 100, as shown in Figure 13-11.

FIGURE 13-11

```
10 FOR X = 1 TO 100
20 PRINT X,
30 NEXT X
40 END
```

When the program is run, a list of all the integers from 1 to 100 is printed.

Now we must write a program to print the squares of those numbers. To do this, we modify line 20 in Figure 13-11 to include both X and X^2. The entire program is shown in Figure 13-12.

FIGURE 13-12

```
10 REM DONA ALVAREZ'S TABLE OF SQUARES
20 FOR X = 1 TO 100
30 PRINT X, X**2
40 NEXT X
50 END
```

When the above program is run, the printout appears as follows.

```
RUN ®
  1     1
  2     4
  3     9
  4    16
  .     .
  .     .
  .     .
100  10000
READY
```

PROBLEM 2

Professor Anna Litik was called by the university athletic director and asked to devise a chart for converting the heights of visiting basketball players from inches to centimeters. Help Dr. Litik by writing a program that will print a table giving the conversions incremented by half-inches from 65 inches to 84 inches.

Solution

In order to solve this problem, the conversion factor 1 inch = 2.54 cm is needed. Thus, 2 inches = 2(2.54) cm, or 5.08 cm and, in general, N inches = $N(2.54)$ cm. We can write a program using FOR-NEXT statements to produce a table for converting heights from inches to centimeters. We let X represent the number of inches starting át 65, increment by 0.5, and end at 84. Between the FOR and NEXT statements, we must print the value of X to represent the equivalent number of centimeters. Because it would be inappropriate to report that a player's height was 196.62 cm, we need to report the heights as integers. One way to do this is through the use of another BASIC special function key

INT word, **INT.** If we use a statement Y = INT(X), the computer will assign to Y the value of the greatest integer that is less than or equal to X. For example, INT(3.25) = 3, and INT(5) = 5. Hence, in our program, we can use INT(X*2.54) to assign an integer number of centimeters to X inches. Notice that the INT function does not round numbers, as discussed in Chapter 7. For example, INT(3.99) = 3.

To write the program, we set the first value of X equal to 65 inches. Next we convert 65 inches to centimeters by multiplying by 2.54 and then choose the greatest integer less than or equal to 65 · 2.54. We then print X and the obtained integer and loop back for the next value of X, which is 0.5 greater than the last value converted. This procedure continues until all values have been converted. The complete program is shown in Figure 13-13(a). In line 50, the PRINT statement is used to provide the desired output in a more readable format. When a PRINT statement is typed with no inputs, a blank line is left between the outputs. It may be helpful to write a flow chart for the problem before writing a program (Figure 13-13(b)).

FIGURE 13-13(a)

```
10 REM THIS PROGRAM WILL PRINT A
20 REM TABLE FOR CONVERTING INCHES
30 REM TO CENTIMETERS
40 PRINT "INCHES", "CENTIMETERS"
50 PRINT
60 FOR X = 65 TO 84 STEP 0.5
70 LET Y = INT(X*2.54)
80 PRINT X,Y
90 NEXT X
100 END
```

FIGURE 13-13(b)

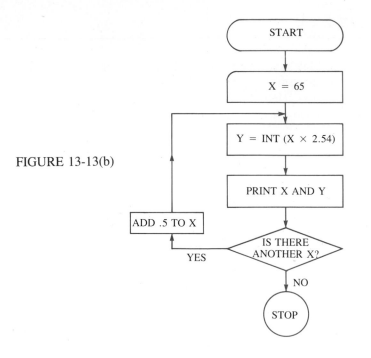

A shortened version of the printout obtained when the program in Figure 13-13(a) is run is given in Figure 13-14. Notice that the space between the headings and the data in Figure 13-14 was obtained from line 50 in the program.

INCHES	CENTIMETERS
65	165
65.5	166
66	167
66.5	168
67	170
67.5	171
68	172
68.5	173
69	175
69.5	176
.	.
.	.
.	.
83.5	212
84	213

FIGURE 13-14

PROBLEM SET 13-2

1. Determine the output for the following programs and then run the programs on the computer to check your answers.

    (a) ```
    10 FOR I = 1 TO 15
    20 PRINT I,
    30 NEXT I
    40 END
    ```

    (b) ```
    10 FOR I = 1 TO 15
    20 PRINT I*10,
    30 NEXT I
    40 END
    ```

    (c) ```
    10 FOR X = 1 TO 4 STEP 0.2
    20 PRINT X,
    30 NEXT X
    40 END
    ```

    (d) ```
    10 FOR X = 15 TO 1 STEP -1
    20 PRINT X,
    30 NEXT X
    40 END
    ```

    (e) ```
    10 LET X = 100
    20 PRINT X
    30 LET X = X - 1
    40 IF X < 0 THEN 70
    50 PRINT X
    60 GOTO 20
    70 END
    ```

    (f) ```
    10 LET X = 10
    20 LET X = X + 1
    30 PRINT X
    40 IF X < = 10 THEN 20
    50 END
    ```

2. Write a program to print all whole numbers from 1 to 500.

3. Determine the outputs of each of the following programs. Why are the outputs different?

    (a) ```
    10 PRINT "HEY YOU OUT THERE"
    20 LET K = K + 1
    30 IF K > 5 THEN 50
    40 GOTO 20
    50 END
    ```

    (b) ```
    10 LET K = K + 1
    20 PRINT "HEY YOU OUT THERE"
    30 IF K > 5 THEN 50
    40 GOTO 10
    50 END
    ```

4. Write a program to find the sum of the first 100 positive integers.

5. Modify the two-number addition program in Figure 13-9 to do two-number multiplications.

6. Write and run a program to print the list of numbers from 1 to 10, their square roots, and their squares.

7. Write a program to determine if any positive integer N is a prime number.

8. Devise a program to convert meters to centimeters for any given input. (1 m = 100 cm)

9. Write a program to convert degrees Fahrenheit to degrees Celsius, using the formula $C = \dfrac{(F - 32)5}{9}$.
   Make the program print the Fahrenheit temperature with the corresponding Celsius temperature for the temperatures from $^-40°F$ to $220°F$ with intervals of $10°F$.

10. Write a program to calculate the area, A, and the circumference, C, of a circle for any radius, R, which is input. Use $A = \pi R^2$ and $C = 2\pi R$, with $\pi = 3.14159$.

11. Write a program to verify that
    $$1^3 + 2^3 + 3^3 + \cdots + N^3 = (1 + 2 + 3 + \cdots + N)^2$$
    is true for the first ten natural numbers.

12. Write a program to compute the sum of the first 1000 odd natural numbers.

13. Write a program to compute and print out the value of the cube and the cube root of the first 20 natural numbers.

★ 14. Write a program to compute $N!$ where N is any natural number.
    $$N! = 1 \cdot 2 \cdot 3 \cdot 4 \cdot \ldots \cdot (N - 1) \cdot N$$

★ 15. Write a program to generate the first N Fibonacci numbers where N is any natural number. The Fibonacci sequence 1, 1, 2, 3, 5, 8, 13, 21, . . . is obtained by starting with 1, 1 and generating each successive term by summing the two previous terms. Check your program by finding the first ten Fibonacci numbers.

★ 16. Imagine that you are paid 1¢ on the first day, 2¢ on the second day, 4¢ on the third day, 8¢ on the fourth day, and, in general, 2^{n-1} cents on the nth day. Each day's salary is double that of the previous day. Compare the salary on the fifteenth day with the sum of the salaries for the first 14 days.

★ 17. In the game of baseball, an important statistic is the pitcher's earned run average (ERA). It is computed by multiplying the number of earned runs, R, by 9 (since there are 9 innings in a game) and then dividing this product by the natural number, I, of innings pitched. If the number of runs and innings pitched are known for each of the pitchers in the Pioneer League, write a program to determine each pitcher's ERA as the data are input.

★ 18. Suppose candy sells for 15¢ a bar in a certain machine. Suppose also that the machine will accept nickels, dimes, quarters, half-dollars, and dollars, and that it will give nickels, dimes, and quarters as change. Write a program that will calculate the number of quarters, dimes, and nickels returned for any amount placed in the machine.

★ 19. The program in Figure 13-13(a) converts inches to centimeters. However, the centimeter values printed represent the largest integer value less than the given number. Write a program in which the centimeter values are rounded to the nearest centimeter.

13-3 LOGO: INTRODUCING THE TURTLE

Turtle graphics, a part of the computer language Logo, are especially suited for teaching geometry. Students learn Logo by giving instructions to a creature known as a *turtle*. The turtle, a triangular-shaped figure, can leave a trail on a display screen as it moves according to given instructions. (The turtle can also move without leaving a trail.) The following discussion refers to MIT Logo run on an Apple computer. Most commands also work in Apple Logo, a slightly different version of the language. If commands differ, the Apple Logo version is shown in parentheses.

NODRAW

DRAW

A computer accepts instructions for the turtle in the NODRAW, DRAW, and EDIT modes. The first mode that appears on the screen is the NODRAW mode. A question mark and a flashing cursor appear as the computer awaits instructions. To execute turtle graphics commands, we enter the DRAW mode by typing **DRAW** (in Apple Logo, CLEARSCREEN (CS)) and pressing the RE-TURN key. To return to the NODRAW mode, we type **NODRAW** (in Apple Logo, TEXTSCREEN). In the DRAW mode, the turtle appears in the center of the screen, as shown in Figure 13-15.

FIGURE 13-15

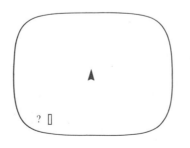

The question mark at the bottom left of the screen indicates that the computer is ready to accept instructions or commands. Logo reserves four lines at the bottom of the screen for user's commands and the computer's responses. The remainder of the screen is used for drawing.

primitives

FORWARD BACK

To make the turtle change position, we use commands called **primitives,** such as **FORWARD** and **BACK.** These commands, followed by a space and a numerical input, tell the turtle how far to move. For example, typing FORWARD 100 and pressing the RETURN key causes the turtle to move forward 100 "turtle units" in the direction it is pointing and may cause it to leave a trail, as shown in Figure 13-16(a). Similarly, the BACK command with a numerical input causes the turtle to move the specified number of turtle units backwards. Most screens are approximately 239 turtle units by 279 turtle units. Giving the turtle too great an input causes the turtle to "wraparound" to the other side of the screen.

RIGHT

LEFT

To make the turtle change direction, we use the commands **RIGHT** and **LEFT.** The RIGHT and LEFT commands, along with numerical input values, cause the turtle to turn in place the specified number of degrees. For example, typing RIGHT 90 and pressing the RETURN key causes the turtle to turn 90° to the right of the direction it previously pointed. A sequence of moves illustrating these commands is given in Figure 13-16.

FIGURE 13-16

FD, BK, RT, LT

To eliminate unnecessary typing, Logo accepts abbreviations for most of its commands. The abbreviations for the four basic commands, FORWARD, BACK, RIGHT, and LEFT are **FD, BK, RT,** and **LT,** respectively. Logo also accepts a sequence of commands written on one line. For example, Figure 13-16(e) could have been drawn by pressing the RETURN key after typing the following.

```
FD 100 RT 90 FD 125 LT 45 BK 75
```

PENUP (PU)
PENDOWN (PD)

To make the turtle move without leaving a trail, the command **PENUP,** abbreviated **PU,** may be used. To make the turtle leave a trail again, the command **PENDOWN,** abbreviated **PD,** may be used.

To start a new drawing with a clear screen, we type DRAW (in Apple Logo, CLEARSCREEN (CS)). This returns the turtle to its initial position and direction in the center of the screen and clears the screen. When the turtle is at "home" in the middle of the screen, it is pointing straight up. Any time the turtle points straight north (up), we say it has heading 0. A heading of 90 is directly east, 180 is directly south, and 270 is directly west. The screen could be marked as shown in Figure 13-17.

FIGURE 13-17

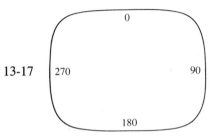

HOME

To return the turtle to the center of the screen with heading 0, the command **HOME** may be used. However, a trail to the center of the screen will be drawn from the position the turtle occupied before HOME was typed unless the command PENUP is used before HOME.

A summary of all commands with possible correct and incorrect examples is shown in Table 13-3.

TABLE 13-3

Command	Abbreviation	Correct Example	Incorrect Example
DRAW*		DRAW	D
NODRAW†	ND	ND	NO DRAW
FORWARD	FD	FD 50	FD50
BACK	BK	BK 60	BK60
RIGHT	RT	RT 90	RT90
LEFT	LT	LT 45	LT45
PENUP	PU	PU	P U
PENDOWN	PD	PD	P D
HOME	HOME	HOME	

*The command in Apple Logo is CLEARSCREEN (CS).
†The command in Apple Logo is TEXTSCREEN (CTRL-T).

The commands in Table 13-3 can be used to write programs. However, before writing programs, people studying Logo are encouraged to "play turtle" and act out their commands. For example, to draw a square, we may play turtle and walk around the square by moving forward 50 units, turning right 90°, moving forward 50 units, turning right 90°, moving forward 50 units, turning right 90°, and finally moving forward 50 units. The sequence of commands for these moves is summarized in Figure 13-18(a), with the resulting square and final position of the turtle in Figure 13-18(b).

FIGURE 13-18

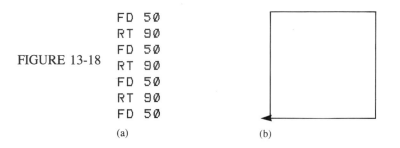

```
FD 50
RT 90
FD 50
RT 90
FD 50
RT 90
FD 50
```
(a)   (b)

Notice that the turtle's position in Figure 13-18(b) is the same as its initial position, but its heading is different. It is often convenient to have the turtle's final state be the same as its initial state. In Figure 13-18(b), to return the turtle to its initial state, we turn it right 90° by adding the line RT 90 at the end of the sequence of commands in Figure 13-18(a). The new sequence of commands is given in Figure 13-19(a), with the resulting square and turtle state as shown in Figure 13-19(b).

FIGURE 13-19

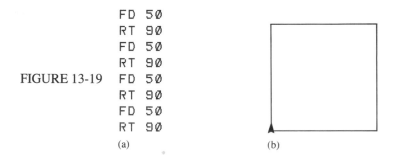

```
FD 50
RT 90
FD 50
RT 90
FD 50
RT 90
FD 50
RT 90
```
(a)   (b)

REPEAT

The sequence of commands in Figure 13-19(a) contain the instructions FD 50 and RT 90 repeated four times. Logo allows us to use the **REPEAT** command to repeat a set of instructions. For example, to draw the square in Figure 13-19(b), we could type the following.

```
REPEAT 4[FD 50 RT 90]
```

In general, REPEAT takes two inputs: a number and a sequence of commands in brackets. The commands in the brackets are repeated the designated number of times. (To obtain brackets on some computers, the SHIFT M and SHIFT N keys must be used.)

Example 13-5

Sketch the following outputs, indicating the initial and final turtle states. Then check your answers using a computer.

(a) FD 100
    RT 135
    FD 100
    RT 45
    FD 100
    RT 135
    FD 100
    RT 45

(b) REPEAT 2[FD 100 RT 135 FD 100 RT 45]

(c) REPEAT 8[FD 50 RT 45]

Solution

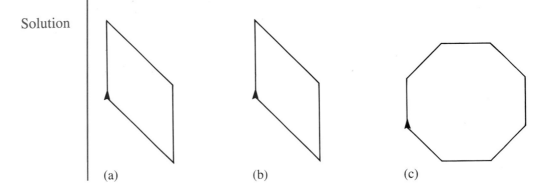

(a)   (b)   (c)

Defining Procedures

The sequence of commands in Figure 13-19(a) told the turtle to draw a square. If the screen is cleared, the figure is lost. To redraw the square, the entire sequence of commands must be retyped. Fortunately, with Logo it is possible to store any instructions in the computer's memory by creating a **procedure.**
        One way to create a procedure is to type **TO** followed by the name we wish to use for the procedure and press Return. (The name for a procedure must start with a letter.) When Return is pressed, the computer enters the EDIT mode. In this

procedure

TO

mode, the lines which follow are not executed but are stored in memory under the given name. For example, to create a procedure to draw a square, we type the instructions in Figure 13-20. To signify the end of a procedure, it is good practice to type END in the last line of the procedure.

FIGURE 13-20
```
TO SQUARE
REPEAT 4[FD 50 RT 90]
END
```

CTRL-C

Different versions of Logo define and store a procedure in different ways. For example, in MIT Logo the C key must be pressed while holding down the CONTROL key to define the procedure after it is typed. This is called a **CTRL-C.** Students should check their specfic Logo manuals to determine exactly how to define a procedure. After the procedure has been defined, typing the name of the procedure and pressing the RETURN key causes the computer to enter the DRAW mode immediately and execute the instructions in the procedure. In the remainder of the text, we assume that the above SQUARE procedure and all subsequent procedures are stored in the computer and can be reused.

Example 13-6

Predict what figures will be drawn by defining and executing the following procedures.

(a)
```
TO SQUARE1
RT 90
SQUARE
END
```

(b)
```
TO SQUARESTACK
SQUARE
RT 90
SQUARE
END
```

(c)
```
TO STAIR
SQUARE
RT 180
SQUARE
END
```

(d)
```
TO TURNSQUARE
SQUARE
RT 45
SQUARE
END
```

Solution

(a)

(b)

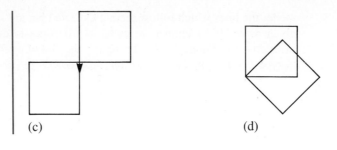

(c)   (d)

PROBLEM 3

Write a procedure for drawing an equilateral triangle whose side is 50 turtle steps long.

Solution

In order to write this procedure, it is helpful to sketch an equilateral triangle and find what angle the turtle needs to turn at each vertex of the triangle. Suppose the turtle starts at point *A* and moves 50 turtle steps to point *B*, as in Figure 13-21. This can be done by telling the turtle to move FD 50.

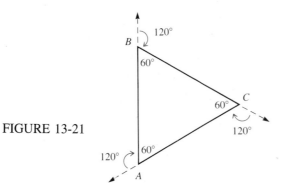

FIGURE 13-21

At point *B*, the turtle still has heading 0. In order to walk on $\overline{BC}$, the turtle may turn 120° to the right. Thus, the next command should be RT 120. The triangle has three sides of equal length. The three turns necessary to achieve the initial turtle state are equal. Repeating the sequence FD 50 RT 120 three times causes the turtle to walk around the triangle and finish in its original position with its original heading. This procedure is given in Figure 13-22.

FIGURE 13-22

```
TO TRIANGLE
REPEAT 3[FD 50 RT 120]
END
```

One of the great advantages of Logo is its ability to use procedures to define new procedures. Consider the following problem.

PROBLEM 4

Write a procedure to draw the "house" in Figure 13-23.

FIGURE 13-23

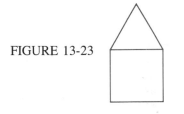

Solution

One way to solve the problem is to use what we already know. We have a procedure for drawing a square and a procedure for drawing a triangle. It may seem that typing SQUARE followed by TRIANGLE will accomplish what we want. The results of this effort are shown in Figure 13-24(a).

FIGURE 13-24

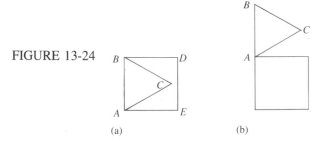

(a)   (b)

Why did this not work? The turtle first drew the square in Figure 13-24(a) and returned to its initial state with heading 0 at point *A*. Typing TRIANGLE causes the turtle to draw triangle *ABC*, as in Figure 13-21. In order to draw the roof, we need the turtle to be at the upper left vertex of the square. This can be achieved by typing FD 50. If TRIANGLE is typed now, we obtain the shape in Figure 13-24(b), which is still not the desired house. Trial and error is an important activity in Logo; it helps to get acquainted with the problem and eventually to find the correct solution. This process of rewriting a program that does not do what we

debugging   want it to do is called **debugging.** To debug the program, we examine how the turtle should walk from the top left vertex of the square in order to draw the roof in Figure 13-25(a). After typing SQUARE and FD 50, the turtle is at point *A* with heading 0. Thus, to walk on $\overline{AB}$, the turtle needs to turn right by 90° − 60°, or 30°. With this heading, typing TRIANGLE causes the turtle to draw the desired roof. The complete procedure, named HOUSE, is shown in Figure 13-25(b).

FIGURE 13-25

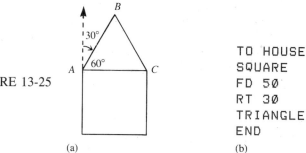

(a)

```
TO HOUSE
SQUARE
FD 50
RT 30
TRIANGLE
END
```

(b)

BRAIN TEASER

Write a procedure for drawing the following figure using a continuous path and without retracing any segment. (Single points may be retraced.)

PROBLEM SET 13-3

1. Sketch figures drawn by the turtle using each of the following sets of instructions. Check your sketches by executing the instructions on a computer.

   (a) FD 50
       RT 90
       FD 50
       RT 45
       FD 50
       RT 135
       FD 50

   (b) FD 50
       RT 90
       BK 50
       RT 60
       FD 50

   (c) FD -50
       FD 50

   (d) BK -50

   (e) FD 30 - 20

2. Sketch figures drawn by the turtle using each of the following sets of instructions. Check your sketches by executing the instructions on a computer.

   (a) REPEAT 8[SQUARE RT 45]
   (b) REPEAT 6[TRIANGLE RT 60]
   (c) REPEAT 36[SQUARE RT 10]
   (d) REPEAT 36[TRIANGLE RT 10]

3. Write procedures to draw each of the following figures.

Rectangle that
is not a square

(a)

Flag

(b)

The letter *Y*

(c)

The letter *V*

(d)

The letter *T*

(e)

A rhombus that
is not a square

(f)

A square with
a smaller square
inside

(g)

A hat

(h)

4. Use any procedures in this section or in Problem 3 to write new procedures that will draw each of the following figures.

(a)

(b)

(c)

(d)

(e)

(f)

(g)

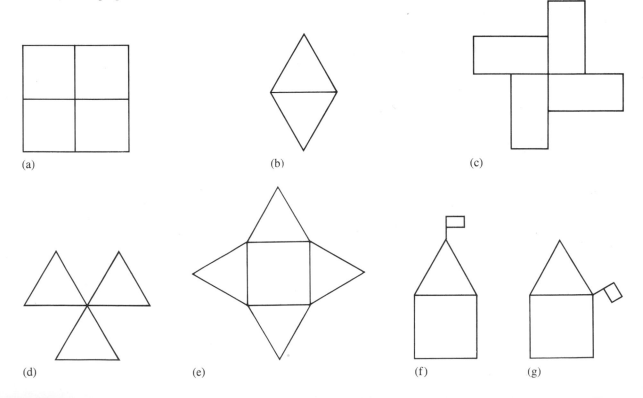

5. Do problems 4(f) and (g) by defining a procedure for drawing the roof shown rather than using the TRIANGLE procedure.

ROOF

6. Write a procedure for drawing the following figure.

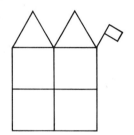

7. Write a procedure for drawing the following.

13-4 PROCEDURES WITH VARIABLES

The SQUARE procedure in Section 13-3 allowed us to draw only squares of side 50. If we want to draw smaller or larger squares, we need to write a new procedure. It would be more convenient if we could write one procedure that would work for any size square. This can be accomplished with Logo by using a variable as input rather than a fixed number, such as 50 in FD 50. We can use variable input in Logo as long as we warn the computer that the "thing" we are going to type is a variable. This is done using a colon. The computer understands that anything that follows a colon is a variable. For example, a variable input to the SQUARE procedure might be called :SIDE, where :SIDE stands for the length of a side of the square. To define a new SQUARE procedure with variable input, we type TO SQUARE :SIDE. Because we would like the turtle to move forward the length of :SIDE instead of 50, we use a new variable square procedure called VSQUARE, as shown in Figure 13-26.

FIGURE 13-26

```
TO VSQUARE :SIDE
REPEAT 4[FD :SIDE RT 90]
END
```

If we want the turtle to draw a square of size 40, we type VSQUARE 40. Notice that we do not type VSQUARE :40 because 40 is not a variable. (In fact, the computer will not understand the instruction VSQUARE :40.)

Remark | We call the new variable square procedure VSQUARE instead of SQUARE because if we attempt to enter the EDIT mode by typing TO SQUARE :SIDE, the computer displays the old SQUARE procedure on the screen for us to edit unless the old procedure has been erased. You should consult your Logo manual for directions on how to edit procedures.

A procedure may have more than one input. For example, consider the equivalent procedures for drawing a rectangle given in Figure 13-27. Two variables are used so that two inputs can be accepted.

FIGURE 13-27

```
TO RECTANGLE :HEIGHT :WIDTH
FD :HEIGHT
RT 90
FD :WIDTH
RT 90
FD :HEIGHT
RT 90
FD :WIDTH
RT 90
END
```

```
TO RECTANGLE :HEIGHT :WIDTH
REPEAT 2[FD :HEIGHT RT 90 FD :WIDTH RT 90]
END
```

Figure 13-28 shows rectangles drawn by either of the RECTANGLE procedures with different inputs for the sides.

FIGURE 13-28

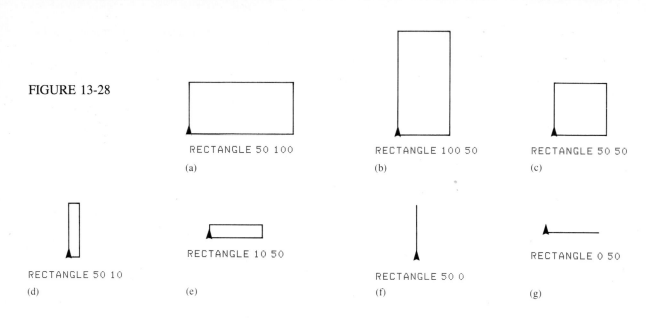

RECTANGLE 50 100

(a)

RECTANGLE 100 50

(b)

RECTANGLE 50 50

(c)

RECTANGLE 50 10

(d)

RECTANGLE 10 50

(e)

RECTANGLE 50 0

(f)

RECTANGLE 0 50

(g)

To instruct the turtle to draw a figure that looks like a circle (*turtle-type circle*). we must tell the turtle to move forward a little and turn a little and then repeat this sequence of motions until it comes back to its original position. If the turtle is told to go forward 1 unit and then to turn right 1°, then this sequence of motions repeated 360 times yields a turtle-type circle. The procedure, which we call CIRCLE1, is given in Figure 13-29 along with its output.

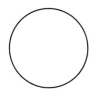

FIGURE 13-29
```
TO CIRCLE1
REPEAT 360[FD 1 RT 1]
END
```

The turtle-type circle determined by CIRCLE1 is actually a regular 360-gon, but it is a close approximation of a circle and is referred to in Logo as a circle. One way to vary the size of the circle is to vary the amount the turtle moves forward. For example, suppose the turtle moves forward 0.5 units rather than 1 unit, or—in general—any number of units, S. In Figure 13-30(a), we define the new procedure and name it CIRCLE2. A new name for this procedure is necessary to distinguish it from CIRCLE1. Notice that CIRCLE2 accepts a variable input :S, while CIRCLE1 does not. Figure 13-30(b) also shows various circles drawn by the CIRCLE2 procedure.

FIGURE 13-30
```
TO CIRCLE2 :S
REPEAT 360[FD :S RT 1]
END
```
(a)

| CIRCLE2 0.8 | CIRCLE2 0.5 | CIRCLE2 0.1 |

(b)

Sometimes it is more useful to draw a circle of a given radius. To write a procedure for drawing a circle of radius R, we utilize the procedure for CIRCLE2. To understand the general case better, we first solve a special case of the problem. Suppose we want to draw a circle with radius 50. What should the side S of the approximating polygon be? We can find the relationship between S and the radius 50 by finding the circumference of the circle in two ways. The perimeter of the polygon is $360 \cdot S$ and the circumference of a circle with radius 50 is $2\pi \cdot 50$. Because $360 \cdot S \doteq 2\pi \cdot 50$, then $S \doteq 50 \cdot \frac{\pi}{180}$, or $S \doteq 0.873$. Thus, CIRCLE2 0.873 will draw a circle with radius approximately 50 units long.

In general, to find a procedure to draw a circle with radius R as an input, we need to find S in terms of R. This can be done as shown below.

$$360 \cdot S \doteq 2\pi R$$

$$S \doteq R \cdot \frac{\pi}{180}$$

$$S \doteq R \cdot 0.01745$$

Hence, a procedure called CIRCLE for drawing a circle whose radius is R can be written as given in Figure 13-31.

FIGURE 3-31

```
TO CIRCLE :R
CIRCLE2 :R*0.01745
END
```

BRAIN TEASER

Write a program that will draw nine dots arranged in a square format, as shown. Then write another program that will connect all the nine dots by a continuous path made of four segments.

```
•   •   •

•   •   •

•   •   •
```

PROBLEM SET 13-4

1. Write procedures that will draw figures similar to those in Problem 3(b)–(h) of Problem Set 13-3 but of variable size.

2. Write procedures that will draw each of the following figures.

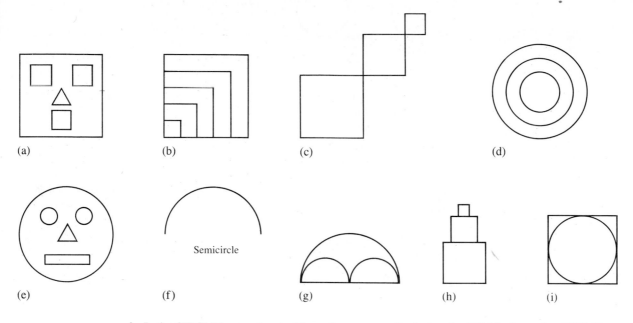

(a)   (b)   (c)   (d)

(e)   (f)   (g)   (h)   (i)

3. In the CIRCLE1 procedure in this section, suppose the instruction RT 1 is changed to RT 5. How does the new figure differ from the original one?
4. If the turtle repeats the sequence FD :S RT 1 fewer than 360 times, it will draw an arc of a circle.
   (a) Write a procedure for drawing an arc when the inputs are the length of a side of an approximating polygon and the number of degrees in the arc.
   (b) Write a procedure for drawing an arc given the radius of the arc and number of degrees in the arc.
5. Use the procedures developed in Problem 4 to write a procedure to draw variable-sized flowers similar to the one shown.

6. Create your own designs using the arc procedure developed in Problem 4(b).
7. Design a procedure to fill in a circle.

13-5   RECURSION

A very powerful feature of Logo is that it enables a procedure to call itself. Recall the procedure CIRCLE1 shown in Figure 13-32.

FIGURE 13-32
```
TO CIRCLE1
REPEAT 360[FD 1 RT 1]
END
```

If we were not sure how many times the instruction [FD 1 RT 1] should be repeated to complete a circle, we could ask the turtle to repeat it indefinitely. This can be achieved using the procedure CIRC, as shown in Figure 13-33. (We call the new procedure CIRC to distinguish it from other circle procedures.)

FIGURE 13-33
```
TO CIRC
FD 1 RT 1
CIRC
END
```

When the computer executes FD 1 and RT 1 in the procedure of Figure 13-33, the turtle moves forward 1 unit and then turns right 1°. The next step in the program is CIRC. However, CIRC is defined in the title line. Thus, the CIRC procedure calls upon the CIRC procedure and the commands FD 1 and RT 1 are repeated. This process goes on unless we use CTRL-G (the control key in combination with the G key), which makes the turtle stop. Notice that the procedure CIRC calls itself. The process of a procedure calling itself is called **recursion.**

CTRL-G

recursion

Recursion is particularly useful when we do not know how many times a certain sequence of instructions should be repeated. Consider the problem of trying to write a single procedure for drawing regular polygons. The shape of a polygon depends upon the size of a side and the angle by which the turtle has to turn, and hence two variables, :SIDE and :ANGLE, are needed. To repeat the instruction FD :SIDE RT :ANGLE indefinitely, we use the recursive procedure in Figure 13-34, which we call POLY.

FIGURE 13-34
```
TO POLY :SIDE :ANGLE
FD :SIDE RT :ANGLE
POLY :SIDE :ANGLE
END
```

To execute the POLY program, we need to type two numbers for the variables, :SIDE and :ANGLE. For example, POLY 100 60 will make the turtle repeat the instruction FD 100 RT 60 forever. The numbers following POLY are assigned in the same order as the variables in the title. Figure 13-35 shows various shapes drawn by POLY with different inputs for sides and angles.

FIGURE 13-35

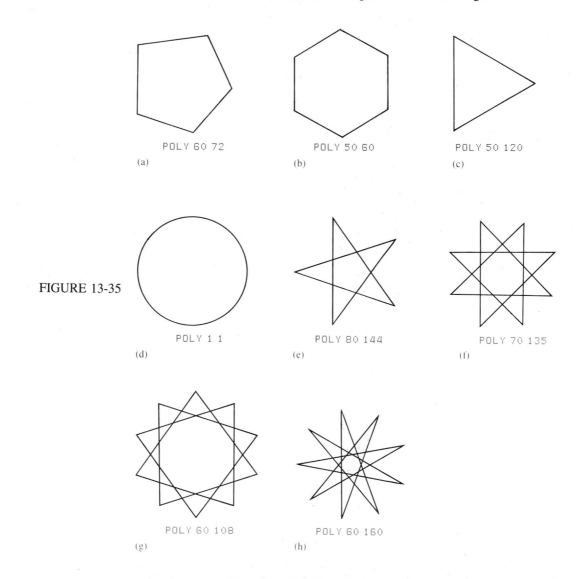

POLY 60 72
(a)

POLY 50 60
(b)

POLY 50 120
(c)

POLY 1 1
(d)

POLY 80 144
(e)

POLY 70 135
(f)

POLY 60 108
(g)

POLY 60 160
(h)

The POLY procedure draws regular polygons in Figure 13-35(a), (b), (c), and (d) and also the star shapes in Figure 13-35(e), (f), (g), and (h).

Are all the figures drawn by POLY closed? Given an angle, is it possible to predict (before the figure is drawn) how many vertices the figure has? And conversely, if we want a POLY with a given number of vertices, what angle will produce such a POLY? These and many other questions concerning POLY and other geometrical figures are investigated in *Turtle Geometry* by Abelson and diSessa.

The turtle graphics features of Logo are particularly suitable for geometric investigations. Suppose that we would like to know what happens when the POLY program is modified so that the recursive call has :SIDE +5 as the variable, a procedure that does this is often referred to as POLYSPI. The POLYSPI procedure appears as shown in Figure 13-36.

FIGURE 13-36

```
TO POLYSPI :SIDE :ANGLE
FD :SIDE RT :ANGLE
POLYSPI :SIDE + 5 :ANGLE
END
```

Figure 13-37 shows different figures drawn by POLYSPI.

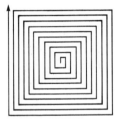

POLYSPI 5 90

POLYSPI 5 120

FIGURE 13-37

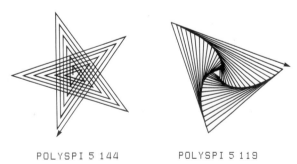

POLYSPI 5 144   POLYSPI 5 119

IF-STOP

Because the lengths of the segments in the POLYSPI procedure increase by five each time the turtle turns, the turtle may eventually get off the screen. It is possible to make the turtle stop by using CTRL-G or by utilizing the commands **IF** and **STOP** in the procedure itself. Suppose we do not want the turtle to walk along any segments longer than 100 units. We could type IF :SIDE > 100 STOP and insert these directions in the procedure given in Figure 13-36. (In Apple Logo, the preceding statement would be written as IF :SIDE > 100 [STOP].) The new procedure, which we call POLYSPIS, is given in Figure 13-38.

FIGURE 13-38
```
TO POLYSPIS :SIDE :ANGLE
IF :SIDE > 100 STOP
FD :SIDE RT :ANGLE
POLYSPIS :SIDE + 5 :ANGLE
END
```

In the procedure of Figure 13-38, the IF statement tests if a side is longer than 100 units. If a side is longer than 100 units, the turtle stops; if not, the turtle executes the next line. What happens if this line is inserted in positions other than immediately following the title line?

Other Logo Commands

Logo provides the basic arithmetic operations of addition, subtraction, multiplication, and division, denoted by $+$, $-$, $*$, and $/$, respectively. As in arithmetic and algebra, multiplications and divisions are performed before additions and subtractions unless parentheses are used, in which case the operations in the parentheses are performed first.

PRINT
    To find the answer to a specific arithmetic problem, the command **PRINT** may be used. For example, if we type PRINT 13*13 + 1, the answer 170 appears. It is possible to write procedures for manipulating numbers using arithmetic operations. For example, to find the average of two numbers x and y, we may define the procedure in Figure 13-39.

FIGURE 13-39
```
TO AVERAGE :X :Y
PRINT (:X + :Y)/2
END
```

SQRT
    Logo also has a square root function, denoted by **SQRT**. To find $\sqrt{100}$, we type PRINT SQRT 100, and the computer prints **10.** Two other commands useful in drawing with the turtle as well as in performing computations are **XCOR** and **YCOR.** These commands give the x- and y-coordinates of the turtle's position on the screen when the x- and y-axes go through the turtle's "home," as shown in Figure 13-40.

XCOR
YCOR

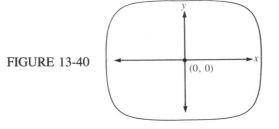

FIGURE 13-40

If we type PRINT XCOR or PRINT YCOR, Logo will print the *x*- or *y*-coordinates of the turtle's position. These commands can also be used along with IF and STOP statements. For example, IF XCOR > 100 STOP. (In Apple Logo, IF XCOR > 100 [STOP].) Other useful Logo commands for coordinate geometry can be found in your manual.

PROBLEM SET 13-5

1. Predict the shapes that will be drawn by the following procedures and then check your predictions on the computer. The procedure for VSQUARE :SIDE has been defined in this section and TRIANGLE :SIDE is defined as follows.

```
TO TRIANGLE :SIDE
REPEAT 3[FD :SIDE RT 120]
END
```

(a)
```
TO FIGURE :SIDE
   TRIANGLE :SIDE
   RT 10
   FIGURE :SIDE
END
```
(b)
```
TO FIGURE1 :SIDE
   IF :SIDE < 5 STOP
   TRIANGLE :SIDE
   RT 10
   FIGURE1 :SIDE - 5
END
```
(c)
```
TO TOWER :SIDE
   VSQUARE :SIDE
   FD :SIDE
   TOWER :SIDE *0.5
END
```

(d)
```
TO TOWER1 :SIDE
   IF :SIDE < 2 STOP
   VSQUARE :SIDE
   FD :SIDE
   TOWER :SIDE *0.5
END
```
(e)
```
TO SQUARE :SIDE
   IF :SIDE < 2 STOP
   VSQUARE :SIDE
   SQUARE :SIDE - 5
END
```
(f)
```
TO SPIRAL :SIDE
   IF :SIDE > 50 STOP
   FD :SIDE
   RT 30
   SPIRAL :SIDE + 3
END
```

2. Type the following procedure on your computer.

```
TO NEWPOLY :SIDE :ANGLE
FD :SIDE RT :ANGLE
FD :SIDE RT :ANGLE*2
NEWPOLY :SIDE :ANGLE
END
```

Run the program by typing each of the following.
(a) NEWPOLY 50 30
(b) NEWPOLY 50 144
(c) NEWPOLY 50 125

3. Type the following procedure on your computer.

```
TO POLYSPIRAL :SIDE :ANGLE :INC
FD :SIDE RT :ANGLE
POLYSPIRAL (:SIDE + :INC) :ANGLE :INC
END
```

Run the program by typing each of the following.
(a) POLYSPIRAL 2 85 3
(b) POLYSPIRAL 1 119 2
(c) POLYSPIRAL 1 100 5

4. Type the following procedure on your computer.

```
TO INSPI :SIDE :ANGLE :INC
FD :SIDE RT :ANGLE
INSPI :SIDE (:ANGLE + :INC) :INC
END
```

Run the program by typing each of the following.
(a) INSPI 10 2 20
(b) INSPI 2 0 10
(c) INSPI 10 5 10

5. Write recursive procedures that will draw figures similar to the following. Use the STOP command in your procedures.

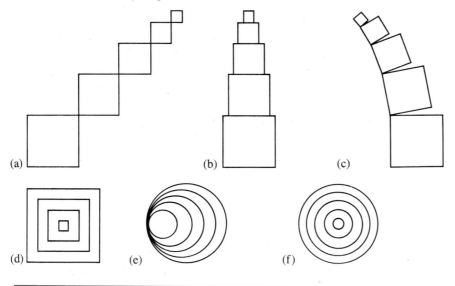

(a) (b) (c) (d) (e) (f)

SOLUTION TO THE PRELIMINARY PROBLEM

Understanding the Problem

A turn-about robot toy car travels some distance in the direction it is facing; then it turns 60° to the right and moves forward in the direction four-fifths of the first distance. At that point, it again turns 60° to the right and moves forward four-fifths of the length of the last segment traveled. This pattern of traveling straight and turning continues until the distance to be traveled is less than 1 cm. At this point, the car stops. A sketch of a possible path for the toy car is given in Figure 13-41. The problem is to find the distance d between the starting and the stopping positions of the car. The distance d is the length of the segment connecting the starting and stopping positions of the car, as shown in Figure 13-41.

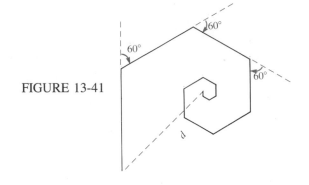

FIGURE 13-41

Devising a Plan

A method of modeling the problem involves the use of a computer. Because drawing a repetitious pattern is involved, using Logo may be suitable for the solution. If we let the turtle make the same moves as the car and represent 1 cm by one turtle step, we could use the XCOR and YCOR commands to find the coordinates of the final position of the turtle. Knowing the starting and stopping coordinates of the turtle will enable us to find the distance d from the initial position to the stopping position. If we let the turtle start at home, its initial position is (0, 0). If the stopping position has coordinates (x, y), as shown in Figure 13-42, it follows from the Pythagorean Theorem that $d^2 = x^2 + y^2$ and hence that $d = \sqrt{x^2 + y^2}$.

FIGURE 13-42

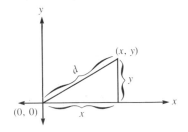

To solve the problem, we need to write a program so that the turtle moves as the car does.

Carrying Out the Plan

The initial distance may vary, so we use a variable for the length of the initial segment along which the car, or turtle, travels. We call the variable :LENGTH. The first set of directions should be FD :LENGTH RT 60. Next, the turtle moves forward four-fifths, or 0.8, of the first length; hence, the next set of directions could be FD :LENGTH*0.8 RT 60. However, since this process continues, we should be able to use recursion. If we call our first attempt TRIP1, we have the procedure in Figure 13-43(a).

FIGURE 13-43

```
TO TRIP1 :LENGTH
FD :LENGTH RT 60
TRIP1 :LENGTH*0.8
END
```
(a)

```
TO TRIP2 :LENGTH
IF :LENGTH < 1 STOP
FD :LENGTH RT 60
TRIP2 :LENGTH*0.8
END
```
(b)

Remark | In Apple Logo, the second line in TRIP2 procedure has to be IF :LENGTH < 1 [STOP].

Following the instruction in Figure 13-43(a), the turtle never stops. To get the turtle to stop when the length of the segment to be traveled is less than one turtle step, we need to modify the program in Figure 13-43(a) by using the IF and STOP commands. The modified procedure is given in Figure 13-43(b). For example, typing TRIP2 100 causes the turtle to simulate the car's path when the initial distance is 100. If we now type XCOR, we obtain the *x*-coordinates of the point where the turtle stops, and if we type YCOR, we obtain the *y*-coordinate of the stopping point. We can find the distance *d* between the starting and stopping position by writing the Logo procedure shown in Figure 13-44. We name this Logo procedure DISTANCE :X :Y, where X and Y are the *x*- and *y*-coordinates of the stopping point.

FIGURE 13-44
```
TO DISTANCE :X :Y
PRINT SQRT (:X*:X + :Y*:Y)
END
```

Looking Back

It is more efficient to write a single procedure that enables us to compute the required distance by typing only the initial length of the segment traveled. This can be accomplished in various ways. For example, we could insert the directions PRINT SQRT (XCOR*XCOR + YCOR*YCOR) just before the STOP command in Figure 13-43(b). The new procedure is shown in Figure 13-45.

FIGURE 13-45
```
TO TRIP :LENGTH
IF :LENGTH < 1 DISTANCE XCOR YCOR STOP
FD :LENGTH RT 60
TRIP :LENGTH*0.8
END
```

Remark | In Apple Logo, the second line in Figure 13-45 must be IF :LENGTH < 1 [DISTANCE XCOR YCOR STOP].

QUESTIONS FROM THE CLASSROOM

1. A student asks if a program can be written partly in BASIC and partly in Logo. How would you respond?
2. A fellow teacher says that BASIC is a better language than Logo because many arithmetical operations possible in BASIC are not built into Logo. For example, in BASIC, unlike in Logo, it is easy to raise a number to any power. How would you respond?
3. A student cites the following program as evidence that the FOR-NEXT statement does not always work. What is your response?

```
10 FOR I = 1 TO 10
20 PRINT "*"
30 I = 10
40 NEXT I
50 END
```

4. A student does not understand why REM statements should be used to document a program when they have no effect on actual running of the program. What do you tell the student?
5. A student claims that since Logo incorporates a RIGHT (RT) primitive, there is no reason for a LEFT (LT) primitive. What is your response?
6. A student asks why the quotation marks in a PRINT statement are not used in BASIC in the same way as in Logo. How do you respond?
7. A student wants to draw a tower and writes the following programs.

```
TO TOWER :S
BOX :S FD :S
TOWER :S - 5
END

TO BOX :S
REPEAT 4[FD :S RT 90]
END
```

When running TOWER 30, the student notices that two towers are drawn on the screen and that part of the second tower is a mirror image of the first tower. The student wants to know why two towers are drawn by the TOWER procedure and why part of the second tower is the mirror image of the first. How do you respond?

CHAPTER OUTLINE

I. Computer **hardware** has three major groups of components.
   A. Input/Output group
      1. An **input unit** is used to get information into the computer. Modes of input include special punched cards, magnetic tapes or discs, and computer keyboards.
      2. An **output unit** sends the obtained information to the user. Modes of output include punched cards, magnetic tapes or discs, a television screen called a **Cathode-Ray Tube (CRT),** and a line printer which prints the computer's responses on paper.
   B. Computing group
      1. The **Central Processing Unit (CPU)** contains an arithmetic logic unit that performs arithmetic and logical operations and a control unit which coordinates all the computer's activities.
      2. The **Internal Memory Unit** is used for temporary storage of programs, input data, intermediate results, and output results.
   C. Auxiliary Storage group
      1. The auxiliary storage unit for a microcomputer usually consists of a cassette recorder or a "floppy disk" system.

II. Computer **software** consists of computer programs.

III. **BASIC** Programming (**B**eginner's **A**ll-purpose **S**ymbolic **I**nstruction **C**ode)

A. BASIC symbols sometimes differ from mathematics symbols. A summary of BASIC operations and equality and inequality symbols is given in the table.

Symbol	Use
+	Addition
−	Subtraction
*	Multiplication
/	Division
** or ↑ or ∧	Exponentiation
=	Is equal to
<	Is less than
<=	Is less than or equal to
>=	Is greater than or equal to
<>	Is not equal to

B. BASIC **system commands** tell the computer to do something immediately. They do not require line numbers.
   1. **RUN** causes a program to be executed.
   2. **LIST** causes the most current version of a program to be displayed.
   3. **CONTROL C, BREAK,** or **STOP** causes the program to halt.

C. BASIC **statements** make up the lines of a program. Statements start with line numbers followed by BASIC **programming commands.** A summary of the commands used in this chapter is given below.
   1. **PRINT**—used to print messages and results.
   2. **LET**—allows program to store data and perform computations.
   3. **END**—tells a computer the program is finished.
   4. **INPUT**—used to obtain values from the keyboard for one or more variables.
   5. **GOTO**—transfers control to another specified line.
   6. **IF-THEN**—transfers control to another specified line under certain stated conditions.
   7. **FOR**—begins a loop.

8. **NEXT**—tells the computer to return to the FOR statement to close the loop.

D. BASIC has several special functions. The following are used in this chapter.
   1. **SQR**—finds the square root of X when used as SQR(X).
   2. **INT**—finds the greatest integer less than or equal to X when used as INT(X).

IV. Logo

A. Logo accepts instructions in the **NODRAW, DRAW,** and **EDIT** modes.

B. The following primitives are used in Logo.

Primitive	Abbreviation
FORWARD	FD
BACK	BK
RIGHT	RT
LEFT	LT
PENUP	PU
PENDOWN	PD
SHOWTURTLE	ST
HIDETURTLE	HT
DRAW*	
NODRAW†	ND
PRINT	PR
HOME	
XCOR	
YCOR	
REPEAT	
IF	
STOP	
SQRT	

*In Apple Logo, this command is CLEARSCREEN (CS).
†In Apple Logo, this command is CLEARTEXT (CTRL-T).

C. Procedures
   1. A set of instructions that Logo can store for future use is called a **procedure.**
   2. To create a procedure, we type **TO** followed by the name of the procedure.
   3. When a procedure calls itself, it is called a **recursive procedure.**

D. Arithmetic

Logo provides basic arithmetic operations, as summarized in the table.

Symbol	Use	Symbol	Use
+	Addition	=	Is equal to
−	Subtraction	<	Is less than
*	Multiplication	>	Is greater than
/	Division		

CHAPTER TEST

BASIC

1. Which of the following are valid BASIC variables?
   (a) 12E
   (b) A
   (c) D5
   (d) 7*

2. Convert each of the following to base 10 notation in standard form.
   (a) 1.25E+07
   (b) 1.659−04
   (c) −4E+07
   (d) −1.5E−03

3. Write each of the following using BASIC symbols.
   (a) $Y = AX^3 + BX^2 + C$
   (b) $V = \frac{4}{3}PR^3$
   (c) $Y = \frac{(AX + B)^2}{C}$
   (d) $Y = \left(X^3 + \frac{W}{2}\right)^3$

4. Evaluate each of the following as a computer would.
   (a) $3^3 + [(3 + 2) \cdot 5]^2$
   (b) $8 - 2 \cdot 3 + (10 \div 2)^2$
   (c) $\frac{1}{2}(5 + 3)^2 - 3$
   (d) $15 \cdot 3 - 2 \cdot 4 + 5 \cdot (4 - 8)$

5. Which of the following are correct PRINT statements?
   (a) 10 PRINT "X" = ; 3
   (b) 20 PRINT A BIT OF BASIC
   (c) 30 "PRINT" X

6. Describe the output, if any, of the following programs.
   (a) 10 PRINT "DAY", "MONTH", "YEAR"
       20 LET D = 4
       30 LET M = 7
       40 LET Y = 1776

```
   50 PRINT D,M,Y
   60 END
```
   (b)
```
   10 FOR N = 1 TO 5
   20 LET A = 2**N
   30 PRINT A
   40 NEXT N
   50 END
```
   (c)
```
   10 LET X = 10
   20 LET Y = 2
   30 PRINT X + Y,X - Y,X/Y,X*Y, Y**X
   40 END
```

7. Write a BASIC program which asks for an input, X, and then computes the value $7X^{10} + 3X^5 - 1000$. If a computer is available, do a run for $X = 3$.

8. Describe the output, if any, for the following program when $T = 2$ seconds.

```
10 REM THIS PROGRAM COMPUTES THE
15 REM DISTANCE AN OBJECT
20 REM FALLS IN FEET AFTER T
25 REM SECONDS
30 PRINT "TYPE IN THE VALUE OF THE ";
35 PRINT "TIME, T, IN SECONDS ";
40 INPUT T
50 LET D = 16*T**2
60 PRINT "AFTER";T;"SECONDS THE
65 PRINT "OBJECT HAS FALLEN ";D;" FEET"
70 END
```

9. Write a BASIC program that will compute and print the sum of the squares of the first ten natural numbers. Run the program, if possible.

10. Write a program that lists the first ten natural numbers and their fourth powers. Run the program, if possible.

11. Write a program to output a table of square roots of the

numbers from 0 to 1 with steps of 0.25. Run the program, if possible.

12. What is the output if the values of 15 and 18 are input for C and M, respectively, in the following program?

```
10 PRINT "TYPE IN THE ";
15 PRINT "CHRONOLOGICAL AGE"
20 INPUT C
30 PRINT "TYPE IN THE MENTAL AGE"
40 INPUT M
50 PRINT
60 PRINT "THE IQ FOR C = ";C;" AND ";
65 PRINT M" =";M;" IS ";M/C*100
70 END
```

13. Write a program such that when any two integers are input, the computer will tell whether the product of the two numbers is positive, zero, or negative.

Logo

14. Sketch figures drawn by the turtle using each of the following sets of instructions.

(a) FD 40
    RT 90
    FD 40
    RT 90
    FD 40
    RT 90
    FD 40
    RT 90

(b) FD 50
    RT 120
    FD 50
    RT 120
    FD 50
    RT 120

(c) REPEAT 6[FD 50 RT 60]

15. Write procedures to draw each of the following figures.

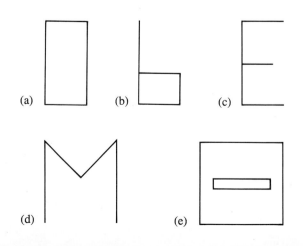

(a) (b) (c)

(d) (e)

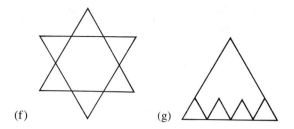

(f) (g)

16. Write procedures to draw each of the following.

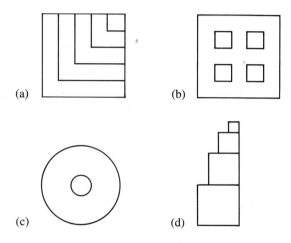

(a) (b)

(c) (d)

17. Write a program for drawing a regular decagon of variable size.

18. Write a recursive procedure to draw a stairway like the one shown.

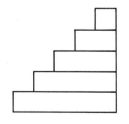

19. Predict the output when the following procedures are run with input 10.

(a) TO SEQ :N
    IF :N > 50 STOP
    PRINT :N
    SEQ :N + 3
    END

(b)
```
TO LOW :N
   PRINT :N
   IF :N = 0 STOP
   LOW (:N - 2)
END
```

20. Predict the output when the following procedure is run with inputs 3, 7, and 5.

```
TO AV :X :Y :Z
PRINT (:X + :Y + :Z)/3
END
```

21. Predict the output when the following procedure is run with input 50.

```
TO DI :SIDE
REPEAT 4[FD :SIDE RT 90]
RT 45
FD :SIDE*SQRT 2
PRINT XCOR
PRINT YCOR
END
```

22. Predict the output when the following procedure is run with inputs 8 and 2.

```
TO GAV :X :Y
PRINT SQRT (:X * :Y)
END
```

INTRODUCTION

In this chapter, a knowledge of the material in the text is assumed, and we introduce problems that require skills from various chapters. This provides an opportunity of looking at problem solving from a broader point of view, one where the problem solver does not know to which specific topics the problem is related.

In the following examples, problem-solving strategies and the motives for various steps in a solution are discussed. Although not specifically indicated, the examples are solved by following the approach of *understanding the problem, devising a plan, carrying out the plan,* and *looking back.* Following these examples is a collection of problems, some of which are nontrivial. Do not expect to solve these problems without some hard work.

Example 14-1

In the circle in Figure 14-1, two perpendicular diameters are shown. From a point C on the circle, two segments $\overline{AC}$ and $\overline{CB}$ are drawn so that quadrilateral $ACBO$ is a rectangle. If the diameter of the circle is 10 cm, find the length of $\overline{AB}$.

Solution

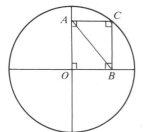

$\overline{AB}$ is the hypotenuse of right triangle AOB. One possible way to find $\overline{AB}$ is to use the Pythagorean Theorem, from which it follows that $(AB)^2 = (AO)^2 + (OB)^2$. Thus, to find $\overline{AB}$, we need to know the lengths of both $\overline{AO}$ and $\overline{OB}$. The lengths of these sides are not given. Moreover, it seems that knowing only the diameter of the circle is not sufficient to determine $\overline{AO}$ and $\overline{OB}$. Thus, using the Pythagorean Theorem does not appear to be a productive strategy.

Our new strategy is to find parts of a triangle using congruent or similar triangles. Triangle BCA is congruent to $\triangle AOB$. However, there is no more information about $\triangle BCA$ than about $\triangle AOB$. Since Figure 14-1 shows no other triangles, we need to draw an additional segment to define a new triangle. The newly constructed triangle should have sides of known lengths. Since the length of the diameter is 10 cm and the radius is 5 cm, the most natural choice is $\overline{OC}$ as shown in Figure 14-2. The diagonals of a rectangle are congruent. (In Chapter 10, this was shown by proving $\triangle ABO \cong \triangle COB$). Thus, $\overline{OC} \cong \overline{AB}$ and $AB = 5$ cm.

FIGURE 14-1

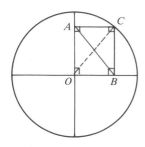

FIGURE 14-2

The solution to Example 14-1 focused on the goal of finding $\overline{AB}$ and relied on previous experiences in solving such problems by trying the Pythagorean Theorem and using congruent triangles. The Pythagorean Theorem approach was abandoned because of insufficient information. Next, a search for appropriate congruent triangles became the focus. This search became the new goal. In the congruent-triangle approach, we used all possible information from the problem along with previous definitions and related theorems. The related theorems gave new information that resulted in a solution.

Example 14-2

The king of Ilusia lost a war and was forced to divide his kingdom into a number of smaller countries, no two the same size. The king also had to distribute all 1000 bars of his gold in such a way that each country received 1 bar more than the next smaller country. No bars could be broken. If the king divided his kingdom into the least number of countries possible and divided his gold as described, how many countries were formed and how many bars of gold did each country receive?

Solution

Each country received one bar more than the next smaller country. Suppose the smallest country received n bars of gold. Then the next larger country received 1 bar more, and the next larger country 2 bars more, and so on. That is, the countries in order of size received $(n + 1)$ bars, $(n + 2)$ bars, $(n + 3)$ bars, and so on. The number of countries is unknown, so we designate that number by k.

Ordering countries according to size from smallest to largest and making Table 14-1 reveals a pattern. The kth country receives $n + (k - 1)$ bars of gold.

TABLE 14-1

Order of Country	Number of Bars Received
1	n
2	$n + 1$
3	$n + 2$
4	$n + 3$
5	$n + 4$
.	.
.	.
.	.
k	$n + (k - 1)$

The total number of gold bars is 1000. Because the total number of bars received by all countries is 1000, we have

$$n + (n + 1) + (n + 2) + (n + 3) + \cdots + (n + k - 1) = 1000$$

Thus, the problem involves finding a sum of consecutive natural numbers.

Recall that in Chapter 1 the similar problem of finding the sum of the first 100 natural numbers was solved by listing the numbers in the following way and computing the sum.

$$
\begin{array}{r}
1 + \quad 2 + \quad 3 + \quad 4 + \cdots + 100 \\
100 + \quad 99 + \quad 98 + \quad 97 + \cdots + \quad 1 \\
\hline
101 + 101 + 101 + 101 + \cdots + 101
\end{array}
$$

There are 100 sums of 101 in twice the desired sum, so we divide by 2 to obtain

$$\frac{100(101)}{2} = 5050.$$

A similar approach can be used to find the sum $n + (n + 1) + (n + 2) + (n + 3) + \cdots + (n + k - 1)$.

$$\begin{array}{cccccc}
n & + & (n + 1) & + & (n + 2) & + \cdots + & (n + k - 1) \\
(n + k - 1) & + & (n + k - 2) & + & (n + k - 3) & + \cdots + & n \\
\hline
(2n + k - 1) & + & (2n + k - 1) & + & (2n + k - 1) & + \cdots + & (2n + k - 1)
\end{array}$$

There are k sums of $2n + k - 1$ shown above and this is twice the desired sum. Hence, we divide by 2 to obtain $\dfrac{[k(2n + k - 1)]}{2}$. This result can be used as follows.

$$n + (n + 1) + (n + 2) + \cdots + (n + k - 1) = 1000$$

$$\frac{k}{2}(2n + k - 1) = 1000$$

$$k(2n + k - 1) = 2000$$

The last equation has two unknowns, k and n. To find k and n, we need another equation involving k and n. Unfortunately, no other condition that yields an additional equation is given in the problem.

A useful strategy in solving any problem is to make sure that no important information is neglected. One condition of the problem states that the number of countries, k, is the least number possible and $k \neq 1$. Also, since no bar can be broken, n and k must be natural numbers. Keeping these conditions in mind, we focus on $k(2n + k - 1) = 2000$. Because k and $2n + k - 1$ are natural numbers, they are factors of 2000. Also, k is the least number possible, so we start with $k = 2$. If $k = 2$, then $2 \cdot (2n + 2 - 1) = 2000$ and $n = 499\frac{1}{2}$, which is not a natural number. Hence, $k \neq 2$. Similarly, if $k = 4$, the next factor of 2000, then $n = 248\frac{1}{2}$, and hence, $k \neq 4$. However, if $k = 5$, then $n = 198$. Thus, the smallest country receives 198 bars of gold, and, consequently, the five countries receive 198, 199, 200, 201, and 202 bars, respectively.

It is easy to check the solution because $198 + 199 + 200 + 201 + 202 = 1000$. Can the problem be solved if there is a different number of bars? What solutions does the problem have if the number of countries is not minimized?

Example 14-3

In the central prison of Ilusia, there were 1000 cells numbered from 1 to 1000. All the cells were occupied, and each had a separate guard. After a revolution, the new queen ordered the guards to free certain prisoners based on the following scheme. The guards walk through the prison one at a time. The first guard opens all 1000 cells. The second guard follows immediately and closes all the cells with even numbers. The third guard follows and changes every third cell starting with cell 3, that is, closing the open cells and opening the closed cells. Similarly, the fourth guard starts at cell 4 and changes every fourth cell. This process continues until the 1000th guard passes through the prison, at which point the prisoners whose cells are open are freed. How many prisoners are freed?

Solution | The strategy of solving a simpler problem is used. Suppose there are only 20 cells. In the queen's scheme, no guard after the 20th touches the first 20 cells.

First, we consider the first 20 cells as the first 20 guards pass through. We denote an open cell by o and a closed cell by c. Table 14-2 shows the state of each cell, as changed by the guards. For example, the fourth guard opens cell 4, opens cell 8, closes cell 12, opens cell 16, and closes cell 20.

TABLE 14-2

Cell Number

Guard Number	1	2	3	4	5	6	7	8	9	10	11	12	13	14	15	16	17	18	19	20
1	o	o	o	o	o	o	o	o	o	o	o	o	o	o	o	o	o	o	o	o
2		c		c		c		c		c		c		c		c		c		c
3			c			o			c			o			c			o		
4				o				o				c				o				c
5					c					o					o					o
6						c						o						c		
7							c							o						
8								c								c				
9									o									o		
10										c										o
11											c									
12												c								
13													c							
14														c						
15															c					
16																o				
17																	c			
18																		c		
19																			c	
20																				c

The table shows that, after 20 guards pass, the only open cells are 1, 4, 9, and 16. Each of these numbers is a perfect square, 1^2, 2^2, 3^2, and 4^2. Will the pattern these numbers suggest continue for 1000 guards and cells? To help answer this question consider cell 25. The cell is opened by guard 1, closed by guard 5, and opened by guard 25, suggesting the answer is yes. (Note that 1, 5, and 25 are the only positive divisors of 25.)

What happened to cell 26 (a nonperfect square)? Cell 26 is opened by guard 1, closed by guard 2, opened by guard 13, and closed by guard 26 and, hence, remains closed. In general, we observe that a cell is changed only by guards whose numbers divide the cell number.

For the final state of a cell to be open, it must be opened one more time than it is closed; that is, the state is changed an odd number of times. For this to happen, the number of the cell must have an odd number of divisors. We can show that the open cells have numbers that are perfect squares by showing that only perfect squares have an odd number of divisors.

Recall that the divisors of a number appear in pairs (see Chapter 5). For example, the pairs of divisors of 80 and 81 are given by the following.

$$80 = 1 \cdot 80 = 2 \cdot 40 = 4 \cdot 20 = 5 \cdot 16 = 10 \cdot 8$$

$$81 = 1 \cdot 81 = 3 \cdot 27 = 9 \cdot 9$$

Thus, 80 has ten distinct divisors or five pairs. On the other hand, the perfect square 81 has five distinct divisors, two pairs of divisors (1, 81 and 3, 27) and a single divisor 9, which is paired with itself. Thus, 81 has an odd number of divisors. By Theorem 5-5 (Chapter 5), if d is a divisor of n, then $\frac{n}{d}$ also is a divisor of n. Consequently, for all divisors d of n, if $d \neq \frac{n}{d}$, then each divisor can be paired with a different divisor and n must have an even number of positive divisors. If, on the other hand, for some divisor d, $d = \frac{n}{d}$, then $n = d^2$, and all the divisors of n are paired with a different divisor, except d. Hence, the number of divisors of n is odd. Because $d = \frac{n}{d}$ occurs only when $n = d^2$, it follows that n has an odd number of divisors if and only if n is a perfect square. As a result, the freed prisoners are in the cells with numbers that are perfect squares less than 1000, namely, 1^2, 2^2, 3^2, 4^2, 5^2, 6^2, . . . , 31^2. Thus, 31 prisoners are freed.

Example 14-4

In a portion of a large city, the streets divide the city into square blocks of equal size, as shown in Figure 14-3. A taxi driver drives daily from point A to P. One day she drove from A to B along $\overline{AB}$ and then from B to P along $\overline{BP}$. If she does not want to cover any distance longer than $AB + BP$, how many possible routes are there from A to P?

FIGURE 14-3

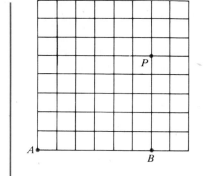

Solution

In order to travel the minimum distance, the taxi driver should only go north (upward) and east (to the right). Two routes are shown in Figure 14-4. For each of the routes, the total length of the horizontal segments is AB. Similarly, the total length of the vertical segments is BP. Thus, the length of each of the taxi driver's routes from A to P equals $AB + BP$.

FIGURE 14-4

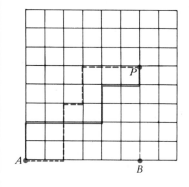

One way to solve the problem is by drawing all possible routes from A to P and counting them. Since that is an enormous task, we try looking for simpler versions of the problem. In Figure 14-5, there is only one possible route from A to C and only one route from A to F. In fact, each of the points on $\overleftrightarrow{AC}$ and $\overleftrightarrow{AF}$ can be reached via only one route.

FIGURE 14-5

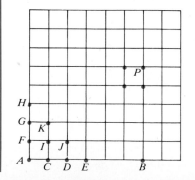

Next, we examine the routes from *A* to *I*. Only two are possible, *A—F—I* and *A—C—I*. From *A* to *J* there are three routes, namely, *A—C—D—J*, *A—C—I—J*, and *A—F—I—J*. Similarly, the number of routes to various other points from *A* can be counted. Figure 14-6 shows the number of possible routes to various points, starting from *A*.

FIGURE 14-6

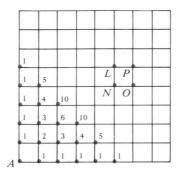

It appears that the number of routes to any given point from *A* is the sum of the number of routes to each of its two neighboring points, one immediately to the left and the other immediately below. If this pattern continues, it would be easy to work from point to point until we reach point *P*. The pattern can be justified because each of the routes from *N* to point *P* in Figure 14-6 can be obtained from the two neighboring points *L* and *O*. Any route from *A* to *P* must pass through either *L* or *O*. The number of routes from *A* to *P* that pass through *L* is the same as the number of routes from *A* to *L* because, for each route from *A* to *L*, there is one single route to *P* that passes through *L*. Similarly, the number of routes from *A* to *P* that pass through *O* is the same as the number of routes from *A* to *O*. Thus, the number of routes from *A* to *P* is the sum of the routes from *A* to *L* and from *A* to *O*. Since the pattern in Figure 14-6 continues, there are 462 routes from *A* to *P*, as shown in Figure 14-7.

FIGURE 14-7

	1	6	21	56	126	252	462
	1	5	15	35	70	*P* 126	210
	1	4	10	20	35	56	84
	1	3	6	10	15	21	28
	1	2	3	4	5	6	7
A	1	1	1	1	1	1	

You may wish to investigate this example further using the concept of combinations discussed in Chapter 8.

Example 14-5

Howie, Frank, and Dandy each tried to predict the winners of Sunday's professional football games. The only team not picked that is playing Sunday was the Giants. The choices for each person were as follows.

Howie: Cowboys, Steelers, Vikings, Bills

Frank: Steelers, Packers, Cowboys, Redskins

Dandy: Redskins, Vikings, Jets, Cowboys

If the only teams playing Sunday are those just mentioned, which teams will play which other teams?

Solution

At first glance, it may appear that there is not enough information to solve this problem, but recording the information in a Venn diagram may provide the insight we need. A Venn diagram with circles H, F, D for each of the pickers is shown in Figure 14-8. The three circles divide the universal set into eight disjoint regions: (a), (b), (c), (d), (e), (f), (g), (h). Each sportscaster picked the Cowboys to win. Since this was the only team that all three picked to win, region (e) consists only of the Cowboys. We can place the Giants in region (h) since none of the three picked the Giants. Howie and Frank both picked the Steelers, so now the Steelers belong in region (b). Howie and Dandy both picked the Vikings, so the Vikings belong in region (d). Frank and Dandy both picked the Redskins, so they belong in region (f). This leaves region (a) for the Bills, region (c) for the Packers, and region (g) for the Jets. This information is given in Figure 14-9. To complete the problem, we must now determine which teams will play each other.

FIGURE 14-8

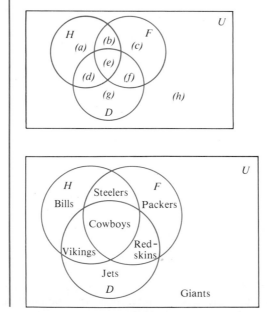

FIGURE 14-9

From Figure 14-9, we know the Cowboys will not play the Steelers, Bills, or Vikings since Howie picked all these teams as winners. Likewise, the Cowboys will not play the Packers or the Redskins since Frank picked all these teams as winners. Similarly, the Cowboys will not play the Jets since Dandy picked both the Cowboys and Jets as winners. This leaves the Cowboys with only one possible opponent, namely the Giants.

Next, we can determine which team the Vikings will play. Since the Vikings are picked by both Howie and Dandy, their opponent must be outside circles *H* and *D*. This means that the Vikings will play the Packers. In a similar manner, we can deduce that the Steelers will play the Jets, and the Redskins will play the Bills. The four games on Sunday will be:

Cowboys vs. Giants

Vikings vs. Packers

Steelers vs. Jets

Redskins vs. Bills

Each team has an opponent and there are no contradictions in the given information. Problems of this type can also be generated from other events, such as baseball, basketball, or even dating, where some type of pairing is used.

PROBLEM SET 14-1

Problems, 19, 20, 21, 24, 25, 32, and 33 are modifications of the following problems from the Mathematical Association of America's Annual High School Mathematics Examination: 9 (1972); 31 (1970); 15 (1971); 23 (1971); 34 (1970); 32 (1970); and 34 (1968). Also, Problems 17 and 18 are modifications of Problems 190 and 153, respectively, taken from the *Comprehensive School Mathematics Program, Elements of Mathematics, Book B, EM Problem Book,* by CEMREL Inc. (1975).

1. A ball bounces 0.8 of the distance from which it is dropped each time it is dropped. If it is dropped from a height of 6 feet, what is the least number of bounces the ball makes before it rises to a height of less than 1 foot?

2. Jim has saved some silver dollars. He wants to divide them among Tom, Dick, Mary, and Sue so that Tom gets $\frac{1}{2}$ of the total amount, Dick gets $\frac{1}{4}$, Mary gets $\frac{1}{5}$, and Sue gets 9 of the dollars. How many dollars has Jim saved?

3. During the baseball season thus far, Reggie has been at bat 380 times and has a batting average of 0.291—that is, his number of hits divided by 380 is 0.291. If he has 60 more official times at bat this season, how many hits must he get in order to end the season with a batting average of 0.300 or better?

4. A race track is 400 feet along the straight section and has a semicircle of radius 50 feet at each end. If one horse runs 10 feet from the inside railing at all times and a second horse runs 20 feet from the railing at all times, what is the difference in distance covered by the two horses in one lap of the track?

5. A circular object $\frac{1}{2}$ inch in diameter is dropped on a large grid consisting of squares that measure 3 inches on a side. If the circular object falls within the grid, what is the probability that it will not touch a grid line?

6. Willie can row 4 miles per hour in still water. If it takes him 2 hours to cover a certain distance rowing upstream and only 1 hour to row the same distance downstream, how fast is the current moving?

7. What is the least number of weights that can be used in order to be able to weigh any amount from 1 ounce to 680 ounces on a balance scale?

8. A computer is programmed to scan digits of successive integers. For example, if it scans the integers 1, 2, 3, 4, 5, 6, 7, 8, 9, 10, 11, 12, it has scanned 15 digits. How many digits has the computer scanned if it scans the consecutive integers from 1 through 10,000,000?

9. Find the remainder when $5^{999,999}$ is divided by 7.

10. A box contains ten red balls and five white balls. One ball is drawn at random from the box and is replaced by a ball of the opposite color. Now if a ball is drawn from the box, what is the probability that it is red?

11. If Tom can beat Dick by 100 m in a 2-km race and Dick can beat Harry by 200 m in a 2-km race, then by how many meters can Tom beat Harry in a 2-km race?

12. Suppose you have one 5-L container and one 3-L container. How can you take out exactly 7 L of water from a well?

13. A single-elimination handball tournament was organized. There were 98 entrants, so in the first round there were 49 matches. In the second round, the 49 players were paired in 24 matches and one player received a bye. In the third round, the 25 players were then paired in 12 matches with one bye. The play and the pairing continued until a champion was determined.
    (a) How many matches were played?
    (b) If n players were entered in the tournament, how many matches would be required?

14. A circular race track for two runners has a 40-m radius for the inside running lane and a 41-m radius for the outside running lane.
    (a) How much of a head start should the outside runner be given?
    (b) How much of a head start should the outside runner be given if the radius of the inside running lane is 80 m and the radius of the outside lane is 81 m?

15. Without using a calculator, find the number of digits in the number $2^{12} \cdot 5^8$.

16. (a) Discover a pattern for the following sequence.

$$\frac{3}{5}, \frac{7}{9}, \frac{11}{13}, \frac{15}{17}, \frac{19}{21}, \cdots$$

    (b) Find the 1000th fraction in the sequence.
    ★ (c) Prove that all the fractions (there are infinitely many) in the sequence are in simplest form.

17. Start with a piece of paper. Cut it into five pieces. Take any one of the pieces and again cut it into five pieces. Then pick one of these pieces and cut it into five pieces, and so on.

(a) What numbers of pieces can be obtained in this way?

(b) What is the number of pieces after the nth experiment?

18. In the figure below, $\overline{BC}$ and $\overline{BE}$ represent two positions of a ladder. How wide is $\overline{AD}$ and how long is the ladder if $AC = 12$ m, $ED = 9$ m, $\overline{CB} \cong \overline{BE}$, and $\overline{CB} \perp \overline{BE}$?

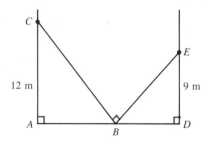

19. Ann and Sue bought identical boxes of stationery. Ann used hers to write 1-sheet letters and Sue used hers to write 3-sheet letters. Ann used all the envelopes and had 50 sheets of paper left, while Sue used all the sheets of paper and had 50 envelopes left. Find the number of sheets of paper in each box.

20. If a number is selected at random from the set of all five-digit numbers in which the sum of the digits equals 43, what is the probability that the number is divisible by 11?

21. An aquarium is in the shape of a right rectangular prism. It has a rectangular face that is 10 in. wide and 8 in. high. When the aquarium is tilted, the water in it just covers an 8 in. by 10 in. end, but only three-fourths of the rectangular bottom. Find the depth of the water when the aquarium is level on the table.

22. From a wire 10 units long, different shapes are constructed: a square, a rectangle with one side 2 units long, an equilateral triangle, a right isosceles triangle, and a circle.
    (a) Find the area of each shape. Which shape has the greatest area?
    (b) Make a conjecture concerning which figure has the greatest area among all figures with a given perimeter.

23. Susan's executive salary increased each of the past 2 years by 50% over the preceding year. Her present salary is $100,000 per year. To the nearest dollar, how much did she make 2 years ago?

24. Teams A and B play a series of games. The odds of either team winning any game are even. Team A must

win two games and Team B must win three games to win the series. Find the odds in favor of Team A winning the series.

25. Find the greatest integer such that when each of the numbers 13,511, 13,903, and 14,589 is divided by this integer, the remainders are the same.

26. Take a two- or three-digit number and create a new number by reversing the digits of the original number. Then, subtract the lesser number from the greater. Observe that the difference is divisible by 9. For example, $561 - 165$ is 396, which is divisible by 9. Is this always true? Justify your answer.

27. What is the angle between the clock hands at 2:15?

28. Given a regular hexagon and a point in its plane, and using only a ruler and a compass, construct a straight line through the given point that separates the given hexagon into two parts of equal area.

29. Find the sum of all the digits in the integers 1 through 1,000,000,000.

30. Two adjacent sides of a parallelogram are on the lines given by $3x - 2y = 6$ and $5x + 4y = 21$. One vertex is at $(2, ^-1)$. Without graphing, find the equations of the lines containing the other two sides and the coordinates of the point where the diagonals intersect.

31. Without graphing, find the center and radius of the circle passing through the points with coordinates $(0, 0)$, $(1, ^-3)$, and $(4, 0)$.

★ 32. Starting at the same time from diametrically opposite points, Linda and David travel around a circular track at uniform speeds in opposite directions. They meet after David has traveled 100 m and a second time 60 m before Linda completes one lap. Find the circumference of the track.

★ 33. With 400 members voting, the House of Representatives defeated a bill. A revote, with the same members voting, resulted in passage of the bill by twice the margin with which it was originally defeated. The number voting for the bill on the revote was $\frac{12}{11}$ of the number voting against it originally. How many more members voted for the bill the second time than voted for it the first time?

★ 34. Lines from the vertices of square $ABCD$ to the midpoints of the sides M, N, O, and P are shown in the following figure.
    (a) Prove that quadrilateral $HGFE$ is a square.
    (b) What is the area of square $HGFE$ if the area of quadrilateral $ABCD$ is 100 cm²? Justify your answer.

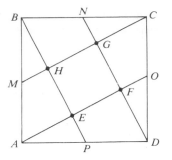

35. The "triangle" pictured below is called the **Pascal triangle,** after the French mathematician Blaise Pascal. Each number in the triangle, except the ones on the "boundary," equals the sum of two immediate neighboring numbers in the preceding row. (Note how the numbers in the triangle compare with those in Figure 14-6.)

									Row
				1					(0)
			1		1				(1)
		1		2		1			(2)
	1		3		3		1		(3)
1		4		6		4		1	(4)
1	5	10		10		5	1		(5)
1	6	15	20		15	6	1		(6)
1	7	21	35	35	21	7	1		(7)

(a) Continue the triangle by finding two more rows.
(b) Find the sum of the numbers in the first row, the second row, the third row, and the fourth row. Do you notice a pattern? Can you predict the sum of the numbers in the tenth row? Make a general conjecture for the sum of the numbers in the nth row.
(c) Find the "alternate" sum of numbers in each row after row 1; that is,

$$1 - 1$$
$$1 - 2 + 1$$
$$1 - 3 + 3 - 1$$
$$1 - 4 + 6 - 4 + 1$$

(d) Find other patterns among the numbers in the Pascal triangle.

★ 36. Justify your conjecture in Problem 35(b).

37. In 1983 the number of cars using the Chicago Loop and Inter-Mountain Bypass highways were 220,819,000 and 66,944,000, respectively. If the annual usage growth rates for these two highways were 1.5% and 2.9%, respectively, and if these usage rates were to remain constant, in what year would the number of cars using the Inter-Mountain Bypass equal or surpass the number of cars using the Chicago Loop? Write a computer program to find how many cars would use each highway in that year.

SELECTED BIBLIOGRAPHY

Averbach, B., and O. Chein. *Mathematics, Problem Solving Through Recreational Mathematics*. San Francisco, Calif.: W. H. Freeman Co., 1980

Brousseau, A. *Mathematics Contest Problems*. Palo Alto, Calif.: Creative Publications, 1972.

Charosh, M. *Mathematical Challenges*. Reston, Va.: NCTM, 1965.

Greenes, C., J. Gregory, and D. Seymour. *Successful Problem Solving Techniques*. Palo Alto, Calif.: Creative Publications, 1977.

Greenes, C., R. Spungin, and J. Dombrowski. *Problem-Mathics*. Palo Alto, Calif.: Creative Publications, 1977.

Hill, T. *Mathematical Challenges 11 Plus Six*. Reston, Va.: NCTM, 1974.

Honsberger, R. *Mathematical Morsels*. Washington, D.C.: The Mathematical Association of America, 1978.

Hughes, B. *Thinking Through Problems*. Palo Alto, Calif.: Creative Publications, 1976.

Kordemsky, B. *The Moscow Puzzles,* New York: Charles Scribner's Sons, 1972.

Krulik, S., and J. Rudnick. *Problem Solving: A Handbook for Teachers*. Boston, Mass.: Allyn and Bacon, Inc., 1980.

Krulik, S., and R. Reys. *Problem Solving in School Mathematics, 1980 Yearbook*. Reston, Va.: NCTM, 1980.

Libeskind, S. "A Problem Solving Approach to Teaching Mathematics." *Educational Studies in Mathematics,* 8 (1977): 167–179.

Mira, J. *Mathematical Teasers*. New York: Barnes and Noble Books, 1970.

Pederson, J., and F. Armbruster. *A New Twist*. Reading, Mass.: Addison-Wesley, 1979.

Polya, G. *How to Solve It*. Princeton, N.J.: Princeton University Press, 1957.

Polya, G. *Mathematical Discovery*. 2 vols. New York: Wiley, 1962–1965.

Polya, G. *Mathematics and Plausible Reasoning*. 2 vols. Princeton, N.J.: Princeton University Press, 1954.

Porter, R. *Project a Puzzle*. Reston, Va.: NCTM, 1978.

Salkind, C., and J. Earl. *The Contest Problem Book III*. Washington, D.C.: The Mathematical Association of America, 1973.

Appendix I
Informal Logic

AI-1 STATEMENTS

statement

Logic deals with reasoning and is a tool used in mathematical thinking. In this section we deal with the basics of logic necessary for problem solving. In logic, a **statement** is a sentence that is either true or false, but not both. The following are examples of statements, along with their truth values, where T stands for true and F stands for false:

1. George Washington is currently the president of the United States. (F)
2. $2 + 3 = 7$ (F)
3. $2 \cdot (10 + 5) \leq 30$ (T)
4. Every triangle has four sides. (F)
5. All girls have red hair. (F)
6. Some woman has been on the Supreme Court of the United States. (T)

Expressions such as, "How tall are you," "$2 + 3$," or "Close the door" are not statements since they cannot be classified as true or false. The following expressions are also not statements since their truth value cannot be determined without more information:

1. She has blue eyes.
2. $x + 7 = 18$
3. $2y + 7 > 1$

Each of the preceding expressions becomes a statement if, for (1), "she" is identified, and for (2) and (3), values are assigned to x and y, respectively. However, an expression involving *he* or *she* or x or y may already be a statement. For example, "If he is over 210 cm tall, then he is over 2 m tall," and "$2(x + y) = 2x + 2y$" are both statements since they are true no matter who *he* is or what the values of x and y are.

negation

From a given statement, it is possible to create a new statement by forming a **negation.** The negation of a statement is a statement with the opposite truth value of the given statement; that is, if the statement is true, its negation is false and if the statement is false, its negation is true. Consider the statement "It is snowing." The negation of this statement is "It is not true that it is snowing." Stated in a simpler form, the negation is "It is not snowing." In general, the negation of a simple declarative sentence is formed by negating the verb in the sentence or by using the phrase "it is not true that" to preface the sentence.

Example AI-1 | Negate each of the following statements.

(a) $2 + 3 = 5$
(b) A hexagon has six sides.
(c) Today is not Monday.

Solution | (a) $2 + 3 \neq 5$
(b) A hexagon does not have six sides.
(c) Today is Monday.

Are the statements, "The shirt is blue," and "The shirt is green," negations of each other? To check, we recall that a statement and its negation must have opposite truth values. If the shirt is actually red, then both of the statements are false and, hence, cannot be negations of each other. However, the statements, "The shirt is blue," and "The shirt is not blue," are negations of each other, since they have opposite truth values no matter what color the shirt really is.

quantifiers   Some statements involve **quantifiers** and are more complicated to negate. Quantifiers include words such as *all*, *some*, *every*, and *there exists*. These words are discussed in more detail later in the appendix, but they are discussed here in regard to their negation.

universal quantifiers   The quantifiers *all*, *every*, and *no* refer to each and every element in a set and are called **universal quantifiers.** The quantifiers *some* and *there exists at least one* refer to one or more, or possibly all, of the elements in a set. *Some* and *there exists*

existential quantifiers   are called **existential quantifiers.** Examples with universal and existential quantifiers are as follows:

All numbers less than 10 are less than 100. (universal)

Every student is important. (universal)

For each counting number x, $x + 0 = x$. (universal)

Some roses are red. (existential)

There exists at least one even counting number less than three. (existential)

There exist women who are taller than 200 cm. (existential)

Consider the following statement involving the existential quantifier *some*. "Some teachers at Paxon School have blue eyes." This means that at least one teacher at Paxon School has blue eyes. It does not rule out the possibilities that all the Paxon teachers have blue eyes or that some of the Paxon teachers do not have blue eyes. Since the negation of a true statement is false, neither "Some teachers at Paxon School do not have blue eyes" nor "All teachers at Paxon have blue eyes" are negations of the original statement. One possible negation of the original statement is, "No teachers at Paxon School have blue eyes."

To discover if one statement is a negation of another, we use arguments similar to the above to determine if they have opposite truth values in all possible cases. Some general forms of quantified statements with their negations follow.

Statement	Negation
Some *a* are *b*.	No *a* is *b*.
Some *a* are not *b*.	All *a* are *b*.
All *a* are *b*.	Some *a* are not *b*.
No *a* is *b*.	Some *a* are *b*.

Example AI-2   Negate each of the following statements.

(a) All students like hamburgers.
(b) Some people like mathematics.
(c) No professor has red hair.
(d) Some graduates will not find jobs.

Solution

(a) Some students do not like hamburgers.
(b) No people like mathematics.
(c) Some professors have red hair.
(d) All graduates will find jobs.

Examples of negations of quantified statements involving mathematical expressions are given below:

There exists a counting number x such that $3x = 6$.
For all counting numbers x, $3x = 3x$.

Possible negations of these statements follow:

There does not exist a counting number x such that $3x = 6$.
There exists a counting number x such that $3x \neq 3x$.

Using the symbol p to represent a statement, the negation of the statement p is denoted by $\sim p$. All possible true-false patterns for statements are often shown in truth tables. Table AI-1 summarizes the truth values for p and $\sim p$.

TABLE AI-1

p	$\sim p$
T	F
F	T

PROBLEM SET AI-1

1. Determine which of the following are statements and then classify each statement as true or false.
   (a) $2 + 4 = 8$
   (b) Shut the window.
   (c) Los Angeles is a state.
   (d) He is in town.
   (e) What time is it?
   (f) $5x = 15$
   (g) $3 \cdot 2 = 6$
   (h) $2x^2 > x$

2. Use quantifiers to make each of the following true where x is an integer.
   (a) $x + 8 = 11$
   (b) $x + 0 = x$
   (c) $x^2 = 4$
   (d) $x + 1 = x + 2$

3. Use quantifiers to make each equation in Problem 2 false.

4. Write the negation for each of the following statements.
   (a) The book has 500 pages.
   (b) Six is less than eight.
   (c) Johnny is not thin.
   (d) $3 \cdot 5 = 15$
   (e) Some people have blond hair.
   (f) All dogs have four legs.
   (g) Some cats do not have nine lives.
   (h) No dogs can fly.
   (i) All squares are rectangles.
   (j) Not all rectangles are squares.
   (k) For all integers x, $x + 3 = 3 + x$.
   (l) There exists an integer x such that $3 \cdot (x + 2) = 12$.
   (m) Every counting number is divisible by itself and one.
   (n) Not all integers are divisible by 2.
   (o) For all integers x, $5x + 4x = 9x$.

AI-2   COMPOUND STATEMENTS

compound statement

From two given statements it is possible to create a new **compound statement** by using a connective such as *and*. For example, "It is snowing," and "The ski run is open," together with *and* give, "It is snowing and the ski run is open." Other compound statements can be obtained by using the connective *or*. For example, "It is snowing or the ski run is open." Lowercase letters are used to represent statements. The symbols $\wedge$ and $\vee$ are used to represent the connectives *and* and *or*, respectively. For example, if p represents "It is snowing," and if q represents "The ski run is open," then "It is snowing and the ski run is open" is denoted by $p \wedge q$. Similarly, "It is snowing or the ski run is open" is denoted by $p \vee q$.

The truth value of any compound statement, such as $p \wedge q$, is defined using the truth table of each of the simple statements. Since each of the statements p and q may be either true or false, there are four distinct possibilities as shown in Table AI-2. The compound statement $p \wedge q$ is called the **conjunction** of p and q and is defined to be true if and only if both p and q are true. Otherwise it is false.

conjunction

TABLE AI-2

p	q	$p \wedge q$
T	T	T
T	F	F
F	T	F
F	F	F

disjunction

The compound statement p or q is called the **disjunction** of p and q. In everyday language, *or* is not always interpreted in the same way. For example, "I will go to a movie or I will read a book" usually means that I will either go to a movie or read, but not do both. On the other hand, if a student says, "I will major in mathematics or in education," the student may major in one or the other or both. In the first statement, the *or* was an *exclusive* or while in the second, it was an *inclusive* or. Either of the meanings for *or* could be adopted, but we use the inclusive meaning. Hence, $p \lor q$ is defined to be false if both p and q are false, and true in all other cases. This is summarized by Table AI-3.

TABLE AI-3

p	q	$p \lor q$
T	T	T
T	F	T
F	T	T
F	F	F

Example AI-3

Given the following statements, classify each of the conjunctions as true or false.

p: $2 + 3 = 5$ r: $5 + 3 = 9$
q: $2 \cdot 3 = 6$ s: $2 \cdot 4 = 9$

(a) $p \land q$ (b) $p \land r$ (c) $s \land q$
(d) $r \land s$ (e) $\sim p \land q$ (f) $\sim(p \land q)$
(g) $p \lor q$ (h) $p \lor r$ (i) $s \lor q$
(j) $r \lor s$ (k) $\sim p \lor q$ (l) $\sim(p \lor q)$

Solution

(a) p is true and q is true, so $p \land q$ is true.
(b) p is true and r is false, so $p \land r$ is false.
(c) s is false and q is true, so $s \land q$ is false.
(d) r is false and s is false, so $r \land s$ is false.
(e) $\sim p$ is false and q is true, so $\sim p \land q$ is false.
(f) $p \land q$ is true [part (a)], so $\sim(p \land q)$ is false.
(g) p is true and q is true, so $p \lor q$ is true.
(h) p is true and r is false, so $p \lor r$ is true.
(i) s is false and q is true, so $s \lor q$ is true.
(j) r is false and s is false, so $r \lor s$ is false.
(k) $\sim p$ is false and q is true, so $\sim p \lor q$ is true.
(l) $p \lor q$ is true [part (g)], so $\sim(p \lor q)$ is false.

logically equivalent

Not only are truth tables used to summarize the truth values of compound statements, they are also used to determine if two statements are logically equivalent. Two statements are **logically equivalent** if and only if they have the same truth values. For example, consider $\sim p \vee \sim q$ and $\sim(p \wedge q)$. Table AI-4 shows headings and the four distinct possibilities for p and q. In the column headed $\sim p$, we write the negations of the p column. In the $\sim q$ column, we write the negation of the q column. Next, we use the values in the $\sim p$ and the $\sim q$ columns to construct the $\sim p \vee \sim q$ column. To find the truth values for $\sim(p \wedge q)$, we use the p and q columns to find the truth value for $p \wedge q$ and, then, negate $p \wedge q$.

TABLE AI-4

p	q	$\sim p$	$\sim q$	$\sim p \vee \sim q$	$p \vee q$	$\sim(p \wedge q)$
T	T	F	F	F	T	F
T	F	F	T	T	F	T
F	T	T	F	T	F	T
F	F	T	T	T	F	T

Note that $\sim p \vee \sim q$ has the same truth values as $\sim(p \wedge q)$. Thus, the statements are logically equivalent. The reader will find an analogue to this logical equivalence in Chapter 2. The equivalence between $\sim p \vee \sim q$ and $\sim(p \wedge q)$ along with the equivalence between $\sim(p \vee q)$ and $\sim p \wedge \sim q$ are referred to as **DeMorgan's Laws**.

DeMorgan's Laws

PROBLEM SET AI-2

1. Complete each of the following truth tables.

    (a)
    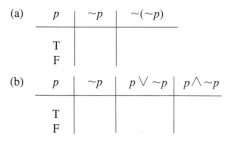

p	$\sim p$	$\sim(\sim p)$
T		
F		

    (b)

p	$\sim p$	$p \vee \sim p$	$p \wedge \sim p$
T			
F			

    (c) Based on part (a), is p logically equivalent to $\sim(\sim p)$?

    (d) Based on part (b), is $p \vee \sim p$ logically equivalent to $p \wedge \sim p$?

2. If q stands for "This course is easy," and r stands for "Lazy students do not study," write each of the following in symbolic form.

    (a) This course is easy and lazy students do not study.

    (b) Lazy students do not study or this course is not easy.

    (c) It is false that both this course is easy and lazy students do not study.

    (d) This course is not easy.

3. If p is false and q is true, find the truth values for each of the following.

    (a) $p \wedge q$ (b) $p \vee q$

    (c) $\sim p$ (d) $\sim q$

    (e) $\sim(\sim p)$ (f) $\sim p \vee q$

    (g) $p \wedge \sim q$ (h) $\sim(p \vee q)$

    (i) $\sim(\sim p \wedge q)$ (j) $\sim q \wedge \sim p$

4. Find the truth value for each statement in Problem 3 if p is false and q is false.

5. For each of the following, is the pair of statements logically equivalent?

    (a) $\sim(p \vee q)$ and $\sim p \vee \sim q$

    (b) $\sim(p \vee q)$ and $\sim p \wedge \sim q$

    (c) $\sim(p \wedge q)$ and $\sim p \wedge \sim q$

    (d) $\sim(p \wedge q)$ and $\sim p \vee \sim q$

6. Complete the following truth table.

p	q	$\sim p$	$\sim q$	$\sim p \vee q$
T	T			
T	F			
F	T			
F	F			

7. Apply DeMorgan's Laws to restate the following in a logically equivalent form.

(a) It is not both true that today is Wednesday and the month is June.

(b) It is not both true that yesterday I ate breakfast and watched television.

(c) It is not raining or it is not July.

BRAIN TEASER

An explorer landed on an island inhabited by two tribes, the Abes and the Babes. Abes always tell the truth and Babes always lie. The explorer met three natives on the shore. He asked the first native to name his tribe and the native responded in his native tongue, which the explorer did not understand. The second native stated that the first native said that he was an Abe. The third native then stated that the first native had said he was a Babe. To what tribes do the second and third natives belong?

AI-3   CONDITIONALS AND BICONDITIONALS

conditionals
implications

Statements expressed in the form "if p, then q" are called **conditionals,** or **implications,** and are denoted by $p \rightarrow q$. Such statements can also be read, "p implies q." Examples of conditional statements follow:

If it is raining, then the grass is wet.

If I pass the final, then I will pass the course.

If you mow the lawn, then you can go to the movies.

A clock striking 12 times implies that it is noon.

An implication may also be thought of as a promise. Suppose Betty makes the promise, "If I get a raise, then I will take you to dinner." If Betty keeps her promise, the implication is true; if Betty breaks her promise, the implication is false. Consider the following four possibilities.

	p	q	
(1)	T	T	Betty gets the raise; she takes you to dinner.
(2)	T	F	Betty gets the raise; she does not take you to dinner.
(3)	F	T	Betty does not get the raise; she takes you to dinner.
(4)	F	F	Betty does not get the raise; she does not take you to dinner.

The only case in which Betty breaks her promise is when she gets her raise and fails to take you to dinner, case (2). If she does not get the raise, she can either take you to dinner or not without breaking her promise. The definition of implication is summarized in Table AI-5. Observe that the only case for which implication is false is when p is true and q is false.

TABLE AI-5

p	q	$p \rightarrow q$
T	T	T
T	F	F
F	T	T
F	F	T

Implications may be worded in several ways:

1. If the sun shines, then the swimming pool is open. (If p, then q.)
2. If the sun shines, the swimming pool is open. (If p, q.)
3. The swimming pool is open if the sun shines. (q, if p.)
4. The sun shines implies the swimming pool is open. (p implies q.)

Any implication $p \rightarrow q$ has three related implication statements.

Statement:	If p, then q.	$p \rightarrow q$
Converse:	If q, then p.	$q \rightarrow p$
Inverse:	If not p, then not q.	$\sim p \rightarrow \sim q$
Contrapositive:	If not q, then not p.	$\sim q \rightarrow \sim p$

Example AI-4

Write the converse, the inverse, and the contrapositive for each of the following statements.

(a) If $2x = 6$, then $x = 3$.
(b) If I am in San Francisco, then I am in California.

Solution

(a) *Converse:* If $x = 3$, then $2x = 6$.
   Inverse: If $2x \neq 6$, then $x \neq 3$.
   Contrapositive: If $x \neq 3$, then $2x \neq 6$.
(b) *Converse:* If I am in California, then I am in San Francisco.
   Inverse: If I am not in San Francisco, then I am not in California.
   Contrapositive: If I am not in California, then I am not in San Francisco.

As Example AI-4(b) shows, a statement and its converse do not necessarily have the same truth value. On the other hand, an implication and its contrapositive do have the same truth value. Table AI-6 shows that, in general, a conditional statement and its contrapositive are logically equivalent and the converse and inverse of a conditional statement are logically equivalent.

TABLE AI-6

p	q	$\sim p$	$\sim q$	$p \rightarrow q$	$q \rightarrow p$	$\sim p \rightarrow \sim q$	$\sim q \rightarrow \sim p$
T	T	F	F	T	T	T	T
T	F	F	T	F	T	T	F
F	T	T	F	T	F	F	T
F	F	T	T	T	T	T	T

biconditional

Connecting a statement and its converse with the connective *and* gives $(p \rightarrow q) \wedge (q \rightarrow p)$. This compound statement can be written as $p \leftrightarrow q$ and usually is read "p if and only if q." The statement "p if and only if q," is called a **biconditional.** A truth table for $p \leftrightarrow q$ is given in Table AI-7. Observe that $p \leftrightarrow q$ is true only if p and q have the same truth values—that is, only if both statements are true or both are false.

TABLE AI-7

p	q	$p \rightarrow q$	$q \rightarrow p$	$(p \rightarrow q) \wedge (q \rightarrow p)$ or $p \leftrightarrow q$
T	T	T	T	T
T	F	F	T	F
F	T	T	F	F
F	F	T	T	T

Example AI-5

Given the following statements, classify each of the biconditionals as true or false.

p: $2 = 2$ r: $2 = 1$
q: $2 \neq 1$ s: $2 + 3 = 1 + 3$

(a) $p \leftrightarrow q$ (b) $p \leftrightarrow r$ (c) $s \leftrightarrow q$ (d) $r \leftrightarrow s$

Solution

(a) $p \rightarrow q$ is true and $q \rightarrow p$ is true, so $p \leftrightarrow q$ is true.
(b) $p \rightarrow r$ is false and $r \rightarrow p$ is true, so $p \leftrightarrow r$ is false.
(c) $s \rightarrow q$ is true and $q \rightarrow s$ is false, so $s \leftrightarrow q$ is false.
(d) $r \rightarrow s$ is true and $s \rightarrow r$ is true, so $r \leftrightarrow s$ is true.

PROBLEM SET AI-3

1. Write each of the following in symbolic form if p is the statement, "It is raining," and q is the statement, "The grass is wet."
   (a) If it is raining, then the grass is wet.
   (b) If it is not raining, then the grass is wet.
   (c) If it is raining, then the grass is not wet.
   (d) The grass is wet if it is raining.
   (e) The grass is not wet implies that it is not raining.
   (f) The grass is wet if and only if it is raining.

2. For each of the following implications, state the converse, inverse, and contrapositive.
   (a) If you eat Meaties, then you are good in sports.
   (b) If you do not like this book, then you do not like mathematics.
   (c) If you do not use Ultra Brush toothpaste, then you have cavities.
   (d) If you are good at logic, then your grades are high.
3. Construct a truth table for each of the following.
   (a) $p \rightarrow (p \vee q)$ (b) $(p \wedge q) \rightarrow q$
   (c) $p \leftrightarrow \sim(\sim p)$ (d) $\sim(p \rightarrow q)$
4. If p is true and q is false, find the truth values for each of the following.
   (a) $\sim p \rightarrow \sim q$ (b) $\sim(p \rightarrow q)$
   (c) $(p \vee q) \rightarrow (p \wedge q)$ (d) $p \rightarrow \sim p$
   (e) $(p \vee \sim p) \rightarrow p$ (f) $(p \vee q) \leftrightarrow (p \vee q)$
5. If p is false and q is false, find the truth values for each of the statements in Problem 4.
6. Can an implication and its converse both be false? Explain your answer.
7. Tom makes the true statement, "If it rains, then I am going to the movies." Does it follow logically that if it does not rain, then Tom did not go to the movies?
8. Consider the statement, "If every digit of a number is 6, then the number is divisible by 3." Which of the following is logically equivalent to the statement?
   (a) If every digit of a number is not 6, then the number is not divisible by 3.
   (b) If a number is not divisible by 3, then every digit of the number is not 6.
   (c) If a number is divisible by 3, then every digit of the number is 6.
9. Write a statement logically equivalent to the statement, "If a number is a multiple of 8, then it is a multiple of 4."
10. A **tautology** is a statement that is always true. Prove that the following are tautologies.
   (a) $(p \rightarrow q) \rightarrow [(p \wedge r) \rightarrow q]$ *Law of Added Hypothesis*
   (b) $[(p \rightarrow q) \wedge p] \rightarrow q$ *Law of Detachment*
   (c) $[(p \rightarrow q) \wedge (\sim q)] \rightarrow \sim p$ *Modus Tollens*
   (d) $[(p \rightarrow q) \wedge (q \rightarrow r)] \rightarrow (p \rightarrow r)$ *Chain Rule*

AI-4 REASONING AND LOGIC PROBLEMS

hypotheses
conclusion
valid

Reasoning situations develop when certain given statements, the **hypotheses,** are used to deduce another statement called a **conclusion.** The reasoning is said to be **valid** if the conclusion follows unavoidably from the hypotheses. Consider the following example.

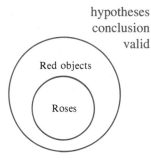

FIGURE AI-1
       Euler diagram

Hypotheses: All roses are red.
                       This flower is a rose.
Conclusion: Therefore, this flower is red.

A circle can be used to represent all roses and another circle to represent all red objects. The statement "All roses are red" can be written as the implication "If an object is a rose, then it is red." The statement can then be pictured with an **Euler diagram,** as shown in Figure AI-1.

The information "This flower is a rose," implies that this flower must belong to the circle containing the roses, as pictured in Figure AI-2. This flower also belongs to the circle containing the red objects. Thus, the reasoning is valid because it is impossible to draw a picture satisfying the hypotheses and contradicting the conclusion.

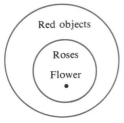

Red objects

Roses

Flower

FIGURE AI-2

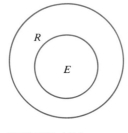

R

E

FIGURE AI-3

Consider the following argument.

Hypotheses: All elementary teachers are rich.
              Some rich people are not thin.
Conclusion: Therefore, no elementary teacher is thin.

Let E be the set of elementary teachers, R be the set of rich people, and T be the set of thin people. Then the statement, "All elementary teachers are rich," can be pictured as in Figure AI-3. The statement, "Some rich people are not thin," can be pictured in several ways. Three of these are illustrated in Figure AI-4.

According to Figure AI-4(c), it is possible that some elementary teachers are thin, and yet the given statements are satisfied. Therefore, the conclusion that "No elementary teacher is thin," does not follow from the given hypotheses. Hence, the reasoning is not valid.

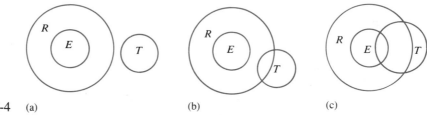

FIGURE AI-4   (a)   (b)   (c)

If a picture can be drawn to satisfy the hypotheses of an argument and contradict the conclusion, the argument is not valid. However, to show that an argument is valid, all possible pictures must be considered to show that there are no contradictions.

Example AI-6

Determine if the following argument is valid.

Hypotheses: All wasps are unfriendly.
              All puppies are friendly.
Conclusion: Puppies are not wasps.

Solution

Let W represent the set of wasps and let U represent the set of unfriendly creatures. Then the first hypothesis is pictured as shown in Figure AI-5(a).

FIGURE AI-5

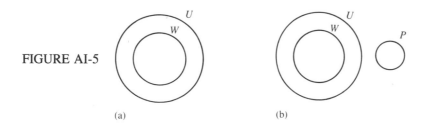

(a)   (b)

Let P represent the set of puppies. Then the second hypothesis may be pictured along with the first hypothesis, as shown in Figure AI-5(b). The intersection between sets U and P is the empty set; because W is a subset of U, then the conclusion that puppies are not wasps is valid.

Law of Detachment

A different method for determining if an argument is valid uses a form of argument called the **Law of Detachment.** For example, consider the following true statements:

If the sun is shining, then we shall take a trip.

The sun is shining.

Using these two statements, we can conclude that we shall take a trip. In general, the Law of Detachment is stated as follows: *If a statement of the form $p \rightarrow q$ is true and p is true, then q must be true.*

The above law can be proved formally using a truth table. (See Problem 10(b) in Problem Set AI-3.)

Example AI-7

Determine if each of the following arguments is valid.

(a) Hypotheses: If you eat spinach, then you will be strong.
                   You are not strong.
    Conclusion: Therefore, you do not eat spinach.
(b) Hypotheses: If Claude goes skiing, he will break his leg.
                   If Claude breaks his leg, he cannot enter the dance contest.
                   Claude goes skiing.
    Conclusion: Therefore, Claude cannot enter the dance contest.

Solution

(a) To utilize the statement "You are not strong," we find the contrapositive of the statement "If you eat spinach, then you will be strong." The contrapositive is "If you are not strong, then you do not eat spinach." Using the Law of Detachment, we see that the conclusion is valid.
(b) By using the Law of Detachment twice, the conclusion is valid.

PROBLEM SET AI-4

1. Investigate the validity of each of the following arguments.
   (a) All men are mortal.
       Socrates was a man.
       Therefore, Socrates was mortal.
   (b) All squares are quadrilaterals.
       All quadrilaterals are polygons.
       Therefore, all squares are polygons.
   (c) All teachers are intelligent.
       Some teachers are rich.
       Therefore, some intelligent people are rich.
   (d) All x's are y's.
       Some z's are x's.
       Therefore, all z's are y's.
   (e) If a student is a freshman, then she takes mathematics.

Jane is a sophomore.

Therefore, Jane does not take mathematics.

(f) If A, then not B.

If not B, then C.

Therefore, if A then C.

(g) All fat people are jolly.

Some thin people are intelligent.

Therefore, no fat people are intelligent.

(h) All x's are y's.

Some z's are x's.

Some z's are not y's.

Therefore, some z's are y's.

2. For each of the following, form a conclusion that follows logically from the given statements.

(a) All college students are poor.

Helen is a college student.

(b) Some freshmen like mathematics.

All people who like mathematics are intelligent.

(c) If I study for the final, then I will pass the final.

If I pass the final, then I will pass the course.

If I pass the course, then I look for a teaching job.

(d) Every eagle can fly.

Some pigs cannot fly.

(e) Every equilateral triangle is isosceles.

There exist triangles that are isosceles.

3. In Problem 1(f), the statements may be translated into symbolic form with p's and q's, as follows.

Hypotheses: $p \rightarrow \sim q$

$\sim q \rightarrow r$

Conclusion: $p \rightarrow r$

The argument may be further symbolized as follows.

$$[(p \rightarrow \sim q) \wedge (\sim q \rightarrow r)] \rightarrow (p \rightarrow r)$$

Write a truth table to test the validity of the argument.

SELECTED BIBLIOGRAPHY

Andree, R., and J. Andree. *Logical Thinking*. Norman, Oklahoma: University of Oklahoma Press, 1977.

Boyer, L. "On Validity and the Use of Truth Tables." *School Science and Mathematics* 69 (March 1969):553–560.

Carroll, L. *The Annotated Alice: Alice's Adventures in Wonderland and Through the Looking Glass*. New York: World Publishing, 1972.

———. *Symbolic Logic and Games of Logic*. New York: Dover, 1958.

Exner, R., and P. Hilton. "Should Mathematical Logic be Taught Formally in Mathematics Classes?" *The Mathematics Teacher* 64 (May 1971):388–401.

Goldberg, D. "Happy Birthday, Alice." *The New Jersey Mathematics Teacher* 24 (October 1966):10–11.

Harnadek, A. *Mathematical Reasoning*, Unit 4, Troy, Mich.: Midwest Publications, 1972.

Kattsoff, L. "Symbolic Logic and the Structure of Elementary Mathematics." *The Mathematics Teacher* 55 (April 1962): 269–275.

Marino, G. "Mysteries of Proof." *The Mathematics Teacher* 75 (October 1982):559–563.

Masse, M. "More Problems Please." *Arithmetic Teacher* 26 (December 1978):11–14.

Poincare, H. "Intuition and Logic in Mathematics." *The Mathematics Teacher*, 62 (March 1969):205–212.

Roberge, J. "Negation in the Major Premise as a Factor in Children's Deducting Reasoning." *School Science and Mathematics* 69 (March 1969):715–722.

Suppes, P. and S. Hill. *First Course in Mathematical Logic*. Boston: Ginn, 1966.

Topics in Mathematics for Elementary School Teachers, Booklet Number 12, *Logic*. Washington, D.C.: NCTM, 1968.

Woodward, E., and J. Tolleson. "Detective Stories in Junior High School Mathematics." *The Mathematics Teacher* 74 (September 1981):434–436.

Appendix II
Calculator Usage

INTRODUCTION

In 1976, the National Council of Teachers of Mathematics (NCTM) adopted the following position on the use of hand-held calculators (see *The Mathematics Teacher*, January 1976, 92–94).

> Mathematics teachers should recognize the potential contribution of mini-calculators as a valuable instruction aid. In the classroom, the minicalculator should be used in imaginative ways to reinforce learning and to motivate the learner as he becomes proficient in mathematics.

In 1980, NCTM published *An Agenda for Action: Recommendations for School Mathematics of the 1980s*. The eight recommendations listed in the *Agenda* reflected the opinions of many sectors of society, both lay and professional. One of these recommendations states:

> Mathematics programs must take full advantage of the power of calculators and computers at all grade levels.

To accomplish this objective, NCTM recommends that "All students have access to calculators and increasingly to computers throughout their school mathematics program."

Concern involving calculator use has revolved around the issue of when and how calculators should be used in relation to basic facts and computational skills. Over 100 research studies have been conducted on the topic. This is more investigation than on almost any other topic, tool, or technique in the last century. The overwhelming evidence is that children's computational skills have not suffered when calculators have been used.

If students are to have increased access to calculators in schools, we as teachers must develop ways for students to use calculators, including ways to communicate with the machine and ways to use it as a tool in problem solving. The savings in eliminating time-consuming computations allows for more time to develop problem-solving skills and enables students to attempt more problems.

Features of Calculators

Once a teacher or school system has decided to use calculators, it is important to determine which calculator best fits the expected uses and which can be integrated into the curriculum with the fewest problems. Manufacturers change models frequently, so it is important to purchase an adequate number of calculators at one time. For ease of classroom use, each student should be using the same model calculator. The choice of calculator depends upon the grade level in which it will be used. There are vast differences in the calculator models available. The discussion below lists some of the features to be considered before purchasing a set of calculators.

Type of Logic

The type of logic built into a calculator determines how a computation is entered into the calculator. For example, the most natural way to enter $2 + 4 \cdot 5 - 4 \div 2$ on a calculator is exactly as it is written. With different types of logic, this may or may not produce the correct computation.

Algebraic Logic.   On some calculators with algebraic logic, the calculator processes the operations in the order in which they are entered. For example,

$$\boxed{2}\ \boxed{+}\ \boxed{4}\ \boxed{\times}\ \boxed{5}\ \boxed{-}\ \boxed{4}\ \boxed{\div}\ \boxed{2}\ \boxed{=}$$

would be evaluated as

$6 \cdot 5 - 4 \div 2$

then as

$30 - 4 \div 2$

and finally as

$26 \div 2 = 13$

Remembering, however, that multiplication and division are done before addition and subtraction, the correct solution to the problem $2 + 4 \cdot 5 - 4 \div 2$ is $2 + 20 - 2 = 22 - 2 = 20$. This type of logic is especially disturbing when we try a computation like $\frac{1}{2} + \frac{1}{4}$ by pushing the keys in the order given—that is, $\boxed{1}\ \boxed{\div}\ \boxed{2}\ \boxed{+}\ \boxed{1}\ \boxed{\div}\ \boxed{4}\ \boxed{=}$. A calculator with this type of logic will evaluate $\frac{1}{2} + \frac{1}{4}$ as 0.375 rather than 0.75. (Do you see why?) This type of algebraic logic is used in many models and is adequate if both teacher and students are aware of the order in which operations must be performed.

algebraic operating system   Many calculators with algebraic logic also include a feature called an **algebraic operating system.** It evaluates parentheses first, then multiplications and divisions, and then additions and subtractions. For example, in the problem $2 + 4 \cdot 5 - 4 \div 2$, if $\boxed{2}\ \boxed{+}\ \boxed{4}$ is entered, the calculator will not perform the addition. If $\boxed{2}\ \boxed{+}\ \boxed{4}\ \boxed{\times}$ is entered, no calculations will be completed. After

2 + 4 × 5 − is entered, the display will show 22. In other words, the calculator performs 4 × 5 before adding 2. A calculator with the algebraic operating system feature will complete the original problem $2 + 4 \cdot 5 - 4 \div 2$ and give the desired answer of 20 if the computation is entered in the order it is written and the = key is pressed.

Reverse Polish Notation.   On a calculator that uses Reverse Polish Notation (RPN), all operations are entered after the numbers have been entered. For example, to find 2 + 4 on a machine that uses RPN, both 2 and 4 must be entered before the operation of addition. There is an ENTER button on a calculator with RPN. To compute 2 + 4, the buttons are pushed as follows:

2 ENTER 4 +

The display shows 6. No = key is necessary since the computation is completed when the operation button is pushed. The absence of an = key is the easiest way to identify a calculator with Reverse Polish Notation. Some of the most advanced scientific calculators utilize RPN. However, calculators with RPN are generally not appropriate for elementary school use.

Arithmetic Logic.   With arithmetic logic, there is no = key. The keys with the "equals" symbol are ± and ≐. An addition like 3 + 4 is entered as 3 ± 4 ±. This logic is confusing for most elementary students and probably should not be used. Arithmetic logic is becoming obsolete and probably will not be found on the majority of calculators.

Number of Functions

The minimum number of function keys a calculator should perform is four. These keys are +, −, ×, and ÷. There are other function keys that are desirable, including % and √, but they are not absolutely necessary. They will be discussed under special keys.

Display

A calculator display should have at least an eight-digit readout. Two types of displays commonly available are the light emitting diode (LED) and the liquid crystal display (LCD). There are various advantages and disadvantages to each of these. An LCD requires some reflected room light to be seen. The LED display can be seen in the dark but is very hard to see in bright light. For classroom purposes a machine must be easily readable from a wide viewing angle, regardless of the type of display. To minimize battery replacement cost, calculators using silver oxide or mercury batteries can provide thousands of hours of computing time and should be considered as an alternative to the purchase of calculators with adaptors. Solar cells are also becoming available at lower costs.

Keys and Keyboard

Each key should have only one purpose and should give some indication that it has been pressed—click, beep, etc. There should be an easily accessible off-on switch. The position of the keys on the keyboard may vary, but they should be adequately spaced and of a large enough size that fingers hit no more than one key at a time. Also, the calculator should have separate clear and clear-entry keys. On some calculators, pressing the clear key once clears the display while pressing it a second time clears the whole calculator.

Decimal Notation

The calculator should have a floating decimal point. For example, when $\boxed{1}$ $\boxed{\div}$ $\boxed{3}$ $\boxed{=}$ is entered, the display should show 0.3333333, rather than 0.33 as some displays do on fixed-point machines. Be aware of how a calculator rounds decimals, if it does. For example, in $\boxed{2}$ $\boxed{\div}$ $\boxed{3}$ $\boxed{=}$, the display with a floating decimal may show 0.6666666 or 0.6666667. If the display shows 0.6666667, the round-off is apparent. If it shows 0.6666666, then we can multiply by 3 and observe the result, which may be either 1.9999998, 1.9999999, or 2. If 1.9999998 appears, there is no round-off by the calculator. If 1.9999999 or 2 appears, there is an internal round-off.

Also, when considering decimal notation, we should determine if the calculator uses scientific notation and, if so, how it works. Recall that in scientific notation a number like 238,000 is written as a number, greater than or equal to 1 but less than 10, multiplied by a power of 10. Thus, $238,000 = 2.38 \times 10^5$. For upper-grade students, scientific notation is desirable. Students should consult their owner's manual to see how scientific notation is displayed.

Error Indicator

There should be some signal on the calculator to indicate when an "illegal" operation is entered. For example, $\boxed{1}$ $\boxed{\div}$ $\boxed{0}$ $\boxed{=}$ should cause the display to show an error. This indicator should also show when the computing limit of the calculator is exceeded.

Special Keys

There are several special keys that are convenient for elementary school usage. The first of these is the constant key $\boxed{K}$, which allows an operation to be repeated without pushing all the buttons each time. For example, the calculator might be designed so that if $\boxed{1}$ $\boxed{+}$ $\boxed{K}$ is entered, then 1 is added to whatever appears on the display each time $\boxed{=}$ is pushed. This allows kindergarten or first-grade students to count by ones. Some machines have constants built into them, rather than a separate constant key. In such cases, the owner's manual should be consulted.

The second of the convenient special keys is a "change the sign" key, $\boxed{+/-}$. This allows for the entry of negative numbers. Normally, each number entered into a calculator is positive. Pushing $\boxed{3}$ $\boxed{+/-}$ changes 3 to $^-3$. This key is especially important if integers are to be studied using the calculator. It is desirable that the negative sign immediately precede a number to denote a negative number rather than leaving a space between the sign and the number, as is done on some calculators.

The third and fourth special keys are the parentheses keys, $\boxed{(}$ and $\boxed{)}$. With parentheses keys, operations may be ordered as desired. A calculator with parentheses keys will perform operations inside the parentheses before any others. For example, there is no confusion in the computation $2 + 4 \cdot 5 - 4 \div 2$ if parentheses are added as shown: $2 + (4 \cdot 5) - (4 \div 2)$.

The fifth special key is the percent key, $\boxed{\%}$. This key may operate in a variety of ways, depending on the calculator. It may change a percent to a decimal. For example, pushing $\boxed{6}$ $\boxed{\%}$ may give 0.06 on the display. On other machines the $\boxed{\%}$ key may be a function key. For example, pushing $\boxed{2}$ $\boxed{\times}$ $\boxed{3}$ $\boxed{\%}$ may yield 0.06 without using the $\boxed{=}$ key. If the $\boxed{=}$ key is used, the display might show 2.06, which is $2 + 2(3\%)$. The user should carefully check how the $\boxed{\%}$ key operates. In many cases, a more thorough understanding of percents takes place by not using a percent key.

Other keys that may be convenient are $\boxed{\sqrt{}}$, the square root key, and $\boxed{x^2}$, the squaring key. There are numerous other keys available that an individual school system or teacher may find useful. Regardless of the type of machine and keys selected, *the teacher should be thoroughly familiar with the owner's manual.*

Memory

The memory feature is particularly important in using the calculator in upper elementary grades. Many calculators use a two-key memory system—$\boxed{STO}$ used for storing a displayed number in the memory and $\boxed{RCL}$ for recalling a number from the memory. This arrangement is adequate for most uses.

Other machines have four-key memories. These are usually memory-plus, $\boxed{M+}$, which allows addition to be performed on the content of a memory register, memory-minus, $\boxed{M-}$, which does subtraction from the content of a memory register, memory recall, $\boxed{MR}$, and memory clear, $\boxed{MC}$.

Other Considerations

There are many other considerations involved in choosing calculators for students. Among these are the size, shape, and weight of the machine, the power source, cost, durability and warranty, and reliability of the vendor and/or the manufacturer. These are individual items upon which the teacher or the school system must decide.

SELECTED BIBLIOGRAPHY

Adkins, B. "Using a Calculator to Find the 'Greatest Common Factor.'" *School Science and Mathematics* 81 (November 1981):603–606.

Aidala, G. "Calculators: Their Use in the Classroom." *School Science and Mathematics* 78 (April 1978):307–311.

Aidala, G., and P. Rosenfeld. "Calculators in the Classroom." *The Mathematics Teacher* 71 (May 1978):434–435.

Bell, M. "Calculators in Elementary Schools? Some Tentative Guidelines and Questions Based on Classroom Experience." *The Arithmetic Teacher* 23 (November 1976):502–509.

Bernard, J. "More Meaning Power to the Zero Power." *The Mathematics Teacher* 75 (March 1982):251–252.

Bestgen, B. "Calculators—Taking the First Step." *Arithmetic Teacher* 29 (September 1981):34–37.

Billstein, R., and J. Lott. "When Does a Fraction Yield a Terminating Decimal?" *Calculators/Computers* 2 (January 1978): 15–19.

Bitter, G. and T. Metos. *Exploring with Pocket Calculators*. New York: Julian Messner (Distributed by Simon and Schuster), 1977.

Bright, G. "Ideas." *Arithmetic Teacher* 25 (February 1978):28–32.

Bruni, J., and H. Silverman. "Let's Do It!—Taking Advantage of the Hand Calculator." *Arithmetic Teacher* 23 (November 1976):494–501.

Caravella, J. *Minicalculators in the Classroom*. Washington, D.C.: National Education Association, 1977.

Davidson, J. *Let's Start to Calculate*. New Rochelle, N.Y.: Cuisenaire Company of America, 1976.

DeMent, G. *Calculator Capers: An Introduction to the Calculator for Primary Grades*. Englewood Cliffs, N.J.: Prentice-Hall Learning Systems, Inc., 1977.

Dolan, D. *Let's Calculate*. San Leandro, Calif.: Lakeshore Curriculum Materials Co., 1976.

Dolan, D. *Let'r Calculate*. San Leandro, Calif.: Lakeshore Curriculum Materials Co., 1976.

Drake, P. "Calculators in the Elementary Classroom." *Arithmetic Teacher* 25 (March 1978):47–48.

Duea, J., and E. Ockenga. "Classroom Problem Solving with Calculators." *Arithmetic Teacher* 29 (February 1982):50–51.

Fisher, B. "Calculator Games: Combining Skills and Problem Solving." *Arithmetic Teacher* 27 (December 1979):40–41.

Fisher, W., and J. Jones. "Large Numbers and the Calculator." In *Mathematics for the Middle Grades* (5–9), 1982 *Yearbook*. Reston, Va.: National Council of Teachers of Mathematics, 1982:130–141.

Gardner, M. "Mathematical Games: Fun and Serious Business with the Small Electronic Calculator." *Scientific American* 335 (July 1976):126–129.

Gawronski, J., and D. Coblentz. "Calculators and the Mathematics Curriculum." *The Arithmetic Teacher* 23 (November 1976): 510–512.

Gibb, E. "Calculators in the Classroom." *Today's Education* 64 (November–December 1975):42–44.

Goldberg, K. *Pushbutton Mathematics: Calculator Math Problems, Examples, and Activities*. Englewood Cliffs, N.J.: Prentice-Hall, 1982.

Goodhue, J. "Calculator Crossword Puzzle." *The Mathematics Teacher* 71 (April 1978):279–282.

Goodman, T. "Calculators and Estimation." *The Mathematics Teacher* 75 (February 1982):137–140, 182.

Gregory, J. "Santa Takes a Calculated Risk." *The Mathematics Student* 22 (December 1974):1–2.

Hobbs, B., and C. Burvis. "Minicalculators and Repeating Decimals." *Arithmetic Teacher* 25 (April 1978):18–20.

Immerzeel, G. "It's in Your Hands." *The Arithmetic Teacher* 23 (November 1976):493.

Immerzeel, G. *Ideas and Activities for Using Calculators in the Classroom*. Dansville, N.Y.: The Instructor Publications, Inc., 1976.

Judd, W. *Games Calculators Play*. New York: Warner Books, 1975.

Judd, W. "Instructional Games with Calculators." *The Arithmetic Teacher* 23 (November 1976):516–518.

Judd, W. "Rx for Classroom Math Blahs: A New Case for the Calculator." *Learning* 3 (March 1975):41–48.

Kerr, S. "Who Is Quickest with Mind and Fingers?" *The Mathematics Teacher* 72 (February 1979):123–126.

Lappan, G., E. Phillips, and M. Winter. "Powers and Patterns: Problem Solving with Calculators." *Arithmetic Teacher* 30 (October 1982):42–44.

Lappan, G., and M. Winter. "A Calculator Activity That Teaches Mathematics." *Arithmetic Teacher* 25 (April 1978):21–23.

Lazarus, M. "Reckoning with Calculators." *National Elementary Principal* 7 (January 1978):71–77.

Meyer, P. "When You Use a Calculator You Have to Think!" *Arithmetic Teacher* 27 (January 1980):18–21.

Michelow, J., and B. Vogeli. "The New World of Calculator Functions." *School Science and Mathematics* 78 (March 1978): 248–254.

Miller, G. "Working Backwards to Achieve Understanding." *Arithmetic Teacher* 29 (September 1981):48.

Miller, W. "Calculator Tic-Tac-Toe: A Game of Estimation." *The Mathematics Teacher* 74 (December 1981):713–716.

Morris, J. "More About Repeating Decimals." *Calculators/Computers* 2 (April 1978):64–68.

Morris, J. "Problem Solving with Calculators." *Arithmetic Teacher* 25 (April 1978):24–26.

Morris, J. *How to Develop Problem Solving Using a Calculator*. Reston, Va.: National Council of Teachers of Mathematics, 1981.

Moursund, D. *Calculators, Computers, and Elementary Education for Teacher Education*. Salem, Ore.: The Math Learning Center, 1977.

Munson, H. "Your District Needs a Policy on Pocket Calculators!" *The Arithmetic Teacher* 25 (October 1977):46.

"Minicalculators in Schools." *The Arithmetic Teacher* 23 (January 1976):72–74. *The Mathematics Teacher* 69 (January 1976): 92–94.

National Council of Teachers of Mathematics *NCTM*. "Position Statements: Use of Minicalculators." *The Mathematics Teacher* 71 (May 1978):468.

Ockenga, E. "Calculator Ideas for the Junior High Classroom." *The Arithmetic Teacher* 23 (November 1976):519–522.

Olson, M. "It's a Factor of Life." *The Mathematics Teacher* 73 (December 1980):681–684.

Olson, M., and V. Sindt. "Examining Rates of Inflation and Consumption." *The Mathematics Teacher* 75 (September 1982):472–473.

O'Neil, D., and R. Jensen. "Let's Do It: Let's Use Calculators." *Arithmetic Teacher* 29 (February 1982):6–9.

Palmer, H. "Minicalculators in the Classroom—What Do Teachers Think?" *Arithmetic Teacher* 25 (April 1978):27–28.

Pollak, H. "Hand-Held Calculators and Potential Redesign of the School Mathematics Curriculum." *The Mathematics Teacher* 70 (April 1977):293–296.

Prigge, G., and J. Gawronski. *Calculator Activities*. Big Spring, Texas: Math-Master, 1978.

Report of the Conference on Needed Research and Development on Hand-Held Calculators in School Mathematics. National Institute of Education and National Science Foundation, 1977.

Reys, R., et al. *Keystrokes: Calculator Activities for Young Students: Addition and Subtraction*. Palo Alto, Calif.: Creative Publications, 1979.

Riden, C. "Less Than Ten on a Calculator." *School Science and Mathematics* 75 (October 1975):529–531.

Schmalz, R. "Calculator Capers." *The Mathematics Teacher* 71 (May 1978):439–442.

Schmalz, R. "Calculators: What Difference Will They Make?" *Arithmetic Teacher* 26 (December 1978):46–47.

Schultz, J. "How Calculators Give Rise to a New Need for Skills in Algebra." *School Science and Mathematics* 78 (February 1978):131–134.

Schultz, J. "Using a Calculator to Do Arithmetic in Bases Other Than Ten." *Arithmetic Teacher* 26 (September 1978):25–27.

Teitelbaum, E. "Calculators for Classroom Use?" *Arithmetic Teacher* 26 (November 1978):18–20.

Usiskin, Z. "Are Calculators a Crutch?" *The Mathematics Teacher* 71 (May 1978):412–413.

Wagner, S. "Fun with Repeating Decimals," *The Mathematics Teacher* 72 (March 1979):209–212.

Wiebe, J. "Using a Calculator to Develop Mathematical Understanding." *Arithmetic Teacher* 29 (November 1981):36–38.

Woodburn, D. "Can You Predict the Repetend?" *The Mathematics Teacher* 69 (December 1976):675–678.

Woodward, E. "Calculators with a Constant Arithmetic Feature." *Arithmetic Teacher* 29 (October 1981):40–41.

Zakariya, N., M. McClung, and A. Warner. "The Calculator in the Classroom." *Arithmetic Teacher* 28 (March 1980):12–16.

Appendix III
Basic Constructions

The following diagrams show how to perform the basic compass and straightedge constructions that were discussed in detail in Chapter 10.

1. Construct a segment congruent to a given segment.

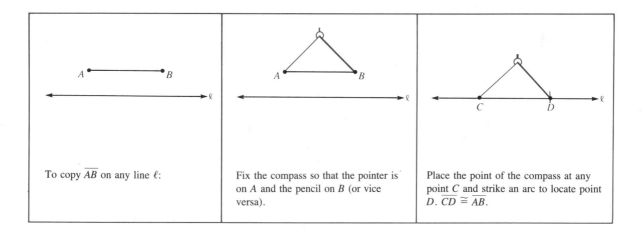

To copy $\overline{AB}$ on any line ℓ:	Fix the compass so that the pointer is on A and the pencil on B (or vice versa).	Place the point of the compass at any point C and strike an arc to locate point D. $\overline{CD} \cong \overline{AB}$.

2. Construct a circle given its center and radius.

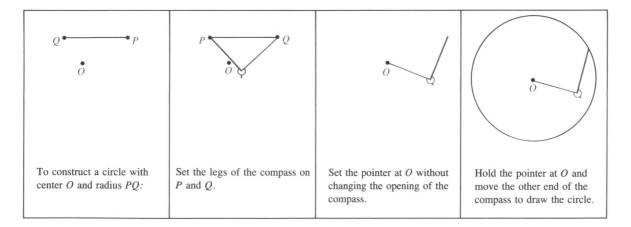

To construct a circle with center O and radius PQ:	Set the legs of the compass on P and Q.	Set the pointer at O without changing the opening of the compass.	Hold the pointer at O and move the other end of the compass to draw the circle.

3. Copy an angle.

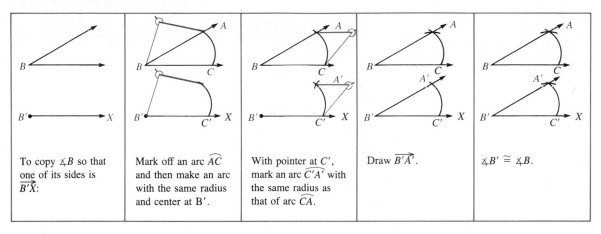

| To copy ∡B so that one of its sides is $\overrightarrow{B'X}$: | Mark off an arc $\overset{\frown}{AC}$ and then make an arc with the same radius and center at B'. | With pointer at C', mark an arc $\overset{\frown}{C'A'}$ with the same radius as that of arc $\overset{\frown}{CA}$. | Draw $\overrightarrow{B'A'}$. | ∡B' ≅ ∡B. |

4. Through a given point P, construct a line parallel to a given line ℓ.

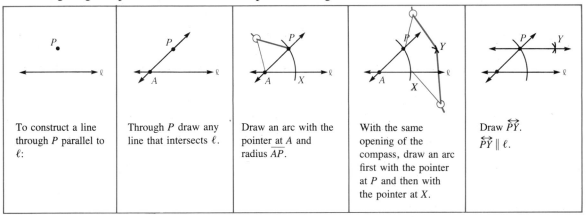

| To construct a line through P parallel to ℓ: | Through P draw any line that intersects ℓ. | Draw an arc with the pointer at A and radius $\overline{AP}$. | With the same opening of the compass, draw an arc first with the pointer at P and then with the pointer at X. | Draw $\overleftrightarrow{PY}$. $\overleftrightarrow{PY} \parallel ℓ$. |

5. Through a given point P construct a line parallel to a given line ℓ, using properties of corresponding angles.

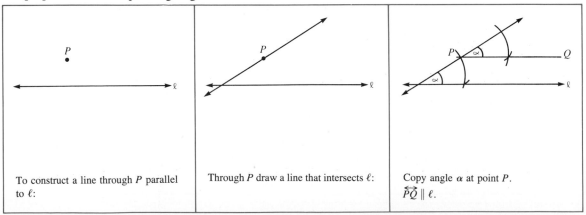

| To construct a line through P parallel to ℓ: | Through P draw a line that intersects ℓ: | Copy angle α at point P. $\overleftrightarrow{PQ} \parallel ℓ$. |

6. Bisect a given angle.

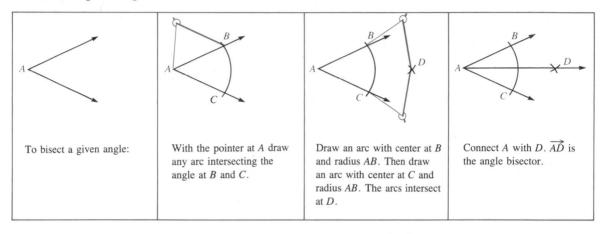

| To bisect a given angle: | With the pointer at A draw any arc intersecting the angle at B and C. | Draw an arc with center at B and radius AB. Then draw an arc with center at C and radius AB. The arcs intersect at D. | Connect A with D. $\overrightarrow{AD}$ is the angle bisector. |

7. Construct a perpendicular to a line ℓ through a point P not on line ℓ.

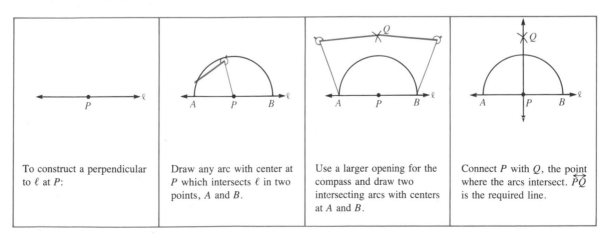

| To construct a perpendicular to ℓ through P: | Draw an arc with center at P that intersects the line in two points. | With the same opening, make two intersecting arcs, one with center at A and the other with center at B. | Connect P with Q. $\overleftrightarrow{PQ}$ is the required line. |

8. Construct a perpendicular to a line ℓ at a point P on line ℓ.

| To construct a perpendicular to ℓ at P: | Draw any arc with center at P which intersects ℓ in two points, A and B. | Use a larger opening for the compass and draw two intersecting arcs with centers at A and B. | Connect P with Q, the point where the arcs intersect. $\overleftrightarrow{PQ}$ is the required line. |

9. Construct the perpendicular bisector of a segment.

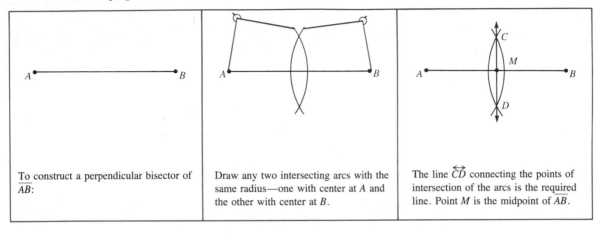

To construct a perpendicular bisector of $\overline{AB}$:	Draw any two intersecting arcs with the same radius—one with center at A and the other with center at B.	The line $\overleftrightarrow{CD}$ connecting the points of intersection of the arcs is the required line. Point M is the midpoint of $\overline{AB}$.

10. Separate a line segment into any number of congruent parts. The following construction illustrates the procedure for three congruent parts.

To separate $\overline{AB}$ into a given number of congruent parts:	Draw any transversal $\overrightarrow{AC}$ such that A, B, C are noncollinear.	Mark off the given number of congruent segments (of any size) on $\overrightarrow{AC}$. In this case, we use three congruent segments.	Connect B with A_3.	Through A_2 and A_1, construct parallels to $\overline{BA_3}$. The points B_1 and B_2 determine the three congruent segments.

Answers to the Odd-Numbered Problems

CHAPTER 1

Problem Set 1-1 **1.** (a) 5×6, 6×7, 7×8
(b) 000000, , 00000000 (c) 45, 41, 37
(d) 15, 20, 26 (e) 26, 37, 50 (f) X, Y, X (answers vary) (g) 1, 18, 1 (h) 34, 55, 89 (i) 111111, 1111111, 11111111 (j) 123456, 1234567, 12345678
(k) $6 \cdot 2^6$, $7 \cdot 2^7$, $8 \cdot 2^8$ (l) 2^{32}, 2^{64}, 2^{128} **3.** (a) 30, 42, 56 (b) $100 \cdot 101 = 10{,}100$ (c) $n(n + 1) = n^2 + n$ **5.** (a) 1, 5, 12, 22, 35, 51 (b) 14,950
7. The resulting sequence is always an arithmetic sequence.
9. (a) 99, $2n - 1$ (b) $50 \cdot 99$ or 4950, $5(n - 1)$
(c) $3 \cdot 2^{99}$, $3 \cdot 2^{n-1}$ (d) 10^{100}, 10^n (e) 5^{101}, 5^{n+1}
(f) 1100, $11n$ (g) 2^{199}, 2^{2n-1} (h) 405, $9 + 4(n - 1)$
or $4n + 5$ (i) 100^3 or 1,000,000, n^3 (j) $2 \cdot 3^{99}$,
$2 \cdot 3^{n-1}$ **11.** 1, 1, 2, 3, 5, 8, 13, 21, 34, 55, 89, 144
13. (a) Yes. The difference between terms in the new sequence is the same as in the old sequence. (b) Yes. If the fixed number is k, the difference of the second sequence is k times the difference of the first sequence.

Problem Set 1-2 **1.** None—there is no dirt in a hole.
3. 4 **5.** 3
7.

9. 1 hour, 20 minutes = 80 minutes **11.** There is no extra dollar since there is no reason for the 2nd column to sum to $50. **13.** $63 **15.** 18
17.

6	7	2
1	5	9
8	3	4

Other variations are possible.
19. One possibility is to turn both of the timers on at the same time. When the 7-minute timer runs out, put the egg in; there are 4 minutes left on the 11-minute timer. After these four minutes run out start the 11-minute timer

again. **21.** 24 **23.** 10 boys, 12 dogs **25.** 16 days
27. (1) Applejack (2) Null Set (3) Fast Jack
(4) Lookout (5) Bent Leg **29.** (a) 11 (b) 63
31. 78; 364 **33.** 35 moves **35.** (a) 260,610
(b) 100,701 (c) 20,503 **37.** Play second and make sure that the sum showing when you hand the calculator to your opponent is a multiple of 3. **39.** Play first; push 3. After that on your turn make the sum 3 plus a multiple of 10. **41.** Play second; use a strategy similar to No. 40 but use a multiple of 4. **43.** $2^n - 1$

CHAPTER 2

Problem Set 2-1 **1.** (c) is well-defined, (a) and (b) are not. **3.** (a) $B = \{x, y, z, w\}$ (b) $3 \notin B$ (c) $\{1, 2\} \subset \{1, 2, 3, 4\}$ (d) $D \not\subseteq E$ (e) $A \not\subset B$ **5.** $\bar{A} = \{x \mid x$ is a college student who does not have a straight A average$\}$
7. (a) $\not\subseteq$ (b) $\not\subseteq$ (c) $\not\subseteq$ (d) $\not\subseteq$ (e) $\subseteq$ (f) $\not\subseteq$
(g) $\subseteq$ (h) $\subseteq$ (i) $\not\subseteq$ (j) $\not\subseteq$ **9.** (a) $2^6 = 64$ subsets;
$2^6 - 1 = 63$ proper subsets (b) 2^n subsets; $2^n - 1$
proper subsets **11.** One, if $B = \varnothing$ **13.** No, $\varnothing \not\subset \varnothing$
15. (a) T (b) F. $\{\varnothing\}$ has one element and hence is not empty. (c) T (d) F. A could equal B. (e) T (f) F. Suppose $A = \{1\}$ and $B = \{1, 2\}$, then $A \subseteq B$, but $A \neq B$.

Problem Set 2-2 **1.** (a) $\{f, i, n, a, l, s, r, e\}$ (b) $\{a\}$
(c) $\{o, v, e, r\}$ or C (d) $\varnothing$ (e) $\{f, i, n, a, l, s, o, v, e, r\}$ or U (f) $\{a\}$ (g) $\{f, i, n, a, l, s, o, v, e, r\}$ or
U (h) $\{f, i, n, a, l, s\}$ **3.** (a) $\bar{B}$ (b) A **5.** (a) $B - A$ or $B \cap \bar{A}$ (b) $\overline{A \cup B}$ or $\bar{A} \cap \bar{B}$ (c) $A \cap B \cap C$
(d) $A \cap B$ (e) $(A \cap C) - B$ or $(A \cap C) \cap \bar{B}$ (f) $(A - B) \cup (C - B) \cup (A \cap C)$ **7.** (a) U (b) U (c) S
(d) $\varnothing$ (e) S (f) U (g) $\varnothing$ (h) S (i) $\bar{S}$ (j) S
9. (a) A (b) $\varnothing$ (c) $\varnothing$ (d) $\varnothing$
11. (a)

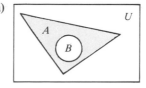

(b)
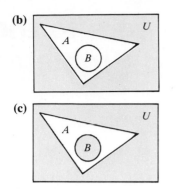

(c)

13. (a) F **(b)** F **15. (a)** No **(b)** No **(c)** No
17. (a) $A \cup B$ $\overline{A} \cap \overline{B}$

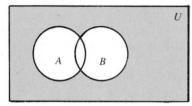

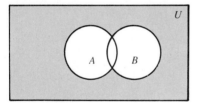

(b) $\overline{A \cap B}$ $\overline{A} \cup \overline{B}$

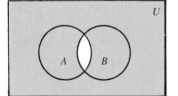

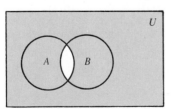

(c) Answers vary.
19. (a) is the set of all students at Paxson School taking band but not choir. **(b)** is the set of all students at

Paxson taking both band and choir. **(c)** is the set of all students at Paxson taking choir but not band. **(d)** is the set of all students at Paxson taking neither choir nor band. **21.** Four have a class in biology but not mathematics.

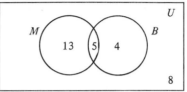

23. (a) 8 **(b)** 8 **25.** $[A \cap (B \cup D)] \cup (\overline{B} \cap C \cap D)$ $\cup (B \cap \overline{C} \cap D) \cup (B \cap C \cap \overline{D})$ **27.** Yes
29. (a) {Massachusetts, Maryland, Mississippi, Minnesota, Missouri, Michigan, Maine, Montana}
(b) $\{x \mid x$ is a state in the United States whose name starts with the letter M$\}$

Problem Set 2-3 **1. (a)** $\{(x, a), (x, b), (x, c), (y, a),$ $(y, b), (y, c)\}$ **(b)** $\{(0, a), (0, b), (0, c)\}$ **(c)** $\{(a, x),$ $(a, y), (b, x), (b, y), (c, x), (c, y)\}$ **(d)** $\varnothing$ **(e)** $\{(0,$ $0)\}$ **(f)** $\varnothing$ **(g)** $\{(x, 0), (y, 0), (a, 0), (b, 0), (c, 0)\}$
(h) $\{(x, 0), (y, 0), (a, 0), (b, 0), (c, 0)\}$ **(i)** $\varnothing$
(j) $\varnothing$ **3. (a)** 3 **(b)** 6 **(c)** 9 **(d)** 20 **(e)** $m \cdot n$
(f) $m \cdot n \cdot p$ **5.** 5 **7.** 12 **9.** 60 **11. (a)** $\{(x, y) \mid y$ $= x^2\}$, ordered pairs vary. **(b)** $\{(x, y) \mid x$ is the wife of $y\}$
(c) $\{(x, y) \mid x$ is the small print letter in the English alphabet and y is the corresponding printed capital letter$\}$ **(d)** $\{(x, y) \mid y$ is the cost of x candies$\}$
13. Answers vary. **15.** Only the pairs (a) and (c).
17. (a) $4 \cdot 3 \cdot 2 \cdot 1 = 24$ **(b)** $5 \cdot 4 \cdot 3 \cdot 2 \cdot 1 = 120$
(c) $n \cdot (n - 1) \cdot (n - 2) \cdot \ldots \cdot 3 \cdot 2 \cdot 1$
19. (a) Cardinal **(b)** Ordinal **(c)** Ordinal
(d) Cardinal **(e)** Cardinal, and then ordinal
21. (a) $\{1, 3, 5, 7, 9, \ldots, 2n - 1, \ldots\}$
$\quad \updownarrow \updownarrow \updownarrow \updownarrow \updownarrow \qquad \updownarrow$
$\quad \{3, 5, 7, 9, 11, \ldots, 2n + 1, \ldots\}$
(b) $\{100, 101, 102, 103, \ldots, n + 99, \ldots\}$
$\quad \updownarrow \quad \updownarrow \quad \updownarrow \quad \updownarrow \qquad \updownarrow$
$\quad \{101, 102, 103, 104, \ldots, n + 100, \ldots\}$
23. (a) Yes, move the guest in Room 1 to Room 1,000,000, the guest in Room 2 to Room 1,000,001, and so on. **(b)** Yes, move the guest in Room 3 to Room 2, the guest in Room 5 to Room 3, the guest in Room 7 to Room 4, the guest in Room 9 to Room 5 and in general the guest in Room $(2n - 1)$ to Room $\dfrac{(2n - 1) + 1}{2}$.
25. Answers vary

27.

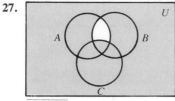

$(\overline{A \cap B}) \cup C$

29. (a) 16 (b) 15 (c) 23 (d) 8 (e) 15 (f) 7
(g) 10 **31.** Cowboys vs. Giants; Vikings vs. Packers;
Redskins vs. Bills

Problem Set 2-4 **1.** (a) $3n - 1$ (b) $n^2 + 1$ (c) $n \cdot$
$(n + 1)$ or $n^2 + n$ **3.** (a) No, 1 is paired with 2
elements, a and d. (b) No, not every element from {1,
2, 3} is paired, namely 2. (c) Yes. (d) No, not every
element from {1, 2, 3} is paired, namely 2 and 3.
5. Yes, each element in the first set is used and each is
associated with only one element in the second set.
7. Range = {5, 41, 45} **9.** (a) No, a and b are paired
with two different elements. (b) Yes, it satisfies the
definition. **11.** (a) Yes (b) Yes (c) No, there is
more than one value associated with the value 2.
13. (a) \$1.70 (b) $C = 20 + 15(W - 1)$ or $C = 15W$
$+ 5$ **15.** \$3.35 **17.** (a) $\{a, b, c, d\}$ (b) $\{a, d\}$
(c) $\varnothing$ (d) $\varnothing$ (e) $\varnothing$ **19.** Answers vary **21.** Answers
vary, for example, $\{a, b, c, d\}$
23. $(A \cup B) \cup C = (\{h, e, l, p\} \cup \{m, e\}) \cup \{n, o, w\}$
$\qquad\qquad = \{h, e, l, p, m\} \cup \{n, o, w\}$
$\qquad\qquad = \{h, e, l, p, m, n, o, w\}$
$A \cup (B \cup C) = \{h, e, l, p\} \cup (\{m, e\} \cup \{n, o, w\})$
$\qquad\qquad = \{h, e, l, p\} \cup \{m, e, n, o, w\}$
$\qquad\qquad = \{h, e, l, p, m, n, o, w\}$

Chapter Test **1.** $\{x \mid x$ is a letter of the English
alphabet} **3.** (a) $\overline{A}$ is the set of people living in
Montana who are less than 30 years old. (b) $A \cap C$ is
the set of people living in Montana who are 30 years or
older and own a gun. (c) $A \cup B$ is the set of people
living in Montana. (d) $\overline{C}$ is the set of people living in
Montana who do not own a gun. (e) $\overline{A \cap C}$ is the set
of people living in Montana who are younger than 30 or
do not own a gun.
5. (a)   (b)

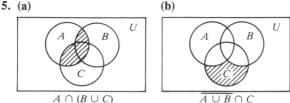

$A \cap (B \cup C)$ $\overline{A \cup B} \cap C$

7. $2^6 - 1 = 63$
9.

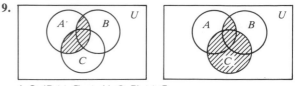

$A \cap (B \cup C) \neq (A \cap B) \cup C$

11. (a) This is a function from $\{a, c, e, f\}$ to $\{b, d, a, g\}$
(b) This is not a function since the elements a and b
are paired with more than one element. (c) This is a
function from $\{a, b\}$ to $\{a, b\}$ **13.** (a) {3, 4, 5, 6}
(b) {14, 29, 44, 59} (c) {0, 1, 4, 9, 16} (d) {5, 9, 15}
15. (a) F. Suppose $A = \{1\}$ and $B = \{a\}$ then A
$\not\subseteq B$ and $B \not\subseteq A$. (b) F. It is not a proper subset of
itself. (c) F. Suppose $A = \{1, 2\}$ and $B = \{a, b\}$, then
$A \sim B$ but $A \neq B$. (d) F. It is an infinite set. (e) F.
Infinite sets are equivalent to proper subsets of
themselves. (f) F. Consider $A = \{1, 2, 3, 4, \ldots\}$ and
$B = \{1, 2\}$. $B \subseteq A$ and B is finite. (g) T (h) F.
Consider $A = \{1, 2\}$, $B = \{a\}$. $A \cap B = \varnothing$. (i) F. $\varnothing$
has no elements. (j) T

CHAPTER 3

Problem Set 3-1 **1.** (a) $\overline{\overline{\text{MCDXXIV}}}$ (b) 46,032
(c) $<$▼▼ (d) ∩ | **3.** (a) Use place value in
columns as done in the Hindu-Arabic system. Group the
numerals in each column and trade symbols and shift
columns if possible. (b) Group all the same symbols
for each number; trade if possible to make the sum using
as few symbols as possible. (c) Add values of symbols
and trade to make the sum as simple as possible.
5. No, $6000 = 1 \cdot 60^2 + 40 \cdot 60 + 0 \cdot 1$ and there is no
numeral in the Babylonian system to stand for the
placeholder zero.
7.

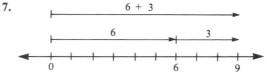

9. Answers vary

Problem Set 3-2 **1.** (a) Hundreds (b) Tens
(c) Thousands (d) Hundred thousands (e) Ten
thousands (f) Hundred thousands **3.** 5 is farther to
left on number line than 7. 6 is farther to right on
number line than 3. **5.** No. If $k = 0$, we would have k
$= 0 + k$ implying $k > k$.
7.

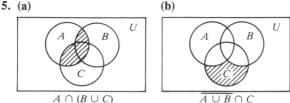

9. (a) Yes **(b)** Yes **(c)** Yes **(d)** No
11. (a) "Siamese cat show" versus "Siamese show cat."
(b) "Going to school I saw the birds" versus "I saw the birds going to school." **13. (a)** 3 **(b)** 3 **(c)** 13
(d) a **(e)** 0 **(f)** {3, 4, 5, 6, 7, 8, 9} **(g)** {10, 11, 12, . . .} **15. (a)** $x = 119 + 213$ **(b)** $213 = x + 119$
(c) $213 = 119 + x$ **17. (a)** X X X X X X X X X X
(b) X X X X X X X X X **(c)** ⬚7 $+ 2 = 9$
⇕ ⇕
0 0
19. (a) $a = b$ **(b)** If $c = 0$, then it is true for all whole number values for which $(a - b)$ is defined. **(c)** $a = 0$
(d) All whole number values of a, b, and c for which $(b - c)$ is meaningful. **21. (a) (i)** $93 + 39 = 132$; $132 + 231 = 363$ **(ii)** $588 + 885 = 1473$; $1473 + 3741 = 5214$; $5214 + 4125 = 9339$ **(iii)** $2003 + 3002 = 5005$ **(b)** Answers vary **23.** 9 pages **25. (a)** 70
(b) 9000 **(c)** 1100 **(d)** 560 **(e)** 3470
27. 9,876,543 **29.** Depends on the individual calculator. **31. (a)** CMLIX **(b)** XXXVIII

Problem Set 3-3 1.

3. $16.00 **5.** $8 \cdot 3 = (6 + 2) \cdot 3$
$= 6 \cdot 3 + 2 \cdot 3$
$= 18 + 6 = 24$
7. (a) 303 **(b)** $ac + ad + bc + bd$
(c) $3x + 3y + 15$ **(d)** $\square \cdot \triangle + \square \cdot \bigcirc$
(e) $x^2 + xy + xz + yx + y^2 + yz$ or
$x^2 + 2xy + xz + y^2 + yz$ **9. (a)** $5x$ **(b)** $14x$
(c) $5(x + 1)$ or $5x + 5$ **(d)** $a(b + 1)$ **(e)** $m(b + c + 1)$
(f) $(2 + x)(x + 3)$
11. $a(b + c + d) = a((b + c) + d)$
$= a(b + c) + ad$
$= (ab + ac) + ad$
$= ab + ac + ad$
13. (a) 6 **(b)** 0 **(c)** 4 **15. (a)** $2 \div 1 \neq 1 \div 2$
(b) $(8 \div 4) \div 2 \neq 8 \div (4 \div 2)$ **(c)** $8 \div (2 + 2) \neq (8 \div 2) + (8 \div 2)$ **(d)** $3 \div 4 \notin W$ **17.** $32
19. 2; 3 left

21. (a)

$\square$	$\triangle$
0	34
1	26
2	18
3	10
4	2

(b) $\triangle = 66$

(c)

$\square$	$\triangle$
25	1
1	25

Also $\square = 5$ and $\triangle = 5$ if $\square = \triangle$.
23. 12 **25.** 30 **27. (a)** 3 **(b)** 2 **(c)** 2 **(d)** 6
(e) 4 **29. (i)** ∩∩∩∩∩∩∩ |||||
(ii) LXXV **(iii)** ▼ ⟨▼▼▼▼▼
31. For example, {0, 1}
33.

Problem Set 3-4 1. (a)

$$\begin{array}{r} 3789 \\ 9296 \\ 6843 \\ \hline 19928 \end{array}$$

(b)

$$\begin{array}{r} 3004 \\ +987 \\ \hline 3991 \end{array}$$

(c)

$$\begin{array}{r} 524 \\ 328 \\ 567 \\ +135 \\ \hline 1554 \end{array}$$

3. The columns separate place value and show that $7 + 8 = 15$ and $20 + 60 = 80$. Finally, $15 + 80 = 95$. **5. (a)** 357; $357 + 79 = 436$ **(b)** 902; $902 + 99 = 1001$ **(c)** 2874; $2874 + 129 = 3003$
7. (a) One possibility

$$\begin{array}{r} 863 \\ +752 \\ \hline 1615 \end{array}$$

(b) One possibility

$$\begin{array}{r} 368 \\ +257 \\ \hline 625 \end{array}$$

9. 434 **11.** 15,782 **13.** 47¢ **15.** Yes; No, not all at dinner **17.** Yes, because a subtraction such as $a - b$ becomes $(a + 10^n) - (b + 10^n)$
19. $8 + 8 + 8 + 88 + 888$ **21. (a)** 34; 34; 34
(b) 34 **(c)** 34 **(d)** Yes **(e)** Yes
23. $5280 = 5 \cdot 10^3 + 2 \cdot 10^2 + 8 \cdot 10 + 0$
25.

27. 1,000,410   **29.** 15

Laboratory Activity

1. (a)

16	3	13
8	1	7
8	2	6

(b)

28	7	21
15	12	3
13	-5	18

Problem Set 3-5

1. (a)

(b)

3. $386 \cdot 10,000 = (3 \cdot 10^2 + 8 \cdot 10 + 6) \cdot 10^4$
$= (3 \cdot 10^2) \cdot 10^4 + (8 \cdot 10) \cdot 10^4 + 6 \cdot 10^4$
$= 3 \cdot 10^6 + 8 \cdot 10^5 + 6 \cdot 10^4$
$= 3,860,000$

5. (a) 5^{19} **(b)** 6^{15} **(c)** 10^{313} **(d)** 10^{12} **7.** 86,400;
604,800; 31,536,000 (365 days) **9.** 1022

11.
```
→ 17 ·    63         63
    8    126     + 1008
    4    252       1071
    2    504
→ 1    1008
```

13. (a) 77 Remainder 7 **(b)** 8 Remainder 10 **(c)** 10
Remainder 91 **15.** 12 km/sec **17.** 8 hours, 12 minutes

19. (a)
```
    762
×    83
 63,246
```
(b)
```
   378
×   26
 9,828
```

21. (a)
```
    37
×   43
   111
  1480
  1591
```
(b)
```
    93
×   36
   558
  2790
  3348
```
(c)
```
   1572
×    21
   1572
  31440
  33012
```
(d)
```
    43
×   56
   258
   215
  2408
```

23. 1; 121; 12,321; 1,234,321. Your calculator may not
produce the pattern after this term, but it continues
through 111,111,111 × 111,111,111. **25. (a)** Yes
(b) Yes **(c)** No **(d)** No **27.** $60; $3600; $86,400;
$604,800; $2,592,000 (30 days); $31,536,000 (365
days); $630,720,000 (approximately) **29.** 19
31. 300,260 **33. (a)** $x \cdot (a + b + 2)$
(b) $(3 + x)(a + b)$ **35.** 724

Problem Set 3-6 **1. (a)** (1, 10, 11, 100, 101, 110,
111, 1000, 1001, 1010, 1011, 1100, 1101, 1110,
1111)$_\text{two}$ **(b)** (1, 2, 10, 11, 12, 20, 21, 22, 100, 101,
102, 110, 111, 112, 120)$_\text{three}$ **(c)** (1, 2, 3, 10, 11, 12,
13, 20, 21, 22, 23, 30, 31, 32, 33)$_\text{four}$ **(d)** (1, 2, 3, 4,
5, 6, 7, 10, 11, 12, 13, 14, 15, 16, 17)$_\text{eight}$ **3.** 20
5. (a) 111_two **(b)** 555_six **(c)** 999_ten **(d)** EEE_twelve
7. (a) ETE_twelve; $EE1_\text{twelve}$ **(b)** 11111_two; 100001_two
(c) 554_six; 1000_six **(d)** 66_seven; 101_seven **(e)** 444_five;
1001_five **9. (a)** 117 **(b)** 45 **(c)** 1331 **(d)** 1451
(e) 157 **(f)** 181 **(g)** 211 **(h)** 194 **11.** 72¢; 242_five
13. 3 quarters, 4 nickels, and 2 pennies **15. (a)** 6
(b) 1 **(c)** 9 **17.** 1 hour, 34 minutes, 15 seconds
19. 4; 1, 2, 4, 8; 5; 1, 2, 4, 8, 16

Laboratory Activity (p. 121) **1. (a)** A computer
2. When a person tells his age by listing cards, he is
giving the base two representation for his age. The
number can then be determined by adding the numbers in
the upper left hand corners of the named cards.

Problem Set 3-7 **1. (a)** 121_five **(b)** 20_five
(c) 1010_five **(d)** 14_five **(e)** 1001_two **(f)** 1010_two
3. (a) 9 hr. 33 min. 25 sec. **(b)** 1 hr. 39 min. 40 sec.
(c) 2 qts., 1 pt., 1 cup
5. 32

   13

   22

   43

   23

   12
  ────
  310_five

7. There is no numeral 5 in base five, $2_\text{five} + 3_\text{five} =$
10_five **9. (a)** 233_five **(b)** 4_five R1_five **(c)** 2144_five
(d) 31_five **(e)** 67_eight **(f)** 15_eight R3_eight **(g)** 110_two
(h) 1101110_two **11. (a)** 450_eight **(b)** 25_eight
Chapter Test **1. (a)** 400,044 **(b)** 117 **(c)** 1704
(d) 11 **(e)** 1448 **3. (a)** 3^{17} **(b)** 2^{21} **(c)** 3^5
5. (a) $3 < 13$ since $3 + 10 = 13$ **(b)** $12 > 9$ since
$12 = 9 + 3$ **7. (a)** 1119 **(b)** $173E_\text{twelve}$
9. (a) 5 remainder 243 **(b)** 91 remainder 10
(c) 120_five remainder 2_five **11. (a)** 3 tens
(b) 3 thousands **(c)** 3 hundreds
13. (a)

(b)

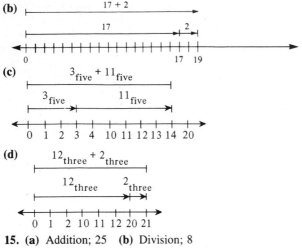

(c)

(d)

15. (a) Addition; 25 **(b)** Division; 8
(c) Multiplication; 72 **(d)** Subtraction; $26.
17. $4380 **19.** $3842

CHAPTER 4

Problem Set 4-1 1. (a) $^-2$ **(b)** 5 **(c)** ^-m **(d)** 0
(e) m **(f)** $-(a + b)$ or $^-a + {^-b}$ or $^-a - b$
3. (a) 5 **(b)** 10 **(c)** 3 **(d)** 7 **(e)** $^-5$
5. (a)

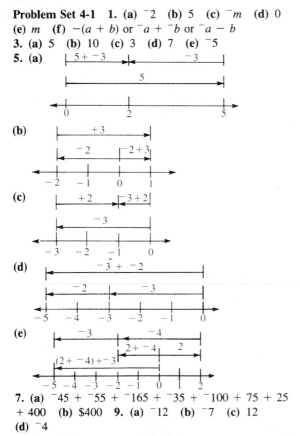

(b)

(c)

(d)

(e)

7. (a) $^-45 + {^-55} + {^-165} + {^-35} + {^-100} + 75 + 25$
$+ 400$ **(b)** $400 **9. (a)** $^-12$ **(b)** $^-7$ **(c)** 12
(d) $^-4$

11. (a)

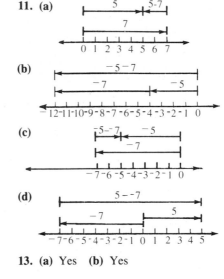

(b)

(c)

(d)

13. (a) Yes **(b)** Yes

15.

2	5	$^-10$	
$^-13$	$^-1$	11	Answers vary
8	$^-7$	$^-4$	

17. $^-269°$ C. **19.** Mileposts 80 or 56 **21. (a)** $^-18$
(b) $^-106$ **(c)** $^-6$ **(d)** 22 **(e)** $^-11$ **(f)** 2 **(g)** $^-18$
(h) 23

Problem Set 4-2 1. (a) 12 **(b)** $^-15$ **(c)** $^-15$
(d) 0 **(e)** 30 **(f)** $^-30$ **(g)** 0 **(h)** 16 **(i)** 30
3. (a) $^-10$ **(b)** $^-40$ **(c)** a if $b \neq 0$ **(d)** $^-10$ **(e)** a
if $b \neq 0$ **(f)** $^-32$ **(g)** $^-5$ **(h)** 0 **(i)** Impossible
(j) $^-4$ **(k)** Impossible **(l)** 13 **(m)** $^-1$ **(n)** $^-9$
(o) $^-2$ **5. (a)** $^-1(^-5 + {^-2}) = {^-1}(^-5) + {^-1}(^-2)$
(b) $^-3(^-3 + 2) = {^-3}(^-3) + {^-3}(2)$ **(c)** $^-5(2 + {^-6}) =$
$^-5(2) + {^-5}(^-6)$ **7. (a)** Yes **(b)** Yes **(c)** Yes
(d) Yes **9.** $^-15°$C **11. (a)** $^-13, {^-17}, {^-21}$ **(b)** $^-12,$
$^-14, {^-16}$ **(c)** $^-9, 3, {^-1}$ **(d)** $^-5, {^-2}, 1$
13. $3(^-1) = {^-1} + {^-1} + {^-1} = {^-3}$
$2(^-1) = {^-1} + {^-1} = {^-2}$
$1(^-1) = {^-1}$
$0(^-1) = 0$
$^-1(^-1) = 1$ by continuing the pattern
15. (a) and **(f)** are always negative; **(b)**, **(c)**, **(g)**, and **(h)**
are always positive **17. (a)** xy **(b)** $2xy$ **(c)** 0
(d) ^-x **(e)** $x + 2y$ **(f)** b **(g)** x **(h)** y
19. (a) $(50 + 2)(50 - 2) = 50^2 - 2^2 = 2496$
(b) $5^2 - 100^2 = {^-9975}$ **(c)** $x^2 - y^2$ **(d)** $4 - 9x^2$
(e) $x^2 - 1$ **(f)** 45,200 **21. (a)** $(3 + 5)x = 8x$

(b) $(a + 2)x$ **(c)** $x(y + 1)$ **(d)** $(a - 2)x$
(e) $x(x + y)$ **(f)** $(3 - 4 + 7)x = 6x$
(g) $x(3y + 2 - z)$ **(h)** $x(3x + y - 1)$
(i) $a(bc + b - 1)$ **(j)** $(a + b)(c + 1 - 1) = (a + b)c$
(k) $(4 - a)(4 + a)$ **(l)** $(x - 3y)(x + 3y)$
(m) $(2x - 5y)(2x + 5y)$ **(n)** $(x + y)(x - y + 1)$
23. (a) $^-81$ **(b)** 184 **(c)** $^-2$ **(d)** 2
25.

```
        -8+(-5)
   |←————————————————|
      -5        -8
   |——————|—|←———————|
   |—|—|—|—|—|—|—|—|—|—|—|—|—|—|
  -13-12-11-10-9-8-7-6-5-4-3-2-1 0
```

27. (a) 14 **(b)** 21 **(c)** $^-4$ **(d)** 22

Problem Set 4-3 **1. (a)** $^-20, ^-13, ^-5, ^-3, 0, 4$
(b) $^-6, ^-5, 0, 5, 6$ **(c)** $^-100, ^-20, ^-15, ^-13, 0$
(d) $^-3, ^-2, 5, 13$ **3. (a)** $\{^-18\}$ **(b)** $\{x \mid x > ^-18,$
$x \in I\}$ **(c)** $\{18\}$ **(d)** $\{x \mid x < 18, x \in I\}$ **(e)** $\{^-18\}$
(f) $\{x \mid x \le ^-18, x \in I\}$ **(g)** $\{^-7\}$ **(h)** $\{x \mid x < ^-7,$
$x \in I\}$ **(i)** $\{^-2\}$ **(j)** $\{x \mid x \ge ^-2\}$ **(k)** $\{^-1\}$
(l) $\{x \mid x < ^-1\}$ **(m)** $\{^-2\}$ **(n)** $\{x \mid x < ^-3, x \in I\}$
5. (a) Yes **(b)** No **(c)** Yes **(d)** Yes **(e)** Yes
(f) No **7. (a)** $\{^-3\}$; $^-2(^-3) + ^-11 = 3(^-3) + 4$
(b) $\{0\}$; $5(0 + 1) = 5$ **(c)** $\{1\}$; $^-3(1) + 4 = 1$
(d) $\{0\}$; $^-3(0 - 1) = 8 \cdot 0 + 3$ **9.** $^-5$ **11.** Nureet is
10; Ran is 14. **13.** 40 lbs. of 60¢ per pound tea and 60
lbs. of 45¢ per pound tea. **15.** 78, 79, 80 **17.** 7, 14
19. (a) Yes. $x^2 + y^2 \ge 2xy$ if and only if $x^2 - 2xy + y^2$
≥ 0 and $x^2 - 2xy + y^2 = (x - y)^2 \ge 0$. **(b)** $x = y$
21. No; $^-5 < 2$ but $(^-5)^2 \not< 2^2$. **23. (a)** $\{^-3, ^-2, ^-1,$
$0, 1\}$ **(b)** $\{^-2, ^-3, ^-4, ^-5, \ldots\}$
25. (a) $^-10$ **(b)** 4 **(c)** $^-4$ **(d)** 10 **(e)** $^-21$
(f) 21 **(g)** $^-4$ **(h)** $^-3$ **(i)** 3 **(j)** $^-4$ **(k)** 7
(l) $^-21$ **(m)** 21 **(n)** 56 **(o)** 15 **(p)** $^-1$

Chapter Test **1. (a)** $^-3$ **(b)** a **(c)** 0 **(d)** $^-(x + y)$
or $^-x + ^-y$ or $^-x - y$ **(e)** $^-(^-x + y)$ or $x + ^-y$ or
$x - y$ **3. (a)** $\{3\}$ **(b)** $\{^-5\}$ **(c)** $\{x \mid x \in I; x \ne 0\}$
(d) $\varnothing$ **(e)** $\{^-41\}$ **(f)** $\{x \mid x \in I\}$
5. (a) $(x - y)(x + y) = (x - y)x + (x - y)y$
$\qquad = (x^2 - yx) + (xy - y^2)$
$\qquad = (x^2 + ^-yx) + (xy - y^2)$
$\qquad = x^2 + (^-yx + xy) - y^2$
$\qquad = x^2 + (^-xy + xy) - y^2$
$\qquad = x^2 + 0 - y^2$
$\qquad = x^2 - y^2$
(b) $(^-2 - x)(^-2 + x) = (^-2)^2 - x^2 = 4 - x^2$
7. (a) $(1 - 3)x = ^-2x$ **(b)** $x(x + 1)$ **(c)** $5(1 + x)$
(d) $(x - y)(x + 1 - 1) = (x - y)x$ **9.** 1010 seniors,
895 juniors, 2020 sophomores, 1790 freshmen
11. $^-7°C$ **13.** 14 lbs **15.** 7 nickels and 17 dimes

CHAPTER 5
Problem Set 5-1

1. (a) T **(b)** T **(c)** T **(d)** T **(e)** T **(f)** F
3. Yes, $9 \not\mid 1379$ **5. (a)** Theorem 5-3 **(b)** Theorem
5-1 (part 2) **(c)** None **(d)** Theorem 5-1 (part 2)
(e) Theorem 5-3 **7. (a)** 5 **(b)** 0 **9. (a)** A number,
N, is divisible by 16 if and only if the number formed by
the last 4 digits is divisible by 16. **(b)** A number, N, is
divisible by 25 if and only if the number formed by the
last two digits is divisible by 25. **11.** Yes **13.** 85,041
15. (a) No. Suppose that the number is divisible by 10;
then it must be divisible by 5, a contradiction. **(b)** Yes;
example $5 \mid 5$ but $10 \not\mid 5$. **17.** Because each digit,
except 0, appears three times, 3 divides the sums of all
like digits. Also $3 \mid 0$, so that 3 divides the sum of all
digits. **19. (a)** Theorem 5-1 part 1: $d \mid a$ means $dx =$
a where $x \in I$. $d \mid b$ means $dy = b$ where $y \in I$. Hence,
$dx + dy = a + b$. Thus, $d(x + y) = a + b$ where
$x + y \in I$. Consequently, $d \mid (a + b)$. Theorem 5-1 part
2: $d \mid a$ means $dx = a$ where $x \in I$. Suppose $d \mid (a + b)$.
Then $dy = a + b$ where $y \in I$. Hence, $dy - dx =$
$a + b - a$ and $dy - dx = b$ or $d \cdot (y - x) = b$. Thus,
$d \mid b$, which is false. Therefore, $d \not\mid (a + b)$.
(b) Theorem 5-2 part 1: $d \mid a$ means $dx = a$, where
$x \in I$. $d \mid b$ means $dy = b$, where $y \in I$. Thus, $dx - dy$
$= a - b$. $d(x - y) = a - b$ where $x - y \in I$. Hence
$d \mid (a - b)$. Theorem 5-2 part 2: $d \not\mid b$ implies $d \not\mid (^-b)$;
Then use Theorem 5-1 part 2. **(c)** Theorem 5-3. $d \mid a$
means $dx = a$, where $x \in I$. Then $k(dx) = ka$,
$d(kx) = ka$. Consequently, $d \mid ka$. **21.** Since $2 \mid 10$,
$2 \mid 10(a_k 10^{k-1} + a_{k-1} 10^{k-2} + \ldots + a_1)$. By
Theorem 5-1, $2 \mid n$ if and only if $2 \mid a_0$. **23. (a)** Yes
(b) Yes **(c)** No **(d)** Yes **(e)** No **(f)** Yes

Problem Set 5-2 **1. (a)** $504 = 2^3 \cdot 3^2 \cdot 7$ **(b)** $2475 =$
$3^2 \cdot 5^2 \cdot 11$ **(c)** $11,250 = 2 \cdot 3^2 \cdot 5^4$ **3.** 73 **5.** 53,
59, 61, 67, 71, 73, 79, 83, 89, 97, 101, 103, 107, 109,
113, 127, 131, 137, 139, 149, 151, 157, 163, 167, 173,
179, 181, 191, 193, 197, 199. **7. (a)** 1×48; 2×24;
3×16; 4×12 **(b)** Only one; 1×47 **9. (a)** 3, 5,
15, or 29 members **(b)** 145 committees of 3; 87
committees of 5; 29 committees of 15; or 15 committees
of 29. **11.** 2^6 or 64 **13.** 27,720 **15.** 3 and 5; 11 and
13; 17 and 19; 29 and 31; 41 and 43; 59 and 61; 71 and
73; 101 and 103; 107 and 109; 137 and 139; 149 and
151; 179 and 181; 191 and 193; 197 and 199. **17.** No;
the student who checked for divisibility by 12 using 2
and 6 is incorrect because $2 \mid n$ and $6 \mid n$ do not imply
that $12 \mid n$. They only imply that $6 \mid n$. **19.** For
example, $6 = 2 \cdot 3$ or $6 = 1 \cdot 2 \cdot 3$. Therefore, 6 would

have at least two prime factorizations. **21.** If any prime q in the set $\{2, 3, 5, \ldots, p\}$ divides N, then $q \mid 2 \cdot 3 \cdot 5 \cdot \ldots \cdot p$. Since $q \nmid 1$ by Theorem 5-1, part 2, $q \nmid (2 \cdot 3 \cdot 5 \cdot \ldots \cdot p + 1)$; i.e., $q \nmid N$.
23. (a) F **(b)** T **(c)** T **(d)** T
25. Let N be a number such that $12 \mid N$.
$$12 \mid N \text{ implies } 12m = N \text{ where } m \in I$$
$$3 \cdot 4 \cdot m = N$$
$$3(4 \cdot m) = N$$
Therefore, $3 \mid N$.

Problem Set 5-3 **1. (a)** 2; 90 **(b)** 12; 72 **(c)** 4; 312
3. (a) 4 **(b)** 1 **(c)** 16 **5. (a)** 160,280
(b) 158,433,320 **(c)** 941,866,496 **7.** 24 **9.** 15
11. (a) ab **(b)** $a; a$ **(c)** $a; a^2$ **(d)** $a; b$ **(e)** 1; ab
(f) $a \mid b$ **(g)** $b \mid a$ **13.** 15 **15.** 36 minutes **17.** 1,
2, 3, 4, 6, 7, 8, 9, 11, 12, 13, 14, 16, 17, 18, 19, 21,
22, 23, 24. **19. (a)** $\frac{7}{12}$ **(b)** $\frac{7}{11}$ **(c)** $\frac{13}{32}$ **(d)** $\frac{1}{4}$ **21.** 2^5
or 32 **23.** 43

Problem Set 5-4 **1. (a)** 3 **(b)** 2 **(c)** 6 **(d)** 8
(e) 3 **(f)** 4 **(g)** Impossible **(h)** 10

3. (a)

$\oplus$	1	2	3	4	5	6	7
1	2	3	4	5	6	7	1
2	3	4	5	6	7	1	2
3	4	5	6	7	1	2	3
4	5	6	7	1	2	3	4
5	6	7	1	2	3	4	5
6	7	1	2	3	4	5	6
7	1	2	3	4	5	6	7

(b) 6; 4 **(c)** Each addition problem. $a - b = x$ can be rewritten as $a = b + x$. Since every number x shows up exactly once in every row and column, no matter what a and b are, then x can be found.

5. (a)

$\otimes$	1	2	3
1	1	2	3
2	2	1	3
3	3	3	3

$\otimes$	1	2	3	4
1	1	2	3	4
2	2	4	2	4
3	3	2	1	4
4	4	4	4	4

$\otimes$	1	2	3	4	5	6
1	1	2	3	4	5	6
2	2	4	6	2	4	6
3	3	6	3	6	3	6
4	4	2	6	4	2	6
5	5	4	3	2	1	6
6	6	6	6	6	6	6

$\otimes$	1	2	3	4	5	6	7	8	9	10	11
1	1	2	3	4	5	6	7	8	9	10	11
2	2	4	6	8	10	1	3	5	7	9	11
3	3	6	9	1	4	7	10	2	5	8	11
4	4	8	1	5	9	3	6	10	3	7	11
5	5	10	4	9	3	8	2	7	1	6	11
6	6	1	7	2	8	3	9	4	10	5	11
7	7	3	10	6	2	9	5	1	8	4	11
8	8	5	2	10	7	4	1	9	6	3	11
9	9	7	5	3	1	10	8	6	4	2	11
10	10	9	8	7	6	5	4	3	2	1	11
11	11	11	11	11	11	11	11	11	11	11	11

(b) 3 and 11 **(c)** On the n-hour clocks on which divisions can be performed, n is prime. **7.** Wednesday
9. (a) 4 **(b)** 0 **(c)** 0 **(d)** 7 **11. (a)** $24 \equiv 0 \pmod 8$ **(b)** $^-90 \equiv 0 \pmod 3$ **(c)** $n \equiv 0 \pmod n$
13. (a) 1 **(b)** 5 **(c)** 10 **15.** Let $N = a_k \cdot 10^k + a_{k-1} \cdot 10^{k-1} + \ldots + a_2 \cdot 10^2 + a_1 \cdot 10^1 + a_0 \cdot 4 \mid N$ if and only if $4 \mid (a_1 \cdot 10 + a_0)$. Proof: $100 \equiv 0 \pmod 4$. Hence, $N = 100(a_k 10^{k-2} + a_{k-1}10^{k-3} + \ldots + a_2) + a_1 10 + a_0 \equiv (a_1 10 + a_0) \pmod 4$. Consequently, $4 \mid N$ if and only if $4 \mid (a_1 \cdot 10 + a_0)$. **17. (a)** For example $2 \cdot 3 \equiv 2 \cdot 1 \pmod 4$, but $3 \not\equiv 1 \pmod 4$ **(b)** For example, $2^2 \equiv 4^2 \pmod 6$, but $2 \not\equiv 4 \pmod 6$

Chapter Test **1. (a)** F **(b)** F **(c)** T **(d)** F **(e)** F
3. (a) 83,160 is divisible by 2, 3, 4, 5, 6, 7, 8, 9, and
11 **(b)** 83,193 is divisible by 3 and 11 **5.** $N = a \cdot 10^2 + b \cdot 10 + c = (99a + 9b) + (a + b + c)$.
Since $9 \mid 9(11a + b)$, then $9 \mid N$ if and only if $9 \mid (a + b + c)$ using Theorem 5.1. **7.** The number must be divisible by both 8 and 3. Since $3 \mid 4152$ and $8 \mid 4152$, then $24 \mid 4152$. **9. (a)** $2^4 \cdot 5^3 \cdot 7^4 \cdot 13 \cdot 29$
(b) $278 \cdot 279$, or 77,562 **11.** 1, 2, 3, 4, 6, 8, 9, 12,
16, 18, 24, 36, 48, 72, 144 **13.** Counting the start, they are together seven times.

CHAPTER 6

Problem Set 6-1 **1. (a)** The solution to $8x = 7$ is $\frac{7}{8}$.
(b) Jane ate seven-eighths of Jill's candy. **(c)** The ratio of boys to girls is seven to eight. **3.** $\frac{4}{18}, \frac{6}{27}, \frac{8}{36}$ **(b)** $\frac{-4}{10}$, $\frac{2}{-5}, \frac{-10}{25}$ **(c)** $\frac{0}{1}, \frac{0}{2}, \frac{0}{4}$ **(d)** $\frac{2a}{4}, \frac{3a}{6}, \frac{4a}{8}$ **5.** Only the fractions in (d) are not equal. **7. (a)** $a = b$ **(b)** $b = c \neq 0$ or $a = 0$ and b and $c \neq 0$. **9. (a)** $\frac{3}{8}$ **(b)** $\frac{1}{2}$
(c) $\frac{1}{6}$ **(d)** $\frac{1}{3}$ **11. (a)** 1 **(b)** $\frac{2x}{9y}$ **(c)** a **(d)** $\frac{a^3 + 1}{a^3 b}$
(e) $\frac{1}{3 + b}$ **(f)** $\frac{a}{3a + b}$ **13.** Only the fractions in (c) are equivalent.

Problem Set 6-2 **1.**

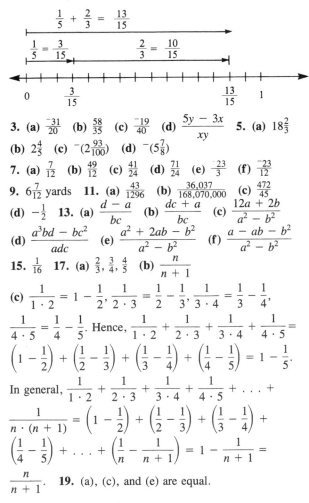

$$\frac{1}{5} + \frac{2}{3} = \frac{13}{15}$$

$$\frac{1}{5} = \frac{3}{15} \qquad \frac{2}{3} = \frac{10}{15}$$

$$0 \qquad \frac{3}{15} \qquad \frac{13}{15} \qquad 1$$

3. (a) $\frac{-31}{20}$ **(b)** $\frac{58}{35}$ **(c)** $\frac{-19}{40}$ **(d)** $\frac{5y - 3x}{xy}$ **5. (a)** $18\frac{2}{3}$
(b) $2\frac{4}{5}$ **(c)** $^-(2\frac{93}{100})$ **(d)** $^-(5\frac{7}{8})$
7. (a) $\frac{7}{12}$ **(b)** $\frac{49}{12}$ **(c)** $\frac{41}{24}$ **(d)** $\frac{71}{24}$ **(e)** $\frac{-23}{3}$ **(f)** $\frac{-23}{12}$
9. $6\frac{7}{12}$ yards **11. (a)** $\frac{43}{1296}$ **(b)** $\frac{36,037}{168,070,000}$ **(c)** $\frac{472}{45}$
(d) $-\frac{1}{2}$ **13. (a)** $\frac{d - a}{bc}$ **(b)** $\frac{dc + a}{bc}$ **(c)** $\frac{12a + 2b}{a^2 - b^2}$
(d) $\frac{a^3 bd - bc^2}{adc}$ **(e)** $\frac{a^2 + 2ab - b^2}{a^2 - b^2}$ **(f)** $\frac{a - ab - b^2}{a^2 - b^2}$
15. $\frac{1}{16}$ **17. (a)** $\frac{2}{3}, \frac{3}{4}, \frac{4}{5}$ **(b)** $\frac{n}{n + 1}$
(c) $\frac{1}{1 \cdot 2} = 1 - \frac{1}{2}, \frac{1}{2 \cdot 3} = \frac{1}{2} - \frac{1}{3}, \frac{1}{3 \cdot 4} = \frac{1}{3} - \frac{1}{4},$
$\frac{1}{4 \cdot 5} = \frac{1}{4} - \frac{1}{5}$. Hence, $\frac{1}{1 \cdot 2} + \frac{1}{2 \cdot 3} + \frac{1}{3 \cdot 4} + \frac{1}{4 \cdot 5} =$
$\left(1 - \frac{1}{2}\right) + \left(\frac{1}{2} - \frac{1}{3}\right) + \left(\frac{1}{3} - \frac{1}{4}\right) + \left(\frac{1}{4} - \frac{1}{5}\right) = 1 - \frac{1}{5}.$
In general, $\frac{1}{1 \cdot 2} + \frac{1}{2 \cdot 3} + \frac{1}{3 \cdot 4} + \frac{1}{4 \cdot 5} + \ldots +$
$\frac{1}{n \cdot (n + 1)} = \left(1 - \frac{1}{2}\right) + \left(\frac{1}{2} - \frac{1}{3}\right) + \left(\frac{1}{3} - \frac{1}{4}\right) +$
$\left(\frac{1}{4} - \frac{1}{5}\right) + \ldots + \left(\frac{1}{n} - \frac{1}{n + 1}\right) = 1 - \frac{1}{n + 1} =$
$\frac{n}{n + 1}.$ **19.** (a), (c), and (e) are equal.

Problem Set 6-3 **1. (a)** $\frac{1}{4} \cdot \frac{1}{3} = \frac{1}{12}$ **(b)** $\frac{2}{5} \cdot \frac{3}{5} = \frac{6}{25}$
3. (a) $\frac{3}{4}$ **(b)** $\frac{3}{8}$ **(c)** $\frac{1}{5}$ **(d)** $\frac{b}{a}$ **(e)** $\frac{-5a}{3b}$ **(f)** $\frac{za}{x^2 y}$
5. (a) $10\frac{1}{2}$ **(b)** $8\frac{1}{3}$ **7. (a)** 27 **(b)** $\frac{8}{7}$ **(c)** $\frac{-6}{7}$ **(d)** $\frac{y}{x}$
(e) $\frac{27}{64}$ **(f)** $\frac{1}{12}$ **(g)** $\frac{32}{21}$ **(h)** $\frac{7}{10}$ **(i)** $\frac{-14}{5}$ **9. (a)** $\frac{21}{8}$
(b) $\frac{1}{5}$ **(c)** $\frac{3}{35}$ **(d)** $\frac{15}{32}$ **(e)** -28 **(f)** $\frac{-45}{28}$ **(g)** $\frac{-56}{5}$
(h) $\frac{-7}{15}$ **(i)** $\frac{-15}{2}$ **11.** 51 and 52 **13.** 45 days
15. $\frac{1}{6}; \frac{1}{1008}$ **17. (a)** 39 uniforms
(b) $\frac{1}{4}$ yard left **19.** 7 oz. **21.** $13\frac{1}{3}$ hours
23. Let $x = \frac{a}{b}, y = \frac{c}{d}, z = \frac{e}{f}$. Then $(x \cdot y) \div z =$
$\left(\frac{a}{b} \cdot \frac{c}{d}\right) \div \frac{e}{f} = \frac{ac}{bd} \div \frac{e}{f} = \frac{ac}{bd} \cdot \frac{f}{e} = \frac{acf}{bde}, x \cdot (y \div z) =$
$\frac{a}{b} \cdot \left(\frac{c}{d} \div \frac{e}{f}\right) = \frac{a}{b} \cdot \left(\frac{c}{d} \cdot \frac{f}{e}\right) = \frac{acf}{bde}$. Hence, $(x \cdot y) \div z =$
$x \cdot (y \div z)$. **25. (a)** First 3, second 4, third 5. Guess 6.
The guess is correct since $(1 + \frac{1}{1})(1 + \frac{1}{2})(1 + \frac{1}{3}) \cdot$
$(1 + \frac{1}{4})(1 + \frac{1}{5}) = 5 \cdot (1 + \frac{1}{5}) = 6$. **(b)** 102
(c) $n + 2$ **27. (a)** 0.1333333 **(b)** 0.0123838 **(c)** 2
29. 120 students

Problem Set 6-4 **1. (a)** $>$ **(b)** $>$ **(c)** $<$ **(d)** $<$
(e) $=$ **(f)** $=$ **3. (a)** $x \leq \frac{27}{16}$ **(b)** $x \geq \frac{115}{3}$
(c) $x < \frac{17}{5}$ **(d)** $x \geq \frac{141}{22}$ **5. (a)** No. Multiplication by bd, which is negative, reverses order. **(b)** Yes. Multiplication by bd, which is positive, retains same order. **7.** 40 **9.** $\frac{3}{2}$ **11.** $\frac{16}{9}$ **13.** 2469 **15.** 270 miles **17.** Let $\frac{a}{b}$ and $\frac{c}{d}$ be two proper fractions where a, b, c, $d > 0$. We need to prove that $\frac{a}{b} \cdot \frac{c}{d} < \frac{a}{b}$. This is true if and only if $\frac{ac}{bd} < \frac{ad}{bd}$. Because $b > 0$ and $d > 0$, the last inequality is equivalent to $ac < ad$, which in turn is equivalent to $c < d$ (because $a > 0$). Now $c < d$ is true because $\frac{c}{d}$ is a proper fraction. Similarly, $\frac{a}{b} \cdot \frac{c}{d} < \frac{c}{d}$.
19. (a) $\frac{a}{b} = \frac{c}{d}$ implies that **(b)** $\frac{a}{b} = \frac{c}{d}$ implies that
$\frac{a}{b} + 1 = \frac{c}{d} + 1$, $\qquad$ $\frac{a}{b} - 1 = \frac{c}{d} - 1$,
$\frac{a}{b} + \frac{b}{b} = \frac{c}{d} + \frac{d}{d}$, $\qquad$ $\frac{a}{b} - \frac{b}{b} = \frac{c}{d} - \frac{d}{d}$,
$\frac{a + b}{b} = \frac{c + d}{d}$. $\qquad$ $\frac{a - b}{b} = \frac{c - d}{d}$.
Using this and part (a)
$\frac{\frac{a - b}{b}}{\frac{a + b}{b}} = \frac{\frac{c - d}{d}}{\frac{c + d}{d}}$ or $\frac{a - b}{a + b} = \frac{c - d}{c + d}$

21. $0 < \dfrac{a}{b} < \dfrac{c}{d}$ so that $0 < \dfrac{1}{2} \cdot \dfrac{a}{b} < \dfrac{1}{2} \cdot \dfrac{c}{d}$. Also, $0 < \dfrac{a}{b} =$
$\dfrac{1}{2} \cdot \dfrac{a}{b} + \dfrac{1}{2} \cdot \dfrac{a}{b} < \dfrac{1}{2} \cdot \dfrac{a}{b} + \dfrac{1}{2} \cdot \dfrac{c}{d} = \dfrac{1}{2}\left(\dfrac{a}{b} + \dfrac{c}{d}\right)$. Similarly,
$\dfrac{1}{2}\left(\dfrac{a}{b} + \dfrac{c}{d}\right) < \dfrac{c}{d}$ and therefore $0 < \dfrac{a}{b} < \dfrac{1}{2}\left(\dfrac{a}{b} + \dfrac{c}{d}\right) < \dfrac{c}{d}$.
23. (a) $\frac{29}{8}$ (b) $\frac{87}{68}$ (c) $\frac{25}{144}$ (d) 1 (provided that
$|x| \neq |y|$). **25.** (a) $x = \frac{-4}{3}$ (b) $\frac{-11}{8}$ (c) $\frac{24}{17}$ (d) $\frac{3}{5}$

Problem Set 6-5 1. (a) $\dfrac{1}{3^{13}}$ (b) 3^{13} (c) 5^{11}

(d) 5^{19} (e) $\dfrac{1}{(^-5)^2}$ or $\dfrac{1}{5^2}$ (f) a^5 (g) a^2 **3.** (a) False.
$2^3 \cdot 2^4 \neq (2 \cdot 2)^{3+4}$ (b) False. $2^3 \cdot 2^4 \neq (2 \cdot 2)^{3 \cdot 4}$
(c) False. $2^3 \cdot 2^3 \neq (2 \cdot 2)^{2 \cdot 3}$ (d) False. $a^0 = 1$ if $a \neq 0$
(e) False. $(2 + 3)^2 \neq 2^2 + 3^2$ (f) False. $(2 + 3)^{-2} \neq$
$\dfrac{1}{2^2} + \dfrac{1}{3^2}$ (g) False. $a^{mn} = (a^m)^n \neq a^m \cdot a^n$

(h) $\left(\dfrac{a}{b}\right)^{-1} = \dfrac{1}{\left(\frac{a}{b}\right)} = \dfrac{b}{a}$ **5.** $2 \cdot 10^{11}; 2 \cdot 10^5$ **7.** (a) $\dfrac{1 - x^2}{x}$
(b) $\dfrac{x^2 y^2 - 1}{y^2}$ (c) $\dfrac{1 + y^6}{y^3}$ (d) $6x^2 + 4x$
(e) $(3a - b)^2$ (f) $8x^2 + 67a^3$ (g) $\dfrac{x^2 y}{y + 3x^2}$
9. (a) $\frac{-3}{5}, \frac{-2}{5}, 0, \frac{1}{5}, \frac{2}{5}$ (b) $\frac{13}{24}, \frac{7}{12}, \frac{13}{18}$
11. (a) $\frac{5}{12}, \frac{6}{12}, \frac{7}{12}$ (Answers vary) (b) $\frac{-3}{36}, \frac{-4}{36}, \frac{-5}{36}$
(Answers vary)

Chapter Test 1.
(a)
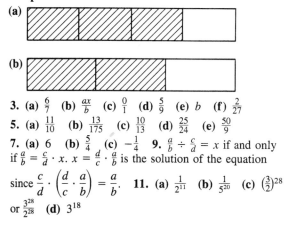
(b)

3. (a) $\frac{6}{7}$ (b) $\frac{ax}{b}$ (c) $\frac{0}{1}$ (d) $\frac{5}{9}$ (e) b (f) $\frac{2}{27}$
5. (a) $\frac{11}{10}$ (b) $\frac{13}{175}$ (c) $\frac{10}{13}$ (d) $\frac{25}{24}$ (e) $\frac{50}{9}$
7. (a) 6 (b) $\frac{5}{4}$ (c) $-\frac{1}{4}$ **9.** $\frac{a}{b} \div \frac{c}{d} = x$ if and only
if $\frac{a}{b} = \frac{c}{d} \cdot x$. $x = \frac{d}{c} \cdot \frac{a}{b}$ is the solution of the equation
since $\dfrac{c}{d} \cdot \left(\dfrac{d}{c} \cdot \dfrac{a}{b}\right) = \dfrac{a}{b}$. **11.** (a) $\frac{1}{2^{11}}$ (b) $\frac{1}{5^{20}}$ (c) $\left(\frac{3}{2}\right)^{28}$
or $\frac{3^{28}}{2^{28}}$ (d) 3^{18}

CHAPTER 7

Problem Set 7-1
1. (a) $0 \cdot 10^{-1} + 2 \cdot 10^{-2} + 3 \cdot 10^{-3}$
(b) $2 \cdot 10^2 + 0 \cdot 10^1 + 6 \cdot 10^0 + 0 \cdot 10^{-1} + 6 \cdot 10^{-2}$
(c) $3 \cdot 10^2 + 1 \cdot 10^1 + 2 \cdot 10^0 + 0 \cdot 10^{-1} + 1 \cdot 10^{-2}$

$+ 0 \cdot 10^{-3} + 3 \cdot 10^{-4}$ (d) $0 \cdot 10^{-1} + 0 \cdot 10^{-2} +$
$0 \cdot 10^{-3} + 1 \cdot 10^{-4} + 3 \cdot 10^{-5} + 2 \cdot 10^{-6}$
3. (a) 536.0076 (b) 3.008 (c) 0.000436
(d) 5,000,000.2 **5.** (a) Yes (b) Yes (c) Yes
(d) Yes (e) Yes (f) Yes (g) No (h) No (i) No
7. (a) 39.202 (b) 230.697 (c) 168.003
(d) $^-390.6313$ (e) 1.49093 (f) 0.0575763
(g) $^-10.4$ (h) 4.681 (i) $^-0.00399$ **9.** (a) 46.3;
4630; 463,000,000 (b) 0.4; 40; 4,000,000 (c) 463;
46,300; 4,630,000,000 (d) 4630; 463,000;
46,300,000,000 (e) 0.0463; 4.63; 463,000
(f) 0.000000463; 0.0000463; 4.63 (g) 7.9; 790;
79,000,000 (h) 62; 6200; 620,000,000 **11.** (a), (c),
and (f) **13.** Answers vary **15.** 0.128 inches/hour
17. \$231.24 **19.** 62.297604 lbs
21. (a) Dime-a-time (b) System B (c) 25
23. Second option; approximately \$4,368,709 better.

Problem Set 7-2 1. (a) $0.\overline{4}$ (b) $0.\overline{285714}$
(c) $0.\overline{27}$ (d) $0.0\overline{6}$ (e) $0.02\overline{6}$ (f) $0.\overline{01}$ (g) $0.8\overline{3}$
(h) $0.\overline{076923}$ **3.** (a) $3.2\overline{3}, 3.\overline{23}, 3.23, 3.\overline{22}, 3.2$
(b) $^-1.45, ^-1.454, ^-1.45\overline{4}, ^-1.\overline{454}, ^-1.4\overline{54}$ **5.** (a) $\frac{1}{1}$
(b) No positive number, k, can be found such that
$0.\overline{9} + k = 1$ or $1 + k = 0.\overline{9}$. (c) $\frac{1}{3} = 0.\overline{3}$ implies $3 \cdot \frac{1}{3} =$
$3 \cdot 0.\overline{3}$ or $1 = 0.\overline{9}$. **7.** (a) 3.25 (b) 462.245
(c) 0.01515 (d) $462.2\overline{43}$ **9.** (a) 3.325×10^3
(b) 4.632×10^1 (c) 1.3×10^{-4} (d) 9.30146×10^5
11. (a) 1.27×10^7 (b) 5.797×10^6 (c) 5×10^7
13. \$37 **15.** (a) 49736.5281 (b) 41235.6789
17. (a) (1) $0.\overline{142857}$ (2) $0.\overline{285714}$ (3) $0.\overline{428571}$
(4) $0.\overline{571428}$ (5) $0.\overline{714285}$ (6) $0.\overline{857142}$ (b) 6
(c) The answers all contain the same digits, 1, 2, 4, 5,
7, and 8. The digits in each answer repeat in the same
sequence, that is, in each case a 1 is always followed
by a 4 which is always followed by a 2 which is always
followed by an 8, etc. In each of the answers in 1–6 the
starting digit is different but the sequence of numbers is
the same. **19.** (a) 21.6 lbs (b) 48 lbs
21. A fraction in simplest form, $\frac{a}{b}$, can be written as a
terminating decimal if and only if the prime factorization
of the denominator contains no primes other than 2 or 5.

Problem Set 7-3 1. (a) 789% (b) 3.2%
(c) 19,310% (d) 20% (e) $83.\overline{3}\%$ or $83\frac{1}{3}\%$
(f) 15% (g) $1.\overline{3}\%$ or $1\frac{1}{3}\%$ (h) 571.43%
approximately or $571\frac{3}{7}\%$ **3.** (a) 2.04 (b) 50%
(c) 60 **5.** \$16,960 **7.** (a) Bill, 221 (b) Joe, 90%
(c) Ron, 265 **9.** Approximately 89.7% **11.** \$5.10
13. Approximately 18.4% **15.** (a) 4 (b) 2 (c) 25

(d) 200 **(e)** 12.5 **17.** $336 **19.** $3,200 **21.** $16.\overline{6}\%$
or $16\frac{2}{3}\%$ **23.** $10.37 **25. (a)** 4% **(b)** 32% **(c)** 64%
27. Answers vary **29.** 97 days **31.** $0.\overline{2}$
33. (a) 3.25×10^6 **(b)** 1.2×10^{-4}

Problem Set 7-4

1.

	I	P	R	T
(a)	540	2000	9%	3
(b)	42	700	6%	1
(c)	1216	8000	7.6%	2
(d)	70	1400	5%	1
(e)	680	4000	8.5%	2

3. $5460 **5.** 3.5% **7.** $64,800 **9.** Approximately
$23,720.58 **11.** $1944 **13.** (c), 13.2%
15. Approximately $5918.41 **17.** $10,935

Problem Set 7-5 1. Answers vary; one possibility is
0.232233222333 . . . **3. (a)** Yes **(b)** No **(c)** No
(d) Yes **(e)** Yes **(f)** Yes **5. (a)** 4.12 **(b)** 2.65
(c) 4.58 **(d)** 0.11 **(e)** 4.51 **(f)** 1.28
7. No; $\sqrt{9 + 16} \neq \sqrt{9} + \sqrt{16}$ **9.** Answers vary; for
example, $\sqrt{2}, \sqrt{3}, \sqrt{5}, \sqrt{6}, \sqrt{7}, \sqrt{8}, 1 + \sqrt{2}$
11. Since $\frac{22}{7}$ is rational and π is irrational and since the
set of rationals and the set of irrationals are disjoint,
these two numbers cannot equal each other.
13. (a) 64 **(b)** $\varnothing$ **(c)** $^-64$ **(d)** $\varnothing$ **(e)** $\{x \mid x > 0\}$
(f) $\varnothing$

15.

	N	I	Q	R
(a)	✓	✓	✓	✓
(b)			✓	✓
(c)				✓
(d)	✓	✓	✓	✓
(e)				
(f)			✓	✓

17. (a) 8.98 seconds **(b)** 20.07 seconds **19.** Suppose
$\sqrt{p}$ is rational where p is a prime. Then $\sqrt{p} = \frac{a}{b}$ where
a and b are integers.

$$p = \frac{a^2}{b^2}$$

$$pb^2 = a^2$$

Since b^2 has an even number of p's in its prime factorization, pb^2 has an odd number of p's in its prime
factorization. Thus, a^2 has an odd number of p's in its
prime factorization and this is impossible. Thus, $\sqrt{p}$ is
irrational. **21. (a)** $0.5 + \frac{1}{0.5} = 0.5 + 2 = 2.5 \geq 2$

(b) Suppose $x + \frac{1}{x} < 2$. Then $\dfrac{x^2 + 1}{x} < 2$. Since $x > 0$,
then

$$x^2 + 1 < 2x$$

$$x^2 - 2x + 1 < 0$$

$(x - 1)^2 < 0$, which is false. Thus, $x + \frac{1}{x} \geq 2$.
23. $\frac{3}{1250}$ **25.** $\frac{24}{99} = \frac{8}{33}$ **27.** $20,274

Problem Set 7-6 1. (a) $6\sqrt{5}$ **(b)** 23 **(c)** $11\sqrt{3}$
(d) $6\sqrt{7}$ **(e)** $\frac{13}{14}$ **(f)** $\frac{7}{14}$ or $\frac{1}{2}$
3. (a) $2\sqrt{3} + 3\sqrt{2} + 6\sqrt{5}$ **(b)** $2\sqrt[3]{5}$
(c) $30 + 12\sqrt{6}$ **(d)** $\dfrac{1}{\sqrt{2}}$ or $\dfrac{\sqrt{2}}{2}$
(e) $17\sqrt{2}$ **(f)** $\sqrt{6}$ **5.** No. $\sqrt{3^2 + 4^2} \neq 3 + 4$
7. (a) 4 **(b)** $\frac{3}{2}$ **(c)** $\frac{-4}{7}$ **(d)** $\frac{5}{6}$

Chapter Test (a) $^-0.693$ **(b)** 31.564 **(c)** 0.2284
(d) 0.032 **(e)** $^-0.097$ **(f)** 0.00000016 **3.** A fraction
in simplest form, $\frac{a}{b}$, can be written as a terminating
decimal if and only if the prime factorization of the
denominator contains no primes other than 2 or 5.
5. (a) $0.\overline{571428}$ **(b)** 0.125 **(c)** $0.\overline{6}$ **(d)** 0.625
7. (a) 307.63 **(b)** 307.6 **(c)** 308 **(d)** 300
9. (a) 25% **(b)** 192 **(c)** $56.\overline{6}$ **(d)** 20% **11. (a)** 0.6
or 0.60 **(b)** $0.00\overline{6}$ **(c)** 1 **13.** $4.7958 \doteq 4.796$
15. If patterns continue, (a), (b), and (e) are irrational;
(c) and (d) are rational. **17. (a)** $\dfrac{1}{2^{11}}$ **(b)** $\dfrac{1}{5^{20}}$ **(c)** $(\frac{3}{2})^{28}$
or $\dfrac{3^{28}}{2^{28}}$ **(d)** 3^{18} **19.** $3.\overline{3}\%$ **21.** $5750
23. Approximately $15,110.69

CHAPTER 8

Problem Set 8-1 1. (a) $\{m, a, t, h\}$ **(b)** $\{1, 2, 3, 4\}$
(c) {Red, Blue} **(d)** $S = \{(1, \text{Red}), (1, \text{Blue}), (2, \text{Red}),$
$(2, \text{Blue}), (3, \text{Red}), (3, \text{Blue}), (4, \text{Red}), (4, \text{Blue})\}$
(e) $S = \{HHH, HHT, HTH, HTT, THH, THT, TTH, TTT\}$
(f) $S = \{(\text{Red}, 1), (\text{Red}, 2), (\text{Red}, 3), (\text{Red}, 4),$
$(\text{Red}, 5), (\text{Red}, 6), (\text{Blue}, 1), (\text{Blue}, 2), (\text{Blue}, 3),$
$(\text{Blue}, 4), (\text{Blue}, 5), (\text{Blue}, 6)\}$ **(g)** $S = \{(1, 1), (1, 2),$
$(1, 3), (1, 4), (2, 1), (2, 2), (2, 3), (2, 4), (3, 1), (3, 2),$
$(3, 3), (3, 4), (4, 1), (4, 2), (4, 3), (4, 4)\}$
3. (b) $P(A) = \frac{5}{10}$ or $\frac{1}{2}$ **(c)** $P(C) = \frac{5}{10}$ or $\frac{1}{2}$ **(d)** $P(D) =$
$\frac{9}{10}$ **5. (a)** $P(\text{Brown}) = \frac{4}{12}$ or $\frac{1}{3}$
(b) $P(\text{Either black or green}) = \frac{8}{12}$ or $\frac{2}{3}$ **(c)** $P(\text{Red}) =$
$\frac{0}{12} = 0$ **(d)** $P(\text{Not black}) = \frac{6}{12}$ or $\frac{1}{2}$ **7. (a)** A person
may both drink and smoke and thus the events are not
mutually exclusive. **(b)** Since these events are
complementary, the probabilities should sum to 1.

(c) Since the population of each state is not the same, the outcomes are not equally likely.   **9. (a)** P(Win on first roll) $= \frac{8}{36}$ or $\frac{2}{9}$ **(b)** P(Lose on first roll) $= \frac{4}{36}$ or $\frac{1}{9}$

(c) P(Neither winning nor losing on first roll) $= \frac{24}{36}$ or $\frac{2}{3}$

(d) Either 6 or 8 has a probability of $\frac{5}{36}$ of occurring again.   **(e)** $P(1) = 0$ **(f)** P(less than 13) $= 1$ **(g)** 10

11. (a) P(Black) $= \frac{18}{38}$ or $\frac{9}{19}$ **(b)** P(0 or 00) $- \frac{2}{38}$ or $\frac{1}{19}$

(c) P(not $1 - 12$) $= \frac{26}{38}$ or $\frac{13}{19}$ **(d)** P(Odd or green) $= \frac{20}{38}$ or $\frac{10}{19}$ **13.** 40

Problem Set 8-2   1. (a) $\frac{1}{216}$ **(b)** $\frac{1}{120}$ **3.** $\frac{1}{30}$

5. (a) $\frac{64}{75}$ **(b)** $\frac{11}{75}$ **7. (a)** $P(\bigcirc\bigcirc) = \frac{1}{5}$ **(b)** P(at least one black) $= \frac{4}{5}$ **(c)** P(at most one black) $= \frac{11}{15}$

(d) $P(\bullet\bigcirc,\bigcirc\bullet) = \frac{8}{15}$ **9.** $\frac{1}{16}$ **11.** $\frac{1}{32}$ **13. (a)** $P(A) = \frac{4}{52}$ or $\frac{1}{13}$; $P(C) = \frac{13}{52}$ or $\frac{1}{4}$; $P(A \cap C) = \frac{1}{52}$; $\frac{1}{52} = P(A \cap C) = P(A) \cdot P(C) = \frac{1}{13} \cdot \frac{1}{4}$ **(b)** $P(A \cup C) = \frac{16}{52} = \frac{1}{13} + \frac{1}{4} - \frac{1}{52}$ **15.** $\frac{1}{256}$ **17.** $\frac{1152}{39,916,800}$ or $\frac{1}{34,650}$ **19. (a)** $\frac{1}{30}$

(b) 0   **(c)** $\frac{19}{30}$

Problem Set 8-3   1. 12 to 40 or 3 to 10; 40 to 12 or 10 to 3   **3.** 15 to 1   **5.** $\frac{5}{8}$ **7.** $.25   **9.** $3.00

11. Approximately 8¢

Problem Set 8-4   1. 224   **3.** 32   **5.** 1352; 35,152

7. (a) T   **(b)** F   **(c)** F   **(d)** F   **(e)** T   **(f)** T   **(g)** T

9. 15   **11. (a)** 24,360   **(b)** 4,060   **13.** 9! = 362,880

15. 45   **17. (a)** 10   **(b)** 1   **(c)** 1   **(d)** 3

19. (a) 12   **(b)** 210   **(c)** 3360   **(d)** 34,650   **(e)** 3780

21. 1260   **23.** 720   **25. (a)** $\frac{15}{19}$ **(b)** $\frac{56}{361}$ **(c)** $\frac{28}{171}$

Problem Set 8-5   1. (a) November, 30 cm

(b) October, 15 cm; December, 25 cm; January, 10 cm.

3. (a)

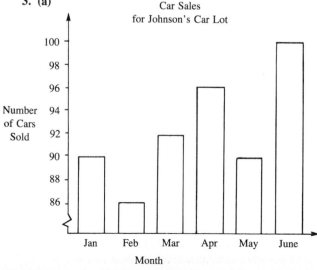

5. (a)

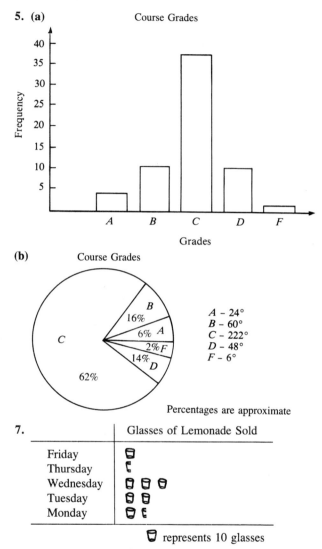

Percentages are approximate

7.

Glasses of Lemonade Sold	
Friday	🥤
Thursday	🥤
Wednesday	🥤 🥤 🥤
Tuesday	🥤 🥤
Monday	🥤 🥤

🥤 represents 10 glasses

9. The horizontal axis does not have uniformly sized intervals and it is not labeled.   **11.** Answers vary.

13. The line graph is more helpful because we can approximate the point midway between 8:00 and 12:00 noon and then draw a vertical line upwards until it hits the line graph. An approximation for the 10:00 temperature can then be obtained from the vertical axis.

15. The year of 1972   **17. (a)** $\frac{16}{27}$ **(b)** $\frac{6}{27}$ or $\frac{2}{9}$ **(c)** $\frac{2}{27}$

(d) $\frac{5}{12}$ **19. (a)** 5040   **(b)** 630

Problem Set 8-6   1. (a) mean = 6.625, median = 7.5, mode = 8   **(b)** mean = 13.$\overline{4}$, median = 12, mode = 12   **(c)** mean $\doteq$ 19.8, median = 18, modes = 18 and 22   **(d)** mean = 81.4, median = 80, mode = 80

(e) mean = 5.8̄3̄, median = 5, mode = 5 **3.** 1500
5. 78.3̄ **7.** Mean = $22,700, median − $20,000, mode
= $20,000 **9.** No, since there may be extreme values.
11. 2.59 **13.** $320 **15.** $41,275 **17. (a)** Range 8,
variance 8, standard deviation 2.8. **(b)** Range 80,
variance 730.4, standard deviation 27.02. **19.** $\frac{68}{100}$
21. (a) 1020 **(b)** 1425 **(c)** 15 **(d)** 7.5 so
approximately 8 **23. (a)** $S = 0$ **(b)** Yes.
25. (a) Approximately 76.81 **(b)** 76 **(c)** 71
(d) Approximately 156.82 **(e)** Approximately 12.52
27. $\frac{15}{36}$ **29.** 1 to 4

Chapter Test **1. (a)** $S = $ {Sunday, Monday, Tuesday,
Wednesday, Thursday, Friday, Saturday} **(b)** $E = $
{Tuesday, Thursday} **(c)** $P(T) = \frac{2}{7}$ **3. (a)** $P(\text{Black}) = $
$\frac{5}{12}$ **(b)** $P(\text{Black or white}) = \frac{9}{12}$ or $\frac{3}{4}$ **(c)** P(Neither red
nor white) $= \frac{5}{12}$ **(d)** $P(\text{Not red}) = \frac{9}{12}$ or $\frac{3}{4}$ **(e)** P(Black
and white) $= 0$ **(f)** P(Black or white or red) $= 1$

5. (a) $P(3W) = \frac{64}{729}$ **(b)** $P(3W) = \frac{24}{504}$ or $\frac{1}{21}$ **7.** $P(L) = $
$\frac{6}{25}$ **9.** $\frac{7}{45}$ **11.** $\frac{3}{3}$ or $\frac{1}{1}$ **13.** 30¢ **15.** 900 **17.** 24
19. 5040 **21.** If it said the average is 2.41 children
then the *mean* average is being used. If it said 2.5, then
the *mean* or the *median* might have been used.
23. (a) mean = 30, median = 30, mode = 10
(b) mean = 5, median = 5, modes = 3, 5, 6

25. (a)

Weight	Tally	Frequency
39	‖	2
40	‖	2
41	‖	2
42	‖‖	4
43	‖	2
44		1
45		1
46		1
47		1
48		1
49	‖	3
		$\overline{20}$

(b)

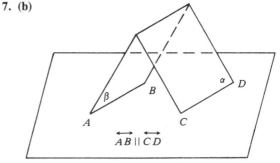

Mass in Kilograms

27.

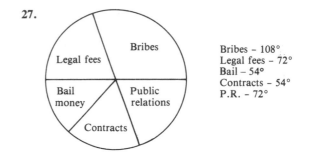

Bribes – 108°
Legal fees – 72°
Bail – 54°
Contracts – 54°
P.R. – 72°

29. $2840

CHAPTER 9

Problem Set 9-1 **1. (a)** C **(b)** ∅ **(c)** C
(d) ∅ **(e)** $\overleftrightarrow{CE}$ **(f)** $\overleftrightarrow{AB}$ **(g)** $\overrightarrow{BA}$ **(h)** $\overrightarrow{AD}$ **3. (a)** $\overleftrightarrow{EF}$
and $\overleftrightarrow{DC}$ **(b)** $\overleftrightarrow{EF}$ and α are parallel **(c)** (i) $\overleftrightarrow{AB}$
(ii) $\overleftrightarrow{BC}$ (iii) $\overleftrightarrow{BD}$ **(d)** No. E, F, and B determine β,
and D is not in β. **5. (a)** An infinite number
(b) One **7. (a)** Yes, if ℓ and m were not parallel they
would intersect in a point common to planes α and β
which contradicts the fact that α and β are parallel.
(b) No, see figure below:
7. (b)

$\overleftrightarrow{AB} \parallel \overleftrightarrow{CD}$

(c) Yes, if the planes were not parallel they would
intersect in a line, ℓ, and at least one of the given lines
would intersect ℓ, and hence the plane α, which
contradicts the fact that the given lines are parallel to α.
9. (a) 3 **(b)** 6 **(c)** 10 **(d)** $1 + 2 + 3 + \cdots + $
$(n - 1) = \frac{n(n-1)}{2}$ **11. (a)** Let ℓ be the line and P be a
point not on the line. Choose any two points Q and R on
ℓ. Let α be the plane determined by P, Q, and R.
Because Q and R belong to α, then ℓ belongs to α. Thus
α is a plane containing ℓ and P. To show α is unique, let
β be any plane containing ℓ and P. Because ℓ is in β, so

are points Q and R. Thus β contains points P, Q, and R. Because α is the only plane containing P, Q, and R, it follows that $\beta = \alpha$.   **(b)** Hint: Choose three noncollinear points on the lines, one of which is the point of intersection. These three points determine a plane.

Problem Set 9-2   1. (a) $\angle ABD$, $\angle DBC$, $\angle EBC$, $\angle EBA$ **(b)** $\overrightarrow{BE}$ **(c)** $\{B\}$ **(d)** $\angle EBC$ **(e)** No
3. (a) $\angle 1$ and $\angle 2$ are adjacent; $\angle 3$ and $\angle 4$ are vertical   **(b)** $\angle 1$ and $\angle 2$ are vertical; $\angle 3$ and $\angle 4$ are adjacent   **(c)** No vertical or adjacent angles marked   **(d)** $\angle 1$ and $\angle 2$ are adjacent
5. (a) 1,2,3,5,6,7,8,9,11,12   **(b)** 1,2,5,7,8,9,11
(c) 1,2,5,7,8,9,11   **(d)** 1,2,7,8,9,11   **(e)** 7,8
(f) 1,2,9,11   **7.** No, two segments will not determine a closed curve.   **9. (a)** $\{E,G\}$ **(b)** $\overline{EG} - \{E,G\}$
(c) $\ell - \overline{EG}$ or $\overrightarrow{EH} \cup \overrightarrow{GK}$ **(d)** $\{F\}$ **11. (a)** Equilateral and isosceles   **(b)** Isosceles   **(c)** Scalene   **13.** 20
15. 20   **17.** (a) and (c) are convex, (b) and (d) are concave.   **19. (a)** $\{C\}$ **(b)** $\overline{BD}$ **(c)** $\overline{AB}$, $\overline{AC}$, and $\overline{AD}$
(d) $\varnothing$ **21.** 6

Problem Set 9-3   1. (a) $42°$ **(b)** $117°$ **3. (a)** $41°\,31'\,30''$ **(b)** $79°\,48'\,47''$ **5.** $m(\angle 1) = 120°$; $m(\angle 2) = 60°$; $m(\angle 3) = 120°$; $m(\angle 5) = 120°$; $m(\angle 6) = 60°$; $m(\angle 7) = 120°$; $m(\angle 8) = 60°$ **7. (a)** Yes, a pair of corresponding angles are $50°$ each.   **(b)** Yes, a pair of corresponding angles are $70°$ each.   **(c)** Yes, a pair of alternate interior angles are $40°$ each.   **(d)** Yes, a pair of corresponding angles are $90°$ each.   **9. (a)** $60°$ **(b)** $45°$ **(c)** $60°$
(d) $60°$ **11. (a)** $540°$ **(b)** $720°$ **(c)** 18
13. (a) $5 \cdot 180° - 360° = 540°$ **(b)** The sum of the measures of the angles in all n triangles is $n \cdot 180°$. Subtracting the measures of all non-overlapping angles whose vertex is P, we obtain $n \cdot 180° - 360° = (n - 2) 180°$.   **15.** 60, 84, 108, 132, 156   **17.** $90°$
19. If the two distinct lines are both perpendicular, then the measures of $\angle B$ and $\angle C$ are both $90°$. This would force the sum of the measures of the angles in $\triangle ABC$ to be greater than $180°$ which is impossible.
21.

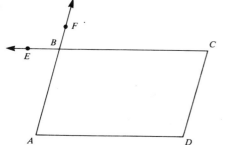

(a) $m(\angle A) = m(\angle FBC)$ (corresponding angles); $m(\angle FBE) + m(\angle FBC) = 180°$ (supplementary angles); $m(\angle FBE) = m(\angle ABC)$ (vertical angles); Thus, $m(\angle ABC) + m(\angle A) = 180°$ (substitution)   **(b)** $m(\angle A) = m(\angle ABE)$ (alternate interior angles); $m(\angle ABE) = m(\angle C)$ (corresponding angles). Hence, $m(\angle A) = m(\angle C)$. Likewise, $m(\angle B) = m(\angle D)$.   **23.** Let $ABCD$ be a quadrilateral with $m(\angle 1) = m(\angle 3)$ and $m(\angle 2) = m(\angle 4)$

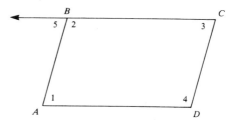

We are given that $m(\angle 1) = m(\angle 3)$ and $m(\angle 2) = m(\angle 4)$. Also, we know $m(\angle 1) + m(\angle 2) + m(\angle 3) + m(\angle 4) = 360°$. Substituting we have $m(\angle 1) + m(\angle 2) + m(\angle 1) + m(\angle 2) = 360°$. Thus $2m(\angle 1) + 2m(\angle 2) = 360°$ or $2[(m(\angle 1) + m(\angle 2)] = 360°$ and so $m(\angle 1) + m(\angle 2) = 180°$. Because $m(\angle 5) + m(\angle 2) = 180°$, then $m(\angle 1) + m(\angle 2) = m(\angle 5) + m(\angle 2)$. Subtracting the $m(\angle 2)$ from both sides, we have $m(\angle 1) = m(\angle 5)$. Now because alternate interior angles are congruent, we have $\overrightarrow{AD} \parallel \overrightarrow{BC}$. Similarly it can be shown that $\overrightarrow{AB} \parallel \overrightarrow{DC}$.
25.

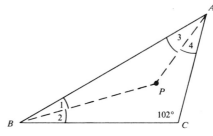

Let $m(\angle 1) = m(\angle 2) = x$ and $m(\angle 3) = m(\angle 4) = y$. Then $m(\angle BPA) = 180° - (x + y)$. In $\triangle ABC$, $2x + 2y + 102° = 180°$ so $2x + 2y = 78°$. Thus $2(x + y) = 78°$ and $x + y = 39°$. Hence $m(\angle BPA) = 180° - (x + y) = 180° - 39° = 141°$.   **27.** 6   **31.** No, adjacent angles share a common side and this cannot happen if the angles are vertical.

Problem Set 9-4.   1. (a) Yes, because m is perpendicular to α, m is perpendicular to every line in α through C. Consequently, $m \perp \overrightarrow{BC}$ and $m \perp \overrightarrow{AC}$ and angles DCB and DCA are right angles. Thus, triangles

BDC and *ADC* are right triangles.   **(b)** No, because △*DPC* will be a right triangle with a right angle at *C*, no other angle can be 90° or more.   **(c)** Yes, because it contains the line *m* which is perpendicular to α.
3. (a) Quadrilateral pyramid   **(b)** Quadrilateral prism
(c) Pentagonal pyramid   **5. (a)** A regular pentagon
(b) An equilateral triangle   **7. (a)** T   **(b)** F   **(c)** T
(d) F   **(e)** F   **(f)** F   **(g)** F   **(h)** T   **9.** Drawings vary

11.

	Pyramid	Prism
(a)	$n + 1$	$n + 2$
(b)	$n + 1$	$2n$
(c)	$2n$	$3n$

(d) Pyramid: $(n + 1) + (n + 1) - 2n = 2$
     Prism: $(n + 2) + 2n - 3n = 2$

13. (a) $V + F - E = 10 + 7 - 15 = 2$
(b) $V + F - E = 9 + 9 - 16 = 2$ **(c)** $V + F - E = 16 + 16 - 32 = 0$, so Euler's formula does not hold.
15. (a) (i) *ABFE* is a parallelogram. $\overleftrightarrow{AB} \parallel \overleftrightarrow{CD}$ and $\overleftrightarrow{CD} \parallel \overleftrightarrow{EF}$, hence $\overleftrightarrow{AB} \parallel \overleftrightarrow{EF}$. Also $\overleftrightarrow{BF}$ and $\overleftrightarrow{AE}$ are parallel because (1) these lines are in parallel planes, and (2) they cannot be skew lines because they are in the plane determined by $\overleftrightarrow{AB}$ and $\overleftrightarrow{EF}$. Thus, *ABFE* is a parallelogram.   **(ii)** *ABFE* is a rectangle. $\overleftrightarrow{AB} \perp \overleftrightarrow{AD}$ because *ABCD* is a square. Likewise $\overleftrightarrow{AB} \perp \overleftrightarrow{AH}$. Because $\overleftrightarrow{AB}$ is perpendicular to two lines in plane *ADE*, it is perpendicular to the plane *ADE*. Thus, $\overleftrightarrow{AB}$ is perpendicular to every line passing through the point of intersection which is *A*. Hence $\overleftrightarrow{AB} \perp \overleftrightarrow{AE}$. Similarly $\overleftrightarrow{AB} \perp \overleftrightarrow{BF}$. It can also be shown in the same manner that $\overleftrightarrow{EF}$ is perpendicular to $\overleftrightarrow{AE}$ and $\overleftrightarrow{BF}$ and so *ABFE* is a rectangle.   **(b)** The planes determined by *ABC*, *DCF*, *HGF*, *ABG*, *ABF*, and *HDC*.   **(c)** Yes, if $\overleftrightarrow{CD}$ intersects the plane *ABF* it must intersect it along $\overleftrightarrow{AB}$ since $\overleftrightarrow{CD}$ is in the plane determined by *ABC* and any point common to both planes is on $\overleftrightarrow{AB}$. This is a contradiction because $\overleftrightarrow{AB}$ and $\overleftrightarrow{CD}$ are parallel.   **17.** No   **19.** 35   **21.** No. If two planes intersect, the intersection is a line.   **23.** 60°
25. (a) T   **(b)** T   **(c)** F. A triangle can have 3 acute angles.   **(d)** F. An angle is not closed.   **(e)** T
(f) F. See figure below.

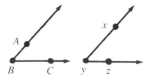

Problem Set 9-5   **1. (a)**, **(b)**, **(c)**, **(e)**, **(g)**, **(h)**, **(j)**, **(k)** are traversable:
(a)

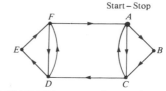

Path: *ABCACDEFDFA*—any point can be a starting point.
(b)

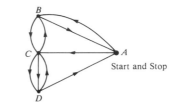

Path: *ABACBCDCDA*—any point can be a starting point.
(c)

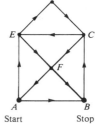

Path: *ABCFAEDCEFB*—only points *A* and *B* can be starting points.
(e)

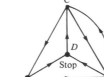

Path: *ABCBDCAD*—only points *A* and *D* can be starting points.
(g)

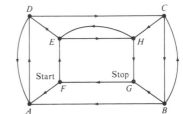

Path: *FADABCBGFEDCHEHG*—only points *F* and *G* can be starting points.

(h)

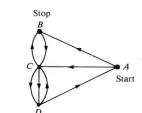

Path: *ACBCDCDAB*—only points *A* and *B* can be starting points.

(j)

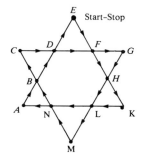

Path: *EFHKLNABDFGHLMNBCDE*—any point can be a starting point.

(k)

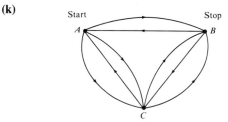

Path: *ABACACBCB*—only points *A* and *B* can be starting points.

3. (a)

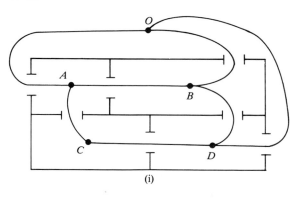

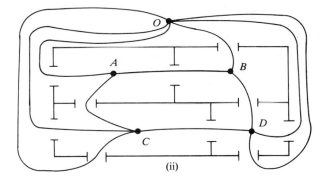

(b) Network (i) is not traversable since it has 4 odd vertices. Network (ii) has 2 odd vertices so it is traversable as shown below.

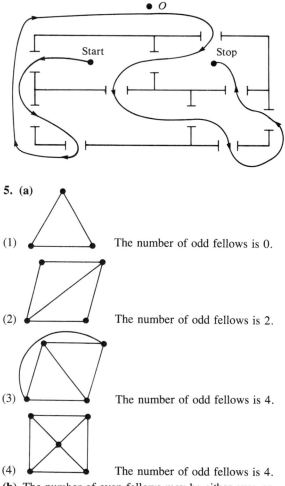

5. (a)

(1)   The number of odd fellows is 0.

(2)   The number of odd fellows is 2.

(3)   The number of odd fellows is 4.

(4)   The number of odd fellows is 4.

(b) The number of even fellows may be either even or odd.

7.

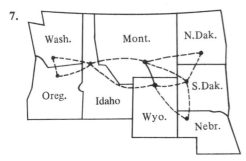

Since all vertices are even, the trip is possible. It makes no difference where she starts.

Chapter Test   1. (a) $\overrightarrow{AB}$, $\overrightarrow{BC}$, $\overrightarrow{AC}$ **(b)** $\overrightarrow{BA}$, $\overrightarrow{BC}$
(c) $\overline{AB}$ **(d)** $\overleftrightarrow{AB}$ **(e)** $\overrightarrow{AB}$ **3. (a)** Three noncollinear points.   **(b)** Two distinct intersecting lines.   **(c)** Two distinct parallel lines.   **(d)** A line and a point not on the line.   **5.** Answers vary.   **7. (a)** No, the sum of two obtuse angles is greater than 180° which is the sum of the measures of the angles in a triangle.   **(b)** No, the sum of the measures of the four angles in a parallelogram must be 360°. If all the angles are acute, the sum would be less than 360°   **9. (a)** Given any convex n-gon, pick any vertex and draw all possible diagonals from this vertex. This will determine $(n-2)$ triangles. Because the sum of measures of the angles in each triangle is 180°, the sum of the measures of the angles in the n-gon is $(n-2) \cdot 180°$.   **(b)** 90 sides.   **11.** 6°   **13. (a)** 60°
(b) 120°   **(c)** 120°   **15.** 48°

CHAPTER 10

Problem Set 10-1   1. (a) Yes; *SAS*   **(b)** Yes; *SSS*
(c) No   **3. (c)** Right triangle   **(d)** Impossible
7. (a) $\angle ABD \cong \angle CBD$; definition of angle bisector.
$\overline{AB} \cong \overline{CB}$; definition of isosceles triangle. $\overline{BD} \cong \overline{BD}$;
$\triangle ABD \cong \triangle CBD$, *SAS*; $\overline{AD} \cong \overline{CD}$; corresponding parts of congruent triangles are congruent (*CPCTC*).
(b) $\angle ADB \cong \angle CDB$, *CPCTC* (using (a) above); $\angle ADB$ and $\angle CDB$ are adjacent; definition of adjacent angles.
$m(\angle ADB) + m(\angle CDB) = 180°$ because $\angle ADC$ is a straight angle. $m(\angle ADB) = m(\angle CDB)$; definition of congruent angles. $m(\angle ADB) = m(\angle CDB) = 90°$.   **9.** If $ABCD$ is such a quadrilateral and F is the intersection point of its diagonals, show that $\triangle AFD \cong \triangle CFB$ and $\triangle AFB \cong \triangle CFD$.   **11.** $\triangle BCD \cong \triangle BCA$ by *SAS* so that $\overline{AB} \cong \overline{DB}$, and DB can be measured.

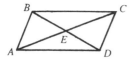

Problem Set 10-2   1. (a) Yes; *ASA*   **(b)** Yes;
AAS   **(c)** No   **(d)** No   **3. (d)** Infinitely many such triangles are possible   **7. (a)** Use *ASA* to show that $\triangle BAD \cong \triangle DCB$ and $\triangle ABC \cong \triangle CDA$.   **(b)** Follows from the congruency of the triangles in (a).   **(c)** Show that $\triangle AFD \cong \triangle CFB$.   **(d)** Show that $\angle DAB$ is congruent to one of the vertical angles formed by $\overleftrightarrow{AB}$ and $\overleftrightarrow{BC}$.
9. (a)

(b) Sum of the angles of a convex quadrilateral is only 360°.   **(c)** No. Any parallelogram with a pair of right angles must have its other pair of angles as right angles and hence be a rectangle.   **11.** Show that $\triangle ABC \cong \triangle ABD$ **13.** Show that $\triangle ABC \cong \triangle BCD \cong \triangle CDE \cong \triangle DEA \cong \triangle EAB$.

Problem Set 10-3   1. (a) Show that $\triangle ABE \cong \triangle CBE$ (The property also follows from problem 7(c) of problem set 10-2).   **(b)** Show that $\triangle DAC \cong \triangle BAC$ and $\triangle ABD \cong \triangle CBD$.   **(c)** Show that $\triangle DAE \cong \triangle BAE$.   **5. (a)** and **(c)** Altitudes should meet at a point in the interior of an acute triangle.   **(b)** Altitudes meet at the vertex of the right angle of a right triangle.   **(d)** Altitudes meet in the exterior of an obtuse triangle.   **7.** Medians meet at a point (centroid).   **9.** Let $ABCD$ be a quadrilateral with $\overline{AB} \cong \overline{CD}$ and $\overline{AB} \parallel \overline{CD}$. $\angle ABD \cong \angle CDB$, alternate interior angles of parallel lines; $\overline{BD} \cong \overline{BD}$, Reflexive property; $\triangle ABD \cong \triangle CDB$, *SAS*; $\angle ADB \cong \angle CBD$, *CPCTC*; $\overline{BC} \parallel \overline{AD}$, congruent alternate interior angles determine parallel lines.   **11.** $\overline{AD} \cong \overline{BC}$ and $\overline{DC} \cong \overline{AB}$ (Opposite sides of a parallelogram are congruent); $\overline{HD} \cong \overline{AH} \cong \overline{CF} \cong \overline{BF}$; $\overline{DE} \cong \overline{CE} \cong \overline{BG} \cong \overline{AG}$; also $\angle A$, $\angle B$, $\angle C$, and $\angle D$ are right angles. Hence, $\triangle DEH \cong \triangle CEF \cong \triangle BGF \cong \triangle AGH$, *SAS*; $\overline{HE} \cong \overline{FE} \cong \overline{GF} \cong \overline{GH}$, *CPCTC*.   **15. (a)** First construct an equilateral triangle.   **(b)** Bisect the angle in (a).   **(c)** Bisect a right angle.   **(d)** Use the fact that $75° = 45° + 30°$.
(e) $105° = 60° + 45°$ **17.** Find the intersection point of the perpendicular bisectors to $\overline{AB}$ and $\overline{AC}$.   **19.** Use the fact that the diagonals of a rhombus bisect all the angles of the rhombus. Then show that all the angles of the figure formed by joining the midpoints of the sides of a rhombus are right angles.   **21.** $\triangle ABC \cong \triangle DEC$ by *ASA* $(\overline{BC} \cong \overline{CE}, \angle ACB \cong \angle ECD$ as vertical angles and $\angle B \cong \angle E$ as alternate interior angles formed by the parallels $\overleftrightarrow{AB}$ and $\overleftrightarrow{ED}$ and the transversal $\overleftrightarrow{EB}$).

Problem Set 10-4   1. (a) Slide   **(b)** Slide   **(c)** Flip
5. Yes, by a slide along a slide arrow perpendicular to ℓ
and m in the direction from ℓ to m whose length is twice
the distance from ℓ to m.   **7.** The final image is
congruent to the original triangle. However, the triangles
are not the same. They can be the same if and only if ℓ
and m are the same line.   **11. (a)** Construct first a 60°
angle by constructing an equilateral triangle.   **(c)** 165° =
180° − 15° or 120° + 45°.   **13.** Prove that the four
triangles formed by the diagonals are congruent.

Problem Set 10-5   1. A circular radio knob is turned
from "off" to "on," a child is swinging, a record
turning.   **3.** Answers vary depending upon how letters
are made.   **5. (a)** 1 vertical   **(b)** 1 vertical   **(c)** None
(d) 1 vertical   **(e)** 5 lines   **(f)** 1 vertical
7.

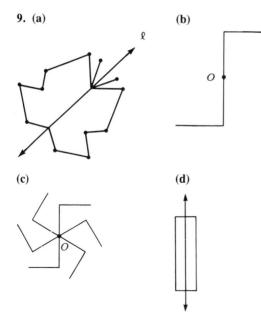

9. (a)   **(b)**

(c)   **(d)**

13. One of the final images can be obtained from the
other by rotation around the point of intersection of the
lines. The rotations are in different directions.

Problem Set 10-6   1. Triangle 3   **3.** This illustration is
one possibility.

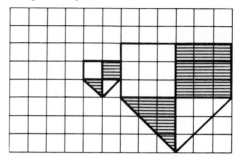

5. (a) $x = 7$ **(b)** $x = \frac{24}{7}$ **(c)** $x = \frac{15}{2}$ **(d)** $x = 10\ m$
7. (a) 9   **(b)** $\frac{14}{3}$ **(c)** $7\frac{1}{2}$ **(d)** 3   **9.** Yes.
Corresponding angles are congruent.   **11. (c)** If in
$\triangle ABC$ and $\triangle DEF$, we have $\dfrac{AB}{DE} = \dfrac{AC}{DF}$ and $\angle A \cong \angle A$,
then $\triangle ABC \sim \triangle DEF$.   **13.** Ratio of the perimeters is
the same as the ratio of the sides.   **17.** $\triangle ABC \sim$
$\triangle BDC$. $m(\angle ABC) = m(\angle ACB)$ (Base angles of an
isosceles triangle are congruent and have the same
measure.) $m(\angle ABC) + m(\angle ACB) + 36° = 180°$;
$2m(\angle ABC) = 144°$; $m(\angle ABC) = 72°$; $\frac{1}{2} m(\angle ABC) =$
$m(\angle DBC) = 36°$; $\angle BAC \cong \angle DBC$. Also $\angle C \cong$
$\angle C$.   **19.** 900 cm   **21. (a)** Turn   **(b)** Turn
(c) Turn   **25.** Show first that $\triangle DEB \cong \triangle FDA \cong$
$\triangle EFC$.

Problem Set 10-7   1. Diameter is the longest chord of a
circle.   **3.** Right triangle.   **5.** No. The tangent line will
intersect one circle in two points.   **7.** Hint: First inscribe
a square in the given circle.   **9.** Hint: The center of the
circle is at the intersection point of the diagonals.
11. Hint: Draw perpendicular from O to ℓ to obtain
radius of the circle.   **13. (a)** Isosceles
(b) $m(\angle 3) + m(\angle COB) = 180°$; $m(\angle 1) + m(\angle 2) +$
$m(\angle COB) = 180°$. Hence, $m(\angle 1) + m(\angle 2) = m(\angle 3)$
(c) $m(\angle 1) = m(\angle 2)$ ($\triangle OCB$ is isosceles). Since
$m(\angle 1) + m(\angle 2) = m(\angle 3)$, it follows that $m(\angle 1) +$
$m(\angle 1) = m(\angle 3)$, $m(\angle 1) = \frac{1}{2} m(\angle 3)$ **15.** The radius
r of the circle is half the distance between the parallel
lines. The center of the circle is on line n parallel to the
given lines and equidistant from these lines. The center
of the required circle can be obtained by finding the point
of intersection of line n with the circle whose center is at
P and whose radius is r.   **17.** Let $m(\angle CAB) = \alpha$ and
$m(\angle ABC) = \beta$. Connect C with O. Since $\overline{AO}$, $\overline{OC}$ and

$\overline{OB}$ are radii, $\triangle AOC$ and $\triangle COB$ are isosceles. Consequently, $m(\angle ACO) = \alpha$ and $m(\angle OCB) = \beta$. In $\triangle ACB$, $m(\angle A) + m(\angle B) + m(\angle C) = 180°$. Since $m(\angle C) = \alpha + \beta$ it follows that $\alpha + \beta + \alpha + \beta = 180$ or $2(\alpha + \beta) = 180°$ or $\alpha + \beta = 90°$. Hence, $m(\angle C) = 90°$. **19.** Show that $\angle EDC \cong \angle AFD$. **21.** $\triangle ADE \cong \triangle CBF$ by SAS. Hence, $\angle DEA \cong \angle CFB$. Since $\angle DEA \cong \angle EAF$ (alternate interior angles between the parallels $\overleftrightarrow{DC}$, $\overleftrightarrow{AB}$ and the transversal $\overleftrightarrow{AE}$) it follows that $\angle EAF \cong \angle CFB$. Consequently, $\overleftrightarrow{AE} \parallel \overleftrightarrow{CF}$. Also, $\overleftrightarrow{EC} \parallel \overleftrightarrow{AF}$ (why?) and therefore $AECF$ is a parallelogram.

Chapter Test 1. (a) $\triangle ABD \cong \triangle CBD$ by SAS
(b) $\triangle AGC \cong \triangle DEB$ by SAS **(c)** $\triangle CBA \cong \triangle CDE$ by AAS **(d)** $\triangle ABC \cong \triangle EDC$ by SAS **(e)** $\triangle ABD \cong \triangle CBD$ by ASA or by SAS **(f)** $\triangle ABD \cong \triangle CBD$ by SAS **(g)** $\triangle ABD \cong \triangle CBE$ by SSS; $\triangle ABE \cong \triangle CBD$ by SSS **(h)** $\triangle ABC \cong \triangle ADC$ by SSS. Possibly others if the pair listed is used to establish corresponding parts of congruent triangles congruent. **3. (a)** Line
(b) Line **(c)** Line, turn, and point

5. (a)

(b)

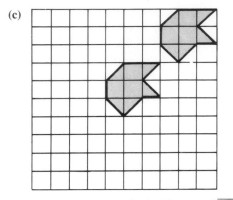

(c)

11. Intersect the perpendicular bisector of $\overline{AB}$ with ℓ. **13. (a)** Show that $\triangle APD \cong \triangle BPC$.
(b) Show that $ABCD$ is a parallelogram and that $\angle BAD$ (or one of the other 3 angles) is a right angle (See problem 17 or Problem Set 10-7).
15. (a) (iii)(iv) **(b)** Any regular convex polygon can be inscribed in a circle. **17.** The point of intersection of the diagonals is the center of the circle. The length of the perpendicular from the center to any side of the square is the length of a radius.

CHAPTER 11

Problem Set 11-1 1. (a) 20; 2 **(b)** 36; 3.6 **(c)** 45; 4.5 **(d)** 5; 50 **(e)** 6.2; 62 **(f)** 7.9; 79
(g) 93; 9.3 **(h)** 11.9; 119 **(i)** 144; 14.4 **(j)** 169; 16.9 **3. (a)** 100 **(b)** 10.0 **(c)** 0.1 **5. (a)** 3.5; 3500 **(b)** 163; 1630 **(c)** 0.035; 3.5 **(d)** 0.1; 10
(e) 200; 2000 **7.** 6 m, 5218 mm, 52 dm, 38 dm, 245 cm, 700 mm, 91 mm, 8 cm **9. (a)** 8 cm
(b) 12 cm **(c)** 9 cm **(d)** 20 cm **11. (a)** 13 cm
(b) $(a + b + c)$ cm **(c)** $3s$ **(d)** $4s$ **(e)** $2l + 2w$
(f) ns **13. (a)** 6π cm **(b)** 6π cm **(c)** 4 cm
(d) $6\pi^2$ cm **15.** πr

Problem Set 11-2 1. (a) cm^2 **(b)** cm^2 **(c)** cm^2
(d) m^2 **(e)** m^2 **(f)** km^2 **3.** Answers vary.
5. (a) 20 cm^2 **(b)** 900 cm^2 or 0.09 m^2 **(c)** 7.5 m^2
(d) 46.5 cm^2 **7.** The area of each triangle is 10 cm^2 since they all have the same base, $\overline{AB}$, and the same height. **9. (a)** 25π cm^2 **(b)** $\frac{8}{3}\pi$ cm^2 **(c)** 3.6π cm^2
(d) 4.5 cm^2 **11. (a)** 2π cm^2 **(b)** $(2 + \frac{\pi}{2})$ cm^2
(c) 2π cm^2 **13.** 24 m^2 **15.** 7π m^2 **17.** 1200
19. (a) $A = 1$, $B = 1$, $C = 4$, $D = 1\frac{1}{2}$, $E = 2$, $F = 3$, $G = 3\frac{1}{2}$, $H = 5\frac{1}{2}$. **(b)** Pick's theorem holds for all polygons in (a), for example, in G, $I + \frac{1}{2}B - 1 = 1 +$

$\frac{1}{2}(7) - 1 = 3\frac{1}{2}$ **21.** Rotate the shaded region 180° clockwise about point E. The area of the triangle is the same as the area of the parallelogram. Thus $A = \frac{h}{2} \cdot b$. **23.** $(50\pi - 100)$ cm^2 or 57.079 cm^2 **25.**

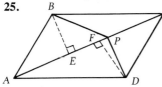

Draw altitudes $\overline{BE}$ and $\overline{DF}$ of triangles BCP and DCP respectively. $\triangle ABE \cong \triangle CDP$ by AAS. Thus $\overline{BE} \cong \overline{DP}$. Since $\overline{CP}$ is a base of $\triangle BCP$ and $\triangle DCP$, and since the heights are the same, the area must be the same. **27. (a)** $(2\pi + 4)$ cm **(b)** $(6 + 5\pi)$ mm

Problem Set 11-3 1. (a) 6 **(b)** $\sqrt{2}$ **(c)** $5a$ **(d)** 12 **(e)** $\sqrt{3}s$ **(f)** $\sqrt{2}$ **(g)** 9 **(h)** 13 **(i)** $\frac{\sqrt{32}}{2}$ or $2\sqrt{2}$ **(j)** $\sqrt{45}$ or $3\sqrt{5}$ **3. (a)** $x = 8, y = 2\sqrt{3}$ **(b)** $x = 4, y = 2$ **(c)** $y = 6$ **5.** $\sqrt{5200}$ km or $20\sqrt{13}$ km or approximately 72.1 km **7.** $\triangle ACD \sim \triangle ABC$. Thus, $\frac{b}{x} = \frac{c}{b}$ implies $b^2 = cx$. $\triangle BCD \sim \triangle BAC$. Thus, $\frac{a}{y} = \frac{c}{a}$ implies $a^2 = cy$. Consequently, $a^2 + b^2 = cx + cy = c(x + y) = c^2$. **9.** The area of the large square is equal to the sum of the areas of the smaller square and the four triangles. Thus,

$(a + b)^2 = c^2 + 4(\frac{ab}{2})$
$a^2 + 2ab + b^2 = c^2 + 2ab$
$a^2 + b^2 = c^2$

The reader should also verify that the smaller quadrilateral is a square. **11.** Yes **13.** $\sqrt{27}$ or $3\sqrt{3}$ **15. (a)**

Draw $\triangle DCB \cong \triangle ACB$. Since all the interior angles in $\triangle ABD$ are 60°, the triangle is equilateral. Hence, $AB = BD = AD$. Since $AC = CD$ it follows that $AC = \frac{1}{2}AD$ and hence $AC = \frac{1}{2}AB$. **(b)** $\frac{\sqrt{3}}{2}c$ **17.** $\frac{5}{3}$ **19.** 0.032 km, 322 cm, 3.2 m, 3.020 mm. **21.** $\frac{25}{\pi}$ m^2

Problem Set 11-4 1. (a) 96 cm^2 **(b)** 236 cm^2 **3. (a)** 4900 square feet **(b)** 1500π square feet **(c)** $32\pi + 16\sqrt{5}\pi$ or $(32 + 16\sqrt{5})\pi$ cm^2

5. 2688π mm^2 **7.** $\frac{16}{36}$ or $\frac{4}{9}$ **9.** Let the radius of the sphere be r and the height of the cylinder h. The area of the sphere is $4\pi r^2$. The lateral surface area of the cylinder is $2\pi rh$. Since $h = 2r$, $2\pi rh = 2\pi r \cdot 2r = 4\pi r^2$. **11.** $(6400\sqrt{2}\pi + 13,600\pi)$ cm^2 **13. (a)** 100,000 **(b)** 1.368 **(c)** 500 **(d)** 2,000,000 **(e)** 1 **(f)** 1,000,000 **15.** $20\sqrt{5}$ **17.** The length of the side is 25 cm. The length of the diagonal is 30 cm.

Problem Set 11-5 1. (a) 8000 **(b)** 0.0005 **(c)** 0.000675 **(d)** 3,000,000 **(e)** 7 **(f)** 2000 **3. (a)** 64 cm^3 **(b)** 120 cm^3 **(c)** 216 cm^3 **(d)** 14 cm^3 **(e)** 50 cm^3 **(f)** 21π cm^3 **(g)** 432π cm^3 **(h)** $\frac{500}{3}\pi$ cm^3 **5.** 1680π mm^3 **7.** It is multiplied by 8.

9.

	(a)	**(b)**	**(c)**	**(d)**
Ht	10	3	20 cm	25 cm
cm^3	2000	6000	4000	7500
dm^3	2	6	4	7.5
L	2	6	4	7.5

11. $253,500\pi$ L **13.** 1.62 L **15.** 32.4 L **17.** 8 cm **19.** 6 cm grapefruit **21.** Approximately 2.2 cm

23. (a) 13,200 cm^2 **(b)** 400 cm^2 **(c)** $\left(1649 + \frac{81\sqrt{3}}{2}\right)$ m^2 **25.** 5 feet

Problem Set 11-6 1. (a) t or kg **(b)** kg **(c)** g **(d)** t **(e)** g **(f)** g **(g)** t **(h)** kg or g **(i)** kg or g **3. (a)** 15 **(b)** 8 **(c)** 36 **(d)** 0.072 **(e)** 4.230 **(f)** 3.007 **(g)** 5750 **(h)** 5.750 **(i)** 30 **(j)** 30,000 **5.** 16,000 g or 16 kg **7.** $0.02 **9. (a)** No **(b)** No **(c)** No **(d)** Yes **(e)** No **(f)** Yes **(g)** Yes **(h)** Chilly **(i)** Hot **11. (a)** 50°F **(b)** 32°F **(c)** 86°F **(d)** 212°F **(e)** 414°F **(f)** ⁻40°F **13. (a)** 35 **(b)** 0.16 **(c)** 400,000 **(d)** 5,200,000 **(e)** 5,200 **(f)** 0.0035 **15.** $\sqrt{61}$ km

Chapter Test 1. (a) 50,000; 5000; 50 **(b)** 3200; 3.2; 0.0032 **(c)** 26,000,000; 260,000; 260 **(d)** 190,000; 19,000; 0.19 **3. (a)** Find the area of $\triangle ADC$ and double it, i.e., $A = 2(\frac{1}{2} \cdot DE \cdot AC)$ **(b)** $A = b \cdot h = DC \cdot FB$ **5.** $8\frac{1}{2}$ **7.** The area of the trapezoid is equal to the area of the rectangle constructed from its component parts. The area of the rectangle is $\frac{h}{2}(b_1 + b_2)$ which is the formula for the area of a trapezoid. **9. (a)** 12π cm^2 **(b)** $(12 + 4.5\pi)$ cm^2 **(c)** 64.5 cm^2 **(d)** 24 cm^2 **(e)** 178.5 m^2 **(f)** 4π cm^2

11. (a) $S.A. = 144 \text{ cm}^2$ **(b)** $S.A. = 96\pi \text{ cm}^2$
$V = 64 \text{ cm}^3$ $V = 96\pi \text{ cm}^3$
(c) $S.A. = 100\pi \text{ m}^2$ **(d)** $S.A. = 54\pi \text{ cm}^2$
$V = \frac{500}{3}\pi \text{ m}^3$ $V = 54\pi \text{ cm}^3$
(e) $S.A. = 304 \text{ m}^2$
$V = 320 \text{ m}^3$
13. (a) L   **(b)** kg   **(c)** g   **(d)** g   **(e)** kg   **(f)** t
(g) mL   **15. (a)** 2000   **(b)** 1000   **(c)** 3   **(d)** 0.0042
(e) 0.0002

CHAPTER 12

Problem Set 12-1   1. (a) $A(2, 2)$; $B(5, 0)$; $C(4, ^-3)$;
$D(0, ^-3)$; $E(^-2, ^-3)$; $F(^-4, 0)$; $G(^-4, 3)$; $H(0, 3)$
(b) $(2, ^-3)$ Answers vary.   **3. (a)** $(0, 2)$ and $(1, 2)$
(b) $(^-1, 1)$ and $(^-1, 3)$ **(c)** $(5, 0)$ and $(6, 0)$
(d) $(0, 1)$ and $(0, ^-1)$ **(e)** $(0, 2)$ and $(0, 3)$ **(f)** $(2, 2)$
and $(3, 3)$ **5. (a)** $x = ^-2$, y is any real number.   **(b)** x
is any real number; $y = 1$.   **(c)** $x > 0$ and $y < 0$; x and
y are real numbers.   **7.** D has coordinates $(4, ^-2)$
9. (a) $x = ^-3$ y **(b)**

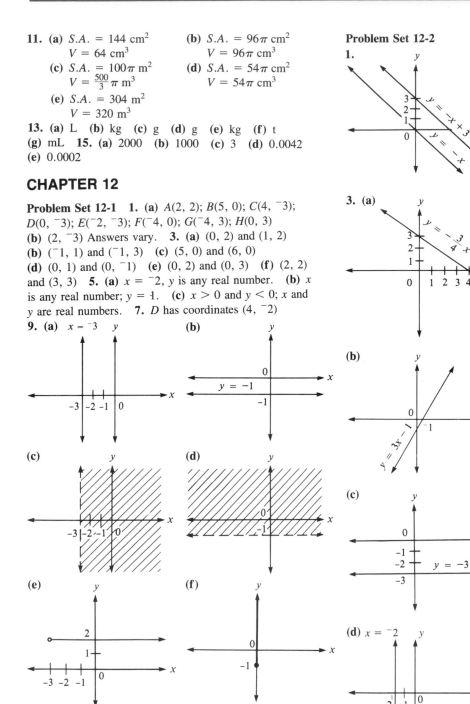

11. (a) $P(3, 4)$; $Q(6, 1)$ **(b)** $N(^-1, 4)$; $M(^-1, ^-1)$
(c) $x = 3$ **(d)** $y = 1$

Problem Set 12-2
1.

3. (a)

(b)

(c)

(d) $x = ^-2$ y

(e)

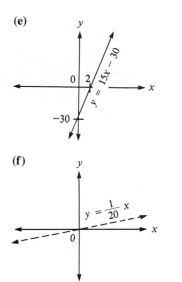

(f)

$y = \frac{1}{20} x$

(c)

(d)

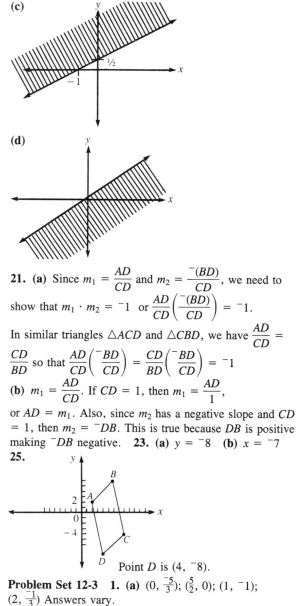

5. (a) $y = \frac{1}{3}x$ **(b)** $y = {}^-x + 3$ **(c)** $y = \frac{3}{4}x + \frac{7}{4}$
(d) $y = \frac{1}{3}x$ **(e)** $y = x$ **7. (a)** $y = {}^-x - 1$
(b) $y = \frac{1}{2}x$ **(c)** $y = 0 \cdot x + 1$ **(d)** $x = 2$ **(e)** $y = x - \frac{1}{2}$ **(f)** $y = 0 \cdot x + 0$ **9. (a)** $y = {}^-2x - 1$
(b) $y = \frac{{}^-2}{3}x + \frac{5}{3}$ **(c)** $x = {}^-2$ **(d)** $y = 3$ **11.** $\sqrt{1616}$
feet   **13.** Slope of $\overline{BC}$ and $\overline{DA}$ is $\frac{1}{2}$ which implies $\overline{BC} \parallel \overline{DA}$. Slope of $\overline{CD}$ and $\overline{BA}$ is 4 which implies $\overline{CD} \parallel \overline{BA}$.
Thus, $ABCD$ is a parallelogram.   **15. (a)** $y = \frac{{}^-1}{2}x - \frac{3}{2}$
(b) $y = \frac{2}{3}x - \frac{11}{3}$ **(c)** $y = \frac{{}^-5}{7}x - \frac{40}{7}$ **17. (a)** $y = {}^-3x - 1$ **(b)** $y = {}^-3x + 1$
19. (a)

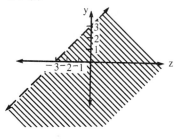

(b)

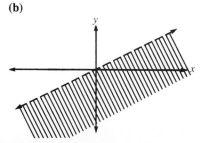

21. (a) Since $m_1 = \dfrac{AD}{CD}$ and $m_2 = \dfrac{{}^-(BD)}{CD}$, we need to show that $m_1 \cdot m_2 = {}^-1$ or $\dfrac{AD}{CD}\left(\dfrac{{}^-(BD)}{CD}\right) = {}^-1$.

In similar triangles $\triangle ACD$ and $\triangle CBD$, we have $\dfrac{AD}{CD} = \dfrac{CD}{BD}$ so that $\dfrac{AD}{CD}\left(\dfrac{{}^-BD}{CD}\right) = \dfrac{CD}{BD}\left(\dfrac{{}^-BD}{CD}\right) = {}^-1$

(b) $m_1 = \dfrac{AD}{CD}$. If $CD = 1$, then $m_1 = \dfrac{AD}{1}$, or $AD = m_1$. Also, since m_2 has a negative slope and $CD = 1$, then $m_2 = {}^-DB$. This is true because DB is positive making ${}^-DB$ negative.   **23. (a)** $y = {}^-8$ **(b)** $x = {}^-7$
25.

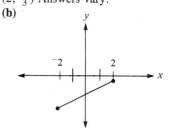

Point D is $(4, {}^-8)$.

Problem Set 12-3   1. (a) $(0, \frac{{}^-5}{3})$; $(\frac{5}{2}, 0)$; $(1, {}^-1)$; $(2, \frac{{}^-1}{3})$ Answers vary.
(b)

(c)

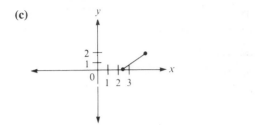

3. (a) ($^-$11, $^-$8) **(b)** ($\frac{^-30}{11}$, $\frac{^-84}{11}$) **(c)** ($\frac{13}{3}$, $\frac{43}{12}$)
(d) ($\frac{^-6}{5}$, $\frac{^-4}{5}$) **(e)** (0, 0) **(f)** ($^-1 + 3\sqrt{2}$, $3 - \sqrt{2}$)
5. The equations of the medians are $y = \frac{1}{2}x$;
$y = 8x - 40$; $y = \frac{^-4}{7}x + \frac{40}{7}$. They intersect at ($\frac{16}{3}$, $\frac{8}{3}$)
7. $\frac{55}{72}$ and $\frac{^-1}{72}$ **9.** $133\frac{1}{3}$ lbs of cashew nut granola and $66\frac{2}{3}$
lbs of golden granola. **11.** \$20,000 and \$60,000
respectively. **13. (a)** \$2,000 **(b)** 6% **15.** 17
quarters and 10 dimes

17.

	Slope	y-intercept
(a)	$\frac{-5}{6}$	$\frac{7}{6}$
(b)	$\frac{-4}{3}$	$\frac{2}{5}$
(c)	3.75	1.85
(d)	0	4

19. (a)   **(b)**

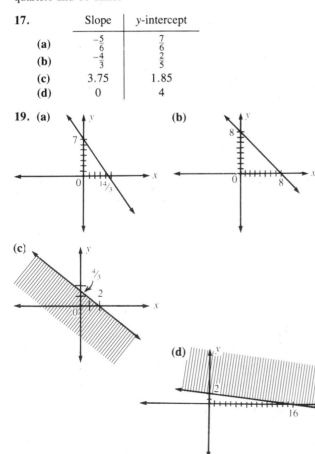

(c)

(d)

Problem Set 12-4 **1. (a)** 4 **(b)** 4 **(c)** 5 **(d)** 5
(e) $\sqrt{52}$ or $2\sqrt{13}$ **(f)** Approximately 3.89 **(g)** 5
(h) 5 **(i)** $\sqrt{68}$ or $2\sqrt{17}$ **(j)** $\frac{\sqrt{365}}{4}$ or approximately 4.78 **3.** The sides have lengths $\sqrt{45}$, $\sqrt{180}$
and $\sqrt{225}$. Since $(\sqrt{45})^2 + (\sqrt{180})^2 = (\sqrt{225})^2$, the
triangle is a right triangle. **5.** $x = 9$ or $x = ^-7$
7. ($^-7$, 11) **9. (a)** $(x - 3)^2 + (y + 2)^2 = 4$
(b) $(x + 3)^2 + (y + 4)^2 = 25$ **(c)** $(x + 1)^2 + y^2 = 4$
(d) $x^2 + y^2 = 9$ **11.** $x^2 + y^2 = 34$
13. $(x + 2)^2 + (y + 2)^2 = 52$ **15.** $(x - \frac{29}{10})^2 + y^2 = (\frac{29}{10})^2$
17. $\pi - 2$ square units **19. (a)** (9, 4) **(b)** ($^-3$, 12)

(c) (1, $^-4$) **21.** M has coordinates $\left(\frac{a}{2}, \frac{b}{2}\right)$;

$$BM = \sqrt{\left(\frac{a}{2}\right)^2 + \left(\frac{b}{2} - b\right)^2} = \sqrt{\frac{a^2}{4} + \frac{b^2}{4}};$$

$$AM = \sqrt{\left(\frac{a}{2} - a\right)^2 + \left(\frac{b}{2} - 0\right)^2} = \sqrt{\frac{a^2}{4} + \frac{b^2}{4}};$$

$$MO = \sqrt{\left(\frac{a}{2} - 0\right)^2 + \left(\frac{b}{2} - 0\right)^2} = \sqrt{\frac{a^2}{4} + \frac{b^2}{4}}.$$

Therefore, M is equidistant from A, B, and O.

23. (a) $y \le \frac{2}{3}x + 7$ **(b)** $y \ge \frac{^-3}{5}x - 10$
25. (a) ($\frac{^-19}{2}$, $\frac{^-13}{2}$) **(b)** No solution

Chapter Test **1.** 16
3. (a)

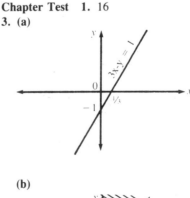

(b)

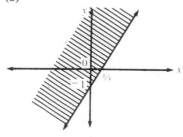

(c)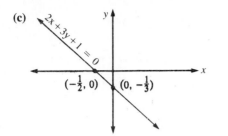

5. **(a)** $y = \frac{4}{3}x + \frac{7}{3}$ **(b)** $y = 5$ **(c)** $(\frac{3}{4}, 5)$ **7.** 80 regular and 30 deluxe

9. **(a)**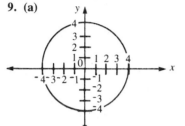

(b)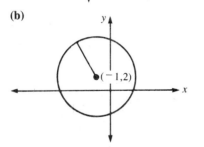

(c)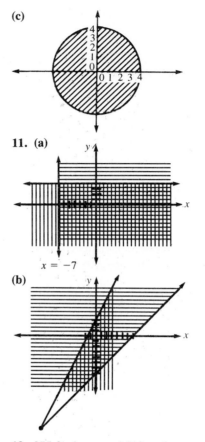

11. (a)

(b)

13. 275 freshmen and 500 sophomores

CHAPTER 13

Problem Set 13-1 **1.** Valid variables are found in (a) and (b). **3. (a)** 7 **(b)** 7 **(c)** 6 **(d)** 3 **(e)** 16 **(f)** -44
5. (a) 5   10 **(b)** A,B **(c)** 5   10 **(d)** 5   10 (format may vary)
(e) No output, or possibly two zeros, since no line number in PRINT statement. **(f)** 5
                                                                                        10
(g) 510 (format may vary)
(h) THE VALUE OF A IS 5 . THE VALUE OF B IS 10. (format may vary)
(i) THE VALUE OF A IS 5   . THE VALUE OF B IS 10   . (format may vary)
7. PRINT 25*0.97**365
9.
```
10 REM THIS PROGRAM COMPUTES THE PERIMETER OF A RECTANGLE
20 PRINT "WHAT IS THE LENGTH";
30 INPUT L
40 PRINT "WHAT IS THE WIDTH";
50 INPUT W
60 LET P = 2*L + 2*W
70 PRINT "THE PERIMETER OF A RECTANGLE WITH LENGTH ";L;" CM AND ";
80 PRINT "WIDTH ";W;" CM IS ";P;" CM"
90 END
```

```
RUN Ⓡ
WHAT IS THE LENGTH? 16
WHAT IS THE WIDTH? 5
THE PERIMETER OF A RECTANGLE WITH LENGTH 16 CM AND WIDTH 5 CM IS 42 CM
```

11. **(a)** `PRINT 100*1.18**25`

  `    6266.863`

  (b)
```
10 INPUT N
20 LET B = 100*1.18**N
30 PRINT "AFTER ";N;" YEARS, THE BALANCE IS $";B
40 END
```

  (The balance in (b) is the same as in (a).)

13. **(a)**
```
10 REM PROPERTY DEPRECIATION
20 PRINT "TYPE THE NUMBER OF YEARS DEPRECIATION";
30 INPUT N
40 LET V = 30000*(1 - 3/100)**N
50 PRINT "AFTER ";N;" YEARS, THE VALUE OF A $30000 PROPERTY";
60 PRINT "WHICH DEPRECIATES AT A 3% RATE IS ";V
70 END
```

  (b)
```
RUN Ⓡ
TYPE THE NUMBER OF YEARS OF DEPRECIATION? 30
AFTER 30 YEARS, THE VALUE OF A $30000 PROPERTY
WHICH DEPRECIATES AT A 3% RATE IS 12030.21
```

Problem Set 13-2   (Formats may vary)

1. **(a)**
```
1  2  3  4  5
6  7  8  9 10
11 12 13 14 15
```
  (b)
```
10  20  30  40  50
60  70  80  90 100
110 120 130 140 150
```

  (c)
```
1  1.2 1.4 1.6 1.8
2.0 2.2 2.4 2.6 2.8
3.0 3.2 3.4 3.6 3.8
4
```
  (d)
```
15 14 13 12 11
10  9  8  7  6
 5  4  3  2  1
```

  (e)
```
100
99
98
 .
 .
 .
1
```
  (f) 11

3. **(a)** `HEY YOU OUT THERE`   **(b)**
```
HEY YOU OUT THERE
HEY YOU OUT THERE
HEY YOU OUT THERE
HEY YOU OUT THERE
HEY YOU OUT THERE
HEY YOU OUT THERE
```

5.
```
10 PRINT "THIS PROGRAM IS TO PRACTICE MULTIPLYING."
20 PRINT "TYPE THE TWO NUMBERS TO BE MULTIPLIED ";
21 PRINT "SEPARATED BY A COMMA."
30 INPUT A,B
35 LET X = X + 1
40 PRINT "AFTER THE QUESTION MARK, TYPE THE PRODUCT."
50 PRINT A;"*";B;"=";
60 INPUT C
70 IF A*B = C THEN 100
80 PRINT "SORRY, TRY AGAIN."
90 GOTO 40
100 PRINT "VERY GOOD. DO YOU WANT TO MULTIPLY OTHER NUMBERS?"
110 PRINT "IF YES, TYPE 1. IF NO, TYPE 2. ";
120 INPUT D
130 IF D = 1 THEN 20
135 PRINT "THE NUMBER OF ATTEMPTED EXERCISES WAS ";X
140 END
```

7.
```
5 REM THIS PROGRAM WILL DETERMINE IF A POSITIVE INTEGER IS PRIME
10 INPUT N
15 IF N = 1 THEN 60
16 IF N = 2 THEN 80
20 FOR A = 2 TO N - 1
30 LET Y = N/A
40 IF Y = INT(Y) THEN 60
50 NEXT A
55 GOTO 80
60 PRINT N;" IS NOT A PRIME."
70 GOTO 90
80 PRINT N;" IS PRIME."
90 END
```

9. A possible program is the following:

```
10 REM THIS PROGRAM CONVERTS DEGREES FAHRENHEIT
20 REM TO DEGREES CELSIUS
30 PRINT "DEGREE FAHRENHEIT","DEGREE CELSIUS"
40 FOR F = -40 TO 220 STEP 10
50 LET C = 5/9*(F - 32)
60 PRINT F,,C
70 NEXT F
80 END
```

11. A possible program is the following:

```
10 REM SUM OF CUBES EQUALS SQUARES OF SUM OF INTEGERS
20 PRINT "1**3 + 2**3 + . . . + N**3","(1 + 2 + 3 + . . . + N)**2"
30 FOR N = 1 TO 10
40 LET Y = N**3
50 LET K = K + Y
60 LET Z = Z + N
70 LET S = Z**2
80 PRINT K,,S
90 NEXT N
100 END
```

```
RUN Ⓡ
1**3 + 2**3 + . . . + N**3        (1 + 2 + 3 + . . . + N)**2
 1                                 1
 9                                 9
 36                                36
 100                               100
 225                               225
 441                               441
 784                               784
 1296                              1296
 2025                              2025
 3025                              3025
```

13. A possible program is the following:

```
10 REM TABLE OF CUBES AND CUBE ROOTS
20 PRINT "NUMBER","CUBE","CUBE ROOT"
30 FOR N = 1 TO 20
40 PRINT N,N**3,N**(1/3)
60 NEXT N
70 END
```

15. A possible program is the following:

```
5 REM THIS PROGRAM PRINTS FIBONACCI NUMBERS
6 PRINT "HOW MANY TERMS OF THE SEQUENCE DO YOU WANT ";
10 INPUT N
20 LET X = 1
30 PRINT X,
40 IF N = 1 THEN 140
50 LET Y = 1
60 PRINT Y,
70 IF N = 2 THEN 140
80 FOR A = 3 TO N
90 LET Z = X + Y
100 LET X = Y
110 LET Y = Z
120 PRINT Z,
130 NEXT A
140 END

RUN Ⓡ
HOW MANY TERMS OF THE SEQUENCE DO YOU WANT? 10
 1   1   2   3   5   8   13   21   34   55
```

17.
```
10 REM PROGRAM TO COMPUTE ERA
20 PRINT "HOW MANY PITCHERS ARE IN THE LEAGUE ";
30 INPUT N
40 PRINT "HOW MANY RUNS AND INNINGS DID PITCHER ";K + 1;" HAVE?"
45 PRINT "TYPE THIS INFORMATION SEPARATED BY A COMMA."
50 INPUT R,I
60 PRINT "PLAYER ID #","RUNS","INNINGS","ERA"
70 LET K = K + 1
```

```
80 PRINT K,R,I,R*9/I
90 IF K >= N THEN 110
100 GOTO 40
110 END
```

19.
```
10 REM THIS PROGRAM WILL PRINT A TABLE
20 REM CONVERTING INCHES TO THE NEAREST CENTIMETER
30 PRINT "INCHES","CENTIMETERS"
40 PRINT
50 FOR X = 65 TO 84 STEP .5
60 LET Y = X*2.54
70 IF Y - INT(Y) >= 0.5 THEN 100
80 PRINT X,INT(Y)
90 GOTO 110
100 PRINT X,INT(Y) + 1
110 NEXT X
120 END
RUN ®
```

INCHES	CENTIMETERS
65	165
65.5	166
66	167
66.5	168
•	•
•	•
•	•
83.5	212
84	213

Problem Set 13-3

5.
```
TO ROOF          TO FLAG                              TO HOUSE1      TO HOUSE2
  RT 30            FD 10                                SQUARE         SQUARE
  FD 50            REPEAT 2[FD 5 RT 90 FD 8 RT 90]      FD 50          FD 50
  RT 120           END                                  ROOF           ROOF
  FD 50                                                 BK 50          LT 90
END                                                     LT 150         FLAG
                                                        FLAG           END
                                                        END
```

Problem Set 13-4

1. (b)
```
TO FLAG :SIDE
  FD :SIDE
  RT 90
  FD :SIDE/2
  RT 90
  FD :SIDE/4
  RT 90
  FD :SIDE/2
END
```

Or, using the RECTANGLE procedure defined in this section:

```
TO FLAG1 :SIDE
BK :SIDE FD :SIDE*3/4
RECTANGLE :SIDE/4 :SIDE/2
END
```

5. Assume that the number of degrees is a whole number.

(a)
```
TO PETAL :D :R          TO FLOWER
   HT                   REPEAT 6 [PETAL 60 1 RT 60]
   ARC :D :R            END
   RT 120               TO ARC :D :S
   ARC :D :R            REPEAT :D[FD :S RT 1]
   END                  END
```

Problem Set 13-5

5. (a)
```
TO STRECH :SIDE
   IF :SIDE < 5 STOP
   VSQUARE :SIDE
   FD :SIDE RT 90
   FD :SIDE LT 90
   STRECH :SIDE - 10
   END
```

(c)
```
TO PIZA :SIZE :ANGLE
   IF :SIDE < 10 STOP
   VSQUARE :SIDE
   FD :SIDE LT :ANGLE
   PIZA :SIDE -5 :ANGLE
   END
```

(e)
```
TO EYE :R
   IF :R < 5 STOP
   CIRCLE :R
   EYE :R*0.8
   END
```

Chapter Test   BASIC   1. (b) and (c) are valid BASIC variables.   **3. (a)** $Y = A*X**3 + B*X**2 + C$
(b) $V = 4/3*P*R**3$ **(c)** $Y = (A*X + B)**2/C$ **(d)** $Y = (X**3 + W/2)**3$ **5.** None of the statements are correct.
7. A possible program is the following:

```
10 PRINT "WHAT IS YOUR VALUE FOR X ";
20 INPUT X
30 LET Y = 7*X**10 + 3*X**5 - 1000
40 PRINT Y
50 END

RUN Ⓡ
WHAT IS YOUR VALUE FOR X? 3
 413072
```

9.
```
10 REM THIS PROGRAM PRINTS THE SUM OF THE SQUARES OF THE
20 REM FIRST 10 NATURAL NUMBERS
30 FOR N = 1 TO 10
40 LET Y = Y + N**2
50 NEXT N
60 PRINT "THE SUM OF THE SQUARES OF THE FIRST 10 NATURAL ";
70 PRINT "NUMBERS IS ";Y
80 END

RUN Ⓡ
THE SUM OF THE SQUARES OF THE FIRST 10 NATURAL NUMBERS IS 385
```

11.
```
10 REM THIS PROGRAM PRINTS SQUARE ROOTS
20 PRINT "N","SQR(N)"
30 FOR N = 0 TO 1 STEP 0.25
40 PRINT N,SQR(N)
50 NEXT N
60 END
```

```
RUN ®
N                    SQR(N)
  0                    0
  0.25                 0.5
  0.5                  0.7071068
  0.75                 0.8660254
  1                    1
```

13. A possible program is the following:

```
10 REM THIS PROGRAM DECIDES IF A PRODUCT IS
20 REM POSITIVE, NEGATIVE, OR ZERO
30 PRINT "INPUT THE VALUES OF A AND B SEPARATED BY A COMMA."
40 INPUT A,B
50 IF A*B < 0 THEN 90
60 IF A*B > 0 THEN 110
70 PRINT A;"*";B;"IS ZERO."
80 GOTO 120
90 PRINT A;"*";B;"IS NEGATIVE."
100 GOTO 120
110 PRINT A;"*";B;"IS POSITIVE."
120 END
```

17.
```
TO DECAGON :SIDE
REPEAT 10[FD :SIDE RT 36]
END
```

19. (a) 10   **(b)** 10   **21.**
         13   8
          .   6
          .   4
          .   2
         49   0   50.
                                              50.

CHAPTER 14

Problem Set 14-1   1. 9 bounces
3. Because $\frac{H}{380} \doteq .291$, then $H \doteq 110.58$. If x is the number of hits he must get by the end of the year, then we must solve the following.

$$\frac{110.58 + x}{440} > .300$$

$$x > 21.42$$

Thus, he must get 22 hits.
5. If the distance between the center of the coin is less than or equal to $\frac{1}{4}$ in., the coin will touch a grid line. If the coin lands within the boundaries of a square that

measures $2\frac{1}{2}$ in. on a side which is located inside each 3 in. square, the coin will not touch. Thus, the probability of the coin not touching a grid line is given by the ratio of the areas of the squares that measure $2\frac{1}{2}$ in. and 3 in. respectively. Hence, the probability is $\frac{6.25}{9}$ or $69.\overline{4}\%$.
7. The minimum number of weights is 10. The weights are 1, 2, 4, 8, 16, 32, 64, 128, 256, 512. Notice that these are just the powers of 2 that are contained in 680.
9. We reduce the problem to simpler cases, look for a pattern and generalize. A table for various exponents and remainders is given below.

Exponent	Remainder	
1	5	
2	4	
3	6	repeating
4	2	block
5	3	
6	1	
7	5	
8	4	
9	6	

To see how many times this block repeats in our problem, we divide 999,999 by 6 to obtain 166,666 with a remainder of 3. Thus, the block repeats 166,666 times and then goes 3 steps further. Because the third number in the repeating block is 6, this is the desired answer.

11. The distances run by each of the runners when Tom and Dick finish the 2 km race are given below.

	Tom	Dick	Harry
(1)	2000 m	1900 m	x m
(2)		2000 m	1800 m

To find x we solve the following proportion:

$$\frac{1900}{2000} = \frac{x}{1800}$$

Thus, $x = 290$ m.

13. (a) The short way to do this problem is to realize that if there are 98 players and only 1 winner, there must be 97 losers. To obtain 97 losers, 97 matches must be played.   **(b)** By similar reasoning, there must be $(n - 1)$ matches.

15. $2^{12} \cdot 5^8 = 2^4 \cdot (2^8 \cdot 5^8) = 2^4 \cdot (2 \cdot 5)^8 = 16 \cdot 10^8$. Hence the number of digits is 10.

17. (a) $1, 5, 4 + 5, 4 + 4 + 5, 4 + 4 + 4 + 5,$ $4 + 4 + 4 + 4 + 5, \ldots$ i.e. $1, 5, 9, 13, 17, 21, \ldots$
(b) $4(n - 2) + 5$ or $4n - 3$.

19. Let x be the number of sheets of paper and y be the number of envelopes. Then for Ann we have: $x - 50 = y$ or $x = y + 50$. For Sue we have $3(y - 50) = x$. Thus $y + 50 = 3(y - 50)$ and $y = 100$, $x = 150$. Thus there were 150 sheets of paper in each box.

21. Let x be the length of the bottom and y be the depth of the water when the bottom is level. The volume of the water is $10xy$. When the aquarium is tilted, the water forms a right triangular prism with an altitude of $10''$. The volume of this triangular prism is $\frac{1}{2} \cdot 10 \cdot 8 \left(\frac{3}{4} \cdot x\right)$ which

is $30x$. Setting the volumes equal we obtain $10xy = 30x$ and therefore $y = 3$. Thus, the water depth is 3 inches.

23. Let x be the amount Susan made two years ago. Because her salary increased 50% each year, her salary after the first year was $1.5x$ and after the second year, $(1.5)(1.5)x$. Thus $(1.5)^2 \cdot x = \$100,000$ and $x = \$44,444.44$ or $\$44,444$.

25. Let d be the integer. Since the remainders are the same, then $d \mid (13903 - 13511)$ and $d \mid (14589 - 13903)$ i.e., $d \mid 392$ and $d \mid 686$. Since GCD(392,686) = 98, then $d = 98$.

27. In one hour, the hour hand covers $\frac{360°}{12} = 30°$. Thus in 15 minutes it covers $\frac{30°}{4} = 7° \, 30'$. Consequently the angle between the hands at 2:15 is $30° - 7° \, 30' = 22° \, 30'$.

29. Pair the numbers as follows:

999,999,998 and 1
999,999,997 and 2
999,999,996 and 3
999,999,995 and 4
999,999,994 and 5

$\vdots$ $\vdots$

500,000,000 and 499,999,999

There are 499,999,999 pairs and the sum of the digits in each pair is $9 \cdot 9$ or 81. The unpaired numbers are 999,999,999 and 1,000,000,000. The sum of the digits in each is 81 and 1 respectively. Hence the total sum of the digits is $499,999,999(81) + 1(81) + 1 = 500,000,000(81) + 1 = 40,500,000,001$

31. Let (x, y) be the center of the circle, then using the distance formula we have $x^2 + y^2 = (x - 4)^2 + y^2$ and $x^2 + y^2 = (x - 1)^2 + (y + 3)^2$. These two equations reduce to $16 - 8x = 0$ and $3y - x + 5 = 0$. Solving these equations we find $x = 2$ and $y = {}^-1$. Hence the center is at $(2, {}^-1)$. The radius is the distance from any point, e.g., $(0, 0)$ to the center $(2, {}^-1)$. Thus $r = \sqrt{2^2 + 1^2} + \sqrt{5}$.

33. Let x be the number that voted against the bill the first time. Then we have the following:

	Against	For
First vote	x	$400 - x$
Second vote	$400 - \frac{12}{11}x$	$\frac{12}{11}x$

Because in the second vote, the bill passed by twice the margin, then

$$2[x - (400 - x)] = \frac{12}{11}x - (400 - \frac{12}{11}x)$$
$$2(2x - 400) = \frac{12}{11}x - 400 + \frac{12}{11}x$$
$$20x = 4400$$
$$x = 220$$

The difference between the "for" votes the first and second time is: $\frac{12}{11}x - (400 - x) = \frac{12}{11}(220) - (400 - 220) = 60$ or 60 votes.

35. (a) 1,8,28,56,70,56,28,8,1; 1,9,36,84,126,126,84,36,9,1   **(b)** $s_1 = 1$, $s_2 = 2$, $s_3 = 4$, $s_4 = 8$. $s_{10} = 512$, $s_n = 2^{n-1}$ **(c)** The alternate sum in each row after row 1 is zero.   **(d)** Answers vary.

37. A computer program for this problem along with its run is given below.

```
10 REM A TRAFFIC PROBLEM INVOLVING THE CHICAGO LOOP AND IM BYPASS
20 LET N = N + 1
30 LET C = 220819000*1.015**N
40 LET I = 66944000*1.029**N
50 IF I >= C THEN 70
60 GOTO 20
70 PRINT "IN ";N + 1980;" THE NUMBER OF CHICAGO LOOP CARS WILL BE ";C
80 PRINT "IN ";N + 1980;" THE NUMBER OF IM BYPASS CARS WILL BE ";I
90 END

RUN Ⓡ
IN 2068 THE NUMBER OF CHICAGO LOOP CARS WILL BE 8.185552E+08
IN 2068 THE NUMBER OF IM BYPASS CARS WILL BE 8.284462E+08
```

APPENDIX I

Problem Set AI-1   1. (a) False statement   **(b)** Not a statement   **(c)** False statement   **(d)** Not a statement   **(e)** Not a statement   **(f)** Not a statement   **(g)** True statement   **(h)** Not a statement   **3. (a)** For all integers x, $x + 8 = 11$ or for no integers x, $x + 8 = 11$.   **(b)** For no integers x, $x + 0 = x$.   **(c)** For no integers x, $x^2 = 4$.   **(d)** For all integers x, $x + 1 = x + 2$ or there exists an integer x such that $x + 1 = x + 2$.

Problem Set AI-2

1. (a)

p	$\sim p$	$\sim(\sim p)$
T	F	T
F	T	F

(b)

p	$\sim p$	$p \lor \sim p$	$p \land \sim p$
T	F	T	F
F	T	T	F

(c) Yes   **(d)** No

3. (a) F   **(b)** T   **(c)** T   **(d)** F   **(e)** F   **(f)** T   **(g)** F   **(h)** F   **(i)** F   **(j)** F   **5. (a)** No   **(b)** Yes   **(c)** No   **(d)** Yes   **7. (a)** Today is not Wednesday or the month is not June.   **(b)** Yesterday I did not eat breakfast or I did not watch television.   **(c)** It is not both true that it is raining and it is July.

Problem Set AI-3 **1.** (a) $p \to q$ (b) $\sim p \to q$
(c) $p \to \sim q$ (d) $p \to q$ (e) $\sim q \to \sim p$ (f) $q \leftrightarrow p$

3. (a)

p	q	$p \vee q$	$p \to (p \vee q)$
T	T	T	T
T	F	T	T
F	T	T	T
F	F	F	T

(b)

p	q	$p \wedge q$	$(p \wedge q) \to q$
T	T	T	T
T	F	F	T
F	T	F	T
F	F	F	T

(c)

p	$\sim p$	$\sim(\sim p)$	$p \to \sim(\sim p)$	$\sim(\sim p) \to p$	$p \leftrightarrow \sim(\sim p)$
T	F	T	T	T	T
F	T	F	T	T	T

5. (a) T (b) F (c) T (d) T (e) F (f) T **7.** No;
Tom can go to the movies or not and the implication is
still true. **9.** Answers may vary; e.g. "If a number is
not a multiple of 4, then it is not a multiple of 8."

Problem Set AI-4 **1.** (a) Valid (b) Valid (c) Valid (d) Invalid (e) Invalid (f) Valid (g) Invalid (h) Valid
3.

p	q	r	$\sim q$	$p \to \sim q$	$\sim q \to r$	$p \to r$	$(p \to \sim q) \wedge (\sim q \to r)$	$[(p \to \sim q) \wedge (\sim q \to r)] \to (p \to r)$
T	T	T	F	F	T	T	F	T
T	T	F	F	F	T	F	F	T
T	F	T	T	T	T	T	T	T
T	F	F	T	T	F	F	F	T
F	T	T	F	T	T	T	T	T
F	T	F	F	T	T	T	T	T
F	F	T	T	T	T	T	T	T
F	F	F	T	T	F	T	F	T

INDEX

FORTRAN, 601
FORWARD (FD), 619, 620, 642
Fractions, 201
  equivalent, 202
  improper, 209, 242
  proper, 209, 242
  real number, 284
  simplest form of, 203, 242
Frequency
  grouped, 336
  polygon, 335, 356
  table, 333, 356
Function, 56, 59, 66
Fundamental Counting Principle, 324, 356
Fundamental law of fractions, 202
Fundamental theorem of arithmetic, 176, 198

Garfield, James, 519
Gauss, Karl, 12, 191, 385, 476
Geometric sequence, 7, 29
Geometry, 361
Glide reflection, 450
Goldbach, Christian, 180
  Conjecture, 180
GOTO, 602, 611, 642
Gram, 541
Graphs, 559
  bar, 334, 356
  circle or pie, 338, 356
  frequency polygon, 335, 356
  histogram, 334, 356
  line, 335, 356
  linear inequalities, 570, 571
  pictograph, 336, 356
Great circle, 478
Greater than, 77, 152
  or equal to, 77
Greatest common divisor (GCD), 184, 198
Grouped frequency table, 336

Half-line, 362, 367
Half-plane, 367
Half-space, 367
Hardware, 600, 642
Hectare, 502
Hecto-, 493, 549
Height
  of a parallelogram, 503
  of a triangle, *See* Altitude
Heptagon, 373
Hexagon, 373
Hindu-Arabic system, 70, 73
Histogram, 334, 356

HOME, 620, 642
Hypotenuse, 514
Hypothesis, 668

Icosahedron, 397
Identity property
  additive, 79, 138, 211, 285
  multiplicative, 87, 146, 217, 285
  set intersection, 43, 66
  set union, 43, 66
IF, 635, 642
IF-THEN, 602, 610, 642
Implication, 665–668
Impossible event, 302
Improper fraction, 209, 242
Index, 288, 294
Inductive reasoning, 4, 29
Inequalities
  properties of, 153, 154, 164
Infinite set, 33, 54
INPUT/OUTPUT group, 600
Input unit, 600, 641
Initialized, 612
INPUT, 602, 603, 642
INT, 615, 642
Integer(s)
  addition, 137
  additive identity, 138
  additive inverse, 138
  associative property, 138, 146
  closure property, 138, 146
  commutative property, 138, 146
  definition, 134, 138
  distributive property, 146, 147
  multiplication, 145, 146
  multiplicative identity, 146
  negative, 134
  subtraction, 138, 139
Interest, 273
  compound, 275, 294
  rate, 273
  simple, 273, 294
Internal Memory, 600, 641
Intersect, 363
Intersection of sets, 38
  definition, 39, 66
Intersection of sets method for GCD, 185
Inverse
  additive, 138, 211, 285
  multiplicative, 217, 285
  of a statement, 666
Invert and multiply algorithm, 222, 223
Irrational numbers, 280, 294

Jordan curve theorem, 372

Kemeny, John, 601
Kilo-, 493, 549
Kline, Morris, 133
Königsberg bridge problem, 403
Kurtz, Thomas, 601

Laboratory Activities
  abacus, 104
  calculator, 95
  coded paper, 121
  computation, 104
  finger multiplication, 114
  geoboard activity, 381
  mass, 546
  Moebius strip, 408
  Napier's bones, 114
  paper cup, 306
  percent, 270
  polyhedra, 399
  regions of plane, 370
  Reese's Pieces, 318
  Tower of Hanoi, 27
Lattice multiplication, 107
Lattice polygon, 511
Law of Added Hypothesis, 668
Law of Detachment, 668, 670
Least common multiple (LCM), 188, 198
LEFT (LT), 619, 620, 642
Legs, 514
Less than, 77
  or equal to, 77
LET, 602, 604, 612, 642
light emitting diode (LED), 674
Line, 361, 410
  coplanar lines, 363
  equation of, 567, 596
  graph, 335, 356
  intersecting, 363
  number, 603
  of intersection, 366
  parallel lines, 362, 410
  parallel to a plane, 366
  perpendicular, 377, 410
  point-slope form of, 570
  segment, 362, 410
  slope-intercept form of, 566
  of symmetry, 454
  skew lines, 365, 410
liquid crystal display (LCD), 674
LIST, 602, 603, 642
Liter, 533
Lobachevsky, Nikolai, 385
Logic, 659, 673
  algebraic, 673
  calculator, 673